TWO ROADS DIVERGE

The dramatic events of Maidan in February 2014 shone a spotlight on the immense problems facing Ukraine. At the same time that Ukraine was undergoing turmoil, its western neighbor Poland was celebrating twenty-five years of postcommunism with a rosy economic outlook and projections of continued growth. How could two countries who shared similar linguistic, cultural, economic, and political heritages diverge so wildly in economic performance in such a short span of time? The main argument of this book is that institutions, and more specifically the evolution or neglect of the particular institutions needed for a market economy, explain the economic divergence between Ukraine and Poland. This book discusses the evolution of key institutions such as property rights, trade, and the role of the executive branch of government to explain the recent relative performance of the two countries.

Christopher A. Hartwell is a leading scholar on the evolution of institutions and president of the Center for Social and Economic Research (CASE) in Poland. He has published in prestigious journals such as the *Journal for Common Market Studies*, *Economic Systems*, *Open Economies Review*, *Post-Communist Economies*, and *Business Horizons*. In addition to his academic work, he has advised governments and the private sector on economic policy issues in Poland, Ukraine, Armenia, Azerbaijan, Georgia, Kazakhstan, Kyrgyzstan, Moldova, Russia, Bosnia, and Kosovo, among others. He holds a Ph.D. in economics from the Warsaw School of Economics and a master's in public policy from Harvard.

Two Roads Diverge

The Transition Experience of Poland and Ukraine

CHRISTOPHER A. HARTWELL

Kozminski University, Warsaw

and

Center for Social and Economic Research (CASE), Warsaw

CAMBRIDGE
UNIVERSITY PRESS

CAMBRIDGE
UNIVERSITY PRESS

One Liberty Plaza, 20th Floor, New York NY 10006, USA

Cambridge University Press is part of the University of Cambridge.

It furthers the University's mission by disseminating knowledge in the pursuit of education, learning, and research at the highest international levels of excellence.

www.cambridge.org
Information on this title: www.cambridge.org/9781107112018

© Christopher Hartwell 2016

First published 2016

Printed in the United Kingdom by Clays, St Ives plc

A catalogue record for this publication is available from the British Library.

ISBN 978-1-107-11201-8 Hardback
ISBN 978-1-107-53098-0 Paperback

This book is dedicated to the brave souls of Maidan and all those who ever stood for institutional change against overwhelming odds.

Contents

Figures

Tables

Motivation and Acknowledgements

This book started life as a short analysis written at the behest of my dissertation advisor, friend, and (without hyperbole) the modern saint of Polish economics, Leszek Balcerowicz. In late February 2014, I was based in Moscow, and Leszek asked me via email to write a five-page analysis for his think tank *Fundacja Forum Obywatelskiego Rozwoju* (FOR, the Civil Development Forum Foundation) on a topic of my choosing. With the events in Ukraine taking an incredible turn, including the Maidan protests and the flight of Ukrainian president Yanukovych to Russia, I thought it made a natural backdrop for a piece of work. Moreover, given FOR's emphasis on Poland and Polish economics, I thought, why not a piece that compared the performance of Poland and Ukraine since transition began? Leszek agreed and encouraged me to start writing, which I did during the month of March 2014, turning in my first draft near the end of the month.

During that month, events moved quickly in Ukraine. Almost immediately at the conclusion of the Sochi Olympics, Russian president Vladimir Putin moved in some of his special forces, in the guise of "little green men," into Crimea to seize it from Ukraine. As the month went on, and as Russia continued to deny any involvement, Crimea was annexed by Russia, followed by similar provocations in the Luhansk and Donetsk regions in the east of Ukraine. By the time I had received my first comments in early April, Ukraine's revolution did not appear to be long for this world. But I was still determined to figure out why it had happened, and what ramifications the past had held for Ukraine's future.

From this short brief, which was finally released by FOR in December 2014, I had come upon the idea to explore this issue more fully. Five pages (or the seventeen pages that the brief ended up becoming) were nowhere near enough space to tell the tale of how Poland and Ukraine had diverged. In fact, I had only begun to scratch the surface of the similarities and differences between the two countries, and I had not even looked prior to 1989. How had the history of Poland and Ukraine shaped their institutional development? As economists, we all say "institutions matter," as the late, great Douglass North showed, but what was the genesis of these institutions? Could we explain the past twenty-five years of transformation in Ukraine and Poland with reference to the institutional development of centuries prior?

After Russia's seizure of Crimea, life in Moscow became intolerable for a foreigner (especially one who explores political economy), and so I leapt at the chance to become president of Poland's oldest and most prestigious economic think tank, the Center for Social and Economic Research (CASE) in Warsaw. This was also a fortunate happenstance for this book, as I attended an event at the University of Warsaw in June on "Institutions, Culture and Long Term Economic Effects." Organized by the excellent Franklin Allen of Wharton at my alma mater, the University of Pennsylvania, it featured luminaries such as James Robinson, Hans-Joachim Voth, Sascha Becker, and Ekaterina Zhuravskaya. With papers exploring the idea of institutional persistence as a legitimate area of economic inquiry, I knew that I had my angle for this book. Irena Grosfeld and Ekaterina Zhuravskaya had already done a paper (presented at the workshop) on how Poland's Partitions had influenced economic outcomes today. It seemed intuitive that the border between Ukraine and Poland would also have a similar effect.

In reality, in both broader institutional economics and in linking economic history to the present, economists have only just begun to explore this issue of the effects of institutional persistence. Thus, with this book I hope to both build on the work that these other authors have been doing, and to expand it over a much longer time frame. And the lessons learned from the past 500 years will have resonance for Poland and Ukraine no matter how the current drama plays itself out. In that sense, by tracing grand historical patterns of institutional evolution, the difference of a year is miniscule.

So, to move to the acknowledgments, thanks are obviously due to the aforementioned researchers, for both laying the groundwork for this book and also for their encouragement while writing it. Thanks should also go to Richard Connolly, Jan Fidrmuc, Janusz Szyrmer, Tomasz Mickiewicz, Oleh Havrylyshyn, and anonymous reviewers who looked over the first proposal and chapters and provided insightful comments. Sincere appreciation goes out to Anders Åslund for agreeing to write the foreword, but more importantly, for discussions we had in Helsinki in December 2013 at the Bank of Finland, just as Yanukovych's regime was starting to unravel. Being able to have these discussions and intellectual debates in real time helped to clarify my thoughts on what was happening, and why it was happening.

In terms of the writing of this book, I am deeply indebted to all those who responded to requests for papers or information, including the great historian Robert I. Frost, on whose work I rely heavily in Chapters 2 and 3. Support was also provided by my employer CASE and especially my boss, Ewa Balcerowicz, as well as a host of interns who obtained some of the data necessary. CASE, as one of the key institutions attempting to help Ukraine reform its own institutions, has been an invaluable resource as my home base, and the current staff and those whose footsteps I followed in are due many thanks, including Marek Dabrowski and my vice president Izabela Styczyńska. My work as an associate professor at Kozminski University in Poland also afforded me access to JSTOR, HeinOnline, EBSCOhost, and other crucial research databases, as well as some critical peace and quiet when I was finishing this manuscript. I hope that the university benefits from having one of their professors publish with Cambridge University Press, a not-unsubstantial accomplishment for a Polish educational institution!

Much of the section on property rights in Ukraine pertaining to land privatization was written in a different (and much less exhaustive) form for a project with the Organization for Economic Cooperation and Development (OECD) in Kyiv, and I am grateful to Coralie David, Yerim Park, and Andrea Goldstein for their support and comments. Additional thanks go to Ukrainian policy makers met during my trips to Kyiv for this project, including the assistance of Vladyslava Rutytska, the deputy minister on European Integration at the Ministry of Agrarian Policy and Food of Ukraine and Viktor Marchenko, the adviser to the Minister of the Ministry of Economic Development and Trade.

Of course, huge gratitude must go out to my editor at Cambridge University Press, Karen Maloney, her assistant Kate Gavino, editorial assistant Kristina Deusch, and content manager Emma Collison for their tireless efforts in getting this book into print. Karen especially has been incredibly understanding of the difficulty of running a multimillion euro think tank and teaching at a university AND writing a scholarly work, so apologies are due to her for missing a deadline (or two). Her support has been invaluable, as was her contribution to my stamina at the 2016 Allied Social Science Associations (ASSA) meetings (in other words, thanks to the

Press for the lunch). The rest of the staff at Cambridge is also to be commended for their excellent work in making this a smooth and enjoyable experience.

As a measure of thanks to the nonacademic support I received during the writing of this book, I must also acknowledge the contribution of Les Claypool in keeping me sane during some frustrating brainstorming and writing sessions, especially towards the end of the book. While I did not enjoy a can of pork soda as Mr. Claypool counseled, I can definitely say that at certain times I was tired and sleepy and he helped me to push through with many a story to tell.

Finally, during the course of writing this book, Mr. Magnus Tadeusz Hartwell, my first-born, entered this world. Much of the end of this book was written to the tune of the music from his baby rocker and in-between fussing and feeding episodes, and I would not have it any other way (Magnus Taduesz also wishes to thank Mr. Claypool for providing a lovely soundtrack while his dad was working). But the biggest thanks must go to my lovely wife Kristen, for both bringing Magnus into this world and helping to take care of him so this book could be completed while there still is a Ukraine to speak of. Without her support, this book would still be just a policy brief, and I would be only half-complete.

Foreword

No comparison of two countries in postcommunist transformation is more obvious than between Poland and Ukraine. Few countries have had as much in common, and few countries have developed more differently in the last quarter century since the end of communism. Interestingly, such a book has not been written before, and that is what Christopher Hartwell gives us in this volume.

In 1989, Poland and Ukraine appeared confusingly similar. They had approximately the same level of GDP per capita whether measured in current prices or purchasing power parities (PPP). Their size is similar, and they are neighbors in the center of Europe. Also their economic structures were similar, with extensive sectors in metallurgy, machine building, mining, chemicals, and agriculture, though small service sectors. Their climate and languages are similar as well. They even have national anthems with the same pessimistic words, claiming that their nations have not perished as yet. Indeed, together with other countries in what historian Timothy Snyder calls the "Bloodlands" in Eastern Europe, these two nations suffered more than anybody else during World War II.

On the basis of these superficial observations, we might have expected to see these two newly free nations to perform approximately as well, or badly, after the collapse of communism, but nothing could be further from reality. Poland has taken off as never before in the last 400 years of its sad history, while Ukraine has stuck to its equally sad history. The economic contrast is extraordinary. At current exchange rates, Poland's GDP is six times larger than Ukraine's, and even at purchasing power parities Poland is three times richer. Rarely have two similar countries diverged this much without war.

The big question, which Christopher Hartwell discusses so well in this book, is why these two neighbors have taken off in completely different directions. It is a question of great importance, because it tells us how a country in crisis can best resolve it, and what really matters for economic, political, and institutional development. The answer lies in the countries' different institutional development. Poland has become a full-fledged democracy, while Ukraine is a struggling democracy; Poland has a well-functioning market economy based on the rule of law, whereas Ukraine has a market economy riddled with severe corruption. Poland has been a member of the European Union since 2004, while Ukraine has only a European Association Agreement. But how did the countries get into such different positions?

Hartwell rightly devotes much attention to the situation before 1989. I travelled extensively in both countries in the 1980s, and the differences in thinking and mentality were striking. Both Poland and Ukraine are old nations, but Poland was an independent state with all state institutions, which Ukraine lacked. In Poland, nobody believed in communism, and millions had spent substantial time abroad. Until Ukraine's independence, the KGB let little true information about the outside world come into the nation. Polish civil society was strong and vibrant, although depressed after martial law was declared in December 1981, whereas Ukraine's civil society was severely repressed, which made it focus entirely on the reinforcement of the Ukrainian nation. Little thought was devoted to democratic state building and none to market economic reform. Needless to say, few Ukrainians spoke foreign languages, and almost nobody had possibility to read foreign academic literature. Poland was also greatly helped by its large private sector under communism. By 1989, Poland was intellectually well prepared for the abandonment of communism, but few Ukrainians had a clue. From this perspective, the differences that evolved appear natural, even if events could have developed differently.

Ukraine devoted its first years of independence to elementary nation building, such as national symbols, the establishment of elementary state institutions, and ascertaining the role of the Ukrainian language. Poland had all that given. Early founding parliamentary elections after a democratic breakthrough are considered vital for democracy building. Neither country did well in terms of timing. Poland had its first parliamentary elections two years after its democratic breakthrough and Ukraine after three years. Poland had a problem with excessive party fragmentation, but Ukraine had parliamentary elections without political parties. Poland did, however, accomplish a democratic consolidation, while Ukraine did not. Its political parties and even constitutional order have stayed in a state of flux. The Polish elite swiftly changed, while Ukraine's old communist elite persisted.

Economic policy contrasted the most between the two countries. Leszek Balcerowicz pursued market economic reforms and macroeconomic stabilization with clarity and stubbornness, and these measures secured a market economic system that was delivering economic growth for Poland by 1992. Ukraine, by contrast, had no economic policy until 1994. The result was vicious hyperinflation of 10,200 percent in 1993 and outrageous rent seeking, leading to permanent corruption. Throughout the 1990s, corrupt gas trade was the main source of top-level enrichment in Ukraine. The country had been caught in an under-reform trap, and it took one full decade before it returned to economic growth.

The differences in economic policy in the early transition set Poland on track not only for economic growth but also for declining corruption, while Ukraine's corruption became rampant and pervasive. Economic policy stands out not only as the greatest difference between the countries, but also the most important policy that could vary across countries. Poland utilized its brief moment of "extraordinary politics," as Balcerowicz has named it, just after its democratic breakthrough, but Ukraine did not.

Nothing succeeds like success. Today Poles often forget how weak and vulnerable their nation was in 1989. It is all too easy to ascribe success entirely to your own virtues, but when a country is down and out even limited assistance from the outside world is vital. Poland benefited greatly from international assistance in its early transition. Its initial stabilization program was sufficiently financed by the International Monetary Fund and Western countries. Early on, the West agreed to write off half of Poland's inherited public debt. The European Union opened its market to Polish goods, which soon encompassed two-thirds of Polish exports. After a few years, EU membership was offered. The Polish reformers had to ask for it all, but they could use the Western assistance as a lever to push through their reforms. Ukraine did not enjoy any of this. It concluded its first IMF program three years after independence. In the 1990s, only one-tenth of its exports went to EU markets, because of rigorous EU protectionism.

The role of old Soviet influences is often ignored, but they are strong and pernicious. In the early 1990s, Ukraine suffered from its membership in the hyperinflationary ruble zone and the maintenance of nonmarket state trade between the former Soviet republics. Thanks to the dissolution of the old Soviet-Bloc trade organization COMECON in 1990, Poland escaped all this. Since that time, Russia's state corporation, Gazprom, has exerted geopolitical pressures and purchased the Ukrainian political elite through its corrupt gas trade. Old KGB agents have remained in place, and they do not work for the new Ukrainian security service but for the old headquarters at the Lubyanka in Moscow.

The essence of this book is that Poland has successfully carried out a major institutional change that Ukraine still needs to go through. Such a change is never easy because it has to be more revolutionary than evolutionary. If the top does not change, little change is possible in any hierarchical system, especially a state. Ukraine has assembled many of the necessary preconditions for a successful transformation. Russian military aggression has compelled the Ukrainian nation to come together. The country has gone through another democratic breakthrough with new parliamentary elections. The new government has attempted to eliminate some of the worst sources of rent seeking and corruption. The West has engaged far more than before. But many conditions need to be in place for Ukraine's transformation to succeed, and this process is nothing for the faint-hearted, as this book so eminently shows.

Anders Åslund
Atlantic Council
Washington, DC

It is clear that to love the neighbor is self-denial, that to love the crowd or to act as if one loved it, to make it the court of last resort for 'the truth,' that is the way to truly gain power, the way to all sorts of temporal and worldly advantage – yet it is untruth; for the crowd is untruth.

But he who acknowledges this view, which is seldom presented (for it often happens, that a man believes that the crowd is in untruth, but when it, the crowd, merely accepts his opinion en masse, then everything is all right), he admits to himself that he is the weak and powerless one; how would a single individual be able to stand against the many, who have the power!"

– Søren Kierkegaard

Introduction

I came from a very poor family and my main dream in life was to break out of this poverty.

– Viktor Yanukovych[1]

Early on the morning of February 22, 2014, approximately twelve miles outside of Kyiv, ordinary Ukrainians began to enter the grounds of Mezhyhirya, Ukrainian president Viktor Yanukovych's palatial estate; first they came in a trickle and then in a flood. Following the extraordinary events of the previous three months, including the Euromaidan protests, actual revolution on the streets of Kyiv over the previous four days, and the killing of over a hundred protestors by state security organs, Yanukovych had apparently fled the estate at 2 a.m. that morning for parts unknown. And now, after extraordinary secrecy in its construction and intense security that kept inquiring minds away for years (in 2012, journalist Tetyana Chornovil scaled a fence to take pictures of the mansion and was detained), Yanukovych's subjects were finally able to get a glimpse of how he and the other leaders of the country lived. As a point of pride, the leaders of the Maidan protests in Kyiv actually invited Ukrainians to the site, to illuminate how their tax dollars had been spent over the previous four years. What had been a guarded compound was now open to all.

The first visitors to Mezhyhirya walked timidly through the manicured grounds, incredulous at what they saw. The opulence on display, while spoken of quietly by Ukrainians before the Maidan revolution, was

---

[1] Spoken to Ukrainian journalists during the 2004 presidential election and quoted in Peter Finn, "Intense campaign down to the wire in Ukraine," *Washington Post*, October 30, 2004, available www.washingtonpost.com/wp-dyn/articles/A10670-2004Oct29.html, accessed June 25, 2014.

unbelievable when actually seen in person. The scale of the excesses at Mezhyhirya rivaled that of other leaders who had a much freer hand in their access to state finances; while not quite on par with the gargantuan palace of Nicolae Ceausescu or Stalin's planned "Palace of the People," Yanukovych's mansion was comparable to the over-the-top tastes of Saddam Hussein, Libya's Muammar Gaddafi, and Zimbabwe's Robert Mugabe. Certainly, as with these other leaders, Yanukovych spared no expense to outfit the mansion and its grounds to his liking, with a replica Spanish galleon that housed a restaurant; a golf course; a zoo stocked with deer, ostriches, peacocks, kangaroos, and wildebeests; and Greek ruins strewn about the compound's 140 hectares (350 acres). The main building itself was rumored to be the largest building made of wood in the world, although Honka, the Finnish company that built the residence, was blocked by Yanukovych personally from submitting this claim to the Guinness Book of World Records.[2]

However, unlike Ceausescu, the supreme leader of communist Romania, or Saddam Hussein, the despot that ruled Iraq for twenty-four years, Yanukovych was the democratically elected president of the independent nation of Ukraine, a country that had seen twenty-two years of independence from the Soviet Union and, at least ostensibly, the same amount of time transitioning its economic system. Moreover, also unlike the Romanian or Arab dictators that came before him, Yanukovych had not been in power for decades, but had been elected only in 2010. Thus, a look at Mezhyhirya could lead one to believe that Ukraine had to be doing something right in its transition to sustain such a lifestyle for its leaders, especially in so short a time. Clearly, people had done well from Ukraine's transition from communism if a humble public servant could have the privilege of dining privately in a galleon on a man-made waterway. Ukraine's system appeared to allow Yanukovych his dream of breaking out of the poverty he was born into.

THE TRAGEDY OF UKRAINE

However, it was not the vast majority of Ukrainians who had benefitted from the fall of the Soviet Union or the much-trumpeted economic transition. Throughout the years of hardship, the halting reforms, the

---

[2] "Monument to corruption: Ukraine's most-wanted man built $75M home on a $25G salary," Fox News, February 24, 2014, www.foxnews.com/world/2014/02/24/monument-to-corruption-ukraine-most-wanted-man-built-75m-home-on-25g-salary/, accessed June 23, 2014.

hyperinflation, and the tug of war between east and west, it seemed that the only people who gained from the volatility of the transition were Ukraine's leaders. Indeed, nothing better illustrates the failures of Ukraine twenty-two years after independence than the contrast between former president Yanukovych's palaces and the life of the average Ukrainian. Rumored at a cost somewhere around US$75–100 million, in a country where the per capita GDP in 2012 was estimated at $2,094 (in constant 2005 US dollars) and where the average monthly salary in 2013 was around US$400, a building like Mezhyhirya would have taken the average Ukrainian 15,500 years to purchase (and only at the low end of the estimates). Even for someone like President Yanukovych, such a palatial estate would have been difficult to attain, as he officially earned a modest salary for his position, estimated anywhere between US$30,000 and US$100,000; in fact, one of Yanukovych's earliest decrees in February 2010 was the public announcement that he was cutting his own salary in half in order to "raise the country's subsistence level and minimum wage."[3]

If the gulf between the average Ukrainian and the opulence of Mezhyhirya was wide, perhaps the justification behind such an impressive work of art was to be found in the health of the Ukrainian government. That is, while the broader economy was still dragging as befitting a lower-income country still undergoing the difficulties of transition, maybe the government had achieved the macroeconomic stability and even fiscal prudence necessary to ensure that its leaders were well compensated for their arduous work. The compound at Mezhyhirya, as well as the estate of ex-prosecutor-general Viktor Pshonka at Gorenichy, the Versailles-like estate of Ukrainian parliament member Yuriy Ivanyushchenko, or the opulent palace of former minister for the environment and natural resources Mykola Zlochevskiy were then just recognition of a job well done, with growth in the broader economy soon to follow. In fact, from a Keynesian perspective, the amount of money that went into each of these homes could be seen as fiscal stimulus to bolster the Ukrainian economy (which might have made more sense if the construction firms weren't all foreign and the luxury goods all imported). Perhaps the rewards that accrued to the leadership of Ukraine were then just a part of Ukraine's broader fiscal policy to jump-start the economy, especially after the hardship of the global financial crisis.

---

[3] "Herman: President Yanukovych halves his salary," Kyiv Post, February 25, 2010, http://www.kyivpost.com/article/content/ukraine-politics/herman-president-yanukovych-halves-his-salary-60442.html, accessed June 30, 2016.

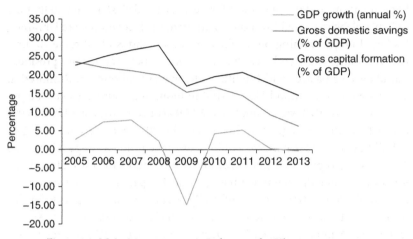

Figure 1.1 Main Macroeconomic Indicators for Ukraine, 2005–2013
Source: IMF and World Bank.

Alas, this too was not the case, as Yanukovych's lavish mansions also stood in stark contrast to the reality of the general finances of the Ukrainian government, a government that just days earlier Yanukovych had headed. It became clearer and clearer that part of the tug of war that Yanukovych fostered between Europe and Russia for Ukraine over the previous three years had been predicated on how much money each side was willing to give to save the country (or, more accurately, to continue to finance Yanukovych's lifestyle). A month after Yanukovych fled Ukraine for the friendly environs of Russia, interim prime minister Arseniy Yatsenyuk went before the Verkhovna Rada (the Ukrainian parliament) and announced that Ukraine was "on the brink of economic and financial bankruptcy."[4] This assessment may have been too mild; even the IMF noted in December 2013, before Yanukovych's ouster, that the Ukrainian "economy has been in recession since mid-2012" with "inconsistent macroeconomic policies generat[ing] deep-seated vulnerabilities and recurrent crises" (IMF 2014: 4). The numbers were indeed grim, with real GDP, investment, and savings already plummeting through 2013 (Figure 1.1), the government deficit at developed-economy levels of 5.7 percent of GDP, and other macroeconomic indicators showing little better progress. With months of continuous protests only just winding

---

[4] Prime Minister Arseniy Yatsenyuk's speech to the Rada, March 27, 2014, http://www.kmu .gov.ua/control/publish/article?art_id=247147805, accessed June 24, 2014.

down, no immediate agreement with Europe on Ukraine's relationship to the EU, and a foreign invasion already underway, the situation for the new interim government seemed even more tenuous.

The blame for Ukraine's dire position was blamed first and foremost on Yanukovych's policies, an argument that had much to recommend it on the evidence of malfeasance at Mezhyhirya alone. Without a doubt, Yanukovych had utilized the state coffers of Ukraine as his personal wallet, with some estimates of the amount stolen from the Ukrainian people by a number of high-ranking officials (including Yanukovych's actual family) placed as high as US$8 to $10 billion *per year*.[5] However, to focus only on four years of Yanukovych-nomics was to miss the deeper currents in place in Ukraine since before the fall of the Soviet Union, both political and economic.

In the first instance, Yanukovych was not the corrupter of the Ukrainian political system – he was a child of it. The institutions and system itself in Kyiv were already broken long before Yanukovych was appointed vice head of the Donetsk 3 Administration in 1996, with the early presidential administrations of the two Leonids (Kuchma and Kravchuk) already placing Ukraine's political system on a dangerous path. The most accurate description of the political jockeying following the independence of Ukraine was "rapacious individualism," a phrase coined by political scientist Martin Shefter (1976), where political institutions are defined by weak loyalties within the political elite, but, paradoxically, strong official powers vested in the executive branch (and especially, in Ukraine's case, in the office of the president). Under this system in Ukraine, there was an incentive for "rampant use of government for personal enrichment" (as amply demonstrated) due to the reality that the "executive was relatively susceptible to defection by allies in the face of perceived vulnerability" (Way 2005: 194). Thus, under such a volatile and short-sighted system, support needed to be shored up immediately, often via extra-legal means, with favors traded and fortunes made quickly. This system also left few politicians in Ukraine untainted, since all had a vested interest in the patronage continuing, a reality that crippled the reformist government of Yushchenko after the Orange Revolution and prevented any meaningful reforms; as Arel (2005) noted, the judicial system in particular continued to

---

[5] Anders Aslund, "Payback time for the Yanukovych 'family,'" *Kyiv Post*, December 13, 2013, www.kyivpost.com/opinion/op-ed/anders-aslund-payback-time-for-the-yanuko vych-family-333567.html, accessed June 24, 2013.

be dominated by politics, with only the political leanings of its targets changed.

In this environment, the political institutions necessary to create a modernized Western democracy were unable to grow, meaning that the transition from Soviet-era structures resulted in a partial institutional vacuum. While some of the trappings of democracy existed (such as elections), and other imported political institutions such as a modern constitution were sought after, for the most part ministries and the state administration followed a particular patron rather than becoming an impartial bureaucracy. Indeed, like many other countries in the post-Soviet sphere (and as in Ukraine's own immediate past), the neglect of proper political institutions was a direct consequence of the primacy of personality in Ukrainian political life; proximity to the leader determined success, and so there was no incentive for creating lasting administrative structures underneath the executive. As throughout the post-Soviet space, initiative was frowned upon and codification discouraged, with informal mechanisms taking the place of democratic institutions. The ministries and administrations and parliament may have been present, but, in the phrasing of Jean Baudrillard (1981), they were only simulacra, empty buildings, masking the absence of reality.

While the corruption and excesses of Yanukovych from 2010 to 2014 were the most visible manifestations of the institutional rot at the heart of the political state of Ukraine, other flaws in the country's institutional structure were rapidly exposed as Ukraine's Maidan revolution segued into foreign invasion. In April 2014, supported by clandestine Russian troops, cities in eastern Ukraine came under assault from heavily armed and trained "pro-Russian separatists." Already, Crimea had been occupied by Russian army regulars and annexed by Vladimir Putin under a similar pretense of "democracy," and now it appeared that the same was going to happen to the eastern, predominantly Russian-speaking regions of the country. Carried out under a shroud of subterfuge and deception, the Russian incursion was made all the easier by the collapse of the organs of law and order in the region.

In post-Soviet Ukraine, it was unclear for years who the police were serving and whom they were protecting, other than themselves (in Ivković's (2003) memorable phrase, it appeared their existence was merely to "serve and collect"). Polese (2008), for example, described the complex transactions that occurred during a routine traffic stop in Ukraine: financial payments are not always necessary, depending upon the situation, but interactions and the possibility of a bribe (or tribute, or "voluntary offer") are conditioned on the broader institutional framework, the personality of the specific officer, and the economic calculations of the officer and the detainee. This scenario played itself out across the country, with opinion polls consistently finding that (next to the judiciary), the police were perceived as the most corrupt institution in Ukraine (Transparency International 2011). This perception even fed back into the public's behavior, as Čábelková and Hanousek (2004) noted that the pervasive view of the Ukrainian police as irredeemably corrupt made it *more* likely for members of the public to offer a bribe.

Thus, years of institutionalized corruption, lack of respect for rule of law, and being enmeshed in a system that offered little incentive for honesty meant that, when the system was called upon to perform its basic functions, it collapsed. As the separatist movement throughout eastern Ukraine gained momentum in early 2014, supported both directly and indirectly by Moscow, local police commanders were at best apathetic and at worst complicit in the unrest. Indeed, rather than enforcing the laws of the country or protecting where they could not arrest, the vast majority of police stood idly by while public buildings were seized or vandalized, violence perpetrated, and the laws of the country broken; or, worse, some defected wholesale to the Russian side.[6] The reality of the hollowed-out institution of the police became apparent for all to see, with the failure to build the proper democratic institutions now threatening the viability of the entire country.

Of course, it wasn't just the political realities that threatened Ukraine, for a stronger and richer country could survive and, in reality, be more attractive to eastern Ukrainians than a sclerotic and authoritarian Russian state. Here too, however, Ukraine had failed to build the economic institutions that were necessary to lead the country from Soviet stagnation to free-market prosperity. All transition countries saw a dramatic drop in output that corresponded with the implementation of reforms, as the new institutions to facilitate a market economy took over from the Soviet-era bureaucracies; termed the "transformational recession" (Kornai 1994), the plummet in growth rates was necessary as the economy reoriented itself and investment began to flow along market-determined, rather than plan-determined lines. In contrast, however, Ukraine's economic underperformance occurred because of

---

[6] Simon Shuster, "Ukrainian policemen stand by as pro-Russian separatists seize control," *Time Magazine*, April 29, 2014, http://time.com/81475/ukrainian-policemen-stand-by-as-pro-russian-separatists-seize-control/.

a *lack* of these reforms. As de Menil and Woo (1994: 9) noted, "Ukraine offers a pure case study of what happens to a transition economy when reform is delayed. Between December 1991 and the autumn of 1994, a succession of [economic] reform plans fell victim to political stalemate." Kaufmann and Kaliberda (1996) were more scathing in their assessment of the transition, correctly highlighting that "until the end of 1994, Ukraine had not had a sustained attempt at economic liberalization ... state-imposed restrictions, interventions and distortions in the foreign exchange, trade, and pricing regimes, were extreme over much of the late-1991 to 1994 period."

The economic stagnation was not just limited to the early transition period, however, as is evidenced by the state of Ukraine's finances by the time Yanukovych had fled to southern Russia. Other economic indicators, beyond the macroeconomic aggregates cited above, were just as abysmal: for example, in the World Bank's Doing Business Indicators, which represent the overall business climate of a country, Ukraine did not fare well, coming in 140th out of 183 countries in the 2013 survey (better than Algeria, ranked at 151st, but worse than countries such as Bangladesh, Cambodia, India, or the Philippines). In terms of overall competitiveness, as compiled by the World Economic Forum's Global Competitiveness Report (GCR), Ukraine's position was also disappointing, with Iran, Lao PDR, and Tunisia coming ahead of Kyiv. Other subjective metrics of economic institutions, some two decades on from transition, continued to lag behind other European countries, with the European Bank for Reconstruction and Development (EBRD) noting that enterprise restructuring in Ukraine had shown little progress in strengthening competition and corporate governance (compared to countries such as the Czech Republic, which graduated out of EBRD assistance altogether). Similarly, the Heritage Foundation's Index of Economic Freedom (IEF) marked Ukraine as a "repressed" economy in 2013, with property rights in particular stagnating at 30 points out of a possible 100.

Clearly, Ukraine's economic prospects by 2014 were not rosy even without revolution and invasion. By any measure, one can see that Yanukovych (and, by extension, the Russians) did not hollow out the independent state of Ukraine in a brief period beginning in 2013, or even from 2010. By virtue of its policies over the previous twenty-three years and stretching back even earlier, the institutions that made up the political and economic system of the country were already hollow. Ukraine was a Potemkin village of what a market economy was supposed to look like but with nothing actually behind it. Institutional rot was the direct reason for the country's predicament, and unless those proper institutions were brought into being, the economy would continue to limp along as a hybrid of capitalism and communism, of law and lawlessness, and reality and simulacra.

FROM SOLIDARITY TO SUBSIDIARITY

Heading west by car, across lands that were formerly Polish but (in an eerie echo of today) annexed by a Soviet dictator in times of crisis, the Polish border is a mere 300 miles away from Kiev. However, crossing the border into Poland may be the equivalent of traveling across worlds, or perhaps, more accurately, across the past and into the future.

The first thing one notices, to be sure, are the roads. The quality improves dramatically on the Polish side of the border; as the former *Financial Times'* head of the Warsaw bureau, Jan Cienski, noted while traveling in the other direction for the Euro 2012 football matches, "the first impression one gets of Ukraine is based on the truly enormous potholes on the main road from the border to L'viv."[7] Expanding more of the differences in infrastructure, Cienski goes on to say,

Although Poland still lags behind Western Europe when it comes to highways, most roads have been modernized and resurfaced – creating a strikingly smoother driving experience. That is in large measure a result of the billions of euros flowing into Poland as part of the EU's structural funds program. The roads in Ukraine look like a lot the ones in Poland two decades ago ... In L'viv, many of the city's streets are a barely-drivable cobblestone that looks to have last been fixed before the war, while ambitious urban transit plans for the tournament look far from ready. East of L'viv, the sight of a horse-drawn cart draws barely a glance, and fields are dotted with farmers walking behind horse-drawn ploughs – views that used to be ubiquitous in Poland but are now a rarity – even in the country's poorest areas.[8]

When one finally traverses the 160-odd kilometers of smooth tarmac to the capital of Poland, the differences with Ukraine expand far beyond merely the quality of the roads. Indeed, coming into Warsaw, the break with the Soviet-ruled past can be seen from nearly every point in the city. From 1955 onward, Warsaw's skyline was dominated by the Palace of Culture and Science (Pałac Kultury i Nauki), a "gift" from the Soviet

---

[7] Jan Cienski, "Poland and Ukraine: miles to go," beyondbrics blog, *Financial Times*, May 2, 2011, http://blogs.ft.com/beyond-brics/2011/05/02/poland-and-ukraine-miles-to-go/, accessed June 28, 2014.

[8] Ibid.

Union that mimicked Stalin's "seven sisters" that proliferate in Moscow. The Palace still stands in Warsaw, across from the train station, but it no longer owns the sky; surrounded by glass skyscrapers that come close to its height, the Palace is now a reminder of worse times that have blessedly passed. Moreover, the building donated by the murderous Stalin himself, the man who helped engineer Poland's dismemberment in World War II and who ordered the execution of tens of thousands of Poles at Katyn alone, has taken a bit of revenge against its upbringing. Besides hosting numerous decadent capitalist rock bands in the years after Stalin's death (the Rolling Stones played the Palace's concert hall in 1967), and housing numerous businesses, cinemas, and pubs inside its brown walls (Murawski 2011), the exterior of the building can also reflect the conscience of the nation; in a bit of irony, the symbol of Soviet domination of the region was lit up in blue and yellow in April 2014 to support the Ukrainians across the border that were still, to some extent, under that domination.

These astonishing changes to Poland in such a short period of time may only be truly evident to people who knew Poland before 1989, when the country was afflicted by the standard communist issues; to the casual observer, Warsaw is just another European capital, slightly poorer than Brussels and not as enormous as Berlin, but otherwise pleasant like a Helsinki or Vienna. The fact that Warsaw *is* just another European capital, however, is a testament to the successful economic transformation of the previous quarter-century. Poland's transformation was not easy, although from the vantage point of twenty-five years and with other postcommunist countries as comparators, it does appear that Poland escaped many of the difficulties of other nations. Key contributors to this success were the policies put in place at the beginning of the transition period. Unlike Ukraine's halting economic changes or its ossified political system, Poland underwent a rapid series of reforms under Finance Minister Leszek Balcerowicz that made the transformation appear irreversible.

The results of these policies can be seen not only in the roads or the Warsaw skyline, but in a battery of impressive economic statistics that stand out on their own. In the first instance, Poland's GDP has grown every year since 1991 (see Figure 1.2), one of the few countries in Europe that can make that boast, in tandem with a wave of foreign investment. While the transformational recession in Poland resulted in a sharp decline in output in the first two years of transition, Poland recovered much more quickly than other countries (indeed, many observers feel that the output decline was overstated due to the notoriously shaky nature of socialist

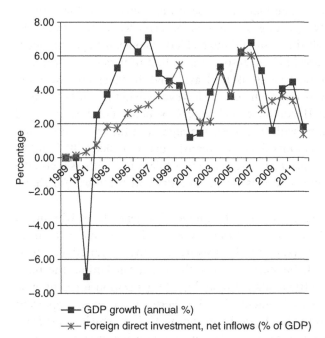

Figure 1.2 Poland, Main Macroeconomic Indicators, 1989–2012
Source: World Bank World Development Indicators.

statistics and the fact that new private sector activity was undercounted in the new statistics). Although Poland's performance in the 2000s has been anything but consistent, this mirrors the rest of Europe, which has seen the boom years of 2003–2007 followed by the global financial crisis. In many respects, looking at the macroeconomic aggregates, Poland is indeed just another European country.

At the microeconomic level as well, Poland has actually transitioned from its communist past. Unlike Ukraine and, further east, Russia, which still has immense issues in creating a conducive business climate, Poland ranks forty-fifth in the world on the World Bank's Doing Business indicators for 2014. Similarly, Poland comes in forty-sixth in the world in the World Economic Forum's Global Competitiveness Report (GCR), ahead of other star transition performers such as the Czech Republic and Lithuania (and ahead of laggard European economies such as Portugal). Perhaps more importantly, there is also a definite cultural shift away from the society that communism engendered. Whereas Ukraine continues to adhere more to Russian social conventions (e.g., less personal space and more winner-take-all), Poland has a more ordered and Western approach to society in general, one that can be seen most sharply in the younger members of society. Queuing is a common occurrence, people move to the side to let others off the tram (although elderly people, brought up under communism, are less likely to respect the notion of personal space), and younger people almost all speak (at least) English. Poles are also more satisfied with the way that their country has evolved: in the EBRD's "Life in Transition" Survey II, conducted in late 2010, 56 percent of those surveyed said they were happy with their lives, the highest in the transition region and an increase of 5 points since the precrisis survey of 2006 (EBRD 2011). Perceptions of corruption are also very low, while trust in others is also the highest in the region and trust in the country's institutions also shows a steady increase.

These changes have translated to a huge divergence from Ukraine in the orientation of the country, toward Western Europe and away from Russia. Poland now stands firmly ensconced in the supranational institutions of the West, including NATO, the European Union, the Bank for International Settlements (BIS), and the Organization for Economic Cooperation and Development (OECD). Perhaps the most important of these organizations has been the European Union, which, apart from the money used to finance the roads, gave the Polish government a goal to strive for after the pain of stabilization had faded away and the country had settled into the normal issues of economic policy. In the first years of transition, the objective was to remove the communist edifice and begin life as a normal capitalist country. With the second decade of transition, the goal became to be a member of Europe and part of the EU.

Poland's transition was impressive by any standard, but perhaps was even more successful because it was so unexpected. Indeed, predictions of the ultimate results that Poland was able to achieve would have seemed farfetched to an observer in the late 1980s, especially in comparison to Ukraine. Poland had gone through the trauma of martial law from 1981 to 1983, with curfews, detentions, and tanks rolling through the streets of major cities. In contrast, the Ukrainian SSR remained stable and without the major disruptions seen even in other Soviet republics throughout the 1980s (such as Armenia, Azerbaijan, Estonia, Georgia, and Lithuania, which all had protests, riots, or outright conflict during the decade). Even at the most basic level, defining the territory of the state, Ukraine's prospects were brighter: Ukraine had been secure in its current borders since the end of the Second World War (and the signing of the Budapest Memorandum in 1994, which denuclearized the country, gave security assurances regarding its territorial integrity). By contrast, it wasn't until 1990 that Poland and the reunified German nation signed a treaty recognizing *de jure* the *de facto* borders that had been in place since the end of World War II.

This is not to say that Poland's transition is complete, nor is it a suggestion that Poland is a picture-perfect example of a functioning market economy. There is some debate as to how much EU membership has helped, and if Poland would have continued along its growth path even if it had not acceded to the EU; as a former advisor at the Ministry of Privatization in the 1990s remarked to me, "Poland has converged with the EU politically, but not economically. It's the worst of both worlds." Moreover, by 2014, the country's political institutions in particular were showing some signs of wear and tear, with politicians being repeatedly exposed for the infelicitous things they said when they thought they were in private; in 2006, a secret recording of former prime minister Józef Oleksy revealed the dirtier side of Polish politics, while in 2014, a similar recording from National Bank of Poland head Marek Belka revealed how much the central bank was planning to interfere in the political life of the country in order to get better economic policy. Even in economics, where Poland was a star performer, there are some low points, including overly stringent labor policies and, most egregiously, a nationalization of half of the private pension funds in the country in order to fill the government's budgetary holes.

Despite the recent issues, Poland continues to outperform Ukraine by any metric. Perhaps there is no greater indicator of Poland's success *vis-à-vis* its eastern neighbor than the preponderance of Ukrainians who have voted with their feet. After a liberalization of Poland's immigration policy, including the development of a new class of temporary worker, in 2012 "Ukrainian citizens were granted over 223,000 permits of this kind and a further 137,000 in the first half of 2013."[9] Additionally, according to the OECD, approximately 10,000 Ukrainians immigrate to Poland every year, with no intention of returning to their homeland. Finally, it is important to note that the stream of immigrants and *Gastarbeiter* is only in one direction: while Ukrainian statistics on this point are hard to come by, as of 2001 (the last census), there were only 1,091 Poles who had immigrated to Ukraine in total, and the Migration Policy Center

---

[9] Marta Jaroszewicz, "Ukrainians' EU migration prospects," OSW (Centre for Eastern Studies, Poland) Commentary, February 25, 2014, http://www.osw.waw.pl/en/publikacje/osw-commentary/2014-02-25/ukrainians-eu-migration-prospects#_ftn2, accessed June 26, 2014.

(2013:2) notes that "evidently the stocks of immigrants have remained consistent since 2001." Poland is a preferred destination, while Ukraine is not.

INSTITUTIONS: THE NEW ECONOMIC REVOLUTION

The key question regarding the divergence of Poland and Ukraine is, of course, why? How could two countries that shared similar linguistic, cultural, economic, and political heritages diverge so wildly in economic performance in such a short span of time? Why did Poland of 1989 become the Poland of 2014, and why did the Ukraine of 1991 not move much beyond this starting point?

The main argument of this book is that institutions, and more specifically the evolution or neglect of the particular institutions needed for a market economy, explain the economic divergence between Ukraine and Poland. Put simply, in Poland the necessary economic and political institutions were put in place or spontaneously emerged at an early time in the country's economic transformation, thus allowing for the creation of a viable and vibrant market. By contrast, Ukraine had an unsuccessful transition, in that it did not transition in the early years at all away from a communist, plan-oriented political and economic system; avoiding stabilization and giving no hint that communism was dead and gone, the necessary institutions for growth and freedom failed to emerge. This has had dire consequences for Ukraine's economy and society. The problems discussed above and the daily news from eastern Ukraine show that the country's very existence may be at stake.

The theoretical framework for this book draws on recent advances in economic theory, as well as a revisiting of some old concepts in economics that had fallen by the wayside during much of the twentieth century. In particular, institutional economics and research into institutions as causes of the wealth or poverty of nations is only just re-emerging after a long slumber to become part of mainstream economic thought. The subdiscipline of institutional economics had its first heyday in the early 1900s, with economists such as Thorsten Veblen, John R. Commons, and Walton Hamilton arguing that "the proper subject-matter of economic theory *is* institutions," indistinguishable from any other conception of economic theory (Walton 1919: 313). As Walton (1919: 314) went on to further explain, institutional economics went beyond the idea of rational actors to include the context in which economic decisions were shaped; he argued:

It is not enough to assert with the neo-classicists that one receives the value of his services in the market; for, if matters subject to control are changed, he will still receive the value of his services, but he may pocket a different sum. He must understand, in addition, the conventions of competition, of contract, of property, of inheritance, of the distribution of opportunity which make incomes what they are.

However, with the advent of the boom of the 1920s and the bust of the 1930s culminating in the Great Depression, neoclassical and Keynesian economics vied for supremacy in explaining the world around us. Institutional economics, more focused on the psychological underpinnings of human economic behavior (Veblen 1898), faded into the background quickly and almost entirely disappeared from the economics mainstream after World War II (Rutherford 2001). Part of the reason for this decline was the descriptive, rather than prescriptive, nature of institutional economics, which made it pale against more activist approaches such as Keynesianism. These other economic schools appeared to be more in tune with the economic *zeitgeist*, as well as offering activist solutions to continuing issues in the developed economies.

But a further issue that surrounded institutional economics was the imprecise nature of the concept. What exactly was an institution anyway? In normal economic parlance, "institutions" were often treated as all-encompassing, slow-moving, but not generally observable, an attitude that made empirical approaches very difficult. Indeed, for too many economists, the concept of "institutions" was the unexplained variance of empirical analysis, the intangible factors that were omitted but still exerted an influence on outcomes. The lack of a consensus definition of institutions at the theoretical level thus hampered the broader influence of institutional analysis within the discipline, as mathematical modeling and econometrics became to be more prominent as tools of economic science. If everything could have been an institution, then it was only proper to think of institutions in an econometric sense as the residual of empirical analysis, rather than try to construct a detailed model for a theoretically vague concept.

Coupling the idea of institutional economics as a descriptive science with a lack of precision, early institutional economists were drawn to a very situational-specific form of analysis, with little scope for generalization; in the words of legendary economist Ronald Coase, the original institutional economists were "men of great intellectual stature, but they were anti-theoretical, and without a theory to bind together their collection of facts, they had very little that they were able to pass on"

(Coase 1998: 72). Put another way, if all institutional development was a specific product of a specific time and place, even the study of, say, institutional genesis in Poland could offer no clues for broader economic development or growth.

The re-emergence of institutional analysis in the 1990s sought to bring more theoretical rigor to the idea of institutions, while continuing the earlier emphasis on the primacy of human behavior in economics. Labeled the "new institutional economics" (or NIE, to separate it from the "old institutional economics" of Veblen, Hamilton, and Commons), this modern institutionalist approach grew from the same soil as old institutional economics, evolving out of dissatisfaction with prevailing economic orthodoxy. However, unlike the old institutional approaches, NIE sought to extend (rather than supplant) neoclassical economics, defining "itself as an attempt to extend the range of neoclassical theory by explaining the institutional factors traditionally taken as givens, such as property rights and governance structures" Rutherford (2001: 187).

Spearheaded by Nobel laureate Douglass North and led by luminaries such as Oliver Williamson, Elinor Ostrom, and Harold Demsetz, NIE retained the old institutionalist emphasis on transactions and transaction costs (given life by Ronald Coase's lifetime of theoretical and empirical work) while adding more theoretical and empirical grounding on institutional change (Hodgson 1998), the idea of bounded rationality (Williamson 2000), and a focus on how institutions are created and why "inefficient" institutions may survive (Acemoglu 2006). Most importantly, the NIE school focused on institutions as "the rules of the game" (North 1990: 3), giving life to new explorations of property rights, other contracting mechanisms, and the interplay of political and economic institutions in determining economic outcomes (Hartwell 2013).

While still nominally a "heterodox" approach to economics, new institutionalist tenets have been broadly adopted by mainstream researchers across the economic spectrum, becoming "one of the liveliest areas in our discipline" (Matthews 1986: 903). Prominent and top-tier journals regularly carry institutional research forward, and to suggest a role for institutions in economic outcomes is so accepted as part of the mainstream that a major debate in the academic literature can erupt among prominent economists Jeffrey Sachs and Dani Rodrik on *how much* institutions matter, not *if* they do (Rodrik et al. 2004; Sachs 2003). By lending insights on the role of culture and history, while filling in the gaps in other approaches to economic analysis, new institutional economics has driven forward our understanding of human action and how it causes an economy to operate.

INSTITUTIONAL SYSTEMS AS A DETERMINANT FOR ECONOMIC OUTCOMES

As the tenets of institutionalist analysis have permeated more deeply into the economics profession, we have also improved our general understanding of the definition, genesis, nature, and especially the complexity of institutions in relation to an economic system. While North's (1990) assertion that institutions are the rules of the game is the classic definition guiding institutional analyses, institutions are in fact much more refined and complex creatures that exhibit not only a framework of rules, but a means to enforce them; as I have noted elsewhere (Hartwell 2013: 17), institutions are different from mere social norms in that they encompass "constraints and behavioral guidelines [that can be] enforced by either formal or informal means external to the individual." To be more formal, as Searle (2005) structured it, institutions exhibit three distinct traits:

1. *Collective intentionality*, or enmeshing the action of an individual in a broader social framework by necessity (Searle uses such simple examples as walking a dog, which is an example of cross-species intentionality, or playing a violin within an orchestra);
2. *Assignment of function*, or the "capacity to impose functions on objects where the object does not have the function, so to speak, intrinsically but only in virtue of the assignment of function" (Searle 2005: 7). In this conception, institutions both embed individuals within a social structure but also allow for the imposition of function on a collective basis, beyond the individual. However, the most important attribute, that takes an institution beyond a mere set of "social facts" is
3. *Assignment of status.* It is not enough that a context be inherent for a specific human action, nor is it sufficient for a physical object to be assigned a specific function. For an institution to be defined as such, it must also "assign functions to objects where the objects cannot perform the function in virtue of their physical structure alone, but only in virtue of the collective assignment or acceptance of the object or person as having a certain status and with that status a function" (Searle 2005: 8). Thus, an institution needs acceptance (status) by the individual, working within a collective, in order to be able to both

influence behavior but also to enforce sanctions against non-compliance with this behavior.

Of course, the exact function of an institution – in regard to which social fact it has coalesced around – is particular to that institution and may even shift as an institution evolves. Moreover, the channels that they operate through are also variegated: depending upon the particular institution, they may either be concerned with constraining human action, as with a police department, or they may be designed to facilitate certain behaviors, as with language, designed to enable communication (Hodgson 2006). In some circumstances, an institution may do both simultaneously: for example, property rights are meant to forestall infringement by another person on one's property (a constraining action), while at the same time they also enable commerce by reducing informational and transactional costs (a facilitating action).

Furthermore, the sphere in which institutions operate is also differentiated by institution, with some institutions overlapping into many different facets of life while others are concerned with narrow and well-defined ends. A simple taxonomy developed by myself in earlier work (Hartwell 2013), building on work from North (1990) and Acemoglu et al. (2005), simplified institutional emphasis into one of three spheres: political, economic, or social institutions. Political institutions are primarily concerned with the distribution of political power in a society and how it is exercised; while these institutions undoubtedly have direct economic consequences, as we shall see throughout this book, as well as indirect effects via shaping economic institutions (as Myrdal (1954) noted), these economic effects are second-order to the power structure they engender. Similarly, economic institutions attempt to maximize the economic utility of the parties to the institution, although their impact may not necessarily be harmonized with broader goals of growth or societal optima, as these institutions may be either "market-creating," "market-stabilizing," or "market-dampening" (Hartwell 2013). Finally, social institutions may also have political or economic effects, but they are not solely concerned with these spheres of influence and instead tend to be focused at the level of the individual. The classic example of a social institution is organized religion (McCleary and Barro 2006), where an institution such as the Catholic Church may have once been a powerful (or the sole) political institution in a country but now throughout most of Europe has been relegated to matters involved in the next life rather than this one.

While Searle's ontology of institutions and my taxonomy of their influence provide us with a useful (if highly theoretical) approach to what an institution is and how it can influence behavior, a much more pressing issue for economists is how institutions actually come to be. That is, if we know that institutions are shapers of individual and collective action, how do specific institutions actually arise? This issue also begins to cut to the heart of the issue at hand regarding Poland and Ukraine, as there was much talk of the "building" of institutions in transition economies (Kołodko 1999, Offe 1998, World Bank 2002). However, "building" institutions is only one way in which institutions come to be, as the reality is that institutions can be built, they can spontaneously arise, or they can start life with one intended function and then mutate suddenly into something very different. In fact, the whole idea of "building" institutions obviously only refers to such formal institutions as parliamentary democracy or a monetary regime, as informal institutions such as language, customary property rights, or civil society spring forward from culture and the prevailing zeitgeist and are very difficult to impose externally. By their very nature, some institutions can only be created or arise along a specific time line, a demarcation that Roland (2004) called "slow-moving" and "fast-moving" institutions.

Finally, institutions are complex creatures in their functioning. As human creations, institutions are influenced by human action, which is rarely linear or even rational (from a strict neoclassical sense, in that it is driven by equilibrium or maximizing utility along only one plane). And institutions are not only burdened by their own history, more importantly they function in a larger institutional system that means that institutions are constantly bumping against, changing, and being changed by other institutions. In any given economic system, there may be institutions that are wholly dependent upon others (such as a central bank, which could not exist without a central government), institutions that arise to service the gaps created between other institutions (one need only look at "payday lenders," which cater to clientele underserved by other financial institutions), and even institutions that exist simultaneously with directly opposite reasons for existence (such as an organized police force versus organized crime).

The complex web of institutions within a society brings us to the key point of this book, in that institutional change (or stagnation) should lead directly to economic outcomes. It is fair to say that most institutions function internally according to economic precepts, the paramount ones being willingness to pay (what are the benefits of enforcement versus their costs?) and transaction costs (how difficult will it be to reform an institution?). But it is also easy to see that all institutions eventually have an economic *impact* within the boundaries of their particular institutional system, be it at the national, regional, or local level. Even just one institution such as the parliamentary assembly or property rights, operating according to its own tenets, influences the way in which transactions are concluded, commercial operations carried out, time and money correctly priced, and savings versus consumption decisions reached. And when taken collectively, this web of institutions has a feedback effect that influences the manner in which an economic system develops. In reality, as this brief overview should show, there is no real distinction between an economic system and the institutions encapsulated therein; they are one and the same. No institution stands outside of the economic system, no matter how much it may try.

EXPLAINING POLAND AND UKRAINE

This reality, that all institutions make up an institutional system which is synonymous with the economic system of a country, which then in turn drives that country's economic outcomes – this is the key idea animating this book. If there is no difference between the institutions that make up a country and that country's economic system, then we come undeniably to the conclusion, as Potts (2007: 341) correctly noted, that "as institutions evolve, so do economic systems."

And it is here that the rise of institutional analysis, its incorporation into mainstream economic theory, and the broader tenets of how institutions at all levels relate to economic outcomes, creates a perfect framework for examining the divergent economic outcomes of Poland and Ukraine. This is simply because transition and the whole concept of economic transition away from communism *was* institutional change, nothing more and nothing less. The end of communism as a political and economic system was not a sudden shift to a higher growth path or an increase in consumption or goods on the shelves; the economic transformation was solely concerned with changing the institutions in the society from those that facilitated central planning (including a single-party state, centralized bureaus directing the economy, communal property, and directed credit) to those that enabled a market economy (private property, a dominant private sector, multiparty democracy, and a capitalist financial sector). Under this reality, transition only occurred where there was this institutional change. If a country kept Soviet-style central planning (such as in Uzbekistan), we can say there was political *independence* but there was no economic *transformation*, and it is the transformation that is the explanatory factor of economic outcomes.

Extending this further, we can then logically see that economic performance, the focus of so much debate in the early transition period, was merely a second-order effect of the transformative process. Economic growth, which should be consistently higher under a market economy due to better resource allocation and efficiency, would return only if the market economy itself was able to grow; that is, the institutions were in place. However, institutional change itself is a disruptive process, as markets continually need to adjust, resource allocations change, and planning and time horizons shift depending upon the credibility of the commitment to institutional change. Where institutional change is a volatile process or, worse still, where institutional change lurches from one direction to another, no economic progress is possible. Institutional change was the crux of transition, but it was a unidirectional change (indeed, no one spoke of "transition" as creating a more perfect communist state or improving the next five-year plan). Stagnation in creating these market institutions meant that transformation was incomplete, but continued volatility and lack of direction in policies and institutional progress meant that the transformation was becoming even harder to achieve.

These insights from the institutional literature, as well as many others regarding the nature of institutional change, the interplay between political and economic institutions, the difficulties of institutional genesis in transition, and the effects of culture on institutions, serve as the backdrop for examining Poland and Ukraine over the past twenty-three years. Drawing on previous empirical work I have done in the economics of institutions in transition (Hartwell 2013), this book will thus examine four overarching themes related to the institutional facets of transition in Central and Eastern Europe:

1. What Were the Initial Conditions of Institutions in Poland and Ukraine?

A large proportion of the early transition literature focused on the differing legacies of the Central and Eastern European (CEE) countries as opposed to the countries of the former Soviet Union (see Åslund, Boone, and Johnson 1996; Popov 2000). Indeed, whether or not a country belonged to the Soviet Union was a huge and accurate indicator of the extent of aggregate distortions in the economy, presumably including institutions. Building on this research, the first portion of this book will focus on the initial conditions in Poland and Ukraine and how institutions were both more and less different from what conventional wisdom would assume.

In the first instance, we will explore the long-term institutional history of Poland and Ukraine, drawing on new research regarding the development of institutions in the nineteenth century and earlier, and highlighting Poland's terrible initial conditions for two centuries (and not just, as Fischer and Sahay (2000) noted, Poland's relative backwardness at the start of transition). More important, we will further clarify "institutions" in a modern market economy (again with reference to Hartwell 2013), examining closely the precommunist era and especially the differing policies pursued in the late Soviet era, and how this may have influenced institutional paths in the late twentieth century. The end result of this inquiry will be to demonstrate that there was "path dependence" for institutional evolution in both countries, as the similar historical and governance factors may have meant very different outcomes in any case due to human action. In short, in line with research done during the second decade of transition (Falcetti et al. (2002) and Fischer and Sahay (2004)), initial conditions and even long-term historical factors were not destiny, but may offer a clue to where and how institutions evolved in the following two decades.

2. How Did Political Institutions Evolve in the Two Countries?

While much ink has been spilled on the political development of Ukraine (Åslund (2009) being the best example), there has been very little examination in a comparative sense between Poland and Ukraine. Indeed, it is in the political institutions, both pre- and postcommunism, that we see some of the biggest divergences, tempered by surprising commonalities: for example, Poland and Ukraine actually share the exact same form of government, the semipresidential model, where the government is appointed by the president (who may be either ceremonial or the source of power), but a prime minister, belonging to a political party, also holds office. Through the chapters on political development, we will delve into the broader political environment in both countries, amalgamating two decades of multidisciplinary research, but looking at the development of politics and government as part of each country's institutional and cultural evolution as well.

Moreover, the examination in this book proposes to look at many different aspects of the political-institutional development of the two countries, including the evolution of democratic processes; an examination of executive constraints; and how Poland was able to rein in its president while Ukraine did not; changes in the constitution and how these came about post–Soviet rule; the relative calm of Poland versus the fits of mob rule in Ukraine; and how the political system in each country was affected by international events over the past two decades. This examination will be examined via both qualitative and quantitative methods, with reference to international indicators of governance and, where possible, econometric examination of policy and institutional volatility. Importantly, the examination of political institutions in the two countries will also focus on the differentiation between the *potential* political institutions represented by the legal framework and the *realized* institutions captured in the administration of the countries. This reality has haunted both Poland and Ukraine, and has been brought into view sharply during the crisis in Ukraine.

3. How Did Economic Institutions Evolve, and What Was the Role of the EU, in the Countries' Transition Paths?

The mirror image of the previous theme, this section will examine the various economic institutions that encompass a market economy and their evolutionary path in Poland and Ukraine. Building on our knowledge of contracting institutions and transaction costs as traced by great thinkers in new institutional economics, and using both standard and novel quantitative indicators, I will examine how property rights evolved in the two countries, how the judiciary (and corruption) operated, how macroeconomic policies contributed to or retarded the growth of institutions, and how the financial sector worked to influence transition. Most important, with a focus on the microeconomic changes that did (not) occur in Poland and Ukraine, I will place the institutional changes in each country in the context of their external environment, specifically how the goal of EU accession both helped and hindered institutional development. How do external institutions influence the growth of internal institutions? Are there cross-cultural currents that can impact institutional development? These ideas, while touched upon in the extant literature, will be brought more clearly into focus here.

4. What Can Be Done Today to Make Ukraine More like Poland?

Of course, while this is a backward-looking book, seeking to explain the divergence of two specific countries as a function of their institutional framework, it will also be firmly focused on the future, and especially in deriving policy guidelines for a (hopefully) transitioning Ukraine. But while the future of Ukraine is still being written – will it be a rump vassal state, at the mercy of Russia, or a re-unified country that is part of the EU? Or a neutral "Finlandized" federal state that is neither? – the recommendations of this book are salient, no matter what the outcome. The underlying theme of this book, made explicit in the final chapter, will be to examine where Ukraine can learn from its history and overcome its legacy to become a prosperous market-oriented economy. In short, if institutions were neglected in the Ukrainian transition, what can be done differently to foster the crucial market institutions? How can the EU, the West, and even Russia help in moving Ukraine along in its too-delayed transition? What does Ukraine have to do to reach Poland's level – and how can Poland stop from regressing back to a Ukraine-like state?

More than just a descriptive retelling of the post-Soviet paths of Ukraine and Poland, and going beyond a broader historical look at the two countries, this book's focus on institutions places it squarely within the realm of economic analysis. Indeed, through an examination of these four overarching questions, we will touch on many of the pressing broader issues in economics, including ideas of growth, institutions and institutional change, the role of culture, and the interplay between politics and economics. Thus, the recommendations derived from this analysis will be applicable not just to two larger-than-average-size countries in Europe but to all transition, developing, and developed economies. Moreover, this book will help to push forward the body of scholarship regarding our understanding of transitions via a much more in-depth qualitative analysis of two similarly situated countries, but also marrying this work with ground-breaking quantitative research. The discipline of quantitative institutional economics may only be in its infancy, but our analysis of Poland and Ukraine will help it to mature, if not to adulthood, at least to get it out of the crib. Finally, given the incomplete transition in the former Soviet countries east of Ukraine, first of all Russia but also including the Central Asian republics and some of the countries of the Caucasus, the examination contained herein will offer a way in which these economies can avoid becoming another Ukraine.

However, to talk about the recommendations in the introduction is to unfairly begin our story with its ending (in the immortal words of Number Two from the British television show *the Prisoner*, "that would be telling"). Like all stories, the institutional evolution of Poland and Ukraine actually begins in the distant past, and it is here where we must begin our journey.

References

Acemoglu, D. (2006). A simple model of inefficient institutions. *Scandinavian Journal of Economics*, 108(4), pp. 515–546.

Acemoglu, D., Johnson, S., and Robinson, J. A. (2005). Institutions as the fundamental cause of long-run growth. In Aghion, P., and Durlauf, S. (eds.), *Handbook of Economic Growth*: Volume 1A. North Holland: Elsevier, pp. 385–472.

Arel, D. (2005). Is the Orange revolution fading? *Current History*, 104 (684), pp. 325–330.

Åslund, A. (2009). *How Ukraine Became a Market Economy and Democracy*. Washington DC: Peterson Institute for International Economics.

Baudrillard, J. (1981). *Simulacra and Simulations*. In Poster, M. (ed.), *Jean Baudrillard: Selected Writings*. Stanford: Stanford University Press (1988).

Čábelková, I., and Hanousek, J. (2004). The power of negative thinking: corruption, perception and willingness to bribe in Ukraine. *Applied Economics*, 36(4), pp. 383–397.

Coase, R. (1998). The new institutional economics. *American Economic Review*, 88(2), pp. 72–74.

de Menil, G, and Woo, W. T. (1994) Introduction to a Ukrainian debate. *Economic Policy*, 9(supplement), pp. 9–15.

European Bank for Reconstruction and Development (2011). *Life in Transition Survey II*. London: EBRD.

Falcetti, E., Raiser, M., and Sanfey, P. (2002). Defying the odds: initial conditions, reforms, and growth in the first decade of transition. *Journal of Comparative Economics*, 30(2), pp. 229–250.

Fischer, S., and Sahay, R. (2000). *The Transition Economies after Ten Years*. IMF Working Paper No 00/30, February.

(2004). Transition economies: The role of institutions and initial conditions. *Festschrift in Honor of Guillermo A. Calvo*, April 15–16. Available at http://citeseerx.ist.psu.edu /viewdoc/download?doi=10.1.1.638.6663&rep=rep1&type=pdf.

Hamilton, W. H. (1919). The institutional approach to economic theory. *American Economic Review*, 9(1), pp. 309–318.

Hartwell, C. A. (2013). *Institutional Barriers in the Transition to Market: Explaining Performance and Divergence in Transition Economies*. Basingstoke, UK: Palgrave Macmillan.

Hodgson, G. M. (1998). The approach of institutional economics. *Journal of Economic literature*, 36(1), pp. 166–192.

(2006). What are institutions? *Journal of Economic Issues*, 40(1), pp. 1–25.

International Monetary Fund (2014). *2013 Article IV Consultation and First Post-Program Monitoring – Staff Report.* IMF Country Report No. 14/145, May.

Ivković, S. K. (2003). To serve and collect: Measuring police corruption. *Journal of Criminal Law and Criminology,* 93(2), pp. 593–650.

Kaufmann, D., and Kaliberda, A. (1996). Integrating the unofficial economy into the dynamics of post-socialist economies. In Kaminski, B. (ed.), *Economic Transition in Russia and the New States of Eurasia.* Vol. 8. New York: M. E. Sharpe.

Kołodko, G. W. (1999). Ten Years of Post-socialist Transition: Lessons for Policy Reforms. *Voprosy Economiki,* 9.

Kornai, J. (1994). Transformational recession: the main causes. *Journal of Comparative Economics,* 19(1), pp. 39–63.

Matthews, R. C. (1986). The economics of institutions and the sources of growth. *Economic Journal,* 96(384), pp. 903–918.

McCleary, R. M., and Barro, R. J. (2006). Religion and economy. *Journal of Economic Perspectives,* 20(2), pp. 49–72.

Migration Policy Centre (2013). *MPC – Migration Profile, Ukraine.* Florence: European University Institute. Available at www.migrationpolicycentre.eu/docs/migration_profiles/Ukraine.pdf.

Murawski, M. (2011). From iconicity to dominationality: The palace of culture and science in contemporary warsaw. *Informationen zur Modernen Stadtgeschichte,* 2, pp. 56–69.

Myrdal, G. (1954). *The Political Element in the Development of Economic Theory.* London: Routledge.

North, D. C. (1990). *Institutions, Institutional Change and Economic Performance.* Cambridge: Cambridge University Press.

Offe, C. (1998). Designing institutions in East European transitions. In Goodin, R.E. (ed.), *The Theory of Institutional Design.* Cambridge: Cambridge University Press, pp. 199–226.

Polese, A. (2008). 'If I receive it, it is a gift; if I demand it, then it is a bribe': On the local meaning of economic transactions in post-Soviet Ukraine. *Anthropology in Action,* 15(3), pp. 47–60.

Potts, J. (2007). Clarence Ayres Memorial Lecture: Evolutionary institutional economics. *Journal of Economic Issues,* 41(2), pp. 341–350.

Rodrik, D., Subramanian, A., and Trebb, F. (2004). Institutions rule: The primacy of institutions over geography and integration in economic development. *Journal of Economic Growth,* 9(2), pp. 131–165.

Roland, G. (2004). Understanding institutional change: fast-moving and slow-moving institutions. *Studies in Comparative International Development,* 38(4), pp. 109–131.

Rutherford, M. (2001). Institutional economics: then and now. *Journal of Economic Perspectives,* 15(3), pp. 173–194.

Sachs, J. (2003). *Institutions don't rule: direct effects of geography on per capita income.* NBER Working Paper No. 9490 (February).

Searle, J. R. (2005). What is an institution? *Journal of Institutional Economics,* 1(1), pp. 1–22.

Shefter, M. (1976). The emergence of the political machine: an alternate view. In Hawley, W. D., et al. (eds.), *Theoretical perspectives on urban politics.* Englewood Cliffs, NJ: Prentice Hall.

Transparency International (2011). *Global Corruption Barometer: Ukraine.* Berlin: Transparency International Press.

Way, L. A. (2005). Rapacious individualism and political competition in Ukraine, 1992–2004. *Communist and Post-Communist Studies*, 38(2), pp. 191–205.

Williamson, O. E. (2000). The new institutional economics: taking stock, looking ahead. *Journal of Economic Literature*, 38(3), pp. 595–613.

World Bank (2002). *World Development Report 2002: Building Institutions for Markets.* Washington DC: Oxford University Press.

Veblen, T. (1898) Why is economics not an evolutionary science? *Quarterly Journal of Economics*, 12(3), pp. 373–97.

2

A Brief Institutional History of Central Europe (Part One): Poland and Its Political Institutions to 1989

The story of Poland and Ukraine's economic divergence over the past twenty-five years begins not with the collapse of the Soviet Union, the first elections in Poland in 1989, or even in the 1980s with the imposition of martial law in Warsaw and the introduction of *glasnost* and *perestroika* to the Soviet Union. The tale of postcommunist economic performance is rooted in the development of institutions in the geographical territories that comprise modern-day Ukraine and Poland. Most important, it is traceable to the manner in which these territories were shaped by both internal cultural factors and the continuous external factors of invasion, partition, redrawn borders, and migration. In short, present-day Ukraine and Poland are a result of both modern policies and the shaping of centuries of institutional development and regression. It is in early modern Europe where the tale of institutional development in Central Europe must begin.

THE POLISH INSTITUTIONAL FRAMEWORK: FROM NOBLE LIBERTY TO COMMONWEALTH

When one considers the difficult road that all transition countries had to traverse, a glance at the history of Poland and Ukraine shows that their case may have been more difficult than most. But this history has been shared by other countries of Central and Eastern Europe, which for centuries have been a highway for invading armies moving either to the west or the east. As Eugeniusz Romer (1917:22) noted in the midst of the cataclysm of the Great War, Poland and the other countries of Central Europe both geographically and politically "figure as the transitional ground between the two great divisions of the Old World, the West and the East." With this shared broader history as a stomping ground for mightier powers, there

28

must thus be specific *internal* issues in each country's development, including the lingering effects of the particulars of successive invasions, which are crucial to understanding the path of institutional evolution in the countries of the region.

The early modern Polish state, beginning from its early years in the fourteenth century through to the Third Partition at the end of the eighteenth century, put in place the very sort of political framework that facilitates the ideas and attitudes necessary for a market economy. In its earlier incarnation as the Polish-Lithuanian Commonwealth, the land now known as Poland set the basis for such fundamental political institutions, including balance of powers and checks on the executive, that are commonly recognized in economic literature as crucial for growth. As Rodrigues (2010:122) correctly notes, the Polish-Lithuanian Commonwealth can be "linked to the institutional building of multi-national states and, subsequently, to the modern right of minorities, the development of regionalism, and federalism in the European states and in the European Union." Put in a more enthusiastic manner, Roháč (2008:209) proclaims that:

If Western Civilization ... rests on the recognition of individual rights that are inalienable and stem from human nature, if it requires a government that is subject to control and accountability, and if necessitates tolerance of people of different races and religions, then the Polish-Lithuanian Republic (1573–1795) offers a fascinating example of Western civilization at its best.

The development of these basic institutions, at a time when much of Europe was enthralled by absolutism, was rooted in the widespread cultural acceptance of the ideas of liberty and efficiency that underpin these institutions. As Anna Grześkowiak-Krwawicz (2012) noted in her recent excellent book on political thought in pre–Partition Poland, the idea of liberty, manifested in a constrained and balanced state, had developed as early as 1505, forming a basis for both political and economic development over the next three centuries. Political philosophers within the Polish-Lithuanian Commonwealth such as Andrzej Wolan (2010[1572]) and Łukasz Górnicki (writing in the late sixteenth century but unpublished until 1616) focused their writing on the idea of *wolność*, or freedom, as the fundamental basis of the Polish state (Gromelski 2013). For these philosophers, pursuit of freedom was based on a simple premise: self-determination, or the right to dispose of one's affairs as one saw fit. Grześkowiak-Krwawicz (2012) also notes that this idea, while driven by philosophers and the ruling elite, was in fact widespread across all social strata in the Commonwealth. Perhaps Polish philosopher Samuel Wysocki (1740) summed it up best when he said, "upon liberty, everyone's freedoms, happiness, and life hinges" (quoted in Grześkowiak-Krwawicz 2012:30).

This deep philosophical attachment to freedom meant that the divine right of kings was eschewed in favor of a focus on individuals and their will within a broader polity, but with the additional obligation of the individual to stand for and participate in freedom. Grześkowiak-Krwawicz (2012:31) correctly highlights this dual nature of Polish ideas of freedom, stressing that Poles cherished "the freedom to determine affairs for one-self *and* one's country" [emphasis mine]. Contemporary accounts from the Commonwealth also stressed the obligation of participating in political life, as, according to political philosopher Łukasz Opalinski (1641:35), "there can be no common good without joint effort and service"; shirking one's duty to defend freedom would result in Poland being "in jeopardy, together with the private freedom that you so love."

This seeming contradiction between self-determination on one hand and the responsibility to participate in the polity on the other was not a contradiction at all for Polish thinkers of the seventeenth and eighteenth centuries (nor for many Greek or Roman philosophers, such as Aristotle and Cicero, to whom Poles paid homage in their own writings). Indeed, in this view, participation in the nation's affairs was a necessary precondition for true freedom, as man could only be free when living in a free republic, invested in and participating in governance, where decisions were made on the basis of consensus rather than coercion.[1] But a free republic needed continuous defense, as there was a pervasive fear among the nobility and philosophers of freedom's evanescence: as another political philosopher of the twentieth century (who would also captivate the Poles) mentioned, "freedom is a fragile thing and is never more than one generation away from extinction."[2] Grześkowiak-Krwawicz (2012) calls our attention to the fact that Poles were overwhelmingly concerned with the republic being under assault

---

[1] A quasi-religious corollary to this argument was noted by Frost (2011), who calls attention to the prevailing idea in the sixteenth-century Commonwealth that man's basest desires caused him to become imprisoned, rather than free. True freedom only sprang from the exercise of self-determination, which included the ability to constrain one's own lustful pleasures. More a libertarian than libertine doctrine, this Polish conception of "political" liberty presaged the works of the American founding fathers, and in particular James Madison, writing in *Federalist* no. 51 on the nature of men and their lack of divinity.

[2] These words are of course from Ronald Reagan, spoken on the occasion of his inauguration as governor of California on January 5, 1967.

by despotism emanating from their own monarch rather than an external enemy (at least during the sixteenth and seventeenth century). This belief in latent tyranny also provided an argument in favor of civic responsibility, as participation in the regular affairs of the nation allowed citizens to protect their state against a capricious monarch.

Moreover, by ensuring that Polish citizens participated in their own governance, whatever policies or laws did arise were the result of the deliberation of free men and not dependent on the "eccentricities of a single autocrat," in the words of Speaker of the Parliament Antoni Małachowski in 1780.[3] To put this in modern terms (following Skinner (1998)), the "negative" liberty of being left alone by the government to pursue one's life was actually conditioned by the "positive" liberty of participating in common governance and freedom to determine the future. And, as an added bonus, such laws created by a free polity were also presumed to be less burdensome because they were enacted by the people themselves (Grześkowiak-Krwawicz draws on the writings of an anonymous politician from 1573 to make this very point).

A key point to note here is, although influenced by trends of the Enlightenment and interacting with the French and British thinkers that were to come later, the cultural bias in favor of liberty was endogenous to Poland and its people, rather than being imposed from abroad. Gromelski (2013) establishes that the Polish thinkers of the sixteenth century were deeply impressed by the humanist school, and, as today, the Polish elite were well-traveled throughout Europe, coming into contact with many different philosophical schools of thought. However, as Stone (2010:7) notes, "democratic ideals came to be typically Polish; democracy was never a foreign import that threatened the moral basis and unity of the Polish nation as it was for European opponents such as French monarchists . . . and Russian Slavophiles."

In fact, the Polish development of the idea of liberty advanced far beyond that of relatively more conservative thinkers in Germany to synthesize a new ideal of freedom independent of other European philosophers. This home-grown philosophy of freedom only grew stronger the more it interacted with an older, reactionary Europe and its increasingly antiquated ideals. As Cole (1999:2065) correctly observed, "each time the Polish people have been left to their own devices – i.e. between invasions by Germans, Austro-Hungarians, Swedes, and Russians – they have established increasingly democratic institutions and protected civil liberties."

---

[3] Quoted in Grześkowiak-Krwawicz (2012:33).

Indeed, perhaps the "Polish suspicion of government" (Stone 2010) was precisely due to their experience with these autocratic regimes as they stormed through Polish lands, upending property and indigenous institutions in service of a foreign master.

Most importantly for our purposes, these cultural and philosophical beliefs that arose in early modern Poland easily translated into broader informal and formal political institutions in the country throughout its history. Indeed, the entire existence of the Commonwealth from 1386 through 1568 was based on an informal political arrangement routed through an entirely social and voluntary contract: the wedding of Jogaila, the Grand Duke of Lithuania, to the reigning Queen Jadwiga of Poland. A prenuptial agreement but so much more, the so-called Union of Krewo laid out the responsibilities not only of the future spouses but their respective political obligations *vis à vis* Poland and Lithuania, forming the basis for the next two centuries of political power. As an informal agreement, it was necessarily vague on details and, more importantly, did not claim to settle centuries of Polish-Lithuanian rivalry overnight. But crucially, the Union of Krewo formed a basis that "was soon replaced by a long series of charters ... which in a process lasting from 1401 to 1569 gradually recognized the full equality of the grand duchy of Lithuania with the kingdom of Poland" (Halecki 1963:434).

Under the overarching and nascent Union of Poland and Lithuania, formal political institutions that were in their earliest forms began to evolve and flourish. Of these, perhaps none was as important as the *Sejm*, or parliament, and the regional bodies and assemblies associated with it. An outgrowth of the *wiec*, an assembly convened to discuss important topics that was popular throughout Slavic lands in the tenth and eleventh centuries, the first *Sejm* is reputed to have taken place in the town of Łęczyca in 1180 (Gloger (1896), although Gumplowicz (1867) notes that it may have taken place in 1179). Throughout the twelfth and thirteenth centuries, well before the unification of Poland (much less the Commonwealth), similar assembly-based political institutions began to proliferate: local assemblies of the nobility (*szlachta* in Polish) began to meet more frequently on matters of state, in parallel with a centralized advisory body for the Crown (the King's Council), which had permanent representation from the *szlachta* and the clergy (Górski et al. 1966). These two institutional strands started to intertwine in 1374 during the negotiations over royal succession at modern-day Košice, with the King's Council brokering the compromise that allowed Jadwiga to ascend the throne. However, as Górski et al. (1966) correctly note, the change in the succession line came at a price, as the *szlachta* of the provinces needed to be considered in any future move to raise revenue (the compromise removed the obligation of the nobility to pay tribute to the monarch). This reality led directly to the creation of "little *Sejms*" (*sejmiki*) in the various provinces, a mechanism for assembly of local nobles to consider royal requests for taxation.

Although the King's Council retained substantial powers in determining matters of state, especially during the reign of King Władysław Jagiełło, the young *sejmiki* became a formal institution via the Nieszawa Statutes in 1454 of King Kazimierz IV Jagiellończyk (Stone 2010). In fact, the Statutes shifted the balance of power away from the Council to the *sejmiki*, abolishing the authority of the castellan's court over the nobility and giving statutory power to the local *sejmiki* in regard to all military expeditions, taxation (Górski et al. 1966), and legislation (Stone 2010). Given the proclivities of Polish kings to deal at a local level (Stone 2001), and coupled with the need for immediate assistance in fighting the Prussians and the Teutonic Order, the decentralization of power to the local assemblies was a win-win situation for both the king and the *szlachta*.

The development of national political institutions did not abate, however, and in fact the development of regional bodies helped to push development of a national parliament (albeit at a much slower pace). With the Council waning in importance, need began to arise for an assembly similar to the *sejmiki* but in Piotrków or Kraków, where representatives of the *szlachta* could be more involved with the daily operations of the state (as well as keep tabs on the monarch). This institution, the true forerunner to the modern *Sejm* at the national level, is generally accepted as having been summoned by King Jan Olbracht in 1493 (Pirie 1995). This new parliament absorbed both of Poland's existing political institutions into a bicameral legislature consisting of a Senate, with eighty-one bishops and dignitaries (the upper house and heir to the King's Council), and a *Sejm*, comprised of fifty-four representatives from local *sejmiki* (the lower house). Regional *sejmiki* continued to operate, as before, but now had permanent representation at the royal court, dependent on their size (the number of envoys from a particular *voivodship* was usually between two and six representatives (Ganowicz 2013)).

The legal equality of the *Sejm* to the Senate and the crown was codified in a historic political document in 1505 at Radom, part of political maneuvers by King Aleksander to align himself with the *szlachta* against the senators (Stone 2001). Since the ascension of Aleksander to the throne, the Senate's members had attempted to secure more rights for themselves *vis à vis* the "ordinary" nobility and the crown, including the sole right to determine future members of the Senate and the ability to appoint lesser officers (Lukowski and Zawadzki 2006). These rights were granted in the Privilege of Mielnik in 1501, a concession that Aleksander set about undermining immediately (having never formally accepted or repudiated them, Górski et al. (1966)). From his absentee rule in Lithuania, Aleksander fomented mistrust of the Senate and a backlash from the nobility that culminated in the general *Sejm* in Radom in 1505 (Stone 2001).

This landmark occasion, much like the Magna Carta in England, created a trilateral balance of political power that we now recognize as placing important constraints on the executive (Rodrigues 2010), as well as between branches of the legislature. Clawing back the privileges granted at Mielnik, Aleksander agreed to elevate the *Sejm* to equal footing as the Senate and the Crown through the enactment of the principle of *Nihil Novi*, or "nothing new." This idea, the bedrock of Polish politics for the next two and a half centuries, in practice meant that the Senate could no longer issue any decisions unilaterally, nor could it force action upon the king without the support of the lower house, the *Sejm*. In fact, the *Sejm* gained powers as the Senate was weakened, with the *Sejm* granted sole responsibility to introduce new laws (Koehler 2012) as well as having an advise and consent role in regard to foreign affairs (Wagner 1954). This transfer of power across institutions, in the words of Ireneusz Ciosek (2009:107), changed "Poland from a medieval to a modern country."

The principle of *Nihil Novi* solidified for a time the cooperation of the king with the *szlachta* against the Senate, the former Crown Council (Górski et al. 1966). Perhaps more importantly, the Constitution of 1505 acted as a formal contract between the "nominal power (the king) against the real power (the nobility)," including the "rights and immunities of the nobility that would never be violated by the king" (Osiatynski 1991:128). The nobility's elevation to equality with the king and the Senate did not give them unfettered rights, however, as steps were also taken to restrain the excesses of the nobility and the Senate in regard to their new powers. Indeed, an oft-overlooked fact is that the Constitution of 1505 also created a dedicated political class among the nobility, by threatening nobles that attempted to become craftsmen with expulsion from the nobility and thus from the *Sejm* (Ludwikowski 1987). Alongside this restriction was a more modern requirement, the *incompatibilitas* principle, originally adopted in 1501 but codified in 1505, that prohibited a noble from holding more than one high state office (McLean 2011). By both of these requirements, nobles were forced to focus on the job of governing rather than collecting titles and offices for pecuniary gain.

While the nobility may have had legal obligations placed on them in regard to their service in the *Sejm*, the newly found powers related to governing the nation expanded steadily throughout the sixteenth century. Emboldened by the seeming ease with which the nobility had been able to break the power of the Senate, and with the king's continued support, the *Sejm* introduced further changes: in 1520, the power of senators to designate deputies at *sejmiki* was cut in half, while in 1540 this right was removed entirely (Opalinski 2005). By 1537, the nobility had moved on to what we would now recognize as the principle of "rule of law" via the Execution of Laws Movement, which sought to compel the king to enforce the legislation that the *Sejm* enacted and forbade the king from publishing laws that were not approved by the *Sejm* beforehand (McLean 2011).

Seen from a modern viewpoint, the Execution of Laws movement was "a disciplined campaign on the part of the nobility against the king to limit the arbitrariness of monarchical authority" (McLean 2004), but it also was one of the world's first public administration improvement projects. In addition to reforming the administration of the state and reducing legal inequalities among the various regions of the realm (Stone 2001), the movement focused on treasury reform in the guise of the reorganization of the distribution of royal lands (Miller 1983). The result of the movement, which continued steadily throughout the century and actually accelerated after the formal union of Poland and Lithuania, was to impose upon the Polish state a nascent legal system complete with administration (elected judicial tribunals), a formalization of the judicial system as Poland moved from customary to codified law (Stone 2001). Perhaps more important, the Execution of Laws movement also began the process of formation of other economic institutions crucial to the development of Poland. In particular, the struggle between the *szlachta* and the Senate over possession of royal lands presaged later arguments about the nature of property, the basis of ownership, and the disposal of property after the death of the owner (Wheeler 2011).

These political changes in Poland were mirrored in the smaller half of the entity, as Lithuania also developed its own parallel parliamentary system. In fact, the separate evolution of independent parliamentary institutions in Poland and Lithuania, as Backus (1963) highlights, created a source of political competition between the two federated entities, although the competition was centered mainly on tangible issues of

territory.[4] This competition was to continue even after 1569 and
the Union of Lublin, where a formal founding document was signed,
bringing forth the new federal entity known as the *Rzeczpospolita* (or
Commonwealth). Indeed, even with an expanded and consolidated
political framework over a broader geographic area, parliamentary development within the two entities was so strong that "the Union ... was
unable to effect a merger of parliamentary institutions; it was compelled
to recognize the stability of the parliaments and provide for their continued existence in the resultant, somewhat more closely united federal
union" (Backus 1963:414).

The Union of Lublin did more than preserve the dual-parliamentary
system, however; it continued the march towards formal political institutions in line with today's best practices. As part of the treaty on Union,
Polish king Sigismund II Augustus extended the above-mentioned rights
of the Polish nobles won over the sixteenth century to Lithuanian and
Prussian lands, while accelerating the pace of "Polonization" in Lithuania
and forging a common currency (the złoty). Ironically, the push for Union
was supported not only at the executive level (due to the increasing threat
emanating from Muscovy), but also at the local level from Polish nobles
who felt that the incorporation of non-Polish lands had been done in an
imperfect and ad hoc legal framework. This continued focus on formal
legal doctrine and limiting the leeway of the king, further expressed
through the *Sejms* of Piotrków and Warsaw over 1562–1564 in order to
extend a legal basis over lands of the crown (Friedrich 2009), underscored
how parliamentary procedure continued to drive the development of
political institutions in the new Commonwealth.

Even with the Polish-Lithuanian Commonwealth formally codified,
there was little slowing of the pace of political reform in the Union
after 1569. Indeed, the most important reforms were still to come in
1572, after the death of Sigismund Augustus, the last of the Jagiellonian
kings. The ensuing interregnum led to the adoption by the *Sejm* of
a far-reaching reform, as Gromelski (2013:223) details:

---

[4] Jakstas (1963) pointed to the rivalry between Poland and Lithuania arising over the regions
of Podolia and Volhynia (in modern-day Ukraine and Belarus) as a source of tension, with
Poland seeking more formal political measures to guarantee sovereignty over these lands.
During this time, the two parliaments were actually acting at cross-purposes, with a strong
lobby within the Polish lands for extension of power to Podolia and Volhynia, and
a correspondingly strong lobby in Lithuania to resist such a move and keep the lands
more closely aligned to Wilno (Vilnius).

Following lengthy debates and negotiations between various factions, it was decided that the king would be chosen from among Polish and foreign candidates by all the szlachta by means of election virtim, or general election. Prior to the coronation the prospective monarch would sign a contract which confirmed all existing "laws, liberties, immunities, and privileges, both public and private," stipulated his duties and obligations towards the body politic and delineated the limits of royal power. The agreement, consisting of the so-called Henrician Articles and Pacta Conventa, sealed the fate of the monarchy in Poland and in a way that of the Polish-Lithuanian Commonwealth.

Elective monarchy had been a principle of Poland since the reign of Kazimierz the Great in 1370, although parliament was governed by the implicit constraint that the elected king must be a Jagiellonian (normally the eldest male heir, as in any normal order of succession (Stone 2001)). The events of 1572 after the power of the Jagiellonians disappeared altered this compact so that the semihereditary succession was now superseded by a free election of all lords and nobles (Podemska-Mikluch 2015).

More important from the viewpoint of constraints on the executive, this package of reforms elevated the principle of rule of law above that of the king's person, allowing the nobles the ability to disobey the king if the order contravened the stipulations of the Pacta Conventa (McLean 2011). In this manner, the election of kings separated the king's person (the all-knowing monarch) from his function as an executive officer (Stone 2001), as well as making clear that the law did not derive from the king but instead from God via the nation itself (Grześkowiak-Krwawicz 2005). And, of course, if the king were a mere man who could be selected by his fellow men, the idea of "divine right of kings," already an idea with little credibility in Poland, was utterly repudiated in favor of a principle that national sovereignty belongs to the whole nation and not to one individual (Brzezinski 1998). In the words of Andrzej Wyrobisz (1989:612), recognizing the king as mortal meant "there were not even the germs of an absolute monarchy in Poland."

This is not to suggest that the evolution of a more open political institution in Poland was done smoothly or that it functioned perfectly. Indeed, even as the trappings of democracy became more institutionalized, the more formal mechanisms created during the sixteenth century may have actually undercut the institution itself. Podemska-Mikluch (2015) is a great proponent of this view, putting forth the idea that the shift from nobles' democracy to royal free elections after the Jagiellonian dynasty died out in 1572 may have appeared more democratic but in reality undermined the previously balanced democratic regime. The shift in balance of power to the nobles perhaps had swung too far, in her view, as it removed incentives from the king to seek noble support (as succession would be entirely out of the monarch's hands). This, in effect, disengaged the king from local politics, allowing for local lords to become the sole powers in their territories, weakening the broader connection between king and country. With the nobility in charge of elections but losing power at home, the direct election of kings may also have created the first institutionalized example of lobbying, as "each successive coronation amounted to something of a royal auction as candidates attempted to surpass each other in placating the desires of the nobility" (Wheeler 2011:28).

However, even as the nobility expanded their privileges *vis à vis* the king, important obligations were placed on the *szlachta* as part of their service. As noted above, Polish political thought linked freedom with the obligation of the individual to defend freedom. Translated into this particular institution, nobles were expected to personally participate in the election of the king upon pain of imprisonment, confiscation of property, or even death, with only small landowners allowed to send a representative (Frost 2011). Their power base may have eroded somewhat within the local *sejmiki*, but the *szlachta* were now ever inextricably more bound to their obligations of legislation. In this manner, and contra Podemska-Mikluch's assertion, the unique Polish philosophical conception of liberty was given more expression via a specific political institution, the election of kings.

The institutions that formed during the sixteenth century have been criticized on the basis that they unnecessarily weakened the executive at a time when the rest of Europe was centralizing and, more importantly, becoming more expansionist. The key institutional mechanism that has come under fire is the *liberum veto*, the principle of unanimity that governed the decision-making processes of the *Sejm*. As Roháč (2008b:117) notes, "there is no clear moment in history when the principle of *liberum veto* was codified . . . it was only in the sixteenth century that the *liberum veto* became a truly binding principle." Under the veto, any legislation that was to pass the *Sejm* required the unanimous consent of all members of the lower house, and any member could prevent the *Sejm* from acting on legislation by announcing "*nie pozwalam*" ("I do not allow it") during a debate (Cole 1999). If any dissent encountered during the reading of a bill could not be smoothed over behind the scenes or in further discussion in the *Sejm*, the procedure of *liberum veto* left no choice but to drop the entire bill (Davies 1984). Indeed, on rare occasions during the seventeenth century (but with a striking increase in frequency in the eighteenth century, see Brzezinski 1998), the veto was even utilized to nullify entire sessions of the *Sejm* (Roháč 2008b).

While the veto is much maligned, it did have some redeeming qualities as a rule for the governance of the legislature. Heinberg (1926) notes that the veto was an important part of the *Sejm*'s power, in that it guarded against a tyranny of the majority from the entire legislature by enabling the *szlachta* further against the Senate. In this formulation, the *liberum veto* was a rational response to the continuing molding of the checks and balances within the Polish government, especially given that the king was supportive of unanimity for his own purposes; in that sense, the veto also represented a way for the executive to try and claw back some of the prerogative that was removed over the previous century. Geremek (1995:44) also correctly notes that "for 200 years, in line with this principle of liberum veto, the Polish Parliament functioned and the Polish Republic had a working parliamentary institution." Thus, while Heinberg (1926) and Brzezinski (1991) may have claimed that the rules of the *Sejm* were messy and not clearly delineated, Geremek makes the exact opposite argument, that the veto was a clear and unequivocal part of the parliamentary procedure that aided the work of the *Sejm* rather than hindered it, at least for a time. As political writer Andrzej Maksymilian Fredro argued in the late 1600s, "thanks to *liberum veto* one wise man could stop a crowd of fools" (quoted in Koehler 2012).

But, *contra* Geremek, the veto may have only functioned "well" for a period of approximately 125 years, until the mid-seventeenth century, when the fragile internal coalition holding the *szlachta* together fractured under various pressures. According to Brzezinski (1991), from 1652 onward, forty-eight out of the fifty-five *Sejm* convened were adjourned as a result of a single person's use of the *liberum veto* (see Table 2.1, from Wheeler (2011), which details the results of the *Sejm* over a sixty-seven-year period). The source of this institutional paralysis can be traced to both external and internal reasons. In the first instance, like all political institutions before and since, the veto became an easy mechanism for purchasing influence. The *liberum veto* was originally seen as a way to guard against the king bribing a simple majority, and thus paving the way to absolutism (Frost 1990). If there were problems in achieving consensus, it was better that these inconveniences exist than enabling a loss of liberty (Lukowski 2004). Ironically, however, the veto also allowed foreign powers such as Russia the ability to bribe legislators to obstruct progress, thus preventing any decisions that could bolster the defense of the realm (Roháč 2008b). Many scholars (see Wheeler 2011) have argued that the ability of foreign

Table 2.1 *Results of the Polish Sejm from 1697 to 1764*

Year	Result	Year	Result	Year	Result
1697	Passed legislation	1720	*Liberum veto*	1738	Filibuster
1698	**Walk-out**	1722	*Liberum veto*	1740	Filibuster
1699	Passed legislation	1724	Passed legislation	1742	Did not assemble
1701	**Envoys dispersed**	1726	Passed legislation	1744	Filibuster
1701–1702	*Liberum veto*	1728	King's illness	1746	Filibuster
1703	Passed legislation	1729	*Liberum veto*	1748	Filibuster
1710	Passed legislation	1730	*Liberum veto*	1750	*Liberum veto*
1712	Passed legislation	1732	*Liberum veto*	1752	*Liberum veto*
1712–13	*Liberum veto*	1733	Cancelled due to king's death	1754	*Liberum veto*
1717	Passed legislation	1735	*Liberum veto*	1756	Did not assemble
1718	Passed legislation	1736	New king elected	1764	*Liberum veto*
1719–20	*Liberum veto*	1736	Passed legislation	1764	New king elected

Source: Wheeler (2011).

monarchs to meddle in Poland's domestic affairs via the *liberum veto* mechanism helped to vitiate the state and make it ripe for division by the rapacious Russians, Prussians, and Austrians who coveted the land.

Even without influence from abroad, it is possible that the breakdown within the legislature would have occurred anyway, due to the increasing fractionalization among the nobility. Brzezinski (1991:59) argues that "as early as the seventeenth century, the *szlachta* became acutely divided, with factions developing based on estate size and ability to hold provincial, crown, or court offices." This increase in "conflict among noble elites, combined with the presence of a weak central ruler, led many of the most powerful elites to adopt a strategy of opposing the state" (Wheeler 2011:30). Such a situation would not be problematic in an institution governed by majority rules, but within the *Sejm* there was not even a manner in which obstruction could be resolved: Brzezinski (1991) notes that, while the veto may have been a point of pride in parliamentary procedure, it was never supplemented with other rules of assembly, including the ability to remove disruptive members or rules of impeachment. Thus, conflict itself became institutionalized in an overarching system that was now built on the principle of parliamentary supremacy.

Finally, an interesting point was noted by Heinberg (1926) on the point at which the veto began to become more problematic. During much of the sixteenth century, there was a chance for "malcontents," or those continually dissatisfied with the course of Polish governance, to vote with their feet and move to the frontier territories of Volhynia or, crucially, Ukraine. That is, rather than obstruct the *Sejm* repeatedly, nobles could move into the newer territories of the realm. However, when this area of Europe became subject to numerous feuds and wars (as in the Polish-Cossack war from 1654–1657) and undesirable for emigration, the closing of the frontier meant that those dissatisfied had nowhere to go. Thus, they remained in the *Sejm* and were more likely to wield the *liberum veto* rather than acquiesce. This thesis is somewhat unproven (it is very difficult to link emigration and voting records from the seventeenth century in Poland given all that has happened since to the records), but it offers an interesting theory into the need for institutional flexibility.

TOWARDS A WARFARE STATE? THE BEGINNING OF POLAND'S DECLINE

Whether or not the need for unanimity in the *Sejm* led to the breakdown of the Polish state is debatable (and has been heatedly debated in the literature), but the reality was that Poland did indeed begin a sustained political and economic decline in the seventeenth century. While various internal forces have been mooted for contributing to Poland's malaise, including the *liberum veto*, the difficulties in transitioning from the feudal system,[5] economic difficulties (more on this below), and the institution of the elective monarchy itself, for the most part, these factors played a subordinate role to the greatest institutional failure of all: war. Poland's decline from the seventeenth century onward was precipitated through external pressure of a sort that went far beyond Russian meddling in the operations of the *Sejm* or bribery of particular legislators, with the Polish state subjected to a series of wars beginning in the mid-seventeenth century. Each of these wars was more draining than the last, which left the central government's treasury bare and the geographic scope of the country smaller and smaller. Perhaps more interestingly for our purposes, much of the conflict that Poland experienced can also be traced to the country's political institutions and how they interacted with the political institutions of neighboring powers.

Poland's external struggles had been ongoing throughout the country's history (and to catalogue all of Poland's wars during this time is far beyond

---

[5] Hobsbawm (1954) is particularly fond of this explanation, couching the entire decline of Europe in his typical Marxist analysis of class struggle.

the scope of this book), but began to accelerate under the Polish-Lithuanian Commonwealth. The increasing damage to the Polish state, eventually culminating in existential threats to the freedom held dearly by the country, began with a long series of wars with Sweden throughout the seventeenth century. The power struggle between Sweden and Poland was precipitated by the Swedish civil war (1597–1598), a struggle within Sweden that led to the deposal of King Sigismund III of Poland from his additional throne as king of Sweden. As part of this turmoil, the lands of Livonia (incorporating portions of modern-day Estonia and Latvia), formally partitioned between Poland and Sweden in 1561 but subjected to strife and war ever since, decided to throw in their lot with Sweden exclusively. Dedicated to regaining his title and asserting Polish sovereignty over Sweden, as well as reclaiming Livonia, King Sigismund oversaw a recurring number of battles fought over Livonia with Sweden from 1600 to 1611.

Throughout his reign, Sigismund proved himself to be no friend of parliamentary procedures, pursuing war over the opposition of both the Swedish *Riksdag* and his own *Sejm*. Having been challenged by the Swedish *Riksdag* since before his coronation, due to the staunch Catholicism which stood in direct opposition to Sweden's overwhelmingly Protestant polity (Benedict 2005), Sigismund saw the Swedish parliament as one more obstacle to overcome; this view was vindicated when it was the *Riksdag* that formally deposed Sigismund from the Swedish throne (Oakley 2005). Similarly, where the Polish nobility were obsessed with restraining the power of the crown from becoming an absolutist in Poland, there was little that could be done about the king asserting these same rights over the Swedish lands. The *Sejm* of 1600 explicitly refused to become embroiled in an issue of dynastic succession, leaving the king to conduct a war on his own devices, finally only voting to provide funding for hostilities at the *Sejm* of 1601 for two years (and only on the king's pledge to cede Estonia to Poland if the Livonian campaign went well, see Reddaway 1971).

But as is so often the case, the expansion of warfare and the need to fund the warfare state led to deleterious consequences for political freedom on the home front (see Davenport 2007 for an excellent discussion of the repressive state throughout history). At the same time that Sigismund was stretching Poland's resources thin in a bid to retain his personal rule over Sweden, he also began a campaign to curtail some of the liberties that *szlachta* had won for themselves over the previous two centuries. In particular, and in an echo of wars of the twentieth and twenty-first century, Sigismund summoned the *Sejm* in 1606 and, according to Reddaway (1971), castigated the parliament for its lukewarm support of his military incursions into Sweden. Frustrated with this "obstructionism," he instead laid out a plan to radically reform the constitution, replacing the *liberum veto* with majority rules, instituting a hereditary monarchy, and providing for both a standing army and a standing annual subsidy from the nobility to the crown (Maciszewski 1960). In short, the king proposed a host of "solutions" that coincided directly with the *szlachta*'s worst fears of an absolutist monarch.

The move of Sigismund III towards absolutism in pursuit of greater political powers abroad and at home led to a watershed moment in the Polish conception of freedom, the Zebrzydowski Rebellion. With Sigismund's political foil Jan Zamoyski having died of a stroke in 1605 (Zamoyski being a loud and consistent opponent to Sigismund's political centralization and foreign aggression), Kraków's palatine (royal governor) Mikołaj Zebrzydowski assembled the *szlachta* in opposition to the king's plans. Utilizing the peculiar mechanism of the *rokosz*, noted by McKenna (2012: 160) as "the right to refuse obedience to a king who violated the laws of the Commonwealth's constitution," Zebrzydowski and his fellow nobility outlined an ambitious list of sixty-seven demands to the king at conventions at Stężyca and Lublin in 1606, including calling for his dethronement (Podemska-Mikluch 2012). Negotiations with the king on these points predictably failed, leading to armed rebellion: raising an army of nearly 10,000, the rebels were finally defeated by the royal army at Guzów in July 1607 (Bussow and Orchard 1994) and formally surrendered to the king via the *Sejm* in 1609. However, the king's plans to move closer to absolutism were stopped and the sanctity of the Polish constitution upheld, with royalty losing the moral prestige it had previously enjoyed (Halecki et al. 1978).

Despite the small victory against absolutism at home, the conflicts abroad continued in a vain attempt to restore Sigismund III as the monarch of Sweden. The results of the continual wars with Sweden over this first decade of the seventeenth century were inconclusive (a truce signed in 1611 could be described in modern terms as a "frozen conflict"), and the Polish monarchy's continually lingering hope to reassert dominion over Sweden instead set the stage for even more bloodshed. As Frost (2014:117) notes while explaining the development of the warfare state in Sweden, Polish king "Sigismund remained notoriously committed to reclaiming his throne, [as he had] invaded once already, and had even managed to seize

Stockholm." Three additional wars followed in rapid succession between Poland and Sweden, in 1617 (again over Livonia) and 1621–1622 and 1625–1629, when the new Swedish king Gustavus Adolphus invaded Polish Prussia and then Polish territory outright (Parrott 2012). The result of three decades of war was merely a codification of what Livonia had already decided thirty years' prior, mainly to ally itself with Sweden, and the Truce of Altmark formally ceded control of the territory to Sweden (Schofield 1969). But still, Livonia remained just a front for the real motive behind the conflict, and Sigismund refused to accept that the political institution of the monarchy, headed by Poland, had been rejected by Sweden.

Abetted by cultural intrigue over the possibility of Poland's "re-Catholicizing" the northern lands (Lockhart 2004), the enmity and power rivalry with Sweden did not easily dissipate, and the Polish hope of returning Sweden to its sphere of influence "obstruct[ed] the conclusion of a lasting peace for some sixty years" (Roberts 1984:13). After a generational pause of approximately twenty-one years, hostilities resumed in the Great Northern War of 1655–1660, the most destructive to Poland yet. Characterized by the "Swedish deluge" and humiliating defeat in the early years of the conflict (as well as the exile of King Jan Kazimierz (Jon Casimir) to the Habsburg lands), the Great Northern War led to occupation of Poland by both Swedish and Russian forces (Frost 2004). After five more years of bloody fighting and Poland's eventually regrouping to evict the Swedish invaders, the Treaty of Oliva finally brought to an end the Polish kingdom's struggle with Sweden. More important, the final renunciation of Poland's claim to the Swedish throne by King Jan II Kazimierz came in 1660 as part of the Treaty, meaning that Poland's ruling class had finally accepted that Sweden was its own sovereign nation. After sixty years of fighting to retain a political institution abroad while subverting it at home, the territory of Poland was almost entirely unchanged, with life and money expended senselessly for little concrete gain. In what was not history's first (nor its last) example of governmental overreach, the desire to keep the scope of a political institution as it was in the previous century instead severely weakened the Polish state and the institutions that remained. In fact, as the Zebrzydowski Rebellion showed, foreign adventurism had weakened democracy in Poland itself.

Unfortunately, the struggle with Sweden was not the last to threaten Poland's political institutions, with the next and larger existential challenges to the kingdom coming (ironically for our purposes) from the hinterlands of Ukraine. Up until this point, we have somewhat avoided the fact that the modern-day lands of Ukraine (previously Ruthenia) were for the most part either directly part of the Polish-Lithuanian Commonwealth or were overseen by Poland from the fourteenth century onward. Since we explore this history in the next chapter in more detail, it is sufficient to note at this point that the two-century-old domination of Ukraine and specifically Kiev by the Polish state had been characterized by severe schizophrenia in Polish policies. As Sysyn (2003:125) notes,

War and violence were endemic in this land where nobles' private wars, Tatar raids, and naval expeditions by frontiersmen across the Black Sea were constant. Its nominal suzerain, the Polish-Lithuanian Commonwealth faced the question of how this territory could be defended and how this periphery could be integrated into that state's political-social system.

Indeed, ever since the Treaty of Lublin and formal creation of the Polish-Lithuanian Commonwealth, Polish sovereigns had vacillated on this very question, with little sense of what to actually do about its Ukrainian territories; whether to annex them and make them part of the Commonwealth (and its institutions) proper, extend the blessings of *szlachta* democracy but keep these territories separate, or retain control over the frontier but only as a buffer state against the already perennial enemy, Muscovy.

The integration of Ukraine had already begun prior to 1569, as Ukraine and the Ruthenian lands were incorporated into the Grand Duchy of Lithuania, but after Union with Poland these lands were nonetheless treated as very distinct entities somewhat outside the formal Commonwealth political and economic structures (Sysyn 1982).[6] This did not mean that some assimilation did not occur, as the nobility in particular saw themselves as part of a community of well-born members of the *szlachta* throughout the Commonwealth and readily adopted the Polish language and cultural mores (Litwin 1987). Moreover, linguistic and cultural assimilation occurred at all strata of society, with only minor and somewhat token resistance (especially in regard to religion, see below and Sysyn 1982). But in regard to the extension of the Commonwealth's political and economic (as opposed to merely cultural) institutions, the Ukrainian frontier was both embraced and kept at arm's length.

[6] For the rest of this chapter, Ukraine and Ruthenia are treated as interchangeable, even though some of the people associated with Ruthenia were precursors of modern-day Belarussians. The vast majority of Ruthenia is associated with today's Ukrainians.

A concrete example of this duality of the Ruthenians within the Commonwealth can be found in the very idea of *szlachta* democracy and its application to the lands of modern-day Ukraine. Prior to the Union of Lublin, there was a hasty initiative to extend Polish administrative to Lithuania, including the cobbling together of a legally equal and unified *szlachta* from the separate classes of the gentry and magnates of the Grand Duchy (Borzecki 1996). The integration of this new *szlachta* into the existing noble arrangement of Poland (coupled with the king's recognition of the freedoms of Orthodox followers in the east on par with the preponderance of Catholics in the west of the country) meant that, on paper at least, the nobility of Ruthenian lands were equal to their Polish counterparts. However, this was far from the case in reality, as the nobility in Ukraine became continually relegated to a second tier, with obligations more onerous in Ukraine than in Poland and much less security of lands *vis à vis* the higher nobility (Subtelny 2009). These disparities in treatment only widened over time, as the nobility of Ukraine were to increasingly decry Polish attempts to change princely titles and shift the burden of defense of the realm to the Ruthenian territories (Sysyn 1982).

In fact, the "legal and administrative peculiarities" of the four Ukrainian provinces (Sysyn 1982:172) meant that they shared common institutions that still remained distinct from the Commonwealth (Pelenski 1998); indeed, a great irony from the incorporation of the Ukrainian provinces is that the attempted extension of Polish political institutions instead forged a national consciousness and national institutions that were absent from the Ruthenian lands prior to the Union of Lublin (Borzecki 1996). An illustration of this comes from Ukraine's primary legal document, the Lithuanian Statute; drafted in 1529 (and updated in 1566 and 1588), the Statute was a body of legislation that incorporated customary laws back to Kievan times and confirmed the rights of Ukrainian nobility. However, whereas the third revision of the Statute was in place from 1588 onward for the Lithuanian portion of the Commonwealth, it was the second version (from 1566, predating the Union of Lublin) that remained the law of Ukraine well into the nineteenth century (Platerus 1965). Despite the importance of the Statute in bringing the idea of legal codification to Ukraine (Subtelny 2009), this was but one example of a "sense of legal distinctness . . . on the one hand, weakened by the unification of political structures in progress, but on the other hand, reinforced through the existence of consciousness of separate historical traditions" (Litwin 1987:59).

While much of the issues connected with the institutional (non-) assimilation of Ukraine fell on the nobility, the policy gyrations from Poland also fell heavy on the "anti-*szlachta*" (Borzecki 1996), the Cossacks. Steppe dwellers of hazy provenance (possibly derived from Turkic-speaking Tatars) and even looser boundaries (including among their ranks escaped serfs from Poland and Russia), the Cossacks have been glorified in hindsight as the true resisters of Polish attempts to "Europeanize" Ukraine (see especially Sawczak (2004) in his discussion of Gogol's writings). But at the time, the Cossacks had been in some sense co-opted onto the Polish side as early as 1523, as the Lithuanian portion of the (not-yet-formed) Commonwealth noted that it would be beneficial to hire Cossacks as a "border guard" (Reddaway 1971). However, the use of Roman Catholicism in a bid to "polonize" the Ukrainian frontier (Wilson 1997) created significant enmity within Cossack ranks, especially as Poland became "once more an output of militant Catholicism" (Lewitter 1948:168); while the co-opting of Ruthenian (Ukrainian) nobility into Catholicism proceeded smoothly, it was vehemently resisted by the peasantry and, especially, the Cossacks (ibid.).

The Cossacks also chafed at measures of more formal political assimilation imposed from Poland, including the process of registration that was begun under King Stephen Bathory. Believing that the Cossacks could be tamed in the service of the crown in order to "make a beneficial use of their enterprising bravery" (Krasinski 1848:16), Bathory required the Cossacks serving with the Polish armies to register with the crown in order to receive their pay and allowances. This registration process also performed a service in building up the Polish defenses against Crimean Tatar raids, as the Cossacks who were drawn into the registration process already appeared to be more "conservative" than their clansmen, selected because they already had property and families (Subtelny 2009). The institution of registration continued to develop in the sixteenth century, with an Act in 1583 placing the Cossacks directly under the king, fostering a sense among the registered Cossacks as a separate class of knights in the service of the crown (Velychenko 1976). As Gordon (1983:97) notes, however,

The register was a failure to the interests of the Polish-Lithuanian state. For the Cossacks, ironically, or at least for the elite, it was somewhat beneficial. It increased their ability to negotiate for privileges and to resist dispersal. It did not limit the growth of cossackdom, nor did it motivate some Cossacks to police others, nor did it create a new armed force loyal to the crown.

Part of this may have been that the register process was itself antithetical to the political ideals of the Commonwealth. As Krasinski (1848:18) notes, "all this organizing of the Cossacks of the Dnieper seemed to be somewhat foreign to the settled institutions of the Polish monarchy, and resembled rather one of those military colonies of ancient Scythians." Indeed, as Gordon (1983) emphasizes, the entire premise behind the registration process was to drive a wedge in the Cossack community, allowing the *rejestrowi* to become accustomed to their privileges and rights, while unregistered Cossacks were then subsumed into the peasantry and driven into serfdom. This was exactly what did happen, as the small number of registered Cossacks (approximately 8,000 were registered by 1630, according to Magocsi (2010)) became wealthy property owners and part of the landed gentry, while unregistered Cossacks from the steppes of Zaporozhia remained wedded to the Cossack traditions. The two sides viewed each other warily, and tensions ran high, although there was some form of income mobility between the two groups (Subtelny 2009). As with the Ukrainian *szlachta*, however, the registered Cossacks soon found that their registration did not confer the "full political equality with the gentry" (Velychenko 1976:24) that they desired, as they too were relegated to a second tier within the Commonwealth. Rather than accessing the noble ideas of political equality based on liberty as espoused by the Polish *szlachta*, the registered Cossacks encountered fierce resistance from "Polish and local Orthodox Rus' magnates [who] could never accept as equals those whom they considered Cossack upstarts and freebooting rabble" (Magocsi 2010:197).

These issues of incomplete social assimilation and diverging national institutions came to a head by the mid-seventeenth century, as the frictions between the *szlachta* in Ukraine and Poland and the grievances of the Cossacks married in a broader resistance to Poland's rule. While the Cossacks had become increasingly restless under the Polish system, with increasingly vocal demands for ennoblement due to their military service (Velychenko 1976) and even outright and repeated rebellions (Gordon 1983, Franz 2005), it was a direct challenge to the Ukrainian *szlachta* that brought together a coalition of nobility against the Commonwealth's monarchy. In perhaps a warning of the dangers of intermingling political institutions with those who hold the commanding heights of the economy, and in a mirror image of Sigismund's earlier machinations in Sweden, the Polish *szlachta* increasingly utilized the power of the state in the east to harass and dispossess even the registered Cossacks of their land.

Indeed, it was such an attempt to threaten the property of a particular Cossack, Bohdan Khmelnitsky, which led to the most famous Cossack revolt and the beginning of the disintegration of Poland's political institutions in 1648.[7] Volumes have been written about the Khmelnitsky uprising, and this book has nothing new to add to this excellent research, but the story of the Cossack rebellion of 1648 merits a special mention here as it touches on our issues of institution-building. While the dramatized version of Khmelnitsky's dissatisfaction with Polish rule relates it to a dispute over a woman, there is agreement that Khmelnitsky's rival in this matter, Daniel Czaplinski, the assistant governor of Chyhyryn, undertook several punitive actions against the Cossack, including raiding and requisitioning his estate at Subotiv (Magocsi 2010). After traveling to Warsaw to put his case before King Władysław and the *Sejm*, Khmelnitsky found that there was little that could be done in his favor, and his pleas for redress went unanswered (Sysyn 2003). Even more of an insult, upon his return to Ukraine he was arrested on the orders of Czaplinski's superior, Alexander Koniecpolski. With the assistance of friends, he escaped and crossed over from his comfortable life as a registered Cossack to join the unregistered majority in the frontier area of the Zaporizhian Sich near the lower Dnieper River (Magocsi 2010).

From this perch in the autonomous regions beyond direct authority of the Polish king, Khmelnitsky forged alliances across the Cossack settlements to the north, and directly challenged an armed force sent by the king to quell the insurrections in April; by May of 1648 Khmelnitsky's force of approximately 8,000 fighters, augmented by assistance from the Tatars and daily increases of warriors sympathetic to the cause (Krasinski 1848), defeated the Polish forces in two separate engagements at Zhotvi Vody and at Korsun (Sysyn 2003). Compounding the Polish disarray was the untimely death of King Władysław in-between the two engagements, leading to political uncertainty at the time that Poland needed certainty the most. As Magocsi (2010:214) succinctly put the extent of Poland's problems, "by the outset of the summer of 1648, two of Poland's leading commanders had been captured, its eastern army had been defeated, its Ukrainian peasant population was in revolt, its Tatar enemies were ravaging the countryside at will, and its king was dead." This turmoil infected the Polish body politic, exerting a strong influence on the election of the

---

[7] Throughout this section, I use the anglicized version of his name rather than the etymologically more correct transliteration of "Khmel'nyts'kyi" that is used by Slavic scholars.

king. Indeed, Jan Kazimierz was catapulted into the king's position due
precisely to the fact that he was perceived as being more willing to
accommodate the rebels and bring the war on the frontier to an end
(Sysyn 2003).

However, the exigencies of being elected in wartime meant that
King Jan Kazimierz's "attempts to assert his authority and to provide
the firm government necessary to defeat Khmelnitsky and his Tartar
allies, and from 1654 his Muscovite allies, brought him into bitter
dispute with magnates" (Frost 1986:188). As Frost (1986) correctly
details, the new king spent much of his energy during the prosecution
of the war with the Cossacks, Sweden, and the Russians intent on
aggrandizing more powers to the executive, first by limiting the life
tenure of some appointments (specifically the Grand Hetmen, or the
commanders of the army of the Commonwealth) and secondly by
instituting a series of secret agreements that bound specific senators
tightly to the king's whims. In this sense, with a perpetual warfare state
apparently in place, King Jan Kazimierz was only following the trends
of his neighbors, as well as proving the *szlachta*'s fears correct; indeed,
"Polish polemical literature of the sixteenth and seventeenth centuries
is full of dismay over the possibility that the concomitant growth of
arbitrary royal power and bureaucracy in Habsburg Austria, France,
and Muscovy could take place in the Commonwealth" (Brown
1982:58).

However, Jan Kazimierz's attempted maneuvering in royal appointments and especially in his parliamentary tactics during the *Sejm* of 1652
led to the first use of the *liberum veto* to nullify an entire session of the
parliament (see above). Frost (1986:193) describes the unprecedented use
of the *veto* as perhaps the only check against an expansion of executive
power that was being increasingly justified by the never-ending wars that
Poland was embroiled in:

*The veto emerged precisely because a large proportion of the szlachta felt
fundamentally threatened by [Jan Kazimierz]'s use of his power and influence.
Had the opposition had a firm majority in the Sejm, there would have been
no need for the principle of liberum veto. It was because the king was clearly
able to exert great influence in the Sejm that the veto became necessary; it
only became finally established in the 1660s, when [Jan Kazimierz] seemed
about to be successful in his efforts to extend royal power by changing the
constitution.*

Thus, in order to prevent internal expansion of monarchical power, the
deputies resorted to the penultimate tactic of legislative sabotage. But even

though this was to have long-term ramifications for perceptions of the *Sejm*, in this instance it was only a speed bump for the king, who was able to get much of what he desired in terms of impeachment of recalcitrant senators and a move towards a more secretive *Sejm* and greater use of the Senate Council rather than the full *Sejm* (Frost 1986). With a continued move towards centralization, internal Polish politics soon scaled up to the last resort, that of full-blown rebellion.

A half-century of war and betrayal of Poland's political ideals on the frontier were washing back in a wave of authoritarianism from that very same frontier. Jan Kazimierz's centralizing tendencies continued to press forward even after the dissolution of the *Sejm* in 1652, and continued external war led him to propose a series of reforms for the coming *Sejm*, including the idea of a *vivente rege* election, or an election for a new monarch while the reigning monarch was still alive. This idea, in line with the constitutional precedent of Polish law (Pernal 1990), was seen by opponents of the king, most notably a faction led by Grand Marshal Jerzy Sebastian Lubomirski, as an attempt for the monarchy to establish a hereditary succession and allow the current king to unduly influence the selection of his successor. A Congress held in Warsaw in 1658 added to the suspicion of the *Sejm*, as specially selected members of the elite floated various proposals to reform the parliament, including the shift towards two-thirds voting (rather than unanimity) required for passage of legislation. Finally, the finance for the road to tyranny had also already been put in place, as part of the king's increasing reliance on the use of his Senate Council to bypass the *Sejm* on day-to-day matters; as an example of this reliance, he decreed in 1656 a tax on beer, mead, and spirits, assuming that such a matter would be ratified at the next *Sejm* (as Frost (1986) notes, this did not happen, but the tax remained). A further tax was created in 1660, also on the authority of the Council rather than the *Sejm*.

Unable to coalesce around a plan for reform, the *Sejm* of 1661 ended with no real plan for augmenting the parliament in this time of foreign crisis and executive expansion. The continued lack of unanimity of the legislative branch may have hastened Jan Kazimierz's impatience with the persistent opposition emanating from Marshal Lubomirski, and, in a sign that the Khmelnitsky affair had taught him nothing, in 1664 the king took steps to impeach Lubomirski and dispossess him of his property. Refusing to submit to the tribunal that had impeached him, and after futilely attempting to have foreign powers Austria and Muscovy intervene in Poland on his behalf, Lubomirski returned to Poland in

1665 under the flag of open rebellion.[8] Lubomirski's rebellion also drained the resources of the Polish army, as his forces first routed Lithuanian troops near Częstochowa, and, after a brief armistice at the beginning of November that collapsed after the *Sejm* of 1666, scored a decisive victory at Mątwy (Pernal 1990).

This victory paved the way for a lasting peace treaty that compelled the king to abandon the idea of *vivente rege* elections, but also "calcified the existing defective representative institutions and the constitutional arrangements" prevailing in Poland well into the next century (Pernal 1990:154). Most modern scholarship tends to agree with this sentiment, regarding the events of the Cossack and Lubomirski rebellions as one of the main causes of the political paralysis in the legislature shown in Table 2.1 above; with the king having attempted to create a reform that benefited only himself and his successors, and with such a strong backlash against such reforms, an atmosphere was created that stifled any serious reform of the *Sejm* for over a century. As Grześkowiak-Krwawicz (2012:55–56) described it, "from at least the mid-seventeenth century onward, the noble society was increasingly convinced that the Polish freedom had already reached its zenith, enshrined in the existing political system, and thus any alterations to that system – that is to say, enacting any new laws – could be dangerous to it."

Perhaps more interesting for our purposes, the real legacy of Jan Kazimierz became not necessarily his weakening of formal political institutions (which did undoubtedly occur), but his effect on the informal political and economic institutions of Poland. The actions of the king struck at the most necessary of informal political and economic institutions, that of trust; while the economic modeling of the necessity of trust for both political agreement and contract-based commerce is only in its infancy (see Bodoh-Creed 2014), there is a growing consensus that societal trust is necessary at a minimum level for formal institutions to operate. This can be seen from the political science literature in the idea of "legitimacy," in that only a government that is trusted can be legitimate

---

[8] An interesting point should be noted here: while historians tend to speak of the Lubomirski "rebellion," the original Polish term (*Rokosz*) refers more to a legitimate confederation of nobles rather than something treasonous. Thus, Lubomirski, wrong-headed as his motives may have been in the eyes of the Polish state, was pursuing a means of redress that was accepted within Poland's polity. Of course, as we have seen, this was not accepted for nationalities on the Polish periphery, nor was the courtesy of "allowable rebellion" extended even to the Polish partners in the Commonwealth, the Lithuanians (Rowell 2001).

(Citrin 1974), and also from numerous works on private property, in that trust allows for commerce beyond one's immediate family due to proper contract enforcement mechanisms (Lorenz 1999, Clague et al. 1999). Unfortunately, the actions of Jan Kazimierz engendered substantial distrust among the populace and created several ossified rival factions in the *Sejm* that were to persist throughout the century (McKenna 2012). In such an atmosphere (and as noted above), the increasing use of the *liberum veto* may have been an imperfect vehicle but it was an equilibrium solution, as it was crucial to blocking the sort of tyranny that was occurring elsewhere in the world. If the trust within the Commonwealth that existed before the reign of Jan Kazimierz had been present at the end of his reign, it is much more likely that the *liberum veto* would not have mutated into the procedural impediment it eventually did. But with a lack of the minimum level of trust that the next king was not actually trying to overthrow the established order, the veto became a first, rather than last resort.

The events of the Cossack rebellion, coupled with the Deluge of the Swedes and the Russians and the political machinations of the king, resulted in a severe weakening of the Polish state and the political system that it encapsulated, and culminated in the abdication of Jan Kazimierz from the throne (Roháč 2008a). The overreach of the king also ultimately created negative feedback into external affairs (as noted above), as the Lubomirski rebellion meant that Polish military efforts were diverted internally rather than directed at the external enemies of the Northern War. This draining of the Polish army meant that Poland, having scored several compelling victories against Muscovy throughout the conflict, was unable to finish off the Russian forces decisively; moreover, facing continued bloodshed at home, Poland was perhaps more eager to end its external hostilities, concluding a truce in 1667 that turned over Kiev to Russian rule. Thus, by 1670, not only had Poland weakened internally and seen one king forced to abdicate, it was now facing an emboldened Russia that was ensconced in much of modern-day Ukraine and was rapidly modernizing its army (Frost 1986).

This state of play was to continue unabated through the rule of Augustus II from 1697 to 1704 and again from 1709 to 1733, where a seemingly never-ending attempt to increase the power of the monarchy led to internal strife and, more importantly, to external occupation. This time around, the flashpoint was King Augustus II's policy of not only quartering soldiers from Saxony on Polish territory (at one point numbering almost 25,000 men), but having a dedicated policy of taxation in order to pay for these troops (Lerski 1996). The founding of the Confederation of Tarnogród in 1715 was the *szlachta*'s response to these perceived transgressions to the social contract, and another year of internal conflict between the "confederates" and the king (supported by the Saxons) ground down the Commonwealth and made it susceptible to foreign intervention. This came quickly in the form of the Russian military where, posing as mediator, Peter the Great sought to broker a peace agreement on favorable terms to Russia. Applying direct pressure in the "Silent *Sejm*" of 1717 in Warsaw (so-called because only a few deputies were allowed to speak, in order to forestall the application of the *liberum veto*; see Jędruch 1998), Russia made the weakened Commonwealth into a vassal state, with ominous consequences for the future of the country's political system. As Davies (2005:460) noted, this *Sejm* "effectively terminated the independence of Poland and Lithuania" as an independent nation-state, meaning that the threat of the absolutist Polish king had finally been extinguished, but replaced by a much more nefarious master.

POLAND IN THE 1700s: FROM POLITICAL INSTITUTIONS TO PARTITION

By the mid-eighteenth century, besieged by opportunistic monarchs from within, distrust of any reforms mooted, constrained by a belligerent and overbearing neighbor, and facing a general tendency within Europe towards absolutism that created many external enemies for Poland, the days of noble liberty appeared to be numbered. And yet, it was during this period that the political philosophy of Polish freedom continued to blossom, even as the physical boundaries of the state continued to recede. Despite continued foreign conflicts such as the Polish-Ottoman wars in the late 1600s (capped by King Jan Sobieski's cavalry charge to rout the Ottoman army at the Battle of Vienna and lift the siege of the city) and a further struggle for monarchical succession from 1704–1706 that resulted immediately in one civil war (and another and an occupation in the coming decade, as just mentioned), the rise of the idea of liberty remained ascendant via the development of other institutions. Grześkowiak-Krwawicz (2012) correctly points to the idea of freedom of speech, which was enshrined in two separate laws enacted by the *Sejm* (in 1669 and then again in 1775). While the *liberum veto* was itself seen as a form of speech of the *szlachta* (in today's parlance, perhaps "speaking truth to power"), Poland went beyond this idea of speech in the exercise of power to guarantee it in the discussions of power as well.

Moreover, while trust in the formal institution of the king may have been lacking, the eighteenth century saw a shift towards a political order shaped more from the networks of the elite. Contra to King Jan Kazimeirz's aims, the rebellions of the mid-1600s and subsequent events of the early 1700s also helped to strengthen specific informal political institutions. Even during the Lubomirski rebellion, word of mouth and reputation playing a large role in spreading and confirming Lubomirski's claims and, according to Rustemeyer (2014), affording the rebel institutions the same legitimacy as those of the Commonwealth. McLean (2011) offers an even more thorough treatment of the rise of informal institutions in the early eighteenth century, noting that the elite networks in Poland from 1750 onward became a mini-state, tied to each other via marriage and family, and lessening the transaction costs of opposition. Indeed, although McLean does not explicitly state it, his thesis of an expanding *szlachta* elite tied together by intermarriage shows that the formal trust that had been broken by the succession of expansionist kings in Poland was rebuilt on an informal level. This process of rebuilding informal linkages, which remained underpinned by a societal consensus on the value of liberty, helped to reform Poland's formal institutions into a coherent defender of liberalism.

Sadly, just as the ideas of political liberty at the informal/theoretical level were beginning to make their way back into the formal levers of government, Poland was to undergo its slow extinction as a state. As Frost (2010) was to say in reviewing a book on the political culture of Poland in the eighteenth century, and as we have seen, "a debilitating cycle of wars fought almost entirely on its own territory ruined [Poland's] economy, depleted its treasury, and left it after 1717 effectively as a Russian protectorate." Continued military weakness, the result of two centuries of conflict, meant that "under Augustus III [1734–1763], Poland periodically served as a transit route for the warring armies of Prussia, Russia, and Austria, even the Ottoman Porte" (Lukowski and Zawadzki 2006:112). Guided from above by the tsar, it is little wonder that Zarycki (2000:862) called Poland "a very weak semi-constitutional monarchy with an almost powerless state apparatus, not only unable to challenge church interests but incapable of sustaining the existence of the state itself." The continued strain on the political system of fighting off absolutism both domestic and foreign culminated in a series of three partitions in the late eighteenth century and the eventual extinguishing of the Polish nation until 1918.

Frost (1986:182) has rightly noted that the Partitions "squat like an incubus over Polish historiography; events before 1795 tend to be evaluated in terms of their 'contribution' to the national disaster." For our purposes, the Partitions are the end of the first phase of Poland's formal political institutions, although the fact that the Partitions occurred as three separate events means that we are still able to trace the further evolution of these institutions. The First Partition, in 1772, was forced upon Poland by an alliance of Catherine the Great of Russia, the Habsburg monarchy, and Prussia, in a pretext of stifling "anarchy" that had erupted in Poland (Schmidt 1926, quoted in Jędrzejewicz 1962). As they had done so often during the previous two centuries, the Polish *szlachta* banded together against the threat of absolutism in an uprising in 1768 known as the Confederation of Bar.

The Confederation, instead of being directed at the internal enemy of the monarch, mounted "a direct challenge to the Russian domination of Polish politics" (Frost 2012:166), eventually encompassing the opponents of King Stanisław August Poniatowski, who was widely seen as a puppet in Moscow's rule (Lerski 1996). Moreover, it also acquired a religious flavor, with Catholicism merging with Polish ideas of patriotism to forge a unified Polish identity; this identity was challenged by Catherine the Great's order that Orthodox Christians should be granted full equality in the Commonwealth, as well as freedom of worship (Skinner 2009). Supported by an odd coalition of Catholic France and the Muslim Ottoman Empire, the confederates of Bar launched a rebellion against Russian occupation that, while initially quickly put down, mutated into a guerilla war lasting for four years (Lukowski and Zawadzki 2006). The strength of Poland's decentralized polity, having resisted monarchical centralization for years, translated into a fighting approach that "ensured that the Russians could not possibly win the war simply by identifying and capturing a small number of targets" (Black 2009:55). However, the Russian forces, displaying tactics that were far beyond their usual staid methods, were able to overcome losses in 1769 and 1770 to end the rebellion in 1772 with a siege of the Wawel in Kraków and the monastery in Zagórz (Corwin 1917).

With the crushing of the Confederation, the stage was set for partition. With Russia becoming more powerful in Central Europe, Habsburg Austria proposed a territorial adjustment at the expense of the Poles to restore a balance in the region (Little 2007). The thievery of the Polish territories was done under arms and the threat of destruction of Warsaw (Corwin 1917), with the so-called Partition *Sejm* eventually acquiescing *de jure* to what had already occurred *de facto*. In the words of Likowski and Zawadzki (2006:122), "the Commonwealth was too weak to resist dismemberment. Its society and army were demoralized, bewildered, humiliated and divided." But as they note, there still was a measure of fight in Poland, as Tadeusz Rejtan blocked "access to the *Sejm*'s debating chamber in a vain protest against the inevitable" (ibid.).

Indeed, even though the First Partition was enabled via a simulacrum of the crucible of legislative power in the Commonwealth, it did not crush the Polish spirit, nor did it quell the development of political institutions capable of translating philosophy into reality. If anything, the First Partition "spurred the Poles to redouble their efforts at reform" (Nabrdalik 2007:653), even in the face of continued foreign intervention. Moreover, it was during the spaces in-between direct intervention, specifically when Russia was occupied by its own foreign adventures, when Poland was able to put in place modern political institutions. Taking advantage of the Russo-Turkish war of 1787–1792, Poland was to embark upon a far-reaching reform that, while short-lived, set the stage for the reemergence of uniquely Polish institutions after 1989.

As noted above, a running theme throughout the development of Poland's political institutions has been its informal nature, with formal institutions such as the direct election of kings sitting alongside informal ideas of liberty, exercise of power of the *szlachta*, and the periodic and perennial call to arms to resist absolutism. It was not until the eve of the last Partitions of Poland that the rhetoric of liberty and the practice of a modern parliamentary institution were complemented by a set of ground rules for the entire political system that codified many of these informal institutions and drew them into the formal legislative system. Indeed, while the continuing development of a parliamentary process (no matter how flawed) and a federal state (no matter how weak) over the previous centuries was an important precursor of modern democracy, perhaps the most tangible institutional demonstration of the Polish idea of liberty manifested itself in the May 1791 Constitution.

The May Constitution has been seen as a "symbol of Polish determination to create a modern democratic state embracing all elements of the Polish nation throughout peaceful, or at least bloodless, action" (Stone 2010:1). Even the king widely perceived to be little more than a puppet of Russia, King Stanisław August Poniatowski, noted the importance of such a document, declaring it "the only method of assuring to Poland the integrity of its possessions, and of preserving it from the ruin which foreign politics were preparing for it" (quoted in Howard 1991:14). Bringing a coalition of reformers together while, as noted, Russia was preoccupied with its own war against the Ottomans, the king convened a special session of the *Sejm* in 1788 that was to become known as the "Four-Year Diet."

Ironically, the process of creating a new charter of the rights of the Polish people and the rights of their government went against the grain of two centuries of legislative practice in Poland, even as the document itself was to encapsulate several hundred years' worth of political thought. In the first instance, the *Sejm* was altered in its composition, called as a "confederacy" so that lawmakers had no ability to use the *liberum veto* (Brzezinski 1991). Despite this alteration of normal (and sacred) parliamentary procedures, the work on the constitution went slowly, and the king also circumvented normal practice by seeking assistance from drafters outside the *Sejm* for the first version of the constitution (Zamoyski 1987). Finally, the draft of the constitution was introduced to the *Sejm* when most of the opposition was away on Easter holiday (Corwin 1917), and the king swiftly enacted the constitution into law without the required unanimity (a fact that was wiped away when the full *Sejm ex post* approved the document).

Despite its somewhat unorthodox provenance, the Polish constitution became the first of its type in Europe and the second codified constitution in the world, a fitting institutional import from the nascent United States of America, where many Polish officers fought for the cause of liberty. Building on seven centuries of Polish political thought prior (Brzezinski 1991), especially related to the constraint of the executive, the constitution had many advantages that even the American one did not. It is worth quoting Grześkowiak-Krwawicz (2012:23) at length on this point:

[Poland] was a country quite uniform in legal and administrative terms, there were no local privileges, and no new uniform structure of power needed to be forged for the entire country. Rather, the functioning of the existing Sejm, sejmiki, and courts merely needed to be streamlined – and this is precisely what the Constitution of the Third of May achieved. Significantly, it likewise precipitated processes of social change: although political power remained vested in the szlachta, by giving the burghers full civil rights and limited political rights and by placing the peasants under the protection of the Republic, a first step was taken towards eliminating the class-based society, replacing the noble nation with

a nation of all Poles. By Polish standards, these changes were revolutionary and were recognized as such by European opinion, which indeed described them as "the Polish revolution."

As evident throughout the history of the Commonwealth, and perhaps more forgivable with looming external threats to Poland, the difficulties in forming institutions that would translate liberty into a functioning system persisted under the Constitution of 1791. As Stone (2010) correctly points out, not every political institution envisioned under the constitution was properly conceived or functioning. There have also been attempts to juxtapose the Polish Constitution with the American one, portraying Poland's as a nondemocratic vehicle meant to serve the interests of a single class rather than extend the benefits of liberty to all (noted in Ludwikowski 1997).

However, the May Constitution did make a monumental contribution to modern political institutions by establishing the now-familiar three branches of government (executive, judicial, legislative) in Poland, as well as replacing the *liberum veto* with majority voting rules. Walking a fine line between the absorption of Enlightenment ideals and the more radical sentiments expressed in the continuing French Revolution, the constitution also included provisions for special sessions of the *Sejm* every twenty-five years to consider changes as necessary (Corwin 1917). In addition to the extension of civil and property rights to burghers noted above by Grześkowiak-Krwawicz (2012), the constitution also reinstated the idea of "religious liberty, and Article V's declaration that all power emanates from the will of the people was rooted in sixteenth-century legislation and the legal/political theories of Frycz Modrzewski, Góslicki, and others" (Cole 1998:17).

While the issues surrounding political institutional development in Poland really appear to enter (and indeed create) modernity at this point, the abruptness of the second Partition (in 1793) and the third and final Partition (in 1795) meant that much of the constitution's institutions were still in their infancy when Poland ceased to exist as a sovereign state. The institutional system that existed beforehand and that had disintegrated in some sense was now being slowly replaced by the empires that partitioned it, albeit not along the same geographic lines (which were substantially redrawn following the Congress of Vienna in 1815, see Wandycz 1974). But more important, the seeds had been planted among the polity in Poland, even if there was no longer a Polish state to implement these political institutions.

INSTITUTIONAL PERSISTENCE WITHOUT A STATE

It was during the time following the final Partition, where the constituent parts of the Polish state were hived off to Russia, Prussia, and Austria-Hungary, that the idea of institutional persistence (Acemoglu and Robinson 2006) or "institutional stickiness" (Krasnozhon 2012) comes into play. Since we will explore this idea more in depth in coming chapters, at this point it is sufficient to note that political institutions especially tend to display an overarching persistence in their functioning as part of their design (Lijphart 1992), even if the mechanisms are subjected to periodic changes at the margin (Alexander 2001). Moreover, even if formal political institutions are subject to less persistence than is normally assumed, informal institutions often display much more resilience and often cause changes in formal institutions if they should move out of alignment (de Soto 2000 uses the United States as an example of how formal political institutions were forced to change to accommodate informal ones).

As noted throughout the overview above, the Commonwealth of Poland and Lithuania sustained a strong, vibrant informal institutional network, with ideas such as executive constraints beginning as informal ideas that eventually percolated into formal institutional arrangements. This vibrant discourse on political arrangements and, perhaps, a reluctance to formally codify political institutions, helped these very same ideas to persist without a formal Polish state. Indeed, institutional persistence in Poland can be typified by the way in which Poland as an idea survived, even if the country itself disappeared off the map. Cultural institutions were crucial in forging the identity of "Polishness," with the Komisja Edukacji Narodowej (KEN, the Commission on National Education) carrying on its work until the 1820s in inculcating Poles with "their responsibility for the country and the nation, care for the well-being of citizens, and observance of law" (Jędrychowska 2014:41). Similarly, Porter (1996:1470) notes how the reality of occupation was overcome via political discourse, with the removal of "the nation from the political mode of discourse within which it had been embedded for decades and transposed it to a social framework. In other words, the nation-as-public-actor became the nation-as-social-collective."

Redefining what made Poland "Poland" helped to resist the forces at work against the political ideas that sustained the state prior to Partition, and created an intellectual barrier against assimilation. This was aided and abetted by the development of Polish print media, which flourished from the 1830s onward (Kawyn 1953), as well as popular culture, music, and art (Berend 2005), and Polish language instruction, which was carried out as a conscious rebellious act against "Russification" in the latter half of the nineteenth century (Bideleux and Jeffries 1998). Finally, the linkages of Roman Catholicism also provided a powerful social (and, at times, political) institution to define the Polish nation; as Jakelic (2012:169) correctly notes, "despite the political crisis and change of diocesan boundaries, the church gained centrality by serving as the sole institutional connection among Poles who lived in Prussia, Russia, and Austria." While only lower-order priests and curates were publicly associated with political movements in Poland (ibid.), the mere continued existence of Catholicism helped to sustain the community of Poles and provide a haven for free thought.

The importance of these social institutions in helping to keep the political ideas that had been formed over several centuries in Poland alive, even as they came under assault from the occupying empires, must not be understated. And when an opportunity arose to put these ideals back into practice, the Poles of the nineteenth century seized upon it. One of the key political actions that survived the Partitions was the idea of the justifiable use of force to resist tyranny, as can be seen in the large number of rebellions and insurrections that occurred during Poland's time of partitions. Even before the Third Partition (indeed, a prime cause of it), in 1794 there was a major uprising led by Tadeusz Kościuszko, an engineer who had cut his teeth in rebel warfare in the American Revolutionary War. Kościuszko's rebellion was inflected by his time in the American colonies (Haiman 1946), as he deviated from previous Polish uprisings, led by the nobility, to foment insurrection among the peasantry and create a broad-based resistance with the goal of social enfranchisement (Wereszycki 1967). Lasting from April to November 1794, Kościuszko was indeed able from the outset to bring peasants to his force of irregulars, where they performed heroically at the Battle of Racławice (Showalter 2013), but the might of the Russian army eventually proved too much. As Wereszycki (1967) rightly points out, the peasantry was not used to fighting for their nation, as this burden had been assumed by the gentry and the *szlachta* for the bulk of Poland's existence (a common occurrence throughout Europe but one especially notable in Poland due to the political decentralization across the *szlachta*).

While it is sometimes difficult to disentangle the reality of Kościuszko from the myth (Micińska 1998), the uprising of the Polish people against their Russian occupiers remained a source of inspiration throughout the Partition years, shaping further political thought and fostering the sense of self-reliance of the Polish people.[9] Moreover, Kościuszko's noble-yet-futile efforts (Kadziela and Strybel 1994) were to be repeated throughout the occupation of partitioned Poland; almost immediately following the Third and final Partition, Jan Henryk Dąbrowski, a general from Kościuszko's rebellion, attached himself to Napoleon's Italian army (with ill-fated consequences, see Wereszycki 1967), while in 1806 the Poles fought against the Prussians and in 1809 the Austrians, as opportunistic participants in Napoleon's march across Europe. The victories engineered via these conflicts came to an end with Napoleon's own fortunes in Waterloo, but the Polish struggle did not leave so easily for exile: a mere fifteen years after the Congress of Vienna, Polish peasants and *szlachta* alike took up arms in the ill-fated November Uprising of 1830–1831. Encompassing the sort of broad-based coalition that Kościuszko had originally planned for and drawing the peasantry into the struggle *en masse* (Milewicz 2010), the disciplined Poles "managed to win some really fine victories. Ultimately, however, less than a year after the outbreak of the insurrection it was defeated, and almost all those who were politically active in the nation, with nearly the whole corps of officers, went into exile" (Wereszycki 1967:113). This was accompanied by wholesale migration from Poland by those who had the means to do so (more on this below).

Following a semiregular cycle, the next insurrection came in 1846 in the "free Republic" of Kraków, one of the last administrative vestiges of Poland from the Congress of Vienna that had long been a hotbed of sedition against the occupying powers. Local uprisings had been occurring sporadically throughout Poland with significant support in Kraków (Corwin 1917), but unfortunately the support for a generalized uprising was misread by Polish exiles and the leader of the insurrection, Jan Tyssowski. Tyssowski, a lawyer with roots in the Habsburg portion of Poland (Tyrowicz 1930), led an attack on Austrian troops in February 1846, and when they withdrew, proclaimed a radical manifesto that utilized themes both from the French Revolution and incipient socialist thought (Lerski 1996). In particular, Tyssowski attempted to incite the peasantry once again into revolution against the Austrian

---

[9] In exile in France after being released by the Russians, Kościuszko himself argued in written work that Poland "could not count on the support of France or of any other foreign power, but must rely exclusively on its own strength and resources" (Sautin 2011:30).

occupation; however, in an eerie foreshadowing of socialist-inspired revolution to come in the next century, the peasantry was instead incited against the Polish aristocracy by the Austrians in an orgy of blood-letting and score-settling (Corwin (1917) and Hahn (2001), although Bideleux and Jeffries (1998) contend that the Austrians were just as clueless in this regard as Tyssowski). In any event, political revolt without popular support, combined with explicitly class-based appeals in the Polish political context had been exposed as a volatile mixture.

With Kraków occupied and officially incorporated into Austrian Galicia, the Polish contribution to the revolutions of 1848 occurring across Europe was directed externally rather than internally, as Poles fought in Italy and Hungary (Hahn 2001). It wasn't until 1863 that another popular uprising, with general support across the territories, was to once again grip the Polish lands. Ironically, Steed et al. (1914:157) note that the underlying catalyst for the "January Uprising" was the relaxation of Russian administration over Poland, which forced Polish nationalists to move towards "'unarmed agitation,' which was in effect a policy of constant provocation designed to bring on measures of repression to be represented to Europe as examples of Russian brutality." Continued protests led to Russians taking this bait, suppressing each fire as it flared up but failing to deal with the underlying spark (Porter 2000). When the pro-Russian head of Poland's civil administration, Count Aleksander Wielopolski, attempted to institute conscription to force radical youths into the Russian army (Zyzniewski 1965), the smoldering rage of Polish society burst into a conflagration.

This uprising became the largest in the recent series of rebellions, mainly "because it drew into its orbit the widest range of social classes, because it lasted longest, and because it covered the most extensive territory" (Wereszycki 1967:114). Hundreds of thousands of Poles across geography and socioeconomic strata took up arms in an extensive guerilla action against the Russians, fighting the regular Russian army across the lands of Poland occupied by Russia, as well as parts of Lithuania and modern-day Belarus and Ukraine (Gentes 2003). As Leslie (1955:57) correctly noted, "a revolt so badly prepared and led by young and inexperienced men might easily have fizzled out, but the Russian military authorities had no clear policy in the crisis." Having to maneuver a numerically superior force over a wide territory and against a hostile population of 5 million Poles, the Russians faced difficulties from the outset (Kieniewicz 1967); coupled with their military structure and distrust of the peasant soldiers forced to fight in a faraway land, Russian officers concentrated their forces rather than retaining the flexibility needed to fight an insurgency (Leslie 1955). These factors perhaps sustained the rebellion long after it should have been torn apart by its own internal fighting.

And there was no end to the dissension within the ranks of the rebels, who were united by a common hatred of the Russian occupation but by little else. Much like the 1846 uprising, the rebellion in 1863 saw an infiltration of socialist ideas into the nationalist struggle, ideas that caused a split among the political class into "Whites" (right-wing) and "Reds" (left-wing) and began to challenge traditional Polish ideas of liberty (Zyzniewski 1965). The actual administration of the insurrection was hampered by these political cleavages, as revolutionary tribunals, internecine struggles, and a left-wing coup that eventually gave way to the dictatorship of Romuald Traugutt (who appropriated many of the leftists' ideas) led to the subduing of the insurrection (Leslie 1955). Coupled with the hope for foreign intervention that never came, and as Marxists were to say later, the revolution collapsed from the weight of its internal contradictions. In the words of Porter (2000:43), "not only did thousands lose their lives, but the defeat seemed to negate the ideals, beliefs, and hopes that had sustained so many for so long."

These repeated insurrections brought stronger and swifter retributions against Poland, making it more difficult for the institutional framework of Poland to survive these external pressures. And while we have seen that Polish political thought and *informal* institutions persisted throughout the Partition period (in addition to the resilience of economic institutions, see below), there is also a growing body of economic and political science research showing how Poland's loss of sovereignty affected the future development of *formal* political institutions. Indeed, as Weeks (2011:53) asserts, "in the nineteenth century the only 'national' institution the Poles retained – in particular in the Russian Empire – was the Catholic Church." It would thus be folly to think that, under foreign subjugation, Polish political thought and institutions could persist indefinitely without being influenced in their evolution; this is doubly true when one considers that, by the late nineteenth century, there was little hope that a country named "Poland" would ever appear again.

In regard to political thought and the development of political institutions, much recent work has shown that *which* empire a Pole was subjected to during the long night of partition had a profound effect on attitudes well into the twentieth century and beyond. As noted above, the Partitions brought together three very different empires on Polish territory, with three very distinct modes of governance and institutional arrangements of their own. Despite the absorption of Kraków into Galicia, there is widespread agreement that on the whole it was preferable for a Pole to be a subject of the Austro-Hungarian Empire, which was much more *laissez-faire* in its approach to administration, than to be subjected to either Russian (Wolf 2007) or, after 1830, Prussian domination (Kann 1974). As Grosfeld and Zhuravskaya (2015:60) correctly summarize, in Austrian Galicia,

Poles were subject to the most liberal law of nineteenth-century Europe. The Habsburgs gave unprecedented administrative and cultural autonomy to their Polish territories. In Galicia, Catholics practiced freely, as the empire was predominantly Catholic, but religious tolerance applied to Jews as well. Polish-language schools were common. Poles were allowed to participate in local administration and to forge a career in government. In the second half of the nineteenth century, Polish became the official language in Galicia and an official self-governance body, Sejm Krajowy, a special parliament made up of Poles, was formed. Censorship was also abolished in the late eighteenth century.

Much of this autonomy came about due to Austria's own weakness, following its defeat in war against Prussia and the subsequent agreement with Hungary to create the dual monarchy. Regardless of the source, however, not only were political institutions that had existed (i.e., the *Sejm*) able to reconstitute themselves somewhat in the Austrian territories, the conditions were created for informal political thought to carry on the banner of noble liberty.[10] This was further strengthened by the lack of sustained German immigration into the region, allowing the Poles to retain their language and identity and avoid assimilation into the Empire (Wandycz 1967). Identity was then passed on by political institutions such as the local school board, which allowed for education along Polish (rather than Austrian) lines from the 1870s onward and ended any half-hearted attempts at "Germanization" (Bialasiewicz and O'Loughlin 2002).

By contrast, the Poles living under the Russian empire (in the so-called Kingdom of Poland) were subjected to the most brutal treatment of any of their fellow countrymen. In the immediate aftermath of the 1863 Uprising, hundreds of rebels were executed by the Russian military, and an estimated 36,459 were deported to the farthest reaches of Siberia (Gentes 2000). In an irony no doubt lost on the Russians or their subjects in Poland, "the

---

[10] Ironically, the ability of Poles to take advantage of these concessions may have been limited by Polish notions of national salvation, and the feeling that the resurrection of the Polish state would come via Warsaw (Kann 1974).

methods of oppression [after the Uprising] were considerably more severe under the reformist Tsar than under his conservative father" (Kappeler 2014:253). The fervent anti-Polish feeling in Russia prevalent after the Uprising, even amongst the liberal intelligentsia, also ensured that policies such as the mandatory teaching of Russian in Polish primary and second-ary schools and the overhaul of education in general along Russian-friendly lines continued unabated (Pogorelskin 1987); these policies were supplemented later in the nineteenth century by policies to expropriate land from the Polish gentry and to erase Catholic and Polish legacies from the "Western territories" (Weeks 2004).

Indeed, over the medium-term, a punitive policy of Russification was also enacted throughout the former Commonwealth, with Russian-language and cultural policies directed at Lithuania from the end of the Uprising through 1868 (Staliunas 2004) and for much longer in the so-called Western territories, encompassing such major centers as Kiev, Minsk, Vilnius, Kaunas, Białystok, Grodno, and Brześć Litewski/Brest-Litovsk (Weeks 1994:28). Scholars agree that Russification was not neces-sarily utilized to the fullest extent against non-Polish nationalities, using cultural policies more as a prophylactic against Polish influence, with some continuing debate on whether or not Russification against Lithuanians, Belarusians, and Ukrainians was explicitly directed by the Tsar and central authorities (Weeks 2001).[11] But against Poland and ethnic Poles, from 1863 onward, the Russian administration and monarchy created a steadily escalating assault on Polish political and cultural institutions, which began to whittle away the political culture that had been building in Poland for centuries.

The first steps of Russification proceeded along the lines of standard Russian practice, even to this day: "to anyone unfamiliar with the Russian system, it is most surprising to learn that many of its most rigorous practices could be put into effect as mere administrative measures, at the whim of an official" (Davies 2005:73). This meant that, rather than ending draconian police practices after the Uprising was thoroughly quashed, the threat of deportation continued throughout the Russian occupation, as did the threat of capricious and arbitrary imprisonment, depending upon the whim of the particular police officer and the judiciary. And while the basis

---

[11] Even if Russification against the "Western territories" was not an explicit goal of the Tsar, many studies (see for example Dolbilov 2004) acknowledge that the intertwining of the Russian administrative and cultural institutions make such nuanced demarcations negligible.

of Polish civil law was retained, the judiciary was replaced with Russian administrators and brought into line with the Russian system (Kappeler 2014). The declaration of Russian as an official language in 1863 also meant that, unless one spoke Russian fluently, the levers of state administration and especially the judicial system were closed off (Pavlenko 2006); much as is true among Russian-speakers today in countries such as Moldova and Ukraine, if given the chance to speak Russian and another language, administrators chose to speak Russian exclusively.[12] Thus, even with the Polish civil legislation retained, access to the formal judiciary was suddenly restricted to those who spoke the language of occupation.

Continuing on this theme, the linguistic and cultural assault on Poland was more subtle than police harassment or closed access to the justice system, but also escalated throughout the occupation. By the 1880s, Russia had forbidden the use of the Polish language in churches and at school, even outside of its ban for use in instruction (Eversley 1915), going so far as to reprimand students who used Polish even on break in-between classes (Pavlenko 2006). A gradual move to the Cyrillic alphabet also meant that many students that were able to obtain Polish-language books from abroad written in the Latin alphabet were not able to read them, a tactic employed by the Tsarist administration to keep literacy down to acceptable (but not rebellion-fomenting) levels (Davies 2005). Even the name of "Poland" was erased from the Russian-occupied areas, instead being re-named the "Vistula region" (*Privislinkii kraii*) for easier administration from St. Petersburg (Kappeler 2014).

The *Kulturkampf* against Poland in the Russian territories extended beyond formal and informal political institutions and encompassed the final "national" institution: the Catholic Church. The Tsar and especially the Russian Orthodox Church led an active campaign to remove Catholicism from the hearts and minds of Poles, equating Catholicism with Polishness and thus treason (Davies 2005). In fact, as Davies (2005) and Grosfeld and Zhuravskaya (2015) were to note, not satisfied with attacking the leaders of the church on Polish territory (whom they worked on corrupting, see Davies 2005), the Russian administration severely

---

[12] I personally heard this assertion in Moldova in May 2015. Moldova, at the time of this writing, has Russian and Romanian as its two official languages. During my talks with Ministry of Economy staff, they said that there were complaints from citizens who dealt with Russian-speaking officials, "because [the officials] only spoke Russian and refused to speak Romanian."

oppressed the lower clergy, sacked the bishops, confiscated the property of the various dioceses, and, most tellingly, isolated the Polish church from Rome by prohibiting any contact with the Vatican (Kappeler 2014).

The sustained assault on institutions in Poland was unsuccessful in utterly destroying said institution only due to an issue that plagues Russia today, the basic incompetence of its state administration. Grosfeld and Zhuravskaya (2015:56) correctly note that "Russia was also character-ized by the least efficient administrative apparatus and the lowest education spending of the three empires"; as shown in Figure 2.1, per capita primary and secondary school enrollment in the Russian Empire was the lowest by far of the three occupying powers, while telegraph density per square mile (a good proxy for technological advancement in the 1800s) also was dwarfed by Prussia and, to a lesser extent, Austria-Hungary. Perhaps this lack of capability led to what Davies (2005:78) characterized as "the machine had several built-in defects [making] the gap which separated the Autocrat's wish from its practical application as vast as the Empire itself." While the Tsar's bureaucracy increased the number of administra-tive subdivisions in Poland, necessitating more administrators (Leslie 1980), this did not necessarily mean that the quality of administration was improved; as Davies (2005) notes at length, corruption permeated the bureaucracy (meaning things could be done for a price), while stringent rules were intermittently applied, and the extreme centralization of the Russian Empire meant that independent thought was discouraged and time could be bought while subordinates waited for orders from their superiors.

The contrast between Russia's extreme political repression and its desultory Russification policies meant that there were spaces in-between where political institutions could continue to grow. In particular, with-out formal political institutions in which to debate and vote, Poles turned to newspapers and meetings (many held in Western Europe) to continue the battle of ideas. Weekly magazines such as *Przegląd Tygodniowy* (Weekly Review) and the literature of Bolesław Prus spear-headed a new political viewpoint under the rubric of "Warsaw Positivism," a direct rebuke to the Romanticism prevalent in Poland during the early Partition. Based on the idea of "organic work" (*praca organiczna*), this school of thought eschewed open and armed rebellion as the way to continue the entity known as Poland, and instead focused on economic and cultural independence, and overcoming the short-comings of the Polish state as it had been operated, as the way to preserve the nation (Blejwas 1982).

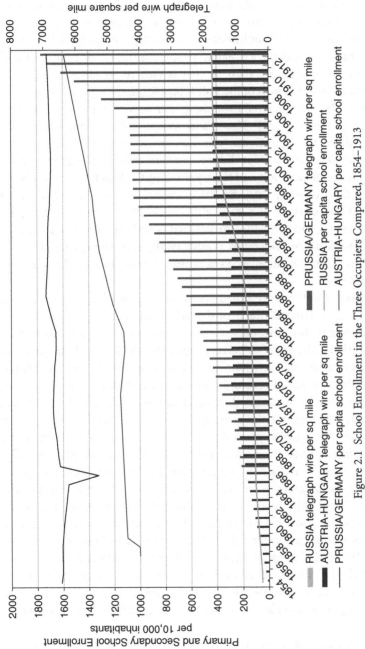

Figure 2.1 School Enrollment in the Three Occupiers Compared, 1854–1913
Source: Banks and Wilson (2015).

In the words of Walicki (2005:10), organic work "consisted in the organization of Polish life through a network of non-governmental institutions – educational, social, and economic, aiming above all at the 'nationalization' of the newly enfranchised peasantry." Because of the formal political oppression in the Russian territories, the idea of organic work took root more strongly there than in Galicia (where, as noted, a *Sejm* was functioning for the benefit of the Polish people), and the proponents of this approach often were derived from the gentry whose land was expropriated by the Tsar (Prizel 1998). This reality meant that, for much of the late nineteenth century, positivism was seen as an upper-class pursuit, with organic work a mission that did not connect with the peasantry; despite preaching social inclusion and rightly stressing the benefits of capitalism in creating this cohesion (Blejwas 2010), even the idea of a Polish nation remained the province of a small elite (Prizel 1998). The lack of popular support for the positivist idea meant that it had dissipated as a coherent intellectual force by the 1890s (Leslie 1980), even though its ideas and tactics were readily adopted as a form of resistance to Russian (and Prussian) rule.

In contrast to the more pragmatic positivist school, the appearance of socialism also changed much of the debate in Poland (as in the rest of Europe) during this time, presenting an alternative to *szlachta* democracy and traditional ideas of political representation. While positivism preached subversion rather than rebellion, and made little inroads with the peasantry, socialism preached revolution and a better life for the working class. The generation of socialists that arose in Poland during the 1870s and 1880s were focused on the growing industrial proletariat and less concerned with the agrarian peasantry, which made them different from their utopian forebearers; more interesting is that the vast majority of Polish socialists came from Russian universities in the borderlands, bringing with them the trappings of secret societies and strong internal organization (Blejwas 2010). Moreover, socialist thought in Poland, as opposed to other countries, was helped precisely by the fact that "the attraction of socialism was not its 'universalism' but its implacable hostility to tsarism" (Prizel 1998:55). Fusing the idea of Polish exceptionalism from the positivists with the Romantic attachment to armed uprising, underground parties such as the Polish Socialist Party (PPS) of Józef Piłsudski were able to appeal to broader segments of society and across socioeconomic classes.

Indeed, where the Russian portion of occupied Poland had focused on crushing internal dissent, instead it had fostered a vibrant underground political movement, essentially split into socialist and National Democratic factions but with common goals of national independence and social reorganization (Kappeler 2014). And while it may have been more difficult for the socialists to reconcile the dreams of the *Internationale* with the desire for an independent Poland (this issue continued to divide Polish socialists well into the twentieth century), the steady policies of Tsarist Russia reconciled many on the left to the need for just such an eventuality. Just as in Russia proper, as would be seen in 1917, the Tsarist Empire planted the seeds for its own destruction across its territories.

Compared to the draconian Russification policies in Warsaw and Russian-occupied Poland and the more laissez-faire approach of Austria-Hungary in Galicia, Prussian-occupied Poland had its own set of policies that seemed to split the difference and create a cacophony of contradictions. Despite a more Austrian approach to the Polish nationality immediately following the Uprising of 1863, Otto von Bismarck's dream of German Empire began to concentrate more on Poland after the three wars Prussia fought to unify Germany (against Denmark, Austria-Hungary, and France) in 1871. By 1873, Bismarck had instituted the *Kulturkampf*, a struggle to solve "the Polish question" that was plaguing Prussia's eastern territories by re-asserting the dominance of Germanic culture. In the Polish territories of Pomerania, Poznania, and Silesia (Zubrzycki 1953), Bismarck's administration attempted to remove "Polishness" via outright legislation, discrimination, and an array of restrictions aimed at breaking the back of Poland's informal institutions.

As Protestant power overseeing a subdued Catholic nation, the *Kulturkampf* against "Polishness" was a difficult task when 10 percent of the Prussian Empire had Polish as its native tongue (Hagen 1972). But following Russia's lead, Germany instituted a set of laws abolishing Polish as a language of instruction, elevating German to the sole language available in the courts and public administration, and, in 1886, even abolishing private language instruction of Polish (Coleman 1934). Unlike anti-Catholicism, as we will see, which abated over time, the attack on the Polish language only escalated, with the Reich Association Law of 1908 forbidding the use of Polish in private clubs and associations (Berghahn 1999). But with each push of the government to eradicate the language, opposition pushed back, with Polish patriots willing to strike, be dismissed from their positions, and even suffer physical violence in order to keep the language alive (Coleman 1934).

Prussian state administration also began to interfere heavily in the daily proceedings of the Catholic Church, with Trzeciakowski (1967) noting that two separate phases can be seen: first, from 1871–1878, where the government attempted to subordinate the clergy to the secular administration, and the second, from 1878–1914, where the influence of the church was neutralized in the community. The first stage had a much more political aspect to it, with government inspectors disrupting religious instruction, dictating which songs could and could not be sung, and closing down theological seminars (Davies 2005). Following on from legislation passed in 1871 prohibiting "dangerous" speech, the pulpit was closely watched as a possible rallying cry for malcontents, an eventuality that the government tried to definitely close down via the "May Laws" of 1873, which gave the government an active and direct role in clerical appointments (Trzeciakowski 1967).

Combined with a general and rising antireligious sentiment in Germany (Arlinghaus 1942), the struggle against the Catholic Church in Poland seemed to be a natural extension of the nationalities issue and anti-Polish legislation, but faced much greater obstacles than anticipated. In particular, and as with the attempted eradication of the Polish language, the Polish clergy practiced a methodical form of civil disobedience. Trzeciakowski (1967:621) emphasizes that the "upper ranks of the Church hierarchy did not observe the May Laws limiting their influence in the filling of clerical posts, and continued to conduct their own personnel policy," with additional measures of dissent undertaken by the lower levels of the clergy. While such disobedience brought punitive measures, including closure of seminaries, fines, and (sporadic) legal action, the reprisals stopped far short of those undertaken in the Russian-occupied territories. The mostly ineffective harsh measures also led to a necessary re-thinking of anti-Catholic policies, which shifted gears by 1878 into the more generalized cultural policies noted above (also taking away Catholic solidarity as a way to forge German-Polish linkages).

The Prussian struggle with Poland during the *Kulturkampf* went far beyond merely culture, however, and began to encompass basic economic institutions as well; under the infamous Colonization Commission (*Ansiedelungskommission*), a total of one hundred million marks were earmarked from the Reich Chancellery in 1886 to buy out Polish lands and redistribute them to German settlers, an amount that was augmented with an additional 100 million marks in September 1898 and another 150 million marks in July 1902 (Drummond 2013). Such a process of "depolonisation" was a barbaric move, but, in comparison with the

Russian policies of expropriation (where by 1853, even before the Uprising, 340,547 of 410,547 gentry were reduced to peasants, see Velychenko 1995), it was relatively mild. At least the Polish were receiving some compensation for their lands, however meager, instead of having them removed outright and being prohibited from acquiring land other than by inheritance, as in the Russian territories (Weeks 1994).

But, as with the Tsar's disastrous policies inculcating socialism in Russia and the Polish territories, Bismarck's cultural strategies short-circuited any chance of co-opting Polish resistance, especially given the predisposition of Polish leaders to Prussia/Germany over the considerately more repressive Russia (Blanke 1974). Instead, similar to life in the Russian-occupied territories, the idea of "organic work" took hold, with political debate and informal institutions flourishing underground (albeit to a much greater extent in the Prussian sector).

As seen already, no sphere of *Kulturkampf* went unchallenged, either from the attack on the Catholic Church (which eventually expanded to Germany proper) or the assault on the Polish language. A key element in supporting these existing institutions was the creation of Polish "self-help" organizations in both the economic (notably the credit unions) and cultural spheres (including libraries and "gymnastic clubs"), providing a meeting point for Poles and keeping a sense of community together even when the *Kulturkampf* was at its strongest (Onslow 1931), and were a consistent part of the landscape well before even the January Uprising (Hagen 1972). The creation of social societies, where one could speak Polish freely even while exercising, became its own form of protest, allowing for dissidence in the most mundane of manners. As Blanke (1974:552) noted, "In some ways the *Kulturkampf* experience actually aided the Polish cause, e.g., by mobilizing previously apolitical sections of the population in a joint national-religious cause and burying an incipient liberal-clerical conflict under a single banner."

Moreover, the Prussian portion of Poland had access to two attributes that were denied to the Russian and Austro-Hungarian territories: first, an industrial heartland that pushed economic growth, and second, the ability to work within the German system and forge alliances within Germany proper. The industrial revolution will be examined in the next section, but more important for the moment is the manner in which ethnic Poles were able to influence internal German politics. The policies of the *Kulturkampf* strengthened Catholic resistance within Germany among Poles and Germans alike, and caused the Catholic Centre Party to benefit immensely (Bowersox 2003). To return to Blanke (1974:552),

As recently as January 1886, Polish Reichstag deputies had joined with German opposition parties to censure Bismarck's expulsion of some 30,000 Poles and Jews from the eastern provinces. During the previous fifteen years of Kulturkampf the Poles had operated in close alliance with the major German opposition party, the Catholic Centre, and Bismarck had been forced to break off his Kulturkampf with no better than a draw.

Indeed, from the 1890s onward, much as in Galicia, Polish deputies were elected to the Reichstag in Berlin and represented Polish interests for the Prussian-occupied territories (Kubiak 1999). This was in stark contrast to the experience of Poles in the Russian-occupied territories, who were explicitly prohibited from holding high-level political offices (Velychenko 1995) and who faced laws forbidding any employment in the government offices of the "Western territories" (Weeks 1994).

Finally, much as Warsaw positivism was supplanted by other modes of resistance, the *Kulturkampf* had also petered out by the 1890s, at least in its most virulent form. The ascension of General von Caprivi to the chancellorship of Germany in 1890 led to a substantial lessening of tensions and relaxation of the most onerous parts of the cultural struggle under a dedicated policy of reconciliation. While this policy only lasted until 1894, due mainly to a perceived lack of advantages from the German side (Blanke 1977), it provided breathing space for the Polish informal institutions that had been under continuous assault for the past century. Moreover, it was a shrewd move for the German authorities, who saw little gain from increasingly stringent policies and, as noted above, the lessening of anti-Catholic policies undercut the collaboration between Poles and the Catholic Centre Party.

And while Bismarck may have blustered from his retirement about the insidious nature of the Pole and how they had to be contained within a strong Germany (Kaminski 1988), and while similarly repressive anti-Polish laws were to resume after von Caprivi's short-lived tenure (Morrow 1936), the failures of the *Kulturkampf* were evident even before von Caprivi's reconciliation. As Davies (2005:96) said, "paradoxically ... the *Kulturkampf* and the Colonization Commission succeeded in stimulating the very feelings which they were designed to suppress. From the Polish point of view, they were the best things that could have happened." Poles closed ranks, built their own informal institutions, and actually thrived; despite the attempt to either expel Poles (as in 1885) or buy their land, between 1896 and 1905 the Poles of Western Prussia actually increased their landholdings by 29,079 hectares (Morrow 1936). By the beginning of the twentieth century, still under partition and viewed with suspicion,

Polish political thought and informal political institutions had withstood an onslaught from all sides and survived.

THE TWENTIETH CENTURY: WAR, INDEPENDENCE, AND A NEW CONSTITUTION

As noted above, the experience of the Partitions have had long-lasting effects on the development of political institutions in modern-day Poland, with the effect different depending upon which of the empires the Polish territory was located in. In terms of political development and the preservation of formal political institutions, Poles located in the Austro-Hungarian Empire undoubtedly fared the best. The ability to access their own formal political institutions in Austria, institutions modeled on pre-existing legislatures, helped this territory of Poland to develop healthy political practices that could transfer over when Poland became independent once again. Becker et al. (2014) recently empirically demonstrated that this is not just a theoretical supposition: Polish citizens who live in the former-Habsburg portion of Poland have a much higher level of trust in the modern-day judicial system and the police than those based in formerly Russian or Prussian territories. Similarly, Grosfeld and Zhuravskaya (2015) find that support for democracy is significantly much higher in the Austrian portion of Poland than in the formerly Russian parts (they also find that the Russian policies against the Catholic Church were more successful than those of Germany, with church-going much lower in the former Russian territories than in either the Prussian or Austrian ones).

However, history, like the value of money, can exert its greatest influence the closer it is to the present day, and it is the experience of the twentieth century that may have shaped many of the formal institutions that now are evolving in both Poland and Ukraine. In 1900, Poland still remained an idea rather than a sovereign state, under Partition but soon to be given its independence via the conflagration of the First World War. Over the first decade of the century, the country saw a continued assault on informal political and cultural institutions in both the Russian and German zones of control; indeed, in many ways, the assault intensified, with the Colonization Commission appropriating more money for German settlement and the new tsar Nicholas II continuing the policies of his father Alexander III in instituting strict new ordinances against private education (Corrsin 1990). Poland and many of its institutions had survived the nineteenth century, but there was no guarantee that it was going to survive the twentieth.

This external repression was coupled by a threat to the institutions of Poland that came from within, the growing cancer of socialism. The idea of socialism had metastasized in the Polish body politic, still supported from its lifeline in Russia, and it began to take over influence in Polish life from, first and foremost, the church. As Blobaum (1988) rightly stresses, the church had adopted a policy of cautious loyalism to the Russian authorities beginning in the 1880s, due mainly to the threat of church closures and other punitive measures. While the retreat of the church from the political sphere, into one that was merely religious or social, may have enabled the organization to survive the worst of the Tsarist anti-Catholic policies; it also increasingly isolated the church from the political issues of the day. The zeal for remaking man in a perfect image thus shifted from the clergy to the revolutionaries, leaving the church out of its normal position as conscience of a nation (a role it only began to resume in the 1970s and 1980s).

Of course, the socialists were not the only political grouping that had coalesced with the retreat of the church from politics. In fact, the retreat of the church coincided with the development of the most modern of formal political institutions, the political party. Another underground political movement, named the National Democratic movement (*Endecja*), was founded in Warsaw in 1893 by Zygmunt Balicki and Roman Dmowski and began to play an informal but increasing role in shaping Polish political thought (Porter 1992). Descended from the "People's League," founded in 1887 with a similar goal to the socialists of independence through armed insurrection, the National Democrats abandoned such ideas early in favor of a radical nationalism that was directed at foreign nationalities (Lithuanians and Ukrainians) and, especially, Jews (Marzec 2015). It coalesced into a formal party by 1897, the National Democratic Party (SND), and, more tellingly, sought out partners in the Prussian-occupied territories, in order to develop a truly Polish-wide movement (Hagen 1972).

However, it was the socialists that were the most successful in their organization, at least up until the First World War. As could be expected in occupied Poland, informal socialist organizations predated the formation of formal socialist political parties, filling the vacuum left by the church, focusing on Polish independence, and calling for a Polish worker's government and social revolution (Szapiro 1929). The advent of an industrial proletariat at the end of the nineteenth century meant that organizations such as the Union of Polish Workers (ZRP) found a ready home in the expanding industrial base of the kingdom. The ZRP "focused on agitation among workers and broadened its movement to all the major industrial pockets of the kingdom" (Zimmerman 2004:18), bringing together various factions and streams of socialist thought under one large umbrella (Leslie 1980). Rather than striking at the political system or Tsarist authorities directly, the ZRP fomented labor actions and strikes such as the one in Łódz in 1892 that left at least 80 dead and 300 wounded (Zimmerman 2004 quotes the number of 80 while Leslie (1980) claims the number was 217 killed).

Even with increased attention of the Russian authorities and repeated crackdowns on socialist organizations, the time had come to transfer public agitation and informal labor organizations into a more formal political organization; this was to become Piłsudski's PPS, an organization that, politically at least, seemed to follow in the Polish tradition of liberty. At the PPS's founding congress in Paris in 1892, a manifesto was drafted that called for such rights as complete freedom of speech, universal suffrage, equality of all citizens under law, and equality of nationalities (Zimmerman 2004), a platform that would have not been out of place in 1830 or 1863. While still formally illegal, the PPS appeared to claim the mantle of a national reform party, given credibility by Piłsudski's continuing troubles with the Russian authorities (going from exile in Siberia to imprisonment in Warsaw's Citadel, see Davies 2005). Indeed, Piłsudski continued to use the language of nationalism, claiming that the "historical role of socialism in Poland is the defense of the west against reactionary Russia" (quoted in Zimmerman 2004:32).

The strains of socialism that mutated from its early beginning in Poland posed a long-term challenge to Poland's traditional political institutions but, paradoxically, in the short term (and with explicitly nationalist goals) it helped to ease the repression in the Kingdom of Poland. This was due mainly not to the exigencies of the Polish socialists, but to the fact that Russia was also infected. With Russia weakened by the Russo-Japanese War of 1904–1905 (an opportunity that leaders such as Piłsudski and Dmowski attempted to exploit in their travels to Japan, see Leslie 1980), the stage was set for resistance in both the Polish lands and in Russia itself. The economic turmoil engendered by the war, including the closing of Asian markets to Polish goods, led to bolder resistance, including demonstrations in Białystok in September 1904 and in Warsaw that November that led to violence, death, and the first open opposition to Russian power in forty years (Davies 2005).

But this opposition in Poland was dwarfed by the events of "Bloody Sunday" in January 1905 in Russia, where the Tsar's forces opened fire on a peaceful demonstration at the Winter Palace in St. Petersburg. The ramifications for Poland were immediate, as "industrial centres such as Łódz, Warsaw or Zagłebie Dabrowskie underwent a complex process consisting of waves of contention" (Marzec 2013:54). Similarly, membership in socialist parties began to grow (from 5,000 to over 100,000, according to Ascher (2004)) and more industrial actions arose throughout the Polish territories, although their spontaneous nature made them very difficult for formal political organizations such as the PPS to coordinate (Hofmann 2004). According to Davies (2005), over 1905–1906, a total of 6,991 work stoppages occurred involving over 1.3 million people, a wave of civil disobedience that accompanied more violent measures, including declaration of martial law in Łódz in May 1905 by the Tsar. This diverted much-needed manpower from the Far East, as the threat of revolution in Poland occupied some 300,000 soldiers that could have been utilized against the Japanese (Ascher 2004).

Weakness at home, including the threat of socialism overcoming the monarchy in Russia and the humiliating loss to the Japanese, forced the Tsar to take a more conciliatory tone towards his domestic, as well as his Polish, subjects. In the Polish territories specifically, the Tsar set aside the stringent anti-Polish language and anti-Catholic laws of the previous four decades, with trade unions legalized, Polish language instruction re-allowed in private schools, and restrictions on land purchases by Poles removed (Davies 2005). And Russia's own fundamental laws were transformed through the creation of a constitution in 1906, allowing for many of the issues called for by the PPS (including universal suffrage) and belatedly creating an all-Russian legislature (the Duma) that had responsibility for a land that had had its own legislature for hundreds of years prior. But, beyond the parliamentary coalitions that Poles had influenced in Prussia but not quite as far as their own *Sejm* as in Austria, under the new constitution, Polish candidates were allowed to stand for the Duma (Thatcher 2011).

In practice, however, the opening of the Duma to Polish candidates meant that only the National Democrats could stand for election (there were to be no socialists from Poland imported back into Russia), and the Duma itself was somewhat impotent as a legislative body, especially by modern standards (Shlapentokh 1999). Moreover, after 1908, Russian nationalism prevailed at the court of the Tsar, meaning that reactionary policies were soon returned to Poland; as Chmielewski (1970:67) noted, "the efforts of the conservative delegates of the Polish *Koło* (Circle) in the Duma to obtain redress of the most conspicuous Polish grievances and win moderate concessions for the Congress Kingdom in the areas of language, schools, and self-governance were ultimately frustrated." The assassination of Russian prime minister Stolypin in 1911 accelerated the punitive measures against Poland, including the removal of Chełm from the Kingdom of Poland in 1912 and its inclusion into the administrative region centered in Kiev (Sadkowski 1998), meaning that Poland's institutions were once again under assault from the Tsar.

The only event able to halt a resurgence of anti-Polish oppression was the worldwide conflict known at the time as the Great War. As volumes have been and continue to be written about the First World War, here is not the place to rehash the travails of Poland as a battleground for warring empires. Moreover, the war itself has little bearing on institutional development in Poland, apart from its influence after the war had ended. In this case, the greatest impact that the Great War had was its restoration of Poland as a sovereign state as part of the Versailles Treaty of 1919, bringing back formal political institutions that had long lain dormant but with a different face.

The road to Poland's independence within the confines of the war began in earnest in late 1917 with the formation of a "Regency Council" (*Rada Regencyjna)* in preparation for the return of the monarch. The German and Austrian occupiers in the Russian zone of Poland created a Provisional State Council (*Tymczasowa Rada Stanu,* or TRS) of fifteen members in January 1917, and the TRS in turn appointed three members of the Council in September to oversee an explicitly pro-German transition to statehood (Szymczak 2009). Creating a cabinet in December of 1917, the Council attempted to prepare the new Polish state for ascension to power, including reinstating the *Sejm* and overseeing how those elections would take place after the war (Karski 2014). Unfortunately, created as it was by the Central Powers, the Regency Council was seen as a puppet government of the Germans. Moreover, the Council lacked the support of the growing socialist movement, which was emboldened by the Russian revolution; from May onward, the Polish socialist parties and especially the PPS saw a growing radicalism as Polish émigrés to Russia returned in waves, with many of these émigrés under direct Bolshevik influence (Holzer 1967). The socialists created a rival provisional people's government in the town of Lublin just four days before the Armistice (November 7, 1918), calling into question which structure would rule an independent Poland.

While these issues of legitimacy and radicalization were to cause problems in the long run, in the short term any potential conflict was rendered moot by the release of Piłsudski from a German prison on November 10, 1918, a mere day before the fighting was to cease. Having spent the war leading Polish troops in alliance with the Austrians against the Russians, Piłsudski cooperated somewhat with the German-backed TRS from 1916 onward, but refused to commit himself fully; when he took to insulting German Warsaw governor Hans von Beseler in late 1917, he was jailed for the duration of the war (Salisbury 2003). The force of his personality was not weakened in any shape, as immediately upon his release, the Regency Council dissolved itself, transferring authority to Piłsudski exclusively. Although expected to side with the Lublin government (on the basis of his previous leadership of the strongest socialist faction in Poland), Piłsudski instead forced the Lublin government to dissolve itself in a show of national unity before assuming the role of temporary head of state himself, with Jędrzej Moraczewski selected as his prime minister (Karski 2014).

Without waiting for a formal settlement of the war, "two months of unpremediated rebellion" (Davies 2005:101) expelled German troops still present on Polish soil at the end of the war, with members of the Polish Military Organization (POW) taking up the fight in Galicia and disarming the passive and broken Austrian garrison (Molenda 1991). Under Piłsudski's leadership, nationalist and pianist Ignacy Paderewski formed a new government as the Polish Republic's second prime minister in January 1919 that was majority right-wing, but still secured the support of five left-wing ministers; despite political intrigues and an attempted right-wing coup in Warsaw at the beginning of January, parliamentary elections were held on schedule later that month (Bernhard 2005). These elections, the first in "postwar" Europe (the war itself had not really ended for Poland), were held in all territories that were Polish-controlled, and as Polish control moved east, additional elections were held (ibid.). As Ajnenkiel (1989) shows, the results of the elections favored the Center and right-wing parties, who together held approximately 75 percent of all representation in the reconstituted *Sejm*. The newly elected *Sejm* (which had not yet formed a government, with Paderewski remaining as the prime minister) met for the first time in February 1919, whereupon it elected a speaker (Wojciech Trąmpczyński) and revoked the temporary powers of leadership granted to Piłsudski (Bernhard 2005).

However, the collapse of the Central Powers (and Russia) did not lead to an automatic transition to independence for Poland, as the exact details of statehood were bargained for in the Halls of Versailles, and the practical matter of the borders was decided by blood on the battlefield. As Karski (2014:28) notes, "Poland still had no definite boundaries because the task of defining them formally belonged to the [Allied] Supreme Council"; the issue of Poland's actual borders was complicated by Piłsudski's insistence on reclaiming Poland's borders of 1795 (as well as hopefully enlisting Ukraine in a fight against Bolshevik Russia; see Rees (2006)) in order to create a multinational bulwark against both German and Russian expansionism (Stachura 2004). The Paris Peace Conference hoped to solve these issues in a final settlement, but instead created many more headaches for the future, especially in denying Poland access to Danzig by declaring it a "free city" under the protection of the League of Nations (but giving Poles a corridor to the city via Pomerania). Similarly, the decision to hold a plebiscite in Upper Silesia kept the status of this region in limbo for two years until it formally joined Poland, but provided another raw spot for relations with Germany going forward for the next twenty years (Cienciala and Komarniski 1984).

The Versailles Treaty created enough problems regarding Poland's western and northern borders, but the unsettled issue of its eastern borders led to repeated conflict with the former borderlands of the Commonwealth. A Polish-Ukrainian war flared up immediately following Polish independence, with Poles from the Galician region supporting a Polish uprising in Lwów against the declaration of a "Western Ukrainian Peoples' Republic" (Frucht 2004). This support of ethnic Poles in Lwów blossomed into a full-blown Polish-Ukrainian war, a "fierce but orderly" conflict that was "fought along established fronts and inflicted relatively little damage on the civilian population" (Subtelny 2009:328). With Polish forces becoming involved by the end of 1918, the outnumbered Ukrainians saw Poland move beyond the original goal of securing Lwów to occupy all of Eastern Galicia up to the Zbruch River by July 1919, putting an end to incipient Ukrainian nationalism (Stachura 2004).

This move immediately began to create friction with Poland's new neighbor, Bolshevik Russia, which had begun a march westward to "set the world aflame" with revolution. Soviet leader Vladimir Lenin's belief that Germany would be the weakest link in the capitalist chain made conflict between the new Polish Republic and the new Soviet Russia inevitable; in order to reach Germany and secure it for socialism, it was necessary to march through Warsaw. Bolshevik forces had begun their westward expansion almost immediately once German forces had withdrawn in 1918, proclaiming a Soviet Socialist Belorussian-Lithuanian

Republic in January 1919, and bumping up against Polish forces that had moved east during the Polish-Ukrainian war (Frucht 2004). Skirmishes and aborted diplomatic overtures between Poland and Russia throughout 1919 (Wandycz 1965) continued to pile upon each other until erupting into a full-scale conflict in April 1920. Early unexpected success and the capture of Kiev, Wilno (Vilnius), and Lwów by Polish troops quickly turned into a Soviet counteroffensive by June that brought the Soviets to the gates of Warsaw and threatened the existence of the Polish Republic once again. Only a brilliant and highly unorthodox counter-counter-offensive from Piłsudski on August 16, 1920 (known afterwards as "the Miracle on the Vistula") was able to rout the numerically superior Soviet army and save Warsaw, pushing Soviet troops back into Belarus and Ukraine until they sued for peace in October (Fiddick 1973).

The defeat of Soviet Russia, the recapture of Western Ukraine, and the (apparently) final demarcation of Poland's borders led to a resumption of formal political institution-building after its long hiatus. As Davies (2001) notes, the interwar period can be delineated into four specific phases of political events: the Second Republic (1918–1921); the Constitutional Period (1921–1926); the *Sanacja* Regime (1926–1935); and the collapse of democracy entirely (1935–1939). The Second Republic, as we have already seen, oversaw the restoration of the *Sejm* and the return of Poland to a physical state within defined borders. In a process harkening back to the final days of Poland before the Partition, the Second Republic also oversaw the creation of a new constitution, the so-called Little Constitution (*Mała Konstytucja*) of February 1919, which endowed the *Sejm* as the highest organ of the state and the initiator of all laws in Poland (Bernhard 2005).

This "interim document was the foundation of government for the next two years" (Brzezinski 1991:72–73) before it was supplanted by the considerably broader March Constitution of 1921. The task of creating this more permanent constitution was borne by all members of society, as those in the newly formalized institutions of the executive and legislative branch, those in academia, and other major political actors offered suggestions for the way forward. Bernhard (2005) offers a fascinating look at the way in which the March Constitution came to be, noting that the original work of the constitution came not from the *Sejm* but from the executive, with Prime Minister Moraczewski opening a Constitutional Office (*Biuro Konstytucyjne*) before the *Sejm* even had its elections in January 1919. Benefiting from possible competition among competing factions, three separate projects were underway simultaneously, including one that would craft an American-like federalist document, one that made a more populist, left-wing constitution, and one that split the difference and was modeled on the French example of the previous century. Paderewski's ascension to prime minister halted these projects and instead handed over work to a hand-picked commission of experts, who fashioned a hybrid model of the American and French constitutions as a basis for Poland going forward (ibid.).

The new *Sejm* seized the initiative from this point on, however, and followed the Little Constitution with the creation of a Constitutional Commission that would examine all proposals going forward (but in practice, the only proposals seriously considered reflected the political make-up of the *Sejm*; that is, more weighted towards centrist and conservatives (Bernhard (2000)). Meeting 106 times over the following 2 years, with discussions taking up 38 sessions of the *Sejm* (Ajnenkiel 1991), constitutional debate was only suspended during the summer of 1920 due to the Russian invasion, and resumed in autumn of that year. The draft that was under consideration was much more closely aligned with the original French draft that came out of the Constitutional Bureau, and while reservations were expressed by many political parties (even after successive readings and tinkering with the language in the *Sejm* in early 1921), the constitution passed overwhelmingly by voice vote on March 17, 1921 (Bernhard 2005).

The Constitution of 1921 as passed was viewed at the time as one of the most progressive and democratic in the world (Fijalkowski 2013). Carrying on the tradition of the 1791 Constitution, the March Constitution "incorporated the wide range of liberal and democratic measures expected of a western-style parliamentary regime, including civil rights, the rule of law, freedom of expression, assembly and religion, and guarantees for ethnic minorities" (Stachura 2004:76). As the founding document of the new Poland, it laid the legal foundation for a multiparty system, party activities, and establishment of a bicameral legislature that included an upper and lower house (with the lower house retaining the name *Sejm* and the upper house being named the Senate (Kubiak 1999)). Also building on the previous constitutional tradition of the country pre-Partition and Poland's traditional adoption of the idea that the nation was separate from the state (and the executive), the early Articles of the Constitution declared that the sovereignty of Poland belonged to its people (Article 2). Perhaps boldly, and for a first in Poland's political history the constitution also rejected the idea of royal rule, thus eliminating in name a political institution that had already been transformed over the previous three centuries (Brzezinski 1991).

However, the constitution also had several changes in the administration of political power in Poland from the manner in which it had been exercised for the previous two years. Despite the reality that the *Sejm* of 1919–1921 had struggled due to lack of experience, polarization of political parties, and the difficulty of overseeing a Poland that was only approximately 70 percent Polish (Główny Urząd Statystyczny (1921); Fijalkowski (2013)), the March Constitution continued to vest the majority of the state's power in the *Sejm*. Unlike the Constitution of 1791, which was consciously modeled on the American Constitution (the only example at the time), the March 1921 Constitution that was selected was fashioned after the French Constitution of the Third Republic (1875), and encouraged factionalism and naked party politics. Elections to the *Sejm* were to be conducted on the basis of "universal, secret, direct, equal, and proportional" processes (Frucht 2004:25), with each of the 444 members of the legislature holding 5-year terms in office; however, a "simple majority vote" of the *Sejm* would be enough to force "a single minister, the whole executive cabinet, or the President to resign" (Fijalkowski 2013:38, quoting Article 58 of the Constitution). This was a definitive shift in the balance of power in favor of the legislature.

In Hawgood's (1939:335) formulation, the constitution preserved the best attributes of Polish *szlachta* democracy and combined "weakness in normal circumstances with strength in the face of national crisis," with the president mostly a figurehead (Cienciala and Komarniski 1984). While the left-wing parties had wanted a strong leader who was directly elected by the people, the center and right parties wanted to vest more power in the *Sejm*, with the National Democratic Party even suggesting that the head of state be chosen by the *Sejm* (making the executive entirely subordinate to the legislative branch; see Fijalkowski 2013). The constitution's strong bias against the executive did not go unnoticed by Piłsudski, who declared he would not abide by such emasculatory rules, and who began his withdrawal from Polish politics (Seton-Watson 1945). In one sense, this had accomplished exactly what many of the political parties behind the constitution had desired, as much of the wording of the constitution and transfer of executive powers to the legislature had been done explicitly to circumscribe Piłsudski and his popularity and avoid his personal takeover of the apparatus of state (Stachura 2004).

The weakness of the executive was a recurring theme in Polish political thought, but need not have doomed the constitution to unworkability.

Unfortunately, the paradox of constitutionalism is that any government strong enough to put together a document limiting its own rights has no ability to bind future governments from abrogating those rights at will. In the case of early twentieth-century Poland, the framers of the March Constitution had every right to be worried about Piłsudski, as he spent the next five years formally out of government planning his return to power.

To be fair, the performance of the *Sejm* during the Constitutional Period gave him much ammunition, as the cleavages in society manifested themselves in the form of extreme political volatility. The legislative elections scheduled for 1922 were delayed due to wrangling within the *Sejm* over the country's electoral law, and how the current members of the *Sejm* would exit power legally via the next election (Bernhard 2000). Once held, the highly contested *Sejm* elections ended in a virtual draw among the major parties (Table 2.2), with

Table 2.2 *Results of the* Sejm *Election of 1922*

	Sejm		Senat	
Electoral List	**Seats**	**%**	**Seats**	**%**
Right				
Chjena	163	36.7	48	43.2
"Polish Centre"	6	1.4	0	0
Subtotal	*169*	*38.1*	*48*	*43.2*
Centre				
PSL "Piast"	70	15.8	17	15.3
NPR	18	4.1	3	2.7
Subtotal	*88*	*19.9*	*20*	*18*
Left				
PPS	41	9.2	7	6.3
PSL "Lewica"	2	0.5	0	0
PSL "Wyzwolnie"	49	11	8	7.2
KZPMiW	2	0.5	0	0
ChSR	4	0.9	0	0
Subtotal	*98*	*22.1*	*15*	*13.6*
Minorities				
Minority Bloc	66	14.9	22	19.8
Other Minority Parties	23	5.2	5	4.5
Subtotal	*89*	*20.1*	*27*	*24.3*
Total	**444**	**100**	**111**	**100**

Source: Bernhard (2000), based on data from Ajnenkiel (1989).

the right-wing having the most support but Gabriel Narutowicz emerging the winner from successive rounds of voting in the *Sejm* due to support from the left, the Minority Bloc, and the centrist PSL "Piast" party. Almost immediately, rioting and protesting began in Warsaw, orchestrated from the right and with a distinctly anti-Semitic tone, only to be met with counter-demonstrations that left two people dead and scores wounded (Brykczynski 2014). The escalating violence culminated in the assassination of the first president of the Second Republic, Gabriel Narutowicz, in December 1922. Narutowicz was in office for just five days before he was killed at an art gallery by an extremist linked to the National Democratic Party. The ensuing institutional crisis following the assassination was described by Bogusław Miedzińsk, a follower of Piłsudski:

After numerous attempts to make contact by phone, we realized that the state institutions had ceased to function. There was no one at the Ministry of Foreign Affairs, the Ministry of Interior, or the State Police Headquarters. We found out that no instructions [for dealing with the crisis] had been issued by anyone to the provincial authorities, diplomatic missions, or the Polish Telegraph Agency. The government had ceased to function (cited in Pajewski 1993).

Despite a tense aftermath in which various factions of the left prepared for revolution on the streets (Brykczynski 2014), calm was eventually restored through the levers of government that had been prepared in the constitution: the speaker of the *Sejm*, Maciej Rataj, called on General Władysław Sikorski, a hero of the Battle of Warsaw, to form a new government, which he duly did (with Piłsudski's acquiescence) in the hours following the assassination. Sikorski simultaneously imposed a state of emergency on the capital (Bernhard 2005), which removed the immediate threat of revolution, but the long-term consequences of the assassination continued to fester, including a growing attraction of proto-fascism and anti-Semitism (Brykczynski 2014). The trend toward right-wing agitation, including the quick rehabilitation of Narutowicz's assassin (whose original target was Piłsudski), led Piłsudski to resign all of his posts in disgust, extending "his bitter condemnation of the National Democrats to the parliamentary system as it then existed in Poland" (Cienciala and Komarnicki 1984:206).

This inauspicious start to the Second Republic mirrored the political divisions within Poland, and the unstable party system saw a cascade of failed governments, with fourteen cabinets rising and then falling between November 1918 and May 1926 (Karski 2014). Moreover, as the early experience of the *Sejm* had shown even before the March Constitution had come into being, the personalities involved in legislation were not up to the task before them:

> the *Sejm* proved incapable of enacting necessary legislation for many areas. Its proceedings all too often degenerated into chaotic tumult which occasionally even spilled over into violent and abusive confrontation. It was brought further into disrepute among the general public by well-founded stories of graft and endemic corruption among the politicians. Too many of them came across as selfish, arrogant opportunists with scant regard for the national interest, however loosely or nebulously that was defined. (Stachura 2004:64).

The years of fragmentation in the *Sejm* and limited reform on economic issues (including an episode of hyperinflation in 1922–1923, see below) appeared to threaten the very independence that Poles had dreamed about for over 120 years. Having railed against the Constitution of 1921 since its inception and criticizing its weight towards the legislature (done with him in mind, as noted above), Piłsudski took the formation of the Center-Right government of "Chjena" and "PSL-Piast" as the final insult (Lerski 1996).[13] Reclaiming the mantle of progress in an attempt to both impose order through a strong executive and to morally "sanitize" the corrupt Polish body politic (Kowalski 2014), Piłsudski engineered a coup in May 1926 and took power after two days of fighting that left over 300 dead (Lerski 1996). This action made the Constitutional Period unfortunately a very short-lived time in Polish history, with Poland drifting from a "mild form of dictatorship" (Bernhard 2005:106) to a much deadlier form in the coming decades.

This is not to say that the constitution or the other newly formed institutions of state disappeared during the time that the Poles call the *Sanacja* regime. The nascent institutions of the Second Republic actually sanctioned the coup, with the *Sejm* voting at the end of May 1926 to offer Piłsudski the presidency, an honor that he declined in favor of his chosen protégé, Ignacy Mościcki (Lerski 1996). The Piłsudski regime also worked within the framework of the constitution by seeking to amend it immediately after assuming power; a team of lawyers created substantial amendments to the constitution, which passed the *Sejm* in August of that year, including giving the president the right to dissolve parliament

---

[13] Donnorummo (1994) also points to the regional nature of opposition to Piłsudski as another reason motivating the coup, noting that resistance from western Poland (especially Poznan and Pomerania) was an important factor in the decision and timing of the coup in May 1926.

and to pass resolutions with the same force of law as legislation originating from the *Sejm* (Kowalski 2014). Other positive institutional measures were also included, such as automatic dismissal of legislators found to be using their office for personal gain and a measure for continuance of government spending in the eventuality that the *Sejm* was unable to reach compromise on a budget (Brzezinski 1991). Even in his framing of the changes to the constitution, Piłsudski was adamant that he was only attempting to save Polish parliamentarianism, not destroy it, promising "a final showdown, and of a brutal type, if [legislators were] to return to their former habits" (quoted in Polonsky 1972:189).

In addition to working within the constitution, the most quintessential essence of democratic theater, the election, was retained in Poland, at least for a time. The scheduled legislative election of 1928 went off as planned, and is generally considered as "free and fair," despite administrative pressure and the disqualification of thousands of votes from the eastern portion of the country (although Kopstein and Wittenberg (2010) note that the point of the election was not to choose a new government but to rally support behind the existing one). Perhaps surprisingly, the Socialists gained in both absolute and relative terms in 1928, but even with the government pushing for national unity, the fragmentation across parties increased as a result of the election (Groth 1964), with twenty-seven parties receiving votes for the *Sejm* (Donnorummo 1994). Even the German party increased its number of seats, from 17 in 1922 to 19 in 1928 (Stachura 2004).

Given the somewhat disappointing results of the (relatively) free elections, and as with all authoritarian regimes (and in a trend that accelerated throughout Europe in the 1930s), the political institutions of democracy in Poland began to erode and become nothing more than a veneer for nondemocratic maneuvering. The *Sejm* elections of 1930 were heavily "managed" by Piłsudski's regime (Kopstein and Wittenberg 2003), and center and left opposition leaders were harassed and jailed before the election even took place (Stone 2010) and interned for years afterwards (Kubiak 1999). Not satisfied with the powers given in the 1926 amendments to the 1921 Constitution, the Piłsudski regime replaced the constitution entirely in 1935, creating a document that subordinated all other branches of government under the presidency. The 1935 Constitution eliminated most of the checks and balances put in place *vis à vis* the *Sejm*, although it did allow for votes of no confidence in government ministers and delineated the *Sejm*'s legislative powers (Brzezinski 1991). The 1935 Constitution all but dismantled any semblance of checks and balances in regard to the judiciary, crushing the idea of judicial independence by giving the executive the right to appoint and dismiss members of the judiciary (Fijalkowski 2013). Finally, in order to ensure continuity of leadership, the president was to be elected for a seven-year term, and there was no provision for term limits in the new constitution.

The Constitution of 1935 sounded the death knell for the March Constitution's vision of democracy in Poland, while keeping many of its trappings intact. But what was the main weakness of the March Constitution, that allowed it to be overpowered so easily (and changed into its opposite just fourteen years later)? If it was explicitly directed against executive overreach, how did that precise problem come to detonate the order it put in place? From hindsight, with knowledge of what was to come in the 1930s, it appeared that (much as during the eighteenth century), Poland's political institutions were going against the trend in Europe, attempting to craft a constitutional parliamentary democracy at a time when the world was becoming more enamored with authoritarian socialist solutions. If Poland had not been wedged between two revanchist powers that were constantly seeking to dominate it, the argument goes, its experiment in parliamentary democracy in such an atmosphere might have succeeded; instead, facing external threats and internal division, it needed a strong hand to guide it to safety.

However, the data does not bear out this assertion, as, unlike the Constitution of 1791, the constitution was working in a favorable international environment. While Italy had fallen under the spell of fascism as early as 1919, Poland's immediate neighbors were on the path towards a modern parliamentary democracy, with countries such as Czechoslovakia and even Germany creating new and open political institutions. This can be seen in Table 2.3, which shows the "polity" index from the Polity IV database, a number scaled from −10 to 10, with higher numbers representing more democracy. For the countries in Central and Eastern Europe, nearly every country fell within the range of "democracy" (6 to 9), with Estonia classified as a "full democracy" and only Hungary classified as a "closed anocracy" (and even this was an improvement from its status in 1919 as an autocracy). It is not until 1926 that any major changes occurred in the region, and not for the better. In fact, to believe Poland to be swept up in an antidemocratic tide is to misread the sequence of events: as Rothschild (1962:241) noted in his study of the May 1926 coup, it was Poland who was the leader of this trend away from democracy, "signal[ing] the failure and death of parliamentarian democracy throughout the area of East Central Europe."

Table 2.3 *Polity IV Scores for Europe, 1919–1926*

	1919	1920	1921	1922	1923	1924	1925	1926
Austria	4	8	8	8	8	8	8	8
Czechoslovakia	7	7	7	7	7	7	7	7
Estonia	10	10	10	10	10	10	10	10
Germany	6	6	6	6	6	6	6	6
Hungary	−7	−1	−1	−1	−1	−1	−1	−1
Latvia		7	7	7	7	7	7	7
Lithuania	4	4	4	4	4	4	4	0
Poland	8	8	8	8	8	8	8	−3

Source: Polity IV Database.

Poland was not carried along by waves of authoritarianism in the region, it was the initiator.

Given that the international setting in which the Second Republic was born was not to blame, it is more instructive to look at the flaws inherent in the constitution as drafted that may have translated into ineffective institutional mechanisms. At the heart of weakness of the constitution was that the institutional mechanisms put in place were less appropriate for a country that was less homogenous than the idea of "Poland" traditionally envisioned it. As noted above, 69.2 percent of the country was Polish, a number that actually declined from 1921–1931, meaning a much more multiethnic state that encompassed nearly 13 percent Ukrainian, 9 percent Jewish, 8 percent Belarusian, and even 2.5 percent German citizens (Tomaszewski 1985). Our overview above showed that the idea of noble liberty, at least as practiced during the seventeenth and eighteenth centuries in Poland, tended to be conferred only upon Poles, with such ideas being transferred to Lithuanians within a political union but never to Ukrainians or other frontier nationalities. But by the twentieth century, the right of representation had been won by the non-Poles in the Republic, and the advent of minority parties based on ethnicity meant that a full 20 percent of the *Sejm* was dedicated to non-Polish citizens. These parties formed a powerful bloc that could bring down governments on its own, a strength that mattered when "centralizing drives of the dominant Polish national group collided with centrifugal tendencies of national/ethnic minorities" (Kubiak 1999:84).

Indeed, the multiethnic state that Poland became as a result of its conflicts and struggle for independence immediately rendered the idea of vesting executive powers in the legislature immediately suspect. In general, legislatures tend to be inappropriate vehicles for carrying out executive responsibilities: as was to be seen during the transition from communism to capitalism, even fairly concentrated legislatures tend to be narrow and provincial institutions that, when given too much power too early, attempt to divvy up a pie that does not yet exist (Hartwell 2013). The Second Republic did not even have this luxury of concentration, however, as over the first four years of the Republic, ninety-two political parties had been founded, and a full third of them had been elected to the *Sejm* in some form (Stachura 2004).

Much of the problems related to this fragmentation came from the mechanism of proportional representation that the constitution's framers selected for Poland. This approach had widespread support across the political spectrum, with both the right and left in favor of proportional representation, but with ethnic minority parties most strongly behind the idea (believing that their small size and dispersed nature could only survive under a proportional system). However, Groth (1964) provides a scathing yet accurate critique of proportional representation in Poland, noting that it made parties indifferent to marginal voters (and vice versa), with parties instead cultivating highly specific support in a system that removed many of the incentives for collaboration prior to an election. Indeed, Growth (1964:112) notes that the main failing of the system was, in order "to win office, parties would require the support of diverse groups which could not be held together very long by a narrow, dogmatic program, so that the tendency would be, if anything, in the opposite direction – toward ideological opportunism, erosion, and 'all things to all men' platforms."

When combined with the strong powers accorded to the *Sejm*, proportional representation made the Polish state directionless and diffuse. The elections of 1922, showing a virtual tie across the political spectrum, meant that executive authority was widely dispersed among several competing factions, some of which had directly opposing ideas on how that power should be wielded. Thus, in the system that the 1921 Constitution created, not only did the president not wield executive power, in a fragmented and fractionalized parliament, *no one* wielded it. This created a power vacuum that a charismatic war hero with popular support could exploit, as indeed Piłsudski did, but even his popularity could not overcome the deficiencies of proportional representation in the 1928 election.

Additionally, as Bernhard (2005:106) noted, the political effects of Poland's Partitions may have also entered into the failings of the 1921 Constitution, as "political development in the three partitions took place under highly repressive (Tsarist Russia) to somewhat permissive (the Habsburg Empire) authoritarian conditions that produced radically different political traditions and three sets of Polish parties." Given the authoritarian nature of Poland's overlords in the nineteenth century, this meant (as noted above) that any political institutions that survived were small-scale and, perhaps more problematic, limited to members or those willing to go against the authorities (thus self-selecting out a small set of people with knowledge of opposition to power but no experience of wielding it themselves). In such an environment, the Polish public did not develop a political consciousness or understand the gravity of what participation in a democracy entailed.

Finally, a note must be added on the collapse of democracy in Poland from the point of view of institutional persistence. While the idea of certain political institutions may have persisted or even been preserved on a small scale in Polish lands during the Partitions, it is crucial to remember that institutions are only mechanisms – organizational structures that very often rely on other institutions for their functioning. Institutions must take into account the state of the world around them, jostling within a complex framework of other institutions in order to be "effective." Because of this, institutions very rarely succeed if they do not evolve within a certain institutional framework from the outset. As I have mentioned elsewhere (Hartwell 2013), it is very difficult to build an institution to operate in a completely different system from the one prevailing at the time. In this sense, despite the lingering idea of what a constitutional order should look like, the design of the actual institutions did not take into account the changes in Poland over the intervening 123 years. This, more than anything else, may have made Poland's interwar experience in constitutional governance a short-lived one.

THE COLLAPSE OF DEMOCRACY, "BLOODLANDS," AND COMMUNIST TAKEOVER

The Constitution of 1935 removed many of the political institutions that the Constitution of 1921 had guaranteed, but it did not create a proto-fascist state in Poland similar to Italy, Germany, or the Soviet Union. In many ways, the 1935 Constitution merely reordered some of the mechanisms of government, while retaining individual rights such as "freedom of religion, freedom of conscience, and the inviolability of one's domicile" (Brzezinski 1991:83–84). As Fijalkowski (2013:44) also rightly notes, this means that "the Polish state of 1935 was not a totalitarian regime in which the state controlled all aspects of public and private life," even though the Constitution of that year was inching towards such an outcome by declaring in Article 7 that "the state was to be an organizer of public life." In fact, as has been seen, the main changes that accompanied the 1935 Constitution were more related to the institutional arrangements of the political system and the reallocation of power away from the legislature to the executive, rather than a move from the people to the state.

Ironically, the man who fought for these expanded executive powers in the 1935 Constitution did not get to utilize them. Josef Piłsudski, the man for whom the constitution was "tailor-made," died of cancer a mere three weeks after the constitution came into being (Cole 1998). Without his strong personality to assemble the fractious parties under the power he had so long coveted, Poland's political morass deepened and the rights of individuals began to suffer. In the words of Haczyński (1975:279), "whether Poland's traditional love of freedom would have kept her from slipping into the totalitarian camp and reduced her to uniformity by employing completely repressive measures cannot be known, but it is fair to say that Poland did don the cosmetics of fascism." Ethnic minorities such as Ukrainians were to feel the brunt of the newly emboldened executive power, but the Jewish population was also targeted; within one month of Piłsudski's death, a massacre of Jews erupted in Grodno, followed by intermittent pogroms up until the German invasion (Midlarsky 2003). With the removal of the institutional mechanism that guaranteed some semblance of equality in the *Sejm*, and coupled with the virulent atmosphere prevailing across 1930s Europe, the national and ethnic minorities in Poland watched their rights and influence vanish.

The collapse of democracy from 1935 to 1939 in Poland was not so abrupt as in the Soviet Union in 1917 nor as it was to be in the Nazi-occupied territories during the Second World War, but was more of a slow disappearance of liberty; it was as if a castle had been built on a swamp and slowly disappeared back into the mire, never to be seen again.[14] Despite the constitution's move to unify Poland internally, the men who were to succeed Piłsudski found their interests diverging over time, which led to a continuous struggle for the enlarged power of the presidency (Haczyński 1975). Moreover, Piłsudski's successors were ill-equipped to deal with the changing international situation, with Germany's remilitarization of the Rhineland, the *Anschluss* of Austria (which Piłsudski himself supported in principle as early as 1933; see Karski (2014)), the occupation of

---

[14] With apologies to Monty Python.

the Sudetenland (which Poland also supported), and the Soviet invasion of Finland all tightening a noose around the Republic's neck. By September 1939, the question of the Second Republic's survival became merely hypothetical, as twin invasions from Germany and the Soviet Union divided up the country once again and lay all that had come before to waste.

The history of Poland in World War Two is well documented, and here is not the place to recount the heroism of the Uprisings or of the atrocities of Nazism and Communism perpetrated on Polish soil. One point does bear highlighting, however, and this pertains to the government-in-exile in London throughout the war. Perhaps mindful of the history of Poland and seeing the signs all around, the Constitution of 1935 contained a special provision that legitimized the continuity of the office of the president even if there was no territorial base, that is, if Poland again ceased to exist (Zamoyski 1987). With the swift dismemberment of Poland in September 1939, a government-in-exile was formed initially in Paris on October 2, 1939, under the leadership of General Wiadysław Sikorski. The government, moving eventually to Angers in Western France and then to London after the Nazi conquest of Paris, relied on the Constitution of 1935 for its legitimacy, claiming the mantle of "true" leadership in a manner that no government under the 1921 Constitution could have (Brzezinski 1991). Unfortunately, the London government also kept many of the other attributes of Polish parliamentary democracy, including, as academic and political advisor Lewis Namier noted in an analysis from the British parliament (quoted in Coutouvidis 1984:422):

One of Sikorski's difficulties is the excessive number of ministers – there are by now more than a dozen when probably four would be sufficient. There are two reasons for their excessive, and still growing, numbers: as this is a government of National Union, the various Polish parties, of which there was always an excess, have to be represented; and the first selection was in some cases rather haphazard – a man of the second rank was included in the government because he was available, and because no one could say whether a more representative member of that party had been, or would be, able to escape from Poland.

Try as it might to keep continuity from prewar Poland, however, the government-in-exile was once again on the outside as the country was being transformed. Poland (and Ukraine, as we will see) occupied the territory subjected to the heaviest, bloodiest, and cruelest fighting seen in the Second World War. The area from Central Poland stretching through to Russia proper was memorably called by Yale historian Timothy Snyder (2010) the "Bloodlands," and from 1930 to 1945 it saw the death of over

14 million people by war, starvation, gassing, political murder, and other means of mass extermination. Unlike Czechoslovakia, which survived the war with much less physical damage than other countries, or the countries of Scandinavia, which saw far fewer deaths per capita, the entire physical fabric and most formal institutions in Poland were rent asunder during this turbulent time. Poland suffered the highest number of deaths as percentage of population and saw its countryside invaded not once, not twice, but three times as the Germans and Soviets mauled each other on Polish land.

The near-extinguishment of Poland yet again (a full quarter of its land was annexed proper to Nazi Germany, while the rest of the country was either under Nazi control as the "General Government" or annexed to the Soviet Union, see Figure 2.2) meant that its postwar incarnation was

Figure 2.2 Poland's Zones of Occupation as Seen from Germany, 1939–1945
Source: "Karte Viertepolnischeteilung" by Sansculotte (2004).

not decided by the precepts of the 1935 Constitution, but by the conflict around it and the reality of power. Indeed, as Cole (1998:25) correctly notes, "Poland was re-constituted, yet again, following World War II. But this time it was not allowed to re-constitute itself; an outside power, the Soviet Union, dictated its political, economic, and constitutional system."

The Yalta conference and ensuing accords, occurring in then-Soviet Crimea in February 1945, was the most visible manifestation of the transfer of power from Polish institutions to Soviet ones, but in reality the fate of Poland had been decided in 1943 when the British decided that Poland lay in the Soviet zone of responsibility and the Soviet army began to reverse the advances of Nazi Germany (Kersten 1991). After the Soviet Union stood by while the Nazis wiped out Warsaw in the Uprising of 1944 and immediately after (despite being right across the river in the suburb of Praga), German forces abandoned the city in January 1945, leaving Soviet forces in control of the capital and shortly afterward the entire country. As the Soviets were to do throughout Central and Eastern Europe in the aftermath of the war, they already had a hand-picked and subordinate political organization ready to move in, the *Polski Komitet Wyzwolenia Narodowego* (Polish Committee of National Liberation, or PKWN), an entirely foreign political institution that was to determine the fate of postwar Poland. Indeed, the Soviet Committee was to act as a gardener, pulling out all of the indigenous political institutions and planting new, Moscow-approved ones.

The PKWN had been formed in Moscow directly on Stalin's orders (Gibianskii and Naimark 2004); led by Wanda Wasilewska, a native Pole who obtained Soviet citizenship in 1939 (and thus missed the bulk of the bloodletting of Stalin's purges), the PKWN was comprised of other Polish communist expatriates and had been operating behind Soviet lines ever since the German invasion of the Soviet Union (Janczewski 1972). The PKWN began its operations on Polish territory in July 1944 in the town of Lublin (it was therefore known as the "Lublin government"), expanding to encompass the communist and leftist resistance groups that remained in Poland during the war (such as the Polish Worker's Party (the PPR), and the Polish Socialist Party (PPS)).

Once in Poland, the PKWN coordinated closely with the Soviet army, helping to disarm partisans who fought with the Home Army but refused to join a "Popular Front" that would fight alongside the Soviet regulars (Reynolds 1981), and standing idly by as Soviet repressive organs such as the NKVD liquidated Home Army resistance (Gibianskii and Naimark 2004). Indeed, in a few short months, as part of the Red Army steamroller east, Stalin was able to outsource the liquidation of the Polish resistance to the Nazis and engage in "mopping up" operations once the Nazis had fled with the willing collaboration of the Polish communists. As Reynolds (1981:637) noted,

The round-ups which began in November continued into spring 1945 on a big scale. Emigre sources claim that as many as 50,000 members of the AK [Armia Krajowa, the Home Army] were arrested and transported to Siberia at this time, but there is no way of course of verifying this figure. Claims that some 8,000 people were incarcerated in Lublin castle at this time are plausible enough in view of official data revealing 1,646 arrests by the UB [Urząd Bezpieczeństwa, the communist secret police] and MO [Milicja Obywatelska, the state police] alone in Lublin province between January and April. In the same operations, over 300 members of the underground were killed.

Gibianskii and Naimark (2004) also provide documentary evidence from the Soviet archives that, at the end of October 1945 (a full five months after the end of the war), 27,000 Poles were still imprisoned in NKVD camps, the vast majority of them interned in 1944 and 1945. Indeed, returnees to Poland from London were often arrested immediately upon setting foot on Polish soil (Manning 1946).

Utilizing Polish versions of Soviet institutions of political repression (the UB was based on the NKVD/KGB and the MO based on the *Militsiya* or internal affairs police from the Soviet Union), the communists who swept west with the Soviets began to diligently create an institutional system that mirrored its patron. These institutions, as well as other organs of communism patterned on the Soviet model, were instituted at first in the territories that had been cleared of Germans, part of a general building of state administration in March 1945 as the PKWN moved its headquarters from Lublin to Warsaw (Kersten 1991). Under the "communization" of the Polish left, the PKWN also attempted to neutralize or at least control the very institutions that had formed linkages between the socialists and the peasantry in the decades prior to the war, namely cooperatives and trade unions, and turn them into carbon copies of the state-directed unions in the Soviet republics (R [Anonymous], 1949).

In the chaos surrounding the end of the war, there may have been some merit to copying some successful institutional structures from abroad (unlike the 1921 Constitution, which copied the patently unsuccessful French Constitution of 1875). The upheaval that Poland was subjected to during the war cannot be understated. As a point of departure, the actual physical territory that Poland now encompassed was substantially different than the Poland of the prewar years, a full 47 percent smaller than the Second Republic (Kubiak 1989). As decided at the Potsdam Conference in 1945, Poland was shifted west at the expense of Germany, with its eastern territories absorbed into Lithuania, Byelorussia, and Ukraine, and resettled by the Soviet Union; of the eastern lands occupied by the Soviets at the end of the war, only the Białystok region was returned to Poland (Tuszynski and Denda 1999). The resulting landmass, unlike the multiethnic Poland of 1922, was made almost entirely homogenously Polish and Catholic, with any remaining Germans in the west expelled during the mass refugee movements accompanying the end of the war. Similarly, in the east, Ukrainians were "evacuated" to Soviet Ukraine on Stalin's orders, with those who refused to go voluntarily discriminated against legally (prohibited from buying land and having their schools closed) and eventually targeted for arrest and murder by the NKVD-controlled internal security forces (Snyder 1999). In such an environment, adapting institutions from one of the victors of the great conflict that just ended may have been a rational response to the institutional vacuum that appeared to exist.

Unfortunately for the communists, at least from the outset of Poland's independence from Nazi rule, there was already a competing institutional conception of postwar Poland emanating from the west, making the idea of an institutional vacuum less plausible than at first glance. While the London government-in-exile was abandoned by the Allies and in particular Franklin D. Roosevelt at Yalta as being "incorrigibly anti-Soviet" (Larsh 1995:267), its recognition as the legitimate government of Poland was not withdrawn from the Allied side until the summer of 1945 (Kacewicz 1979). Until that time, the London government had "functioned as an internationally recognized political centre ... [operating] inside the country a secret parliament united all the major non-communist parties ... [and] above all ... the 'London' camp maintained its social base" (Reynolds 1981:644). While the Soviets would have preferred that the London government had never existed, its presence made reconstituting Poland in the image of the Soviet Union slightly more problematic.

In order to overcome this obstacle, a deal had been struck at Yalta to have the PKWN recognized as the basis from which a "Polish Provisional Government of National Unity" would be formed (Fijalkowski 2013), a *de jure* acceptance of what had already *de facto* occurred in early 1945 (and had already been recognized by the Soviets a month earlier; see

Kacewicz (1979)). As part of the co-optation of the old guard, in June 1945, a month after Germany's surrender, former prime minister of the government-in-exile, Stanisław Mikolajczyk, returned to Poland as vice-premier of the coalition government of National Unity (representing the Peasant's Party). Working under the 1921 Constitution rather than the 1935 version (since the 1935 version had been found to be too closely associated with the London government), the Unity government was bound to call "free and unfettered" elections as soon as was possible (Brzezinski 1991).

However, the Polish communists and Soviets found, just as Piłsudski had, that calling free elections was dangerous if the polity was not already solidly behind the party that was supposed to win. Popular support for the communists had never been very high in Poland before the war: Kopstein and Wittenberg (2003) estimated that communist parties never garnered more than 10 percent of the popular vote, with their main source of support coming from Jewish and Belarusian minorities rather than Poles or Ukrainians. While there was some uptick in favorability for communists at the end of the war, any gratitude that had been owed to the Soviets for liberation from the Nazis dissipated quickly when the Red Army let the Uprising be crushed, moved strongly against the Home Army, and (most egregiously) raped and pillaged its way across the countryside (Goldyn 1998). As a British informant in Poland relayed back to London just before the end of the war, the communists were "generally unpopular throughout Poland as an agent of a foreign power. On a free vote at least 90 percent of Poles would be against them ... Mikolajczyk's name still carried the same prestige and he could count on the support of the great bulk of the peasants" (Foreign Office 1945). Thus, the postwar support for communists appeared to equal their prewar support.

In order to make the conditions more amenable for a communist victory, a number of manipulations of the still-prevailing constitutional order were required. The first ploy was the postponement of elections that had originally been scheduled for spring 1946: realizing that both popular support was weak and the Polish Worker's Party (PPR, the official Communist Party) and other parties on the left were still facing fragmentation, the left supported pushing back elections for as long as possible. Instead, as a second tactic, a referendum was called in June 1946, "consisting of three questions so phrased as to obtain an overwhelming majority of affirmative votes ... [and] give the impression that the communist government enjoyed the support of the Polish population" (Staar 1958:200). The three questions of the referendum asked the public to vote on the abolishment of the Senate from the legislature, validating the new western borders of the country, and approving a plan of nationalization of industry, all pet initiatives of the political left and, for the communists, a stepping stone to greater entrenchment in power (Goldyn 1998).

The referendum itself has become legendary for the "successful" tactics of the communists to subvert a major political institution, that of popular voting (Gibianskii and Naimark 2004). As Mikolajczyk himself was to relate to foreign reporters and, eventually, a much wider audience after the fact (Mikolajczyk 1948), the Communists harassed members of the opposition in the run-up to the polling, confiscated property, censored any support of the opposition, disqualified voters by the thousand, and conducted mass arrests in the countryside (Staar 1958). Even the symbols associated with the old regime were to be swept away, and only new PPR-approved displays of Polish patriotism could be used; a demonstration in Kraków in May 1946 celebrating the anniversary of the 1791 Constitution was broken up by force, and several hundred participants were arrested (Behrends 2009). In the words of Kersten (1991:281), the electorate was so cowed by intimidation and agitation even at the polls, that "going behind the curtain to vote was an act of courage."

Taking no chances, the communists also were hard at work once the votes were cast to make sure that such courage only counted if it was done in their favor. Documentation abounds of PPR functionaries illegally transferring ballot boxes from polling stations to electoral commission headquarters before the votes were actually counted; as Staar (1958: 203–204) recounts, this blatant vote-stealing had a farcical quality about it:

In Kraków, however . . . the communist members of the electoral control commission were reportedly so disturbed by the unfavorable returns that they left the tabulation room in order to telephone Warsaw for advice. The non-communists quickly tallied the ballots and notified the capital by telegraph of the correct results. The percentage of negative votes by question in Kraków was 84 on the first, 62 on the second, and 31 on the third.

This correct result in Kraków was sharply at odds with the "official" results released after the election (Table 2.4), which showed a landslide victory for communist ideals and (especially) communist economics (this experience also brought opprobrium to Kraków as a "bastion of reaction" from the communist-controlled media; see Goldyn 1998). A similar experience to Kraków was had in Janów, where 79 percent actually voted against

Table 2.4 *Official Results of the 1946 Referendum*

Question	"Yes" Votes	Percent	"No" Votes	Percent
1 – Abolishing the Senate	7,844,522	66.2	3,686,029	33.8
2 – Supporting land reform and nationalization	8,896,105	77.3	2,634,446	22.7
3 – Validating the new borders of Poland	10,534,697	94.2	995,854	5.8

Source: Monitor Polski, Warsaw, July 11, 1946, as quoted in Staar (1958).

question number one and 76 percent voted against question number two (with 81 percent in favor of Poland's new borders); as the true numbers revealed a super-majority of 75 percent of voters in the region against communist ideals, the results were falsified with an undercount of approximately 14,500 votes that resulted in an easy win for the communists (Chodakiewicz 2004).[15] As Kersten (1991:281) notes, the exact numbers did not matter in any form, as "Party instructors assigned by the PPR and UB functionaries were to have obtained the real results of voting first and only later substitute an outcome that had been previously prepared by the members of the PPR leadership."

Prazmowska (2000) noted that the referendum of 1946 was a "trial run" for the parliamentary elections of January 1947, to ensure that communists had at least a veneer of legitimacy even if the results themselves were patently false. Indeed, as they were to do repeatedly (and to this day), the left became enamored with the trappings of democracy, appearing to utilize these institutional mechanisms to confirm their broad-based support and present to the rest of the world the appearance that Poland was wholeheartedly embracing communism. The charade continued unabated after the referendum as an Electoral Law was passed in September 1946, as a seemingly necessary piece of enabling legislation was subverted by gerrymandering of districts and the granting of disproportionate representation to the former German territories (on the assumption that these would be more procommunist); additionally, communists appointed their own staff to all fifty-two of the country's electoral commissions, who then

---

[15] In perhaps a sign of communist adherence to symbols and symmetry, across the country, with 327,000 votes invalidated officially, there is also a perfect correspondence of votes and total numbers (i.e., the total number of votes cast for each question is 11,530,551). This means that no one voted partially. Such an outcome is statistically implausible.

in turn appointed all local commissioners, making sure that they were loyal communists (Staar 1958).

Indeed, despite the re-constitution of the *Sejm*, the Electoral Law, and the appearance of a "people's democracy" exercised via referendum, the political institutions of the Soviets in Poland were hollow and the support for the communists non-existent. More importantly, they were manipulated behind the scenes by a foreign power; much as Russia had attempted to do with the *Sejm* and the exercise of the *liberum veto* to keep Poland weak in the seventeenth century, the Soviet Union now resorted to much blunter tactics to overwhelm the *Sejm*. Staar (1958) relates that the planning for the parliamentary elections took place in Moscow, where a strategy of putting forth a bloc of "democratic" parties, coupled with repression of all other parties, was concocted (Mikolajczyk (1948) also notes that Stalin personally decreed that the election should be decided before it was actually run). During the run-up to the election, Soviet security forces also directly intervened to "brand opponents to the Soviet presence as 'bandits,' and killed or intimidated all who could conceivably mount organized resistance" (Brzezinski 1991:87).

The "success" of the referendum in 1946 emboldened the communists to use similar tactics to suppress opposition, once again calculating that their chances of winning actually free elections was still low (Kersten 1991). In addition to the direct Soviet involvement just noted, the Polish communists had a series of other tactics that they utilized, including the banning of other opposition parties (the Labor Party was banned entirely in July 1946 and its board arrested in Katowice) and removing other nonreliable candidates from electoral lists across the country a mere week before elections (Fijalkowski 2013).[16] Mass arrests predictably followed, with over 7,000 members of the PSL Party held in jails just one month before the election (Staar 1958). The Polish army, acting under Soviet orders, was also a key player in the intimidation campaign, with platoon-strength detachments moving randomly across the country to "correct administrative problems" and (immediately prior to the election), inspecting polling stations and "supervising" the vote count (Michta 1989).

---

[16] Ten out of the country's 52 electoral districts had candidates struck from the lists; these ten districts had a population of approximately 5.5 million people, or a quarter of the entire country. In this manner, the communists were able to remove even the illusion of choice.

As can be expected, the results of parliamentary elections also were announced as going precisely in the direction that the Soviet Union wanted, with the communists garnering 80 percent of the vote. Moreover, the groundswell of support for communism was apparently able to bring more voters to the polling stations, as turnout at 89.8 percent far surpassed that of previous elections (15 percent higher than the authoritarian 1930 election and much higher than the 67.9 percent turnout in 1922; see Staar (1958)). Safely entrenched in power, the communists sought to eradicate any chance in the future of true representative democracy returning:

In the aftermath of the fraudulent election of 1947, the communists launched an overt terrorist campaign that eventually destroyed the only organized opposition party.... On the orders of the regime, special military tribunals unleashed state terror against the remaining opposition; in 1947, over 6,000 Poles were sentenced by special military judges, some of them to death, on fabricated charges based on confessions extracted under torture. Terror by the security police and summary trials by military tribunals laid the groundwork for final consolidation of power by Poland's communist party (Michta 1989:42).

As part of the removal of all constituent parts of democracy, the political party system, itself a relatively new phenomenon in Poland, was also dismantled, with the PSL absorbed into the PPR to create the Polish United Workers' Party, the only politically legal entity. With one vestige of democracy eliminated, the communists continued their fundamental transformation of Polish political institutions with major changes to the constitution. The newly-convened *Sejm* in 1947 adopted its own "Little Constitution," based on the 1921 version, which gave all power to the *Sejm* and replaced the office of the presidency entirely with a "Council of State." This Council, elected by the *Sejm*, functioned as the executive power of the country, especially when the *Sejm* was not in session (Brzezinski 1991). In a way, this was an extreme measure of continuing a theme from Poland's past; for centuries the *Sejm* had tried to restrain the executive, and the Council meant that there was no more executive, merely legislators in different roles. However, the Council aggregated to itself the very powers that the *Sejm* had tried to keep out of the hands of first the monarch and later Piłsudski, namely autocracy and untrammeled ability to rule the country. As Kersten (1991) correctly called it, the Council of State was not the continuation of Polish political tradition, but contained the seeds of Soviet institutions that were to grow in the country.

The "Little Constitution" of 1947 was meant to be temporary, and indeed it only lasted through the parliamentary elections of 1952, which saw even more of an official turnout (95 percent of eligible voters were said to have participated). With even the veneer of democracy removed, the government proclaimed Poland a "people's republic" in July 1952, and instituted a constitution (the "Basic Law") that had input from Soviet theorists and was modeled on the Soviet Constitution of 1936, created during the middle of Stalin's purges; that is, a document that enshrined the primacy of the Communist Party in law and proclaimed the irreversible victory of socialism (Osakwe 1979). Just as the Soviet constitution modeled a "fairy tale" of socialist victory that allowed individual rights only if they were exercised "in correspondence with the interests of workers and with the goal of strengthening the socialist system" (Schmid 2010), the Polish constitution of 1952 was a fig leaf that enabled intense concentration of political power at the top with little (if any) restraint (Brzezinski 1991).

As Cole (1998:27) points out, given that the constitution did not require enacting implementing legislation, the document was "entirely without legal force, except to the extent that the Party/state chose to enforce it"; in short, "in People's Poland there was no constitutional *law*, only constitutional *policy* [emphasis in the original]." Under such a system, the *Sejm* was nothing more than a "rubber stamp" to the whims of the Party (Simon 1996), while the judiciary was entirely and utterly subordinated to the Party as well, given that any measure of judicial review would infringe upon the rights of the *Sejm* to issue laws (Brzezinski 1991). In fact, the entire process of the constitution's genesis showed that even the Party itself was subordinate to the Soviet Union, as Stalin himself inserted sections and edited the draft constitution before it was adopted (Persak 1998).

Cole (1998) also rightly notes that the Constitution of 1952 did not create a system where the Communist Party dominated (the constitution did not actually explicitly mandate the monopoly of power of the Party, see Rapaczynski 1991), it merely reflected communist hegemony and enshrined the institutions that accompany a Leninist political order. Poland's Communists now set about further nurturing the political institutions under such an order, including strengthening the power of the secret police and attempting to destroy the power of the church (arresting believers and monks and engaging in show trials; see Kemp-Welch (2008)). Indeed, in many respects, to speak of institution-building under communism in the political sphere is to misspeak, as communism only dismantled political institutions during its time rather than build them up. The *Sejm* was subordinated to the Party, elections were turned into a charade, the constitution was neutered, and political parties were consolidated until one party ruled all. The only political institution that communism engendered in Poland, apart from the secret police, was to create a political class in service of a foreign power: Behrends (2009) also points to the historical parallels between the Soviet domination of Poland at the time of the Partitions, noting that, while Russification was not attempted as it was in the nineteenth century, "Sovietization" was crucial to the communist order and only those who wholeheartedly embraced the Soviet Union and its institutional structure could thrive.

For the most part, the formal political institutional structure put in place in Poland by 1952 survived the Cold War with little alteration, at least until the Solidarity movement of the 1980s. Khrushchev's denouncement of Stalin at the Twentieth Party Congress in 1956 created a ripple effect in the Polish Communist Party as well, but the re-ascendance of Władysław Gomułka to the head of the Party brought no real political changes (no matter the effect it had on society). From this point onward, the political mold had been cast and changes within the leadership of the communists in Poland were as academic as asking a condemned man if he preferred to be shot or electrocuted. This is not to say that changes did not occur, although they were mainly of a negative nature. In fact, minor changes at the margins were enabled in the basic institutions surrounding the dictatorship, including an amending of the 1952 Constitution in 1976 to formally recognize the monopoly on power of the Communist Party and to further emphasize the unbreakable role of the Soviet Union in guiding Poland's future. In the words of Cole (1998:27), "the 1976 amendments accomplished what was seemingly impossible: they further discredited Poland's Communist Constitution."

The backlash against the 1976 amendments was, somewhat surprisingly for a Soviet satellite, very vocal and public, and pointed to the institutional changes that actually *were* occurring in Poland under communism in the informal sphere. As under the Partitions, communist (and some would say Soviet-occupied) Poland continued to foster clandestine informal institutions, albeit in a much more muted form than those of the nineteenth century. These informal institutions, whether related to an underground press, small-scale gatherings of intellectuals, or (as will be seen) labor organization outside of the communist apparatus, grew much more slowly than under the Partitions, mainly due to the efficacy of the one novel political institution of communism, the state secret police. To be involved in any dissent against the system, especially in the Stalinist years of

1947–1953, was to risk one's own life (and possibly the lives of families, neighbors, friends, and co-workers), and thus the development of informal institutions was to remain smaller scale until the 1960s. As under the Partitions, however, the best-organized social institution that could serve as a "midwife to civil society" (Borowik 2002:241) remained the Roman Catholic Church.

As noted above, under the three Partitions the church became more than a social institution for the salvation of souls, focused solely on the next life. Across a country divided, the church became a repository of knowledge and symbolism of a nation, guarding the entire idea of "Polishness" and, in many instances in the late nineteenth century, the Polish language. In the words of Valkenier (1956:305), the church was "a powerful institution" that "enjoyed constitutional guarantees of its privileged position, and managed an extensive and well-knit ecclesiastical organization, together with numerous charities, schools, and a sizeable press." As an institution so closely associated with what it meant to be a Pole, under Partition, the church was under constant assault from both Protestant Prussians and Orthodox Russians, with churches closed, religious instruction banned, and priests harassed or harmed. In this environment, attending Mass became its own form of protest; to declare oneself a Catholic was to stand up for freedom from oppression and independence for Poland (Eberts 1998).

The church was to see itself under a similar sustained assault from within starting in 1947, but the communists were perhaps more savvy than the Russian before them, seeking not to destroy religion *per se* but to bring the institutional apparatus entirely under the power of the state (Valkenier 1956). However, such a co-optation was difficult in Poland due to both the inextricable link between Polishness and Catholicism, but also due to the paradoxically decentralized nature of Catholicism in Poland: as Byrnes (1997) catalogued, the parish priest in Poland under communism was often not just at odds with Warsaw and Moscow in his teachings, he was also at odds with his own hierarchy and the Vatican, who were seeking to temper some of the radical nationalism at the grassroots in favor of passive resistance. Moreover, as Kenney (1997) astutely notes, the church itself had avoided taking the bait of the communists and engaging in class warfare, ministering to its adherents as "Catholics" and "Poles" rather than as "workers." By refusing to meet communists in their chosen arena, the church was able to identify itself with something permanent and immutable, rather than the evanescent class distinctions of this life.

But the existence of the church was enough to make it a symbol of resistance to communism, as the whole conception of a Leninist state was that only sanctioned political institutions could exist. As Byrnes (2002:28) eloquently put it, "the Church's persistent identification with, and the support for, the interests of an autonomous Polish nation was the backbone of the Church's political role in the years leading up to the fall of communism." Walaszek (1986:118) put it even more bluntly: "The Roman Catholic Church serve[d] as an alternative legitimate system within Communist Poland. It is an authority system that is not constitutionally recognized, but in real terms it functions as if it were and coexists with the Communist authorities." This reality enabled the church to play a valuable role in mobilizing dissent against the regime from the 1970s onward, a trait that accelerated after the creation of Solidarity and the imposition of martial law in 1981 (Frentzel-Zagorska 1990). In fact, Walaszek (1986) provides data to show that, far from buckling under the pressure of the communists and Moscow, the church grew in strength during the 1960s and 1970s, with 2,631 more priests in 1980 than in 1967 and 1,312 more places of worship.

While the church was involved in supporting and mediating worker's strikes that occurred with increasing frequency (including condemning the violent repression of the strikes in 1970), it was the changes in the constitution in 1976 that really began to push the church away from a passive role in facilitating dissent to actively supporting the democratic opposition (Kennedy 1992). Moreover, this shift united all factions within the church, as the Catholic hierarchy also pushed back publicly against the changes in the constitution, led by Cardinal Karol Wojtyla of Kraków, a man shortly destined for a more active role in Polish dissent. Combined with additional workers' strikes in 1976 against proposed food price increases, the events of that year created "a united and nationally-based organization [which was] making fundamental political and economic demands" (Brzezinski 1998:74), one that fused the generally anticlerical left with leaders within the church (Bernhard 1993). The church remained at the vanguard of this movement by advising the opposition, providing physical space for meetings, connecting priests via the clerical network, and contributing intellectually to a movement that was not exclusively Catholic but that touched on the main themes of Christianity (Kennedy 1992).

The broad-based opposition that the church as an institution facilitated created a nascent civil society in Poland, a safe space outside of the Party's all-encompassing reach, which gathered together all resistance to the regime (Arato 1981). Moreover, and most importantly, this civil society sought to challenge the Party on its efficacy in taking care of the working class. If the communists could not even take care of the workers, their sole reason for existence and their fundamental goal, what then was the reason for the Party? By attacking the roots of the communist institutions at their very heart, by striking at their legitimacy, the opposition was able to use a fundamentally nonpolitical institution (such as the church) for intense political ends. This attack on the legitimacy of the state was also carried out using a very novel approach, one that also involved the church, especially after Karol Wojtyla was elevated as Pope John Paul II in 1979: rather than use the language of class warfare in explaining the plight of the workers, the new pope and the opposition in Poland utilized phrases that expressed concern for human dignity and truth (Kennedy 1992). As a universal movement (Catholic Christianity) that also emphasized the role of Poland in Christian Europe (Byrnes 1997), the church provided a viable alternative to the prevailing political institutions *in pursuit of the same goals*, starting a process that would eventually lead the unraveling of the communist state in Poland.

The church, despite providing an alternative to restoring the dignity of the worker, needed allies in its struggle against atheist Marxism, and this came (in a delicious irony) from the working classes themselves. An umbrella Committee in Defense of Workers *(Komitet Obrony Robotników* or KOR) was set up after the workers' strikes in 1976 had been violently repressed, creating another group independent from the state but that supposedly pursued the same goals as the Party. KOR ostensibly was a charity organization, supporting the workers imprisoned after the strikes and offering legal aid, but its leaders (Jacek Kuron and Adam Michnik), prominent intellectuals, also provided underground information via an independent publication, *Robotnik* ("the Worker"; see Raymond 1999). This organization played a valuable and symbiotic role with the church in fostering opposition to the regime, "produc[ing] an entire oppositional network, including underground, uncensored publications (the 'second circulation'), lectures by the 'flying university,' and the nuclei of independent workers' and farmers' organizations" (Payerhin 1996:186–187). In this manner, KOR was able to coalesce the workers' frustration and lay the groundwork for the association that was to become *Solidarność* (Solidarity).

Solidarity sprang to life from the assembled bits and pieces of civil society that had grown since 1976, but was catalyzed by the strike at the Lenin Shipyards in Gdańsk (and across Poland) in August 1980; as Bernhard (1993:316) asserts, "it is only with the strikes of the summer of

1980 that we can talk about the reconstitution of civil society in Poland. The massive working-class strike waves accomplished something that the opposition movements of the 1970s did not." The Founding Committee of Free Trade Unions of the Coast (CFTU), an offspring of KOR, were able to seize yet another increase in food prices in July 1980 as an opportunity to turn out the working class against the regime. While Gdańsk was somewhat isolated from the strikes that gripped Poland (Barker 2009) their grasp of factory-level issues (Payerhin 1996) and the sacking of one of their own led to an eruption of support for a general strike, which then spread across the city (Barker 2009). Once again, the workers had set themselves up as part of a movement that was opposed to the one legal political institution charged with taking care of the workers, the Party.

In many ways, Solidarity and the church as institutions were two sides of the same coin; as Walaszek (1986:119–120) notes, "Solidarity can be considered as the manifestation of societal aspirations in the political domain that were part of a broader manifestation of national aspirations embedded in the adherence of Poles to their Catholic Church." Much as the church threatened communism by its existence, the presence of Solidarity undermined the legitimacy of the state and its activities (Mason 1989). Solidarity also carved out another public space of dissent, not physical as with the church's facilities, but metaphysical in the fostering of a free press and free thought (Frentzel-Zagorska 1990). And while Solidarity began as a limited set of demands, mostly tied to local grievances and economic issues, it soon blossomed into much more. Calls for democracy, representation, and purging corruption from the body politic (Mason 1989) were all heard during the (first) fifteen months that Solidarity was a force in Polish politics, a trait that helped Solidarity specifically and civil society in general "consolidate[] against the system and its ruling elite" (Frentzel-Zagorska 1990:769).

Striking a nerve with the broader public, Solidarity garnered popular support across the country: Curry (2004) notes that Solidarity had membership of nearly one-third of the country during this period (although Mason (1989) notes that this support was mainly "soft"). Solidarity's strength, apart from its opposition to the power elite, was that it allowed for the forging of broad-based coalitions across class lines, as it encompassed intellectuals, workers, peasants, and clergy in a manner that had not been seen before in Poland (Walaszek 1986). Moreover, Solidarity also had organizational abilities that had been lacking in earlier unorganized protests, creating its own legal and institutional structures to perpetuate the movement (Frentzel-Zagorska 1990). Coupled with the difficult economic straits in which Poland increasingly found itself (see next chapter), the Communist PZPR was forced to allow Solidarity some measure of autonomy, and from mid-1980 to the end of 1981, this independent group played a major role in the country's political fortunes.

However, such popular support provided a direct threat to the monopoly of power that was the basis for the Communist Party and the entire Leninist state. And as 1981 progressed, Solidarity became much more strident in its demands, going from "explicitly eschewing any attempts to oust the ruling Polish United Workers Party ... [to], by late 1981 calling for free elections and an end to communist rule" (Biezenski 1996:261). Such an equilibrium in a communist context was highly unstable, and unlikely to continue so long as the monopoly of violence that the PZPR held was unchallenged. As Mason (1989:48) noted, "Solidarity recognized that it could not challenge the Party head on, both because of the possible civil violence that might entail and because of the ever-present threat of Soviet intervention on behalf of the Party." This impasse between the two sides was broken in December 1981 when, ostensibly acting to prevent an armed insurrection by Solidarity across Poland, General Wojciech Jaruzelski declared martial law and sent in the tanks against any and all enemies of the state.

Volumes have been written and continue to be written about the imposition of martial law in Poland, given the controversy surrounding the decision and the possible alternatives; General Jaruzelski, having only been in power for two months as First Secretary of the Communist Party, later argued that martial law was necessary to avoid Soviet intervention, an assertion which may have weighed heavily on the minds of the military in 1981 but was in actuality not a threat, as archival evidence has shown (Mastny 1999). For our purposes, the era of martial law shows once again the schism between formal political institutions in Poland and their informal brothers, as the formal institutions of the Party (much as the Russians and Prussians before it) sought to eradicate the informal institutions that kept alive the idea of Poland.

A major change that came from martial law, however, was that the power of formal institutions had shifted from the secret institutions of the police to the overt force of the military. As Spielman (1982:23), in an otherwise laughable rant in hindsight, pointed out, "far from a typical communist, [Jaruzelski] is much more a typical general. He does not aspire to re-create a political order based on the personal rule of the Party apparatchiks, whom he detests and whose vehicle of domination is the

Polish Communist Party. He seeks to create an order based on his army, directed by a loyal following of a supra-Party elite." Even class warfare was practiced by the new-look Polish government, with workers arrested during martial law treated much more roughly than the intelligentsia, housed in separate housing, and political activities among workers targeted with particular zeal (Kennedy 1992). Thus, where the Communist Party sought to keep the reins of power via subterfuge and mass terror, Jaruzelski instead wanted a straightforward power projection to crowd out all others. In this sense, the pretense of democracy, using elections for Kabuki Theater, was dropped in order to preserve the formal power structure.

This did not mean that the trappings of democracy were ignored, however. Perhaps oblivious of the effects that the formal political institutions were having on the informal institutional landscape, the Communist Party pushed through additional amendments to the constitution in 1982, in the wake of martial law. The two most important changes were the introduction of a Constitutional Tribunal, to perform judicial review of statutes and regulations, and the creation of a Tribunal of State, designed to hold state officials accountable for malfeasance (Cole 1998). While these institutions were circumscribed in their abilities (for example, the Constitutional Tribunal could only examine laws that were promulgated after the Tribunal came into existence, and not review laws on the books), they did contribute to a dilution of the Party's monolithic power by introducing a semblance of balance across government (Brzezinski 1991). While the *Sejm* was transformed into a rubber stamp parliament under communism, these amendments gave some autonomy to the legislature as a check on the executive (Cole 1998).

More important, the creation of the Tribunal of State meant that Solidarity's critique of corruption actually had some impact on formal institutions, with the government realizing it had to take the lead in fighting the issues that civil society would continue to raise. For perhaps the first time in a Warsaw Pact state (but not the last), an independent movement had forced the communist government to amend its own procedures in order to satisfy the polity. In an important move for Poland's future, "the notion of the contractual state began to reemerge in Poland, with the ruling Party slowly becoming attentive to the duties accompanying state positions of authority" (Brzezinski 1991:101). Although the Tribunal of State was also limited in its scope, the mere fact that the PZPR felt it had to create such an organ perhaps showed that one can only play at democracy for so long before it starts becoming reality. Indeed, Jaruzelski's moves began to separate the Party from the state, structuring a government of institutions that were ruled over by the Communist Party but that had an institutional framework separate from the Party apparatus (Poznański 1996). Finally, by creating such an institution, Jaruzelski's regime "tacitly repudiated a fundamental tenet of communism: that a communist state would be devoid of social and political discord" (Cole 1998:28).

Unfortunately, tanks continued to display the might of the Party and the military, with martial law only lifted in 1983 (and many Solidarity supporters remaining in prison until 1986). Martial law "essentially froze political change for the first half of the 1980s and left the society bitterly split" (Curry 2004:21–22), isolating hardline PZPR members who found themselves trapped between democratic forces in civil society and military leadership that were more along the lines of a traditional junta than a progressive vanguard. As under the Partitions, martial law was able to somewhat limit the growth of opposition and prevent any transformation of informal institutions into formal ones, leaving only small-scale resistance and dissidence (as Buchowski (1996:83) called them, "microstructures form[ing] a network of tightly knit interest groups"). But the overall goals of martial law were not attained (Frentzel-Zagorska 1990), as Solidarity was not crushed (if anything, its antiregime bona fides were strengthened); the church and especially the person of Pope John Paul II continued to exercise a powerful influence in opposition to communism; and the further self-organization of society continued because the ideas unleashed during 1980–1981 could not be contained.

More reforms continued from the end of martial law in 1983, including changes in the electoral law to allow for limited political participation by noncommunist parties (but without challenging the monopoly on power of the PZPR) and the creation in 1987 of an Office of the Commissioner for Citizens Rights, an early ombudsman-type office (Brzezinski 1991). These changes, while reflecting the resilient strength of informal institutions, also showed a continuing absorption of ideas from civil society and perhaps an attempt to co-opt their ideas for the state. Regardless, Solidarity and its alliance with the church had become too powerful to be co-opted in such a manner, with the church in particular gaining strength from the visits of Pope John Paul II (his second visit in 1983 pointedly praised Solidarity; see Kubik 2010). When another economic crisis struck in 1987–1988, workers' strikes forced the regime's hand to come to the bargaining table and negotiate a way forward. With substantial changes occurring in the Soviet Union, the external force that still ruled over Poland and colored all decisions both political and economic, the threat of intervention had subsided. Time had come for the informal to swap places with the formal, and for a foreign-occupied Poland to once again attempt to build its own independent institutions.

SUMMING UP: THE IMPACT OF HISTORY ON POLITICAL INSTITUTIONS

As this overview shows, Poland's political institutional development over the past 500 years has been conditioned by many different factors, both internal and external, but they display a remarkable continuity. This reality, of an unbroken history of political debate, is directly contra to Longworth's (1994:7) assertion that "the nations of Eastern Europe had no tradition of democracy in the Western sense . . . . if one regards Soviet Communism as a disease, then it seems that Eastern Europe may have had a pre-disposition to the infection." The only disease that consistently reared its head is one that continues to plague every country, and that is the attempt of politicians to aggregate power to themselves. From King Jan Kazimierz's attempt to neuter the *Sejm* to Josef Piłsudski's military coup to the communist takeover, Poland has grappled with designing the appropriate institutional mechanisms to restrain the executive but often failing to contain the desires of men who were not angels. While Polish political debate accurately recognized what the threat was to the liberty of the *szlachta* and, in turn, the individual, there was no successful mechanism created to constrain this threat, apart from the possibility of armed rebellion every decade or so. While an effective check against tyranny, lurching from crisis to crisis was no way to engender stability in either the political or (as we will see) the economic sphere.

The history of political institutional evolution in Poland has also been conditioned by external forces, a reality that was to continue into the postcommunist times and until today. Much of the time which Poland could have utilized under the Constitution of 1791 to refine its formal institutions along the lines of the United States was lost to foreign occupation, and the resulting constitutions were at once too weak or too authoritarian to be matched by "good" effective political institutions. The brief period of independence between the wars saw institutional evolution also mightily influenced by the international drift towards fascism (although, as we saw above, Poland played a major role in pushing Central Europe in that direction). Under such pressure, political institutions remained reactive to the world around them, either taking cues from external powers (e.g., the Soviet Union) or straining for more power in order to challenge external threats (e.g., Augustus II's attempt to raise taxes and quarter a standing army).

A further challenge to the development of Polish institutions has been the fact that Poland itself has continually changed geographic and ethnographic borders. Most institutions are created or arise to deal with a specific set of boundaries, especially institutions in the political sphere. But the continual recreation of Poland as a physical entity made this difficult, especially when "Poland" began to encompass Lithuanians, Ukrainians, and Belarusians in varying proportions, and especially when the political discourse in Poland had not caught up to the idea of extending noble liberty to other nationalities. Political institutions that may have relied on common goals and a unified society (as in the Constitution of 1921) suddenly became inadequate in a multiethnic country with a fragmented polity. In this sense, the relative stability forced upon Poland's borders by the Soviet Union at the end of the Second World War has contributed to the development of formal institutions, albeit not before communism itself had been defeated.

Finally, and perhaps most important from this overview, where Poland's formal institutions have failed, the vacuum has been filled by informal ones. While these institutions may have necessarily been small scale, as under the Partitions or under the Stalinist regime of Bolesław Bierut, they have kept the political debate within Polish society churning. From the power of the church in retaining national identity during the Partitions to Solidarity providing an alternative to the class rhetoric of the communists, informal institutions have been able to challenge the ruling orthodoxy. In this way, these informal institutions also helped to inculcate a healthy distrust of authority as a check on formal institutions, a persistent theme in Polish political life. And with the fall of communism, the fact that there had been an independent civil society in Poland, drawing on themes that had existed for centuries, was to play a major role in constituting the postcommunist political order. It also helped to revive the capitalist system, a theme that is the subject of the next chapter.

References

Acemoglu, D., and Robinson, J. A. (2006). De facto political power and institutional persistence. *The American Economic Review*, 96(2), pp. 325–330.

Ajnenkiel, A. (1989). *Historia Sejmu Polskiego: Volume 2*. Warsaw: PWN Publishers.
  (1991). *Polskie Konstytucje*. Warsaw: Wydawnictwo Szkolne I Pedagogiczne.

Alexander, G. (2001). Institutions, path dependence, and democratic consolidation. *Journal of Theoretical Politics*, 13(3), pp. 249–269.

Arato, A. (1981). Civil society against the state: Poland 1980–81. *Telos*, 47, pp. 23–47.

Arlinghaus, F. A. (1942). The Kulturkampf and European Diplomacy, 1871–1875. *Catholic Historical Review*, 28(3), pp. 340–375.

Ascher, A. (2004). *The Revolution of 1905: A Short History.* Palo Alto, CA: Stanford University Press.

Backus, O. P. (1963). The problem of unity in the Polish-Lithuanian State. *Slavic Review*, 22(3), pp. 411–431.

Banks, A.S., and Wilson, K.A. (2015). *Cross-National Time-Series Data Archive.* Databanks International. Jerusalem, Israel. Available at www.databanksinternational.com.

Barker, C. (2009). Fear, laughter, and collective power: The making of solidarity at the Lenin Shipyard in Gdansk, Poland, August 1980. In Goodwin, J., Jasper, J.M., and Polletta, F. (eds.), *Passionate Politics: Emotions and Social Movements.* Chicago: University of Chicago Press, pp. 175–194.

Becker, S. O., Boeckh, K., Hainz, C., and Woessmann, L. (2014). The empire is dead, long live the empire! Long-run persistence of trust and corruption in the bureaucracy. *Economic Journal.* Accepted article, http://onlinelibrary.wiley.com/doi/10.1111/ecoj.12220/abstract.

Behrends, J. C. (2009). Nation and empire: Dilemmas of legitimacy during Stalinism in Poland (1941–1956). *Nationalities Papers*, 37(4),pp. 443–466.

Berend, I. T. (2005). *History Derailed: Central and Eastern Europe in the Long Nineteenth Century.* Oakland: University of California Press.

Berghahn, V. R. (1999). Germans and Poles, 1871–1945. In Bullivant, K. (ed.), *Germany and Eastern Europe: Cultural Identities and Cultural Differences, Vol. 13.* Amsterdam: Rodopi Publishers, pp. 15–36.

Bernhard, M. (1993). Civil society and democratic transition in East Central Europe. *Political Science Quarterly*, 108(2), pp. 307–326.

(2000). Democratization by direct constitution in Weimar Germany and interwar Poland. *Journal of European Area Studies*, 8(2), pp. 221–245.

(2005). *Institutions and the Fate of Democracy: Germany and Poland in the Twentieth Century.* Pittsburgh, PA: University of Pittsburgh Press.

Bialasiewicz, L., and O'Loughlin, J. (2002). Reordering Europe's eastern frontier: Galician identities and political cartographies on the Polish-Ukrainian border. In Kaplan, D.H., and Häkli, J. (eds.), *Borderlands and Place: European Borderlands in Geographical Context.* Lanham, MD: Rowman & Littlefield, pp. 217–238.

Bideleux, R., and Jeffries, I. (1998). *A History of Eastern Europe: Crisis and Change.* New York: Routledge.

Biezenski, R. (1996). The struggle for solidarity 1980–81: Two waves of leadership in conflict. *Europe-Asia Studies*, 48(2), pp. 261–284.

Black, J. (2009). *War in European History, 1660–1792.* Lincoln, NE: Potomac Books.

Blanke, R. (1974). The development of loyalism in Prussian Poland, 1886–1890. *Slavonic and East European Review*, 52(129), pp. 548–565.

(1977). An "era of reconciliation" in German-Polish relations (1890–1894). *Slavic Review*, 36(1), pp. 39–53.

Blejwas, S. A. (1982). Warsaw positivism – patriotism misunderstood. *Polish Review*, 27(1/2), pp. 47–54.

(2010). New political directions: A transition toward popular participation in politics, 1863–90. In Biskupski, M.B., Pula, J.S., and Wróbel, P.J. (eds.),

The Origins of Modern Polish Democracy. Athens: Ohio University Press, pp. 23–59.

Blobaum, R. (1988). The revolution of 1905–1907 and the crisis of Polish Catholicism. *Slavic Review,* 47(4), pp. 667–686.

Bodoh-Creed, A. (2014). *Endogenous Institutional Selection, Building Trust, and Economic Growth.* Paper presented at the Annual Meeting of the International Society for New Institutional Economics, Durham, NC, June 19–21. Available at http://faculty.haas.berkeley.edu/acreed/PVP.pdf, accessed June 29, 2015.

Borowik, I. (2002). The Roman Catholic Church in the process of democratic transformation: The case of Poland. *Social Compass,* 49(2), pp. 239–252.

Borzecki, J. (1996). The Union of Lublin as a factor in the emergence of Ukrainian national consciousness. *Polish Review,* 41(1), pp. 37–61.

Bowersox, J. D. (2003). 'Loyal sons of the church and fatherland'? Center-Polish relations in Upper Silesia, 1871–1907. *Canadian Journal of History,* 38(2), pp. 231–257.

Brown, P. B. (1982). Muscovy, Poland, and the seventeenth century crisis. *Polish Review,* 27(3/4), pp. 55–69.

Brykczynski, P. (2014). Anti-Semitism on trial: The case of Eligiusz Niewiadomski. *East European Politics & Societies,* 28(2), pp. 411–439.

Brzezinski, M. (1991). Constitutional heritage and renewal: The case of Poland. *Virginia Law Review,* 77(1), pp. 49–112.

   (1998). *The Struggle for Constitutionalism in Poland.* Basingstoke: Palgrave Macmillan.

Buchowski, M. (1996). The shifting meanings of civil and civic society in Poland. In Hann, C., and Dunn, E. (eds.), *Civil Society: Challenging Western Models.* New York: Routledge, pp. 79–98.

Bussow, C., and Orchard, E. (1994). *Disturbed State of the Russian Realm.* Montreal: McGill-Queen's Press.

Byrnes, T. A. (1997). The Catholic Church and Poland's return to Europe. *East European Quarterly,* 30(4), pp. 433–448.

   (2002). The challenge of pluralism: The Catholic Church in democratic Poland. In Wilcox, C. (ed.), *Religion and Politics in Comparative Perspective: The One, the Few, and the Many.* Cambridge: Cambridge University Press, pp. 27–44.

Chmielewski, E. (1970). The separation of Chełm from Poland. *Polish Review,* 15(1), pp. 67–86.

Chodakiewicz, M. J. (2004). *Between Nazis and Soviets: Occupation Politics in Poland, 1939–1947.* Lanham, MD: Lexington Books.

Cienciala, A. M., and Komarnicki, T. (1984). *From Versailles to Locarno: Keys to Polish Foreign Policy, 1919–25.* Lawrence: University Press of Kansas.

Ciosek, I. (2009). Universalism and particularity of Polish political thought. *Dialogue and Universalism,* 19(6/7), pp. 105–114.

Citrin, J. (1974). Comment: The political relevance of trust in government. *American Political Science Review,* 68(3), pp. 973–988.

Clague, C., Keefer, P., Knack, S., and Olson, M. (1999). Contract-intensive money: Contract enforcement, property rights, and economic performance. *Journal of Economic Growth,* 4(2), pp. 185–211.

Cole, D. H. (1998). Poland's 1997 constitution in its historical context. *Saint Louis-Warsaw Transatlantic Law Journal*, 1, pp. 1–43.

(1999). From Renaissance Poland to Poland's Renaissance. *Michigan Law Review*, 97, pp. 2062–2102.

Coleman, A. P. (1934). Language as a factor in Polish nationalism. *Slavonic and East European Review*, 13(37), pp. 155–172.

Corrsin, S. D. (1990). Language use in cultural and political change in pre-1914 Warsaw: Poles, Jews, and Russification. *Slavonic and East European Review*, 68 (1), pp. 69–90.

Corwin, E. H. L. (1917). *The Political History of Poland*. New York: Polish Book Importing Company.

Coutouvidis, J. (1984). Lewis Namier and the Polish government-in-exile, 1939–40. *Slavonic and East European Review*, 62(3), pp. 421–428.

Curry, J. L. (2004). Poland's ex-communists: From pariahs to establishment players. In Curry, J.L., and Urban, J.B. (eds.), *The Left Transformed in Post-Communist Societies: The Cases of East-Central Europe, Russia, and Ukraine*. New York: Rowan & Littlefield, pp. 19–60.

Davenport, C. (2007). State repression and political order. *Annual Review of Political Science*, 10, pp. 1–23.

Davies, N. (1984). *God's Playground: A History of Poland (Volume 1)*. New York: Columbia University Press.

(2001). *Heart of Europe: The Past in Poland's Present*. Oxford: Oxford University Press.

(2005). *God's Playground: A History of Poland (Volume 2: 1795 to the Present)*. New York: Columbia University Press.

de Soto, H. (2000). *The Mystery of Capital*. New York: Basic Books.

Dolbilov, M. (2004). Russification and the bureaucratic mind in the Russian Empire's northwestern region in the 1860s. *Kritika: Explorations in Russian and Eurasian History*, 5(2), pp. 245–271.

Donnorummo, R. (1994). Poland's political and economic transition. *East European Quarterly*, 28(2), pp. 259–280.

Drummond, E. A. (2013). In and out of the Ostmark: Migration, settlement, and demographics in Poznania, 1871–1918. *Itinerario*, 37(01), pp. 73–86.

Eberts, M. W. (1998). The Roman Catholic Church and democracy in Poland. *Europe-Asia Studies*, 50(5), pp. 817–842.

Eversley, G. S.-L. (1915). *The Partitions of Poland*. London: T. Fisher Unwin, Ltd.

Fiddick, T. (1973). The "miracle of the Vistula": Soviet policy versus Red Army strategy. *Journal of Modern History*, 45(4), pp. 626–643.

Fijalkowski, A. (2013). *From Old Times to New Europe: The Polish Struggle for Democracy and Constitutionalism*. Surrey, UK: Ashgate Publishing, Ltd.

Foreign Office (1945). Correspondence of the UK Foreign Office, Document PRO FO 371 47585 N3581/6/G55.

Franz, M. (2005). Powstanie kozackie 1637 roku i bitwa pod Kumejkami w polskiej historiografii wojskowej [The Cossack uprising of 1637 and the Battle of Kumejki in light of Polish military historiography]. In B. Miśkiewicz (ed.), *Studia z dziejów polskiej historiografii wojskowej*. Poznań: Wydawnictwo naukowe Uniwersytetu im. Adama Mickiewicza.

Frentzel-Zagorska, J. (1990). Civil society in Poland and Hungary. *Europe-Asia Studies*, 42(4), pp. 759–777.

Friedrich, K. (2009). Citizenship in the periphery: Royal Prussia and the Union of Lublin 1569. In Friedrich, K., and Pendzich, B.M. (eds.), *Citizenship and Identity in a Multinational Commonwealth: Poland-Lithuania in Context, 1550–1772*. Leiden, the Netherlands: Brill Publishing, pp. 49–70.

Frost, R. I. (1986). 'Initium Calamitatis Regni'? John Casimir and monarchical power in Poland-Lithuania, 1648–68. *European History Quarterly*, 16(2), pp. 181–207.

—— (1990). "Liberty without licence?" The failure of polish democratic thought in the seventeenth century. In Pula, J.S., and Biskupski, M.B. (eds.), *Polish Democratic Thought from the Renaissance to the Great Emigration: Essays and Documents*. New York: Columbia University Press, pp. 29–54.

—— (2004). *After the Deluge: Poland-Lithuania and the Second Northern War, 1655–1660*. Cambridge: Cambridge University Press.

—— (2010). Review of *Disorderly Liberty: The Political Culture of the Polish-Lithuanian Commonwealth in the Eighteenth Century* (review no. 1044). www.history.ac.uk /reviews/review/1044, accessed June 29, 2015.

—— (2011). Ut unusquisque qui vellet, ad illum venire possit. In Leonhard, J., and Wieland, C. (eds.), *What Makes the Nobility Noble?: Comparative Perspectives from the Sixteenth to the Twentieth Century*. Göttingen: Vandenhoeck & Ruprecht, pp. 142–163.

—— (2012). Book Review: Making ukraine. Studies on political culture, historical narrative, and identity by Zenon E. Kohut. *Eighteenth-Century Studies*, 46(1), pp. 164–166.

—— (2014). *The Northern Wars: War, State and Society in Northeastern Europe, 1558–1721*. New York: Routledge.

Frucht, R.C. (2004). *Eastern Europe: An Introduction to the People, Lands, and Culture*. Oxford: ABC-CLIO Publishers.

Ganowicz, E. (2013). History of Polish Parliamentary System. *Вісник Львівського університету. Серія: Міжнародні відносини*, 32, pp. 137–146.

Gentes, A. A. (2003). Siberian exile and the 1863 Polish insurrectionists according to Russian sources. *Jahrbücher für Geschichte Osteuropas*, 51(2), pp. 197–217.

Geremek, B. (1995). Parliamentarism in Central Europe. *Eastern European Constitutional Review*, 4(3), pp. 43–48.

Gibianskii, L. I., and Naimark, N. M. (2004). *The Soviet Union and the Establishment of Communist Regimes in Eastern Europe, 1944–1954: A Documentary Collection*. Washington, DC: National Council for Eurasian and East European Research.

Gloger, Z. (1896). *Słownik rzeczy starozytnych*. Warsaw: Gebethner.

Główny Urząd Statystyczny (1921). *Pierwszy Powszechny Spis Ludności* [First General Census]. Warsaw: GUS.

Goldyn, B. (1998). Disenchanted voices: Public opinion in Cracow, 1945–1946. *East European Quarterly*, 32(2), 139–165.

Gordon, Linda (1983). *Cossack Rebellions: Social Turmoil in the Sixteenth-Century Ukraine*. Albany: State University of New York Press.

Górnicki, Ł. (1616). *Droga do zupełnej wolności*. Kraków: Jakub Siebeneicher.

Górski, K., Raczyńska, V., and Raczyńska, C. (1966). The origins of the Polish *Sejm*. *Slavonic and East European Review*, 44(102), pp. 122–138.

Gromelski, T. (2013). Liberty and liberties in early modern Poland-Lithuania. In Skinner, Q., and van Gelderen, M. (eds.), *Freedom and the Construction of Europe, Volume 1*. Cambridge: Cambridge University Press.

Grosfeld, I., and Zhuravskaya, E. (2015). Cultural vs. economic legacies of empires: Evidence from the partition of Poland. *Journal of Comparative Economics*, 43(1), pp. 55–75.

Groth, A. J. (1964). Proportional Representation in Prewar Poland. *Slavic Review*, 23(1), pp. 103–116.

(1965). Polish Elections 1919–1928. *Slavic Review*, 24(4), pp. 653–665.

Grześkowiak-Krwawicz, A. (2005). Anti-monarchism in polish republicanism in the seventeenth and eighteenth centuries. In Van Gelderen, M., and Skinner, Q. (eds.), *Republicanism: Volume 1, Republicanism and Constitutionalism in Early Modern Europe: A Shared European Heritage*. Cambridge: Cambridge University Press, pp. 43–59.

(2012). *Queen Liberty: The Concept of Freedom in the Polish-Lithuanian Commonwealth*. Leiden, the Netherlands: Brill Publishing.

Gumplowicz, L. (1867). *Prawodawstwo polskie względem Żydów*. Berlin: Himmelblau.

Haczyński, L. J. (1975). Review of wynot, polish politics in transition: the camp of national unity and the struggle for power 1935–1939. *Canadian Journal of History*, 10(2), pp. 278–280.

Hagen, W. W. (1972). National solidarity and organic work in Prussian Poland, 1815–1914. *Journal of Modern History*, 44(1), pp. 38–64.

Hahn, H. H. (2001). The Polish Nation in the Revolution of 1846–49. In Dowe, D. (ed.), *Europe in 1848: Revolution and Reform*. New York: Berghahn Books, pp. 170–185.

Haiman, M. (1946). American Influences on Kosciuszko's Act of Insurrection. *Polish American Studies*, 3(1–2), pp. 1–4.

Halecki, O. (1963). Why was Poland partitioned? *Slavic Review*, 22(3), pp. 432–441.

Halecki, O., Polonsky, A., and Gromada, T. (1978). *A History of Poland*. New York: Routledge.

Hartwell, C.A. (2013). *Institutional Barriers in the Transition to Market: Explaining Performance and Divergence in Transition Economies*. Basingstoke: Palgrave Macmillan.

Heinberg, J. G. (1926). History of the majority principle. *American Political Science Review*, 20(1), pp. 52–68.

Hobsbawm, E. J. (1954). The general crisis of the European economy in the seventeenth century. *Past and Present*, 5, pp. 33–53.

Hofmann, A. R. (2004). The Biedermanns in the 1905 revolution: A case study in entrepreneurs' responses to social turmoil in Łodź. *Slavonic and East European Review*, 82(1), pp. 27–49.

Holzer, J. (1967). Attitude of the Polish Socialist Party and Polish Social-Democratic Party to the Russian Revolution of 1917. *Acta Poloniae Historica*, 16, pp. 76–90.

Howard, A. E. D. (1991). The essence of constitutionalism. In Thompson, K.W., and Ludwikowski, R.R. (eds.), *Constitutionalism and Human Rights: America, Poland, and France – A Bicentennial Colloquium at the Miller Center*. Lanham, MD: University Press of America.

Jakelic, S. (2012). *Collectivistic Religions: Religion, Choice, and Identity in Late Modernity*. Surrey, UK: Ashgate Publishing.

Jakstas, J. (1963). How firm was the Polish-Lithuanian Federation? *Slavic Review*, 22(3), pp. 442–449.

Janczewski, G. H. (1972). The origin of the Lublin Government. *Slavonic and East European Review*, 50(120), pp. 410–433.

Jędruch, J. (1998). *Constitutions, Elections, and Legislatures of Poland, 1493–1977: A Guide to Their History*. New York: Hippocrene Books.

Jędrychowska, J. (2014). Cursed with patriotism. The educational potential of enslavement (Polish society in the Russian Partition of Poland in the first half of the nineteenth century). *Czech-Polish Historical and Pedagogical Journal*, 6(1), pp. 40–47.

Jędrzejewicz, W. (1962). Review: A Soviet history of Poland. *Polish Review*, 7(2), pp. 111–116.

Kacewicz, G. V. (1979). *Great Britain, the Soviet Union and the Polish Government in Exile (1939–1945)*. Amsterdam: Springer Netherlands.

Kadziela, Ł., and Strybel, R. (1994). The 1794 Kościuszko Insurrection. *Polish Review*, 39(4), pp. 387–392.

Kamiński, A. (1977). The Cossack experiment in *szlachta* democracy in the Polish-Lithuanian Commonwealth: The Hadiach (Hadziacz) union. *Harvard Ukrainian Studies*, 1(2), pp. 178–197.

Kaminski, T. M. (1988). Bismarck and the Polish question: The "Huldigungsfahrten" to Varzin in 1894. *Canadian Journal of History*, 23(2), pp. 235–250.

Kann, R.A. (1974). *A History of the Habsburg Empire, 1526–1918*. Oakland: University of California Press.

Kappeler, A. (2014). *The Russian Empire: A Multi-Ethnic History*. New York: Routledge.

Karski, J. (2014). *The Great Powers and Poland: From Versailles to Yalta*. New York: Rowan & Littlefield.

Kawyn, S. (1953). *Polska publicystyka postepowa w kraju*. Wrocław: Zakład Narodowy im. Ossolińskich.

Kemp-Welch, A. (2008). *Poland under Communism: A Cold War History*. Cambridge: Cambridge University Press.

Kenney, P. (1997). *Rebuilding Poland: Workers and Communists, 1945–1950*. Ithaca, NY: Cornell University Press.

Kersten, K. (1991). *The Establishment of Communist Rule in Poland, 1943–1948*. Oakland: University of California Press.

Koehler, K. (2012). The heritage of Polish republicanism. *Sarmatian Review*, 2, pp. 1658–1665.

Kopstein, J. S., and Wittenberg, J. (2003). Who voted communist? Reconsidering the social bases of radicalism in interwar Poland. *Slavic Review*, 62(1), pp. 87–109.

(2010). Beyond dictatorship and democracy: Rethinking national minority inclusion and regime type in interwar Eastern Europe. *Comparative Political Studies*, 43(8), pp. 1089–1118.

Kowalski, G. M. (2014). The Amendment of August 1926 to the first Polish Constitution of the Second Republic. *Krakówskie Studia z Historii Państwa i Prawa*, 7(2), pp. 317–322.

Krasinski, H. (1848). *The Cossacks of the Ukraine*. New York: AMS Press.

Krasnozhon, L. A. (2013). Institutional stickiness of democracy in post-communist states: Can prevailing culture explain it? *Review of Austrian Economics*, 26(2), pp. 221–237.

Kubiak, H. (1999). Parties, party systems, and cleavages in Poland: 1918–1989. In Lawson, K., Römmele, A., and Karasimeonov, G. (eds.), *Cleavages, Parties, and Voters: Studies from Bulgaria, the Czech Republic, Hungary, Poland, and Romania*. Santa Barbara, CA: Greenwood Publishing.

Kubik, J. (2010). *Power of Symbols Against the Symbols of Power: The Rise of Solidarity and the Fall of State Socialism in Poland*. University Park, PA: Penn State Press.

Larsh, W. (1995). Yalta and the American approach to free elections in Poland. *Polish Review*, 40(3), pp. 267–280.

Lerski, J. J. (1996). *Historical Dictionary of Poland, 966–1945*. Westport, CT: Greenwood Publishing.

Leslie, R. F. (1955). Politics and economics in Congress Poland, 1815–1864. *Past and Present*, 8, pp. 43–63.

——— (1980). *The History of Poland Since 1863*. Cambridge: Cambridge University Press.

Lewitter, L. R. (1948). Poland, the Ukraine and Russia in the seventeenth century. *Slavonic and East European Review*, 27(68), pp. 157–171.

Lijphart, A. (ed.) (1992). *Parliamentary versus Presidential Government*. Oxford: Oxford University Press.

Little, R. (2007). *The Balance of Power in International Relations*. Cambridge: Cambridge University Press.

Litwin, H. (1987). Catholicization among the Ruthenian nobility and assimilation processes in the Ukraine during the years 1569–1648. *Acta Poloniae Historica*, 55, pp. 57–83.

Lockhart, P. D. (2004). *Sweden in the Seventeenth Century*. Basingstoke, UK: Palgrave Macmillan.

Longworth, R. (1994). *The Making of Eastern Europe*. Basingstoke, UK: Palgrave Macmillan.

Lorenz, E. (1999). Trust, contract and economic cooperation. *Cambridge Journal of Economics*, 23(3), pp. 301–315.

Ludwikowski, R. R. (1987). Two firsts: A comparative study of the American and the Polish Constitutions. *Michigan Yearbook of International Legal Studies*, 8, pp. 117–156.

——— (1997). *Constitution-Making in the Region of Former Soviet Dominance*. Durham, NC: Duke University Press.

Lukowski, J. (2004). Political Ideas among the Polish nobility in the eighteenth century (to 1788). *Slavonic and East European Review*, 82(1), pp. 1–26.

Lukowski, J., and Zawadzki, H. (2006). *A Concise History of Poland*. Cambridge: Cambridge University Press.

Maciszewski, J. (1960). *Wojna domowa w Polsce, 1606–1609*. Wrocław: Zakład Narodowy im. Ossolińskich.

Magocsi, P. (2010). *A History of Ukraine: The Land and Its Peoples*. Toronto: University of Toronto Press.

Manning, C. (1946). The Soviet Union and the Slavs. *Russian Review*, 5(2), pp. 3–9.

Marzec, W. (2013). The 1905–1907 Revolution in the Kingdom of Poland: Articulation of political subjectivities among workers. *Contention: The Multidisciplinary Journal of Social Protest*, 1(1), pp. 53–72.

(2015). What bears witness of the failed revolution? the rise of political antisemitism during the 1905–1907 revolution in the kingdom of poland. *East European Politics & Societies*, Online First, April 24, doi: 10.1177/0888325415581896.

Mason, D. S. (1989). Solidarity as a new social movement. *Political Science Quarterly*, 104(1), pp. 41–58.

Mastny, V. (1999). The Soviet non-invasion of Poland in 1980–1981 and the end of the Cold War. *Europe-Asia Studies*, 51(2), pp. 189–211.

McKenna, C. J. (2012). *The Curious Evolution of the Liberum Veto: Republican Theory and Practice in the Polish-Lithuanian Commonwealth, 1639–1705.* Unpublished doctoral dissertation, Georgetown University; Washington DC.

McLean, P. D. (2004). Widening access while tightening control: Office-holding, marriages, and elite consolidation in early modern Poland. *Theory and Society*, 33(2), pp. 167–212.

(2011). Patrimonialism, elite networks, and reform in late-eighteenth-century Poland. *Annals of the American Academy of Political and Social Science*, 636(1), pp. 88–110.

Michta, A. A. (1989). *Red Eagle: The Army in Polish Politics, 1944–1988.* Palo Alto, CA: Hoover Institution Press.

Micińska, M. (1998). The myth of Tadeusz Kościuszko in the Polish mind (1794–1997). *European Review of History*, 5(2), pp. 191–196.

Midlarsky, M. I. (2003). The impact of external threat on states and domestic societies 1. *International Studies Review*, 5(4), pp. 13–18.

Mikolajczyk, S. (1948). *The Pattern of Soviet Domination.* London: Samson Low, Marston and Company.

Milewicz, P. (2010). National Identification in pre-industrial communities: Peasant participation in the November Uprising in the Kingdom of Poland, 1830–1831. *Jahrbücher für Geschichte Osteuropas*, 58(3), pp. 321–352.

Miller, J. (1983). The Polish nobility and the renaissance monarchy: The "execution of the laws" movement: Part one. *Parliaments, Estates, and Representation*, 3(2), pp. 65–87.

Molenda, J. (1991). The formation of national consciousness of the Polish Peasants and the part they played in the regaining of independence by Poland. *Acta Poloniae Historica*, 63–64, pp. 121–148.

Morrow, I. F. (1936). The Prussianisation of the Poles. *Slavonic and East European Review*, 15(43), pp. 153–164.

Nabrdalik, B. (2007). How a nation outlived its state – Polish partitions and their impact on the citizens of the former commonwealth. *Journal of Slavic Military Studies*, 20 (4), pp. 653–678.

Oakley, S. P. (2005). *War and Peace in the Baltic: 1560–1790.* New York: Routledge.

Onslow, R. W. (1931). Polish self-help under Prussian Rule, 1886–1908. *Slavonic and East European Review*, 10(28), pp. 126–137.

Opalinski, E. (2002). Civic humanism and republican citizenship in the Polish Renaissance. In van Gelderen, M., and Skinner, Q. (eds.), *Republicanism: Volume 1, Republicanism and Constitutionalism in Early Modern Europe: A Shared European Heritage.* Cambridge: Cambridge University Press, pp. 147–168.

Opalinski, Ł. (1641). Rozmowa plebana z ziemianinem albo Dyskurs o postanowieniu teraźniejszym Rzeczypospolitej i o sposobie zawierania *sejmów*. In Kamykowski, L. (ed.), *Pisma Polskie*. Warsaw: Wyd. Kasy im. Mianowskiego-Instytutu popierania nauki, 1938.

Osakwe, C. (1979). The theories and realities of modern Soviet constitutional law: An analysis of the 1977 USSR Constitution. *University of Pennsylvania Law Review*, 127(5), pp. 1350–1437.

Osiatynski, W. (1991). The constitution-making process in Poland. *Law & Policy*, 13(2), pp. 125–133.

Pajewski, J. (1993). *Gabriel Narutowicz: Pierwszy Prezydent Rzeczypospolitej*. Warsaw: Książka i Wiedza.

Parrott, D. (2012). The Military Revolution (1560–1660). In Martel, G. (ed.), *The Encyclopedia of War*. Oxford: Blackwell Publishing.

Pavlenko, A. (2006). Russian as a lingua franca. *Annual Review of Applied Linguistics*, 26, pp. 78–99.

Payerhin, M. (1996). Terms of endearment: Intellectuals and workers mobilizing for a social movement. *Communist and Post-Communist Studies*, 29(2), pp. 185–212.

Pelenski, J. (1998). *The Contest for the Legacy of Kievan Rus'*. New York: Columbia University Press.

Pernal, A. B. (1990). The Lubomirski rebellion in 1665–66: Its causes and effects on the diet and the constitution of the Polish-Lithuanian commonwealth. *Parliaments, Estates and Representation*, 10(2), pp. 145–155.

Persak, K. (1998). Stalin as editor: The Soviet dictator's secret changes to the Polish Constitution of 1952. *Cold War International History Project Bulletin*, 11, pp. 149–154.

Pirie D. P. A. (1995). Constitutional Developments 1180– 572 (The Inexorable Political Rise of the *szlachta*). London. http://de.szlachta.wikia.com/wiki/Privilegien-1180– 1572. Accessed January 20, 2015.

Plateris, A. (1965). Codification of the law in the Grand Duchy of Lithuania. *Lituanus*, 11–2, www.lituanus.org/1965/65_2_03_Plateris.html. Accessed June 24, 2015.

Podemska-Mikluch, M. (2012). *The Lost Consensus: Unanimity Rule in the Institutional Context*. Available at SSRN: http://ssrn.com/abstract=2175984.

(2015). Elections vs. political competition: The case of the Polish-Lithuanian Commonwealth. *Review of Austrian Economics*, 28(2), pp. 167–178.

Pogorelskin, A. E. (1987). Vestnik Evropy and the Polish question in the reign of Alexander II. *Slavic Review*, 46(1), pp. 87–105.

Polonsky, A. (1972). *Politics in Independent Poland*. Oxford: Oxford University Press.

Porter, B. A. (1992). Who is a Pole and where is Poland? Territory and nation in the rhetoric of polish National Democracy before 1905. *Slavic Review*, 51(4), pp. 639–653.

(1996). The social nation and its futures: English liberalism and Polish nationalism in late nineteenth-century Warsaw. *American Historical Review*, 101(5), pp. 1470–1492.

(2000). *When Nationalism Began to Hate: Imagining Modern Politics in Nineteenth-Century Poland*. Oxford: Oxford University Press.

Poznański, K. (1996). *Poland's Protracted Transition: Institutional Change and Economic Growth, 1970–1994*. Cambridge: Cambridge University Press.

Prazmowska, A. J. (2000). The Polish Socialist Party, 1945–1948. *East European Quarterly*, 34(3), pp. 337–359.

Prizel, I. (1998). *National Identity and Foreign Policy: Nationalism and Leadership in Poland, Russia and Ukraine*. Cambridge: Cambridge University Press.

R (Anonymous) (1949). The fate of Polish socialism. *Foreign Affairs*, 28, pp. 125–142.

Rapaczynski, A. (1991). Constitutional politics in Poland: A Report on the Constitutional Committee of the Polish Parliament. *University of Chicago Law Review*, 58(2), pp. 595–631.

Raymond, W. (1999). Poland – The Road to 1989. *Polish Review*, 44(4), pp. 397–400.

Reddaway, W. F. (1971). *The Cambridge History of Poland*. Cambridge: Cambridge University Press.

Rees, S. (2006). Bloody lances & broken sabers. *Military History*, 23(1), pp. 54–60.

Reynolds, J. (1981). 'Lublin' versus' London'-The Party and the underground movement in Poland, 1944–1945. *Journal of Contemporary History*, 16(4), pp. 617–648.

Roberts, M. (1984). *The Swedish Imperial Experience 1560–1718*. Cambridge: Cambridge University Press.

Rodrigues, D. (2010). The Polish-Lithuanian Commonwealth: A new look on a peculiar type of federalism. *Regioninės Studijos*, (5), pp. 121–130.

Roháč, D. (2008a). 'It Is by unrule that poland stands': Institutions and political thought in the Polish-Lithuanian Republic. *Independent Review*, 13(2), pp. 209–224.

(2008b). The unanimity rule and religious fractionalisation in the Polish-Lithuanian Republic. *Constitutional Political Economy*, 19(2), pp. 111–128.

Romer, E. (1917). Poland: The land and the state. *Geographical Review*, 4(1), pp. 6–25.

Rothschild, J. (1962). *Piłsudski's Coup d'Etat*. New York: Columbia University Press.

Rowell, S.C. (2001). The face beneath the snow: The Baltic region in the seventeenth and eighteenth centuries. *Historical Journal*, 44(2), pp. 541–558.

Rustemeyer, A. (2014). Transnational representations of revolt and new modes of communication in the mid-seventeenth century Polish-Lithuanian Commonwealth: Jerzy Lubomirski's Rebellion against King Jan Kazimierz. In Griesse, M. (ed.), *From Mutual Observation to Propaganda War: Premodern Revolts in Their Transnational Representations*. Bielefeld, Germany: Transcript Verlag, pp. 159–180.

Sadkowski, K. (1998). From ethnic borderland to Catholic Fatherland: The Church, Christian Orthodox, and state administration in the Chełm Region, 1918–1939. *Slavic Review*, 54(4), pp. 813–839.

Salisbury, C. G. (2003). For your freedom and ours: The Polish question in Wilson's peace initiatives, 1916–1917. *Australian Journal of Politics & History*, 49(4), pp. 481–500.

Sansculottes (2004). *Karte viertepolnischeteilung*. https://commons.wikimedia.org/wiki/File:Karte_viertepolnischeteilung.png#/media/File:Karte_viertepolnischeteilung.png.

Sautin, V. (2011). The Polish Question: An apple of discord between Napoleon Bonaparte and Alexander I. *West Bohemian Historical Review*, 2, pp. 27–51.

Sawczak, P. (2004). Europe as object of aversion and desire: Cultural antinomies in Gogol''s 'Taras Bul' ba'. *Australian Slavic and East European Studies*, 18(1–2), pp. 17–39.

Schofield, A. N. E. D. (1969). Anglo-Polish Relations in the seventeenth century: A contemporary memorandum. *Historical Research*, 42(106), pp. 234–239.

Schmid, U. (2010). Constitution and narrative: Peculiarities of rhetoric and genre in the foundational laws of the USSR and the Russian federation. *Studies in East European Thought*, 62(3–4), pp. 431–451.

Schmidt, O. (1926). Большая советская энциклопедия *[Great Soviet Encyclopedia]*. Moscow: State Publishing House.

Seton-Watson, H. (1945). *Eastern Europe Between the Wars, 1918–1941*. Cambridge: Cambridge University Press.

Shlapentokh, D. (1999). Reassessment of the relationship: Polish history and the Polish question in the imperial duma. *East European Quarterly*, 33(1), pp. 115–135.

Showalter, D. (2013). *Revolutionary Wars, 1775-c. 1815*. New York: Amber Books.

Simon, M. D. (1996). Institutional development of Poland's post-communist *Sejm*: A comparative analysis. *Journal of Legislative Studies*, 2(1), pp. 60–81.

Skinner, B. (2009). Khmelnitsky's shadow: The confessional legacy. In Friedrich, K., and Pendzich, B.M. (eds.), *Citizenship and Identity in a Multinational Commonwealth: Poland-Lithuania in Context, 1550–1772*. Leiden, the Netherlands: Brill Publishing.

Skinner, Q. (1998). *Liberty before Liberalism*. Cambridge: Cambridge University Press.

Snyder, T. D. (1999). "To resolve the Ukrainian Problem once and for all": The ethnic cleansing of Ukrainians in Poland, 1943–1947. *Journal of Cold War Studies*, 1(2), pp. 86–120.

(2010). *Bloodlands: Europe Between Hitler and Stalin*. New York: Basic Books.

Spielman, R. (1982). Crisis in Poland. *Foreign Policy*, 49, pp. 20–36.

Staar, R. F. (1958). Elections in Communist Poland. *Midwest Journal of Political Science*, 2(2), pp. 200–218.

Stachura, P. (2004). *Poland, 1918–1945: An Interpretive and Documentary History of the Second Republic*. New York: Routledge.

Staliunas, D. (2004). Did the government seek to Russify Lithuanians and Poles in the Northwestern Region after the Uprising of 1863–64? *Kritika: Explorations in Russian and Eurasian History*, 5(2), pp. 273–289.

Steed, H. W., Phillips, W. A., and Hannay, D. (1914). *A Short History of Austria-Hungary and Poland*. London: The Encyclopaedia Brittanica Company.

Stone, D. Z. (2001). *The Polish-Lithuanian State, 1386–1795*. Seattle: Washington University Press.

(2010). An Introduction to Polish Democratic Thought. In Biskupski, M.B., Pula, J.S., and Wróbel, P.J. (eds.), *The Origins of Modern Polish Democracy*. Athens: Ohio University Press, pp. 1–22.

Subtelny, O. (2009). *Ukraine: a History*. Toronto: University of Toronto Press.

Sysyn, F. E. (1982). Regionalism and political thought in seventeenth-century Ukraine: The Nobility's grievances at the Diet of 1641. *Harvard Ukrainian Studies*, 6(2), pp. 167–190.

(2003). The Khmel'nyts'kyi Uprising: A characterization of the Ukrainian revolt. *Jewish History*, 17(2), pp. 115–139.

Szapiro, J. (1929). Poland and Pilsudski. *Journal of the Royal Institute of International Affairs*, 8(4), pp. 376–385.

Szymczak, D. (2009). *Między Habsburgami a Hohenzollernami. Rywalizacja niemiecko-austro-węgierska w okresie I wojny światowej a odbudowa państwa polskiego* [Between Habsburg and Hohenzollern. The German and Austro-Hungarian rivalry during WW1 and the making of the Polish state]. Kraków: Avalon Publishing.

Thatcher, I. D. (2011). The First State Duma, 1906: The view from the contemporary pamphlet and monograph literature. *Canadian Journal of History*, 46(3), pp. 531–561.

Tomaszewski, J. (1985). *Rzeczpospolita wielu narodów* [A Republic of Many Nations]. Warsaw: Czytelmk Publishers.

Tuszynski, M., and Denda, D. F. (1999). Soviet war crimes against Poland during the Second World War and its aftermath: A review of the factual record and outstanding questions. *Polish Review*, 44(2), pp. 183–216.

Tyrowicz, M. (1930). *Jan Tyssowski, dyktator Krakówski r. 1846: Działalność polityczna i społeczna, 1811–1857*. Warsaw: Kasy im. Mianowskiego Instytutu Popierania Nauki.

Valkenier, E. (1956). The Catholic Church in Communist Poland, 1945–1955. *Review of Politics*, 18(3), pp. 305–326.

Velychenko, S. (1976). The origins of the Ukrainian Revolution of 1648. *Journal of Ukrainian Studies*, 1(1), pp. 18–26.

(1995). Identities, loyalties and service in imperial Russia: Who administered the borderlands? *Russian Review*, 54(2), pp. 188–208.

Wagner, W. J. (1954). Treaties and executive agreements: Historical development and constitutional interpretation. *Catholic University Law Review*, 4, pp. 95–111.

Walaszek, Z. (1986). An open issue of legitimacy: The state and the church in Poland. *Annals of the American Academy of Political and Social Science*, 483(1), pp. 118–134.

Walicki, A. (2005). Polish conceptions of the intelligentsia and its calling. *Slavica Lundensia*, 22, pp. 1–22.

Wandycz, P.S. (1965). Secret Soviet-Polish peace talks in 1919. *Slavic Review*, 24(3), pp. 425–449.

(1967). The Poles in the Habsburg Monarchy. *Austrian History Yearbook*, 3(2), pp. 261–286.

(1974). *The Lands of Partitioned Poland, 1795–1918*. Seattle: University of Washington Press.

Weeks, T. R. (1994). Defining us and them: Poles and Russians in the "Western Provinces," 1863–1914. *Slavic Review*, 53(1), pp. 26–40.

(2001). Religion and Russification: Russian language in the Catholic Churches of the "Northwest Provinces" after 1863. *Kritika: Explorations in Russian and Eurasian History*, 2(1), pp. 87–110.

(2004). Russification: word and practice 1863–1914. *Proceedings of the American Philosophical Society*, 148(4), pp. 471–489.

(2011). Religion, nationality, or politics: Catholicism in the Russian empire, 1863–1905. *Journal of Eurasian Studies*, 2(1), pp. 52–59.

Wereszycki, H. (1967). Polish insurrections as a controversial problem in Polish historiography. *Canadian Slavonic Papers*, 9(1), pp. 107–121.

Wheeler, N. C. (2011). The noble enterprise of state building: Reconsidering the rise and fall of the modern state in Prussia and Poland. *Comparative Politics*, 44(1), pp. 21–38.

Wilson, A. (1997). *Ukrainian Nationalism in the 1990s: A Minority Faith*. Cambridge: Cambridge University Press.

Wolan, A. (2010). *De libertate politica seu civili (O wolności Rzeczypospolitej albo ślacheckiej) [1572]*. Warsaw: Neriton Publishing.

Wolf, N. (2007). Endowments vs market potential: What explains the relocation of industry after the Polish reunification in 1918? *Explorations in Economic History*, 44(1), pp. 22–42.

Wyrobisz, A. (1989). Power and towns in the Polish Gentry Commonwealth. *Theory and Society*, 18(5), pp. 611–630.

Wysocki, S. (1740). *Orator polonus: Primò aliquot instructionibus de comitijs, legationibus, militia, politica: deinde occasionibus ibidem dicendi, modis, materijs, exemplis & supplementis informatus: illustr. juventuti scolas pias frequentanti in exemplar propositus*. Warsaw: Typis S.R.M. & Reipublicae in Collegio Scholarum Piarum.

Zamoyski, A. (1987). *The Polish Way: A Thousand-Year History of the Poles and Their Culture*. New York: Hippocrene Books.

Zarycki, T. (2000). Politics in the periphery: Political cleavages in Poland interpreted in their historical and international context. *Europe-Asia Studies*, 52(5), pp. 851–873.

Zimmerman, J. D. (2004). *Poles, Jews, and the Politics of Nationality: The Bund and the Polish Socialist Party in Late Tsarist Russia, 1892–1914*. Madison: University of Wisconsin Press.

Zubrzycki, J. (1953). Emigration from Poland in the nineteenth and twentieth centuries. *Population Studies*, 6(3), pp. 248–272.

Zukowski, R. (2004). Historical path dependence, institutional persistence, and transition to market economy: The case of Poland. *International Journal of Social Economics*, 31(10), pp. 955–973.

Zyzniewski, S. J. (1965). The futile compromise reconsidered: Wielopolski and Russian policy in the Congress Kingdom, 1861–1863. *American Historical Review*, 70(2), pp. 395–412.

3

A Brief Institutional History of Central Europe (Part Two):
Poland and Its Economic Institutions to 1989

The previous chapter concentrated solely on the political institutional development of Poland for a simple reason; as Djankov et al. (2003:284) correctly note, "most crucial institutional differences among countries – whether regulating markets or regulating politics – are governmental." As shown in our extensive-yet-not-exhaustive overview of political development in Poland over five centuries, there were indeed sweeping and visible changes in the governmental apparatus from 1386 to 1988 that had profound effects on the country's economic system. Yet, at the same time, there still was a consistent framework of political thought and even some consistency of structure in political institutions in Poland. The development of executive constraints and primacy of the *Sejm* throughout Poland's history played out through various institutional permutations but was never gone for very long, even during the time of Partitions.

However, it is a fallacy to believe that institutional change begins and ends with the political arena, especially when we are considering the evolution of an economic system. While the political institutions explored in the last section may have been necessary (but not sufficient) prerequisites for understanding the creation of the modern market economy in Poland, for our purposes, the development of economic institutions is perhaps more crucial. As we will see in this chapter, even during the era of informal political institutions in Poland, formal economic institutions flourished, while, under communism, informal economic institutions continued to operate even though they were outlawed by the formal political institutions. Thus, only through understanding the mechanisms that mediate exchange and the normal human propensity for commerce can we truly understand the development of the Polish economy throughout its history and to today.

This chapter and the following ones will explore a variety of economic institutions and how they developed alongside Poland's political structures, concentrating on the institutions that have been proven to be integral to the development of a successful market economy (Hartwell 2013). In particular, we will examine the evolution of property rights; the development of labor market institutions; the creation of a sustainable financial sector and its corresponding monetary institutions; and the formal and informal institutions surrounding trade. Each of these institutions, evolving separately and in tandem with the others, is necessary to sustain a flourishing market economy, and their creation and progression over the past few centuries will give a glimpse into their (re-)introduction in Poland and Ukraine after the fall of communism.

PROPERTY RIGHTS

The most important institution for a functioning market economy is property rights, a building block for all other facets of economic exchange and a key determinant of the wealth of nations. Indeed, the presence of and unimpeded exercise of property rights has been proven to influence the subsequent path of all other economic institutions in an economy, a fact we will see in later chapters in the transition context and has been proven empirically by Hartwell (2013). While I have written at length elsewhere about the determinants of property rights and their interactions with other institutions in a country (Hartwell 2014), it is still important to give a brief synopsis of the workings of property rights before moving on to examining their development in Poland pre-1989.

Anderson and Hill (1975:163) offer perhaps the best definition of the institution of property rights, noting that it encompasses "the sanctioned behavioral relationships among men which governs their interaction and their use of resources. Such rights may be formal or informal, expressed or implied, written or unwritten but do not refer solely to real property."[1] These rights can encompass many different facets of ownership of particular resources, and in general can be thought of as having three distinct attributes:

---

[1] However, the issue of *intellectual* property rights is an entirely different creature and kept distinct from other types of property rights.

1. *Assignment and management of rights:* the right to obtain and utilize physical property as one sees fit, free of hindrance in either its acquisition or its management. This attribute of property rights also includes the right of exclusion; that is, the right to prevent others from using a resource or property (Ostrom and Hess 2010).
2. *Enforcement of rights:* the right to seek and obtain redress for any violations against the property or resource that is owned. This right may also allow for the protection of property rights against expropriation and the "grabbing hand" of the state (Hartwell 2015).
3. *Transference of rights:* the right to dispose of property in any manner chosen by the rights holder (Tietenberg 1992).

For the most part, while these facets are separate, they are often thought of as indivisible, as the inability to sell land after acquisition means that property rights are in fact severely circumscribed. This is not entirely the case, however, particularly in the area of enforcement, which often also involves other institutions in a society; indeed, property rights enforcement relies on the judiciary, which needs to be independent from political pressure to properly rule on transgressions of rights within a country's legal framework. Thus, when we trace the evolution of property rights, the differences across legal systems, countries, and territories (or even within a single country) tend to come down to differences in enforcement, with assignment/management and transference of rights defined under a basic framework law or constitution. Of course, this is not always the case, as there may be changes to that very framework law, as with the prohibition of property under communism or its reinstatement after 1989 and the fall of communist regimes across Europe. However, the bulk of differentiation across countries in terms of property rights can be traced to enforcement and not to an aversion to property rights in their entirety (Figure 3.1).

Given this description of what property rights *are*, a crucial question is thus how these formal rights *come to be* in a particular country (that is, how is the basic framework for property rights established). A long and rich literature on the determinants of property rights has come from many other disciplines, including anthropology (Hann 1998) and political science (Sened 2008), with the economics literature notable in lagging somewhat on theories of the emergence of property rights. The seminal work in this area came from Demsetz (1967), who argued that all property rights institutions are created when the benefits of their creation exceed their costs, but they only become formal when the

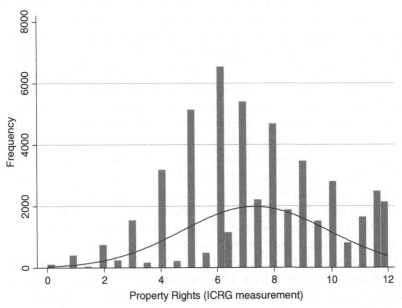

Figure 3.1 Dispersion of Property Rights across Countries, 1984–2014
Note: This shows the dispersion of the International Country Risk Guide's (ICRG)
measure of "investor profile" across 146 countries from January 1984
to July 2014. The ICRG index measures property rights from a scale of 0–12,
with 0 being no rights and 12 being the best protection. As this shows, the
countries having no property rights are very small across time and space.
Author's calculations based on ICRG data.

calculus of their benefit becomes accepted by gradual changes in social
mores (that is, when informal and formal institutions align). As further
elaborated by North (1971:123), the economic approach also correctly
believes that the formalization of such basic rules as property rights
creates a very high barrier to their alteration, with such costs to (for
example) changing the constitution a reflection of "the sanctity with
which such basic customs are regarded."

While the economic approach is elegant for providing a calculus of
institutional genesis, it still may not provide the reason behind an institution's transformation from informal to formal; just because social mores
have shifted does not necessarily mean that property rights will become the
law of the land. Two alternative approaches to the determination of
property rights, catalogued by Mijiyawa (2013), address this deficiency,
and are characterized as either the "political approach" or the "cultural
approach." The "political approach" draws from the assertion of

Djankov et al. (2003:284) that "it is impossible to understand the formation of institutions, their consequences for performance, or their appropriateness for the circumstances without understanding the political forces that drive institutional evolution." Under this approach, it is believed that institutions such as property rights are chosen by the individuals who control political power to maximize their personal payoffs (Sonin (2003) and Sened (2008)), with formalization only occurring when the benefits to such rights can payoff directly for the specific politician. Until that threshold is reached, it is likely that less efficient institutions will rule the day, mainly because they do not charge the same costs as broader-based protection, nor do they provide the same narrow benefits. As Mahoney (2004:110) notes, "distributional conflicts present political risks to politicians, giving these politicians incentives to propose regulations that do not seriously upset status quo rankings and that offer only limited relief from property rights economics inefficiencies."

On the other hand, the "cultural approach" is based on the assumption that different societies have different cultures that reflect different beliefs, which then translate into different political and economic institutions (Acemoglu et al. 2005). Under this conception, there may be inherent cultural traits that influence institutional development, meaning that certain institutions may be inherently at odds with the prevailing culture of a nation (Weber 1958). Thus, the establishment of a particular institution, in this case property rights, occurs only if the institution reflects political or societal beliefs about potential benefits for society at large (Grief 1994). This approach has a very strict corollary to it, as noted by Mijiyawa (2013), in that it presupposes that a society will not choose inefficient institutions but rather choose institutions that help society to prosper. In this sense, the cultural approach is in some ways the institutional version of Lange's (1936) idea of "market socialism," in that a society (the analogue to Lange's central planners) would utilize trial and error to create the best institutions for that society, discarding those that failed along the way.

Both of these theories rely on an assumption that elites play the critical role in formalizing property rights in legislation, with one crucial difference: the political approach assumes that elites will formalize what already exists when it suits their own economic calculation, while the cultural approach could allow for elites to *deny* formal property rights if they felt such rights were not in line with society. The difference is thus a matter of Type I versus Type II error, with cultural approaches possibly incorrectly rejecting necessary property rights on the basis of "culture" and political approaches failing to reject inefficient institutions that do not provide as many benefits as property rights.[2]

Although some support can be found for both of these approaches across countries and at different times in a country's life, recent evidence from Mijiyawa (2013) appears to give more credence to the political approach. Using a sample of 142 countries over 1970–2005, he finds that, statistically, the political approach performs best in explaining the determination of property rights. Even though this is an incredibly short time-span when one is concerned with the development of such a fundamental institution as property rights, this econometric work does provide empirical support for the idea that North (1981) formulated in his "neoclassical theory of the state"; namely, that even fundamental economic institutions are subjected to political forces and the whims of the political actors within the system.

And, as we will now see, the history of formal property rights in Poland also appears to have been determined almost entirely by political forces prior to 1989. In particular, the early years of *szlachta* democracy and the beginnings of the Polish-Lithuanian Commonwealth evidenced the development of formal property rights directly as a way, as Sonin's (2003) model would predict, to ensure the economic rights of the nobles to their lands. In the words of Ogilvie and Carus (2014:420), in Poland of the fifteenth and sixteenth centuries, a society

in which the wider institutional system endowed wealth holders with coercive privileges giving them large economic rents, these wealth holders used those rents to obtain representation in parliament. They then used their control over parliament to intensify their own privileges in such a way as to redistribute more wealth toward themselves, even at the expense of the rest of the economy. Under such circumstances, parliamentary control over the executive choked off growth rather than encouraging it.

Indeed, according to Malinowksi (2015:4), the *szlachta* "used its influence to accumulate land and gain special property rights," forcing through legislation that would protect noble property, with corresponding broader benefits only occurring as a by-product. An example of such a mechanism was related to the practice of partible inheritance, a system that had been followed in Poland since the Piast dynasty and preserved after the collapse of that dynasty in the late fourteenth century (Friedrich 2006). Partible

---

[2] Acemoglu (2006) provides a good glimpse into inefficient institutions and why they persist; Sonin (2003) gives an example of this reality in the context of postcommunist Russia.

inheritance meant that the death of a male landowner would result in a partitioning of land amongst the next of kin, a situation that dissipated the stored wealth accumulated over a lifetime to avoid creating economic dynasties. This system of inheritance began to take a toll on all classes of society in Poland, affecting the largest families as well as the Mazovian small land-holders (ibid.). To avoid the loss of economic power that such a partitioning created, the *szlachta* fought to have their estates attain the status of "entailment" (*ordynacja*), a "legally protected set of landholdings that could not be separated" (Malinowksi 2015:17). Such a decree created a permanent and indivisible trust upon the death of the noble owner, allowing for passage of the land to the first-born male heir (Jakubowska 2012). The entailment system was rarely used, given that it required the *Sejm* to approve each exception, and Frost (1995) notes that it was only utilized seven times due to the fact that it came with entangling strings attached (limiting the flexibility of use and thus rendering the land less valuable). But the fact remained that only the upper nobility were entitled to access this mechanism, leaving lesser nobility and landowners to hope that they were survived by "one, well-married son" (Blackburn 2004:12).

However, the drive by the *szlachta* to preserve their own rights did not mean that the formation of broader-based property rights was precluded; in line with Adam Smith's invisible hand, the pursuit of self-interest by the *szlachta* in garnering protection against the state resulted in positive externalities for all.[3] In fact, perhaps the most important role that the *szlachta* served was to establish a precedent of such protection of property from expropriation, a precedent that was set in the early years of modern Poland: in 1422, King Jagiełło, needing the military services of the nobility, was forced to pledge "not to confiscate property of a member of the *szlachta* without prior judicial determination, thus establishing a right to private property" (Brzezinski 1991:53). This protection mirrored trends in property rights throughout Europe by the sixteenth century, enabling the creation of new investment opportunities such as the printing press, which represented a major outlay of capital (Angeles 2011).

These rights did not just apply to the nobility, as Kamiński (1975:267) notes that, from the time of Kazimierz the Great in 1348, "a peasant . . . had full rights of ownership of movable property, and in some cases he could

---

[3] This is in distinct and unequivocal contrast to the pursuit of self-interest that leads to granting of favors from the state, which leads to distortions and inequities.

buy, sell, and bequeath land." The right to acquire something does not necessarily mean that the means are available, however, as peasants in the Polish territories found it more difficult to physically acquire capital or land due to limited income mobility. Indeed, peasants tended to remain peasants in Poland unless they fled to the towns, and even then, the nobility attempted to use the political process to stymie this outlet, with the *Sejm* issuing more than sixty laws in the sixteenth and seventeenth centuries against peasants taking flight (Żytkowicz 1972).[4] The lack of economic opportunities in the early modern era led to a concentration of landholdings in Poland that began to increase in the mid-fifteenth century, as "medium owners of one, two, or three manors often disappeared, giving way to larger estates" (Mączak 1968:86).

While acquisition of property became more difficult under inefficient labor market institutions (as we will discuss below), property rights development in Poland thus mostly concentrated on the aspects of management, enforcement, and disposal. Similar to the genesis of political institutions, which flourished even if the ruling elite in Kraków or Warsaw did not favor their formalization, property rights concentrated around management and enforcement of existing property began as informal arrangements and became formalized via rules and procedures at the local level. According to Guzowski (2014:116), in "the late middle ages the first contracting institutions appeared in Poland, which were similar in character to their west European counterparts, and written contracts quickly became the basis of economic interactions among the representatives of the largest social group: the peasants." These small-scale contracting and protection institutions in Poland were, unlike England around the same time (Libecap 1986), driven from below rather than from above by the gentry.

Moreover, these contracting institutions thrived as small-scale enforcement mechanisms due to "Poland-Lithuania's long tradition of decentralized, local control" (Murphy 2012: 388). The dispersion of Poland's population during the late medieval period and well into the seventeenth century was concentrated in villages and towns rather than cities (Wyrobisz 1989), meaning local institutions played a much more important role in everyday life than those ruling from a far-off capital. Royal towns (i.e., those under the purview of the king, distinguished from "private towns" run by a noble) followed a Germanic code of self-governance based on the

---

[4] This issue of "second serfdom" will be explored below in our look at labor market institutions.

Magdeburg Laws, which enabled the establishment of property rights for its citizens (Murphy 2012), creating judicial mechanisms beholden to a broader law but implemented via local means.[5] With the further advent of sanctions such as the community responsibility system, which imposed damages on individuals if they violated property rights in an intercommunity (-town or –village) transaction, protections against property right infringement became more substantial (Greif 2006). And the development of the judiciary as an "independent, inter-provincial legal system" (Brzezinski 1991:56) created legitimacy that enforcement would be impartial. As Guzowski (2014) shows, these local-level enforcement mechanisms and their implementing institutions such as village courts became a crucial and effective means for securing transactions and providing a foundation for basic financial institutions. In this way, property rights were formalized, but in a decentralized manner across Poland.

Although these smaller-scale contracting institutions were very effective in underpinning the local economies of Polish towns and villages, they were also subject to prey from political forces, almost immediately threatened by the exigencies of Polish foreign policy; as detailed in the previous chapter, Poland underwent a near-continuous series of wars from the late sixteenth century onward, a reality that brought these tenuous self-enforcement mechanisms to the brink of extinction. The growth of executive power accompanying the warfare state in Poland, although mainly thwarted at the central level (as shown previously), was shifted instead to local administration. Without a centralized mechanism for maintaining an army, the *szlachta* were relied on for funding and staffing of the military to engage in these conflicts, and in turn they continued to extract political concessions from the king.

The king's increasing reliance on the nobility to finance foreign adventures led to an accumulation of land and an increase of the political power of the *szlachta*, a volatile cocktail where "the increasing administrative power of the Polish landlords enabled them to gradually expropriate rights from the peasants" (Grief 2007:24). Mainly this was conducted via the re-enserfment of peasants, but the expansion of private towns over this time frame also allowed the *szlachta* to control the urban landscape, as well as the rural. According to Wyrobisz (1989), 90 percent of the towns founded in Poland in the sixteenth and seventeenth century were founded by the gentry and big nobles, with only nineteen new settlements created by

---

[5] As we will see below in the section on labor market institutions, the "private towns" created some of their own disincentives to growth via their enforcement mechanisms.

the kings of the Commonwealth. Within these towns, formal institutions were eschewed in favor of the whims of the local noble, with little formal protection of property rights, especially if they conflicted with the desires of the nobility. In the words of Gourevitch (1978:426), "the weak central government," an explicit goal of the *szlachta* all along, "was unable to protect peasants from the imprecations of lords." In this sense, one may speak of the success of executive constraints at the central level in pre-Partition Poland, but a failure to restrain the executive at the local level, or, to put it into the language of the economic approach to property rights, the threshold of marginal benefits for support of property rights in Poland had been attained by the sixteenth century at the executive level, but it had not yet been reached at the local level. In fact, as Grief (2007:42) noted in a different context, the "constitutional institutions benefitting the elite can be socially harmful exactly because they are 'good' at fostering intra-elite cooperation"; in the Polish case, the cooperation extracted from the king by the *szlachta* continued to alter the calculus of the benefit of broad-based property rights for the nobility, delaying them even further.

We can confirm this assessment using data from Acemgolu et al. (2002), who examined the level of central executive constraints and protection of private property throughout Poland's history. Based on the Polity IV ranking system, where a country's executive constraints are coded from 1 to 7 depending upon the level of constraints (higher numbers meaning more constraints), Acemoglu et al. (2002) determined that Poland peaked at a level of "slight to moderate limitation on executive authority" as early as the year 1300 and held this level of central executive constraint until 1750 (Table 3.1). Indeed, if anything, the Acemoglu et al. (2002) ranking understates the level of constraint placed on the central executive, as the ranking of 3 corresponds to the ability of the legislature to block implementation of executive acts and decrees and prevent the executive from changing constitutional restrictions; a ranking of 5 after 1600 appears to be more in order, given that this ranking corresponds to the ability of the legislature to refuse funds to the executive. However, Acemoglu et al. (2002:34) recognize this fact by noting that the total sum of constraints in Poland was lower than would at first appear, given that "there was relatively little protection for urban merchants – most of the rights rested with the nobility." As there is little to no historical data on executive constraints for subnational units in Poland, this approach is perhaps our best approximation of the influence of the *szlachta* on the overall political system.

Table 3.1 *Economic Indicators for Poland, 1000–1850*

Year	Urbanization (percent of Population)	GDP per capita (millions of 1990 international $)	Constraints on the Executive	Protection for Capital
1000	0.00	.	1	1
1100	.	.	2	1
1200	1.02	.	2	1
1300	0.94	.	3	1
1400	2.84	.	3	1
1500	4.43	462.00	3	1
1600	7.72	516.00	3	1
1700	3.30	566.00	3	1
1750	4.36	.	3	1
1800	5.51	636.00	1	1
1850	6.88	871.00	1	1

Source: Acemoglu et al. (2002).

But more important for this section is the effect that this lack of local executive constraint had on property rights, and Acemoglu et al. (2002) are also perhaps the only ones to attempt to quantify protection of capital (a valid proxy for property rights) in Poland over this time frame. Acemoglu et al. (2002:34–35) note that their measure of protection of capital, "depends on the formal rights given to urban merchants, particularly their protection in the event of a dispute with the nobility or monarch. A code of 1 indicates that these merchants have no effective protection against arbitrary confiscation by the ruler (e.g., as was the case in most absolutist regimes)." As can be seen in the last column of Table 3.1, the lack of local constraints in Poland meant that this was precisely the case, as the country as a whole made little progress in protecting capital or property rights formally. This quantification is reinforced by the observations of contemporaries, such as Jean-Jacques Rousseau (1972:32),

Each depositary of a portion of this [executive] power sets himself, by virtue of that portion, wholly above the magistrates and the law. He does … recognize the authority of the [Sejm]; but since that is the only authority he does recognize, when the diet is dissolved he no longer recognizes any; he despises the courts of law and flouts their judgments. Each is a petty despot who, without exactly usurping the sovereign authority, constantly oppresses the citizens in specific cases, and sets a fatal and too frequently imitated example of unscrupulous and fearless violation of the rights and liberties of individuals.

This of course did not mean that property was threatened uniformly across Poland, for, as we have seen, protection of property rights was effective in an environment where they were surrounded by other supporting institutions (e.g., the royal towns). Nevertheless, on the whole, the march of the *szlachta* meant that one set of political developments (weakening the central executive) led to a specific effect on economic institutions (low protection of rights *ceteris paribus*).

As with formal political institutions, however, the state of affairs regarding property rights was changing for the better on the eve of the final Partitions, and for the same reason. The Constitution of 1791, taking a page from the U.S. Constitution, made a big leap forward for property rights protections in Poland at the same time that Poland was in danger of losing its land. In the first instance, as Topolski (1987) notes, the Constitution of 1791 was the first in Europe to base entrance to the political system on property ownership rather than on birth status, allowing for income mobility. Beyond the acknowledgement of the importance of property, the constitution also protected the rights garnered by the *szlachta* in Article II and pledged to "preserve sacred and intact the rights to personal security, to personal liberty, and to property, landed and movable." In the *Sejm* act accompanying and incorporated into the constitution, "Our Free Royal Cities in the States of the Commonwealth," the idea of property rights were expanded further in regard to the royal towns, with Article II.5 explicitly noting "every townsman may henceforth acquire landed and other property as hereditament, own it entirely, and bequeath it to his heirs as his rightful successors, possess property by succession or *iure potioritatis*." While the constitution and its supporting act still applied to royal, and not private, towns, the move towards a codification of all facets of property rights was a major step towards their protection. It is likely that, had Poland remained independent, the blessings of economic liberty would have been extended to all citizens of the country (much as it was in the United States).

Alas, as we have already discussed in the previous chapter, even the tangible progress made in the formal, central political system in holding back autocracy was lost in the Partitions, as Poland was spread amongst three separate monarchies, which had centralized decidedly market-unfriendly institutions. Given that, as noted, the two attributes of executive constraint and formal legal protection go hand in hand for guarding property rights, the loss of executive constraints at the center dealt a heavy blow to all types of formal property rights protection in the country. In fact, as Poland has so often been subjected to in her history, the pendulum had swung widely the other way, with an exchange of limited central power for a decimation of the local nobles' power during the Partitions. Whereas Poland needed to couple its executive restraint at the central level with restraint at the local level, the exchange of foreign tyrants for local ones did not contribute to the development of property rights throughout the three Partitions.

Of course, the exact degree to which property rights were hindered during the Partition Era was determined, as with the country's political institutions, by which particular side of the border a person was located in. Being under the administration of foreign powers, the Polish territories imported formal economic institutions that were exogenously created, meaning that the extent of property rights that a Polish individual could access was thus determined in Vienna, St. Petersburg, or Berlin. Moreover, given the varying practices of these three occupying powers, this meant that there was also wide dispersion in the property rights institutions that were imported, as well as dispersion in their evolution during the time of Partition.[6]

As in the political realm, the Austro-Hungarian portion of the Partition, in Galicia, remained more liberal towards property rights protection than elsewhere in partitioned Poland, backing Polish tradition with a rule of law secured by Austrian force of arms (Kuninski 1997). Although many of the important reforms to property rights did not occur until after the revolutions of 1848, and were tied to a feudal system of labor, peasants did have land held in usufruct that was both inheritable and inalienable (Komlos 2014). However, the economic peculiarities of the Galician region also created difficulties in transitioning to an Austrian system of property rights, creating friction in meshing local traditions within the Polish villages under Habsburg rule with a modern legal-based rights structure. The Polish territories that were under Habsburg rule were generally much poorer than the rest of Poland, economically backward and dominated by small-scale agriculture (Pobog-Malinowski 2004). Due to this emphasis on the productive nature of land, there was widespread peasant insistence that property rights derived from land use rather than formal title transfer; such insistence continued to frustrate attempts to codify land laws throughout

[6] And as with political institutions, the effects of Partition linger in regard to property rights as well. For example, Becker et al. (2014) show a positive correlation between faith in courts and a belief in property rights being upheld in territories that were on the Habsburg side of the border.

the Partition period, because peasants considered laws regulating inheritance to be illegitimate (Stauter-Halsted 2004). An additional source of continued miscommunication concerned lands that did not actually yield crops (e.g., forests and pastures), which were viewed as communal by peasants but subjected to the same rights of property as any other piece of land (Leslie 1955).

Despite these issues, the protection of rights in the Habsburg Partition was ahead of property rights elsewhere on the lands of Poland, which were less secure in either the Russian portion (the "Kingdom of Poland") or in the Prussian portion. The Prussian administration for a time observed formal property rights for Poles, even contributing to the creating of a Polish middle class, which had been conspicuously absent under *szlachta* democracy (Clapham 1966). According to Leslie (1954), the processes of gradually rolling out property rights to all strata of society also continued under Prussian rule, as the Prussian emancipation edict of 1823, narrowly tailored for the former Polish lands, granted full property rights to the highest level of the peasantry if they were able to compensate their former landlords. This was in addition to the introduction of the Prussian Civil Code of 1807, which codified these rights for the nobility, as well (Kochanowicz 2006a). In this sense, the move towards universal property rights in Poland was still continued after the dislocation of the Partitions and the influence of the Napoleonic wars; coupled with the effective levers of Prussian administration, including an independent judiciary, peasants were enjoying more personal freedom than ever before (Wysokinska 2011). As Ogilvie and Carus (2014:422) note, "the economic policies pushed through forcibly against parliamentary protest by the autocratic Prussian state abolished the regime of privileges and rents for special-interest groups, creating better (if not perfect) incentives for the economy at large."

However, as with the *Kulturkampf* and the erosion of political liberties, the property rights of Poles also underwent degradation under continuous Prussian rule, beginning with differential property taxation (Poles were forced to pay higher rates on their land than German settlers; see Kirby (2014)). Moreover, the continuous increase in the number of Poles soon led to a backlash in Berlin against the apparent failure of Germans to keep pace, leading to the founding of the Settlement Commission, which attempted to purchase Polish land for German settlers. While not an outright violation of property rights in the sense of expropriation (or other means which the Germans were to use in the twentieth century), the Commission sought explicitly to purchase large estates and subdivide

them for German settlers, implicitly restricting the amount of land available for the growing Polish population. Ironically, this ended up restricting
the turnover of land transactions in the German-occupied lands, as Polish
landowners created a boycott of sales to the Commission, in order to keep
the lands in Polish hands (Eddie 2004). This resistance in turn then led to
more draconian measures as Poland moved into the twentieth century,
including restricting any rights of sale to blood relatives, creating a series of
permits to keep new building restricted via bureaucratic means, and,
finally, in 1908, authorization for outright expropriation of 70,000 hectares
of land (Kaczmarczyk 1945).[7]

Finally, in the Russian Partition, again similar to the development of
formal political institutions, property rights were highly restricted,
although there were some positive moves towards protecting the rights
of both the nobility and the lower classes in the early days of the Partition.
As Murphy (2011) noted, Russia's move towards centralization meant
placating and assimilating the nobility, and in order to do this their
property rights needed to be upheld (Murphy also notes that in a battle
between noble property rights and town autonomy, property rights won
the day, with the practice of town ownership effectively ended by 1867).
Such co-optation of the nobility began even before Poland ceased to be,
during the Partition of 1772, as Catherine the Great ensured that Polish
nobility still dominated the administration (chiefly the courts) of the area
that is present-day Belarus (Thaden 2014). At the other end of the class
ladder, and in another political ploy to win back the peasantry after the
1863 Uprising, peasants were also given full property rights to their land via
an emancipation decree in 1864. This decree cancelled all serf obligations
and offered compensation to landlords of amounts less than offered in
Prussia or Galicia, hoping to pacify the large peasant population of the
Lands of the Vistula (Wandycz 1974).

As with the other two Partitions, however, Russia also had few problems
in restricting or eliminating property rights if it suited the tsar. While the
nobility was courted in the early years of the Congress Kingdom, running
from approximately 1815 to 1832, the upper classes refused to be assimilated, and supported both the Uprisings of 1830 and 1863 against Russian
rule *en masse* (Kappeler 2014). The retribution following the first uprising
in 1830 led to the "Great Emigration" (more on this below), while the
punitive measures enacted after the 1863 rebellion struck primarily at the

---

[7] Eddie (2004) notes that the Commission only ever utilized this authorization in 1912, to
expropriate 1,656 hectares of land from four properties.

heart of the nobility and their property rights; Kochanowicz (2006b) points out that those who survived the reprisals after the uprising or who were not exiled to Siberia had their property confiscated outright. Even the political currying done to the peasantry through the emancipation decree was done in a manner to weaken the power of the nobility, attempting to explicitly play off the *szlachta* against the peasantry (Kappeler 2014). And of course, the most encompassing of property rights restrictions was enacted after the Uprising of 1863 in the current lands of Ukraine and Belarus, where Polish nobles were forbidden to purchase land. This restriction would return in the twentieth century in a different manifestation, but suffice it to say at this point, from the mid-nineteenth century onward, the Russian administration of Poland had stymied nearly all facets of property rights.[8]

In sum, the Partition had a similar effect on the economic institution of property rights as it did on political institutions, forcing through some beneficial changes when the occupying powers had a light touch, but seeing these institutions wither on the vine after a century of partition. This interplay of political institutions and property rights once again highlights the fact that the state may, in some instances, be a guarantor of property rights, creating "market-guaranteeing federalism" in Weingast's (1995) memorable phrase, but far too often it instead acts as a block on these rights. The experience of Poland both pre- and post-Partition gives more evidence for the political approach to property rights, however, as in each instance of expanded rights, they only came in response to a perceived gain on the part of the ruling elite, whether they were Polish or foreign. But there also may be a case of diminishing marginal returns to institutions, as the rights that once provided the elite with comfortable rents become more of a hindrance the longer they are in place. Under this scenario, ruling elites would seek a rollback of these rights once they had gone "too far," using political institutions to circumscribe property rights or limit them to politically connected favorites.

Given this hypothesis, it is perhaps ironic that the fact that formal Polish political institutions were not present may have actually enabled the idea of property rights to continue to develop longer than they would have otherwise (especially in the ordinary political storm that was

---

[8] Even where property rights were allowed to continue, there still remained problems. As in Galicia, the issue of common pastures and forests also bedeviled administrators, creating conflict between peasants and the Russian occupiers (Kochanowicz 2006a).

characteristic elsewhere in nineteenth century Europe). Much as the idea of liberty was retained during the Partitions, the idea of property rights gained momentum throughout the nineteenth century in a manner that had not been accepted prior to the Constitution of 1791. But it may have been easier to believe in an ideal, unencumbered by reality, than it was to actually fashion a system that protected all facets of property rights, a fact that is the mirror image of what occurred in the building of the political system of an independent Poland after the First World War.

And indeed, these two processes went hand in hand, as the difficulties in political institution-building had a serious effect on property rights in the new Republic after 1918. As Andonova (2003) has noted, the structure of a country's political system can substantially influence the evolution of property rights protections once these rights have been legally codified (i.e., have gone from informal to formal). In particular, a country that is polarized socially tends to have substantially reduced property rights due to this tension, a threat to rights that grows with the level of polarization (Keefer and Knack 2002). Andonova (2003) built a model that demonstrated this reality, showing that parliamentary regimes with majority rules provide better protection, due to the uncertainty of what happens when one is out of power, but proportional voting allows parties to defend their own rights within the government. Thus, there is less incentive to guarantee broader rights protections, as the narrow interests of a specific party can be protected within government. With Poland beginning to have political parties when it had no political system for them to operate in, the idea of broader property rights survived and even flourished in the Partitions, becoming another form of opposition to occupation. In short, there was no way for these political parties to actually put their ideas into practice, as they were (for the most part) informal.

But what happened once the Poles were back in charge of their own fate? Andonova's (2003) model appears to be vindicated by the events in reunified Poland under proportional representation. Property rights came under sustained assault in the new Polish Republic, a reality that began almost from the moment of independence, but occurred under the rubric of actually creating property rights rather than abnegating them. The Constitution of 1921 in Article 99 claimed that private property was "one of the most important bases of social organization and legal order," but Poland began a comprehensive land reform process as early as 1919 (implemented beginning in July 1920), in an effort to minimize social conflict regarding the concentration of large-sized land holdings (Pronin

1949).[9] The land reform limited property ownership, capping the maximum holding size of any one piece of land at 300 hectares in the eastern provinces, while industrial areas had maxima set between 60 and 180 hectares (Zawojska 2004). Additional reforms were introduced in 1925 and 1927 which somewhat relaxed these restrictions, increasing the maximum size of allowable holdings; however, these changes were accompanied by a requirement for "the distribution of a minimum of 500,000 acres annually over a period of ten years" (Pronin 1949:136), threats to owners of compulsory expropriation if they did not sell, and compensation regulations that limited sales prices to 50 percent of its market value (Zawojska 2004). In fact, the land reforms had an insidious motive behind them as well, as the "distribution" of land was created to entice the Prussian/German settlers who had come to Poland during the Partition years to once again head "home" (Gosewinkel and Meyer 2009).

Starting off on such a bad footing, property rights in the reunified Republic never really recovered, and, indeed, they were pushed aside in favor of nation-building and the integration of lands in the east (Pronin 1949). But if the goal was to complete the distribution and consolidation of land first and then fashion a workable system of property rights later, as so often happens, the political forces in the country sidetracked this formal protections of rights. As noted in the previous chapter, the move away from market-friendly economic institutions was foreshadowed by the political movements within the country, including Piłsudski's military coup and the 1935 Constitution, which placed "social solidarity" as a priority over individual rights. In fact, while the Constitution of 1935 explicitly retained Article 99 of the 1921 Constitution on property rights, the first ten articles of the constitution placed all forms of caveats to such property rights, including "the duty of the citizens to be loyal to the State" (Article 6), "the State extends protection over labor and supervises its conditions" (Article 8.2), "no activity shall be counter to the aims of the State, as expressed in its laws" (Article 10.1), and "in case of resistance the State applies means of compulsion" (Article 10.2). All of the clauses, interpreted broadly, could be utilized as an infringement on property rights, and, while there was not enough time before the German and Soviet invasions in 1939 to see the outcome of this prioritization of the commune in practice, it is likely that this approach toward property rights would have enabled a fascistic economy.

---

[9] A hint as to the importance that the new Republic would place on property rights can perhaps be found in the fact that 98 Articles of the Constitution occurred before property rights were mentioned.

The dual invasions accompanying World War Two of course led to some of the gravest and ultimate infringements upon property rights, and thus do not need to be discussed in detail here, apart from to mention that the systems instituted in the two occupied halves of Poland once again mirrored their occupiers. Soviet-occupied eastern Poland became the graveyard of many property owners, who were executed, exiled, or forcibly expropriated (or some combination of the three), while the German-occupied zone allowed for some estates to continue on, but gradually expropriation by Germans became more commonplace (Zawojska 2004). With the end of the war and the Soviet installment of a communist government, however, the idea of property rights was very swiftly rendered traitorous for the Polish mind, in line with the tenets of Marxist-Leninist ideology.

Under communism, property rights were ostensibly denied to all as private property was assumed to be the source of all of man's exploitation (Riha 1996); or rather, as Williamson (1991:181) notes, "ideally, property rights under socialism belong to the people."[10] But even under the communist system, one could see the merits of applying a political approach to establishment of property rights, as certain narrow rights did in fact exist and were created and endowed by the system: however, they were only reserved for the party elite (Winiecki 1990), who used such privileges to punish nonconformers and reward cronies, as well as enrich themselves from the means of production (Walder 1994). This repeated a pattern seen across socialist countries from the founding of the Soviet Union in 1917, memorably mocked in Orwell's *Animal Farm* as "some animals are more equal than others," as apparatchiks used their positions to obtain property that was denied to ordinary citizens. While this use of property rights was nowhere near as absolute as to encompass all facets of rights noted above – apparatchiks had little ability to dispose of property and were severely constrained by their fellow autocrats in their management of bureaucracies or factories – the fact that they were able to acquire domain over movable and immovable property ran directly counter to purist Marxist ideals on the abolition of property.

In terms of practical application of such ideology to Poland, the Soviets moved forward on a broad front against property rights. First, they immediately extended the very same "agrarian reform" that they had carried out between 1939 and 1941 in the eastern portions of the country (now parts of

---

[10] I use "communism" and "socialism" interchangeably here; although the People's Republic may have been a socialist state, it was run by a Communist Party.

Soviet Belarus and Ukraine) to the rest of Poland, resulting in deportations, executions, arrests, and, mildest of all, confiscation (Pronin 1949). As with the earlier, prewar regulations, maximum landholdings were set, and land was redistributed from large landowners to smaller ones, with some large (formerly German) estates remaining intact to be used by state agricultural enterprises (Zawojska 2004). Second, with the rewriting of the Polish Constitution in 1952, even the vestiges of Article 99 from earlier constitutions were removed, including any mention of a right to property (Cholewinski 1998), with "social justice" instead inserted as the guiding principle of the People's Republic. And finally, throughout the entire economy, private ownership was denigrated in favor of state-owned and collective enterprises, "subject to centralized, complex, and highly politicized control" (Wellisz and Iwanek 1993:345). Property in the Polish People's Republic became a matter of property for the "state," where only the government had the right of exclusion (Carson 1974), although a fruitful literature sprang up trying to explain the property rights that were held on the factory floor by managers under socialism (Furubotn and Pejovich 1972).

However, unlike other parts of the Soviet bloc, the extent of socialist envelopment of the economy was not as extensive as elsewhere in the region (Table 3.2). Small-scale farms remained in private hands in Poland, with as much as 76 percent of all acreage (not just agricultural)

Table 3.2 *Degree of Socialist Envelopment of the Economy,*
1953 and 1960

	Percent of agricultural land		Percent of national income produced
	1953	**1960**	**1960**
Soviet Union	94	97	100
Bulgaria	56	91	100
Czechoslovakia	54	87	99
Hungary	39	77	91
Albania	13	85	88
East Germany	5	90	85
Romania	21	84	83
Yugoslavia	37	10	73
Poland	19	13	63

Source: Harrison (2012).

still nominally private throughout the communist era (Ho and Spoor 2006). Continuing to hold ownership, in spite of desultory moves towards collective farms which faced stern resistance, remained an act of political opposition, "an important battlefield in Polish society's fight for its independence ... crippl[ing] the Communist system in Poland, making it incomplete and weaker than in many other countries where the Communists seized power" (Gorlach 1989:23).[11] In fact, a survey undertaken in 1993 examining the extent of confiscations showed that only 7.6 percent of Polish respondents' parents had land confiscated that they owned as of 1948, while 18.4 percent of businesses were confiscated (Hanley and Treiman 2004). This was by far the lowest across the six transition countries surveyed, with a high of 53.7 percent businesses confiscated in the Czech Republic and 69 percent of land expropriated in Hungary from 1948 onward. This survey data also comports with (admittedly shaky) macroeconomic data from official communist sources (quoted in Brus 1986), which showed that only 13 percent of agricultural land in Poland was socialized as of 1960, and only 63 percent of national product came from the socialized sector, lowest among all Soviet bloc countries (shown in Table 3.2).

But even these concessions to immovable property in Poland could not wipe away the fact that all other aspects of broad-based property rights had been removed or degraded as part of the designed transition to communism. As noted in the previous chapter, the judiciary under communism became just another arm of the executive, wholly dependent upon the Communist Party for its direction and decisions. This reality made any hope of contract enforcement futile, unless it could be proved that someone was acting to the detriment of the Party or the People's Republic. Similarly, transfer or disposal of property was highly discouraged, with farmers encouraged to hand over their land to the state instead; under this coercion, much as under Prussian rule, turnover instead remained minimal and inheritance once again became the prime source of land transfers (Halamska 2001). Even the economic crises of the 1970s led to only small changes in the overall official attitude towards property rights, with more autonomy given to enterprises but little thought given to restoring the rights of the individual (Wellisz and Iwanek 1993).

---

[11] As Fałkowski (2013) also notes, holding property remained a status symbol in rural Poland, even in the supposedly classless People's Republic.

Given the direct opposition of communist ideology and the machines of government to property rights, it wasn't until the mid-1980s, after decades of stagnation, that popular and elite attitudes towards broad-based private ownership began to turn favorable (Tarkowski 1990). But even this change in culture meant little until the political leadership was either brought around or, as we will see, changed entirely; Litwack (1991:255) noted in the Soviet context that the biggest failure of reform in the 1980s was "the reluctance of the leadership to decree large-scale nongovernment property rights." Thus, while Poland was better placed than other communist states that were politically much more repressive or missing even the saving grace of small-scale private ownership (Wu 1990), it was up to history to see if the full panoply of property rights could be recovered in the country postcommunism. By the mid-1980s, with communism still hanging on politically, if not economically, there was no guarantee that they would.

LABOR MARKET INSTITUTIONS

The development of labor market institutions in Poland prior to 1989 followed a path very similar to that of property rights; indeed, in many ways, the evolution of labor markets and property rights was an inextricable process. Much of this comes down to the inherent nature of labor market institutions, as they function as an enabling mechanism for one particular form of property rights, the ability to own and thus dispose of one's labor as one sees fit.[12] Thus, an economic system should have adequate labor market institutions to enable the use of labor for productive means, matching supply and demand of labor and enabling the transfer of value from worker to process to product.

As the discipline of labor economics encompasses very many attributes of this transfer of value, so too must an examination of labor market institutions. From the meta-institutions of labor markets and their organization to the more micro-oriented formal legislation governing labor contracts or trade unions and collective bargaining, labor institutions are varied and many. And, as with property rights and other institutions we have already mentioned, labor market institutions can also manifest as formal, as in a national Labor Code, or as informal, as in employment not determined through formal contracts; moreover, labor market institutions

---

[12] Such a right is an integral part of human freedom, something on which capitalists and Marxists agree!

can be innately tied to national cultural characteristics, as evidenced by much of European business shutting down in August while workers are on holiday versus still at their desks in the United States.[13]

However, the very concept of labor market institutions is relatively new, generally associated with the Industrial Revolution and the rise of division of labor in the nineteenth century. Such institutions as labor codes, employment protection legislation, or unemployment insurance (to say nothing of pensions) simply did not exist prior to the 1800s. For much of Poland's (or even the world's) existence, the development of the labor market was instead tied to agriculture and the structure of the broader economy, which lent itself to very specific labor arrangements and different contractual arrangements than the now-familiar labor market institutions just noted. As Wyrobisz (1989:611) remarked in a discourse on Poland in the sixteenth century, "the Polish economy was based almost exclusively on extensive exploitation of natural resources, and on an equally extensive agricultural and breeding production, with almost complete neglect of industrial production." Such a structure of the economy led necessarily to very specific labor market institutions that, to this day, are prevalent throughout the country.

In fact, the major labor market (meta-) institution that blossomed across Europe in the fifteenth century, occurring concurrently with a spike in formalized legislation (and, in Poland, as Topolski (1974) notes, a demographic boom), was serfdom. Gorecki (1983:14) notes that "Poland completed the transition from an economy based on force and warfare to one based on intensive agriculture and craft specialization in the twelfth and early thirteenth centuries," meaning a move towards land-holding and regular labor. In tandem with this shift in labor forms, the expansion of nobility and especially of local nobility in Poland led to increases in estate size and changes in distribution of ownership; as Blum (1957) pointed out, Poland on the eve of the German colonization of the twelfth century had already seen a decreasing number of peasants who owned their own lands, and were absorbed into larger noble estates. Gorecki (1983:35) notes that Polish peasants, especially under the king, had advantages perhaps not available elsewhere in Europe, as they were already beginning to specialize in their labor:

The Polish peasants of the later twelfth century were burdened by customary services and tribute to the monarch but were mobile and enjoyed access to the monarch to

---

[13] Similarly, work-life balance is also another cultural attribute that may shift depending upon the particular country or even subregion.

press grievances against wealthier and more powerful members of society. They held land in familial settlements from which they could not be arbitrarily dispossessed and which they defended vigorously before the monarch's court. Each peasant household performed a variety of economic tasks; the households which became particularly proficient at a specific task often executed their customary obligations to the monarch in their areas of specialization. Hence we find a category of the peasantry performing a variety of specialized agricultural and nonagricultural services to the royal household.

Throughout the fourteenth and fifteenth centuries, however, in conjunction with the rise of the *szlachta*, the rights of the peasantry became less beholden to the monarch and more dependent upon the local lord. The German colonization accelerated the consolidation of noble estates, and the imitation and codification of German seigniorial law in Poland led to acceptance of more restrictive labor arrangements (Małowist 1966). Indeed, the localization of executive power, as with property rights, disrupted the free provision of labor throughout the kingdom, creating more demesne labor arrangement and institutionalizing the rights of lords over those of peasants (Kamiński 1975).[14]

This move towards "neo-"or "second" serfdom came to characterize the labor markets of Poland (and Lithuania) from the sixteenth to the eighteenth centuries, and its growing power stifled both labor and capital mobility; as Millward (1982:524–525) correctly summarized, "peasant families were effectively prevented from leaving their holdings without the lord's permission, deprived of all rights in the location, quantity, and disposition of their labor time." Poland was at the forefront of this Europewide trend, as "Poland banned seasonal migration by non-landowning peasant farmers" (Dittmar 2011:25) while at the same time passing a law to stop lords from poaching peasants off of each other's lands. In conjunction with the reduction of the power of the king (as shown in the previous chapter), the *szlachta* successfully lobbied in the *Sejm* to have grievances against lords from the peasantry heard at the local level, rather than by the crown (Trethewey 1974). Peasants became little more than cattle that could be traded, with the "right to transfer the peasants from one

---

[14] Kamiński (1975) does correctly note that, in a world of second-best alternatives, private feudalism was better than state feudalism, as lords had much more of an economic incentive to protect their renters and maximize the profitability of their land than the crown, which often tried to extract as much as possible during a short lease period. However, as seen in the previous section, the level of the unfettered executive did not matter much in Poland when it came to trampling economic freedom, no matter the economic incentives.

holding to another or to deprive them of parts of their holdings was recognized as belonging to the Polish landowner" (Makkai 1975:232).

A large debate rages in the political science literature regarding the reasons behind and the effects of the second serfdom in Poland, especially regarding whether re-feudalization accompanied the agricultural boom of the sixteenth century or preceded it (Denemark and Thomas 1988). For our purposes, while an interesting intellectual exercise, it is more important to understand how feudalism impacted labor markets in Poland, and how this translated to development of other labor market institutions. The economics literature has grappled with an appraisal of the efficiency of serfdom (and especially the second serfdom), with some early work from North and Thomas (1973) arguing that serfdom was an efficient institution due to its ability to allocate labor contractually. More recent work from Hagen (2007) also takes up this theme in regard to the Prussian peasantry, echoing Kamiński's (1975) point that profit-maximizing lords would have better ability to allocate capital than free peasants. Ogilvie (2007:668) however makes a convincing case, from a more institutional framework, that serfdom was a very inefficient form of allocation; in her words, "serfdom distorted labor markets by entitling overlords to levy coerced labor, compel serfs to work at below-market wages for privileged employers, prevent serfs from migrating freely, and force them to migrate against their will." In fact, Ogilvie explicitly states that serfdom only survived, not because it provided better allocation of labor and capital, but because it created rents that lords could then reap. Finally, Dennison (2006) makes a similar case in an examination of eighteenth and nineteenth century Russia, where he concludes that serfdom did provide some benefits in lowering transaction costs and creating nascent property rights, but they were extremely localized and nontradeable. Thus, the facilitating effects of serfdom were minimal, especially when coupled with the reality that the system was designed to prevent mobility.

Empirical evidence is thin on these points but can be teased out from existing data of labor markets during this time period. Table 3.3 provides one glimpse of the effects of neoserfdom through the sixteenth and seventeenth centuries, comparing nominal wage rates of laborers in grams of silver per day across Europe. In the first instance, it is interesting to note that Kraków and Gdansk had much higher wages than Warsaw from 1500 to 1800, befitting the status of these cities as the seat of government and seat of economic power respectively. Second, Polish wages were consistently the lowest amongst Europe, only surpassing Italy and Vienna to 1850 (and Italy again from 1900 to 1913). But the most important trend shown in

Table 3.3 Nominal Wages across Europe (grams of silver per day)

	1500–1549	1550–1599	1600–1649	1650–1699	1700–1749	1750–1799	1800–1849	1850–1899	1900–1913
Antwerp	3.0	5.9	7.6	7.1	6.9	6.9	7.7	12.7	32.4
Amsterdam	3.1	4.7	7.2	8.5	8.9	9.2	9.2	16.3	48.6
London	3.2	4.6	7.1	9.7	10.5	11.5	17.7	31.2	71.5
Southern English towns	2.5	3.4	4.1	5.6	7.0	8.3	14.6	25.4	57.9
Florence	2.9	3.8	4.7				3.1	10.8	25.0
Milan			5.9	4.1	3.2	2.9	3.8	7.3	22.4
Naples	3.3	3.5	5.3	4.8	4.8	3.8			
Valencia	4.2	6.6	8.8	6.9	5.7	5.1			
Madrid		6.3	8.0		5.1	5.3	8.0	9.7	19.0
Paris	2.8	5.5	6.6	6.9	5.1	5.2	9.9	21.4	52.2
Strasbourg	3.7	3.4	4.3	3.1	2.9	3.3	8.1	9.3	0.0
Augsburg	2.1	3.1	4.0	4.7	4.2	4.3			
Leipzig		1.9	3.5	3.9	3.7	3.1	4.4	14.8	51.6
Vienna	2.7	2.6	4.4	3.5	3.2	3.0	2.1	4.2	43.5
Gdansk	2.1	2.1	3.8	4.3	3.8	3.7	4.8		
Krakow	1.9	2.9	3.4	2.9	2.2	2.9	2.4	7.1	24.1
Warsaw		2.5	3.2	2.7	1.9	3.4	4.9	9.1	26.3

Source: Allen (2001).

Table 3.3 is within Poland itself, where wages saw growth until 1649, and then fell in Kraków and Warsaw for the next hundred years (Gdansk starting its decline from 1650 and not recovering until 1800–1849). This trend illustrates the dampening effect that serfdom had on wage rates, as reduced labor competition and prohibited mobility allowed for monopoly pricing of labor by nobles (Stanziani 2010), holding prices firm even in the face of declining rents.

As with all economic institutions, however, not every aspect of the second serfdom was distortive, mainly (as was seen in the twentieth century in regard to communism) because serfdom was neither uniform nor all-encompassing. Kamiński (1975:257) strenuously argues that serfdom "never gained complete control of the entire territory of the Commonwealth, and its level of development ranged from areas with the 'Dutch' model of rich peasants, strong cities, and hired labor to those where long distances from market outlets and adverse natural conditions … made the organization of grain-producing, market-oriented demesne-*robot* farms not a profitable venture." This diversity of serfdom could perhaps be seen in the dispersion of wages in Table 3.3, with the agrarian south experiencing much more of an impact than the trading-intensive north. In fact, Frost (1995) points out that peasant labor under serfdom in the seventeenth and eighteenth centuries only provided between 40 and 50 percent of the labor required on Polish estates during the summer, leading to a reliance on hired and contract labor. Perhaps because of this, Małowist (1959) contends that peasants may have had more bargaining power than they realized, but chose to eschew their monopsonistic position because increases in feudal obligations only came when agricultural prices were already advantageous to peasants. Finally, Kamiński (1975) also points out that serf labor arrangements were most common in the biggest estates, which belonged to the king, the church, and the richest magnates, and thus to speak of the *szlachta in general* as relying on demesne labor is a fallacy. In labor markets as well as in executive power, what mattered was not necessarily the level of government involved in the execution of power but its concentration.

Serfdom in Poland, like much of Eastern Europe, continued well into the nineteenth century in the different Partitions and, as noted in the previous section, was not actually ended until Poland ceased to be a sovereign state. But even before the official end of serfdom in the three Partitions of the country in the mid-nineteenth century, Poland underwent a mass disloca-tion of labor that altered the region's labor markets. The crushing of what was perhaps Poland's most propitious chance to obtain independence in

1830–1831 led directly to the start of the "Great Emigration," as Poles began to leave their homeland for other parts of the world (Zubrzycki 1953).[15] As Kuninski (1997:241) notes, Poland at the turn of the nineteenth century "had a pre-industrial social structure with a huge peasant class, a limited middle class composed to a large degree of ethnic minorities, and a slowly developing working class, together with strong class differences and restricted vertical and horizontal mobility." Thus, bounded by serfdom behind and foreign occupation in front, and with little hope of change after 1831, the only way for many Polish citizens to pursue their livelihood (or their dreams of democratic Poland) was to exit the country (indeed, for many, this was the only form of "labor mobility" allowed). This trend, of exodus as a way to cope with labor market failures, increased notably throughout Poland's occupation and peaked on the eve of the First World War (Massey 1988).

The thesis that these emigrants were pushed out by the labor market practices of the time is given a boost when one considers their socio-economic status, which Greene (1961) notes was almost uniformly from the lower classes or agricultural laborers. However, the geographic origin of these emigrants (i.e., which Partition they came from) was not as uniform, and indeed appeared to crest in waves. Zubrzycki (1953) has perhaps the most comprehensive examination of the migration of Poles during the Partitions, calling our attention to the population boom of the nineteenth century, which occurred in each Partition. Prussian Poland had the earliest spike in population, with a growth of 79 percent from 1816 to 1849, while over this same time frame, the population of the Congress Kingdom (the Russian Partition) increased by 50 percent, while Galicia saw growth of only perhaps 15 percent (difficult to extrapolate, as the earliest source of data on the population of Galicia is 1827).[16] This population boom, in this sequence, was a major contributor to the large increase in emigration from Poland:

- As Greene (1961) catalogues, Polish emigration from Prussia peaked in the 1870s, when the youngest cohort of the baby boom of the previous decades would have reached their twenties. This would correspond with the years in which a person is most likely to emigrate, between the ages of twenty-one and twenty-eight by Gibson and

---

[15] Although the phrase "Great Emigration" refers generally only to the political exiles after the Uprising, it works well in the context of the emigrations from Poland that began in 1831 and continued until the reconstitution of Poland as an independent state.

[16] All calculations in this section are based on data provided in Zubrzycki (1953).

McKenzie (2011) in the Pacific context. Polish emigration from Prussia tapered off in the 1880s, at the same time that the overall population of the Partition decreased (Zubrzycki 1953).

- Galicia took the lead in Polish emigration in the 1880s, following its own demographic increase of approximately 30 percent from 1850 to 1880, also corresponding with the coming-of-age of many agricultural laborers. Given the relative poverty of Galicia compared to the other two Partitions, there may not have been the means for more agricultural workers to emigrate, accounting for its relatively low showing in aggregate numbers.

- Finally, in the Congress Kingdom, the late abolition of serfdom led to the creation of a landless proletariat who, facing uncertain employment prospects and a concerted effort against revolutionary tactics (especially after the Uprising of 1863–1864), began to head elsewhere: Zubrzycki (1963) estimates that 9,000 Poles left the Russian partition annually by the 1890s and reached a total of 90,000 Poles annually by 1910 (for a total of 1.25 million over 1870–1914). This tracks neatly with the 39 percent increase in the population from 1880 to 1900, meaning that a large cohort was coming of age and immediately heading to the United States.

Moreover, this wave of emigration also coincides exactly with the sequence in which serfdom was abolished on the Polish territories. However, it is interesting to note that, while serfdom may have contributed to emigration due to limited labor mobility, it was not until serfdom was abolished, and modern labor institutions did immediately not fill the vacuum, that emigration began to spike. Serfdom was eliminated in Prussian Poland as early as 1807 (under Napoleon), but it was not until the *Kulturkampf* and the attempts to deprive Poles of their property rights that an exodus began. Similarly, Polish Galicia had been free of serfdom since 1848, but it was not until thirty-two years later that emigration began to increase. And in the Congress Kingdom, serfdom was abolished the latest (in 1864), and it was a similar lag between this decree and the spike in emigrants. Thus, one may conclude (as Zubrzycki (1953) does) that the abolition of serfdom led to a demographic boom; but once this generation of the postserfdom boom had come of age, the lack of opportunities in the Polish labor markets caused them to seek their fortune elsewhere.

This is not to say that modern labor market institutions were not developing in Poland during the nineteenth century across its Partitions, as the end of serfdom and the rise of industrialization did have an impact on labor markets and forced evolutionary institutional change. However, the exigencies of foreign occupation played an important role in the path dependency of this evolution, as the normal iterative processes of learning were disrupted by exogenous events.

The shift from an agrarian economy in Poland to one of industry happened in a rather abrupt manner, and was by no means homogenous across all three Partitions; in fact, all sections of Poland remained fairly tied to agriculture even in the late nineteenth century, and for a time immediately following the abolition of serfdom the only collective labor organizations were thus those connected with agriculture (Chloupkova et al. 2003). The rise of industrial and professional labor organizations took much longer to develop than these deep-rooted agricultural institutions, and, as with all organic institutions, did so in an ad hoc and haphazard manner. Schofer (1972:454) notes that workers in the late 1880s tended to protest that the rules of the game, that is, basic governance of labor contracts, were not respected, with workers complaining "that they did not know what the work rules were. More particularly, they protested that when paid by the shift and not by piecework some of their shifts were not recorded if the demanded 'normal production' was not delivered." Schofer also notes that other practices, such as forced overtime and creative fines (including temporary demotion to poorly paid positions) also disrupted the contractual relationship between employer and employee.

The translation of these desires via an institutional mechanism was also somewhat desultory in the early years of organized labor in the partitioned country and offered a glimpse of how institutions interact with each other in the broader economy. As noted in the previous chapter, workers' strikes were beginning to gain traction as an informal labor institution, particularly in the Russian and Prussian Partitions, presenting management with demands (often vague) to improve working conditions or lower working hours (Żarnowska 1980). Żarnowska (1984) notes that the earliest labor protests in Poland were tied to very specific bread-and-butter causes; a prime example of this was the week-long strike of 1883 in Żyrardów, a factory town founded in 1833 and the largest factory in the Russian sector of Poland (Wandycz 1974), where workers protested against wage cuts but made no specific political demands (Żarnowska 1980). Similarly, a strike in Lwów in 1870 from typographers had a very narrow goal of a collective agreement and nothing more (Rojahn 1990). In short, the desires of the working class had yet to find an institutional mechanism to be expressed through.

An interesting, and overlooked, aspect of the development of labor market institutions in Poland comes from Schofer (1972), who notes that many of the frictions that came about between labor and management stemmed from the fact that the proper managerial institutions had not evolved yet, either. While not using this exact terminology, Schofer (1972: 454–455) details how owners and factory stewards had little experience in dealing with an emancipated workforce, and indeed continued to display a paternalistic attitude towards workers; he relates the story of "the directors of the government mines run by the Berginspektion Königshütte comment[ing] that workers, particularly unskilled ones, complained of inadequate wages not because wages were too low but because they squandered their money – thus the workers' 'laziness' and 'disorderly life.'" Such an attitude was likely a holdover from serfdom, where labor relations were based on familiarity and long-term living arrangements, rather than modern capitalist labor, where impersonal contractual agreements were meant to eliminate the need for close personal knowledge and intertwining of one's personal and professional life. And, just as organized labor was learning via an iterative process how to harness its own market powers (and understand what could and could not be achieved), so too did management need to understand which attitudes towards workers were appropriate and which were not. In both instances, only time and practice, repeated interactions, could have reached an institutional equilibrium.

Unfortunately, the end of the nineteenth century was not a time where gradual adjustments and the evolution of labor market institutions were possible. This iterative process of institutional learning was disrupted by both foreign occupation and the ideology of socialism; indeed, given the fact that Poland was still splintered into three parts, it is perhaps no wonder that the growth of formal labor market institutions for employees took a more languid pace than elsewhere in Europe. But they did evolve, as the idea of the labor union began to coalesce as precisely the institutional mechanism needed to express the desire of workers to management. Schofer (1972:447) correctly points out, "it is important, however ... to avoid focusing on the labor union as the sole standard by which to measure the character of industrial workers' life and as the unique avenue of legitimate labor protest," and we will try to avoid that mistake here. But the movement towards organized labor and in particular the advent of the union, whether in agriculture, mining, or industrial production, does offer a glimpse into a concrete labor market institution that was designed to facilitate better economic outcomes for its members. Thus, some examination is necessary of this institution, in order to better understand the development of labor markets in partitioned Poland in the nineteenth century for, as we will see, the development of organized labor was different in each Partition.

As with political institutions, formal trade bodies or societies in German Poland and Galicia began manifesting themselves at the same time that informal (and underground and illegal) labor unions began to take hold in the Congress Kingdom. While Germany was less fertile ground for creating native Polish labor organizations, due to the access Poles had to German political parties (the SPD) and their associated labor unions (Dziewanowski 1951), by the 1880s, unions linked to Christian associations and the Catholic Church had begun to coalesce in Upper Silesia. The largest and most popular for a time was the *Związek Wzajemnej Pomocy Chrześcijańskich Robotników Górnośląskich* (ZWP ChRG, the Upper Silesian Christian Workers' Mutual Aid Society), created in 1889 as an accompaniment to a year-long series of miners' strikes in the region (Hojka 2006) as an advocate for better working conditions and the eight-hour day (Rojahn 1990). This Society grew from 5,000 members in 1890 to 14,000 by 1900 (Gasiorowska-Grabowska 1962) before merging with other trade unions in Germany in 1908 to form the Polish Professional Union (as noted in Dziewanowski (1951)). As Rojahn (1990) notes, the structure of trade unionism in Upper Silesia was generally driven by antipathy towards German officials, but the labor market institutions were designed to work within the Bismarckian system rather than oppose it from the outside.

Similarly, in Austrian Galicia, the relative liberalism of rule allowed for the development of freely organized labor organizations, even more so than in Prussia and much more (as we will see) than in the Congress Kingdom (Polach 1955). Derived from worker's aid societies, and led by typographers in Lwów, these small-scale organizations transformed into modern labor organizations in the 1870s and eventually became a part of the Social Democratic Party from Austria proper (Rojahn 1990). The growing labor movement resulted, as in Prussia, in consolidation of the Christian trade unions in 1913 into an umbrella organization, the *Polskie Zjednoczenie Chrześcijańskich Związków Zawodowych* (PZChZZ, Polish Union of Christian Trade Unions); in the same year, a socialist trade union known as the "Central Polish Trade Union" was also founded, with approximately 30,000 members (Gardawski et al. 2012). In addition to the creation of formal labor organizations, labor protests among Poles in the region became increasingly more common, with a miner's strike in 1900 and a strike in the Galician oil fields in 1904 showing remarkable discipline on the part of workers (Polach 1955); however, Rojahn (1990) correctly notes that the prevailing leaders of the overall labor movement in Galicia, who were more likely to be craftsmen than laborers, meant that the social democracy route was favored for change instead of revolution. The development of village co-operatives also undercut the immediate impetus for revolution from agricultural laborers, although, as noted in the previous chapter, this did not stop Austrian authorities from manip- ulating the peasantry in Galicia and initiating a bloody rebellion against landowners in the 1846 uprising (Wandycz 1980). Moreover, additional tension in the labor movement was also derived from nationalist fervor (as we will explore in the next chapter), with Ukrainian farmers taking up the call for land redistribution from "wealthy" Polish landowners (Blobaum 2010).

Finally, in tandem with the growth of nationalist sentiments in Poland in the nineteenth century, particularly fertile ground for labor organization could be found in the Russian sector. Described by Dziewanowski (1951:513) as "politically and nationally the most handicapped part of the country," the Congress Kingdom did not see wage growth or oppor- tunities for organization as in Silesia, nor did workers have German counterparts that they could join to agitate for better working conditions. Moreover, the increasing anti-Polish measures after the suppression of the 1863–1864 Uprising meant that any thought of labor organizing was out- lawed on grounds of subversion; according to Rojahn (1990:512), "there was never any question of building up a legal workers' organization" in the kingdom, and thus the stage was set for more underground and militant labor actions.

Here is normally the point in any historical or political analysis of nineteenth-century Poland where the inevitable tale of socialism, socialist ideology, and Polish socialist parties in each Partition is elaborated, usually in the sort of excruciating detail that can only come in describing socialist meetings. We have already touched upon the effects of socialism on the political order in Poland in the previous chapter, and the voluminous literature on socialist agitation in Poland prior to the First World War need not be repeated. A few key points need to be brought forth, however, as socialist thought really took root only in the Congress Kingdom, rather than in the other two Partitions, with underground left-wing political parties driving the labor movement in the late nineteenth century. This receptiveness to socialism can be attributed in the first instance to the rapid economic growth in the Russian-occupied zone, where an increase in output and the industrial power of the region (especially compared to the rest of the Russian Empire) created economic dislocations unparalleled in the history of Poland. Development of industrial might in the textile, iron, coal, and leather sectors led to increased urbanization, as cities such as Łódź saw its population go from 28,000 people in 1860 to 325,000 in 1900 while Warsaw saw a population increase of 317 percent over the same period (based on data from Zubrzycki 1953). The combination of poor working conditions, coupled with a huge influx of laborers abruptly shifting from rural agriculture to urban industry, suddenly made socialist labor market solutions, with their focus on heavy industry and the industrial proletariat, viable.[17]

Secondly as Dziewanowski (1951) notes, the interconnectedness between Russia and Poland during this time meant that Marxist ideas, which had been gaining currency in Russia as a reaction to authoritarian tsarist practices, were also finding their way to Poland. This increase of connectedness between Poland and Russia was literal by the late nineteenth century, while, although the kingdom had much lower railway density than the other Partitions, the building of railway lines linking the country to Russia increased substantially. Moreover, as part of a strategy of protection, the tsarist authorities made sure that the infrastructure faced overwhelmingly towards Russia, with only small connections with Galicia and a conscious decision not to link with the Prussian partition (Zukowski 2004). This meant that the moderate, social-democratic approaches of Prussia and (to a lesser extent) Galicia were prevented from entering the country, bringing only the radical left-wing rhetoric that was bubbling underground in Russia.

The absorption of this socialist revolutionary rhetoric, rather than the more moderate and within-the-system approach of labor in Galicia and Upper Silesia, led directly to much more strident labor standoffs in the kingdom, as well as different forms of labor organization. In particular, one only need look at the mass strikes of 1892 in Łódź, when 60,000 textile workers walked off their posts in protest against deplorable work conditions and subpar salaries (Pytlas (1993) estimates that workers in Łódź made only 65 percent of the national industrial average wage). In a real sense, the strike was also a manifestation of the unhappiness

---

[17] This was not the case from 1830 to 1850, as socialist thinkers attempted to overcome the fact that Poland remained highly agrarian but never sufficiently offered a satisfactory path away from this reality (Dziewanowski 1951).

with Russian administration, as this administration had led directly to the workers' grievances:

Whereas in mainland Russia provincial authorities shared certain anti-capitalist and anti-industrial bias and were prone to somehow support the basic worker's claims in terms of living conditions, it was certainly not the case in Poland, where national tension prevented governors from extending such sympathy. . . .. In addition, due to class-national divisions usually the local bourgeois lacked national solidarity with their employees and were quite willing to cooperate with the Russian – seemingly foreign – administration (Marzec and Zysiak 2014:14).

Underscoring the inextricable nature of labor market and political institutions, the "revolt" in Łódź was violently suppressed by the Russian authorities, with a death toll over two hundred. As Wandycz (1974:296) remarked, this showed that "while industrialists were willing to make concessions, the authorities were not." In fact, the reality of a dual struggle against Russia and managers meant that the next step to advancing labor's demands, beyond uncoordinated labor action, was the creation of trade unions. Such organizations fused the need for improved working conditions with the desire for independence from Russia, blurring the line between nationalism and class antagonism; as Tych (1970:172) put it,

It was evident from the essence of the working class movement's political platforms that they had also to relate to the fate of the whole nation and not the vindication of the proletariat alone. No revolutionary group of Poland's proletariat had ever limited itself from the very beginning of their existence, even in their programs, to the day-to-day economic struggle for an improvement in the workers' material situation; fundamental political transformations within the country were the primary target, which obviously was of nation-wide concern.

Given the lack of existence of formal political channels in which to express these sentiments, as well as the explicit anti-Russian nature of their goals (meaning that working within the system was impossible), the labor movement in the kingdom manifested itself in underground politico-labor parties. The first to come was the Social Revolutionary Party Proletariat, a group inspired by the "national" socialism of writers such as Limanowski and Mendelson and, as claimed by Deutscher (1984), the group behind the Żyrardów strikes of 1883 mentioned above. While the Proletariat Party only lasted from 1882 to 1886, due to thorough infiltration by tsarist secret police and its odd antipatriotic stance (it called for revolution across Russia, not just in the Polish-Lithuanian-Byelorussian lands), it laid the groundwork for later organizations.

As shown in the previous chapter, the mantle of labor was taken up by the Polish Socialist Party (PPS) and its splinter (and more radical) group, *Socjaldemokracja Krolestwa Polskiego i Litwy* (Social Democracy of the Kingdom of Poland and Lithuania, or SDKPiL). PPS led a drive for winning the minds (if not the hearts) of workers in the Congress Kingdom through information campaigns, a direct result of its genesis as part of the exiled intelligentsia with roots in Western European socialism; as Dziewanowski (1951:512–513) observed, "until the end of the third quarter of the nineteenth century, the centre of gravity of the Polish Socialist movement lay outside the country, in small groups which were overwhelmingly intellectual in character." However, the Polish and patriotic nature of the PPS soon began to encompass many more adherents, becoming a more broad-based organization, while the SDKPiL (founded in 1894) became associated mainly with radical intelligentsia and Jewish leaders, with a slight pro-Russian orientation that built on the Proletariat Party (Kubiak 1999). Indeed, as Rojahn (1990:515) notes, it was the nature of the institution of PPS that contributed to its success, as it trimmed "its forms of organization and action to fit the political system ... [seeing] no point in continuing trade union work under these circumstances [and instead] confin[ing] themselves to building up a cadre organization." While explicitly avoiding the broad-based aspirations of the SDKPiL, which attracted attention to itself via its fiery pronouncements and high profile (its precursor SDKP was closed down in 1895 by the secret police), the PPS soon found itself successful across strata of Polish society in the kingdom.

But as with political institutions, the direct prohibition on labor organization in Russian-occupied Poland meant that all such political and labor institutions remained small-scale in the kingdom, with socialist organizations having no more than a few hundred formal members on the eve of the 1905 revolution (Żarnowska 1965). Perhaps mindful of the continuous agitation occurring against working conditions, and the threat that this could pose to the political order, the tsarist authorities applied both carrots and sticks to the labor market in the late nineteenth century. Crago (2000:24), speaking of the riots and suppression of 1892, noted that "the 1892 demonstrations in Łódź provoked tsarist authorities to intervene directly in the factory lives of textile worker," mainly in a rudimentary attempt to provide worker training and skills upgrading. In this manner, the Russian authorities pursued very active labor market policies (in modern parlance) with an explicit goal of increasing the managerial acumen of Poles; it was felt that this labor market improvement would also quell both nationalist and socialist feelings. Additional timid labor market reforms came about in Russia proper but were rarely transferred over to the Congress Kingdom, and the tsarist authorities had no real coherent strategy for dealing with labor market strife, preferring to convene commissions and discuss options rather than take up opportunities (Zelnik 1971). In addition, carrots such as welfare reform were only a small part of the Russian authorities' approach to labor, however, as the main tactic was "police socialism," or the co-opting of the labor movement by official organs of the state (Mavor 1914) via the "deceit of unions sponsored by the state" (Palat 2007:307).

The half-measures taken by the tsars in Russia and in Poland, and even the progress made in the other Partitions, did nothing to halt labor unrest, and in 1905 massive strikes across the country (in tandem with those in Russia) showed that revolutionary action could be successful (Żarnowska 1980). In particular, in the Russian partition, trade unions were legalized, and workers' pay and conditions both began to improve (Lukowski and Zawadzki 2006). In the memorable words of Żarnowska (2001:99), "in the years of the [1905] Revolution, Congress Poland was the scene of a far-reaching democratization of political life, which was most intensive in working class circles." At the same time, these actions also proved the staying power of formal native labor market institutions, as membership of unions spiked across all Partitions after the events of 1905–1906: trade unions affiliated with PPS in the Russian partition counted 45,000 members as of 1907; trade unions in Galicia (both socialist and Catholic) numbered over 35,000; and consolidations within the Prussian trade unions resulted in a significantly strengthened *Zjednoczenie Zawodowe Polskie* (Polish Trade Union or ZZP) and membership of over 77,000 by 1912, in addition to 30,000 in Catholic workers' aid societies (Rojahn 1990).

As everywhere around the world, the formation of formal labor market institutions was artificially halted by the First World War, where class antagonism took a backseat to nationalism (apart from in Russia, where a vanguard of intelligentsia overthrew the government and attempted to enact radical labor market and other policies). The re-unification of Poland after 1918 (and throughout the entire interwar period) brought renewed emphasis on the protection of workers' rights and building appropriate labor market institutions, albeit such a project was now to be accomplished within the confines of the Polish government rather than by other governments or by underground political parties. Indeed, one of the challenges facing the new state was the diversity of employment and social institutions that co-existed on the territories of Poland. In the Prussian (German) partition, the "cradle-to-grave" welfare of the Bismarckian system was present, as the region was integrated into the civil administration of Prussia/Germany. Polish Galicia was also moving in this direction, having enacted legislation in 1887 covering occupational injury and disability, in 1888 regarding employee sickness, and in 1906 for establishing pensions (Świątkowski 2010). By contrast, the absence of any protections in the Russian partition represented the other extreme of institutional thought, as tsarist prohibitions did not allow formation of even informal labor institutions such as these.

Blending these three experiences, the new Polish government sought to follow the other nations of Europe in laying the foundations for the welfare state. In the Constitution of 1921, Article 102 declares that "every citizen has the right to state protection for his labor," while also noting that social insurance will be available on the basis of a separate statute. The very next article also prohibits child labor, making it illegal to employ those under the age of fifteen, while setting out rigid conditions for female employment, and Article 108 continued the reality of late-era partitioned Poland by noting that unions were legal in the Rzeczpospolita. Secondary legislation followed on from the basic constitution in the coming years, including government insurance for worker sickness (1920), the creation of unemployment insurance in 1924 (Burns 1945), government disability and injury insurance (also 1924), government-funded old-age pensions in 1927, and paid maternity leave in 1933 (Tomka and Szikra 2009).[18] These disparate portions of the social safety net were brought together in the "Unification of Social Security Schemes Act" in 1933, which sought to consolidate the various labor market institutions that had been layered on by successive governments (Świątkowski 2010).

In the early years of the re-unified Polish state, the labor market institutions put in place became the most comprehensive in the region (Inglot 2008), even if the implementation of these institutions was problematic: as Świątkowski (2010) notes, rather than creating indigenous institutions, the government simply extended legislative blessings from one partition across

---

[18] As Świątkowski (2010) notes, the original design of unemployment insurance at first only covered blue-collar workers before public opinion forced it to be extended to all a mere few months later in 1925.

the entire country (as was done with injury insurance in 1924, which was merely the Austrian legislation extended to the formerly-Russian partition). In other instances, extension was not done precisely because of existing Partition practices, as with the region of Upper Silesia, which kept its German insurance scheme and was not a part of the supposedly-comprehensive Unification of Social Security Schemes Act of 1933 (ibid.). And throughout each of these legislative mechanisms, intense bargaining for coverage occurred via the political process, with agricultural workers being exempt (or excluded) from the vast bulk of labor legislation and government employees enjoying a much higher level of coverage than the private sector (Tomka and Szikra 2009). Additionally, lobbying by the business community prior to the Unification Act of 1933 resulted in lower levels of coverage than existed previously for sickness benefits, as well as its duration (Świątkowski 2010). Finally, as is often a problem in a state with low capacity but lofty goals, the legislation did not always translate to reality; the Polish government's "Polish Research and Information Service" (PRIS) noted in 1948 that the interwar period saw frequent violations of labor law, especially those connected with the eight-hour work day (PRIS 1948). It is possible that this was compounded by the decentralization of the administration of social security enforcement, which was much higher in Poland than elsewhere in the region (Tomka and Szikra 2009).

As with the political system, the development of indigenous labor market institutions was going to require time to adapt, a luxury that interwar Poland did not have. Similar issues as in the political realm began to hamper the development of trade unions, as nine union federations existed after independence in addition to the government Union of Trade Unions, with over a thousand branches of these various unions active throughout the country (Wróbel 2014). These unions fought, splintered, combined, fragmented, and recombined, leading to a decided lack of unity on issues of interest to labor. Moreover, the administration of social security schemes also took much longer to develop than imagined at the creation of the system, as by 1936, only 14 percent of the population was covered by social insurance, as opposed to 43 percent in the United Kingdom and 25 percent in France; this number was even after a great uptick in those claiming benefits due to the effects of the Great Depression (Świątkowski 2010).

In fact, the collapse of the world economy from 1929 onward put great strains on the burgeoning social welfare system in Poland, as the number of unemployed registered with the state (in relation to workers) ballooned to

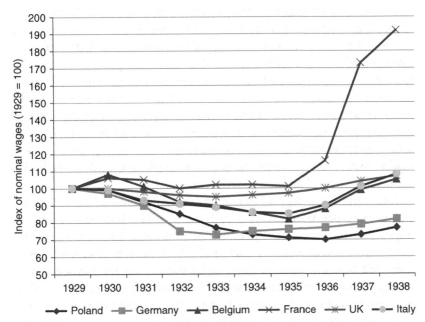

Figure 3.2 Nominal Wage Declines during the Great Depression (1929=100)
Source: Eichengreen and Hatton (1988).

43.5 percent in 1934 from a low of 3 percent in 1929 (Sułek 2007). This in and of itself had a severe strain on the entire fabric of society, as Poland as a country had little actual experience of the phenomenon of "unemployment"; throughout centuries of serfdom, agricultural work could always be done if no other work was available, and it was not until the advent of capitalist labor market institutions in tandem with urbanization that the prospect of not finding a job became reality. At the same time, hourly earnings also plummeted, meaning even those who could find a job found their livelihoods being eroded (Figure 3.2). This problem was the worst in countries that had Bismarckian safety nets (although it is superficial to say that these safety nets were the only cause), and Poland took a much longer time to recover than any of its neighbors to the west. Thus, unlike the safety of serfdom, where wages did not decline and only obligations increased, the labor market institutions of the early twentieth century appeared to facilitate uncertainty.

Indeed, perhaps this dislocation, from paternalistic serfdom (which, as shown above, many employers still used as their attitude towards workers) to uncaring contract labor also made the workers themselves more willing to accept governmental institutions as a solution. Zawadzka (2007:30), in a sociological study of worker memoirs during the 1930s, notes that the common thread running through these writings was that while "the unemployed ... were often dissatisfied with the general situation in the country, they respected the authorities and placed their hopes in the government." Other work that Zawadzka (2007) details express similar sentiments to labor today, railing against technology as "stealing our jobs" and calling for restrictions on machinery. In such an environment, it is little wonder that labor market institutions were moving towards more market-distorting traits, with the government taking the role of the lord of the manor, rather than market-facilitating ones.

Such a trend was only accelerated by the communist takeover after the end of the Second World War, as the Soviet system of labor institutions was imposed from above onto the Polish state. Whereas under Piłsudski, the government was playing the maternal role of providing support during a difficult time for workers, communist Poland saw the introduction of a paternal system where commands were meant to be obeyed and workers were enjoined to listen to their betters. Modern capitalist labor market institutions were eliminated entirely, and the veneer of social democratic ones was put in their place, such as the creation of a single Central Trade Union Committee, highly centralized and subordinated to the Communist Party (Ascherson 2011). As Kochanowicz (1997:1450) correctly noted, in contrast to western labor market institutions, where evolution was anticipated, under communism, "the social system – including welfare provisions – was treated as close to perfect and not subject to critique; at the most only the particularities of implementation could have been put in doubt."

Unfortunately, the Polish Constitution of 1952, while producing a laundry list of workers' "rights," gives little indication of the institutional mechanisms that will enable such important pronouncements as "Citizens of the Polish People's Republic have the right to rest and leisure" (Article 59, Section 1). Along these lines, Article 60 promises the whole panoply of social safety net mechanisms, including sickness insurance, old age pensions, disability, sanitation services (Section 2), hospitals, fire services, and other services not normally thought of as part of the social safety net. Given the very large promises made by the communist constitution, the vagueness of the manner in which these promises were to be realized was perhaps understandable (Świątkowski 1995). As with the interwar Polish safety net, however, the overall labor institutions retained a "policy of particularities and privileges rather than that of universalism," offering some classes and individuals (especially Party functionaries) better coverage than others (Tomka and Szikra 2009:24). While Berend (1996) claims that the widening of labor market institutions occurred fairly quickly after the demise of Stalin, it was not until the 1970s that independent agricultural workers were able to access the public pension system (Tomka and Szirka 2009). Moreover, the unrealistic aspirations of the communist planners meant that the entire bureaucratic apparatus was overextended (and had no incentive to improve), "resulting in poor quality and bad management. Waiting lines were growing longer, bribes became universal, and whoever could afford it, exited the system, preferring services offered by the parallel economy" (Kochanowicz 1997: 1447).

Even where the constitution appeared to grant straightforward "rights" that could have little problem in translation, even here there were different interpretations by the government for implementation. For example, Article 58 grants citizens the right to "work, that is, the right to employment paid in accordance with the quantity and quality of work done ... ensured by the social ownership of the basic means of production, by the development of a social and co-operative system in the countryside, free from exploitation; by the planned growth of the productive forces; [and] by the elimination of sources of economic crises and by the abolition of unemployment" (Sections 1 and 2). In practice, this "right" to work became an obligation, with the abolition of unemployment created by treating those who did not work as criminals, parasites, or worse (Kochanowicz 1997). Similarly, Article 72 promised the free creation of unions, although this was a narrowly circumscribed freedom in reality, as the political crackdowns in the 1970s and martial law in 1980 showed. Hanging over all of these "rights" was a series of caveats, as in Article 72, where it was noted that "the setting up of, and participation in, associations the aims or activities of which are directed against the political or social system or against the legal order of the Polish People's Republic are forbidden." With no definition of what might fall under this heading, virtually all independent labor associations were potentially at risk.

This is precisely what happened under Solidarity, which, as seen in the previous chapter, went from illegal organization to tolerated partner to criminals to tolerated legality in the span of fifteen years. Of course, no discussion of labor market institutions would be complete without understanding the trade union that put in motion the end of communism in this one country. As already noted, the years under communism still had their share of labor unrest, including violent suppression of strikes in 1956 in

Poznań, the strikes and riots in 1970 in northern Poland, the strikes in Radom and Warsaw in 1976, and of course, the formation of Solidarity and the strikes at the Lenin Shipyards in 1980. Despite repeated attempts at reforming the legislative framework around labor relations, including instituting a Labor Code in 1974 and various legal amendments in 1981 regarding staff management (Matey 1986), the interconnectedness of labor to the broader economy (and its institutions) meant that such legal maneuvering would never satisfy the independent labor movement without more fundamental reform. Moreover, as Kochanowicz (1997) accurately notes, the labor market institutions of communism were never permitted to evolve, as institutions should, meaning that what was appropriate for the era of industrialization in the 1950s seemed outdated and antiquated by the 1970s. With labor market institutions impervious to criticism and resistant to change, it was only through the creation of informal unions that the status quo could be challenged.

The history of labor market institutions in Poland prior to 1989 can be seen as an evolutionary process of learning within broader economic systems. Indeed, more than any other institution, labor market institutions were highly dependent upon the prevailing political and economic institutions surrounding them, with little power to evolve independently. Under serfdom and within the feudal system, labor markets were distorted along with other crucial institutions (e.g., property rights and trade), and it was only with the ending of serfdom across Partitioned Poland that new and modern labor market institutions began to arise. However, Poland had little time to develop the indigenous institutions necessary to adapt to capitalist labor relations, due to fragmentation of the country, the growing allure of socialism in the Congress Kingdom, and then repeated, massive international conflict. When Poland finally emerged from the cataclysm of war in 1945, it was provided with a frozen institutional arrangement that dictated labor relations and allowed no room for evolution of labor institutions. It was only in the 1970s that labor market institutions proved themselves capable of transforming the system, as inflexible communist labor modalities set the stage for informal labor institutions that eventually toppled the system in the 1980s. Having struggled under the paternalistic restrictions of serfdom, to the revolutionary rhetoric and crackdowns of socialism, to the collective solutions of the Polish Republic, and then to the heavily enforced strictures of communism, it was the challenge for Polish labor institutions post-1989 to perhaps recapture the evolution that ended abruptly in 1939.

MONETARY AND FINANCIAL SECTOR INSTITUTIONS

As any growth economist will eagerly explain, the Solow growth model posits that the determinants of the growth of nations are threefold, encompassing technology (the residual), labor, and capital/savings/investment. However, such a simple growth accounting framework deals only with the endowments (and their proportions) in a particular economy, and offers little guidance as to the utilization of these three attributes or which policies can set the stage for growth. It is only the institutional economist who describes how these various facets of an economy may be channeled into productive use, how they come to be, how they are renewed or propagated, or, in far too many cases, how they are destroyed. Up to this point, we have already touched upon the institutions that mediate technology (property rights) and explored those that determine labor supply and demand (labor market institutions); it is only fitting that we now turn to the third member of the Solow triad and examine the evolution of institutions that facilitate the creation and usage of capital.

When considering the complex web of institutions that facilitate (or hinder) capital, we need to take care to focus on two specific groupings of institutions, each of which plays a crucial role in determining the manner in which an economy facilitates the creation and utilization of capital. This first grouping of institutions refers to the mechanisms that move existing capital, generated by the private sector, from lower-value to higher-value usage, while simultaneously alleviating information asymmetries and transaction costs. In this sense, I am speaking of the financial sector itself, comprised of banks, nonbank institutions (such as credit unions), capital markets, and the entire panoply of lending and borrowing institutions. These institutions are able to pool capital and aid an economy by creating scale effects; at the same time, these institutions reduce costs to capital transactions by aggregating diligence and informational services that otherwise would have needed to be carried out by individual holders of capital. Finally, financial institutions also reflect the time value of money, and the calculations of the market about the benefits of transactions today versus those of tomorrow, via the interest rate mechanism. Given all this, it should be self-evident that, if the lifeblood of a market economy is investment, banks and a thriving financial sector are the heart that keeps this blood moving.

The second group of institutions that matter for the intermediation of capital is less concerned with the informational and efficiency attributes of banks, and is more predicated on defining the rules of the game (and how

scoring is kept) for these other institutions. Here, I am referring to monetary policy institutions and the institution of money itself, which "is the
general medium of exchange, the thing that all other goods and services are
traded for, [and] the final payment for such goods on the market"
(Rothbard 1978:144). In a world of fiat money, where the value of money
is tied to reputation, government policies, and expectations, the capital
denominated in the financial sector is fully prey to the whims of monetary
policy institutions. And, over the past hundred years, these central monetary authorities have also been where the policies governing the financial
sector have been determined, including the oversight of fractional reserve
banking via reserve requirements, and where societal determinations of the
time value of money have been imposed. Therefore, the development of
a country's financial sector is also intimately tied to the development of
money and the institutions that control this money.

Much like labor markets, the growth of modern financial institutions
that can mediate capitalist exchange has a shorter pedigree in Poland than
political institutions or property rights, although the use of money and
monetary institutions does stretch back centuries. Indeed, the history of
the financial sector in Poland can be linked with the development of
modern banking in general, especially throughout Europe. The minting
of silver coins reached Poland from elsewhere in Europe around the tenth
or eleventh century (Lannoye 2005), with the first Christian king of Poland
Mieszko I and his son, Bolesław I (the Mighty) introducing coinage that
was closely modeled on English pennies but quickly petered out in usage
(Craig 1953).[19] It was only under Bolesław II (between 1058 and 1079) that
Poland acquired its first "permanent" coinage, and archaeological evidence
puts the use of coins as a medium of exchange as beginning around the
same time (Spufford 1989).

Almost immediately upon obtaining this coinage, however, the currency was subjected to political pressure under successor King Bolesław
III, as the idea of *renovatio monetae*, or exchange of coinage, became
a common occurrence in Poland (and elsewhere in Europe). *Renovatio
monetae* (literally the renovation of money) involved the sovereign
declaring that previous coins issued were invalid and that they must
be exchanged for new ones in order to remain legal tender. Under such
an exchange, revenue was raised for the crown through fees charged for

---

[19] Majkowski (1934) and Craig (1953) both note King Bolesław was so enchanted with the
English design that he copied it wholesale, right down to having the bust and name of the
English king (Aethelred II) featured on the coin.

the physical exchange (i.e., having an exchange rate more favorable to the crown), and the popularity of such a method meant that it was utilized as often as twice a year in other parts of Europe; in Poland, King Bolesław III held against the temptation to do this with irregular recoinages occurring every third to seventh year, but temptation later overcame him, and the recoinage became far more frequent (Svensson 2013). Unlike modern-day (and earlier) debasement, however, the monetary impact of these frequent "re-mints" of coins was somewhat limited, as the coinage remained of relatively small denomination even into the fourteenth century, and silver ingots were used for large payments (Spufford 1989).

The introduction of coinage, along with the use of specie as a means of settling transactions, coincided with the development of the first formal financial institutions in Poland. As was common throughout Europe, credit institutions and in particular money-lending services became concentrated within the Jewish community; records exist of Jewish lending from as early as the thirteenth century, while there are much more copious records of lenders to the nobility, including King Kazimierz himself, with extension of credit as an advance against future revenue streams (Weinryb 1973). The increase in money lending, including the numerous accounts of Jewish women taking up the practice (Bogucka 2003), was accompanied by regulations to prohibit usurious practices, including a privilege granted to Jewish lenders in 1347 to demand rates of up to 54 percent (but only 25 percent if loaned to a student) and a further decree in 1364 to set a higher ceiling on interest rates (Weinryb 1973). Even with these high limits, Weinryb (1973) notes that, in practice, lending rates secured against real estate were generally in the 10–20 percent range in the fourteenth century across Poland, decreasing to a maximum of 8 percent in the late fifteenth century (however, rates in Warsaw remained in the 43 to 86 percent range, as Warsaw at this time was outside of the rule of the other statutes governing Poland). And rates within Poland in general came down as a result of competition, as the relatively small number of Jewish moneylenders from the fifteenth century was eased out of the business by 1600 by a much larger number of Christians looking to derive some profit from the business (Stone 2001).

The entry into the market of Christian moneylenders did not dramatically enlarge the burgeoning credit markets in the kingdom, and the pool of finance in Poland remained relatively small at the beginning of the seventeenth century. Part of this reality can be attributed to events out of Poland's control, including the Spanish default of

1557, which set off a European-wide financial crisis and all but decimated the capital markets in Kraków (Wallerstein 1974). But a large part of the struggling financial sector in Poland can be attributable to the broader institutions within the Polish economy, specifically the lingering attachment to serfdom. As has been repeatedly noted in the economics and finance literature (see Claessens and Laeven 2003, for example), secure property rights are a prerequisite for higher-order financial intermediation, allowing for use of collateral and instilling confidence in investors that their capital will not be arbitrarily expropriated. While we noted above that serfdom may have been a suboptimal institutional arrangement that nevertheless afforded a modicum of property rights, its small scale (limited by the size of the estate) and additional distortions ensured that it could never facilitate broader financial intermediation.

However, serfdom did operate as an intermediate step between moneylenders and larger-scale, pooled credit institutions, channeling capital from the wealthy nobles and magnates who had it to those who needed it (and in a more organized manner than the money lending of previous centuries). The extension of credit to the peasantry was linked to tasks demanded of the serfs by the manor, adding additional obligations on top of the annual labor and tribute obligations that serfs were bound by. In most instances, credit was extended in a nonmonetary manner, as with the lending of grain and livestock, although monetary sums were also transacted, with their size dependent upon the financial resources of the lord of the estate (Rutkowski 1991). The benefit of such credit extension was related to transactional and informational costs, as there was intimate knowledge regarding the ability of creditors to repay (relationships were long-lasting, resulting in the so-called friend trade), and the intricacies of the serf relationship meant that labor could be seized as collateral if money was not available (Seppel 2004). This extension of monetary credit by lords and even by relatively better-off tenants (Mączak 1976) also fed into other institutions, as Millward (1982) notes that there is evidence of land sales being financed by credit in Poland in the sixteenth century, especially from the larger estates. Finally, the generation of credit under serfdom was not only limited to lords and peasants, as "credit was also used by the magnates on a very large scale as a tool of their domination over the lesser nobility" (Mączak 1976:96). The vast majority of lending by the largest estates involved loans to each other, but loans for property were also prevalent, as evidenced by records from annual fairs in Lwów.

But, as with serfdom's distortionary influence on labor and land markets, there is also ample evidence that the utilization of the rigid class relationship as a source of credit created much higher interest rates than would have been found in a voluntary credit market. As Mączak (1976:94) pointed out, "in extreme cases – and these were by no means rare – credit (or usury) offered peasants the only, if dearly bought, chance of survival.. . . But credit was hardly ever cheap and the peasantry was at the mercy of usurers of various kinds." From this brief description it is hard to tell if interest rates were actually priced accordingly (i.e., in an environment where demand is high and capital is scarce, it should be more expensive), but even if this were the case, the economic imbalances inherent in serfdom were sure to keep a higher risk premium than in a system based on free labor and property rights. Moreover, it was common throughout Europe's feudal manors that debts attached not to individuals, but to the household, meaning that debts unpaid on the death of the holder transferred to the next head of household; much like formal restrictions on labor mobility, this weight of debt helped to restrict any upward income mobility as well (Seppel 2004).

Even with the "second serfdom" in Poland, larger-scale credit institutions began to develop during the sixteenth and seventeenth centuries, spurred on by two developments: the growth of trade and commerce and their supporting institutions, and the growth of towns and cities across the country (increased urbanization). In regard to commerce, which we will explore in depth below, the expansion of the international grain trade in the fifteenth and sixteenth centuries led to the accumulation of large sums of money for investment and lending. Małowist (1959) notes that, despite regional disparities, Poland had achieved a unified national market by the fifteenth century precisely to facilitate the production and trade of agriculture and dairy products, and such a barrier-lowering scheme had grand benefits: between 1550 and 1650, ships carried approximately 60,000 to 80,000 cartloads (approximately one to two tons) of grain for export from Gdańsk in peak years (Stone 2001), while Dutch cloth, salt, wines, spices and silks flowed into Poland from abroad (additionally, there was a substantial re-exporting business carried out, as Western goods flowed through Poland to Turkey, Hungary, Russia, and points further east; see Małowist 1958).

All of these opportunities drove up the demand from traders for financial intermediation, as well as increasing the supply of capital available for lending. In the most obvious example, Gdańsk by the mid-sixteenth century, enormous profits from the grain trade led to a surplus of capital and a concomitant boom in finance, with Stone (2001) estimating that approximately 30 percent of all merchant capital was dedicated to lending operations. This had additional effects on the surrounding economy, where manors dedicated to feeding the grain trade "used hired labor [instead of serfs] and made extensive use of credit" (Kochanowicz 2006a:41) in an attempt to satisfy the demands of the markets. The rapid expansion of credit also led to an increase in financial innovation beyond standard credit arrangements prevailing at the time, which Mączak, (1970) notes were fairly rudimentary; in an example of early technical assistance programming (albeit one pursued by the market and not by well-meaning governments), much of this nascent banking sector in Gdańsk was driven by immigrants, chiefly specialists from Amsterdam, who helped to introduce to Poland letters of credit and bills of exchange (Bogucka 1983).[20]

In tandem with the expansion of trade, the move away from the agrarian manor to freely organized towns and cities also led directly to an expansion of demand for financial services (especially in Gdańsk, which had become a hub of the Baltic grain trade). Poland remained highly agrarian, and indeed the riches to be had via the expansion of commerce came from dealing in agriculture, but the nexus for the merchants in this trade was in the cities, due to their infrastructure and function as a transit point. Even Polish economic thought of the time, as reflected in the writings of Anzelm Gostomski, reflected the belief that towns could also be a source of income, creating scale for trade in agriculture from the surrounding countryside (Wyrobisz 1989). And while urbanization was much slower in Poland than elsewhere in Europe – Broadberry and Gupta (2006) note that only 0.4 percent of Poland lived in towns of over 10,000 inhabitants in 1600, as opposed to 4 percent in Germany and 19 percent in Belgium – it was on an upward trend throughout the seventeenth century, with Gdańsk seeing growth of perhaps as much as 30 percent from 1550 to 1600 and a further 40 percent by 1650 (based on estimates from Miller (2013)). Additionally, while the average size of towns in Poland was much smaller than European averages, their higher proliferation meant that more people were living in an urban environment than elsewhere on the continent (Goryński 1967). The growth in commerce across Poland also attracted peasants to the cities

---

[20] Even offshore, financial innovations were accompanying the spread of commerce, as from the Dutch side, freighters were sold as stocks, with investors able to purchase portions of ships rather than the whole vessel (Jonker and Sluyterman 2001).

and towns, abandoning agriculture for the promise of industrial work (Małowist 1959).

In regard to the effect this had on financial intermediation, the geographic agglomeration of wealthy burghers and merchants, finding their riches from industry and trade, resulted in economies of scale for capital, as well as reducing the transaction costs necessary for lending on a dispersed scale; in short, the pooling of the population also pooled available capital and made it easier to match demand with supply. Across Poland, increased urbanization led to more finance, with even provincial Warsaw seeing a growth of money lending in the mid-sixteenth century alongside wealthier Kraków and Gdańsk (Stone 2001). On the other side of the ledger, demand for such financial services also increased during this time, as the gentry were interested in spending or investing their riches from agriculture in a much more civilized and comfortable environ than the countryside (Wyrobisz 1989). And as noted above, Guzowski (2014) showed how the various institutions at the village level (i.e., in towns and not on agricultural estates) contributed mightily to the creation of credit institutions in the seventeenth century. Indeed, a case can be made that, with the promise of lucrative returns, trade and then finance also helped to drive the creation of better town administration, creating a virtuous institutional cycle that further enhanced urbanization. But from the point of view of financial institutions, by providing the correct supporting institutions (property rights and a judiciary) and relying on free association rather than bonded labor, village administration also enabled financial intermediation on a scale unavailable in the agrarian countryside.

Alongside the expansion of commerce and urban space, monetary institutions were also beginning to evolve beyond the basic level of the fourteenth century into more modern structures by the sixteenth century. Further shenanigans involving money had persisted throughout the fifteenth and early sixteenth centuries, with a move towards debasement (diluting the metallic content of a coin) rather than reminting (striking the same coin but exacting a fee for the exchange). Conflict in the early 1500s between the Teutonic Order of Prussia and Poland led the authorities of Gdańsk to issue coins containing only trace amounts of bullion in an effort to raise seignorage for the conflict, leading to severe economic and social issues in the surrounding areas (Volckart 1997). The conclusion of the war and the creation of a Prussian-Polish monetary union led to a grander series of monetary reforms from King Sigismund I, including a shift to consistent gold coinage in Poland in 1528 and creation of a bimetallic monetary system similar to that which already existed for two centuries in Bohemia and Hungary (Frost 2015).[21] As part of this reform, new denominations and larger coins (still based on silver) also came into circulation, solidifying the use of gold as a store of value in its own right and moving away from its previous perception in Poland as nothing more than a precious commodity (Spufford 1989). Moreover, a growing sophistication regarding the role of money in the economy was beginning to appear at this time. In fact, it was in Poland that notable advances in monetary theory were born; Volckart (1997) notes that advisors to King Sigismund realized that increases in money in circulation corresponded to high prices, thus establishing the quantity theory of money as early as 1542.

However, the process of controlling the money supply continued to undergo a trial and error process in Poland during the early modern era, with the seventeenth century showing that nothing had been learned from the re-coinage episodes of the fourteenth century or the debasement of the sixteenth century. Both Poland and its Prussian monetary brother underwent a series of competitive debasements in the 1600s that was colloquially named *Kipper- und Wipperzeit*, from the German slang for clipping coins along their edges (*Kipper*) and sliding the weight back and forth (*Wipper*) to cheat those trying to exchange money (Kindleberger 1991). As Bogucka (1975) relates, in reality two monetary crises took place in the century, with the first occurring between 1620 and 1623 as the coinage was continuously debased; Bogucka notes that the actual content of silver in Polish coins went from 0.67 grams in 1580 (under the money law) to a mere 0.30 grams by 1623 (and was further set at 0.27 grams in 1630). Kindleberger (2005) claims that this debasement came about due to private currency competition, as private owners of mints debased their coinage in order to stay ahead of rivals.

However, in reality, such debasement had many causes; more often than not it was official rather than private. In the first instance, a diminution of the supply of silver coming from the Ottoman Empire occurred throughout the seventeenth century, with flows from the new world not able to make up for the decline in supply (Pamuk 1997). Although this cessation of supply hit its bottom in 1640, the flow of silver slowed to a trickle well before then, making new coinage difficult (Bogucka (1975) notes that

---

[21] Frost (2015) also notes that a Polish gold coin had been in circulation since the early 1500s, but it was part of a "half-hearted" package of reforms and was re-denominated almost immediately.

minting almost entirely ceased in Poland by the 1630s). Beyond the technical aspects of minting, the motivation behind debasement may also have been a *reaction* to the political volatility and the continuous wars of the seventeenth century, which created adverse conditions for all involved, rather than a *precipitant*. Sadowski (1959) is one of the main proponents of this interpretation, noting that the currency debasement of the early seventeenth century was related to poor global economic conditions, as price shifts abroad made Polish goods worth less and imports correspondingly more expensive (we would now call this a deterioration in the country's terms of trade). Thus, coinage debasement was an early form of currency devaluation and a reaction to price increases abroad, "forcing" the government to debase the currency (Bogucka 1975:41). Occurring in the context of the Thirty Years' War and the need to finance foreign adventurism, the monetary debasement served a dual purpose as a means of economic warfare for the *szlachta* against foreign states. From the point of view of merchants, the debasement also served as a way to keep more precious metal for themselves in case of disaster accompanying the war (Supple 1957).

As in modern times, the monetary manipulation that was rampant throughout the seventeenth century hit hardest those who were reliant on cash and without the means to hedge themselves against such debasement. Bogucka (1975) relates how Gresham's Law had a spatial component, with "good" (i.e., high-metal content coinage) crowns being held with the bankers and the "bad" crowns being exported to Silesia, Kraków, and Lwów; Kindleberger (1991) supports this by noting that debasement occurred most slowly in the area where merchants had the most to lose, mainly in the bustling port of Gdańsk. But where nobility in the country were able to hoard precious jewels and materials as a hedge against continued instability, peasants, villagers, and lesser nobility were not, causing erosion in their purchasing power, which had already been undercut by the Price Revolution and inflation of the mid-sixteenth century (Gigliotti 2009). Amongst town-dwellers, real wages began to fall, while in the fields, serfs were forced to take payment in debased coinage, also lowering their purchasing power (Bogucka 1975).

Debasement also led, as predicted a hundred years earlier at the king's court, to substantial inflation, increasing the burden on salaried workers by skyrocketing prices on basic foodstuffs (Kindleberger 1991). As Figure 3.3 shows, the prices of staples for a peasant fluctuated in a manner that would be unthinkable today. Just looking at tallow (for

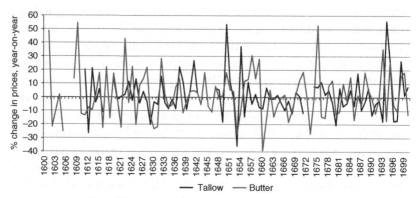

Figure 3.3 Annual Price Changes of Tallow and Butter in Gdańsk, 1600–1700
Source: Author's calculations from data provided by Jacks (2004).

candlewax, a measure of energy use) and butter, a basic source of protein, shows unimaginable annual gyrations; as an example, during the *Kipper und Wipperzeit*, by 1622 the price of butter had risen 43 percent from its price in 1621, while tallow increased 11.6 percent from 1622 to 1623. In 1650, the price of tallow increased 53 percent before falling 35 percent in 1653 ... only to increase 37 percent in 1654! In such an environment, rational price calculations would have been incredibly difficult for businesses and consumers, especially (as Jacks (2004) shows) in an era where wages were stagnant).

This trend unfortunately continued throughout the century, as the continual wars of the seventeenth century offered no respite for either the banking or the monetary sector. In fact, the monetary crisis of the latter half of the century was explicitly linked to the ruin visited upon Poland by its enemies, including the disruption of trade and finance. The need to pay mercenaries for continuing the battle against Sweden and the Cossack uprising, combined with political pressure for the national mint to turn a profit, led to continuous monetary debasement from 1650 onward (Bogucka 1975). The use of silver, heretofore still the basis of most small Polish coinage, was replaced wholesale by copper, mirroring the debasement of money across Europe to finance the continent's conflict; Spooner (1972) notes that Poland minted seven million copper gulden (*boratynek* in Polish) from 1659 to 1663 and even more from 1663 to 1666, resulting in a depreciation of one gulder from a worth of 30 grosz to approximately 12 grosz (a fall of 60 percent). The silver value of the grosz itself once again fell, with Bogucka (1975) noting that it contained merely 0.23 grams of silver by

1685, a third of what it did a century previously. Gdańsk, having been on a de facto "silver standard" to this point, was squeezed by the lack of silver and increasing prices in the crisis of 1619–1623, but the devaluation of 1661–1663 was too much for it to take and it effectively detached its monetary policy from the rest of Poland (Spooner 1972).

Archival data on the state of the banking sector in Poland during this time is severely lacking, which directly translates into similar deficiencies in the economic history literature; this means we must be somewhat creative in attempting to ascertain the reality of banking in the kingdom during the late seventeenth and eighteenth centuries. Homer and Sylla (2005) provide an excellent compilation of interest rates across Europe during this time, noting that market rates for loans in England went from 8 percent in 1688 to between 4 percent and 6 percent by 1688, and with the executive-constraining events of the Glorious Revolution behind them, a further drop to about 4.5 percent by 1698. Similarly, rates in the Dutch Republic, a prime trading partner with Poland, were seen as even less risky (due to the booming Dutch economy), with data for commercial rates as low as 3 percent by the late 1600s. However, with the decline of Gdańsk as a major trading port by the end of the 1600s and the continued disruption in Polish commerce caused by repeated wars, Poland was likely seen as a much higher liability than the rest of Europe for cost of capital, likely closer to the Habsburg Empire than the Dutch.

According to Dickson (1987), there was a wide dispersion of loans in Austria at the beginning of the eighteenth century, ranging from 6 to a maximum of 20 percent in 1700. By the end of the eighteenth century, after the Partitions, there is anecdotal evidence that even the largest of Polish landowners, Prince Czartoryski, was lending 10 percent on deposits lodged with him by lesser nobles, a high rate imposed by the "very primitive credit conditions in Poland" (Lukowski 2003:91). Given all of this bracketing evidence, it is quite likely that the cost of capital in Poland in the late seventeenth and early eighteenth centuries was closer to 15 percent on average, with likely spikes around the time of the Swedish and Cossack invasions closer to 30 percent (Homer and Sylla (2005) note that rates on Dutch sovereign debt quadrupled after the French invasion in 1672). Such a high cost of capital in an era of price volatility and monetary manipulation meant that, in the tension between town and country, the serf-based country model was winning over the town-based modern financial system. Thus, the financial system in Poland remained fairly small-scale, informal, and tied to personal wealth rather than formal and based on impersonal intermediation, simply because the wealthy non-landed class of the cities continually saw their wealth wiped out in inflationary bursts.

These bursts became quite frequent in the run-up to the Partitions as, similar to the modern fiat money era, the continual alteration of the currency in Poland, combined with seemingly perpetual conflict, created a series of boom and bust cycles in credit markets, exacerbated by political intervention abroad. More perniciously for the development of the economy, this institutionalized the use of inflation as a political tool, well before John Maynard Keynes was even born. In one such example, Reinhart and Rogoff (2008) were able to obtain data on inflation in Poland in the eighteenth century, going back to 1704, and their results are somewhat astounding: for fully 43.8 percent of the ninety-six years between 1704 and the end of the century (a total of forty-two years), Poland saw inflation over 20 percent per annum. Furthermore, in nearly thirty-one years of the century, inflation was running at over 40 percent per annum, with a maximum annual inflation of 92.1 percent in 1762! This comports with data from Edvinsson (2010), who, using the silver-backed (and stable) Hamburg currency as a benchmark, shows that the Gdańsk florin continuously fell in value *vis à vis* Hamburg, with the biggest drop starting in 1756 and bottoming out in 1762 due to monetary debasement. As Figure 3.4 shows, there was also a substantial drop in silver content in

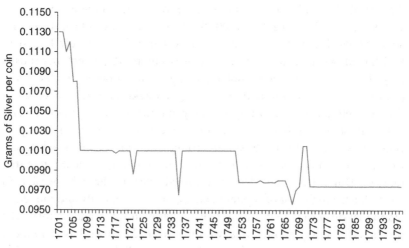

Figure 3.4 Silver Content in the Lwów Grosz, 1701–1798
Source: Derived from Jacks (2004).

the grosz as used in Lwów, starting at the beginning of the eighteenth century and recurring every ten to twenty years thereafter.

Eerily similar to the development of political institutions in Poland, it was not until the cusp of the Partitions when modern, broad-based financial institutions began to develop in the country, as the great surge of capitalism engendered by the Second Industrial Revolution occurred just as Poland was breaking apart. The late seventeenth and early eighteenth centuries saw some early financial instruments such as debentures and the issuing of bearer documents attempted in Gdansk (1701) and Elblag (1758), but the lack of a Polish legislative framework governing these instruments meant that German law was applied (Koziński 2000). Such a framework underscoring a modern capitalist financial system did not develop until the late eighteenth century, with the Bill of Exchange Act implemented by King Stanisław August Poniatowski in 1775 allowing for the establishment of banks as we know them today (Kopyściański 2015). Up until this point, and indeed throughout the eighteenth century, capital markets in Poland continued to be ruled by magnates, although income mobility and liberal economic policies in trade also allowed a number of foreigners to tap the Polish market (notably amongst them the Scottish). Wealthiest amongst these was Piotr Ferguson-Tepper, the son of a fur trader from Brandenburg, who owned a trading house in Warsaw and also opened Poland's first "department store" (Rogowski 2002). Ferguson-Tepper eventually built a financial empire that financed industrial endeavors, provided credit and money exchange services, and supported the government and the king with much-needed finance (Bajer 2012). Such banking services were still limited to men of means, but the mechanisms and instruments that were pioneered here were soon to proliferate throughout Poland.

Of course, the political volatility of the Partition process, coupled with the Polish backlash and revolution of 1794, undercut this nascent formal financial system terribly and resulted in a large number of bank failures and a general loss of confidence in the formal banking system (Reddaway 1971); Tepper's financial empire itself was decimated by a panic in 1793, where his shareholders demanded a full 18 million zloty payment immediately, and he was killed one year later by an angry mob (Bajer 2012). But in the years following the Partitions, the financial sector throughout the Polish territories began an upward trajectory unseen in Polish history, with the individual path of institutional development colored by each Partition. Perhaps part of this development was due to the reality that monetary policy was entirely removed from the hands of the Polish government and delegated to an occupying power, but it more likely was attributable (as noted) to the greater industrialization of Poland during this time, along with an influx of foreign capital. Demand for longer-term finance beyond consumer lending (as under serfdom) underpinned capitalist modes of production, challenging financial sectors in Western and Central Europe to transfer this capital from savers to investors.

In the Prussian Partition, foreign capital flowed into Poland from Prussia proper, due to the new availability of land, a general economic boom from economic liberalism (Hagen 1976), and, important for investors, an interest rate differential that favored Prussian investors over Polish ones (Reddaway 1971 notes that the rates in Poland were 2 percent higher than in Prussia, which were in the 4–6 percent range in the late 1700s – this means, based on our estimations above, that Polish rates had settled down after the Partitions). However, continued expenditures on the military and a defeat at the hands of Napoleon created a sovereign financial crisis in Prussia, which spread to the Duchy of Poland, as cross-border lenders suddenly needed to call in their debts to cover losses imposed by the "haircut" decreed by the government (Kindleberger 2005).

As with the underground political institutions that began to flourish during the late nineteenth century, so too did financial institutions in the Polish lands under Prussian rule come to acquire a nationalist flavor, especially in the wake of the contagion of the early nineteenth century. Kuninski (1997:242) points out that there was a "politically motivated economic competition with Germans," which eventually translated into the institutional sphere; in particular, the "establishment and development of Polish financial institutions" allowed for Polish investments in agriculture and industry in Poznań and a means to push back against the well-funded Prussian settlers. Such an idea had been gestating since the revolutions of 1848, when Polish political thinkers began stressing the need for formatting savings and loan banks by Poles and for Poles (Hagen 1972). In particular, agricultural cooperatives began to blossom in Poland in the nineteenth century as a way of pooling capital and leveraging Polish resources, with the establishment of the Hrubiewzów Agricultural Association in 1816, an early attempt at farmer-owned financing (Chloupkova et al. 2003). The first formal, full-fledged, and voluntary cooperative was established in Poznań in 1861 (Zabawa and Bywalec 2013), but began to blossom during the *Kulturkampf* of the 1870s (Hagen 1972). Accumulating large reserves that could then be lent against, these organizations became the basis of an "efficient and well-organized network of cooperative associations [which] made it possible to register progress even with modest funds" (Wandycz 1974:286). Moreover, the cooperative system allowed Poles to compete with larger Prussian enterprises, often financed by the state, creating flexibility that government finance could never match and allowing for the growth of both a middle class and smaller industries (Zukowski 2004). This financial power only accelerated during the years of Prussian rule, reaching a zenith in the early twentieth century.

Where the Prussian Partition saw the development of self-sufficient and small lenders creating native industry, the trend in the Kingdom of Poland, under Russian rule, was in the exact opposite direction. The kingdom saw its first steps toward modern central banking taken in 1828, as Finance Minister Lubecki established a national bank in order to service debt, finance industry, and be a source of neo-mercantilist trade credits (Wandycz 1974). Combining a commercial bank with a guarantor of the monetary system, Bank Polski was subjected to political interference by Russian authorities from the outset (including in the insurrection of 1830–1831, where the funds of the Bank were put under seal to prevent them being used by the rebels, see Lewak (1930)). Continued political unrest and the final policies of Russification by the end of the nineteenth century made intervention even more overt, eventually leading to the Bank being subsumed into the Russian Imperial State Bank in 1886 (Jedlicki 1999).

While the Congress Kingdom did not see the creation of a modern independent central bank, it did foster a financial system that bloomed in tandem with the Second Industrial Revolution and the abolition of serfdom. With Polish industry beginning to power the whole Russian empire, the need for long-term investment created a series of large formal banks in Warsaw and in Łódź, including "Bank Handlowy in Warsaw (1870, the biggest financial institution in the kingdom), Bank Dyskontowy (1871), Bank Handlowy in Łódź (1872), and Bank Kupiecki in Łódź" (Kochanowicz 2006b:14). Unfortunately, also in tandem with Russian cultural policies, these institutions tended to be staffed with Russians rather than Poles, as only 15 percent of Polish intelligentsia found employment in banks and similar institutions (Micińska 2009), with the vast majority of upper-level positions reserved for Russians. Unlike Prussia, there were few other opportunities for Poles in finance; it was not until after the events of 1905 that smaller cooperative societies such as in the German Partition began to take hold in the kingdom, with the founding in 1908 of the Union of Consumer Cooperatives (*Zwiazek Spóldzielni Spozywców*) in Warsaw (Chloupkova et al. 2003).

The Russian Partition was also home to that most modern of capitalist institution, the stock exchange, with development of equity markets in Poland beginning fairly early in the nineteenth century. In 1817, a mere twenty-five years after the creation of the New York Stock Exchange, the Russian occupiers had established the forerunner of today's Warsaw Stock Exchange, the *Giełda Kupiecka w Warszawie* (Warsaw Mercantile Exchange). The original Exchange, befitting the mostly agrarian and light-industrial nature of Poland at the time, was heavily weighted toward trades in bonds and debt instruments with only a few equity securities listed (Wąsowska and Obłoj 2013). However, the use of the exchange gathered momentum alongside the economy, with the first public security issued in 1826 from *Towarzystwo Kredytowe Ziemskie* (the Agrarian Credit Association) and the first major industrial security in 1840 from *Kolei Warszawsko-Wiedeńskiej*, the joint stock company building the Warsaw-to-Vienna railway (Łagowski 2013). With industrialization came the need for more and different types of equity financing, and the increase in equity trading at the Exchange led to an additional Commodity Exchange being hived off in 1873, at the same time that the Vienna stock exchange was crashing, coinciding with the financial crisis in the United States (Schwartz 1987). On the original Exchange, financial innovations, in line with international best practices, also continued to develop, including the publication of the first company prospectus in Poland in November 1894 from the joint-stock furniture company "Wojciechow." In a landscape of battered institutions, especially in the financial sphere, the Stock Exchange stood out as a fairly consistent innovator.

Finally, Polish Galicia, as the poorest and most agrarian Partition, saw correspondingly slow growth in the financial sector, although it did become a magnet for Austrian capital from the mid-century onward. As in the development of many other institutions, the Galician partition had an odd blend of Russian and German approaches. With increasing economic activity from the 1870s, a centralized approach similar to Russia was attempted for increasing credit in the region, with the creation of a Provincial Bank (*Bank Krajowy*) in 1883 (Wróbel 1994) and the development of a "Bank of Industry" in 1910 specifically to cater to heavier and larger industrial concerns (Reddaway 1971). However, smaller-scale agricultural cooperatives also began to coalesce in Galicia in the 1880s and 1890s, led by the Polish Society of Farmers' Associations (*Towarzystwo Kolek Rolniczych* or TKR) in 1885. The TKR was founded explicitly as a credit union to provide easier access to finance for its members, as well as to lower transaction costs by eliminating the need for (mostly Jewish) middlemen (Wróbel 1994). In the wake of the TKR's founding, other small cooperatives began to proliferate across the Galician landscape, focused mainly on savings and credit along the Austrian *Raiffeisen* model, rather than following the supply cooperative model of Prussia or the consumer cooperative model in the Kingdom of Poland (Chloupkova et al. 2003).

As with the disparate political and other economic institutions coming together in a unified Poland post-1918, the merging of financial institutions also saw some difficulties. In the first instance, monetary policy was returned to Polish control: almost immediately with the independence of the Republic, a plan was put in place to revive the Bank Polski as the central monetary authority of the reunified country, with an interim "National Loan Office" passing from German to Polish hands in 1918 having responsibility for issuing notes of legal tender. The monetary outlook was complicated by the reality that there were at least five currencies in circulation on Polish territory, including the German mark, the Austrian crown, the Russian ruble, the Polish mark in the Kingdom of Poland (an equivalent to the German mark, introduced after the Germans captured the Russian partition) and the "*ost-rubel*" on the territory of "*Ober Ost*," which included Lithuania and Białystok-Grodno (Wolf 2005). To overcome this monetary confusion, the Polish mark was introduced as a parallel currency wherever it was not already in circulation, while the other currencies were gradually withdrawn by the central authorities, a hugely important step that was accomplished by early 1920 (Landau 1990). While a better approach may have been to spread the currency that was accepted the most as a solid store of value or even to let the currencies continue to fight it out in the marketplace (the Polish mark was chosen because it was the one currency that the Warsaw government could control), the accomplishment of unifying the currency in such a short time after decades of other currencies in use was a monumental achievement.

However, the impressive success of currency unification soon took a backseat to the issue of financing the new government and, in the midst of the Soviet invasion, paying for the conflict that was thrust upon the new state. Perhaps showing how it would have behaved if it were a sovereign state during the Great War, the new Polish government followed the experience of other countries and began to run the printing press nonstop. Although Roszkowski (2008) calls the experience of 1918–1922 an episode of "moderate inflation," more accurate scholarship at the time from Zdziechowski (1925) shows that "the money supply increased between 1918 and 1919 by 519 percent, in the following year by another 929 percent, to reach in 1923 more than 12,000,000 percent (!) of the level in 1918" (Wolf 2005:417). The inflation was in reality not moderate from the outset, but instead moved from incredibly high to stratospheric levels well after the Russians were repulsed from the gates of Warsaw, financing the higher and higher deficits that the new government took on (Sargent 1982). Table 3.4 shows the dramatic extent of this rise on a monthly basis: with the new Polish government perhaps needing to listen to the king's advisors from the 1540s, one can easily see a huge increase in the quantity of money (notes in circulation, leading to corresponding rises in the wholesale price index. Over the "moderate" years of 1921 and 1922, notes in circulation increased by 316 percent (in 1921) and a further 231 percent in 1922, leading to a increase of over a hundred percent in the wholesale price index in just four months in 1922 (July to October). The numbers from that point on, both price indices and notes in circulation, are simply too large for the human brain to grasp.

The havoc wreaked by such monetary profligacy was enormous. A false sense of security was purchased with inflated marks in the early years of the Second Republic, with even scholars in the late twentieth century claiming that the inflation led to a competitive devaluation, while government loans for reconstruction, occurring in a depreciating currency, created implicit state subsidies of industry (Landau and Tomaszewski 1984). However, the reality was that the hyperinflations created by the Polish government did not have a competitive effect, even an evanescent one, as they occurred in tandem with the same disastrous policy in Hungary, Austria, and of course Weimar Germany. Moreover, the combination of huge government expenditures and monetary insanity from the new government put the newly-independent Poland on a very bad footing from the outset. The hyperinflation was only broken with the creation of a new złoty as legal tender in 1924 by the new Bank Polski, which took over from the National Loan Office and established a gold and foreign paper reserve to back the new currency (Sargent 1982). The Bank itself, modeled on British experience and presaging modern central banking, was set up as a joint stock company in order to retain some independence from the government in setting monetary policy (Landau and Tomaszewski 1984). Prices began to stabilize immediately in the wake of the new currency, with a brief spike in the new notes in circulation that stabilized by January 1925, as people began to clamor after currency that had 100 percent backing from bullion and hard currency (Sargent 1982). Polish unemployment also spiked at this point, not because of some ephemeral Philips Curve relationship, but

Table 3.4 *Prices and the Money Supply in Hyperinflationary Poland, 1921–1924*

Year	Month	Wholesale Price Index	Notes in Circulation	Year	Month	Wholesale Price Index	Notes in Circulation
1921	January	25.14	55,079.50	**1923**	January	544.69	909,160.30
	February	31.83	62,560.40		February	859.11	1,177,300.80
	March	32.88	74,087.40		March	988.50	1,841,205.60
	April	31.71	86,755.30		April	1,058.92	2,332,396.80
	May	32.64	94,575.80		May	1,125.35	2,733,794.10
	June	35.39	102,697.30		June	1,881.41	3,566,649.10
	July	45.65	115,242.30		July	3,069.97	4,478,709.00
	August	53.10	133,734.20		August	2,594.68	6,871,776.50
	September	60.20	152,792.10		September	7,302.20	11,197,737.80
	October	65.54	182,777.30		October	27,380.68	23,080,402.20
	November	58.58	207,029.00		November	67,943.70	53,217,494.60
	December	57.05	229,537.60		December	142,300.70	125,371,955.30
1922	January	59.23	239,615.30	**1924**	January	242,167.70	313,659,830.00
	February	64.45	247,209.50		February	248,426.60	528,913,418.70
	March	73.47	250,665.50		March	245,277.90	596,244,205.60
	April	75.11	260,553.80		April	242,321.80	570,697,550.50
	May	78.63	276,001.10				
	June	87.69	300,101.10				
	July	101.59	335,426.60				
	August	135.79	385,787.50				
	September	152.37	463,706.00				
	October	201.33	579,972.70				
	November	275.65	661,092.40				
	December	346.35	793,437.50				

Source: Sargent (1982). Price index is set at 1914=100.

because the firms that had been subsisting only through implicit state subsidies suddenly went bust when facing a hard budget constraint.

Even with the halt of hyperinflation, inflation still remained very high (approximately 16 percent annually), and the ramifications of the monetary policies of the government fed directly into the development of the banking sector in the Second Republic. Establishment of a modern financial system began in earnest from the early days of independence, and in 1921 there also began work on a law on bills of exchange to underpin the credit system (Kopyściański 2015). However, Taylor (1926) noted that the banking sector in Poland, perhaps having evolved in an era of cheap money and government credit, immediately began to take on a series of undesirable traits, including a cavalier disregard for capital reserves (keeping them far too low for lending operations), bloated staff and employee lists akin to government agencies rather than private sector firms, and high costs of administration. This reality translated directly to a major banking crisis in 1925 once the inflationary "good times" ended, with a massive liquidity crunch and (perhaps blessedly) promises of central bank assistance that never materialized (Morawski 2008). According to Rydel (1925), the effects of the banking crisis included severely undercutting public trust in formal financial institutions, although such damage was likely already done by the hyperinflation of the year previous.

Moreover, the inflationary boom had also gravely impacted the other major formal financial institution in Poland, the Warsaw Stock Exchange, which had run uninterrupted since its inception in 1817 and stood ready to provide capital for the transition to independence. The hyperinflation and ballooning money supply, as is always the case, translated directly to huge gains in the securities traded on the Exchange, gains that suddenly and precipitously reversed with the currency reform of 1924. Indeed, Polish equity markets, despite having a long pedigree, fared poorly throughout the Second Republic, having never recovered from this first great shock; according to Jorion and Goetzmann (1999), the return to equity in Poland over the whole period from 1921 to 1939 for someone pursuing a "buy and hold" strategy would have yielded a real return of negative 4 percent. While real returns were high year on year over this period (approximately 14 percent), the volatility of the Polish stock market was the highest in Europe, approximately 2.5 times higher than in Hungary and 5 times higher than in Czechoslovakia. In addition, Poland remained closed to international capital markets – not by Poland's choice – as only two external bond issues were created in the period between independence and the coup (Bandera 1964). As with the political institutions, which were in a constant state of flux, the underlying problems of the real economy fostered massive uncertainty in equity markets and also created difficulties for firms to secure long-term financing outside of the state apparatus.

Having created a difficult situation at a point when much of the rest of the world was enjoying the peace dividend from the end of the war, there were only approximately three years of "good economic conditions" (Roszkowski 2008:47) before the stock market crash in the United States ushered in the Great Depression in 1929. But even this rosy appraisal of the financial markets is not quite accurate, as the Piłsudski coup of 1926 created more difficulties, including a drop in the złoty exchange rate of 51 percent from January to May 1926 right after the coup (Landau and Tomaszewski 1984). Although the currency stabilized in the second half of the year, the Polish economy had been through three major crises in just over eight years, an unenviable track record that, it was assumed, the new regime would address. But with an emphasis on national renewal rather than economic specifics, the policies followed by the new *Sanacja* regime were oddly consistent from the previous government. In particular, attracting foreign (mainly American) capital was emphasized at all strata of government and from private sector economists, with government organs such as the Bank for the National Economy working with foreign financiers to loan money to regional Polish towns for development (Landau 1982). An additional major loan was negotiated between Bank Polski and the Bank of England and the New York Federal Reserve to create a fund for stabilization of the złoty, committing the government to monetary soundness, ensured with the addition of an American advisor to the Bank, Charles Dewey (Landau and Tomaszewski 1984); the loan finally stabilized the złoty in 1927, allowing for perhaps two years of economic stability before the Depression.

A key attribute of this stabilization loan was the integration of Poland into the gold-exchange standard prevailing in the world, a position that Poland was to hold from October 1927 until 1936, long after the United States, Britain, and Germany had abandoned the standard. While the standard utilized was not a pure gold standard, and gold coins were withdrawn from circulation in all major economies and concentrated in the vaults of central banks (Cassel 1936), it represented a major change for the inflation-prone Polish economy. With the advent of the industrial contraction that was to become the Great Depression, however, the gold standard soon became the policy of a smaller and smaller coterie of

countries. There are conflicting views on the effect that the gold standard
had on Poland during the Depression, with Eichengreen (1992), among
many others, arguing that the restrictions created by the gold standard kept
Poland's economy down more so than devaluation and a resumption of
inflation would have. However, the arguments that the gold standard
depressed industrial production are not borne out by the evidence, as
even Bernanke and James (1991), two authors not known for their support
of the gold standard, show that industrial production had recovered year-
on-year in Poland by 1933, a full three years before Poland abandoned its
gold peg. Declining prices in Poland were also likely still wringing out the
excess liquidity and inflation from the early 1920s, and by 1935 the price
level was only slightly below its 1929 level. In practice, it was more likely the
uncertainty in the global economy that came from the abandonment of the
gold standard, and the "last-mover" effect that Poland suffered from, that
continued to create difficulties in the Polish economy, and not the gold
standard per se (see Ferderer and Zalewski (1994) for an excellent discussion of the effects of uncertainty).

Also interesting from the point of view of institutional development is
the reason that Poland continued to be on the gold standard: Wolf (2007a)
attributes this stance to political and military considerations rather than
monetary ones, as Poland both feared the return of hyperinflation and the
loss of French capital, which was crucial for rebuilding the Polish military
(France remained on the gold standard until 1936 as well). Eichengreen
(1992) also notes that the lack of democracy in Poland, which had just
suffered under proportional representation, meant that the regime had
more to lose from inflation, and thus was likely to stay on the gold standard
than a majority representation polity, which would vote itself inflation and
then vote it away (Eichengreen also notes that fiscal stabilization necessary
for the gold standard was more difficult under a proportional regime).
In this case, the correct monetary institution (the gold standard) may have
been adhered to simply because of poor functioning of political institutions, with both being subsumed by international events outside Poland's
control. This provides an interesting case of institutional interaction, in
that good institutions do not necessarily beget good institutions; the
example of Poland on the gold standard also shows that serendipity may
play a role in institutional development.

But, as too often in Poland's history, promising institutional development was ruined by conflict, first economic and then actual. The escalating
and competitive currency wars that were unleashed by the world going off
the gold standard led Poland to adopt a series of draconian and misguided

financial policies, including foreign exchange controls in April 1936 and additional capital controls and penalties in 1937 and 1938 to try and keep scarce capital locked in the country (Bandera 1964). None of these proto-fascist moves helped, nor did actual fascism: the Second World War decimated Poland's financial architecture, with the Stock Exchange ceasing to exist in 1939 and Polish banks being forced into ruin (Łagowski 2013). There is unfortunately little to say from this point onward, as the communist system that was imposed on Poland in the aftermath of the war was directly antithetical to the modern financial system that Poland had instituted in the Second Republic, and, indeed, was a system designed to do away with capital entirely. The Soviet-imposed communist model from 1946–1989 utilized the monobank structure common to all socialist countries, with the National Bank of Poland (NBP) created in 1945 as a successor to the Bank of Poland (which had formally moved to London in 1939 and was now deemed liquidated) in order to regulate both currency and credit, aggregating to itself the role of central planner of credit for the entire economy (Podolski 1973). While existing state, municipal, and cooperative banks began to reconstitute themselves in the immediate aftermath of the war, using the prewar legislative framework (which had not been repealed yet), the same was not to be the case for private banks, which were never given permission to re-open and thus the system was nationalized by inactivity (ibid.). Under this system, monetary policy as well was reduced from a primary role in the maintenance of the economy to a mere accounting exercise, with the złoty an inconvertible unit for measuring production. As with other institutions under communism, some flexibility began to be introduced in the 1980s: relaxation of plan targets for credit in 1982 was followed by the much more important step of creating a savings bank from the monobank in 1987 (Thorne 1993). However, it was not until the transformation of the regional branches of NBP into commercial banks in February 1989 that Poland returned to a capitalist financial system, resuming its growth of financial institutions that had been on hold for fifty-two years.

TRADE

The final series of institutions we will examine is trade, which can be taken as a proxy for economic freedom more general (freedom to exchange is often one of the first freedoms that a government restricts), while also mirroring the development of Poland's economy (countries that are more prosperous trade more, and vice versa). While libraries have been written in the political science, history, and economics literature about the volume of trade that Poland has generated (especially during the fifteenth through seventeenth centuries), this section is not concerned with the actual size, composition, or destination of trade from Poland; instead, as we have done throughout this chapter, we will focus on Poland's trade institutions, the mechanisms and organizations that have helped to facilitate international exchange. Many of these underlying institutions we have already touched upon, as the economics literature has shown that institutions such as property rights and rule of law are necessary to reap the gains from trade (Levchenko 2007) or even to make trade possible (Ranjan and Lee 2007), while other institutions such as (overly restrictive) labor markets can dramatically influence the volume of trade (Borrmann et al. 2006). But there are other institutions that are specifically concerned with trade, including tariff regimes and trade policy institutions, guilds, customs, and infrastructure provision, some of which we will tackle in this section.

Poland's physical geography, at least during its early years, facilitated transport of goods, and the outlet to the Baltic Sea was conducive to the development of healthy trade relations with the world. Situated in the center of Europe and on trade routes from Western Europe to the Middle and Far East, Poland also was blessed with situational advantages for fostering pass-through trade. Simply put, as Poland's neighbors grew richer, there was a greater chance that Poland would be able to benefit from this, as was seen in the heavy trade with the Netherlands in the fourteenth through sixteenth centuries. But history is replete with countries blessed with natural advantages and wealthy neighbors that never turn these into trade success. Thus, Poland's specific trade institutions, in tandem with its natural advantages, hold the key to understanding the country's trade relations in the centuries prior to 1989.

One of the earliest such trade institutions, an early counterpart to unions in the labor market, was the guild, an institution that pervaded Poland beginning with craft guilds in the twelfth century, followed by merchant guilds in Kraków in the fourteenth century (Carter 2006). As formal institutions, guilds consisted of organizational structures and procedures that set out manufacturing processes and production techniques, set conditions of sale and in many instances prices, and regulated the competition amongst members (Lerski 1996). In many towns, the guilds also fulfilled other functions, including as "religious brotherhoods, social organizations, welfare societies, and as citizens militias to aid in the town's defense" (Sedlar 2011:126). Their true power, however, came from their interaction with other institutions, most prominently the crown, as the king was able to grant privileges to certain guilds and deny the access of small traders or other merchants to commerce, while also allowing guild members some say in local administration (Stone 2001). These privileges were granted early in Polish history to Kraków by King Kazimierz, who sought to "deny merchants from Torun access to Russia and Hungary," so that the Kraków guild could "take control themselves of the trade between these countries and western Europe" (Michaud 2000:750). King Kazimierz also gave substantial privileges to Gdańsk (which already had the ability to undertake its own administration), where the traders of the region were allowed to trade throughout Poland and Lithuania (Lindberg 2009).

In regard to their economic impact, guilds have benefitted from historical revisionism over the past two decades, with many emphasizing their role in creating the conditions for trade. According to Guinnane (1994), craft and merchant guilds played a role in disciplining their members via the threat of exclusion (much as was done by the Catholic Church), with this discipline creating codes of conduct, reputational risk, and informal modes of dispute settlement; this intraorganizational development then translated into a way to enable trade, either by reducing information asymmetries from producers to consumers (Gustafsson 1987) or by creating a safe space for innovation (Epstein 1998). While Ogilvie (2007) takes great umbrage at celebration of the second- (or third-) best efficiency characteristics of these guilds, Gelderblom and Grafe (2010:478) note that the guilds were an "institutional response to the fundamental problems of long-distance trade" that complemented other coping mechanisms such as towns.

However, much like unions, guilds existed solely to advance the interests of their members, functioning according to hierarchical and nonmarket principles, with an explicit goal of stifling competition that could harm the guild. They were also sensitive to political winds, given that their status was based on political privilege, and could have the same exclusionary principles they utilized turned against them: for example, in 1405, Polish merchants were prohibited by the Hungarian king to trade with his kingdom (Carter 2006), at the same time these merchants were given a monopoly within Poland. Thus, Ogilvie (2007) is entirely correct in noting that the guild system was a highly imperfect institution that existed in an imperfect institutional system (serfdom, communes). In fact, the existence of guilds in Poland may have made it more difficult to transition to a free-market system due to their ability to create rents behind walls of permissions, restrictions, and privileges.

It was this precise attribute of guilds, the ability to create rents, which created their downfall over the coming centuries. In a market system, rents are a signal for new participants to enter the market, and even in an imperfect market, such as political markets, this signaling function is intact. As early as the fifteenth century, the *szlachta* grew jealous of the privileges afforded to the merchant guilds and attempted to limit their activities in towns and cities across Poland; interestingly, as Wyrobisz (1989) notes, the *szlachta* stopped their demands short of outright abolition, for that would have harmed their own tax base. This schizophrenia in regard to guilds is typified in a law created by King Jagiełło in 1423 to abolish guilds altogether, but the law was never promulgated, and guilds continued their increase unabated (Stone 2001). Moreover, Ogilvie (1995) noted that it wasn't just the political competition for rents that undermined the guild system, as cheap rural competition undercut the dominance of the guilds. In this manner, the collection of urban merchants in a guild was attacked from both above and below, leading to a cessation of their importance by the eighteenth century and their outright abolition early in the Partitions (Lerski 1996).

While the guild system deteriorated in the towns and for internal trade, however, across the Baltic, merchant guilds retained a monopoly on foreign trade well into the eighteenth century or even later (Lindberg 2007). Part of this longevity of the guild system in regard to foreign trade was the fact that the rents for trade were much higher, and thus guilds fought more tenaciously to protect them. The rents that could be garnered from a monopoly on trade were impressive indeed, as starting in the fourteenth and fifteenth centuries, Poland became a major exporter of wheat and wood products to the Low Countries (where they were then re-exported to England and France); as the population of Europe rebounded from the Black Death and began to increase substantially by the sixteenth century, the market expanded exponentially for Polish goods (Wallerstein 1972). While statistical data is scarce, Małowist (1959) asserts that approximately 10,000 lasts of grain were exported annually from Gdańsk to the west at a minimum during the booming fifteenth century, whereas more concrete data derived from the customs point at Wloclawek on the Vistula river shows that 19,000 lasts of grain were exported via this point in 1555, fluctuating between 6,416 lasts in 1558 to a high of 24,826 lasts in 1562.[22] Continued specialization in agricultural production in the fifteenth and sixteenth century concentrated Poland's agricultural might into the grain trade, and while technical progress in agriculture was confined to northern and western portions of Poland (Zukowski 2004), absolute volumes and high demand from Dutch and Belgian consumers created a steady stream of revenue for Polish merchants (Unger 1983).

Perhaps more important, however, the status of Gdańsk as a nearly-independent city-state within Poland meant that these rents were more protected from the predations of the king and other Polish *szlachta*, allowing the guilds to survive via distribution of these rents. To put it another way, as noted, merchant guilds throughout Poland were subjected to institutional competition from the nobility, the crown, and even from Jewish merchants and peddlers who circumvented the system (Stone 2001). In Gdańsk, with the merchant guilds in charge of revenue and administration, and with no need to pay tribute to the rest of the country, the guild was able to secure this lucrative revenue stream as a monopoly, in collusion with local nobility but without any loyalty to other nobility (Małowist 1959). As Bogucka (1983:51) relates, "Duke Francisco de Mendoza, who came to Poland in 1597 as an envoy of King Philip II of Spain . . . argued, that trading ties between Poland and the Netherlands were so strong that the both countries could hardly get along without each other." Such a vote of confidence from abroad also strengthened the hand of merchant guilds in the north and gave them political cover to survive any potential encroachments. In this sense, the weak central state of the Polish-Lithuanian Commonwealth was a boon to merchants (but not necessarily to consumers), much as the decentralized institution of serfdom was a boon to landlords (but not necessarily to peasants).

Małowist (1959:38) sums up this state of affairs, placing emphasis on the nobility's role in trade but, for our purposes, more accurately showing the collaboration between businesses (guilds) and government (nobility) that distorted prices and trade:[23]

---

[22] A "last" was the standard measure of grain utilized by the Dutch and accepted internationally, equivalent to approximately 3,004 liters or a weight of nearly 2,280 kilograms of wheat or 2,160 kilograms of rye (see De Vries 2012).

[23] It is important to note that there is a definite dividing line between nobility and merchants during this time. In 1633 the *Sejm* passed an act that declared that any nobles engaging in commerce would forfeit their noble privileges (Klimesz 1970).

In Poland the trade favoured above all the interests of Gdansk and of the nobility, partly also of the large merchants. The interests of the peasants (whose resistance to the growing enserfment was for a time weakened by the general boom in the demand for grain), and of the mass of townsmen – craftsmen, small traders, etc. – were sacrificed. The country was constantly drained of large quantities of foodstuffs and raw materials, and simultaneously flooded by quantities of industrial and luxury goods, thus weakening small and middling crafts and traders, who had neither the skill nor the capacity to resist, and changing the social structure in the aristocracy's favour. Thus we observe a growing tendency towards a uniquely agrarian development which helped to turn the country into an agrarian and raw-material producing colony of the West. It is tempting to see certain similarities – perhaps rather remote ones – with the development of systems of monoculture in the colonial countries of the nineteenth and twentieth century.

Małowist's (1959) analysis is far off in terms of his understanding of economics – as a historian writing during the communist era, this might be excused – especially in his neo-mercantilist view of raw materials being "drained" for export while damnable luxury goods were imported from abroad, thus taking local jobs (in modern parlance). But his point regarding the skewed composition of trade is well taken, given that trade has been subjected to political pressures since time immemorial that has diverted it from its "natural" flows. It is entirely plausible that demand might have been different had peasants been able to access more purchasing power, and thus the flow of goods to Gdańsk would have also been different. In this manner, there was not so much a liberalization of trade in Poland during this time, but a mere reshuffling of which political entity was imposing its preferences. Political favoritism hardly constitutes support of free trade.

Of course, the monopolization of trade routes would not have created riches unless there had been institutions supporting infrastructure to help facilitate trade; without infrastructure, a port is just a beach. Poland's infrastructure development in the early modern era in the Baltic helped to supplement the technological specialization occurring in agriculture and better-positioned the region for foreign trade. Lenartowicz (1924) points to the important communication links that were established in Gdańsk with the outside world, in particular the postal system, which was created in the fourteenth century and operated autonomously until being subsumed into the Polish postal system in 1654. And van Tielhof (2002:47) notes (a crucial point for later chapters),

The existence of connections between districts in Poland-Lithuania and Danzig or other Baltic ports like Königsberg or Riga was largely decisive for the evolution of cereal production for export. The fertility of the soil and climactic conditions were less

important than transportation routes. That is why, for example, most parts of the extremely fertile Ukraine did not export grain to western markets in the period under consideration; they lacked the essential infrastructure of waterways.

Gdańsk, as the prime trading port in Poland, obviously gets much of the attention regarding trade and trade infrastructure, but it was just one example of how the infrastructural fabric all across Poland developed to support trade. In particular, the increasing urbanization of the country from 1400–1600 (as shown in Table 3.1) led to the development of better roads, bridges, waterways, and the creation of cities as the nodes for international trade networks (Antrop 2004). The king was involved in this process as well, using a mechanism that today would be called a "public-private partnership," investing state funding on building the roads but subcontracting out the toll services to Jewish "toll farmers," who paid the state for the right to be a collector and reimbursed their expenses via collections (Stone 2001). Purely private infrastructure was also provided throughout the country at the time, but it was often small scale and done via labor obligations of serfdom rather than as part of the profit motive.

Finally, an important point must be made here regarding Poland's overall trade policies during this period. While the internal trade structures that mediated trade may have been distortionary, the overall trade institution that underpinned the grain trade was salutary. Especially compared to England during the sixteenth and seventeenth centuries, Poland had a very laissez-faire tariff policy, "imposing only minor tariffs as purely revenue-raising measures and exempting even these modest tariffs for the Polish clergy, land-owners and their serfs" (Way 2012:14). This point is reinforced by Friedrich (2006), who notes that the tariff structure of Poland, supported by the nobles (and granted by King Kazimierz), was an incredible improvement on the complex and high-tariff impositions of the Teutonic Order, leading to increased integration with neighboring Prussian cities. Thus, Poland's trade institutions were not uniformly effective or ineffective, as the overall attitude towards trade was beneficial for increasing volumes and choice amongst the populace. It was only in conjunction with other institutions in the system, including property rights, labor market institutions, and paramount above them all, political institutions, that Poland's trade institutions diverged from optimality.

In tandem with geopolitical changes, transitions were imminent in Poland's trade by the 1600s. As with every other economic institution we have examined here, the grain trade in the seventeenth century suffered as a result of Poland's constant wars, with the occupation of broad swathes of the country during the Swedish-Polish War from 1655 to 1660 creating the biggest disruptions to agricultural production (van Tielhof 2002). According to data provided by Van Zanden (2005), per capita output in agriculture fell by 33 percent between 1570 and 1800, contributing to a precipitous decline in GDP per capita over the same period that only began to rebound after the Partitions. The effect of external conflict also meshed well with internal policy difficulties, with Mączak (1970) noting that the inflationary episodes detailed above had an enormous impact on agricultural trade, which requires long-term capital investment and much longer time-horizons than retail or small-scale manufacturing. With interest rates and prices in flux, normal economic calculations were increasingly difficult, disrupting agriculture produced for export.

Thus, the continuous conflict of the seventeenth and early eighteenth century steadily disrupted trade routes, destroyed infrastructure, and created uncertainty regarding borders and policies. From the point of view of Poland's competitiveness, external humiliation owing to military defeat and mismanaged institutions internally also allowed for old competitors to triumph in the international trade arena. Małowist (1959) notes that Poland and Russia, as with every other aspect of their existence, were locked in a rivalry for trade during the fifteenth and sixteenth centuries, with the destruction wrought on Poland by the Northern Wars allowing Russia to gain the upper hand. Similarly, Stone (2001) relates how the development of St. Petersburg, willed into being by its monarch, populated by force and *diktat* (Braudel 1982), and untouched by invasion, was able to re-route the forest trade that had previously transited Poland and Lithuania, depriving the Commonwealth of a source of revenue. Indeed, even in the sixteenth century, Russia wielded trade as a weapon for geopolitical gain, whereas Poland saw trade as a way to enrich certain strata of the population (neither interpretation being correct, obviously); with the grain trade directed and controlled by the government, any lessening of Polish influence was a gain for the centralizing Russian state (Cherepnin 1964).

The diminution of Poland's geopolitical power in the eighteenth century, with its neighbors encroaching on and eventually seizing its territories, also presaged a change in Poland's trade institutions. Ironically, the grain trade began to recover in Poland after the destruction of the seventeenth century around 1720 (Stone 2001), with increasing grain prices and a general European peace contributing to increased demand. At the same time, incipient financial markets also helped to hedge the uncertainty of agricultural production, although this was more evidenced in advanced markets (London and Amsterdam) than in Poland (Neal 1987). Within Poland, communications and infrastructure were also improving, with improved internal waterways linking the country to the east and with easier access to the ports on the Baltic, and by 1764 the last vestiges of internal tariffs had been abolished, creating a much more coherent and standardized internal market (Stone 2001). Even regionally, Poland was becoming more integrated in the grain trade with German cities across the border (Baten and Wallusch 2005), and even mining and refining was beginning to come back on-line during the era of relative prosperity and stability (Stone 2001).

However, the Partitions put an end to the beneficial development of Polish trade institutions, just as it had done with political and economic institutions explored earlier. The integration process with Prussia was shut down completely by the Partitions, as the first Partition in 1772 smothered the north of Poland via Prussian customs policies: as an example, Gdańsk withered under the protectionist policies of its Teutonic neighbor, with a mere 65 ships leaving its harbor in 1792, a far cry from the 1,100 per year that landed before the Partitions (Brand 2007). Further evidence of the collapse of the Baltic trade comes from Swedish-Polish shipping, where, based on data from Cieślak (1983), the tonnage of ships coming from Sweden to Poland decreased by 87 percent from 1769 to 1793, even as average tonnage went up. The adoption of foreign (and alien) trade institutions such as high protective tariffs forced still-independent Poland into looking north to Scandinavia and south to the Black Sea for more profitable trading opportunities between 1772 and 1795 (Ardeleanu 2014:33), before the flame of independence was snuffed out entirely and Poland no longer had a say in its trade.

As should be obvious by now, the development of trade institutions in Poland was supplanted post-1795 by the institutions of the Partitioning countries. The development of trade institutions in the Polish lands was made more difficult, however, by the fact that the three partitioning powers were diametrically opposed to each other in their trade relations, and, indeed, used their trade policies to harm each other to the maximum extent (Müller 2015). Prussia, already having shown its preference for high tariffs, continued such an approach in the Polish territories; liberal trade policies in Prussia proper were introduced in 1780 and quickly discarded due to an unfortunate and poorly timed economic crisis

(Helleiner 2002), and thus Polish territory was acquired as Prussia was at the height of a protectionist mania. This protectionist mindset was accelerated by the drive for German unification, as, after all internal barriers were abolished in Prussia in 1818 (Henderson 1962), the creation of the *Zollverein* (customs union) in 1834 re-erected substantial barriers to trade externally. Statistics bear out this antipathy of the Prussian ruling class to unfettered trade, with trade openness (defined as exports plus imports as a percentage of GDP) at levels 10 percentage points less than that of the UK and four times lower than the Netherlands by 1850 (Daudin et al. 2008). Indeed, tariff policies within Prussia only changed somewhat as part of the rivalry with the Habsburgs over which country was to lead German integration (Gallarotti 1985), and once the German Empire was formed in 1871, protectionism once again ruled the day (it is safe to say that none of the minor liberalization moves taken by Prussia in the 1860s reached the Polish territories). However, while the tariff regime was more restrictive in the Prussian Partition, the territories under Prussian control had much higher levels of urbanization and railway density twice that of the Austrian Partition and nearly three times that of the Congress Kingdom (Zukowski 2004). Thus, as in independent Poland, the trade institutions were not all working in the same direction in Prussian Poland.

Austria-Hungary, despite its relative liberality in other spheres, was closer to Prussia during the Partitions and remained protectionist (and thus, by extension, so did Polish Galicia). In general the Habsburgs went against a European-wide trend for falling tariffs and retained high protectionist walls: Austria-Hungary's openness in 1850 was the lowest in Europe except for Spain, at a paltry 13.2 percent of GDP involved in trade, half the percentage of tiny Belgium (Daudin et al. 2008). Indeed, Austria-Hungary defined its trade policy in opposition to its German rival, with mild liberalization in 1861 occurring as part of the political rivalry with Prussia and the protectionism of the 1870s onward imposed as a reaction to German agricultural tariffs (Müller 2015). Moreover, Polish Galicia suffered without even the benefit of the infrastructure that Prussia provided, as the Habsburgs in general had little interest in railway technology and little understanding of the benefits it could provide to the monarchy (Keller and Shiue 2008).

Finally, in the Russian-occupied lands of the kingdom, there was a creeping economic absorption of Poland that underwent several fits and starts, with even a customs tariff imposed at the border between Russia and the Kingdom of Poland in retaliation for the events of

1830–1831 (Kochanowicz 2006b). From 1851 onward, however, the Kingdom of Poland was fully incorporated in Russia's tariff structures, totally removing the determination of trade pricing from Warsaw's hands (Kochanowicz 2006a). This high tariff structure allowed for the development of Polish industry during the Second Industrial Revolution, with cities such as Łódź luring weavers and craftsmen from the Prussian Partition with the promise of protected work and a thriving local market (Kochanowicz 2006b). As with the other two Partitions, however, policies in the late 1800s were predicated on tit-for-tat retaliation against Prussia and Austria, with an all-out tariff war between 1891 and 1893 that permanently closed some markets to goods from the Russian Empire and the Congress Kingdom (Müller 2015). And as in Austria, trade infrastructure was much poorer than in Prussia, with the Polish lands under Russian control having the lowest railway density and highest transportation costs of all three Partitions (Zukowski 2004).

The wresting of trade institutions back from foreign control after the First World War created a whole new set of difficulties for the reborn Polish nation. The creation of the Second Republic, in addition to the issue of currency unification noted above, confronted Poland's trade institutions with a dual transition: not only was Poland seeking to establish its own foreign economic relations as a sovereign nation, it also faced the task of lowering the trade barriers that had been erected across the country during the Partitions. In this sense, the reunification of Poland in 1918 was more than a political merger; it was also the creation of a common internal market across three disparate entities that had been independent from each other in theory, if not in absolute reality. Wolf (2005, 2007b) showed just how daunting a task this was, demonstrating empirically that internal barriers were still coming down as late as 1934, with the internal liberalization stalled as a result of the Great Depression. Thus, Poland's internal barriers, which had been removed entirely only in 1764, were re-erected in 1795 and still persisted through at least 1934 and likely until the Second World War. In this sense, it is perhaps easier to say that Poland had a long experience of restrictive trade institutions internally, with only brief periods of liberalization punctuating centuries of internal rifts. As Nitsch and Wolf (2013) have shown, such internal barriers are generally easy to put up, but can influence trade for decades afterwards.

Externally, Poland did not have an easy road ahead either, as trade, perhaps more than any other economic institution, had deep and lasting effects from the Partitions. In fact, the experience of Poland's external trade institutions during the twentieth century emphasizes Roland's (2004) point on relative speeds of institutional development, in that some institutions simply cannot evolve as fast as others. This was entirely the case after reunification in 1918 for Poland. Miletić (2014) cites data that shows that, prior to the founding of the Second Republic, the Kingdom of Poland had 90 percent of its exports go to other parts of Russia, while the German partition sent 77 percent of its goods to Germany and received 80 percent of its imports from the same source; linkages across Poland and across Partitions, when they existed at all, were very low. These ties that bound the Partition to the partitioning country were not just evident in *ex post* flows radiating outward from Poland, but also in the orientation of trade, as the Congress Kingdom had nearly its entire infrastructure and trade pointed towards Russia, while the Prussian Partition was well-integrated with Germany's economy.[24]

Policy, like infrastructure, was also slow-moving and difficult to change, as the rampant protectionism that each Partition had practiced against the other (Poland was ranked highest in the world in protection in 1913, presumably referring to the Congress Kingdom) was maintained after the war by the new government (Poland remained highest in the world in tariff levels in 1927 and 1931, according to Liepmann (1938)). This protection was uneven, as Poland's tariff levels on manufacturing were actually quite low by European standards in the interwar period, but the government utilized many other means beyond mere tariffs to stifle trade, including an emphasis on several types of nontariff barriers from 1919 to 1924 (Miletić 2014). In fact, rather than moving back towards a policy of laissez-faire, trade continued to be an instrument of national policy rather than a treasure to be defended. With such an approach towards trade, consistent under foreign powers and Poles themselves, trade institutions were bound to develop in a manner antithetical to free trade and oriented towards managed trade. Such a situation was typified in the Polish-German tariff war in 1925.

By 1925, approximately 45 percent of Polish trade was still concentrated with one of its former occupiers, due to an agreement under the Treaty of Versailles that allowed for the free flow of trade from Germany to Upper Silesia (through January 1925) and a further agreement made in Geneva in 1922 that allowed for duty-free export of coal and other goods from Poland

---

[24] An additional barrier was noted by Heinemeyer (2007), who called attention to the fact that the railways in the Congress Kingdom, in addition to being oriented exclusively towards Moscow, also had the Russian broad gauge which was incompatible with railways across the rest of Poland.

to Germany (Karski 2014).[25] However, issues unrelated to trade (specifically concerning the German minority within Polish borders and continuing dissatisfaction with the Versailles borders) led to an economic blockade on each side, as Germany suddenly refused Polish coal imports originating from Upper Silesia, and Poland retaliated by blocking German imports (Kruszewski 1943). The tariff war lasted for nine long years, and while Rothschild (1963) claims that the trade war created rising unemployment and great hardship for the Polish economy, Bandera (1964) notes that it was more the monetary policy of Poland at the time that was to blame. Kowal (2002) also points out that the tariff war was somewhat circumvented by informal trade, as German and Polish firms forged relationships with each other and also lobbied their respective governments to end the bickering; thus, formal trade institutions were acting directly counter to the trade flows and informal trade linkages that already existed, a situation that was difficult to fathom for a new government supposedly dedicated to restoring Poland's glory. Additionally, more recent scholarship also makes a convincing case that Germany was more debilitated by the sanctions and Poland actually was able to craft new trade linkages and bolster domestic production, breaking its dependency on its colonial masters (Karski 2014).

Regardless of the possibly salutary effects that the tariff war had in terms of trade orientation, it was a disaster in terms of trade institution-building. In the first instance, such a system of prohibitions and bureaucratic determination of trade required an apparatus to deter trade, and Poland instituted a system of licensing and state controls that effectively made trade another purview of the state (Miletić 2014). These controls outlasted the stabilization of the złoty and were in place until Poland was torn apart in the Second World War (de Ménil and Maurel 1994), and expanded to include import quotas and other draconian measures (Păun et al. 2009). And for a country that was still learning to build trade institutions after a long night of protectionism, the German tariff war merely continued the policies of the occupiers. Whereas previous policies had cut bits of Poland off from each other (Heinemeyer (2007) points to the Russian tariffs that prevented Warsaw from using Upper Silesian coal and instead forced Poland to import it from Donetsk), the

---

[25] Heinemeyer (2007) also notes that Russia's prohibitive tariffs and turn towards autarky after the Bolshevik takeover effectively shut down Russo-Polish trade and forced Poland to turn to Germany.

new Polish government was cutting Poland off from the world voluntarily. During this time, some of its major formal trade institutions, above all customs administration, were suffering from volatile trade policies, inadequate personnel, and the political uncertainty engendered by other economic institutions (Miletić 2014). Indeed, as already seen, Poland in many ways eschewed the explicit development of trade institutions, using other economic considerations to guide policy; for example, Poland remained on the gold standard as long as it did only because France was a main trading partner and was also on the gold standard, while the Polish government utilized exchange controls to regulate trade rather than develop a separate trade apparatus in the government (Irwin 2011). In the Second Republic, the development of trade was thus similar to other economic institutions, especially post-1926, with economic institutions subordinated to the nationalist (and later, proto-fascist) goals of a greater Poland, rather than openness for its own sake.

To be fair, as with many economic and political institutions, this state of affairs was not solely the doing of the military junta under Piłsudski or his successors. Indeed, by the 1930s, the whole concept of free trade was in retreat internationally, and even perceived bastions of liberalism such as the United States were being sucked down the socialist rabbit hole. In this sense, Polish policy makers discussing inward-oriented development in 1931, eschewing trade in favor of the import substitution that would become fashionable in the 1950s and 1960s or even in today's Russia (Szlajfer 1990), was not an aberration but part of a broader trend. Even Poland's largest trading partner in the 1930s and fellow gold-standard-bearer, France, began to impose quantitative restrictions on imports in an attempt to artificially induce competitiveness (Irwin 2011). The Polish government, perhaps looking to the corporatism that National Socialism in Germany offered, took it upon itself to centralize trade institutions and create four-year plans. Massive state-directed projects such as the *Centralny Okręg Przemysłowy* (Central Industrial District) were begun, ostensibly to rapidly industrialize but also including a focus on securing an armaments industry (Williamson 2011). In either case, the Polish government after the Constitution of 1935 also began to ape the Soviet model of heavy industry above all else. In this sense, the influence of Germany and Russia (now the Soviet Union) continued to negatively impact Poland's trade institutions.

This slide into utilitarian trade was taken to its logical extreme with the communist takeover in Poland after the Second World War. As with all other economic institutions in the communist era, trade institutions in the People's Republic may have the same outward appearance as their capitalist counterparts but were wholly unrecognizable in terms of their organization, incentive structures, or objectives. In many ways, trade functioned similarly to the financial system under socialism, acting as an accounting exercise for fulfilling the plan according to the needs of the specialists in the Central Committee rather than a voluntary exchange guided by comparative advantage. Indeed, the creation of the Council of Mutual Economic Assistance (COMECON), the trade zone of Soviet bloc states founded in 1949, was just an enlargement of the plan's space across international borders, allowing communist countries to manage their trade more easily and split up production amongst countries. And as with all other political and economic institutions, foreign trade was monopolized by the Communist Party, with state trading "corporations," inconvertible currencies, an array of restrictions and licenses, and trade agreements that were actual plans rather than statements of intent (Holzman 1976). In practice, this trade system protected capital at the expense of land and labor, an interesting irony for a system that was designed to categorically oppose capitalism, creating rents for Party officials (Brada 1991).

The failure of the COMECON system to allow Poland to trade its economic faults away manifested itself not only in a dearth of consumer goods, but also in a very concrete macroeconomic manner. Poland in the late 1930s had relied heavily on foreign investment and capital to build the economy, reaching a peak of 44.8 percent of all share capital in the country in 1935 (Hehn 2005). During the communist era, foreign investment was negligible, as the state did not (theoretically) allow private enterprise or encourage investors to put their capitalist dollars in Poland. But with the state taking on the role of engine of growth, this meant financing still had to be done, although it would be on a state-to-state basis rather than in the form of foreign direct investment. Thus, the Polish government took on massive quantities of debt, beginning with credits from Western banks in the 1970s, to finance modernization and subsidize the growing and unexpected trade deficit that the country had contracted (Rynarzewski 1986). As Frentzel-Zagorska (1990:764) notes, "the failure of [Polish leaders] Gomulka and Gierek to implement economic reform . . . resulted in periods of stagnation and a fall in living standards, leading in the late 1970s to economic catastrophe, which was preceded by a short period of spurious prosperity financed by foreign borrowing." By the late 1980s, Poland (along with Bulgaria and Hungary) was in the unenviable position of being one of the most indebted countries in the world (Elster et al. 1998).

Poland's trade institutions show a definite path across time and space, and their development may have been more linear than other economic institutions shown in this section. In particular, Poland was starting to capture the laissez-faire spirit of the late eighteenth century in regard to its trade, but had this stifled by autocratic rule that treated trade as a weapon. Unfortunately, Poland never really lost this faith in government-directed trade, moving from a complex system of licenses and restrictions in the Second Republic to completely state-dominated "trade" under Soviet rule. The intricacies of trade institutions, and in particular their reliance on other economic institutions such as property rights and monetary institutions, meant that, unless these other institutions were reformed, trade would remain an accounting exercise and not a source of wealth.

CONCLUSION: POLAND AS AN ECONOMIC BEING

This overview of the history of Poland's economic institutions serves as a counterpart to the previous chapter, where we saw the evolution of democratic thought over the centuries. In contrast to the political institution-building explored earlier, the building of economic institutions in Poland followed a somewhat different path, although the exact course taken was differentiated by the particular institution. Where all political institutions, formal and informal, were animated by a specific thought, that of "noble liberty," the development of economic institutions was more opportunistic: either these institutions developed as directed by prevailing political institutions (property rights and trade), in tandem with the existence of other economic institutions (labor market development under serfdom), as a response to external factors (as with the development of agricultural cooperatives in Prussian Poland), or even were imported from abroad but quickly took on a distinctly Polish flair (such as the Warsaw Stock Exchange).

The reason behind the more desultory course of economic institution-building is obviously in part due to the variegated nature of the institutions involved, but thinking about the economic institutional system of Poland as a whole, there are other reasons that can be ascertained for the evolution detailed here. One of the key causes may be the differing philosophical approach to economics than to politics in Polish history, an approach that has been far less unitary than the idea of "noble liberty." As Kuninski (1997:242) correctly notes, "the political tradition and experience of the main political class, the gentry, were basically democratic rather than liberal, based on the notion of collective and political liberties rather than individual freedom." Indeed, the Polish idea of liberty somewhat diverged from what is commonly thought of in a modern sense as "economic liberty"; one must remember that the Polish conception of liberty from the fifteenth to the eighteenth century referred specifically to the obligations of noble men to participate in the political process, and thus was less a call for economic *laissez-faire* and more of a license to form a polity.

This is not to say that classical liberalism, while never having a wide acceptance in Poland as noble liberty, had no advocates throughout Poland's long history, especially during the time of Partitions. Wincenty and Bonawentura Niemojowski from the border town of Kalisz (originally part of Prussia's portion but annexed to Russia after Napoleon's defeat) were public agitators for laissez-faire economics and were highly opposed to the tsar's centralizing economic reforms (Kuninski 1997). Similarly, Adam Heydel of Jagiellonian University in Kraków was an avowed free-market proponent at a time when Poland was turning away from free markets and towards fascism (Machaj 2015). However, Szacki (1995) notes that liberalism in Poland was very rarely coherent and instead coalesced around fragments of thought imported from elsewhere, while being labeled a "liberal" merely meant one was advocating for greater economic freedom (i.e., more relative change rather than higher absolute levels, as a classical liberal would argue).

This lack of a foundational *economic* philosophy, unlike with the political system, may be somewhat to blame for the somewhat uneven building of economic institutions, but, as shown above, it is more likely that the incorrect implementation of *political* philosophy stunted the growth of necessary economic institutions. Continued failures to restrain the executive, at either the central or local level, led to uneven protection of property rights and various restrictions on trade enforced by the same nobility who claimed political freedom, while conflict directed from above led to monetary shenanigans that affected the entire economy. And, of course, the experience of nationalism and communism in the twentieth century, with its emphasis on centralization of power, created the same turmoil in Poland as they did elsewhere, from Germany to the United States to Asia and all points in-between. The difficult circumstances of the Second Republic, compounded by increasing executive powers, began to degrade Poland's economic institutions almost immediately from reunification: the banking sector, which had been fairly stable in providing financial intermediation, suffered greatly from its internal failings and external situation, while the new Polish government also conducted monetary policy from 1918 to 1924 in a manner anathema to growth and stability. Similarly, property rights, the most important institution for a market economy, came under assault fairly rapidly via land reform and a constitution that downplayed these rights, while trade was used as a weapon rather than a tool for prosperity.

These accumulated difficulties culminated in the communist era, where the most crucial institutions were wiped out entirely or forced into small-scale informality under Moscow's heavy hand. This did not mean that, like under the Partitions, ideas of market-oriented institutions did not persist. Indeed, communist economic institutions had less fertile ground in Poland than elsewhere in the Warsaw Pact: as Wiles (1957) noted, there was no widespread acceptance of Marxian economics and, even after the imposition of communism, communist economics did not hold Polish econo-mists in thrall; they knew that the ration/price system was irrational and unworkable. Regardless of this fact, however, the Soviet Union and its willing Polish servants sought to impose communism in its entirety, targeting the specific institutions needed for a market economy for extinc-tion. In such a manner, it appeared that the political approach of institu-tional creation was finally triumphant: the political elites had decided that capitalism was bad for the masses (and definitely bad for themselves), and thus Marxist-Leninist economic institutions would be the only permissible ones on the territory of Poland.

However, the extreme concentration of political power led to predictable results in terms of economic performance, with the Polish economy under communism subjected to the recurring crises, which, ironically, were supposed to be endemic to late-stage capitalism. Curiously, these economic failings of communism in the 1970s appeared to be the main cause of the political collapse of the system in the 1980s. To put it another way, as communists believed and as we showed above, the history of Polish economic institutions has mostly been about the influence that political institutions have had in shaping these economic institutions; this has not been always the case, of course, as can be seen above with the Warsaw Stock Exchange and, additionally, as Zukowski (2004) notes, Poland's Partitions almost perfectly mirrored the level of development and thus economic institutions that had already existed in the unitary state (reinforcing rather than creating these divisions). For the most part, however, the role of the central executive or of the local politician played a primary role in deter-mining the path of property rights, the extent of trade, the types of labor contracts and relationships, and the state of the financial system and its ownership. But with the advent of the 1980s, economic reform from the grassroots led directly to political dissent and the unraveling of the system. Fifty years of economic failings helped to precipitate the assembling of independent economic organizations (trade unions), which, when coupled with explicitly economic actions (strikes) "made society realize that outbursts or upheavals could be effective" (Frentzel-Zagorska 1990:764). In the space of a decade, the political approach to institutional formation was replaced almost entirely by the economic approach, as the benefits of keeping communist economic institutions was far outweighed by the costs. Of course, as we will see, there needed to be political acquiescence before property rights or free trade could return, but it was economic factors that suddenly took the drivers' seat in fostering change rather than elite calculations about what was best for them.

This abrupt shift showed that, despite the lack of a coherent philosophy of economic liberalism from the elites of society[26] and despite periods of extreme political centralization, Poland might still be able to create many of the building blocks of a modern market economy. Indeed, many of these building blocks had already evolved during the country's long history, including the innovation in the financial sector that occurred under (and even flourished during) the Partitions, as well as Poland's success in trade in the fifteenth and sixteenth centuries and the brief experiment with the gold standard from 1927 to 1936. Even in property rights, although by no means protected as firmly as in other countries, there was some success in protecting these rights against the predations of the king and external aggressors. And while the staying power of economic institutions examined above was also variable – the gold standard lasted for just 9 years, while the stock exchange lasted for 122 years, took a 52-year pause, and then started up again – the fact that they did take root in Poland meant that they created an institutional memory for policy makers to access and an experience to be passed through the culture. As noted with property rights above, the historical experience of economic institutions in Poland did not necessarily mean that their (re-) introduction would be a success, but the fact that an institution had existed or thrived in the past made their existence more probable (as scholarship from Becker et al. (2014) and Grosfeld and Zhuravskaya (2015) has shown). On the other hand, where an institution never existed, it was difficult to create it out of whole cloth and have it accepted by the populace. It is precisely this legacy, of economic

---

[26] Indeed, the collapse of communism came about in direct opposition to these elites, who never had reform on their agenda (Frentzel-Zagorska 1990).

institutions that have never existed before, that has been weighing on modern-day Ukraine, as the next chapter will show.

References

Acemoglu, D. (2006). A simple model of inefficient institutions. *Scandinavian Journal of Economics*, 108(4), pp. 515–546.

Acemoglu, D., Johnson, S., and Robinson, J. (2002). *The Rise of Europe: Atlantic trade, Institutional Change and Economic Growth.* National Bureau of Economic Research Working Paper No. W9378.

(2005). Institutions as the fundamental cause of long-run growth. In Aghion, P., and Durlauf, S. (eds.), *Handbook of Economic Growth: Volume 1A.* North Holland: Elsevier, pp. 385–472.

Allen, R. C. (2001). The great divergence in European wages and prices from the Middle Ages to the First World War. *Explorations in Economic History*, 38(4), pp. 411–447.

Anderson, T. L., and Hill, P. J. (1975). The evolution of property rights: a study of the American West. *Journal of Law and Economics*, 18(1), pp. 163–179.

Andonova, V. (2003). *Property Rights and the Structure of Political Competition.* Universitat Pompeu Fabra, mimeo, https://www.researchgate.net/profile/Veneta_Andonova/publication/228557139_Property_Rights_and_the_Structure_of_Political_Competition/links/0046351e5a26c9d61c000000.pdf.

Angeles, L. (2011). Institutions, property rights, and economic development in historical perspective. *Kyklos*, 64(2), pp. 157–177.

Antrop, M. (2004). Landscape change and the urbanization process in Europe. *Landscape and Urban Planning*, 67(1), pp. 9–26.

Ardeleanu, C. (2014) The opening and development of the Black Sea for international trade and shipping (1774–1853). *Euxeinos*, 14, pp. 30–52.

Ascherson, N. (2011). *The Polish August.* Edinburgh: A&C Black Publishers.

Bajer, P. P. (2012). *Scots in the Polish-Lithuanian Commonwealth, Sixteenth to Eighteenth Centuries: The Formation and Disappearance of an Ethnic Group.* Leiden, the Netherlands: Brill Publishers.

Bandera, V. N. (1964). *Foreign Capital as an Instrument of National Economic Policy: A Study Based on the Experience of East European Countries between the World Wars.* Leiden, the Netherlands: Martinus Nijhoff Publishers.

Baten, J., and Wallusch, J. (2005). Market integration and disintegration of Poland and Germany in the eighteenth century. *Economies et Sociétés*, SerieHistoire Economique Quantitative, 33, pp. 1233–1264.

Becker, S. O., Boeckh, K., Hainz, C., and Woessmann, L. (2014). The empire is dead, long live the empire! Long-run persistence of trust and corruption in the bureaucracy. *Economic Journal.* Accepted article, http://onlinelibrary.wiley.com/doi/10.1111/ecoj.12220/abstract.

Berend, I. (1996). *Central and Eastern Europe, 1944–1993: Detour from the Periphery to the Periphery.* Cambridge: Cambridge University Press.

Bemanke, B., and James, H. (1991). The gold standard, deflation, and financial crisis in the Great Depression: An international comparison. In Hubbard, R.G. (ed.),

Financial Markets and Financial Crises. Chicago: University of Chicago Press, pp. 33–68.

Blackburn, C. (2004). Marriage, inheritance, and family discord: French elite and the transformation of the Polish *Szlachta. World History Review,* 1(3), pp. 2–19.

Blobaum, R. E. (2010). The rise of political parties, 1890–2014. In Biskupski, M. B. B, Pula, J. S., and Wróbe, P. J. (eds.), *The Origins of Modern Polish Democracy.* Athens: Ohio University Press, pp. 60–93.

Blum, J. (1957). The rise of serfdom in Eastern Europe. *The American Historical Review,* 62(4), pp. 807–836.

Bogucka, M. (1975). The monetary crisis of the xviith century and its social and psychological consequences in Poland. *Journal of European Economic History,* 4(1), pp. 137–152.

 (1983). The Baltic and Amsterdam in the first half of the seventeenth century. In Wiering, W.J. (ed.), *The Interactions of Amsterdam and Antwerp with the Baltic region, 1400–1800.* Amsterdam: Springer Netherlands, pp. 51–58.

 (2003). Women and credit operations in Polish Towns in early modern times (xvith-xviith centuries). *Journal of European Economic History,* 32(3), pp. 477–486.

Borrmann, A., Busse, M., and Neuhaus, S. (2006). Institutional quality and the gains from trade. *Kyklos,* 59(3), pp. 345–368.

Brada, J. C. (1991). The political economy of communist foreign trade institutions and policies. *Journal of Comparative Economics,* 15(2), pp. 211–238.

Brand, H. (2007). Baltic connections: Changing patterns in seaborne trade (c. 1450–1800). In Bes, L., Frankot, E., and Brand, H. (eds.), *Baltic Connections Archival Guide to the Maritime Relations of the Countries around the Baltic Sea (including the Netherlands) 1450–1800, Vol. I.* Leiden, the Netherlands: Brill Publishing, pp. 1–18.

Braudel, F. (1982). *Civilization and Capitalism, 15th–18th Century: The Perspective of the World.* Oakland: University of California Press.

Broadberry, S., and Gupta, B. (2006). The early modern great divergence: Wages, prices and economic development in Europe and Asia, 1500–1800. *Economic History Review,* 59(1), pp. 2–31.

Brus, W. (1986). Institutional change within a planned economy. In Kaser, M.C. (ed.), *The Economic History of Eastern Europe, 1919–1975, vol. 3.* Oxford: Clarendon Press.

Brzezinski, M. (1991). Constitutional heritage and renewal: The case of Poland. *Virginia Law Review,* 77(1), pp. 49–112.

Burns, E. M. (1945). Unemployment compensation and socio-economic objectives. *Yale Law Journal,* 55(1), pp. 1–20.

Carson, R. (1974). Property rights. In Mesa-Lago, C., and Beck, C. (eds.), *Comparative Socialist Systems: Essays on Politics and Economics.* Pittsburgh, PA: University of Pittsburgh Press.

Carter, F.W. (2006). *Trade and Urban Development in Poland: An Economic Geography of Cracow, from its Origins to 1795.* Cambridge: Cambridge University Press.

Cassel, G. (1936). *The Downfall of the Gold Standard.* Oxford: Oxford University Press.

Cherepnin, L. V. (1964). Russian seventeenth-century Baltic trade in Soviet historiography. *Slavonic and East European Review,* 43(100), pp. 1–22.

Chloupkova, J., Svendsen, G. L. H., and Svendsen, G. T. (2003). Building and destroying social capital: The case of cooperative movements in Denmark and Poland. *Agriculture and Human Values*, 20(3), pp. 241–252.

Cholewinski, R. (1998). The protection of human rights in the new Polish constitution. *Fordham International Law Journal*, 22(2), pp. 236–291.

Chor, D. (2005). Institutions, wages, and inequality: The case of Europe and its periphery (1500–1899). *Explorations in Economic History*, 42(4), pp. 547–566.

Cieślak, E. (1983). Aspects of Baltic sea-borne trade in the XVIIIth century. The trade relations between Sweden, Poland, Prussia and Russia. *Journal of European Economic History*, 12 (2), pp. 239–270.

Claessens, S., and Laeven, L. (2003). Financial development, property rights, and growth. *Journal of Finance*, 58(6), pp. 2401–2436.

Clapham, J. H (1966). *The Economic Development of France and Germany, 1815–1914*. Cambridge: Cambridge University Press.

Crago, L. A. (2000). The "Polishness" of production: Factory politics and the reinvention of working-class national and political identities in Russian Poland's textile industry, 1880–1910. *Slavic Review*, 59(1), pp. 16–41.

Craig, J. (1953). *The Mint: A History of the London Mint from A.D. 287 to 1948*. Cambridge: Cambridge University Press.

Daudin, G., O'Rourke, K. H., and De La Escosura, L. P. (2008). *Trade and Empire, 1700–1870*. Paris: Documents de Travail de l'OFCE No. 24.

De Ménil, G., and Maurel, M. (1994). Breaking up a customs union: The case of the Austro-Hungarian Empire in 1919. *Weltwirtschaftliches Archiv*, 130(3), pp. 553–575.

De Vries, J. (2012). *Taxing the Staff of Life: The Dutch bread tax, 1574–1855*. Paper for presentation to Yale Economic History Seminar, 23th April.http://economics.yale .edu/sites/default/files/files/Workshops-Seminars/Economic-History/devries-120423.pdf, accessed August 27, 2015.

Demsetz, H. (1967). Toward a theory of property rights. *American Economic Review*, 57(2) pp. 347–359.

Denemark, R. A., and Thomas, K. P. (1988). The Brenner-Wallerstein debate. *International Studies Quarterly*, 32(1), pp. 47–65.

Dennison, T. K. (2006). Did serfdom matter? Russian rural society, 1750–1860. *Historical Research*, 79(203), pp. 74–89.

Deutscher, T. (1984). In memoriam: Proletariat Party, 1882–1886. *New Left Review*, 1 (143), pp. 109–119.

Dickson, P. G. M. (1987). *Finance and Government under Maria Theresa, 1740–1780*. Oxford: Oxford University Press.

Dittmar, J. (2011). *Cities, Markets, and Growth: The Emergence of Zipf's Law*. Princeton, NJ: Institute for Advanced Study. http://www.jeremiahdittmar.com/files/ Zipf_Dittmar.pdf.

Djankov, S., La Porta, R., Lopez-de-Silanes, F., and Shleifer, A. (2003). Appropriate institutions. In Pleskovic, B., and Stern, N. (eds.), *Annual World Bank Conference on Development Economics 2003: The New Reform Agenda*. Washington, D.C.: World Bank, pp. 283–298.

Dziewanowski, M. K. (1951). The beginnings of socialism in Poland. *Slavonic and East European Review*, 29(73), pp. 510–531.

Eddie, S. M. (2004). Ethno-nationality and property rights in land in Prussian Poland, 1886–1918. In Engerman, S. L., and Metzger, J. (eds.), *Land Rights, Ethno-nationality and Sovereignty in History*. New York: Routledge, pp. 56–86.

Edvinsson, R. (2010). Foreign exchange rates in Sweden 1658–1803. In Edvinsson, R., Jacobson, T., and Waldenström, D. (eds.), *Historical Monetary and Financial Statistics for Sweden: Exchange Rates, Prices, and Wages, 1277–2008*. Stockholm: Sveriges Riksbank.

Eichengreen, B. (1992). The origins and nature of the Great Slump revisited. *Economic History Review*, 45(2), pp. 213–239.

Eichengreen, B., and Hatton, T. J. (1988). Interwar unemployment in international perspective: An overview. In Eichengreen, B., and Hatton, T.J. (eds.), *Interwar Unemployment in International Perspective*. Berlin: Springer Science & Business Media.

Elster, J., Offe, C., and Preuss, U. K. (1998). *Institutional Design in Post-Communist Societies: Rebuilding the Ship at Sea*. Cambridge: Cambridge University Press.

Epstein, S. R. (1998). Craft guilds, apprenticeship, and technological change in pre-industrial Europe. *Journal of Economic History*, 58(3), pp. 684–713.

Fałkowski, J. (2013). *Does it matter how much land your neighbour owns? The functioning of land markets in Poland from a social comparison perspective*. Factor Markets Working Document No. 59, August. Available at http://aei.pitt.edu/58600/1/Factor_Markets_59.pdf.

Ferderer, J. P., and Zalewski, D. A. (1994). Uncertainty as a propagating force in the Great Depression. *Journal of Economic History*, 54(4), pp. 825–849.

Frentzel-Zagorska, J. (1990). Civil society in Poland and Hungary. *Europe-Asia Studies*, 42(4), pp. 759–777.

Friedrich, K. (2006). *The Other Prussia: Royal Prussia, Poland and Liberty, 1569–1772*. Cambridge: Cambridge University Press.

Frost, R.I. (1995). The nobility of Poland-Lithuania, 1569–1795. In Scott, H. M. (ed.), *European Nobilities in the 17th and 18th Centuries: Northern, Central and Eastern Europe*. Basingstoke: Palgrave-Macmillan, pp. 266–310.

——— (2015). *The Oxford History of Poland-Lithuania*. Volume 1: *The Making of the Polish-Lithuanian Union, 1385–1569*. Oxford: Oxford University Press.

Furubotn, E. G., and Pejovich, S. (1972). Property rights and economic theory: A survey of recent literature. *Journal of Economic Literature*, 10(4), pp. 1137–1162.

Gallarotti, G. M. (1985). Toward a business-cycle model of tariffs. *International Organization*, 39(1), pp. 155–187.

Gardawski, J., Mrozowicki, A., and Czarzasty, J. (2012). History and current developments of trade unionism in Poland. *Warsaw Forum of Economic Sociology*, 3(1), pp. 9–50.

Gasiorowska-Grabowska, N. (1962). *Zrodla do dziejow klasy robotniczej na ziemiach polskich II* [Sources on the history of the working class in the Polish lands, Volume II]. Warsaw: Wydawnictwo Naukowe PWN.

Gelderblom, O., and Grafe, R. (2010). The rise and fall of the merchant guilds: Re-thinking the comparative study of commercial institutions in pre-modern Europe. *Journal of Interdisciplinary History*, 40(4), pp. 477–511.

Gibson, J., and McKenzie, D. (2011). The microeconomic determinants of emigration and return migration of the best and brightest: Evidence from the Pacific. *Journal of Development Economics*, 95(1), pp. 18–29.

Gigliotti, J. (2009). The role of high inflation in the decline of sixteenth century Poland-Lithuania's economy. *Polish Review*, 54(1), pp. 61–76.

Gorecki, P. (1983). Viator to Ascriptititus: Rural economy, lordship, and the origins of serfdom in medieval Poland. *Slavic Review*, 42(1), pp. 14–35.

Gorlach, K. (1989). On repressive tolerance: State and peasant farm in Poland. *Sociologia Ruralis*, 29(1), pp. 23–33.

Goryński, J. (1967). *Problemy gradostroitelstwa v svete sovremennoi urbanizatsii* [The nature and character of the urbanization process]. Warsaw: Polish Academy of Sciences.

Gosewinkel, D., and Meyer, S. (2009). Citizenship, property rights and dispossession in postwar Poland (1918 and 1945). *European Review of History – Revue européenne d'histoire*, 16(4), pp. 575–595.

Gourevitch, P. (1978). The international system and regime formation. *Comparative Politics*, 10(3), pp. 419–438.

Greene, V. R. (1961). Pre-World War I Polish emigration to the United States: Motives and statistics. *Polish Review*, 6(3), pp. 45–68.

Greif, A. (1994). Cultural beliefs and the organization of society: A historical and theoretical reflection on collectivist and individualist societies. *Journal of Political Economy*, 102(5), pp. 912–950.

(2006). History lessons: the birth of impersonal exchange: The community responsibility system and impartial justice. *Journal of Economic Perspectives*, 20(2), pp. 221–236.

(2007). *The Impact of Administrative Power on Political and Economic Development Toward Political Economy of Implementation.* Monograph, available at: http://papers.ssrn.com/sol3/papers.cfm?abstract_id=1004394.

Grosfeld, I., and Zhuravskaya, E. (2015). Cultural vs. economic legacies of empires: Evidence from the partition of Poland. *Journal of Comparative Economics*, 43(1), pp. 55–75.

Guinnane, T.W. (1994). A failed institutional transplant – Raiffeisens credit cooperatives in Ireland, 1894–1914. *Explorations in Economic History*, 31(1), pp. 38–61.

Gustafsson, B. (1987). The rise and economic behaviour of medieval craft guilds. *Scandinavian Economic History Review*, 35 (1), pp. 1–40.

Guzowski, P. (2014). Village court records and peasant credit in fifteenth-and sixteenth-century Poland. *Continuity and Change*, 29(1), pp. 115–142.

Hagen, W. W. (1972). National solidarity and organic work in Prussian Poland, 1815–1914. *Journal of Modern History*, 44(1), pp. 38–64.

(1976). The Partitions of Poland and the crisis of the Old Regime in Prussia 1772–1806. *Central European History*, 9(2), pp. 115–128.

(2007). *Ordinary Prussians: Brandenburg Junkers and Villagers, 1500–1840.* Cambridge: Cambridge University Press.

Halamska, M. (2001). Farmers and land: Between myths and reality. *Wieś i Rolnictwo* [Village and Agriculture], 4 (113), pp. 27–40.

Hanley, E., and Treiman, D. J. (2004). Did the transformation to post-communism in Eastern Europe restore pre-communist property relations? *European Sociological Review*, 20(3), pp. 237–252.

Hann, C. M. (1998). *Property Relations: Renewing the Anthropological Tradition.* Cambridge: Cambridge University Press.

Harrison, M. (2012). *Communism and Economic Modernization.* Competitive Advantage in the Global Economy (CAGE) Online Working Paper Series No. 92. Available at: http://wrap.warwick.ac.uk/57860/1/WRAP_92.2012_harri son.pdf.

Hartwell, C. A. (2013). *Institutional Barriers in the Transition to Market: Explaining Performance and Divergence in Transition Economies.* Basingstoke: Palgrave Macmillan.

(2014). Do (successful) stock exchanges support or hinder institutions in transition economies? *Cogent Economics & Finance,* 2(2).

(2015). Property rights. In Hoelscher, J. (ed.), *Palgrave Dictionary of Emerging Markets and Transition Economics.* Basingstoke: Palgrave Macmillan, pp. 193–215.

Hehn, P.N. (2005). *A Low, Dishonest Decade: The Great Powers, Eastern Europe and the Economic Origins of World War II.* Edinburgh: A&C Black Publishers.

Helleiner, E. (2002). Economic nationalism as a challenge to economic liberalism? Lessons from the 19th century. *International Studies Quarterly,* 46(3), pp. 307–329.

Heinemeyer, H. C. (2007). The treatment effect of borders on trade. The Great War and the disintegration of Central Europe. *Cliometrica,* 1(3), pp. 177–210.

Henderson, W. O. (1962). *The Genesis of the Common Market.* Chicago: Quadrangle Books.

Ho, P., and Spoor, M. (2006). Whose land? The political economy of land titling in transitional economies. *Land Use Policy,* 23(4), pp. 580–587.

Hojka, Z. (2006) *Polski ruch zawodowy w województwie śląskim (1922–1939): Oblicze polityczne* [Polish Trade Union Movements in the Silesian Voivodship (1922–1939): A Political Face]. Katowice: Wydawnictwo Uniwersytetu Śląskiego.

Holzman, F. D. (1976). *International Trade Under Communism: Politics and Economics.* London: Macmillan Press.

Homer, S., and Sylla, R. (2005). *A History of Interest Rates.* London: John Wiley & Sons.

Inglot, T. (2008). *Welfare States in East Central Europe, 1919–2004.* Cambridge: Cambridge University Press.

Irwin, D. A. (2011). *Trade Policy Disaster: Lessons from the 1930s.* Cambridge: MIT Press.

Jacks, D. (2004). Market integration in the North and Baltic Seas, 1500–1800. *Journal of European Economic History,* 33(3), pp. 285–329.

Jakubowska, L. (2012). *Patrons of History: Nobility, Capital and Political Transitions in Poland.* Surrey, UK: Ashgate Publishing.

Jedlicki, J. (1999). *A Suburb of Europe: Nineteenth-century Polish Approaches to Western Civilization.* Budapest: Central European University Press.

Jonker, J. and Sluyterman, K. (2001). *At Home on the World Markets: Dutch International Trading Companies from the 16th Century Until the Present.* Montreal: McGill University Press.

Jorion, P., and Goetzmann, W. N. (1999). Global stock markets in the twentieth century. *Journal of Finance,* 54(3), pp. 953–980.

Kaczmarczyk, Z. (1945). *Kolonizacja niemiecka na wschód od Odry [German Colonization east of the Oder].* Poznań: Instytut Zachodni.

Kamiński, A. (1975). Neo-serfdom in Poland-Lithuania. *Slavic Review,* 34(2), pp. 253–268.

Kappeler, A. (2014). *The Russian Empire: A Multi-ethnic History.* New York: Routledge.

Karski, J. (2014). *The Great Powers and Poland: From Versailles to Yalta.* New York: Rowan & Littlefield.

Keefer, P., and Knack, S. (2002). Polarization, politics and property rights: Links between inequality and growth. *Public Choice,* 111(1–2), pp. 127–154.

Keller, W., and Shiue, C. H. (2008). *Institutions, technology, and trade.* National Bureau of Economic Research Working Paper No. w13913.

Kindleberger, C. P. (1991). The Economic Crisis of 1619 to 1623. *Journal of Economic History,* 51(1), pp. 149–175.

——— (2005). *A Financial History of Western Europe.* Oxford: Taylor and Francis.

Kirby, D. (2014). *The Baltic World 1772–1993: Europe's Northern Periphery in an Age of Change.* New York: Routledge.

Klimesz, H. (1970). Poland's trade through the Black Sea in the eighteenth century. *Polish Review,* 15(2), pp. 55–80.

Kochanowicz, J. (1997). Incomplete demise: Reflections on the welfare state in Poland after communism. *Social Research,* 64(4), pp. 1445–1469.

——— (2006a). *Backwardness and Modernization: Poland and Eastern Europe in the Sixteenth–Twentieth Centuries.* Surrey, UK: Ashgate Publishing.

——— (2006b). *Polish kingdom: Periphery as a leader.* Presentation to the Fourteenth International Economic History Congress, Helsinki, Finland, August 21–25. Available at http://www.helsinki.fi/iehc2006/papers3/Kochan.pdf.

Komlos, J. (2014). *The Habsburg Monarchy as a Customs Union: Economic Development in Austria-Hungary in the Nineteenth Century.* Princeton, NJ: Princeton University Press.

Kopyściański, M. (2015). Genesis of institution of bill of exchange and bill of exchange law. In Blažek, J. (ed.), *System of Financial Law: Financial Markets Conference Proceedings.* Brno: Masaryk University Faculty of Law.

Kowal, S. (2002) Economic co-operation between Poland, the former partition states and their successors in the inter-war period. In Müller, U., and Schultz, H. (eds), *National Borders and Economic Disintegration in Modern East Central Europe.* Berlin: Berlin Verlag, pp. 143–154.

Koziński, M. H. (2000). Rodzaje Akcji [Types of Shares]. In Bączyk, M., Koziński, M. H., Michalski, M., Pyzioł, W., Szumański, A., and Weiss, I. (eds.), *Papiery wartościowe* [Securities]. Kraków: Kantor Wydawniczy Zakamycze.

Kruszewski, C. (1943). The German-Polish Tariff War (1925–1934) and its aftermath. *Journal of Central European Affairs,* 3, pp. 294–315.

Kubiak, H. (1999). Parties, party systems, and cleavages in Poland: 1918–1989. In Lawson, K., Römmele, A., and Karasimeonov, G. (eds.), *Cleavages, Parties, and Voters: Studies from Bulgaria, the Czech Republic, Hungary, Poland, and Romania.* Santa Barbara, CA: Greenwood Publishing.

Kuninski, M. (1997). Liberalism in Poland: What is left? *Studies in East European Thought,* 49(4), pp. 241–257.

Łagowski, P. (2013). Geneza rynku papierów wartościowych w Polsce [The genesis of the securities market in Poland]. *Ekonomia – Wrocław Economic Review,* 19(4), pp. 69–79.

Landau, Z. (1982). The inflow of foreign capital into Poland after the coup d'état of May 1926. *Acta Poloniae Histórica,* 46, pp. 159–78.

(1990). Integracja Gospodarcza Polski w Latach 1918–1923 [Polish economic integration in the years 1918–1923]. *Studia Historyczne*, 33(1), pp. 63–76.

Landau, Z., and Tomaszewski, J. (1984). Poland between inflation and stabilization. In Feldman, G. D., and Bouwsma, W. J. (eds.), *Die Erfahrung der Inflation im internationalen Zusammenhang und Vergleich*. Berlin: Walter de Gruyter, pp. 270–294.

Lange, O. (1936). On the economic theory of socialism I. *Review of Economic Studies*, 4 (1), pp. 53–71.

Lannoye, V. (2005). *The History of Money for Understanding Economics*. Brussels: Le Cri Publishers.

Lenartowicz K. (1924). *Historia królewskiej poczty w Gdańsku od r. 1654 do 1793 pisana na podstawie niemieckich źródeł historycznych* [The history of royal mail in Gdansk from 1654 to 1793 written on the basis of German historical sources]. Gdańsk: Towarzystwo Akcyjny Drukarnia Gdańska.

Lerski, J.J. (1996). *Historical Dictionary of Poland, 966-1945*. Westport, CT: Greenwood Publishing.

Leslie, R. F. (1954). Left-wing political tactics in Poland, 1831–1846. *Slavonic and East European Review*, 33(80), pp. 120–139.

(1955). Politics and economics in Congress Poland, 1815–1864. *Past and Present*, 8, pp. 43–63.

Levchenko, A. A. (2007). Institutional quality and international trade. *Review of Economic Studies*, 74(3), pp. 791–819.

Lewak, A. (1930). The Polish Rising of 1830. *Slavonic and East European Review*, 9(26), pp. 350–360.

Libecap, G. D. (1986). Property rights in economic history: Implications for research. *Explorations in Economic History*, 23(3), pp. 227–252.

Liepmann, H. (1938). *Tariff Levels and the Economic Unity of Europe*. Edinburgh: George Allen & Unwin.

Lindberg, E. (2007). Merchant guilds and urban growth in the Baltic Sea area. In Brand, H., and Müller, L. (eds.), *The Dynamics of Economic Culture in the North Sea and Baltic Region in the Late Middle Ages and Early Modern Period*. Hilversum, the Netherlands: Uitgeverij Verloren.

(2009). Club goods and inefficient institutions: Why Danzig and Lübeck failed in the early modern period. *Economic History Review*, 62(3), pp. 604–628.

Litwack, J. M. (1991). Discretionary behaviour and Soviet economic reform. *Europe-Asia Studies*, 43(2), pp. 255–279.

Lukowski, J. (2003). *The European Nobility in the Eighteenth Century*. Basingstoke: Palgrave Macmillan.

Lukowski, J., and Zawadzki, H. (2006). *A Concise History of Poland*. Cambridge: Cambridge University Press.

Machaj, M. (2015). Liberal economics in Poland. *Econ Journal Watch*, 12(2), pp. 233–241.

Mączak, A. (1968). Export of grain and the problem of distribution of national income in Poland in the years 1550–1650. *Acta Poloniae Historica*, 18, pp. 75–98.

(1970). The balance of Polish sea trade with the West, 1565–1646. *Scandinavian Economic History Review*, 18(2), pp. 107–142.

(1976). Money and society in Poland and Lithuania in the 16th and 17th centuries, *Journal of European Economic History*, 5(1), pp. 69–104.

Mahoney, J.T. (2004). *Economic Foundations of Strategy*. London: SAGE Publications.

Majkowski, E. (1934). Coins struck by Boleslav the Mighty, Duke of Poland (992–1025), with bust and name of Aethelred II of England. *Numismatic Chronicle and Journal of the Royal Numismatic Society*, 14(55), pp. 168–182.

Makkai, L. (1975). Neo-serfdom: Its origin and nature in East Central Europe. *Slavic Review*, 34(2), pp. 225–238.

Malinowski, M. (2015). *Freedom and decline: Polish state formation and rye market disintegration, 1500–1772*. University of Utrecht monograph. Available at https://www.academia.edu/9107881/Freedom_and_decline_Polish_state_formation_and_rye_market_disintegration_1500–1772.

Małowist, M. (1958). Poland, Russia and Western Trade in the 15th and 16th centuries. *Past and Present*, 13, pp. 26–41.

    (1959). The economic and social development of the Baltic countries from the fifteenth to the seventeenth centuries. *Economic History Review*, 12(2), pp. 177–189.

    (1966). The problem of the inequality of economic development in Europe in the Later Middle Ages. *Economic History Review*, 19(1), pp. 15–28.

Marzec, W., and Zysiak, A. (2014). Days of labour: Topographies of power in modern peripheral capitalism. The case of the industrial city of Łódź. *Journal of Historical Sociology*, Early View online, DOI: 10.1111/johs.12080.

Massey, D. S. (1988). Economic development and international migration in comparative perspective. *Population and Development Review*, 14(3), pp. 383–413.

Matey, M. (1986). The prospects for labor law reform in Poland. *Northwestern Journal of International Law and Business*, 7(4), pp. 621–632.

Mavor, J. (1914). *An Economic History of Russia*. Vol. 2. London: JM Dent & Sons, Ltd.

Michaud, C. (2000). The kingdoms of Central Europe in the fourteenth century. In Jones, M. (ed.), *The New Cambridge Medieval History* Vol. 6: *c. 1300 – c. 1415*. Cambridge: Cambridge University Press, pp. 735–763.

Micińska, M. (2009). The Polish intelligentsia in the years 1864–1918. *Acta Poloniae Historica*, 100, pp. 171–206.

Mijiyawa, A. G. (2013). Determinants of property rights institutions: Survey of literature and new evidence. *Economics of Governance*, 14(2), pp. 127–183.

Miletić, A. R. (2014). De-globalization in the periphery – Tariff protectionism in Southeast and East-Central Europe 1914–1928. *Tokovi istorije*, 3, pp. 69–87.

Miller, J. (2013). *Urban Societies in East-Central Europe, 1500–1700*. Surrey, UK: Ashgate Publishing.

Millward, R. (1982). An economic analysis of the organization of serfdom in Eastern Europe. *Journal of Economic History*, 42(3), pp. 513–548.

Morawski, W. (2008). *Od marki do złotego. Historia finansów Drugiej rzeczypospolitej* [From mark to złoty: The history of finance in the Second Republic]. Warsaw: Wydawnictwo Naukowe PWN.

Müller, U. (2015). The concept of regional industrialization from the perspective of the economic history of East Central Europe. In Czierpka, J., Oerters, K., and Thorade, N. (eds.), *Regions, Industries, and Heritage: Perspectives on Economy, Society, and Culture in Modern Western Europe*. Basingstoke: Palgrave Macmillan, pp. 90–113.

Murphy, C. G. (2011). *Progress without consent: Enlightened Centralism vis-à-vis Local self-government in the towns of East Central Europe and Russia, 1764–1840*.

Dissertation, Georgetown University. Available at https://repository.library .georgetown.edu/bitstream/handle/10822/558068/Murphy_georgetown_0076D_ 11517.pdf?sequence=1.

(2012). Burghers versus bureaucrats: Enlightened centralism, the royal towns, and the case of the Propinacja Law in Poland-Lithuania, 1776–1793. *Slavic Review*, 71(2), pp. 385–409.

Neal, L. (1987). The integration and efficiency of the London and Amsterdam Stock Markets in the eighteenth century. *Journal of Economic History*, 47(1), pp. 97–115.

Nitsch, V., and Wolf, N. (2013). Tear down this wall: On the persistence of borders in trade. *Canadian Journal of Economics/Revue canadienne d'économique*, 46(1), pp. 154–179.

North, D. C. (1971). Institutional change and economic growth. *Journal of Economic History*, 31(1), pp. 118–125.

(1981). *Structure and Change in Economic History*. New York: W. W. Norton.

North, D. C., and Thomas, R. P. (1973). *The Rise of the Western World: A New Economic History*. Cambridge: Cambridge University Press.

Ogilvie, S. (1995). Institutions and economic development in early modern Central Europe. *Transactions of the Royal Historical Society*, 5, pp. 221–250.

(2007). 'Whatever is, is right'? Economic institutions in pre-industrial Europe. *Economic History Review*, 60(4), pp. 649–684.

Ogilvie, S., and Carus, A. W. (2014). Institutions and economic growth in historical perspective. In Aghion, P., and Durlauf, F. (eds.), *Handbook of Economic Growth*. Vol. 2A. North Holland: Elsevier, pp. 403–513.

Ostrom, E., and Hess, C. (2010). Private and Common Property Rights. In Bouckaert, B. (ed.), *Encyclopedia of Law & Economics*. Cheltenham, UK: Edward Elgar, pp. 53–106.

Palat, M. K. (2007). Casting workers as an estate in late imperial Russia. *Kritika: Explorations in Russian and Eurasian History*, 8(2), pp. 307–348.

Pamuk, Ş. (1997). In the absence of domestic currency: Debased European coinage in the seventeenth-century Ottoman Empire. *Journal of Economic History*, 57(2), pp. 345–366.

Paun, N., Corpădean, A. G., & Păun, D. (2009). World economy and the Depression years: Mechanisms. National and worldwide tactics. *Studia Universitatis Babes-Bolyai-Studia Europaea*, 3, pp. 5–19.

Pobog-Malinowski, W. (2004). *Najnowsza Historia Polityczna Polski*. Krakow: Wydawnictwo Platan.

Podolski, T.M. (1973). *Socialist Banking and Monetary Control: The Experience of Poland*. Cambridge: Cambridge University Press.

Polach, J. G. (1955). The beginnings of trade unionism among the Slavs of the Austrian Empire. *American Slavic and East European Review*, 14(2), pp. 239–259.

Polish Research and Information Service (PRIS) (1948). *Social Legislation in Poland*. New York: PRIS.

Pronin, D. T. (1949). Land Reform in Poland: 1920–1945. *Land Economics*, 25(2), pp. 133–143.

Pytlas, S. (1993). Przemyslowcy łódźcy a kwestia robotnicza w II polowie XIX wieku. In Samuś, P. (ed.), *'Bunt łódźki' 1892 roku*. Łódź: Wydawnictwo Uniwersytetu Łódzkiego, pp. 61.

Ranjan, P., and Lee, J. Y. (2007). Contract enforcement and international trade. *Economics & Politics*, 19(2), pp. 191–218.

Reddaway, W. F. (1971). *The Cambridge History of Poland*. Cambridge: Cambridge University Press.

Reinhart, C.M., and Rogoff, K.S. (2008). *This Time Is Different: A Panoramic View of Eight Centuries of Financial Crises*. National Bureau of Economic Research Working Paper 13882.

Riha, T. J. (1996). The origins of private property and wealth in post-communist society. *International Journal of Social Economics*, 23(4–6), pp. 245–268.

Rogowski, W. (2002). *Fergusson-Tepper's Falenty: The episode of free banking in Poland in the 18th century*. Paper for the National Bank of Poland Conference 2002, available at https://www.nbp.pl/konferencje/falenty2002/esej_en.pdf. Accessed August 21, 2015.

Rojahn, J. (1990). Poland. In Van der Linden, M., and Rojahn, J. (eds), *The Formation of Labour Movements, 1870–1914: An International Perspective*. Leiden: Brill Publishers, pp. 487–521.

Roland, G. (2004). Understanding institutional change: Fast-moving and slow-moving institutions. *Studies in Comparative International Development*, 38(4), pp. 109–131.

Roszkowski, W. (2008). Reflections on Poland's Development after 1918 and after 1989. *Polish Quarterly of International Affairs*, 1, pp. 41–54.

Rothbard, M. N. (1978). Austrian definitions of the supply of money. In Spadaro, L. M. (ed.), *New Directions in Austrian Economics*. Kansas City, MO: Sheed Andrews and McMeel, pp. 143–156.

Rothschild, J. (1963). The ideological, political, and economic background of Pilsudski's coup d'état of 1926. *Political Science Quarterly*, 78(2), pp. 224–244.

Rousseau, J.-J. (1972). *The Government of Poland*. Indianapolis: Hackett Publishing (original work published 1772).

Rutkowski, J. (1991). *The Distribution of Incomes in a Feudal System*. Wrocław: Ossolineum.

Rydel, E. (1925). Kilka słów o sytuacji bankowej [A few words on the banking situation]. *Gazeta Bankowa*, 5(18), pp. 365–366.

Rynarzewski, T. (1986). *The debt crisis in Poland: Causes, consequences, prospects*. Kiel Working Papers No. 257.

Sadowski, Z. (1959). *Rozprawy o pieniadzu w Polsce pierwszej polowy XVII wieku* [Treatises on money in Poland in the first half of the 17th century]. Warsaw: Państwowe Wydawnictwo Naukowe.

Sargent, T. J. (1982). The ends of four big inflations. In Hall, R. E. (ed.), *Inflation: Causes and Effects*. Chicago: University of Chicago Press, pp. 41–98.

Schofer, L. (1972). Patterns of worker protest: Upper Silesia, 1865–1914. *Journal of Social History*, 5(4), pp. 447–463.

Schwartz, A.J. (1987). Real and pseudo-financial crises. In Schwartz, A. J. (ed.), *Money in Historical Perspective*. Chicago, University of Chicago, pp. 271–288.

Sedlar, J. W. (2011). *East Central Europe in the Middle Ages, 1000–1500*. Seattle: University of Washington Press.

Sened, I. (2008). *The Political Institution of Private Property.* Cambridge: Cambridge University Press.

Seppel, M. (2004). The assistance of manors to peasants in cases of subsistence crisis in seventeenth-century Livonia. *Acta Historica Tallinnensia,* 8, pp. 3–19.

Sonin, K. (2003). Why the rich may favor poor protection of property rights. *Journal of Comparative Economics,* 31(4), pp. 715–731.

Spooner, F. C. (1972). *The International Economy and Monetary Movements in France, 1493–1725.* Cambridge,: Harvard University Press.

Spufford, P. (1989). *Money and Its Use in Medieval Europe.* Cambridge: Cambridge University Press.

Stanziani, A. (2010). Revisiting Russian serfdom: Bonded peasants and market dynamics, 1600s–1800s. *International Labor and Working-Class History,* 78(1), pp. 12–27.

Stauter-Halsted, K. (2004). *The Nation in the Village: The Genesis of Peasant National Identity in Austrian Poland, 1848–1914.* Ithaca, NY: Cornell University Press.

Stone, D. Z. (2001). *The Polish-Lithuanian State, 1386–1795.* Seattle: Washington University Press.

Sułek, A. (2007). The Marienthal 1931/1932 Study and Contemporary Studies on Unemployment in Poland. *Polish Sociological Review,* 1(157), pp. 3–25.

Supple, B. E. (1957). Currency and commerce in the early seventeenth century. *Economic History Review,* 10(2), pp. 239–255.

Svensson, R. (2013). *Renovatio Monetae: Bracteates and Coinage Policies in Medieval Europe.* London: Spinks Publishing.

Świątkowski, A. (1995). Employment and collective labor law in post-communist Poland. In Frankowski, S., and Stephan III, P. B. (eds.), *Legal Reform in Post-Communist Europe: The View from Within.* Leiden, the Netherlands: Martinus Nijhoff Publishers.

(2010). *Social Security Law in Poland.* Alphen aan den Rijn, South Holland: Kluwer Law International.

Szacki, J. (1995). *Liberalism after communism.* Budapest: Central European University Press.

Szlajfer, H. (1990). *Economic Nationalism in East-Central Europe and South America: 1918–1939.* Paris: Librairie Droz.

Tarkowski, J. (1990). Endowment of nomenklatura, or apparatchiks turned into entrepreneurchiks, or from communist ranks to capitalist riches. *Innovation: The European Journal of Social Science Research,* 3(1), pp. 89–105.

Taylor, E. (1926). *Druga inflacja Polska. Przyczyny – przebieg – środki zaradcze* [The Second Inflation in Poland. Causes – Course – Remedies]. Poznań: Gebethner i Wolff.

Thaden, E.C. (2014). *Russia's Western Borderlands, 1710–1870.* Princeton, NJ: Princeton University Press.

Thorne, A. (1993). Eastern Europe's experience with banking reform: Is there a role for banks in the transition? *Journal of Banking & Finance,* 17(5), pp. 959–1000.

Tietenberg, T. H. (1992). *Environmental and Natural Resource Economics.* New York: Harper Collins.

Tomka, B., and Szikra, D. (2009). Social policy in East Central Europe: Major trends in the 20th Century. In Cerami, A., and Vanhuysee, P. (eds.), *Post-Communist*

Welfare Pathways: Theorizing Social Policy Transformations in Central and Eastern Europe. Basingstoke: Palgrave Macmillan, pp. 17–34.

Topolski, J. (1974). The manorial-serf economy in Central and Eastern Europe in the 16th and 17th centuries. *Agricultural History*, 48(3), pp. 341–352.

(1987). *An Outline History of Poland.* New York: Hippocrene Books.

Trethewey, R. (1974). The establishment of serfdom in Eastern Europe and Russia. *American Economist*, 18(1), pp. 36–41.

Tych, F. (1970). Some conditions and regularities of development of the Polish working class movement. *Acta Poloniae Historica*, 22, pp. 158–179.

Unger, R. W. (1983). Integration of Baltic and Low Countries grain markets, 1400–1800. In Wiering, W. J. (ed.), *The Interactions of Amsterdam and Antwerp with the Baltic region, 1400–1800.* Amsterdam: Springer Netherlands, pp. 1–10.

van Tielhof, M. (2002). *The "Mother of All Trades": The Baltic Grain Trade in Amsterdam from the Late 16th to the Early 19th Century.* Leiden, the Netherlands: Brill Publishing.

Van Zanden, J. L. (2005). Early modern economic growth: A survey of the European Economy, 1500–1800. In Prak, M. (ed.), *Early Modern Capitalism: Economic and Social Change in Europe 1400–1800.* New York: Routledge, pp. 67–84.

Volckart, O. (1997). Early beginnings of the quantity theory of money and their context in Polish and Prussian monetary policies, c. 1520–1550. *Economic History Review*, 50(3), pp. 430–449.

Walder, A. G. (1994). The decline of communist power: Elements of a theory of institutional change. *Theory and Society*, 23(2), pp. 297–323.

Wallerstein, I. (1972). Three paths of national development in sixteenth-century Europe. *Studies in Comparative International Development (SCID)*, 7(2), pp. 95–101.

(1974). *The Modern World System.* Vol. 1, *Capitalist Agriculture and the origins of the European world-economy in the sixteenth century.* Bradford, UK: Emerald Group Publishing.

Wandycz, P.S. (1974). *The Lands of Partitioned Poland, 1795–1918.* Seattle: University of Washington Press.

(1980). *The United States and Poland.* Cambridge: Harvard University Press.

Wąsowska, A., and Obłoj, K. (2013), Resource based determinants of internationalization of Polish companies. *Journal of International Doctoral Research*, 2(1), pp. 8–34.

Way, E. D. (2012). *Why rich nations fail: Explaining Dutch economic decline in the 18th century.* Mimeo, http://works.bepress.com/edwin_way/1/. Accessed August 28, 2015.

Weber, M. (1958). *The Religion of India.* Glencore: Free Press.

Weingast, B. R. (1995). The economic role of political institutions: Market-preserving federalism and economic development. *Journal of Law, Economics, & Organization*, 11(1), pp. 1–31.

Weinryb, B. D. (1973). *The Jews of Poland: A Social and Economic History of the Jewish Community in Poland from 1100 to 1800.* Philadelphia: The Jewish Publication Society.

Wellisz, S., and Iwanek, M. (1993). The privatization of the Polish economy. *Eastern Economic Journal*, 19(3), pp. 345–354.

Wiles, P. J. (1957). Changing economic thought in Poland. *Oxford Economic Papers*, 9(2), pp. 190–208.

Williamson, D. C. (2011). *Poland Betrayed: The Nazi-Soviet Invasions of 1939.* Mechanicsburg, PA: Stackpole Books.

Williamson, O. E. (1991). Economic institutions: Spontaneous and intentional governance. *Journal of Law, Economics, and Organization*, 7(special issue), pp. 159–187.

Winiecki, J. (1990). Why economic reforms fail in the Soviet system – A property rights-based approach. *Economic Inquiry*, 28(2), pp. 195–221.

Wolf, N. (2005). Path dependent border effects: The case of Poland's reunification (1918–1939). *Explorations in Economic History*, 42(3), pp. 414–438.

(2007a). Should I stay or should I go? Understanding Poland's adherence to gold, 1928–1936. *Historical Social Research/Historische Sozialforschung*, 32(4), pp. 351–368.

(2007b). Endowments vs. market potential: What explains the relocation of industry after the Polish reunification in 1918?. *Explorations in Economic history*, 44(1), pp. 22–42.

Wróbel, P. (1994). The Jews of Galicia under Austrian-Polish rule, 1869–1918. *Austrian History Yearbook*, 25, pp. 97–138.

(2014). *Historical Dictionary of Poland 1945–1996.* Westport, CT: Greenwood Publishing.

Wu, Y. S. (1990). The linkage between economic and political reform in the socialist countries: A supply-side explanation. *Annals of the American Academy of Political and Social Science*, 57, pp. 91–102.

Wyrobisz, A. (1989). Power and towns in the Polish Gentry Commonwealth. *Theory and Society*, 18(5), pp. 611–630.

Wysokinska, A. (2011) *Invisible Wall: Role of Culture in Long-Term Development.* Ph.D. dissertation, University of Warsaw.

Zabawa, J., and Bywalec, M. (2013). Development of cooperative banking in Poland. In Druhov, O. and Bula, P. (eds), *The Development of the Financial Systems of the Countries of Central and East Europe.* L'viv: L'viv Institute of Banking.

Żarnowska, A. (1965). *Geneza rozłamu w Polskiej Partii Socjalistycznej 1904–1906* [Genesis of the split in the Polish Socialist Party 1904–1906]. Warsaw: Państwowe Wydawnictwo Naukowe.

(1980). Determinants of the political activity of the working class in the Polish territories on the turn of the 19th century. *Acta Poloniae Historica*, 42, pp. 97–110.

(1984). Working-class culture or workers' culture: The problem of working-class culture in Poland at the turn of the 20th Century. *Acta Poloniae Historica*, 50, pp. 231–256.

(2001). Some aspects of the democratization of political life in Congress Poland at the beginning of the 20th century. *Acta Poloniae Historica*, 84, pp. 79–100.

Zawadzka, A. (2007). The unemployment in the inter-war period and at the end of the 20th century: Problems, attitudes, narratives. analysis of the memoirs of the unemployed. *Polish Sociological Review*, 1 (157), pp. 27–43.

Zawojska, A. (2004). Process of land reform in Poland. *Electronic Journal of Polish Agricultural Universities*, 7(1). Available at http://www.ejpau.media.pl/volume7/issue1/economics/abs-01.html.

Zdziechowski, J. (1925). *Finanse Polski w latach 1924 i 1925* [Polish finance in the years 1924 and 1925]. Warsaw: Instytut wydawniczy "Bibljoteka polska."

Zelnik, R. E. (1971). *Labor and Society in tsarist Russia: The Factory Workers of St. Petersburg, 1855–1870*, Vol. 1. Palo Alto, CA: Stanford University Press.

Zubrzycki, J. (1953). Emigration from Poland in the nineteenth and twentieth centuries. *Population Studies*, 6(3), pp. 248–272.

Zukowski, R. (2004). Historical path dependence, institutional persistence, and transition to market economy: The case of Poland. *International Journal of Social Economics*, 31(10), pp. 955–973.

Żytkowicz, L. (1972). The peasant's farm and the landlord's farm in Poland from the 16th to the middle of the 18th century. *Journal of European Economic History*, 1(1), pp. 135–154.

4

A Brief Institutional History of Eastern Europe: Ukraine and Its Institutions to 1989

The previous two chapters have taken an in-depth look at Poland and the evolution of its political and economic institutions in the centuries prior to the fall of communism in 1989. In order to understand the relative performance of Poland *vis-à-vis* its eastern neighbor after the collapse of the command economy, it is now time to turn our gaze to Ukraine, performing a similar analysis as in Chapters 2 and 3 for the institutions centered on the city of Kyiv and its territories. How did Ukraine's political institutions develop during the years 1400 to 1989, and were there similarities with its Polish neighbors? More important for the development of a market economy, did Ukraine's economic institutions protect private property and commerce?

However, unlike the Polish-Lithuanian Commonwealth, which had a defined (although shifting) set of borders and a persistent linguistic and political lineage, the idea of "Ukraine" had no such consistency. Indeed, Von Hagen (1995) famously asked, "Does Ukraine have a history?" as, for much of the millennium, Ukraine was a frontier land, trapped between Polish kings and Russian tsars. Whereas Poland had both a nation *and* a state, Ukraine was adrift without a common identity, encompassing Ruthenians, Byelorussians, Cossacks, and even Hungarians and other Uralic peoples. At times, the only common factor of the peoples on Ukrainian territory was a definition in opposition to the "other," noting what Ukraine was *not* (usually, defined in relation to Russia) but with little explicit definition of what Ukraine *was* (Kuzio 2001). In the words of Szporluk (1997:86), "the national identity of modern Ukrainians was formulated by those who, in defining Ukraine, rejected both the Russian identity and the Polish identity."

Moreover, for a substantial portion of the period under examination here, Ukraine's borders were also a theoretical exercise, as parts of

227

modern-day Ukraine were joined together within the Polish-Lithuanian Commonwealth, parts were autonomous, and other parts were aligned with or physically absorbed into the Russian Empire. Von Hagen (1995:668) has gone so far as to claim that "historians of modern Ukraine cannot establish firm state or institutional continuity from the pre-modern period," given the fact that (like Poland) it ceased its own autonomous political development at the precise moment that the rest of Europe was forging the modern nation-state. *Contra* von Hagen, however, this does not mean that there is no thread of institution-building that cannot be discerned. Rather, like Poland and as explored in the previous chapters, with no coherent nation nor independent state of their own, Ukraine's institutional development was much more dependent upon the path that outsiders chose for it throughout its history.

This reality gives us an early clue as to tracing the path of Ukraine's recent institutional evolution, in that many institutions that are needed to function as a market economy have only shallow roots in the чорнозем (black earth) of Ukraine. For the purposes of this chapter, it also means that our examination of the territory of Ukraine and its predecessors, especially in the development of political institutions, will necessarily be truncated somewhat, as compared to the long Polish history that we have already analyzed. Regardless, the fact that outside influence has been predominant in shaping Ukrainian institutional development also highlights the truth, shown during Poland's Partitions, that *who* the outsider was that was doing the influence matters for institutional evolution.

POLITICAL INSTITUTIONS IN UKRAINE: FROM EARLY SUCCESS TO STAGNATION?

The basis for modern Ukraine, the Kievan Rus', was in many respects a forward-thinking monarchy that established various political institutions still in play today in advanced economies. Under the reign of Yaroslav the Wise in the late tenth and early eleventh centuries, the proto-Ukrainian monarch created the *Руська Правда* (*Rus'ka Pravda*) or the first code of law known to Eastern Slavs. Drawing from the customary laws already in place in the Kievan lands, the code made important alterations to harmonize rules across the kingdom and reflected "the increasing involvement of the ruler in the lives of his subjects" (Subtelny 2009:20). The law had three iterations, evolving over two centuries, with a "short" (*kratkaya*) version appearing first, a full (*prostrannaya*) version incorporating the short version and expanding the basis of rights being codified in 1036, and an "abridged" (*Sokrashchennaya*) version, which appeared in the second half of the twelfth century (Badalova 2013). As Antonovych (2010) also notes, an underlying basis of the code was a respect for human rights and acknowledgement of the individual as opposed to clan-based interests. This shift towards individual responsibility meant that tribal customs such as blood tribute were replaced in the code with monetary payments and penalties, while capital punishment was also abolished (with the strictest penalty being banishment for arsonists and horse thieves). However, in keeping with its status as an early precursor of modern law, there were no accompanying institutions along with the law that we would recognize today, as a permanent court system or even a legal profession remained unheard of (Smith 1996).

But from its high point of power as Kievan Rus' in the twelfth century, where Ukraine was the seat of Slavic power, Ukraine lost its independence to the Mongol Golden Horde in the early thirteenth century. A series of battles starting in Crimea and working its way to Kyiv (which was abandoned ahead of the Mongol invasion; see Halperin 1987) decimated the empire from 1237 to 1240, laying waste to the great city of Kyiv and leaving hundreds of thousands dead and no more than two hundred homes still standing (Paszkiewicz 1983). While the strength of the Horde would have made resistance difficult for any ruler, the Kievan Rus' was weakened by the issues surrounding Yaroslav's succession, as the normal hereditary succession was jettisoned in favor of a rotation scheme where Yaroslav's four sons would advance towards ruling Kyiv in the event of the death of another. This system floundered almost immediately in the face of a popular revolt that threw Yaroslav's son, and hand-picked ruler of Kyiv, Izislav off the throne; Izislav only returned to power through an armed intervention with the assistance of Poland (Subtelny 2009). But such internecine feuding weakened the monarchy from resisting outsiders, as well as creating political rents (such as land ownership) which were then distributed in an effort to shore up support for succession. This political marketplace weakened the agriculturally based economy and vitiated the wealth of the kingdom (Riasanovsky 2000).

The years under Mongol domination insulated the lands of Ukraine from the constitutional and institutional innovations occurring elsewhere in Europe, and instead created a system of public law based on the supremacy of the state and its need for revenue extraction; such a system was useful when the power of Eastern Slavs shifted from Kyiv to Muscovy after the Mongol occupation (Smith 1996). This time was to come in the late fourteenth century, as the Mongols had both overextended themselves and undergone their own series of internal power struggles, allowing for military encroachments against the Horde by both the Poles and Lithuanians to begin to bear fruit. In particular, the Lithuanian monarchy, led by Grand Duke Gediminas, scored victories against the Mongols and secured large swathes of Belarus and Kyiv, although Lithuania continued to play off the Golden Horde against Muscovy and the Poles for the next forty years (Rowell 2014). The Piast dynasty also was able to succeed militarily against the Mongols, with the Poles occupying the region of Galicia–Volhynia in the 1340s and eventually absorbing these lands into the Polish kingdom under King Kazimierz. With the personal union of Władysław II Jagiełło and Queen Jadwiga in 1386 cementing the relationship between Poland and Lithuania, there was a vast consolidation of the Ukrainian lands under the Polish banner, although the lands of eastern Ukraine were nominally a part of Lithuania and not Poland. This state of affairs lasted until the Union of Lublin in 1569, which detached the Ukrainian lands annexed in the fourteenth century and annexed them to Poland proper (Sysyn 1982).

The gradual loss of sovereignty to first the Mongols and then the Poles and Lithuanians meant an abrupt change in Ukrainian political institutions, from the established monarchy that ruled during the Kievan Rus', to the brutal subjugation under the Mongols, to a stark division between northern and southern Ukrainian lands in the fourteenth and fifteenth centuries. The Tatar states, and in particular the Crimean khanate, emerged from the rule of the Golden Horde entrenched in the Crimean peninsula; independent until 1475, the khanate (along with similar ones in Kazan and Astrakhan) came under the suzerainty of the Ottoman Empire, forming a Muslim outpost in Eastern Europe (Rudnytsky 1987a). Even before its loss of independence, the Crimean khanate adopted the Ottoman form of rule to its Mongol roots, with a strong central ruler and a state built on extraction. Much as in Poland, however, the power of the khan was limited by the strong influence of the nobles (*boyars*), who remained economically independent and thus had less reliance on the khan than, say, the average prince in Moscow had on the tsar (Khodarkovsky 2002). The nobles themselves were organized as in the rest of the Golden Horde territories, with the four noblest families making up the *qarachi beys* (or Council of State), the organization from which the khan of Crimea was chosen. As Williams (2001) notes, the *beys* system reflected the Crimean Tatars' strong attachment to clans and clergy, with lesser attachments to the ruling khan and the Ottoman sultan, meaning that traditional tribal law was strongly embedded in the informal institutions throughout Crimea.

This illiberal state of affairs was to persist even beyond the khanate's conquest by the Russians in 1771, as many of the political institutions of the khanate were absorbed by Moscow and given a Russian equivalent (Ostrowski 2000).

The noble families of Crimea may not have been beholden to the khan for their legitimacy or for their political organization, but they were heavily reliant on the slave trade, undertaking raids against the rest of Ukraine and Russia for three centuries and enslaving an estimated 2 to 2.5 million people in Ukraine alone (Katchanovski 2005). The constant pressure of the raids forced the rest of Ukraine into more concentrated settlements and off the steppes, shrinking the actual area that was "Ukrainian" (Rudnytsky 1987a); at the same time, the slave trade provided a steady stream of income that contributed to the urbanization of the khanate itself (Fisher 1978). This emphasis on human trafficking offers some clue to the overall political environment of the khanate as, despite the relative dispersion of political power, life in Crimea was anything but liberal. Formal political institutions demanded absolute loyalty to the khan and his nobles, with Muslims elevated above Christians and Jews in terms of their place in society. While nominally protected as "people of the Book," informal political institutions throughout the Crimea discriminated against non-Muslims and either allowed for their enslavement or indentured servitude (Katchanovski 2005). These political institutions, both formal and informal, became more concentrated in the khanate until the Russian conquest, as the decline in Ottoman administrative capacity meant increasing concentration of power in the hands of the khan (Fisher 1979).

In the non-Muslim lands of northern Ukraine, the political institutions that existed under the Kievan Rus' began to take on a distinctly Polish flavor. The boyars of the Rus' turned from trader-warriors in the twelfth century into landowners with hereditary rights, merging with the princely retinues to create a separate class of economic and political power second only to the princes (Katchanovski et al. 2013). While nominally vassals to the grand prince and servants of their own local princes, in reality, the boyars were highly independent from any central authority. Part of this was due to the fact that membership in the boyar class was open to all, as one who distinguished himself in the service of a prince or obtained great wealth was able to become a boyar; similarly, being a boyar conferred no special rights per se apart from their economic importance, and thus there was little reliance on the grand prince for privileges (Blum 1964). In fact, given the independent wealth of most boyars, they were able to participate independently of the grand prince in the affairs of state via the *Boiarska Rada* or Council of Boyars. The Rada, a political institution similar to the *qarachi beys* in Crimea, advised the grand prince on legislation and foreign policy, acting as an early House of Lords for a small subset of the boyar class (Subtelny 2009). This formal institution supplemented the prominent role that the boyars as a whole took in determining military and political policies informally in the Kievan Rus' (Blum 1964).

With the annexation of Ukraine into its neighbors, the boyars were removed from their advisory role in the political process and their prominent role in society, but in a manner that was differentiated by the geographical location of the nobility. Sysyn (1982:171) claims that, due to the geographical dispersion of the Ukrainian people, "prior to 1569, the institutional and historical bases for Ukrainian regionalism were weak and in neither state were the Ukrainian lands a united entity with a 'political nation' of nobles." While this may have been true prior to the fourteenth century, given the local power held by the boyars and their lack of fealty to the grand prince, this blanket statement was only true of half of the lands of the Kievan Rus'. As noted above, the absorption of Ukraine into the Polish-Lithuanian Commonwealth proceeded in two distinct phases. The first stage integrated the western Ukrainian lands into Poland in the fourteenth and fifteenth century; as part of this process, the Ukrainian nobility also began to assimilate into the Polish nobility, with boyars located closer to the Polish frontier (as in Lwów) finding that "polonization and Catholicization offered the easiest route to preserving and advancing their status and fortunes" (Lukowski and Zawadzki 2006:33).

Most importantly, the Ukrainian nobility was establishing itself as a distinct class within the Polish kingdom at the exact same time that the *szlachta* was coming into its own in Poland. The Nieszawa Statutes in 1454 (see Chapter 2) enabled the *szlachta* to make great strides in the political arena in Poland, establishing the idea of "noble liberty," and the Ukrainian boyars (those that polonized, that is) became part of this process. As Litwin (1987:58) correctly noted, "for outside nobility [i.e., the Ukrainians] the most attractive component of Polish culture and civilization was the political system and the ideology of liberty," drawing attention to the fact that a large part of the polonization process involved becoming politically active in the Polish kingdom. Tazbir (1982:321) also confirms this assertion, stating that "the concept of a noble nation contributed greatly to the nobility's integration throughout the whole territory of the Commonwealth. Within several decades, noble privileges brought about a community of language and customs, which in turn caused the relatively rapid polonization of the Lithuanian, Belorussian, and Ukrainian nobility." Thus, *contra* to Sysyn's (1982) assertion, the Ukrainian boyars in the west were indeed developing as a political force in tandem with (and feeding off of) their Polish counterparts, continuing the political involvement in their new nation that boyars had participated in during the Kievan Rus'.

In contrast, in the eastern lands of Ukraine, assimilation was much more problematic and more in line with Sysyn's conclusion. Indeed, according to Sysyn (1982:167), "linguistic and cultural assimilation proceeded with relatively minor resistance" in the west, but regional pockets located to the east such as Livonia and Volhynia held out much longer against the cultural tidal wave. The reasons behind this focus on two separate issues, first the state and second the church. In regard to the state, the second stage of Ukraine's absorption joined eastern Ukrainian lands to the Grand Duchy of Lithuania as part of the Union of Krewo in 1386, concurrent with the absorption of western Ukraine into the Polish kingdom. With Ukrainian lands made a part of Lithuania, King Władysław II Jagiełło proceeded to dismantle the existing administrative boundaries in the Ukrainian lands and gave rule of the new territories over to Catholic (Polish) boyars and their newly-catholicized counterparts in Lithuania. Lithuania, as an independent grand duchy from the years 1386–1569, had its own legal system, political administration, and proud lineage that placed them as equals to Poland (Tazbir 1982). Under the arrangement of the Union of Krewo, thus, the boyars of Ukraine were integrated into Lithuania's social mores and administrative institutions rather than into those of the driving force of the Union, Poland. Combined with the reality that Lithuania itself was becoming integrated into Polish structures, Ukrainians assimilating to the political court were undergoing integration into a system that was itself changing yet considered Ukrainians as second-class citizens (Magocsi 2010). This atmosphere made it much more difficult for Ukrainian nobility to take on the attributes of Lithuania than for those who were in Crown Poland (Litwin 1987).

The second key sticking point in this assimilation process in the heart of the Kievan Rus' centered not necessarily on cultural differences in the grand duchy and the kingdom of Poland, but instead on the adaptation to a major social institution that also played a role in the political evolution of Ukraine. The struggle between the Roman Catholic Church (championed by Poland and Lithuania) and the Orthodox Eastern variant of Christianity (common throughout eastern Slavdom) had begun as early as

1386, where Lithuania's nobility was admitted to the Polish court only if they were Roman Catholic. As Magocsi (2010:134) notes, to further reinforce our earlier point of discrimination, even though administrative equality was established in 1434 between Catholicism and Orthodoxy in Lithuanian Ukraine, "it was clear that social and political advancement would be severely limited for non-Catholics." This state of affairs was even more intense in the Galician portions of Ukraine and specifically in Kyiv, where Polish gentry and the church itself were given large tracts of land to settle and dispose of as they wished, thus undercutting the indigenous nobility (ibid.).

However, it was not until the Union of Lublin and the joining of the Ukrainian lands of Kyiv and Volhynia to Poland rather than Lithuania that issues regarding assimilation (both cultural and religious) began to arise in a systematic way. The political joining of the core of Kievan Rus' into the Polish noble kingdom meant the extension of new administrative and legal structures, again tied to religious affiliation; in this way, "in the course of some two generations following 1569, nearly all Ukrainian aristocratic families and a large portion of the middle gentry converted to Catholicism" (Rudnytsky 1987a:50). At the peasant level, however, the mass movement into Catholicism precipitated a backlash, one intensified by King Sigismund III's moves after the Union of Brest in 1596. The Union placed the Ukrainian Rus' churches under the authority of the pope, signifying a break with other Eastern Orthodox churches and aligning it more closely with the Polish state as the Uniate Church. The Polish crown took the Union a step further, however, by declaring that it was binding on all Christians in the Commonwealth, including those who wished to remain Orthodox (Goldblatt 1986). This move led directly to a sustained assault on Orthodoxy in the Ukrainian lands, closing churches and monasteries from 1596 to 1620, denying recognition to the Orthodox Church, and transferring Orthodox assets to the newly fashioned Uniate church (Backus 1963). Regarded as "the gravest violation of the ancient Ruthenian liberties and ancient laws" (Chynczewska-Hennel 1986:383), the assault on Orthodoxy also dovetailed with the perceived cultural assault on the Ukrainian/Ruthenian language, fostering the perception that Ruthenian traditions were under assault (Hrushevskiy 2012).

So whereas western Ukrainian lands may have had an easier time in assimilating to the Polish-Lithuanian Commonwealth, due to repeated exposure and similarities in language and religion, inhabitants further east began to experience their own cultural reaction, with the Unions of Lublin and Brest awakening a nascent Ukrainian "national consciousness" and "allegiance to the Ruthenian community within the Crown Poland" (Borzecki 1996:37). This national awakening manifested itself in various ways throughout the political system for, while the first two centuries of incorporation into Poland may have seen Ukrainians becoming more Polish to enter Polish political institutions, the next century saw a concerted effort to make the institutions more Ukrainian (or at least Ukrainian-friendly). Chynczewska-Hennel (1986) highlights the fact that Ruthenian/Ukrainian nobles began to express themselves more frequently in official documents in terms of the Ukrainian nation after the Union, referring to "our Ruthenian voivodships" (in contrast to Polish ones) and drawing a distinction between Poland proper and Ukrainian lands. Similarly, banding together in political expression of nationalist desires, Ukrainian nobles spoke in the *Sejm* as "one united bloc in defense of their religious and regional privileges, such as the retention of the Ruthenian language in communications with the King" (Borzecki 1996:51). These concrete expressions of Ukrainian interest in political institutions were backed by advances in political theory, as the Ukrainian nobility began to assert its independence within the crown framework. One (factually misguided but interesting) theory that was floated at the beginning of the seventeenth century claimed that the merger of Ukrainian lands into Poland was done on a contractual basis, as a free union between the nobility of Ukraine and the nobility of Poland (Sysyn 1980), thus making Ukrainian political participation a Ukrainian choice rather than a Polish concession.

As in Poland, the missing link in the political institutional-building of Ukraine was the classes below the nobility, namely the peasantry. As already mentioned, while the nobility may have assimilated to life in the Polish Commonwealth in order to preserve their privileges, rural peasants and urban dwellers had no such incentive to polonize and thus resisted assimilation. As noted in Chapter 2, the Polish peasantry had little access to the political process, and Chapter 3 noted that this was due mainly to the "second serfdom" and use of the political process to stifle development of economic institutions. With its incorporation into the Commonwealth, the Ruthenian/Ukrainian lands also had the somewhat more repressive Lithuanian estate system extended to its own lands, notably through the *Voloky Ustav* of 1557, which made labor obligations of peasants to nobles the law of the land (Subtelny 2009). As Gordon (1983) notes, the differentiation between social classes in Ukraine started off with a wider gap than in Poland and only grew over time, with Ukraine having much larger estates than elsewhere in Europe, due to land grants from the

Polish kings; given this concentrated land ownership, even the lesser gentry found itself in a state of vassalage, and upward mobility was severely limited (Subtelny 2009). The political strata in Ukraine began to be dominated by a few wealthy families, including the Ostrozhskys, the Vishnevetskys, and the famous thirteen nobles of Volhynia, all of whom came to dominate local government but derived their power from their polonization and the privileges dispensed by the king of Poland (Magocsi 2010). As Melnichuk (2014) notes, the loss of a uniquely Ukrainian political entity with the rush of the gentry to polonization, combined with the concentration of political power in their hands, meant that the peasantry was alienated from their own elites. This vacuum was filled through the emergence of a new political "elite," the Cossacks, who came bearing ideas of democratic self-rule and full equality (Borzecki 1996).

The Cossack rebellion of 1653–1654 was covered in the previous chapter, in regard to the shock waves it sent through the Polish monarchy. But in addition to the political shifts in Poland in response to the external threat of the Cossacks, and despite the longing for peace that initially brought Kazimierz to the throne in Poland, more troubles were to come for Ukraine as a result of the Cossack rebellion. Although Khmelnitsky may have been satisfied with his initial successes as a way of redressing the legal wrongs done to him and never set out to overthrow the established social and economic order in Ukraine (Borzecki 1996), the rebellion had taken on a life of its own. Portrayed after the fact in literature as a struggle between the carefree Cossack life and the strictures of Polish living (Sawczak 2004), the Cossack rebellion transformed into something antithetical from its original aims (as many revolutions are wont to): rather than a call for legal reform or an attempt to rectify perceived injustices against the Cossacks, many factions such as "Cossack colonel Maksym Kryvonis led a fierce campaign against the established order. The social war, accompanied by looting and brigandry, took the lives of numerous landlords, Catholic clergymen, and Jews" (Sysyn 2003:119). The end result of "six years of inconclusive fighting" was that "Khmelnitsky abandoned his Tartar allies for Tsar Alexei of Muscovy" in 1654 (Frost 1986:181), a result that precipitated yet another Russian-Polish war (1654–1657), only one theatre in the Northern War against Sweden spoke of in Chapter 2.

The Zaporozhian Host eventually reached an accord with the Polish Commonwealth in 1658 with the Treaty of Hadziacz, coming a year after the death of Khmelnitsky and his failed attempt to create a broader anti-Polish alliance (which instead led mainly to bickering between Ukrainians and Transylvanians about territory in Galicia and Volhynia; see Frost (2000)). The Treaty, concluded by Khmelnitsky's successor Ivan Vyhovskyi, actually made a turn back in favor of Poland, proposing substantial autonomy for the Ukrainians within their own state of equal status to Poland and Lithuania; with an independent judicial system and abolition of the Uniate Church, the Treaty was meant to move the Commonwealth from a dual-kingdom to a triad (Magocsi 2010). But while the new hetmanate (named after the Cossacks' political leadership position) was envisioned as working within a reconstituted Commonwealth, in reality, the Treaty led to the establishment of an independent Cossack Ukraine established on the Left Bank of the Dnieper River, with Polish nobility cleansed from the region and Cossacks taking over the reins of state administration from the *szlachta* (Baran 1982). The odd combination of suzerainty under Moscow and not-quite-final divorce from Poland led to the Hetmanate being accurately described by Von Hagen (1995:668) as "at best . . . a proto-state, especially when compared with the absolutist national states that were emerging in contemporary western Europe."

With such a tenuous existence, once it had pushed out the noble liberty of Poland, the hetmanate was not long for this world, as Poland's own diminished stature after a half-century of war, coupled with substantial unrest from the rank and file against Vyhovskyi's "selling out" to Poland, led to little opposition to the ascendance of Muscovy and its own designs on the region. The former and future rulers of Ukraine went over the heads of the Ukrainians to delineate their own spheres of influence, with the Treaty of Andrusovo in 1667 between Poland and Russia pledging joint protection of the Ukrainian lands but in reality splitting the country into two separate halves, delineated by the Dnieper River (Magocsi 2010). Poland's rapid decline after the Northern Wars, however, meant that the ascendant tsar was to play the more important role in Ukraine's institutional development going forward. As noted above, the tsar had already been allowed into the hetmanate's workings during the original Uprising via the Treaty of Pereyaslav, where Khmelnitsky had pledged Ukraine under the nominal suzerainty of Moscow. Ukraine was soon to find that this deal pulled it out of the proverbial (and relatively cooler) frying pan in Poland and exposed it instead to the fire of Imperial Russia. Indeed, almost immediately after establishing themselves as the hetman state, independent of the Polish crown, the Russian authorities provoked civil conflict in Ukraine between 1663 and 1674 in a bid to avoid Ukraine returning to the Polish fold (Pritsak and Reshetar 1963). This time of ruin was followed by repeated Russian encroachments, the destruction of the hetmanate's rule on the right bank of the Dnieper, and the eventual dismantlement of the hetmanate as a quasi-independent state by 1709 (Gajecky 1978). While the hetmanate limped along until 1783 as an administrative division of Russia, it was for all intents and purposes wholly absorbed by the Russian Empire at the start of the eighteenth century.

From the point of view of Ukraine, this assimilation into Russia was a step back from the relative liberality of the Commonwealth and into a system that retained serfdom for another 200 years. Despite the rhetoric of the Cossacks and the reality of peasant life throughout Europe, the Ukrainians were ensconced in a fairly liberal Polish political system, including a long period of time where Ukraine had some measure of decentralized political autonomy (Rodrigues 2010). Additionally, while Ukrainian nobles were likely to be polonized and assimilate into the Polish political landscape, Polish peasants who colonized Ukrainian lands were more likely to go the other way, becoming "Ruthenized" and learning the local language (Tazbir 1982). Moreover, Łobodowski (1980) points out that the heights of culture and liberality under the Kievan Rus' had been destroyed during the Mongol occupation, and it was only Poland that functioned as an intermediary to help channel the new ideas of the Renaissance to the Ukrainian lands. As Ukrainian author Bohdan Lepky aptly phrased it, "Ukraine gave Poland her men, and received in exchange, ideas" (quoted in Łobodowski 1980).

In particular, the key ideas that were transmitted regarded political institutions and the role of the individual *vis-à-vis* the collective. In the first instance, Poland introduced the idea of the nation to Ukrainian thinkers, which is why the Ukrainian terms for "nation" and "fatherland" were adopted from Polish words (Sysyn 1986). By the simple act of incorporating the entirety of Ukrainian lands into Poland, the Poles gave a collective identity to these territories, conceptualizing them as their own distinct entity (Sysyn 1982). But perhaps more importantly, the idea of noble liberty that Poland practiced (and that Polish political thought continued to develop) had a very real effect on Ukrainian society. While noble liberty may have built on the proto-institutions of the Kievan Rus', it extended them far beyond what the Ukrainians had ever implemented into a practical political institution for Poles, Lithuanians, and Ukrainians. In particular, the underlying ideology of a contractual relationship meant that citizens were expected to play a role in their own governance; as Borzecki (1996) notes, in the Commonwealth this translated into the *szlachta* expressly encouraging the Ukrainian nobility to participate in political life. And while there were real and substantial flaws in the practice of noble liberty in Poland (explored in the previous two chapters), it was a major improvement on the centralized patrimonial system of Kievan Rus', where the nobility never had a chance to develop an interest in political life (Pritsak 1986). By contrast, in the Commonwealth, the Ukrainian nobility had begun to develop into a political elite, with all of the responsibilities that entailed.

The benefits that integration into the Polish-Lithuanian Commonwealth may have conferred on Ukraine thus make it difficult to understand the full extent of rage unleashed under the Cossack rebellion, until one considers the context in which the Cossacks operated. In fact, it may have precisely been this liberality of the Polish regime that the "anti-*szlachta*" of the Cossacks rebelled against; as Kamiński (1977:182) notes, a longer-term goal of the rebellion may have been recentralization along the lines of the Golden Horde, as, in a letter "promising Jan Kazimierz support for his candidacy to the Polish throne, Khmelnitsky simultaneously urged him to change the political system of the Commonwealth. In effect, the hetman of the Zaporozhian Host wanted the Polish king to become an absolutist ruler." In this sense, the Cossack rebellion really was a clash of political ideologies, and, in the medium-term, the true illiberal ideas of the Cossacks (far removed in practice from their theoretical calls for self-rule and democracy) were to triumph over the Polish *szlachta* democracy. Even in the brief interregnum between Polish integration and Russian domination, the hetmanate was characterized by what was essentially a military administration, with the leading general (the hetman) taking over as national leader and his staff generals fulfilling the role of a cabinet (Gajecky 1978). While Pritsak and Reshetar (1963) note that the initial Uprising brought magnates and gentry alike to the Cossack Ukraine to assist in the administration of the new state, Gajecky (1978) shows clearly that the hetmanate never stopped being a military dictatorship, with little in the way of modern organizational practices, no semblance of public financial management, and decreasing ability to offer government lands to buy loyalty (Subtelny 2009). In the words of Subtelny (1980:2), "the Zaporozhian Host saw itself as a military fraternity in which every fighting man was an equal [but] in reality, it was a hierarchically organized military estate whose leadership – the *starshyna* – was in the process of becoming a hereditary territorial elite." With broader consequences for today, this illiberality and desire for a "strong man" to lord over subjects led to substantial political changes in the lands of Ukraine and Russia, none for the better.

In another important turn of events, the Cossack move towards Russia did not aid the political aspirations of the oppressed peasantry, and in fact their prospects became much more dire over time. Despite the early promises of freedom, and even the release of the peasantry from the second serfdom during the Rebellion, the process of state-building led to the "Cossack officer class . . . push[ing] for the renewed enserfment of the peasants" while the Cossacks curried favor from the elites in Moscow (Yekelchyk 2007: 203). Subtleny (2009) is direct on the reasoning behind this, noting that the Cossack warriors did not want to create an egalitarian political society, but instead to expel the Poles and their nobility and replace it with a native Ukrainian one (presumably on the theory that home-grown exploitation is preferable to foreign exploitation). His point on the political incentives in the Cossack hetmanate is worth quoting in full:

For [the Cossacks,] a society without an elite was unthinkable and unworkable. Because of their relatively high status, extensive military and political experience, and wealth, many Ukrainian nobles and well-established Cossacks attained positions of leadership in the Zaporozhian Host. And they used these positions to retain and expand their status and wealth. Moreover, they frequently transformed the public lands attached to their offices into their own private property. Since hetmans frequently emerged from the officer class and greatly relied on its support, they not only failed to prevent its aggrandizement of power and wealth but actively encouraged it with generous land grants and appointments. As this new elite evolved, it pushed for sharper delineation of the classes in Ukrainian society and it increased its demands upon the peasants and common Cossacks. The latter responded to these attempts to deprive them of the gains of 1648 with growing animosity and even open resistance. As a result, a bitter and eventually fatal cleavage developed in the newly formed society of Cossack Ukraine (Subtelny 2009:142).

Indeed, as we have seen, the Cossack hetmanate swapped out one form of foreign domination for another, more pernicious one. And not only was there little improvement in the material status of ordinary peasants under the hetmanate, "the Russian government reintroduced full-fledged serfdom in Left-Bank Ukraine in the 1780s, simultaneously with the abolition of the remnants of the country's autonomy" (Rudnytsky 1980:115).

The hetmanate experience shows, unlike von Hagen's (1995) assertion, that there was institutional continuity in the Ukrainian lands, with the only bone of contention being the question of who was to lord over the political system. The assimilation into Muscovy of the left bank of the Dnieper was accelerated by the early eighteenth century, despite repeated rebellions from Cossacks and peasants alike throughout the second half of the seventeenth century, after the final defeat of the revolt of Hetman

Mazepa at Poltava in 1709. The cultural and religious revolution against the Ukrainians had already begun in waves, with the tsar first subordinating the Kievan church to the patriarch in Moscow in 1686 and then outlawing the use of any language but Russian in official church texts (Goldblatt 1986). In the political realm, by 1665 the tsar had claimed direct rule over a majority of Ukrainian cities, including Kyiv, and ordered that all taxation raised on the Ukrainian lands be remitted directly to the Imperial Treasury (Magocsi 2010). But the crushing of armed resistance in 1709 meant that the process of russification could be completed and the fiction of a separate state of "Little Russia" (the preferred Muscovy term for Ukraine) erased. By destroying "forever the idea of a Rus' principality" via a series of repressive measures under Tsar Peter I, Russia was able to hasten "the decline of all independent political thought" in Ukraine (Pritsak and Reshetar 1963:229).

In one sense, however, political institutions became informal, much as they were to do in the Polish kingdom in the following century. In the first instance, the hetmanate survived as its own territorial administration, albeit in a much vitiated form. More important, Antonovych (2010) notes that Ukraine had its first experience of a democratic constitution in 1710, with the Constitution of Hetman Pylyp Orlyk setting the boundaries for human rights and political order within the newly subjugated territories. The Constitution of 1710, signed in April of that year, placed the Cossacks as the rightful heirs of the Kievan Rus' while also laying out a tangible plan of administration for the hetmanate, including the executive and judicial branches (Katchanovski et al. 2013). Much like the Polish Constitution of 1791, the Ukrainian Constitution was a document that had more basis in idealism than reality, coming immediately before foreign subjugation that was to render the document itself worthless; additionally, given that Hetman Orlyk only ruled on the Right Bank of the Dnieper (still under Polish protection) and promulgated the Constitution in Ottoman lands, now part of Moldova (Pritsak 1998), the document had the same legal enforceability as Lincoln's Emancipation Proclamation in the United States a century and a half later.[1]

But despite the latent stirrings of political institutions, in reality Left-Bank Ukraine became wholly absorbed into the Russian Empire's political

---

[1] U.S. President Abraham Lincoln's Proclamation freed the slaves but only in the territories that had seceded from the Union and were currently at war with the Washington, DC–led regime. As such, Lincoln had no legal authority to free the slaves in the states that had not seceded.

and administrative machinery. While the country was effectively cut in two in 1667 between Russia and Poland, Russia's expansion in the eighteenth century absorbed large swathes of Ukrainian territory in waves, much as Poland was partitioned at the end of the century. First to go was Sloboda Ukraine, the small area of land encompassing Kharkiv and parts of modern-day Donetsk oblast, which was a haven for refugees from the Left and Right Banks and was integrated into Russia in 1765 (Magocsi 2010). This was followed by Zaporozhia in 1775, when, after the Russian army emerged triumphant from the Russo-Turkish War of 1768–1774, it turned to the Zaporozhian Sich and destroyed its vestiges of autonomy (Kappeler 2014). Formally annexed by decree from Catherine the Great in August of that year, the Cossacks from the region of the lower Dnieper were resettled along the Kuban River in the north Caucasus and the region became reorganized as the Novorissyan Governate (*Новоросси́йская губе́рния*). Finally, the hetmanate was fully absorbed over 1781–1785, in tandem with Catherine the Great's decree of 1783, which prohibited the Ukrainian peasantry from leaving their lands, thus reintroducing serfdom. In a bid to co-opt the Cossacks into the Russian political system, Catherine the Great granted the Cossacks of the hetmanate noble privileges in 1785 (Yekelchyk 2007). This was the logical consequence after the Cossacks had been tamed by their own inertia, with their leaders having gone from revolutionary goals to attempting to "maintain a satisfactory relationship with the tsar and, as members of a rising Cossack elite, to consolidate their socioeconomic gains *vis-à-vis* the common Cossacks and peasants" (Subtelny 2009:159–160).

On the right bank of the Dnieper, as well, the polonization of the nobility was to resume after a fifty-year hiatus. Poland was promised influence in Right-Bank Ukraine in the Treaty of Andrusovo in 1667, a right that was confirmed via the "Eternal Peace" treaty of 1686 with Russia (which also took away the promise of joint administration of Kyiv from the Treaty of Andrusovo and replaced it with Russian domination (Solchanyk 2000)). However, the weakness of the Polish crown and the uneven administration of economic institutions (see below) led to a half-century of limbo for Ukraine until Poland itself was carved up by greater powers. Indeed, Poland's influence was anything but guaranteed, as restive Cossacks, war with Ottoman Turkey, and both Hetman Ivan Samoilovych and his successor Hetman Mazepa's "*izmena*" (where the right bank was briefly occupied) made Polish power in the region fairly thin throughout the seventeenth century. *De facto* occupied by the Ottomans from 1672 through 1699, it took until the Treaty of Prut in 1711 for the

Cossacks to be suppressed, and the administrative apparatus of the Commonwealth was extended back into the Ukrainian lands. As Magocsi (2010) notes, the Poles extended the voivodship (*wojewoda*) system back into Ukraine after 1714 with a palatine appointed by the king, but, as in the Commonwealth, the real seat of power in Ukraine belonged to the nobility and their seats in the *Sejm*. Polonized Ukrainians and Polish noble families began to reclaim land in the region, and even undertook a large (and successful) resettlement plan to repopulate the strife-torn region with peasants (Rudnytsky 1987a).

Repeated Cossack rebellions resisting Poland's domination did not cease with the extension of administration from Warsaw, in some sense taking up where they had left off in the seventeenth century. The *haidamak* movement, a broad-based insurgency comprising free Cossacks and disaffected members of the peasantry, arose in Volhynia after 1725 and soon spread to Kyiv and other parts of Right-Bank Ukraine (Katchanovski et al. 2013). Targeting Polish nobility and named after the Turkish word for brigand (Skinner 2005), the *haidamak* undertook regular raids with detachments of up to 200 or 300 men, seizing property and murdering with impunity (Katchanovski et al. 2013). Occasionally, these raids flared up into major conflicts, which occurred from 1734 to 1737, in 1750, and, the bloodiest of them all, in the *Koliivshchyna* of 1768–1769 (Thaden 2014). Skinner (2005) has produced an excellent summation of the roots of the *Koliivshchyna* rebellion, focusing on the land leases that were utilized to entice peasants to settle the Right-Bank of Ukraine; as an incentive to bring population to the depopulated lands, Polish nobility offered twenty-year no-obligation leases for settlers, which came to an end throughout the 1750s and the 1760s. For many peasants, overnight their burden went from "no obligations" to "total obligations," meaning a reinstatement of serfdom. At the same time, the Confederation of Bar (see Chapter 2) began military campaigns to preserve the rights of the *szlachta*, but with the unfortunate consequence of the Polish military abusing Ukrainians and destroying Orthodox churches on their way to fight the Russians (Katchanovski et al. 2013). All of these factors led to rebellion in mid-1768, which was only put down by a joint Polish-Russian force, seeking to keep the peace in their sphere of influence. Before the end of the rebellion, massacres had occurred on both sides, with the death toll ranging from a conservative estimate of tens of thousands to an almost-unthinkable two hundred thousand fatalities (Skinner 2005).

The reality that Poland required Russian assistance to quell the rebellion in Right-Bank Ukraine (as it did in many of the previous rebellions) shows just how impotent Poland had become by this time in influencing the path of Ukraine. In fact, the story of Ukraine's formal political institutions for the most part ends here at the end of the eighteenth century, as Poland was no longer in the position to protect against Russian expansionism or to provide a credible institutional alternative. Indeed, Poland was removed entirely from Ukraine by the Partitions, as the First Partition (1772) separated Galicia from Poland and gave it to the Habsburgs, while the Second Partition (1793) led to all of Right-Bank Ukraine being annexed by the Russian Empire, and the Third Partition (1795) saw the final piece of the puzzle, Volhynia, incorporated into Russia. The Russians took advantage of these territorial gains to centralize administration, a tactic (then as now) utilized heavily by Moscow to bring the Ukrainian lands to heel. From 1775 onward, Ukrainians were ruled the same as any other subject of the tsar(ina), as Catherine introduced a standardized administrative process for all of Russia that placed all power for the state apparatus in her hands and left little to no autonomy for the regions (Magocsi 2010). As Kappeler (2014:68) accurately notes, "in the eyes of the Russian government, the Ukraine on the left bank of the Dnieper had become part of the Russian core, and the Ukrainian polity created by the Dnieper Cossacks had been eliminated." It appeared that, in tandem with Poland's extinction, the same fate was about to befall Ukraine. However, while the reality in Partitioned Poland and Ukraine seemed to be closely related,

the similarity in the situations of dependent Poland and Ukraine was close to the surface. More deep-seated, and weighing more in the historical balance, were the great disparities between the two nations – in social structure, in cultural heritage, and, deriving from these, in their treatment at the hands of the dominating powers. Although nineteenth-century Europe knew no independent Poland, no one ever questioned the existence of a separate Polish nation. European public opinion, and the partitioning powers themselves, took for granted the existence of a distinct Polish nationality. The governments of Russia, Austria, and even Prussia made important political and cultural concessions to the Poles at various times. In contrast, tsarist Russia consistently denied the very existence of a Ukrainian nationality, and treated the "Little Russians" as a tribal branch of the Russian nation. Consequently, the tsarist government suppressed even quite innocuous, non-political expressions of Ukrainian cultural identity, considering them subversive of the unity of Russia (Rudnytsky 1987a:70).

In reality, the stretch where Ukraine could truly be called independent lasted only approximately six years, from 1648 to 1654, as the conclusion of a treaty with Moscow immediately aligned the hetmanate with another country that did not believe in Ukrainian independence (as Rudnytsky notes in the quote above). Without a long history of existence as an independent state, Ukraine's claims were seen as somehow less legitimate than those of Poland. In addition, Ukraine's political institutions were snuffed out at the exact moment when modern political institutions were being formed (von Hagen 1995), thus leaving only memories of premodern institutions and rule akin to the Golden Horde rather than a golden throne. Finally, and although Rudnytsky does not explicitly mention it he would likely be in agreement with it, the fact that Ukrainian independence only came about because of wild frontiersmen instead of the nobility (as it did in so much else of Europe) also probably lessened the perceived legitimacy of the Ukrainian state. If the noble, well-bred, and most intelligent strata of society could not be bothered to agitate for an independent state, what right did steppe-dwelling ruffians on horses have? Indeed, whereas prior to the Cossack hetmanate (and afterwards in the Right Bank) the Ukrainian nobility aspired to status within the Polish political and class structure, after the hetmanate, the Cossack *starshyna* in Left-Bank Ukraine did the same within Russia, continually leaving Ukraine without an indigenous ruling class. Grassroots change was virtually unthinkable in Europe in the early-to-mid-eighteenth century, and thus the lack of a "Ukrainian" nobility meant the lack of a "Ukraine" as well.

These problems persisted well into Ukraine's own absorption into foreign powers for, unlike Poland, which had the gentry to sustain its politics informally and unite around the idea of Poland, Ukraine's lack of a political elite meant that nation-building fell on cultural institutions such as the writing of poets and nationalist authors (Yekelchyk 2007) or on social institutions such as the Orthodox Church (von Hagen 1995). This too was an uphill battle, as the division of Ukraine that was enshrined in treaties in 1667 and 1686 had split the country culturally as well as territorially. In particular, Kyiv and the environs of the east (Left-Bank Ukraine) were more easily assimilated into Russian administration than the provinces of the west (Right-Bank Ukraine), which continued to see the dominance of Polish culture and Polish noble traditions (Yekelchyk 2007). However, much as the Poles had come to reclaim their "Polishness" under foreign domination, the same occurred for Ukraine under the Russians, as "beginning with the 1840's and until the 1917 Revolution, there was an uninterrupted chain of groups and organizations, formal and informal, that were committed to the idea of the Ukraine's cultural and political regeneration as a separate nation." An example of the formal institutions that arose to fill the gap in Ukraine's national consciousness, although they had a strong influence for only a short time, included educational institutions. For example, the first university in Ukraine under Russian rule was founded in Kharkiv in 1805, funded by private sources and "fueled by local patriotism and a desire to raise the cultural level of Ukraine" (Subtelny 2009:223). For approximately twenty-nine years, until supplanted by St. Vladimir's University in Kyiv (an explicit attempt by Russia to begin the process of cultural assimilation of Ukrainians), Kharkiv University remained a prominent way to create an indigenous Ukrainian intelligentsia.

Unfortunately, the route of formal instruction was never going to be enough to engage the Ukrainian masses, as the relatively small reach of the universities could not overcome the relative backwardness of the population: as late as 1897, approximately 93 percent of the country could still be classified as peasants (Magocsi 2010). Moreover, the educational system was utilized by the tsar to inculcate Russian values, using the schools as a method of assimilation and a way of blurring any distinctions between Ukrainians and Russians (Yekelchyk 2007). Given this reality, the way to reach the relatively uneducated was not through higher learning, but through folklore and the power of the printed word, and this is precisely how the idea of a Ukrainian nation did indeed spread in the nineteenth century. In particular, nationalist feelings were strongest in the areas where the Cossack influence was strongest (Rudnytsky 1963:201), and nationalist organizations tended to rely heavily on the Cossacks as the romantic core of a nascent Ukrainian national consciousness. As Sysyn (1991:848) notes, "for the Ukrainian national movement of the nineteenth and twentieth centuries, the Cossacks and their political entities, the Zaporozhian Sich and the hetmanate, have served as a focus for national self-identification." As Lieven (1995:617) adds, "life under Nicholas I's authoritarian and bureaucratic regime provided ample incentives to invoke the myth of the freedom-loving Cossack as Ukraine's ancestor and the symbol of its identity." Taras Shevchenko, now revered as Ukraine's national poet, was the foremost progenitor of the romantic view of the Cossacks, creating a concrete link between the Cossacks, the hetmanate, and the Ukrainian identity. Shevchenko also transformed himself into a national icon by refusing to bow to tsarist rule and writing in Ukrainian, as well as referring to his country as *Ukrainia* rather than *Malorossiia*, thus simultaneously establishing the country's national myth and settling any dispute on what the name of the country might actually be (Pritsak and Reshetar 1963).

Unlike Poland, however, these informal cultural institutions did not have the same success in creating informal political institutions that could be implemented once independence was achieved (in Magocsi's (2010) memorable phrase, they were stuck in the "heritage-gathering" stage). While the foundation was laid for a national myth and a national narrative built on historical symbolism, they did not necessarily build a state apparatus-in-waiting. As part of the Russian Empire, Ukraine faced the same centripetal pull that other far-flung regions succumbed to, with "political power ... highly centralized and vested in the person of the emperor, who saw no need to take into account the views or desires of his subjects" (Subtelny 2009:201). And this political centralization was able to triumph over informal cultural awakening mainly due to the fact that the tsar also had weapons to use culturally as well as politically. Indeed, Russification began earlier and was much more intense in Ukraine than in Poland, mainly because the ruling Russian class (and likely the peasantry) saw Ukrainians as "little Russians" and not a distinct nation. Thus, cultural assimilation was not seen as bringing to heel an external threat, as it was in Poland, but rather, as Catherine II said in 1793, the recovery of what was torn away (quoted in Subtelny 2009). More accurately, as Kohut (1986:566) put it, "From the Muscovite point of view, Little Russian rights and liberties were gifts of the tsar and could be rescinded whenever he wished."

The strategy of Russification proceeded on several fronts. Bureaucratic expansion so that "no differences would remain" between Ukraine and Russia was begun by Catherine the Great, accelerated under Paul I (Subtelny 1980:12), and expanded under the highly autocratic rule of Nikolai I. As Szporluk (1997:94) noted, "Especially in Catherine II's reign (1762–1796), St. Petersburg held the view that the elimination of Little Russia's traditional institutions was just one element of a larger state- and nation-building project and thus required a variety of measures, the aim of which was to achieve the complete integration of Little Russia into the Russian state and Russian society." In order to eliminate these institutions, a key component of establishing tsarist rule was extensively reorganizing Ukraine's administrative divisions to make it easier to govern from Moscow:

Ukraine was divided into ninety-six districts (uezd) and nine provinces (guberniia). Kiev, Chernihiv (Chernigov), Poltava and Katerynoslav (Ekaterinoslav) provinces were carved out of Cossack Ukraine in the early 1800s and made part of three non-historical entities, ruled for most of the century by governors-general with extensive powers: the South-Western Lands (1796–1914), Little Russia (1801–56) and New

Russia (1796–1874). Chernihiv and Poltava provinces were under the Kievan Governor-General from 1856 to 1879, and the Kharkiv Temporary Governor-General from 1879 to 1889. Katerynoslav and Taurida provinces were under a Military Governor based in Mykolaiiv (Nikolaev) from 1803 to 1828 and from 1879 to 1882 they were supervised by a Temporary Governor-General in Odessa (Velychenko 1995:189).

Imperial Russia had only recently begun, under Peter the Great, to separate out the idea of the state from the tsar, creating "an expanded and reinvigorated government machinery to serve it" (Kohut 1986:566). Such a sweeping reorganization in Ukraine would require sending armies of bureaucrats into these frontier lands in order to administer the myriad of rules and regulations, and this is precisely what occurred in the nineteenth century. Unlike Ukraine, which had no centralized state apparatus to speak of and whose only experience with a bureaucracy consisted of military officers, Russia had developed a professional cadre of very homogenous administrators who held their jobs for life, mostly noblemen who had become bureaucrats or former military officers (Pinter 1970). These administrators were beholden to the governors of each of the nine territories, who in turn were chosen directly by the tsar. However, their loyalty was fickle, given that the Russian state paid very little, and led to the importing of the institution of corruption into Ukraine from Russia; as Subtleny (2009:220) rightly notes, "while Russians were more accustomed to this burdensome bureaucratism, it was still a new and strange phenomenon for Ukrainians in the nineteenth century." With little experience of central state apparatus in Ukraine, it was thus odd that the creation of such an apparatus would require multiple payments and personal connections in order to achieve what a citizen needed under the law. But, as Velychenko (1995:189–190) correctly pointed out, "Russia had a government of men, not of laws, [and so] policy depended greatly on personality, and interests could find expression within the nominally unified administrative system.... Autocracy could ensure that this diversity did not express itself as bureaucratic nationalism, but graft, corruption, bribery, venality, nepotism and red tape riddled the bureaucracy, and ignoring directives was so widespread that, in practice, self-rule was the rule."

In addition to the extension of "normal" political institutions and the export of Russia's corrupt bureaucracy, the Russian Imperial State also innovated in creating new political institutions to suppress any Ukrainian thoughts of independence. For example, the military had a conspicuous presence in the country, with garrisons and forts across the country and conscription introduced in 1797; added to this was the establishment of military colonies between 1816 and 1857, in which "every aspect of family life, including permission to marry and the timing of children, was regulated by strict and detailed instructions" (Subtelny 2009:203). Beyond the obvious military presence, Nikolai I not only expanded the bureaucracy throughout Ukraine but also created a secret police to keep an eye on subversives. Started in 1825 in Russia as *III отделение собственной Е.И.В канцелярии* (the Third Department of His Imperial Majesty's Chancellery), the secret police were to play a large role in Ukraine over the next 150 years in regard to any perceived moves towards rebellion. Indeed, from the 1840s onward, the imperial administration also began to take a dim view of cultural institutions, equating Ukrainian pride with subversion and anti-Russian sentiment (Magocsi 2010).

The key example of this cultural threat came from Shevchenko's secretive Brotherhood of Cyril and Methodius, an organization created in Kyiv in 1845 to discuss a platform of economic equality, abolition of serfdom, and a Slavic brotherhood of free association (Yekelchyk 2007). Like most Ukrainian nationalists, their goals "rested on the concept of ethnic nationality and of ethnic-linguistic frontiers [which] did not necessarily imply political separatism" (Rudnytsky 1987a:72). However, the mere existence of an organization outside of the official spheres of Russian political institutions was perceived as a threat by the tsarist authorities, and the ringleaders were arrested and shipped off deep into Imperial Russia (Allen 2014). Correspondingly, censorship, already on an upswing, was tightened throughout Ukraine, and by 1848 (in a reaction to the revolutions happening throughout Europe) a series of decrees were enacted that gave censors broad leeway to forbid anything that could be perceived as injurious to the Russian state (Velychenko 1989). Having been shut out of the political process and with no parliament to express their grievances, the tsarist authorities then took away any notion of a free press as well, with "special committees closely inspecting everything that appeared in print" (Subtleny 2009:233). Moreover, these restrictions were to get worse over the rest of the century, including the Valuev Decree of 1863 and the Ems Ukaz of 1875 (Velychenko 1989) outlawing the use of the Ukrainian language, reforms that occurred in tandem with the accelerated Russification policies in the Kingdom of Poland and the increase of internal threats to the Russian political order.

As Magocsi (2010) notes, Ukrainian political institutions under the Russian Empire were dormant until the 1890s, when the radicalization of the intelligentsia began to blossom in tandem with an incipient socialist movement. As with the Kingdom of Poland, Ukraine also had a dalliance with socialist and revolutionary thought, as the ideas created throughout Russia proper spread to Ukraine even more easily than they did to Poland. However, the relative backwardness of the country and its lack of industrialization made Ukraine an even less-promising garden for socialism, with a recognizable proletariat only coming into being in the last decade of the nineteenth century and even then only constituting approximately 7 percent of the total labor force (Subtelny 2009). Socialism in Ukraine also faced another obstacle beyond the lack of willing adherents, as the promulgators of socialist ideology saw themselves as bringing radical social change to the Russian Empire and not to an independent Ukrainian state: as Pritsak and Reshetar (1963:230) noted, "the socialist element [in Ukraine] devoted its energies to opposing the Ukrainization of the nobility and the emerging bourgeoisie and in this way hindered the process of advancing the Ukrainian nation to a state of 'completeness.'" In this manner, socialists were going with the cultural tide and accepting Russian domination of Ukraine rather than agitating for political separatism; on the other hand, perhaps the poverty of Ukraine convinced socialist theorists that any radical change had to start in the belly of the beast, in Moscow and St. Petersburg.

Instead of factory workers pushing for an independent and socialist Ukraine, as elsewhere in the world (including today), the utopian ideals of socialism found favor especially amongst students. The first acknowledged informal Ukrainian political institution under Russian rule was the Taras Brotherhood, a secret society created in 1891 by students from Lviv, which called for political autonomy for Ukraine (Katchanovski et al. 2013) and the removal of social inequalities, a platform that was distinctly influenced by socialist ideas (Reshetar 1952). Operating somewhat in the open, the founding members were soon arrested, although affiliated members continuing operating until approximately 1898 (Katchanovski et al. 2013). Following on this early attempt at political organization, in 1900, an informal political party was finally created in the Ukrainian lands of the Russian Empire, the Revolutionary Ukrainian Party (RUP).[2] Founded by university students in Kharkiv (Magocsi 2010), the RUP encompassed several ideologies but was less concerned with Ukrainian independence than with a much more socialist-inflected platform, including social revolution and economic advancement (Lamis 1978). This absence of a Ukrainian-centric program also led to the founding of splinter groups that eventually grew into formidable forces in their own right, including

---

[2] As we will see below, this was not the first political party of Ukrainians.

the Ukrainian Social-Democratic Union, which was heavily influenced by the radical Leninist strain of socialism (Magocsi 2010). Breaking with the trend towards socialist agitation, the Ukrainian People's Party (UPP) of Mykola Mikhnovsky also splintered from the RUP, as Mikhnovsky felt there should be more agitation for Ukrainian statehood and an appeal to antiforeigner passions (as well as a need to jettison the socialist rhetoric of the RUP).

The early years of the twentieth century were fruitful for Ukrainian political institutions as, much as throughout the Russian Empire in the run-up to the Revolution of 1905, political consciousness was awakening. The hodgepodge of informal political parties created a dialogue on which path was appropriate for Ukraine to take economically, how much autonomy was desired, and what was really meant by "Ukraine." Mykhailo Hrushevsky, one of the great chroniclers of Ukrainian history and a driving force of Ukrainian nationalism in the early twentieth century, stressed that building a nation was difficult work, requiring a "pan-Ukrainian" approach that developed a common language in order to avoid the fate of the Croats and the Serbs (Szporluk 1997). However, and somewhat ironically, it was not until the events in St. Petersburg in 1905 that truly pan-Ukrainian political organizations had a chance to move into action, with strikes breaking out across Ukraine in support of the protests in Mother Russia. As Katchanovski et al. (2013:505) note, "peasant unrest engulfed more than half the gubernias of Ukraine," while opposition political parties began to operate openly and in defiance of the tsarist authorities. The most memorable act of the Revolution came in June 1905, as sailors mutinied on the battleship *Potemkin* in Odessa harbor, an act that caused countless other military units to rebel throughout Ukraine (including the cruiser *Ochakov* in Sevastopol) and saw unrest continue well into the autumn. Voluntary associations such as *Prosvita*, an educational society already established in Galicia but unknown in Russian Ukraine, also began to proliferate, as civil society began to fill the vacuum held in place by tsarist authorities for so long (Himka 1993).

In addition to these informal political institutions, the tsar's October reforms, in a grudging attempt to calm the revolution, established the Russian Duma and allowed Ukrainian participation, thus giving Ukrainian nationalists a formal voice for the first time in their long history under the Russian Empire. However, the empire would not go quietly and arranged for counter-demonstrations and pogroms throughout Ukraine, with Russian-sponsored groups such as the *Chernosotentsy* (the "Black Hundreds") conducting mass violence against socialists and, especially,

Jews (Weinberg 1993). These counter-revolutionary groups, standing for autocracy and anti-Ukrainian vitriol, also were able to manipulate the nascent political institutions in the region and stood for the Third State Duma, with the Black Hundreds and their affiliated institutions winning every single seat in the Kyiv and Volhynia gubernias in 1907 (Markus and Struminsky 1984). Given that these Dumas were subject to the Imperial Manifesto of June 1907, which drastically reduced the representation of the peasantry and altered the power structure from the first two Dumas,[3] the Ukrainian representation thus was far less nationalistic than the populace as a whole and represented Russian interests rather than those of Ukraine (Lotots'kyi 1934). This state of affairs was to persist until the First World War, with the informal political parties formed during the previous decade remaining underground and, in some sense, diametrically opposed to the formal institution that the tsar had graciously allowed.

Before turning to the aftermath of World War One, it is important to note that Ukraine was actually split between two empires during the nineteenth and early twentieth centuries, with the poor and ethnically heterogeneous region of Galicia under Habsburg rule. Much as with the Polish Partitions, the Ukrainians living under Austrian rule found a much easier time than those under Russia, even though their socioeconomic status was much lower than in Kyiv or Kharkiv. Part of the reason for the relatively better life under the Habsburgs was the continuity of rule in Galicia, which remained semigoverned by noble Poles who dominated the Galician administration on behalf of the Habsburgs, having already made "a compact with Vienna in 1868" (Himka 1979:4 – see also Chapter 2). While "a common administration for Pole and Ukrainian was of no profit for a nationality that already in 1772 had no nobility of her own, but consisted of illiterate peasant serfs and of a poor and far from numerous bourgeoisie and clergy" (Andrusiak 1935:163), as was shown in Chapter 2, the continued Polish administration of the region had a much lighter touch than a Russian one would have (or, indeed, would in the twentieth century). Moreover, the "lopsided autonomy" that Galicia retained within the Austro-Hungarian Empire after 1867 also contributed to the region's political development for the better, coming as it did on the heels of constitutional reforms within the empire from 1860 to 1867 (Himka 1998:13). As Rudnytsky (1963:203) noted, "after the 1848 Revolution, Galician Ukrainians took part in elections,

---

[3] The text of the Manifesto can be found at:
  http://academic.shu.edu/russianhistory/index.php/Manifesto_of_June_3rd,_1907_ (Dissolution_of_the_Second_Duma), Accessed October 17, 2015.

possessed a parliamentary representation, a political press, parties, and civic organizations." Finally, the liberality of Galicia, even under Polish administration in a multiethnic empire, also allowed for Ukrainian nationalist sentiments to coalesce more easily than under the tsarist secret police's gaze, confirming Rundytsky's (1963:203) assessment that "conditions in the Russian Empire were such that an overt political life on a nongovernmental level was also impossible."

These nationalist sentiments were still slow to develop in Galicia, however, due to the backwardness of the region and the tide of history which nationalists were swimming against. Where national consciousness was blooming in the Russian Ukraine over the second half of the nineteenth century in a highly clandestine manner (and in direct opposition to Russification), the lands of Galicia were still heavily Polish in culture and attitudes and actually became more Polish over the century: a steady migration of Poles into traditional Ukrainian lands "transformed much of eastern Galicia, especially the cities, into oases of Polish culture" (Magocsi 2010:429). The Polish nobility of the region used this demographic edge to their advantage, convincing the authorities in Vienna that Galicia was essentially Polish in character and blocking attempts in parliament to separate out Ruthenians from Poles territorially or even culturally (Andrusiak 1935). As Rudnytsky (1987a:65) said, "the aristocratic bias of the Austrian constitution and the policies of Vienna favored the Polish element [and thus] the Poles used their dominant position to deny the Ukrainians parity and to impede their civic, economic, and cultural advancement." These attempts to retain a Polish administration in Galicia were aided by the reality that Ukrainians in Galicia were separated from their brothers in the Russian Empire by religion as much as their culture, as they remained Greek Catholic rather than Orthodox. There also was a split amongst Ukrainians in Galicia in regard to their preferred approach to resisting Polish rule, with a division along the lines of Russophile organizations, which believed that salvation lay in the arms of their Slavic brothers, and Ukrainian nationalists, who were wedded to a revival of their own language as a distinct and sustainable alternative to Moscow (Andrusiak 1935).

This is not to say that Galicia did not see a revival of Ukrainian heritage, as, perhaps due to its relative liberality, the proliferation of societies and underground nationalist parties began somewhat sooner than with its brothers to the east. Himka (1982) points out that the currents of radicalism in Ukrainian Galicia started as early as the 1870s, but it was not until 1890 (ten years before the first political party in Russian Ukraine) that the

Ruthenian-Ukrainian Radical Party (URP) of Mykhailo Drahomanov was founded in Lviv. Previous attempts by Ukrainians to influence the formal political system, by working through the parliament, had been blocked by Polish nobles, including a petition in 1868 to overturn the current electoral law that limited Ukrainian representation to half of what it should have been, based on population size (Andrusiak 1935). With continued attempts at compromise floundering throughout the following decades, the URP discarded the earlier ideas of representation within the Austro-Hungarian Empire to advocate political separatism and an independent Ukrainian state. Although their efforts were ultimately unsuccessful and, as in the case of Russian Ukraine, depended upon external events, the URP did spark a revival in Ukrainian language publications, building on the *Prosvita* educational societies that were created three decades before they arrived in eastern Ukraine (Himka 1982). As Himka (1998) was to note, this political consciousness also filtered through to the peasantry and began to impact cultural institutions such as the church, leading to mass strikes and protests for universal suffrage in the 1900s.

In fact, the Greek Catholic (Uniate) Church in Galicia was to play a similar role as the Roman Catholic Church in Poland during the Partitions and later under communism. As Smolka (1917:228) noted, the role of the Uniate Church had become thoroughly entangled with the idea of a Ukrainian nation, so much so that "even unbelievers love the national church which they regard as a vehicle of incomparable efficacy in the political struggle." Himka (1979) calls our attention to the fact that the relatively unhindered role of the clergy in Galicia, distinct from that of Russia, allowed for the priesthood to act as transmission belts of nationalist ideas from the intelligentsia to the peasantry. Also highly active in the informal *Prosvita* societies, clergy also were instrumental in setting up an entire array of informal political institutions that we would now recognize as "civil society." In this manner, the church helped to foster national consciousness by providing a safe space away from the regulated and Polish-dominated sphere of politics (Himka 1998), while also creating a sort of lesser gentry for a region that was lacking in nobility (Rudnytsky 1963). More important, the experience of informal institutions meant that, unlike their brethren to the east, Galician Ukrainians were actively putting in place the building blocks for a coherent state. In this sense, the church had been instrumental in creating the nation, as, thanks to the church, "the Galician Ukrainians were already, before 1914, a fully crystallized national community" (Rudnytsky 1963:213). And while these institutions were not necessarily meant to replace the church, but in reality, this is what they did:

"the priest's historical mission in the village – to put this in grand nineteenth-century terms – was to replace himself with institutions. In other words, the priest was important in the very first phase of the villages' transformation, in the initial germination of the movement to found institutions and read newspapers; but once the movement in a village passed this primary stage and began to run on its own momentum, the priest became an expendable part of the process" (Himka 1979:9). Thus, the creation of informal political institutions began to lessen the importance of the cultural institutions that had functioned as the only avenue for political expression for so long.

The experience of both parts of Ukraine up until the twentieth century in regard to political institutions was one that both tracked and diverged from Poland's experience. In particular, unlike Poland, which experienced independence as a sovereign commonwealth for hundreds of years, Ukraine was subjected to a tug of war by external forces almost continuously. From a high point under Kievan Rus', Ukraine's political institutions always lay in another country; even when Ukraine had successfully rebelled against its masters in a show of national consciousness, the reality of a Ukrainian state dissipated quickly as the Russian Empire forcefully moved in. And also unlike Poland, even the semblance of informal political institutions such as underground organizations and political parties were delayed until the beginning of the twentieth century, much later than elsewhere in the world. Even the concession of a parliament in Russia only lasted for two years before its betrayal, meaning that Ukraine's own ambitions were once again inextricably linked to that of its imperial master; this was also seen in the Galician portion of Ukraine, where the Polish nobility thwarted Ukrainian ambitions that were moderate and sensible. It was not until the conclusion of the First World War and the October Revolution in Russia that Ukraine was to see another major shift in its fortunes. Unfortunately, like those that had gone before, it ended in its absorption into a Russian-dominated imperial state.

Poland saw a new republic forged from the crucible of war in 1918, but Ukraine's experience, given its incorporation into the Russian Empire and proximity to Moscow, meant that it was destined to have a different path. In February 1914, a compromise was finally reached in Galicia regarding representation between Ukrainians and Poles, finally breaking the monopoly of Polish nobles on the political process (Rudnytsky 1977). However, the outbreak of the war in August halted any implementation of the compromise and instead wiped away the Habsburgs entirely (Rudnytsky 1987a). With Ukraine split between two warring parties, the loyalties of

Ukrainians were also divided, as approximately 3.5 million Ukrainians fought with the Imperial Russian Army during the war while 250,000 Galician Ukrainians fought for the Austro-Hungarian side (Subtelny 2009). Moreover, much of the war in the Eastern Front was fought on Ukrainian land, first as the Russians pushed east in late 1914, then, after the October Revolution in Russia, a massive counter-push by the Germans conquered all of Ukraine and brought their armies to within 100 miles of Petrograd (Moore and Kaluzny 2005). The liberation of Ukrainian lands from the Russians, now represented by the Bolsheviks, was seized upon by Ukrainian nationalists, who declared an independent Ukrainian state in January 1918. The Treaty of Brest-Litovsk in early 1918, between the Germans and the Bolsheviks, obliged the new Soviet government to give up Ukraine and acknowledge the new state as independent.

Like the hetmanate before it, the new Ukrainian state was plagued by many institutional deficiencies and the danger of its neighborhood. As Rudnytsky (1977:154) correctly noted, "the war and the subsequent revolution accelerated the nation-building process but at the same time placed the young nation under a tremendous burden which exceeded its strength." A key issue that was to harm the young nation was similar to that in neighboring Poland, where the experience of governing was all but extinct and new political parties vied for a power that was as yet undefined. Whereas Poles were united by their belief in the idea of Poland, the state of Ukraine was formed around a polity that had only just come around to the idea that they were a nation. Moreover, the prewar cleavages surrounding nationalism and socialism rose to the fore, as it was the socialist revolution in Russia that allowed for Ukrainian independence, but such an economic policy was opposed by pure Ukrainian nationalists. New organizations that came into being in March 1917, upon arrival of the news of the tsar's deposal, spanned the political spectrum from the Kyiv Executive Committee to various socialist worker's committees and the Central Rada, a collection of nationalists and prewar Social Democrats (but dominated by leftists) that was to play a key role in the country's next four years (Magocsi 2010). By the time of independence in January 1918, the stage was set for a tug-of-war on the country's political future and what sort of political institutions it should actually have, a struggle that Russia was determined to influence.

Heady with their success in Russia, the Bolsheviks immediately went about setting the world aflame with revolution, and pushed hard to subvert the Central Rada and establish a Ukrainian Soviet Republic. For nearly a month, the Rada had its members forced out of Kyiv by Bolshevik forces, who set about establishing a terror that they were to perfect in Moscow in the coming years; archives show that between 2,000 and 5,000 "class enemies" were summarily executed by the Bolsheviks, with more sent into exile in Russia (Yekelchyk 2007). Reasoning that "the enemy of my enemy is my friend," the Rada called for German intervention into Ukraine to push back the Bolsheviks, a plea that was taken up by the Central Powers to the tune of 450,000 men pouring over the Ukrainian frontier. With breathing space established for the Rada by the German and Austrian advance towards Russia, by April 1918 a provisional government based on the Rada had come into place (although the Ukrainian Soviet "government" in exile in Russia, having hastily abandoned Kyiv in the face of the German invasion, continued to agitate from afar; see Eudin (1941)). However, the German occupation had created tensions between the impatient Central Rada, which was eager to establish a Ukrainian state free of foreign interference, and the German army, which saw Ukraine as an important source of raw materials for the continuing war effort. Despite agreements between the Rada and the German occupiers, the Rada had difficulties in establishing an administration to deliver grain as promised, and the Germans first took over the railways and then started meddling in legislative details (Yekelchyk 2007). With numerically superior forces, the Germans finally lost patience with the leftist Rada and swept it aside, establishing a new hetmanate under Russian-born Ukrainian Pavlo Skoropadsky in April 1918 (Eudin 1941).

Pavlo Skoropadsky was a direct descendant of the last man to hold the title of hetman in Ukraine in the eighteenth century, and his own considerable military prowess was proven throughout the Great War. In a turn of events that the Central Rada was sure to regret, he offered the Rada in summer 1917 a corps of 40,000 battle-hardened men to help protect the new Ukrainian nation only to be rejected on the basis of socialist ideology (Subtelny 2009). Skoropadsky's reign, coming as it did only because of German might, failed to secure the legitimacy that a brand new Ukrainian state would require. However, as Yekelchyk (2007) correctly notes, Skoropadsky was not just a German puppet but represented much of the prewar Ukrainian elites, including the military, industrialists, and upper-middle-class urban dwellers. Despite these credentials, the peasantry was not convinced, and its representative organization, the Ukrainian Peasant Congress, began issuing decrees calling for more revolutionary tactics and resistance against the revived hetmanate (Khristyuk 1921). In response to the growing unrest, Skoropadsky cancelled every single one of the Rada's (somewhat toothless) laws, forbade public demonstrations, and reinstituted censorship of antigovernment publications (Yekelchyk 2007). Setting a trend that was to be copied throughout Europe in the coming decades, Ukraine eschewed the development of three branches of government in favor of centralized authority in the hetman, as Skoropadsky cancelled promised elections and took on dictatorial powers (Magocsi 2010).

And yet, Skoropadsky did have some success in creating a Ukrainian state from its fragmented pieces. As Subtelny (2009) notes, Skorpadsky overcame the lack of support from the Ukrainian nationalists to create an effective bureaucracy that replaced all Central Rada appointees, and he was also able to restore order with the creation of a police force. The neo-hetmanate also took important steps to forge a Ukrainian identity, printing Ukrainian-language textbooks and reorganizing the educational system to promote Ukraine (including the creation of new universities) and opening 150 new secondary schools (Yekelchyk 2007). As a rare island of stability in the region, the newly-independent Ukraine also became a beacon for the nonsocialist intelligentsia of Russia, which fled *en masse* to Ukraine to escape the Bolshevik bloodshed (Subtelny 2009). Taken together, all of these changes could have made a stable basis for a new Ukrainian state, independent of foreign powers and able to create a semblance of normalcy.

Unfortunately for Ukraine, the hetman was unable to parlay these successes into sustainable governance, continuing to rely on German might to suppress the increasingly violent guerilla warfare that engulfed the country. Led by the Bolsheviks but with other support, the opposition was able to kill the man in charge of Ukraine from the German side, Field Marshal von Eichhorn, in addition to attempting to assassinate Skoropadsky (Eudin 1941). While the violence was never enough to dislodge the Germans from Ukraine, with the Armistice in November 1918, Germany's presence was removed, and Ukraine entered another bloody chapter. A grouping of leftist political parties and assorted supporters (including, crucially, the Sich Riflemen) that came to be called "the Directory" coalesced three days after the Armistice to plot the overthrow of the hetmanate (Katchanovski et al. 2013). Within ten days, the Directory's forces were besieging Kyiv, despite Skoropadsky's last-minute attempts to rally support from the Russian elements in Ukraine (Subltelny 2009), and were able to enter the city and re-establish the Ukrainian National Republic, which had been deposed months earlier. As Magocsi (2010:495) remarked, "the Directory had few concrete plans for governing the country," trying to walk the fine line between revolutionary rhetoric and the reality of the need for governance and, especially, public order. As in Russia, there was little enthusiasm for order, and instead the Directory called for mass expropriation of the land of any previous institution (including the state, church, and large-peasant lands) while simultaneously attempting to shut down any opposition from the gentry (Subtelny 2009).

Academic arguments about which class was the rightful vanguard of the proletariat were quickly overtaken by events, as, despite reuniting with the West Ukrainian National Republic (ZUNR in Ukrainian) of Galicia, the Republic saw a repeat invasion of the country by the Bolsheviks in December 1918.[4] With French forces in Odessa ready to support the White forces in the Don against the Bolsheviks in the widening civil war, Ukrainian leaders made an appeal to yet another foreign power to save them from the predations of the Russians. While the Directory made changes to curry favor with the French (Subtelny 2009), what actually ensued was two years of anarchy and disorder that bloodied the Ukrainian state. Bolshevik forces, aided and augmented by peasants who had little idea of what they were actually fighting for (Magocsi 2010), had a steady string of victories that brought them into Kyiv in February and over most of Ukraine by June. Aided by large-scale desertions from leaders who were already quite sympathetic to the Soviets and the Bolshevik terror, the Bolsheviks ironically took over a country that was in the midst of implementing Soviet policies and its own Russification (Subtelny 2009). At this point, Ukraine became an additional front in the Russian civil war, as White armies under General Denikin invaded the Left Bank of Ukraine and forced a collapse of the Bolsheviks, who had held control of the cities but had little influence in the countryside (Magocsi 2010). The Directory's forces had regrouped but had undergone several changes of leadership, harming their cause and expending energies uselessly in the interim through large-scale anti-Jewish pogroms; despite returning to Kyiv in August 1919, their army was immediately expelled by Denikin, who had already proven his mistrust of Ukrainians (Katchanovski et al. 2013).

---

[4] Ukrainian nationalists had seized power in eastern Galicia on November 1, 1918, and proclaimed the West Ukrainian National Republic. This too saw the start of violent confrontation, as street battles in Lviv precipitated the opening of the Polish-Ukrainian war (Rudnytsky 1987).

The anarchy of 1919 and 1920 meant that Kyiv changed hands several times between all manner of warring parties, and no political institutions were able to be built. Moreover, the Ukrainian state was fighting on almost all fronts, as the apparent sideshow of eastern Galicia, now the West Ukrainian National Republic, had drawn the Poles into a battle that sapped Ukrainian forces at the exact time they were needed to repel Bolshevik invaders (Bocheński 1937). Unlike the proto-Bolsheviks (the Directory) or proto-fascists (Skoropadsky, Denikin) in Kyiv, the leadership of the ZUNR was a good model for a united Ukrainian state – according to Katchanovski et al. (2013:749), "the political culture of the ZUNR, shaped by decades of Austrian constitutionalism, made for a stable and orderly administration whose institutions functioned reliably" – which was a double tragedy for the country when they were swept away by Polish might. Even though the Ukrainians had numerical superiority in Galicia, the Poles had both military superiority (in regard to the entire Ukrainian armed forces, but especially in Galicia) and diplomatic advantages, as the victorious Entente allowed Poland a relatively free hand in its east (Magocsi 2010). The Polish-Ukrainian war in Galicia lasted for only a few months during the chaos of 1919, with Polish forces successfully pushing out the ZUNR by November 1919; however, by July, members of the West Ukrainian military had already abandoned Galicia to fight against the Bolsheviks in eastern Ukraine, and were helping to create an effective fighting force. Indeed, the Galician influence in the east meant that, "for the first time, a semblance of law, order, and stability appeared on the Directory's territory" (Subtelny 2009:372). However, continued strife amongst the Ukrainian military leaders led to the Galicians placing themselves under the command of the Whites while the Directory's forces reorganized as partisan units to fight the Bolsheviks.

As noted in Chapter 2, the Polish-Soviet war came on the heels of the war with Ukraine, as, after agreeing to cede Galicia to the Poles, the remnants of the Directory's army under Symon Petliura agreed to team up with the Poles against the Bolsheviks. With the Poles seeing great successes, followed by the advance of the Red Army to the gates of Warsaw, and the miracle on the Vistula throwing the Soviets back, Ukrainians once again saw foreign invaders sweeping across their lands. In a betrayal that was to have dramatic repercussions for Ukraine, in the peace accord between Poland and the Soviet Union signed in Riga in 1921, the Polish political classes abandoned Petliura and the Ukrainians and instead made an arbitrary division of Ukraine and Belarus between Poland

and Russia (Subtelny 2009).[5] With Polish politicians intent on not absorbing lands that were not "historically Polish" (Boemeke et al. 1998), this demarcation left Dnieper Ukraine, including Kyiv, in the hands of the Bolsheviks, while retaining the more Catholic provinces (and 5 million ethnic Ukrainians) within Polish borders (Wright 1945). Derided as a "new Andrusovo" by Volodmyr Kedrovskyi (1936), the Treaty of Riga resulted in Bolshevik victory and the establishment of the Ukrainian Soviet Socialist Republic (SSR). While the Poles had held back the scourge of world revolution for twenty years, their nationalist impulses, implemented by those who had little experience of governance themselves, handed over the incipient Ukrainian state to Russia while absorbing the Ukrainians who could have made a difference in their homeland.

It is here that the political institutional history of Poland and Ukraine begins a severe divergence. Unlike Poland, which had the experience of twenty-one years of independence before it was obliterated by the Nazis and the Soviets, only returning to a quasi-independence after the Second World War (but actually under the Soviet thumb), Ukraine was absorbed whole into the Soviet Union by 1922. The effect that this had on Ukraine's economic institutions will be explored below, but this series of events meant that Ukraine's political institutions ceased to operate despite the appearance of being fully functional. The weakness of the Bolsheviks in the early years of the Ukrainian SSR may have prompted many Ukrainians to view the 1920s as a "golden age" (Subtelny 2009), mainly due to Ukraine's apparent independence, ability to conduct its own (Russian-aligned) foreign policy, and the use of Ukrainian in official proceedings ("Ukrainization"). Rudnytsky (1987b:463) called the early years of the Ukrainian SSR a *de facto* political compromise that worked to the favor of Ukrainians, where "Russia retained political control over Ukraine and, by virtue of that, the position of the paramount power in Eastern Europe [and] Ukraine preserved, from the shipwreck of her greater hopes, the status of a nation (denied to her by the tsarist regime) and a token recognition of her statehood in the form of the Ukrainian SSR."

In reality, however, the brief weakness of the Soviets up to and immediately following Lenin's death meant that steps needed to be taken cautiously in regard to the fragile Ukrainian Soviet state; when

---

[5] In reality, the border was not as arbitrary as I may have made it appear; Wandycz (1969) details how the border was actually meticulously drawn in regard to ethnicities. What I meant above is that the border was drawn with little heed to Ukrainian claims.

the requisite power had been found, Stalinism and the destruction of national autonomy followed swiftly. The deliberate starving of the countryside in the Holodomor in the 1930s (which will be explored more below) broke the backs of any Ukrainian resistance, while the Great Terror exterminated millions of Ukraine's best and brightest in an attempt to crush Ukrainian nationalism (Katchanovski et al. 2013). From approximately 1928 to 1941, Ukraine was brutally subjugated and absorbed into the Soviet apparatus in Moscow, meaning that any desired move towards political development was pushed back by a tidal wave of blood. Ukrainian political institutions continued to operate on a nominal level, but they were entirely and wholly orchestrated by Moscow, and when the orders came to reverse Ukrainization or purge key Ukrainians, the Communist Party in Kyiv duly complied (Subtelny 2009). As Rudnytsky (1987b:465) accurately said,

Soviet Ukraine lacks the most essential trait of any self-governing state: the ability to formulate and pursue policies of its own. The power of the central government in Moscow is all-pervasive, and it does not leave the organs of the Ukrainian Republic any sphere of independent jurisdiction. Any decision made in Kiev can always be overruled by Moscow. Thus the supposedly sovereign Ukrainian SSR reveals itself in practice as an administrative subdivision of a monolithic empire, endowed with a modicum of linguistic-cultural autonomy. And even the latter is being subverted by strong Russification pressures.

The German invasion of the Soviet Union in 1941, aided by the forward position they were given in Poland by Stalin and the Molotov-Ribbentrop Pact, visited continued unspeakable crimes on Ukraine (as it did in Poland and Belarus). Moreover, at the end of the war, with the victorious Red Army covering ground as far west as Berlin, Stalin was determined to expand the borders of the Soviet Union outward. As part of the Yalta agreements (see Chapter 2), Ukraine as an administrative territory (and the Soviet Union as a country) expanded westward, with the Galician and Volhynian lands of Poland, including Lviv, absorbed into the Ukrainian SSR. Whereas these lands once held the biggest promise for an independent Ukraine, due to their institutional affinities for Western Europe, they were now Sovietized in a brutal fashion, with the Greek Catholic Church liquidated, the Ukrainian Insurgent Army (UPA) crushed by NKVD detachments, and the Polish minority forcibly deported to the new frontier of Poland (Subtelny 2009). Worried of lingering nationalist sentiment, as well as unreliability in these newly acquired lands, Stalin also set about a new phase of collectivization and purges that lasted until his death in 1953 (Magocsi 2010).

From the ascendance of Nikita Khrushchev through to the end of the Cold War, Ukrainian political institutions remain as dormant as they did during the late tsarist era, and for the same reason. Any upwardly mobile Ukrainian leaders were soon to seek their fortune in Moscow rather than Kyiv, as "Ukrainian elites were once again assimilated, this time to the dominant and largely Russified Soviet political and cultural norms" (von Hagen 1995:668). As "second among equals," Ukraine did rather well in securing its place within the Soviet leadership, with four Ukrainians eventually becoming members of the Politburo and countless others rising through the ranks of the military, although this was due more to their association with Khrushchev rather than their Ukrainian nationality (Subtelny 2009). Other issues that were to become much more important in recent years also originated from Moscow, such as the gifting of Crimea to the Ukrainian SSR, and were done as purely political moves from Khrushchev to solidify his own position in the Party (Kramer 2014). Finally, even within the Ukrainian SSR, the political climate encouraged stagnation, as evidenced by the two Communist Party leaders under Brezhnev, Petro Shelest and Volodymyr Shcherbytsky. Shelest encouraged Ukrainian nationalism and defended Ukraine within the Soviet Union during his tenure (1963 to 1972), but he was hardly the salvation of the country, ardently defending the Soviet invasion of Czechoslovakia in 1968 and pushing for even more heavy industrialization (Subtelny 2009). Shcherbytsky, eased into position after Shelest was ousted, reversed Shelest's nationalist policies, and carried out mass arrests against any members of the intelligentsia that dared to dissent from Soviet policies as officially stated. Having proven his bona fides to Moscow, Shcherbytsky was to remain in power in Ukraine until 1986.

The political institution-building in Ukraine thus ends here, as even cosmetic changes towards political institution-building, such as the introduction of a new constitution in 1978 (to replace the Soviet one from 1937), did little to alter the entrenched power structure or the punishment for going against the Soviet model (Horbulin et al. 2010). However, two important events must be noted briefly: the growth of the dissident movement in the Soviet Union more generally and the Chornobyl disaster in 1986. Throughout the Soviet Union, the growth of *samizdat* publications and especially the linkages to the Helsinki processes in the mid-1970s encouraged a separate space from the state, using the language of human rights. A Ukrainian Helsinki group began work in 1976, operating in the open as a civic organization apart from the Communist Party; while the group only lasted for four years before 75 percent of its members were imprisoned, its existence was revolutionary, as was its advocacy of rule of law and civil rights (Subtelny 2009). But while the effects of the Helsinki process were limited to intelligentsia and professional dissidents, the trauma of Chornobyl especially exposed the leadership of Ukraine and the Soviet Union more generally as incapable of meeting even the most basic needs of the populace (Solchanyk 1986). In the words of Wanner (2010:33), the inept Soviet response to the catastrophe made even Russian residents of Ukraine see "their republic as a colony for the first time." In parallel with Mikhail Gorbachev's dual processes of *glasnost* and *perestroika*, the feelings unleashed by the disaster were to prove a powerful impetus for Ukrainian political separatism, with even the sacrifice of Shcherbytsky to the political gods unable to appease the populace (Subtelny 2009). For once, Ukrainians were able to see the system itself as the problem.

But even the dramatic nature of Chornobyl was not enough to bring down the Soviet system in Ukraine. Indeed, these events throughout the 1970s and the 1980s, with the exception of Chornobyl, were happening in parallel across the Soviet Union, once again showing that the idea of a Ukrainian history separate from Moscow is impossible. As so often in Ukraine's history, it took an exogenous event – the fall of the Soviet Union from centrifugal and external forces throughout 1991 – for Ukraine to actually find itself independent. It was only then that political institution-building, in a truly Ukrainian state, could begin anew and build on the history of Kievan Rus', the brief hetmanate of the seventeenth century, and, hopefully, the experience of the Galician Ukrainians in 1918 and 1919. Unfortunately, as we will see in the next chapter, the allure of the Golden Horde and the Muscovy approach to governance remained strong in Kyiv even after the Russians had left.

ECONOMIC INSTITUTIONS

Despite the long history of domination by other empires and the relative inexperience of Ukrainians with developing their own political institutions, it can be plausibly argued that Ukraine had a much more successful experience in building economic institutions. In fact, the original basis for a Ukrainian state was economic, as Kievan Rus' was founded in the ninth century by a nobility that took advantage of location on several major trade routes to the east to enrich itself, in the process transforming itself from a warrior class into merchants and creating vital trade institutions. The expansion of trade-and-craft settlements in the tenth century led to proto-urbanization, as villages housing both long-range traders and the craftsmen that they depended upon began to agglomerate throughout the Rus' (Dolukhanov 2014).

From this early vantage point, Ukraine appeared to have laid a solid foundation for economic growth; however, the fluidity of political institutions over the thousand years after the fall of the Kievan Rus' meant that there was often intense pressure on economic institutions to change to fit new political climates. A key issue that was to recur throughout Ukraine's history was that, apart from a short time under the Polish-Lithuanian Commonwealth, in general economic institutions in Ukraine were developed to enrich the political elite. Whereas the *szlachta* in Poland demanded more political rights in order to protect their property and rights from the predations of rulers, in Ukraine, it appeared that political power was sought precisely to institute those very same predations. As with Poland, however, this story is not uniform across all economic institutions, as many have persisted even despite the constant raids from political institutions and different rulers. But for every economic institution that persisted at an informal scale, there are still others that were entirely demolished during Soviet rule. Indeed, the history of rapacious rulers in the Ruthenian lands, engineering economic institutions for their own good, is sadly a story that has been consistent in Ukraine, amplified during the tsarist era, and perfected under communism.

As with political institutions, the history of economic institutions in Ukraine prior to 1989 must necessarily be narrowly focused due to Ukraine's fleeting periods of independence, which meant there was little indigenous development of institutions (and the relevant foreign institutions have been dealt with elsewhere in this book). In particular, the building of monetary and financial sector institutions was, for the most part, absent in Ukraine prior to 1989, as monetary policy was ruled from either Warsaw or Moscow during the modern era. Similarly, it is useless to speak of Ukrainian banking in the 1800s or under the Soviet period, because financial intermediation was either undertaken via Polish moneylenders, dominated by Russian financiers, or laboring under the communist credit allocation system shown in the previous chapter. Thus, in order to really home in on the economic institutional development of Ukraine, we are forced to limit ourselves to property rights and labor market institutions, two sides of the same coin in the land-rich but peasant-poor land of Ukraine, and trade, which was to play a large part in Ukraine's early existence.

Property Rights and Labor Market Institutions

We start the look at Ukraine's economic institutions, as in the previous chapter, with the paramount economic institution, the right of private property. However, the history of property rights in Ukraine is inextricable from labor markets, especially the institution of serfdom, which determined so much of the rights of the peasantry for hundreds of years in Ukraine. For that reason, we treat both of these institutions here.

Somewhat paradoxically, Ukraine's early experiences with property rights were favorable, despite a long history of scholarship that claims the opposite (Pipes 1990). Blum (1964) points to the substantial private ownership of land during the Kievan Rus' era, competing with independent peasant communes for the majority of landholdings throughout the land now known as Ukraine. Weickhardt (1993) also makes a strong case that Byzantine law, which was enforced across the Kievan Rus', had an influence on attitudes towards property rights, allowing for contracts and directly informing customary law in the territory, even if it was not formalized in later legislation. Dewey and Kleimola (1984) also point to the creation of individual suretyship, which acted as a form of bail or a bond in legal proceedings, as another basis for contract enforcement, as it could be utilized in case of violation of contract. Finally, the *Ruska Pravda*, in addition to its legal provisions noted above, formally recognized customary property rights by allowing for penalties against plowing beyond one's boundaries, while also establishing a system to punish theft of property and resolve ownership disputes (Weickhardt 1993).

The end of the medieval era and the gradual incorporation of portions of Ukraine into the Polish-Lithuanian Commonwealth meant that changes to this basic framework of property rights protection were inevitable, and in time the framework transformed to encompass the Polish estate system. The shift was not immediate, and indeed took approximately two hundred years to coalesce as economic forces were in favor of the peasantry in the sparsely populated Ukraine. Subtelny (2009) notes that the peasantry in fourteenth-century Ukraine had won extensive rights to property due to the relative scarcity of labor versus land; the effects of the plague throughout Europe had reduced the labor force and increased the relative demand for workers, giving them substantial bargaining power and in turn the ability to extract the right to sell or bequeath land, with only light labor obligations attached to land ownership/rental. However, the extension of the estate system from Poland, with rigid socioeconomic stratification amongst classes (nobility, burghers, and peasants) meant that there was a trend away from broad-based property rights and towards concentration of those rights at the top of the social/political pyramid. Moreover, the depopulation of the fifteenth century also created a countervailing pressure for the land rights of the peasantry, as the prospect of deserted villages and scarce labor put an end to the push from Polish nobles to "colonize" the Ukrainian lands. This meant in practice that nobles sought profit not through expansion of land but through consolidation of what they already owned, meaning an erosion of property rights of the peasantry (Trethewey 1974).

As shown in the previous chapter, even in a Poland of laws and limited central executive power, property rights began to suffer by the sixteenth century; in fact, it was perhaps due to the laws themselves that property rights became the exclusive purview of the nobility, as the *szlachta* were able to utilize strong local executive power to codify their privilege in legislation. This process gained momentum in tandem with the formalization of political rights in the Polish-Lithuanian Commonwealth. As noted in the previous section and in Chapter 3, much of Ukraine was originally hived off to Lithuania rather than Poland during the period after 1386 but before the Union of Lublin in 1569. This meant that property rights protections in most of Ukraine were originally subjected to Lithuanian jurisdiction rather than Polish, especially in regard to serfdom and the ability to dispose of one's landholdings. But it was not until the key reform in Lithuania noted above, the *Voloky Ustav* of 1557, was originally introduced in order to facilitate property rights by standardizing land measurements, but instead was utilized to enforce ever more stringent labor obligations on peasants (Subtelny 2009). As part of this reform, property rights were denied to the peasantry and reserved to the gentry, with restrictions on transfer of property gradually tightened over the following decades until codified into the Third Lithuanian Statute in 1588 (Gordon 1983).[6] While Subtelny (2009) rightly notes that the Lithuanian Statutes provided a firm basis for legally guaranteed rights, and the concept that natural rights can be protected by the state, it also created a way in which political institutions could conquer economic ones.

---

[6] Legally, by this time the restrictions should have fallen on a smaller portion of Ukraine, due to the reassignment of boundaries as part of the Union of Lublin. However, the inconsistencies between this Statute and the Treaty agreed to at Lublin persisted for many years even after the right of approval was given to both the *Sejm* and the Diet of Lithuania (Plateris 1965).

The administrative transfer of much of Ukraine to Poland proper after the Union of Lublin accelerated the process of limiting broader property rights, with the development of such restrictions in Ukraine evolving hand in hand with the move towards greater serfdom, as the restriction of rights of peasants came in tandem with the expansion of the Polish landed gentry into Ukrainian territories (Subtelny 2009). But, as with political control, the application of the Polish estate system was also quite uneven in Ukraine. The lands that were annexed to Poland under the Union of Lublin, including the more western provinces of Ukraine and Galicia, were to see extensive integration into the Polish manorial system due to their proximity and the relative desirability of these lands (Baten and Szoltysek 2014). However, to the east, according to Gordon (1983:47), "not only did freeholding continue in these frontier lands, but squatting intensified in the late sixteenth century, and peasants in service continued to labor under a multiplicity of different tenant relationships." Thus, much as Ukraine was to see divisions between its western and eastern halves in terms of political institutions, property rights also had an uneven distribution; the difference, of course, from nearly every other institution was that property rights were more widespread across social strata in the east than in the west, although the legal framework was more developed in the west (as noted, to protect the *szlachta*'s privileges).

The story of property rights in Ukraine exhibited little change in the early seventeenth century, as the *szlachta* and, more importantly, the Ukrainian nobility continued to consolidate their privileges at the expense of the peasantry and defended their own rights from pressure from above. Indeed, the crucial nature of the Ukrainian magnates in the estate system in Ukraine cannot be understated as, in a very real sense, property rights flowed from their largesse rather than from the *Sejm* in Warsaw for both peasants and the lesser nobility (the *starshyna*). Of course, the influence of the magnates on the peasantry is well known, as the large landowners were even able to influence town-dwellers and demand obligations or threaten them with expropriation (Subtelny 2009). But as Kamiński (1977:179) noted, "even some Crown officials who possessed extensive *latifundia* sought protection from one of these Ukrainian 'kinglets.' For without such protection, neither life nor property was assured." The source of this power for the magnates came from their integration into the *szlachta* system (whereas the *starshyna* remained on the outside), as well as the Polonization of many of the magnates (with the most famous of them all, the Wiśniowiecki family, having polonized their name from the original Vyshnevetsky). Given such extensive land-ownings and acting as regents in their domain, property rights were available only as a whim of the magnates rather than, as in the rest of Poland, legislatively determined as part of the "execution of laws" movement. In fact, this movement barely penetrated Ukraine (Miller 1983).

With a series of rebellions in the early 1600s underscoring the growing power of the Cossacks and their popularity amongst the peasantry, the great Ukrainian magnates of the incorporated Ukrainian lands undertook draconian policies to keep their serfs in line and avoid further troubles; as Subtelny (2009:123) correctly judged it, "some of Europe's most exploitive feudal lords confronted some of its most defiant masses." Grievance fed upon grievance, until the major Cossack rebellion of 1648 upended the Polish control of the estate system and threatened the largest Ukrainian landowners. Kamiński (1977) notes – perhaps in eerie prescience of the events of Maidan – that entire strata of society underneath the great magnates joined in the rebellion, which was not only directed against Polish administration but against the oligarchy that de facto ruled over the Ukrainian lands. As part of the rebellion, and in an irony that should not be lost, the ultimate deciders of property rights in Ukraine were robbed of their own rights wholesale, as magnate estates were taken over by the Cossacks.

The gains of the Cossacks, as noted above, were not destined in the long run to favor the peasantry or even the existing *starshyna*, as the hetmanate was merely a way to replace the Polish nobility with an indigenous, Ukrainian one drawn from the Cossacks' ranks. In the short term, the Cossack rebellion was seen as a victory for property rights across the whole spectrum of society, as they immediately restored the rights of land transfer to the peasantry and removed the labor obligations that had been imposed (Subtelny 2009). But the legal basis for property rights remained mired in the hodgepodge of laws extended to Ukraine over the previous two centuries, informed by the same estate ideology and without a reflection of the shifting circumstances that brought the Cossacks to power. Indeed, perhaps because the hetmanate was still nominally part of the Commonwealth, the Cossacks relied on previous legislation for determining property rights, including the Lithuanian Statute and the Magdeburg Laws, but tailored them for Ukrainian usage. Furthermore as part of the Treaty of Pereyaslav with the tsar, the rights of the Ukrainian nobility to own land and the inviolability of land ownership was guaranteed but there was no mention of the peasantry or even a thought of extending these rights to them at this point in time (Myronenko 2013). Additional confirmation of the property rights of the nobility also occurred in the ceding of Smolensk to the Russian Empire via the Treaty of Andrusovo in 1667, where the nobility were guaranteed their continued property (although this was to change rapidly in the eighteenth century; see Kappeler (2014)). By utilizing these pre-existing laws and the additional codicils in the treaties concluded in the mid-seventeenth century, the Cossack leadership was able to arbitrarily grant estates to Cossack noblemen as a reward for faithful service, as well as to codify various rights of inheritance of property (Myronenko 2013).

The encroachment of the Russian Empire after the initial Cossack dealings with the tsar, and the *de facto* split of the country after 1667, led to a steady loss of property rights across every class in the new Ukraine, a process that began almost immediately after the final subjugation of the Cossacks by Imperial Russian forces in 1709; as Subtelny (1980:11) noted, "within weeks of their arrival in the Ukraine, the Russian regimental commanders initiated a reign of terror in the land. Confiscations of property, interrogations, executions, and exile were the fate of anyone not only slightly associated with Mazepa's '*izmena*,' but even suspected of uttering an uncomplimentary remark about the Tsar." Such an inauspicious start to formal Russian occupation of Ukraine was formalized with the region's incorporation into the Russian administrative structure, a move that increased administrative burdens and led to a corresponding threat of arbitrary seizure of property by the state (Velychenko 1995). Subtleny (2009:202) summarized the approach of the Russian administrator as follows: while "the nobles – both Ukrainian *starshyna* and Polish *szlachta* – who dominated Ukrainian society in the eighteenth century . . . acted on the principle of the less government, the better, the imperial bureaucrats who governed in the nineteenth century believed that the more rules and regulations they imposed on society, the better off society would be." This love of administration translated directly to lower levels of property rights, as administrators subscribed to the belief that "the nation was the property of the monarch" (Szporluk 1997:104), meaning that all other property rights were malleable. Whereas property rights had been tenuous at the local level prior to 1654, they were now in danger of abrogation from Moscow directly.

It is perhaps unfair to blame the Russian administration of Ukraine for the diminution of property rights, as, for the most part, the incorporation of Ukraine into the tsar's bureaucracy continued a long-standing policy of rights for the privileged. For example, before the office of the hetman was formally abolished in 1783, there were still conflicts within the Cossack ranks over issues of private property, including a major skirmish in 1768 precipitated by widening socioeconomic conditions amongst the Cossack nobility and the rank-and-file; as Subtelny (2009:181) correctly notes, by the mid-eighteenth century "less than 1 percent of the population controlled close to 50% of the land." But the Russian oversight of Ukraine set these disparities into overdrive, as rulers in St. Petersburg could see the benefits of supporting such inequalities to strengthen their own rule over Ukraine. In this manner, the Russian administration was wholeheartedly behind attempts by the Cossack nobility to limit the mobility of the peasantry and circumscribe the property rights of the peasantry (Subtelny 2009). This included Cossack-initiated reforms as late as 1786 (even though the office of hetman no longer existed) where the Cossack hierarchy defined perpetual grants to land and blocked off large swathes of Ukrainian estates from ever being disposed of. In tandem with Catherine's strict enserfment of the peasantry in 1783, even the ancient tradition of right via presence (squatting) was revoked by the Cossack elite (Myronenko 2013). Land administration from Russia also did not just play itself out in subtle support for indigenous policies, as the tsars and tsarinas were also quite happy to intervene directly where needed. As an example, Tsarina Catherine was said to have gifted 800,000 serfs and their lands to her noble friends during her tenure on the throne, making it obvious why "her reign [would] become known as the golden age of the serf-owning nobility" (Volin 1943:47).

As with Poland, it was only during the eighteenth and early nineteenth century that the idea of property as an inviolable right for all began to take hold in Ukraine. First mentioned in the Constitution of Pylyp Orlyk from 1710, the issue of the right of property regardless of class still had little support amongst the Cossacks or the Russians throughout the eighteenth century. A slight move towards greater property rights for the peasantry occurred in the 1840s under the heading of "inventory reform," where Tsar Nikolai I ordered a ceiling set on labor obligations in Ukraine; however, while it was trumpeted as a step towards freedom, the perception of the inventory was overwhelmingly negative, and over 300 peasant disturbances broke out (Leonard 2011). It was likely that this reform was too little, too late, and that more drastic measures were required. But it was not until two decades later, with the removal of serfdom across the Russian Empire in 1861, that the right of ownership was transferred to the peasantry. But the autocracy was not about to let political devolution accompany this process, and the granting of property rights was manipulated by those who were already advantaged by the political system:

Generally speaking, peasants emerged from the reforms with less land at their disposal than they had had prior to 1861. In the Russian north, peasants lost about 10% of their former plots. In the Left Bank and in southern Ukraine their holdings were reduced by almost 30%. Thus, whereas the average size of peasant holdings in the empire was about 27 acres per family, in the Left Bank and in southern Ukraine it was only 18 acres per family. Landlords in Ukraine appear to have fared especially well in the bargain. Through the use of various tactics during the period of negotiation and redistribution of land, they appropriated forests, meadows, and ponds that had previously been considered common property. Invariably, they kept the most fertile areas for themselves and sold inferior land at inflated prices. In the course of redistribution, they often forced peasants to move, thereby imposing additional expense upon the poor. To be sure, these practices were common throughout the empire, but, in Ukraine, where competition for land was keenest, they were especially widespread. As a result, the peasants of the Left Bank and southern Ukraine fared much worse than their Russian neighbors (Subtelny 2009: 255–256).

As with so many policy shifts in Russia, even the institution of private property was carried out in order to be as advantageous as possible to the Russian state. In contrast to the Left Bank and its relative disadvantages immediately following the end of serfdom noted above, the Russian government supported property rights fully in the Right Bank, granting much larger concessions to the peasantry and larger land plots than elsewhere in Ukraine. The reason behind this was simple, as it was seen as a way to buy the loyalty of the peasantry *vis-à-vis* the Polish nobility who still tended to dominate economically, granting more power to the peasants to counterbalance the enemies of the tsar (Volin 1943). Such an approach gained a sense of urgency with the Uprising in the Kingdom of Poland in 1863, where the rebels promised the Ukrainian peasantry larger land allotments and a cancellation of any redemption fees in exchange for their support (Finkel et al. 2015).

Similar issues, and a similarly cynical use of property rights, were to be found in the Galician lands under Austrian rule. While we have spoken already in depth on property rights in Galicia in Chapter 3, it is important to note here that property rights were established after the revolutions of 1848 in Galicia before being extended throughout the empire in order to undercut the Polish nobility (Struve 2008), who were already under assault from the collusion between Habsburg authorities and Ukrainian peasants (Leslie 1955). But, as noted in the previous chapter, the rush to removing serfdom also left open the issue of "common" land, and a controversy over usage of land such as meadows and forests festered well into the nineteenth century. More importantly, the conflicts over land use between "manorial estates" (i.e., nobility) and peasants that ended up in the formal judicial system seemed to be resolved overwhelmingly in favor of the manors (Struve 2008). Thus, while property rights were officially available to all, the class distinctions present before the end of serfdom continued to manifest themselves in the enforcement of those rights after abolition.

Even with the abolition of serfdom in both Galician and Russian Ukraine, the latter half of the nineteenth century did not see greater codification of property rights, at least not in the way we would understand such rights from today's vantage point. A trend in the Russian Empire writ large was to not quite make the leap to the idea of individual property rights, with the tsarist authorities instead emphasizing "communal property rights," where land was allotted to communities rather than households. Under this system, "authority over the use-rights to open-field arable plots in repartitional communities was vested in the commune itself, and communal authorities could and did reorganize the division of arable land and redistribute specific plots among member households" (Nafziger 2015:6). More important, the repartitional system, emphasizing communal exercise of property rights, was plagued by the same institutional inefficiencies as other forms of communal ownership (the "tragedy of the commons"), reducing incentives for agricultural efficiency and tending to stifle productivity (Nafziger 2008). Moreover, as Williams (2013) points out, all decisions regarding agricultural production, including timing on grazing, were made at the collective level, placing constraints on choice of crops or harvesting. While this system was almost unheard of in Right Bank Ukraine, making up only 14 percent of all land holdings, it was more prevalent in Left Bank Ukraine, making up nearly 49 percent of land, closer to the average of 80 percent across the Empire.

There may have been a longstanding attachment to private property in Ukraine as opposed to Russia, with homesteads being much more prevalent than larger communal properties, but the economic position of the former serfs in Right Bank Ukraine was not dramatically improved by the abolition of labor obligations (Subtelny 2009). Part of the reason for this lack of improvement, apart from the insider advantages noted above, was that labor markets remained very rigid throughout Ukraine (and the Russian Empire in general). Migration amongst regions was severely curtailed and subject to administrative approval in the form of internal passports, and it wasn't until the turn of the twentieth century, when such restrictions were removed, that growth of peasant land-holding (as measured by land purchases) began to boom (Leonard 2011). But other economic trends at this time also began to weaken the push for formal property rights: in the first instance, the Second Industrial Revolution led to an increase in manufacturing and urbanization, lessening the need for land rights in the agricultural sphere. At the same time, the industrialization of Ukraine (and the Russian Empire in general) meant that Ukraine's bountiful supply of coal in the Donbas was in high demand, also creating opportunities in the labor market for unskilled laborers (Portal 1966). This desire for point-source resources paradoxically may have also vitiated the expansion of individual property rights, as the need for capital-intensive extraction reinforced the dominant "communal property rights" paradigm of the Russian Empire. Put another way, given that resources such as coal came from readily identifiable sources under large tracts of land, and given that energy was seen (then as now) as a matter of national security, it was more desirable to have such resources under a communal/state-owned property regime rather than a private property one (where the land would have had to be purchased piecemeal). This approach was also markedly different from the approach towards oil in Galicia, where oil was designated as the private property of the landowner where the oil emerged (Frank 2006).

A further impediment to enforcement of property rights in Russian Ukraine in the nineteenth century was very similar to that noted in Galicia above, namely the issue of the judiciary. There was little tradition in Russia of the concept of a *Rechtsstaat*, with an independent judiciary constituted to protect citizens against infringements on their property or liberties, with social class instead considered the basis for the system of "justice" (Plank 1996). This point of view was broadly held throughout society, as Engelstein (1993:346) notes, even "the radical intelligentsia [of the Russian Empire] was resolutely anti-legal, the mirror image of this relentlessly inconsistent autocratic state." This different view of what the legal system was meant to accomplish meant that, for most of the eighteenth and early nineteenth centuries, the judicial system in Russia was an appendage of the monarchy, with trials conducted in secret and courts expected to enforce but not interpret the law. It was not until the Judicial Statutes of 1864 that the formal conception of the judiciary in the Russian Empire changed, allowing for "independent public courts, an oral adversary procedure, and the jury system" as a way to limit "the tyranny of the police" (Wortman 2011:2). However, even this momentous change in legislation was of limited usefulness in the area of property rights, as special "peasant" (*volost*) courts were exempted from the new regulations, meaning that the vast claims of former serfs were held in these courts under different (and less transparent) procedures (Plank 1996). For non-Russian nationalities such as Ukrainians, access to the new independent courts was even more difficult, meaning that property claims were adjudicated in a "business as usual" manner in Kyiv.

The turn of the twentieth century and the revolution of 1905 also had a considerable impact on property rights as well as the political system, with the institution of a right to individual property ownership in 1906. Introduced as part of the Stolpyin reforms to revitalize the agrarian sector in Russia (of which Ukraine was an integral part), the codification of property rights came under a "constitutional haze," being first introduced by a *ukaz* from the tsar in November 1906, confirmed in a statute four years later, and further elaborated in an additional statute in May 1911 (as Williamson (2013:114) notes, this was due to the fact that there was not broad-based support in the Duma for such a measure). The reforms introduced a land-titling process that greatly undermined the communal property approach, shifting the Russian Empire over a period of nine years to a title-based system. In Ukraine, this meant a large change in the Left Bank, as by 1914 communal property was prevalent only in Kherson and Kharkiv, and even then 200,000 households in the two oblasts combined had switched to individual landowning (Guthier 1979). Agricultural productivity also increased, as was the ultimate end goal of the reforms, and inefficient communes were dissolved under competitive pressures (Krasnozhon 2004). These reforms also encouraged a large migratory shift throughout the Empire, as, unshackled from their lands, peasants were able to move away from Ukraine and towards the Asian portion of Russia in search of their fortune (Chernina et al. 2014).

Unfortunately, the arrival of property rights in Russia approximately 125 years after its pinnacle in the U.S. Constitution only lasted for a mere eleven years, as the Bolshevik Revolution of 1917 was intent on destroying all forms of private property and returning Ukraine (and the rest of the Soviet Union) to communal property. It took years before this became reality, however, as the independence of Ukraine during the civil war years, as noted above, resulted in several different governments, none of whom was able to form a coherent approach towards private property. The Central Rada had no preconceived notions about the desirability of private property, although they were likely less than predisposed to it given their leftist leanings, a reality that was irrelevant given the short time they were in power. Institutional instability ruled the day throughout the rest of 1918 and 1919, as the hetmanate proclaimed the primacy of private ownership, but the Directorate reversed course and made plans for expropriation of land to be turned over to "the people" (Dzera 2012). The schizophrenia regarding private property even continued into the early years of the Ukrainian SSR, as from 1919 to 1921 property was outlawed, a reality put into law in the Land Code of the USSR in October 1922. This legal nicety was quickly undercut by the needs of the New Economic Policy (NEP) (Bandera 1963), and the Civil Code of the Ukrainian SSR a mere two months later, which allowed for some forms of private ownership (Dzera 2012). The concessions the peasantry received under the NEP allowed for private farming, "aimed at increasing marketable agricultural output by inducing the peasants to pursue their self-interests" (Bandera 1963:268). But by 1927, the immediate crisis facing the young state was over, and the Soviet Union returned to its zeal for removing property rights as a tool of "exploitation" of the working class.

In addition to the loss of political independence that Ukraine suffered as a constituent republic of the Soviet Union, the toll on its economic institutions and, as a consequence, human life was enormous. The key (or at least one of them) to this carnage in Ukraine was collectivization, the removal of all forms of individual ownership in the countryside and replacement with collective farming. As Subtelny (2009:405) accurately put it, "the plan aimed, in effect, at transforming the entire labor force in the countryside as well as the city into employees of state-controlled enterprises." Collectivization not only involved the eradication of private property, but it involved the forced requisition of the labor that had been put into the land; thus, not only were Ukrainians under labor obligations more onerous than those ever imposed under serfdom, but the food that they were able to produce under an inefficient system was then taken and sent elsewhere in the Soviet Union. In this manner, the Soviet leadership hoped to procure the bountiful grain that was necessary for the successful fulfillment of other aspects of the first Five-Year Plan, above all rapid industrialization.

Although the experience with war communism and collectivization during the civil war (primarily 1919 to 1921) was a total failure, such empirical evidence did not deter the Bolsheviks and especially Stalin. After initial setbacks and a brief pause to the killing, Stalin attempted to make individual farming economically unfeasible, aggregating the best farmland for collective farms and ordering all sorts of prohibitions against peasants who dared to leave the collectives (including not allowing them to take their equipment or livestock with them; see Subtelny 2009). With the second phase of collectivization, however, Stalin identified the source of past failures as "saboteurs," and specifically the influence of the nefarious "kulaks," the mythical moneyed class that was the root of all obstacles to realizing communism. Thus, moving beyond liquidating the right to own property, Stalin set out to liquidate all those who advocated private property, a project that met with much success through the liquidation of capitalists, people who looked like capitalists, people who may have once known capitalists, or people who may or may not have known what capitalism was.[7] As a consequence of Stalin's direct orders, the elimination of private property via collectivization from 1928 to 1933 wiped out a huge portion of Ukraine's human capital and resulted in the greatest tragedy to hit Ukraine. The Holodomor took the life of an estimated 3.3 million Ukrainians (Snyder 2010) as a lower bound and, perhaps more likely, 5 to 7 million as the higher bound (Conquest 1987), a lost generation who were tossed aside as part of a misguided belief that too many property rights in Ukraine's history was the reason for the poverty of the peasantry. Of course, and as noted earlier in this chapter, the deliberate starvation of so many Ukrainians was a consequence of the eradication of property rights, but the fact that the killing went on as long as it did was that it also served a political purpose for Stalin, eliminating any opposition and turning Ukraine into an "exemplary republic" of the USSR.[8]

With the Holodomor and the following Great Terror and purges of the population, private property in the Ukrainian SSR was driven far into the underground, with any small-scale private enterprise in the 1930s punishable by death or deportation. As the governing framework for the next fifty years of the Soviet Union, the "Stalin Constitution" of 1936 (adopted wholesale in 1937 in the Ukrainian SSR) made it clear in Chapter I, Article 6 that all basic property such as "the land, its natural deposits, waters, forests, mills, factories, mines, rail, water and air transport, banks, post, telegraph and telephones, large state-organized agricultural enterprises (state farms, machine and tractor stations and the like) as well as municipal enterprises and the bulk of the dwelling houses in the cities and industrial localities" was "state property," belonging to all of the people. In this manner, the legal consolidation of communal property rights was

---

[7] Despite the excellence of the Bolsheviks in killing people, Hessler (1998) makes a well-reasoned point that the private sector never went away in the USSR, even during its darkest times. Perhaps some ideas are immune to bullets.

[8] Stalin wrote this in a letter to Lazar Kaganovich, the First Secretary of the Communist Party of the Ukrainian SSR and later a Secretary of the Central Committee of the Communist Party, in 1932. Quoted in full in Snyder (2010).

codified and all forms of private ownership, with the exception of "small" plots of land for collective farmers for their personal use (Chapter I, Article 7). And despite the re-acceptance of some private ownership during the Second World War and in the months immediately following (Hessler 1998), the tightening of Stalinist policies, in tandem with the expansion of communism throughout Central and Eastern Europe, meant that large-scale, formal and individual property rights had indeed been eradicated in Ukraine.

However, this reality was not uniform across the entire Ukrainian state, which, as noted earlier in this chapter, had expanded to include the formerly eastern Polish lands at the end of the Second World War. Indeed, Volhynia and Galicia managed to escape the Holodomor by dint of their being part of Poland, and were spared communist policies until being forcibly incorporated into Ukraine in 1939 by Stalin as part of the Molotov-Ribbentrop Pact. The outbreak of hostilities amongst the former friends in 1941 put on hold any plans Stalin had for extending collectivization to the new territories of Ukraine, although changes to land tenure laws in March of that year restricted the size of private landholdings (Marples 1984). It was not until after the war that collectivization was slowly implemented in the Western Ukraine, a difficult task for a region where armed resistance to the Soviet presence continued for years after the defeat of Germany and where private farming had a much longer pedigree than in the east of the country (Marples 1985). Despite these challenges, and perhaps due to twenty more years of experience with the collectivization process, the Soviets were able to complete collectivization by 1951, with nearly all of the region's 1.5 million peasants concentrated on 7,000 collective farms (Subtelny 2009). This did mean, however, that western Ukraine had only approximately forty years of experience with collectivization, as opposed to eastern Ukraine, which had nearly sixty-three years (dating back to the start of collectivization in 1928), in addition to western Ukraine's much longer experience with private property as part of Poland (Swinnen and Heinegg 2002). The disparity between the two parts of Ukraine was perhaps most vividly illustrated by the onset of the collectivization process in 1948 and 1949, where resistance by peasants was overcome via an influx of technocrats from eastern Ukraine (Marples 1985).

With both halves of the country subjugated, the reality of collective rights rather than individual ones was to persist for the rest of the Soviet Union's existence. Ukraine, governed by the monopoly of the Communist Party and under such legal documents as its constitution, reverted to a quasi-communal approach to property rights, with the only forms of contracts that were entered into under the planned economy utilized amongst various economic units, such as factories and suppliers. In fact, the loosening of the Soviet economy after the death of Stalin was predicated not on large-scale property rights, but on the gift of more autonomy to firm and factory-level managers to enter into contracts (Pejovich 1969). However, as a long literature detailing the failures of communism has noted (see McFaul 1996), the contractual arrangements entered into were concluded out of necessity in serving the plan, leaving very little room for individual initiative, and, most damningly, the contracts themselves also were very rarely fulfilled (or even based on any sane economic rationale). It was only at the upper echelons of the Party that anything resembling property rights based on personal interest existed, where the rights of the *nomenklatura* allowed them to maximize their rents at the expense of the property and liberties of the rest of the country (Winiecki 1990).

Similarly, other supporting institutions crucial for property rights protection were turned on their head in order to support the communal rights idea. The most important of these, the formal judicial system, had been under pressure ever since the Tsar's Reforms of 1864, "sow[ing] conflict between executive and judicial authorities, as the autocrat became increasingly distrustful of the independent judiciary" (Wortman 2011:3). As noted above, this distrust was misplaced in the arena of property rights, where peasants were under a different legal regime and had far less recourse to address infringements of these rights. However, such distrust of all other poles of authority led to a radical reform of the judiciary under the Soviet system: rather than setting up the judiciary as a bulwark against infringement of the rights of Soviet individuals and expanding the reforms of 1864 to cover all individuals, the court system of the USSR was expressly set up to protect the state from its citizens. This was made explicit in Chapter X, Article 131 of the 1936 Soviet Constitution, where individuals who committed offenses against socialist or public property were deemed "enemies of the people." Thus, the court system once again became an enforcer of the laws, rather than an interpreter, guarding the communal rights of the Soviet Union (and the state) against any attempts to return to a capitalist system. In this manner, even the formal judiciary became a tool for denying individual property rights, bringing the weight of the state to bear on those who challenged the state's notions of property.

The fact that Ukraine was actually a part of the administrative apparatus of the Soviet Union, and with a twenty-five year head start on Poland in implementing communism, also meant that Ukraine had much less experience with informal property rights and contracting (although, as just noted, these were more prevalent in the west of the country).[9] Indeed, as a way to shift workers away from property and towards system-specific communal assets, the state instead provided for labor-market outcomes such as job security or generous (on paper) benefits, filling the void of personal property with guarantees from the government (Pejovich 2012). This did not mean that informal institutions did not exist and persist throughout the Soviet period, as a survey taken in 1977 of Soviet émigrés estimated that Ukrainians earned 40 percent of their income from the shadow economy (Grossman 1989). As with elsewhere in the Soviet Union, the small-scale informal rights exercised in Ukraine relied on personal connections and networks, reverting to a "clan" mentality in order to conclude informal contracts and enforce promises (what Ledeneva (1998) called reputation-based informal networks with "favors of access"). Without such networks and connections, one's property rights, as is the design in a communal rights system, were directly dependent upon the acquiescence of every other person in the system or, more accurately, on the elites (Heller 1998). Ironically, this created a large collective action problem not just throughout the country but even at the local level; Crowley (1994) details worker grievances in the Donbas in the late 1980s and notes that miners would have been able to exercise power for small-scale reform if they had banded together informally (and outside the state union mechanisms), but faced severe sanctions if they were not united. This problem was replicated throughout the Soviet Union. So long as the Communist Party retained its political monopoly, the idea of voluntary contracts, enforced by an independent judiciary, was unthinkable, as was the expansion of private property beyond personal effects.

However, the gradual thawing of economic control in the 1980s under the heading of *perestroika* weakened Moscow's control of the economy and brought a measure of political decentralization which, while it did not change the small-scale nature of property rights in Ukraine, increased the number of such contractual arrangements. Informal institutions rushed to fill the void left by the retreat of the Communist Party throughout the Soviet Union, with the "defensive mechanisms" of the shadow economy

---

[9] Unfortunately, given the difficulty of obtaining data in a closed society such as the Soviet Union, much less on its constituent republics, there is little scholarly work done in English or Russian on informal property rights in Ukraine. Much of the work that has been done has related to the entire Soviet system, but even this work relies on anecdotes or surveys of émigrés (as noted above in Grossman (1989)).

multiplying to provide goods and services that the planned economy patently could not (Gel'man 2004). These arrangements, including the aforementioned clan mentality, only increased in an atmosphere where even the repressiveness of the authorities suddenly became more uncertain. At first, these informal contracting arrangements built a bridge for survival, but at the same time they weakened bonds throughout society, enabled nonoptimal behaviors such as criminal networks (Wedel 2003), and atomized larger potential markets into ones reliant on first-hand knowledge of the other parties to a transaction (Raiser 2001). These difficulties intensified as it became more certain that the Communist Party would have to make some drastic economic reforms in order to save the system, meaning possibly more political reforms (and further loss of control) as well. With knowledge that the system was to change but no sense of its timing, firms and especially collective farms were able to use informal contracts to create deals in anticipation of a restitution of full property rights (Mathijs and Swinnen 1998). The longer it took towards this dramatic reform by the elites, the more the informal contracting arrangements became entrenched in Ukraine and elsewhere throughout the Union.

It was not until these elites of the Communist Party allowed alternative forms of property ownership via the Ukrainian Supreme Soviet's resolution on land reform of 1990 that the actors in the economic system could reorient themselves to a new set of property rights institutions. Buttressed by the newly independent Ukraine introducing its own law on land ownership in January 1992 (Lerman 2001), legislation finally caught up with both western Ukraine's history and the informal contracting arrangements in place during the last decade of the Soviet Union. However, as we will see in the next chapter, building the supporting institutions of formal property rights remained problematic for the new country, as the legacy of informal institutions designed to overcome the Soviet economic system's weaknesses took on a life of its own and contributed to opposition to the new state.

Trade

The other key economic institution to influence Ukrainian development, trade was the original economic basis of the Kievan Rus'. While Ukraine did not have the luxury of an extensive coastline to launch seafaring trade, as did Poland, it did have the benefit of advantageous geography, being located on several major trade routes to the east and linking southern, northern, and eastern portions of Europe and beyond. Transit trade beginning in the ninth century with the Byzantine Empire and Khazaria created a lucrative source of income, allowing the indigenous Ruthenian nobility to enrich and transform itself from a warrior class into merchants by the early eleventh century. Multiple trade treaties concluded in the tenth century (one in 911 and another in 944), generally as part of military excursions, institutionalized the rights for Ukrainian merchants to trade in the Byzantine lands, providing a coherent summation of privileges and obligations related to trade (Martin 1995). At the same time, Ukrainian participation in trade, generally in agriculture but also in fur, honey, and other products on the fringes of agricultural processing, also contributed to an incipient urbanization movement, with individual homesteads being knitted together to create towns and eventually cities (Dolukhanov 2014). The development of both the interior of Russia and the continued expansion of Constantinople and trade along the "highway" from Regensburg to Khazaria meant accessible markets and increasing demand, a fortunate combination of circumstances that helped Kyiv to attain status as a major commercial center by the 1100s (Pritsak 1977). Indeed, Subtelny (2009) asserts that the quest for control of this trade was in fact the prime impetus for the existence of the Kievan Rus' itself, as the nobility was well served by fashioning a political "conglomerate" to oversee the collection of tribute in a more formal manner.

Reliance on transit trade for both the merchants and politicians of Ukraine created difficulties when global trade patterns shifted, however, and the sacking of Byzantium during the Fourth Crusade in the thirteenth century marginalized Constantinople and vitiated the existing trade routes running through Ukraine (Curtis 1996). This in turn weakened the Rus' from within by undercutting its economic clout, a situation that was to prove disastrous in the following decades. The Mongol invasion and time spent under the Golden Horde in the thirteenth and fourteenth century took advantage of this weakness to conquer the lands of Ukraine, at the same time continuing to severely disrupt the trade and commerce that was the basis of Ukrainian wealth; in particular, depopulation, punitive political measures by the Mongols, and the slave trade robbed the land of peasants to work it (Halperin 1987), skewing investment decisions away from long-term planning to short-term survival. By the time of the expulsion of the Horde in the late fifteenth century, Ukrainian merchants would have to deal with a whole new external environment and their absorption into the Polish-Lithuanian Commonwealth, while still facing the threat of raids from Crimean Tatars, which would continue until well into the seventeenth century (Kotilaine 2005).

The basis for the growth of trade during the early years of liberation from the Mongol yoke came from the continued expansion of towns and villages, and specifically the political and economic decentralization enjoyed by these settlements under the Magdeburg Law, which was based on Flemish law and was brought to the east by German colonists in the fourteenth century. It constituted a body of privileges afforded to settlements including the "right to self-administration, exclusion from the jurisdiction of Polish governors (*wojewody*), [and] the right to organize guilds for craftsmen and trade" (Nadel-Golobič 1979:351). In contrast to the Lübeck Law, which was found mainly in the cities of the Hanseatic League that traded along the Baltic coast, the Magdeburg Law was less focused on powers of governance and administration and more on guilds and rights connected to trade, preferring to let municipal councils emerge organically (Sedlar 2011) and in a manner very different from in Western Europe (Katchanovski et al. 2013). And as a symbol of rule of law and a welcome change from the capricious rule of the Mongols, the principles of the Law spread rapidly through Poland and especially into eastern Poland, reaching now-Ukrainian towns such as Volodymyr-Volynskyi around 1324, Sianik in 1339, and Lwów (L'viv) in 1356 (Tkach 1968).

As with many other institutional developments in Ukraine, there was a decided divide between the east and the west of the country, with the Magdeburg Law concentrated in the west, taking until 1494 to reach Kyiv and later to spread elsewhere in the country (Korostelina 2013). However, there were also differences in the application of the law's provisions in reference to the citizenry across the Ruthenian lands. In particular, the portions of Ukraine attached to Lithuania after 1386 generally extended equality of participation in town administration and ability to enter commerce for all, incorporating Ruthenian standards and administrative practices into town governance (Stone 2001). By contrast, in the Polish towns of what is now western Ukraine, the Magdeburg Law was often applied only to Catholic burghers, meaning that large minorities such as Ukrainians, Jews, and even Armenians suffered discrimination and were treated as second-class citizens, with limited civil rights, in contravention of the royal privileges bestowed by King Kazimierz (Sysyn 2003). Ironically, this state of affairs was to play out in Ukraine as it did elsewhere in the world; with no real way to influence the political process, ethnic minorities went into business, often becoming leading merchants and financiers and dominating the economy of a nation that refused to accept their membership. This was especially true in the eastern Polish/western Ukrainian lands, with Lwów standing as the main example of a municipality where Armenians and Jews together became the commercial heart of the city (Nadel-Golobič 1979). As middlemen in the agricultural trade, working with Polish landlords, such minorities and especially the Jews became more identified with the ruling Poles than with the Ukrainian peasants (Magocsi 2010).

Despite the uneven application of the Law across East Central Europe, the extension of its principles to at least a part of the Ukrainian lands helped to foster both basic trade institutions such as guilds, as well as to create a necessary framework for both governance and finance of trade. More important, where early trade formalities had been conducted at a highly centralized level (as in the trade treaties from the Kievan Rus' in the tenth century), the autonomy granted under the Magdeburg Law allowed for decentralized development of trade according to comparative advantage. While Polish-Lithuanian authorities, aware of the lucrative possibilities of the towns and villages, attempted to extract tribute and regulate trade routes, the increase in trade around the towns was too meteoric to be hampered by these regulatory burdens, personified in the growth of Lwów. As Subtelny (2009) notes, by the mid-1400s Lwów had a population over 10,000, comprising 36 different professions spread across 14 craft guilds (in contrast to Kyiv, whose population had dwindled due to repeated Tatar attacks originating from Crimea). Part of this growth had also been due to government regulation in the fourteenth century: Hrytsak (2000) notes that, during a period of joint administration with Hungary, Lwów was under a law stipulating that all merchants passing through the town had to remain for fourteen days in order to offer their wares, allowing for the merchants of the town to have a great say in the trade with the east. With cultural and ethnic diversity in the town unlike elsewhere in the Commonwealth, Lwów was to remain a major trading center until the middle of the seventeenth century.

As with property rights, the history of trading institutions in Ukraine from this point until the Partitions closely follows the Polish path, although the geographic dispersion of the country and its position between two powers meant that there also was a different evolution between east and west. Indeed, Ukraine is the border of Wallerstein's (1972, 1974) thesis that the global trading system of the sixteenth century had its "ins" (of which Poland was one) and its "outs" (including Muscovy and the Ottoman Empire). Depending upon which part of Ukraine is under discussion, it is easy to see that trade radiated in very different directions; for example, as Gordon (1983) correctly notes, southeastern Ukraine served very different markets from the polonized west, with one branch sending grain to Scandinavia and Moscow and the other shipping agricultural products to the south and India, bypassing Gdańsk entirely. More obviously, parts of Ukraine that had been incorporated in the Polish-Lithuanian Commonwealth focused their trade towards Western Europe (and especially the Netherlands), utilizing the seafaring trade routes that were to vitiate the overland routes in later years and cause economic dislocation to Ukrainian cities (Hrytsak 2000). But even here, as Nadel-Golobič (1979) shows, the trade was not limited in one direction, as Lwów saw trade radiating towards Moldova, Crimea, Turkey, Flanders, Kraków, and Gdańsk (but relatively little with Lithuania and Muscovy).

Of course, one attribute of trade that both western and eastern Ukraine shared was the main commodity it traded, namely agricultural products and specifically grains such as wheat. With the increase in grain prices occurring throughout Europe during the sixteenth century, more and more production was required to feed expanding demand, meaning that more and more resources were drawn into agriculture in East-Central Europe. Here, the institutions of trade, labor, and private property all become entangled, as the development of Ukraine's agricultural trade during this period was intimately connected with both the extension of serfdom and the grab for land in the east. With space freely available, (Millward (1982) notes that population density in Ukraine was only approximately three people per square kilometer), the challenge for merchants and nobles was to entice peasants into the east to help cultivate the land and satisfy the burgeoning demand globally. Polish nobles, having won concessions to large tracts of land throughout Ukraine granted by the crown after the incorporation of these lands in 1569, promising lessened or suspended labor obligations for those who helped to colonize Ukraine and turn a profit in grain (Kamiński 1975). While transportation infrastructure was still lacking and was to continue to lack for many more years (van Tielhof 2002, noted in the previous chapter), the trade in grain had its own vertical processes well in place, with Polish landlords often subcontracting out oversight of the manorial system but holding control over agricultural processing (Magocsi 2010). This process continued as grain prices continued to rise, especially in wheat but also in rye and, more variably, in oats (Figure 4.1).

In addition to the grain trade, more mobile and less-capital-intensive trade also began to occur in the hinterlands of Ukraine, driven by the Cossacks of the Zaporozhian Sich. Many of the peasants who had already shifted to the Dnieper basin during the late fifteenth and early sixteenth

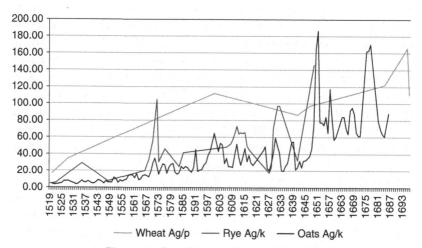

Figure 4.1 Grain Prices in Lwów, 1519–1696
*Source: Hoszowski (1954). Measurements are grams of silver (Ag) per polmiarek
(38.93 litres) or per kloda (311.45 litres). Series for wheat and to some extent rye
extrapolated from data over longer (twenty-year) time-spans.*

century were economic refugees, moving to escape the "second serfdom"
and take their chances on the borderlands in-between empires (the name
"Ukraine" is actually an Anglicization of Україна (*Ukrayina*), which
means "frontier" or "borderland" in early Slavic). As frontiersmen,
much like in the myth of the American West, these colonists brought
a rugged individualism with themselves, settling untamed lands and
believing themselves to be under obligation to no man (Subtelny 2009).
Coalescing into the Cossack nation and its concomitant political institutions, the Cossacks of the frontier also became involved in trade.
With a more nomadic lifestyle, Cossack trade focused on mobile assets,
including livestock and furs, without aspiring to higher value-added
production; as Guillaume de Beauplan (1990:5), a French military
engineer who served in Poland during the seventeenth century, noted,
"the fertile land produces grain in such abundance that they do not know
what to do with it . . . they prefer to borrow goods for their comfort from
their good neighbors, the Turks, rather than take the trouble to work
for them." In reality, the Cossacks tended to be facilitators of trade,
providing protection against Tatar raids, rather than those intensely
engaged in it (Katchanovski et al. 2013).

The Cossack behavior observed by de Beauplan appeared to be sympto-
matic of the somewhat idiosyncratic development of the entrepreneurial

class in Ukraine since Kievan Rus' times. As Korzhov (1999) explored in detail, Ukrainian merchants under the Rus' and then the Golden Horde displayed a (perfectly natural) aversion to risk-taking, based on the need to keep trade at a small scale and informal. Given the highly uncertain nature of their external environment, especially under Mongol domination, Ukrainian merchants restricted their trade channels to the familiar and the well-known, eschewing market dominance (growth) in pursuit of profits. Jancec (2013) offers some empirical evidence on the effects of these shifting borders in Ukraine, showing how repeated conquests engendered lower levels of trust, which in turn likely made it difficult to expand production and trade networks. Korzhov (1999:511) also draws our attention to the fact that Ukrainian merchants became less likely to band together in pursuit of their own interests, as even the guilds or brotherhoods that Ukrainian merchants engaged in in the sixteenth and seventeenth centuries avoided collective political or social action in favor of a "self-imposed restriction to innovation." While much of this aversion to collective action was forced upon Ukrainians in the west, with Polish burghers explicitly prohibiting Ukrainian membership in guilds, even the "brotherhoods" that sprung up as a reaction to this prohibition were dependent upon a few individuals (Subtelny 2009). As Katchanovski et al. (2013) note, the guild system in Ukraine was also less exclusive than in Western Europe, more focused on governance than on increasing the standards of products and the reach of members.

With the Cossack Uprising, as with so many other institutions, the trade routes of Ukraine took a decided turn eastward, with tsarist impositions closing down the "natural" trade routes with Poland and artificially reorienting trade towards Muscovy (Hisrich et al. 2006). Moscow's control over trade at first was less than total, as in the words of Kotilaine (2003:280), "seventeenth-century Muscovy was a state heavily dependent on foreign trade, yet in a very weak position *vis-à-vis* the foreign merchants who made this trade possible." As an example, Magocsi (2010) notes that the Cossack hetmanate also had its own flourishing trade with the Ottomans (as de Beauplan was to note), a trade that actually dominated Russian trade flows until the eighteenth century. Kotilaine (2005) also goes into great detail on the trade between Ukraine and Russia in the early seventeenth century, noting that only liquor and tobacco were the main exports of Ukraine to the tsar, and even then much of this trade occurred illicitly (contradicting de Beauplan's assertion that Cossack's did not know what to do with their abundant grain, as evidently they distilled it into high-proof alcohol). Showing that the small volumes of trade went both ways, only furs and hides came back across the border to Ukraine, as well as likely larger amounts of illicit salt, forbidden by the tsar for trade with Ukraine but still smuggled across the frontier anyway (Braudel 1982). Trade only began to increase by the late 1640s, at the time of the rebellion, including in trade in livestock and horses, despite attempts by the Ukrainian authorities to shut this down in the interest of national security (Kotilaine 2005). Thus, for the greater part of the fifteenth through seventeenth centuries, the only trade institutions operating between Russia and both parts of Ukraine were informal, designed to circumvent formal trade policies rather than to support them.

However, as with the other frontier lands that Moscow conquered over the seventeenth and eighteenth centuries, complete assimilation into the tsarist empire did eventually come, with the major trade institutions of Poland-Lithuania that may have existed in Left-Bank Ukraine being overcome by the extremely centralized Russian model. Cossacks willingly joined in this process of trade-based *Anschluß* with Russia from the period of 1648–1709, using their own social cleansing of Polish nobility as a way to impose ideas about the structure of trade and commerce as well. In particular, Cossacks during the rebellion may have killed up to 50 percent of the Jewish community (approximately 18,000–20,000 people) living in Ukraine, barring those who survived from living under Cossack control and forcing them to flee towards Poland proper (Stampfer 2003). This effort, while not necessarily systematic or organized as later campaigns of extermination would be, erased the predominant merchant class in the region, leaving behind only small-scale traders. In order to fill the void left behind, the hetmanate invited Greek merchants and gave them privileges, including their own courts, if they would settle in the Cossack lands (Magocsi 2010). A fair number of Cossacks of the Zaporozhian Sich also began to turn in their warrior clothes for those of merchants, much as their forbearers did during the Kievan Rus', entering into affiliated trades such as metalwork or boatmaking (Subtelny 2009).

Unfortunately, the attempt of Ukraine to create its own indigenous merchant class, perhaps supplemented by co-religionists, was stymied by relentless pressure from tsarist Russia and, perhaps even more so, by the global economy. External economic events also conspired to shift the trade routes and institutions within Ukraine, as the great grain price boom of the sixteenth century came to an abrupt end by the mid-seventeenth century (Fischer 1996), just as the hetmanate was establishing itself as independent from Poland. With the near-constant conflict of the seventeenth century, typified in the Thirty Years' War from 1618 to 1648, land-based trade infrastructure was also utterly devastated around Europe, precipitating a further shift towards sea-based trade. Such a global change in trade supply modes was destined to impact Ukraine negatively, given the aforementioned lack of a coastline; in an example of disastrous timing for Ukraine's leaders, the hetmanate cut itself off from Polish shipping outlets such as Gdańsk and turned towards the Russian Empire, which had no warm-water port, precisely when global trade began to rely more on shipping. As Kotliane (2005:412) accurately noted, when combined with "periodic famines and perennial social conflicts – especially the rise of the Cossacks ... the development of Ukrainian trade in the first half of the seventeenth century lagged significantly behind its potential. Indeed, compared to Russia, Ukraine appears to have been a relatively closed economy."

Other internal institutional issues were also pressing against the hetmanate's trading abilities, including the role of monetary policy institutions. Monetary policy has been deliberately passed over in this chapter mainly because Ukraine has little modern experience of its own, independent monetary policy institutions, continually under the sway of Poland's institutions (as detailed in the previous chapter) or, as will be seen, under Russia's. But in the time of transition from the Polish-Lithuanian Commonwealth to the tsarist empire, monetary conditions suddenly became more pressing for the development of foreign trade (Moshenskyi 2008). In particular, as Kotilaine (2005) notes, the trade links between Poland and Ukraine meant that there was a much bigger need for Polish currency, and throughout the latter half of the seventeenth century Polish copper coins predominated, even in Left-Bank Ukraine. This dual-currency system, based on both Polish and Russian coinage, was further complicated by differing exchange rates between Ukraine and Russia, as Moscow fixed the rate of the thaler (an international monetary unit) while Ukrainian authorities allowed it to float; combined with a prohibition on export of silver and gold coinage from Ukraine but continued export of precious metals for minting coins from Ukraine to Russia, the monetary situation in Ukraine was a morass of contrasting rules and regulations (Moshenskyi 2008). Poland's own difficulties in debased coinage also further affected Ukrainian trade, as low-value Polish silver coins, allowed to come into the country but not leave contributed to price fluctuations, thus hindering longer-term credit markets. As Moshenskyi (2008) notes, credit activity for foreign trade did not exist at all in the hetmanate, skewing trade into small-scale and provincial activities, and in some instances, barter was still the preferred coin of the realm, in order to guard against currency debasement or arbitrageurs.

As Left-Bank and eventually Right-Bank Ukraine became more assimilated into the Russian Empire in the late seventeenth and early eighteenth century, eventually monetary issues gave way to the trade issues that were also to plague Poland as part of its absorption into Russia. Foreign trade under the tsar was governed by a philosophical approach that saw trade as the right of the sovereign, to be managed at will: as O'Brien (1949:167) put it, the tsar felt that "the right to possess and cultivate land and to engage in trade came from above," an attitude that comported well with the Cossacks' own highly centralized and mercantilist approach to trade (Magocsi 2010). This philosophical underpinning translated into administrative, policy, and institutional difficulties that began to emerge in Ukraine during the time of "the Ruin" and multiplied with each passing year. The most visible manifestation of this approach came in the institution of a restrictive tariff and customs regime based on the Russian model.

As a semisovereign state, the hetmanate had the right under the Treaty of Pereyaslav of 1654 to impose its own tariffs, a task it set about doing almost immediately (Pritsak and Reshetar 1963); indeed, the Cossacks relied on trade as a source of revenue, and thus paradoxically tried to "stimulate" it at the same time they were discouraging it via taxation (Magocsi 2010). While the Polish-Lithuanian Commonwealth had its own intricate series of customs tolls and duties, with a continual ratcheting of rates, abortive attempts to raise revenue at the port of Gdańsk in the mid-seventeenth century (Stone 2001), and a focus on private duties levied by the *szlachta*, the hetmanate and, later, the Russian approach towards trade policy was comparatively very simple. In the words of Subtelny (1980:15), "an elaborate and stringent system of import duties was set up on the Ukraine's western borders . . . designed to prevent the import of finished products which might compete with Russia's fledgling industry." The hetmanate set this process in motion by centralizing the customs and tariff system away from the decentralized Polish system, abolishing private duties and imposing a state duty on foreign goods, as well as attempting to renegotiate earlier treaties that Ukraine had entered into (Holubnychy and Ohloblyn 1993). Additionally, the hetman set up formal customs posts at the borders of Russia and the Ottoman Empire, governing their operations under the "Universal of 1654" (Babirad-Lazunin 2013:14).

But as the Cossack state was increasingly absorbed into Russian administrative structures, the level of trade barriers began to increase, with an imposition of transit duties in 1677 having an immediate and negative impact on trade oriented towards the south (Kotilaine 2005). By the time of Peter I's crushing of the Cossacks and Swedes at Poltava in 1709, this absorption was complete, leading to

a disastrous effect on Ukrainian trade. Formerly, Ukrainian merchants were free to trade wherever they wished and many of them developed extensive contacts in the Baltic region and in Western Europe. In 1714, they were suddenly ordered to shift their business, regardless of the losses this entailed, to Russian or Russian-controlled ports such as Arkhangel'sk, Riga and finally, St. Petersburg. In 1719, the export of Ukrainian wheat to the West was forbidden. This allowed the Russian government to buy up the wheat for its own use at a very low price (Subtelny 1980:15).

As can be seen from Subtelny's description above, an arcane system of permissions and licenses or permits, overseen by draconian prohibitions when the tsar so decreed it, ruled Ukrainian trade policy. Again, this approach started in the hetmanate, as explicit permission was needed from the Cossack leadership for Ukrainian businesses to export or import, much as such permission was needed from the tsar (Kotilaine 2005). However, the tsar's increasingly direct interventions into Ukraine's major source of export earnings, grain, created massive dislocations in the Ukrainian rural economy. In the first instance, the price interventions had a dampening effect on agricultural productivity in the countryside, which was already quite low by European standards; while only 65 percent of Ukrainian fields were common-use by the end of the eighteenth century, as opposed to 80 to 95 percent in Russia proper, there were the same "small yields, soil exhaustion, and the inefficient methods of cultivation used by the peasant" in both Ukraine and Russia (Blum 1960:3). According to Subtelny (2009:179), in Ukraine "typical harvests of wheat were only three to four times greater than the amount of grain sown," a yield far below that of Western Europe (and miles behind England, see Brunt 2004). With prices held down by fiat, there was little incentive to either innovate, increase wheat yields, or to invest in existing land, rather than just moving on to a new parcel. Moreover, land that could have been producing grain for food or for livestock feed was instead going into the production of alcohol, with districts averaging 500 distilleries a piece by 1750 (Subtelny 2009).

This state of affairs was supplemented by the formal policies setting tariffs and duties on Ukrainian trade, which also were put in place to advantage ethnic Russians in favor of Ukrainians.

Finally, Russian merchants were given preferential treatment in the export of their goods to the Hetmanate, while Ukrainians had to pay duties of 10–37 percent for the goods they sent to the north. Taking advantage of the situation, such men as Menshikov and the Stroganovs became heavily involved in Ukrainian trade, forcing many local merchants out of business (Subtelny 1980:15).

The tariff border between Russia and Ukraine was abolished entirely in 1754 (Holubnychy and Ohloblyn 1993), but this only turned the frontier of Ukraine into the frontier of the tsarist Empire. With customs posts now taken up by Russian bureaucrats, this added the indignity of duties collected at the Ukrainian border bypassing Ukraine altogether and going straight to St. Petersburg (Rudnytsky 1963). In this manner, not only were Ukrainian businesses disadvantaged by increased taxation and imperial prohibition, the money that was collected was not even returned to the region to help in development. The total effect of these policies was to turn Ukraine into a semicolonial outpost of the tsar, useful as a source of low-cost agriculture that could not be procured elsewhere and a source of revenue from taxation, but still a primitive backwater of the empire.

The evolution of Ukraine's trade institutions during the era of Russian dominance, from approximately 1709 through to the mid-nineteenth century, is thus rather stagnant; Kotilaine (2005) accurately notes that Ukraine's shift toward Moscow had an element of trade creation in it, although it is folly to think that this trade was not a function of external economic forces (such as the increase in wheat prices or global agricultural market integration) but instead of tsarist trade policies. Tariff policy was very uneven over the early eighteenth century in what it covered, but there was a consistent trend towards higher duties, including the move towards import substitution under the Petrine tariff of 1724, which set rates up to 75 percent on some manufactured goods (Kahan and Hellie 1985). Similarly, in tandem with the abolition of the internal tariff border between Ukraine and Russia in 1754 came the imposition of a tariff that dramatically increased duties on foreign goods, specifically in order to make up for the loss of internal revenues collected at the Russo-Ukrainian border (ibid.). At the same time, Peter the Great's mercantilist policies, prohibiting export of raw materials (something that Ukraine had in abundance) and directing the minutiae of trade from Moscow, remained in effect, harming Ukraine's trade flows (Leonard 1993).

Some attempts at reforming this system were made in Russia in the 1760s, as both Peter III and then Catherine II saw the ruin that Russia's mercantilist policy was creating. Building on her attempts to rectify the empire's difficulties through the convening of a "Commission on Commerce" in 1763 (Alexander 1988), a *nakaz* issued in 1767 from the tsarina attempted to address some of the issues with the country's trade institutions. Moving to reform the "antiquated customs system" that restricted domestic trade and hampered external commerce, Russia introduced a more liberal tariff schedule, and the tsarina herself railed against policies that involved too much bureaucracy or that limited trade (Dmytryshyn 1960:2). However, Catherine's subsequent tariff policy "rejected the notion of government abandonment of an active role in influencing the patterns and conditions of foreign trade," and the 1766 tariff also directly hampered the development of Ukraine (and the rest of the empire) by prohibiting the import of primary products that were the equivalent of Russian exports (Kahan and Hellie 1985:238). In this manner, the Russian state remained supreme in the determination of trade, removing any hope of building adequate free trade institutions in Ukraine and consigning the countryside to a consistent state of backwardness.

The Partitions of Poland also played a major role in disrupting Ukrainian trade institutions and flows. Even with the creeping absorption of Ukraine into the tsarist Empire and the reorientation by fiat of trade links east instead of west, the Polish Partitions created additional international barriers where there previously had been a free trade zone. The first Partition of Poland in 1772 hived off Galicia to the Austro-Hungarian Empire, and the final partition 1795 erected an international border between the Russians and the Austrians, separating Ukrainians from Kyiv, the Donbas, and Crimea from their country-mates in Lwów. Kuzmany (2011:71) describes the effect that this had on one border town, the town of Brody northeast of Lwów:

The new political borders established in 1772 threatened Brody's role as a hub of European trade. Before, as Poland's import tariffs were very low and Berdyčiv was also part of the Polish-Lithuanian Commonwealth, Brody's merchants had been able to transport their goods between the various partner cities almost without paying duties. Now the traders had to clear their wares at the Silesian-Galician border, bring them to Brody where they would be unpacked and sold further, because few of the goods were intended for consumption in the city itself or in Galicia. When leaving Brody, merchants once again had to pass a customs boundary—this time between Austrian Galicia and Polish Volhynia. Transport of goods through Galicia hence became very expensive after 1772.

As Kuzmany (2011) hints at, assimilation into the Habsburg Empire was also to harm the development of Ukrainian trade institutions. Unfortunately, where Austria-Hungary had been more liberal in many of its political policies, there was a similar mercantilist bent towards the trade institutions that it imposed on Ukrainian Galicia. With the region itself incredibly poor and its Ukrainian citizens mired in poverty, an open trade regime, supported by effective exporters for Galician goods, could have brought wealth to the region and lifted many out of poverty. Indeed, an interesting coda to the story of Brody detailed above is that the Habsburgs realized the difficulties inflicted on the town and by 1779 had created a "free trade zone" around it; such a designation increased trade through the elimination of further duties, but this only lasted until approximately 1811 and the adoption of protectionist policies in Russia, followed shortly by the Habsburgs (ibid.).

The particular brand of protectionism that the Austro-Hungarian Empire was to pursue in the early nineteenth century appeared to follow the tenets of comparative advantage, but the ultimate determination of such advantages were made politically in Vienna rather than determined on the ground in Lwów or Kraków. The Habsburgs were convinced that their empire needed to be a self-sufficient economic entity, with portions of the realm supporting other areas in supplying raw materials. As part of the eastern "agricultural" zone, Galicia was not encouraged to industrialize but to instead remain a low-cost provider of agricultural goods to the rest of the empire (Magocsi 2010). This did not always help Galicia in providing for its residents, as, compared to Russian Ukraine, there was less possibility of large crop yields and poorer soil (and in the mid-nineteenth century, potato blight forced import of grain from abroad; see Komlos 2014). Favoritism towards the western provinces of the Habsburg Empire manifested itself in other ways, including tariff differentials that disadvantaged Galicia, meaning that by the end of the nineteenth century, 95 percent of the population was engaged in agricultural and a mere 0.2 percent in trade (Subtelny 2009). Landlocked and cut off from its natural markets elsewhere in Poland by international boundaries, the city of Lwów declined as a trade center, and Galicia withered economically, having the third-lowest GDP per capita (behind Dalmatia and Bukovina) in the entire Habsburg Empire (Schulze 2007).

It was only with the beginning of the Second Industrial Revolution, in tandem with the emancipation of the serfs in 1861, that trade institutions in Russian-dominated Ukraine and in Ukrainian Galicia were able to begin a slow modernization. Part of this was linked to the expansion of infrastructure, which helped (somewhat) in reducing transaction costs across Ukraine. Infrastructure in the frontier land was notoriously bad from the seventeenth century onward (Subtelny 2009), a reality that forced merchants into large-scale trade fairs so as to minimize need for travel (Kotilaine 2005). The advent of railroads in the nineteenth century allowed for better transportation for both freight and, to a much lesser extent, passengers, linking Kyiv and the south of the country, especially the port of Odessa (Metzer 1974). Indeed, even prior to the expansion of railroads, geopolitical moves by Russia in the mid-eighteenth century helped to open up new sea routes to the rest of the world, with the subjugation of the Crimean khanate during the 1770s (and annexation in 1783) removing a large source of instability and permitting free use of the Black Sea for trade. With the concomitant increase in grain production following global price rises, the port of Odessa saw trade volumes increase a whopping *2200 percent* between 1764 and 1793 (Subtelny 2009). As van Tielhof (2002) noted, the increase of Ukrainian grain production actually began to push out Baltic grain on world markets, with the bulk of this grain going to Italy, France, England, and the Netherlands. However, Subtelny (2009) makes a very important point, and that is that the Ukrainian grain trade during this time did not have widespread roots throughout Ukraine, instead being dominated by a tiny segment of the nobility and involving a relatively small percentage of the population. "Sugar barons," coming from Polish, Ukrainian, and Russian nobility, also oversaw much of the sugar beet production in Ukraine, a crop that became a prime export earner for the empire in the mid-to-late 1800s.

Alongside basic infrastructure improvements and global price signals, the move towards industrialization in Ukraine following the emancipation of the serfs had a similar effect on the economy (and thus trade) of the region as it did in the Kingdom of Poland. Global demand and price shifts marked a shift in production patterns in Ukraine, with the rich coal mines of the Donbas coming on-line and growing exponentially from 1870 onward (Subtelny 2009). Ukrainian society also began to implement small-scale and informal financial institutions (such as cooperatives and mutual credit associations) to support the increasing number of Ukrainians entering the trade field, filling the small-scale informal financial role that larger state-owned Russian banks would not or could not do (Magocsi 2010). Part of the shift towards trade in Russian Ukraine during this time was aided and abetted by a change in trade policy in Russia, which, between 1850 and 1877, pursued a policy of lower tariffs and some tentative trade liberalization (Knowles 2013). Mikhail Khristoforovich Reutern, the minister of finance in the mid-nineteenth century, identified Russia's formal trade policies as a large impediment to industrialization, and took the already-impressive steps of the Tariff Act of 1857 further in 1868 with the abolishment of nearly all export duties and reduction of most import duties (Crisp 1976). As any student of taxation and the Laffer curve would predict, the reforms of this period boosted customs revenue while at the same time increasing imports, providing Ukraine with much needed materials for industrialization (Barnett 2014).

However, Russian trade policy soon reverted to type in the late nineteenth century, with tariffs increasing from 1877 through the First World War, with Russia having the highest customs duties in the world by 1891 (World Customs Organization 2003). Especially hit by Russian duties were basic materials of industrialization, including pig iron and chemicals, which saw ad valorem rates from a low of 17 percent to a high of 50 percent imposed from 1877 onward (Dormois and Lains 2006). The last decade of the nineteenth century also saw extreme centralization of Russia's trade policies in an attempt to industrialize, with Russian finance minister Sergei Witte advocating for the "state taking on large infrastructural projects, subsidizing private enterprises, [and] erecting tariff walls" (Waterbury 1999). While presenting themselves as defenders of Russian industry, the tsar and his government instead were seeking revenue from trade, extracting surplus from the agricultural sector located in Ukraine to pay for the industrialization of the rest of the empire. Indeed, Goldsmith (1961), working off available data, shows that agricultural output grew at a rate consistently slower than the rate of growth of exports of agriculture, meaning that agricultural consumption in the empire (and especially in Ukraine) actually declined; trade, directed from above, was being forced to provide for the tsar's imperium rather than acting as a source of innovation and enrichment. Whereas the rest of Europe had accepted free trade and globalization as an engine of economic growth, with Great Britain leading the way in market-determined trade (Howe 1997), Russia had tasted it and decided it was not to its liking.

The consequences of this for Ukraine were catastrophic, as, unlike Western Europe, which had a perch of free trade to fall from during and after the Great War, Ukraine was continually mired in protectionist thinking. Small-scale cooperative institutions and some industrialization could not compensate for the low level of trade institutions, meaning that the economy of the country was very fragile even before the bloodshed started. And the years of Ukrainian "independence," first under the Germans and then during the Russian Civil War and the revolving door of governments, did not help to create these institutions, as the constant political instability stymied formal trade and kept the country at a subsistence level. Even where trade channels were opened and goods began to flow, as between the Ukrainian Democratic Republic and Turkey in 1918, they were soon closed off by successive governments (Kirimli 1998), and institutions that were imported from abroad, such as a Bank for Trade and Industry, set up by the Germans in 1919, soon were lost in a sea of Bolshevik red (Healy 2003).

The final subjugation of Ukraine under the Soviet Union meant that there was little chance that any free-trade-oriented institutions would develop, even though it was private trade that kept the population of Ukraine alive during the final years of the Civil War (Banerji 1997). While the NEP allowed for some measures of internal trade, as with all private commerce in general, it was exceedingly small scale and was subject to reversals (Ball (1984) notes that Lenin's attitude towards private enterprise in Ukraine was unfavorable, as he called for heightened vigilance against Ukrainian shopkeepers). In fact, the trade institutions that emerged under the NEP were little more than a small-scale privatization of socialist property, with a Cheka agent noting in 1920 that "nearly all goods sold on the free market originate in Soviet institutions [with] petty speculation ... fueled almost exclusively by theft from transport or the transportation agencies" (quoted in Hessler 2004:32). Apart from this re-requisitioning of property for private commercial use, trade under the early Soviet period followed all other facets of the planned economy, with the requisitioning of grain as needed, consequences be damned, and a hybridized version of the Austrian and Russian mercantilist models ruling the day: in particular, the Soviets continued the tsarist tradition of protection and trade ordered from above, while adopting the Austrian idea of specialization across the empire. Under this schema, Ukraine was once again to be a breadbasket for the Soviet Union, while the east of the Republic was to continue to churn out coal for the glorious Five-Year Plans. At no point was there any consideration of anything but a monopoly on foreign trade by the Soviet government, nor any sense that internal trade would follow anything but the plan.

This reality was to persist throughout the postwar years and until the collapse of the Soviet Union in 1991, with Ukraine tightly integrated into the Soviet production machine, which in turn was enmeshed (like Poland) in the Council for Mutual Economic Assistance (COMECON) trade bloc. Perhaps reflecting the damage that had been done in the previous century to Ukraine's trade institutions, the Ukrainian SSR generally had a very small percentage of the Soviet Union's exports (Clement 1999), with much of the materials supplied for export concentrated in metallurgy and chemicals (Gillula 1983).[10] Even this small amount of trade for the Ukrainian SSR was subjected to the Soviet Customs Code of 1928, the legislative basis for tariff schedules for the whole Union and, not incidentally, the trade institutions of the country. A somewhat embarrassing document put in place on the eve of Stalinism and at the tail end of the NEP, the Soviet Customs Code of 1928 was successively not acknowledged as a real "law" (Lavigne 1992) even though it guided all institutional development of trade, highlighting the schizophrenic nature of the Soviet leadership to foreign trade in general. It was not until May 1964 that this code was replaced by a new *Tamozhennyi Kodeks*, which allowed for inspection of every single good (including personal effects) crossing the Soviet frontier by the customs administration (de Jong 1985). And, of course, the borders of Ukraine, being the borders of the Soviet Union with similarly socialist Poland, were overseen by the central Customs Administration in Moscow and staffed with Russians as well as Ukrainians and other ethnic minorities of the Union. Most importantly, reaffirming the Soviet monopoly on trade, the Customs Code of 1964 was to remain in force up until the moment the Soviet Union was dissolved, as even during the 1980s Gorbachev was determined to keep this monopoly even as other powers were hived off to the constituent republics (Gleason 1992). It was not until Ukraine declared independence in August 1991 that the issue of foreign trade being separated from Moscow was even raised. As we will see in the next chapter, the trade institutions of the newly independent Ukraine often did not know that such independence even existed.

CONCLUSIONS

This chapter has extended our analysis of economic and political institutions from Poland to Ukraine, examining the historical roots of Ukraine's institutional development prior to 1989. Many similarities exist between the two countries, not least because of the fact that, for much of the period under discussion, large portions of Ukraine were under Polish control. Like Poland, the development of the country's institutions were highly path dependent and influenced by external events, although there was less of an ability to self-organize in the Ukrainian lands due to the greater number of

[10] Grain was of course held back for feeding the other republics of the Soviet Union.

external conflicts, which kept the Ukrainian peoples continually engaged. Also like Poland, Ukraine was handicapped by the fact that much of modernity, and by extension modern political and economic institutions, was to arrive globally at the exact same time that the country was partitioned among other powers. Even the brief periods of independence, in both the 1600s and in the twentieth century, were far too short to set the country on a different path, as they often just replaced foreign dysfunctions with ones created domestically. Finally, Poland and Ukraine were both to suffer, although to different extents, from being under the suzerainty (Poland) or direct control (Ukraine) of the Russian Empire in the nineteenth century and the Soviet Union in the twentieth. Radical moves towards communal property, disadvantageous tariff policies, and stifling of cultural and political institutions by tsarist authorities were a hallmark of the time Poland and Ukraine spent under Russian occupation, as, it must be noted, was the advent of the Second Industrial Revolution and the emancipation of the serfs. Thus, the two countries saw a similar timeline for external pressures corresponding to how those events played themselves out in Moscow or St. Petersburg.

However, there are many important differences in Ukraine's institutional development from Poland, which will be important to keep in mind for the next two chapters. In the first instance, in contrast to Poland's well-developed intellectual history regarding freedom, the area spanning the modern-day nation of Ukraine had little philosophical experience of liberty or freedom. A large part of this can be attributed to its small experience of independence, as constant subjugation under different empires left no real support of liberty or even respect for merchants. Manifestations of support for the administrative trappings of freedom, such as the Constitution of Pylyp Orlyk, occurred just as all hope was lost and Ukraine was about to disappear as a sovereign entity. And where some philosophical basis for economic organization along the lines of liberty did exist, it was imported, mainly from Poland, and then only because "noble liberty" offered a worldview to ensure that Ukrainian nobility retained its perquisites of power. But the long experience of absorption into the Russian Empire and its administrative structures, which perhaps experienced only a twenty-year experiment with classical liberalism in the nineteenth century (and only then in trade), meant that Ukraine could not even import sound institutions from elsewhere in the empire. Without a philosophical basis for market orientation and with hundreds of years of directed trade and little respect for property, there is little wonder that neither political nor economic institutions had fertile ground to grow in.

Another key attribute of Ukraine to note, one that is incredibly important for today, is that, despite fluid borders, there has always been an institutional divide between the east and the west. This division was not just visible in the now-Ukrainian cities that were part of Poland for centuries, such as Lwów (L'viv), but also manifested itself in the Left Bank/Right Bank of Ukraine, with Kyiv as the dividing line. Interestingly, the division of Ukraine in terms of its institutions was not always consistent in the sense that western Ukraine was more modern and eastern Ukraine was more autocratic, as the untamed east and expansion of colonists into the region could have created the rugged individualism necessary to survive the market economy. Similarly, the east's earlier industrialization, at a time when elsewhere in Ukrainian lands (such as Galicia) industrialization was explicitly avoided by political fiat, also could have allowed it to create a constituency in favor of pro-market economic institutions. However, as with Poland, the ruling empire that prevailed in each locale was to have a substantial effect on the development of particular institutions; in particular, the centripetal tendencies of the Russian Empire and its subordination of nascent (and potential) economic institutions ensured that these institutions developed along a mercantilist, protectionist, and planned route rather than a market-determined one. The economic outcomes that then followed these policies irrevocably split along an axis marked by the boundaries of empires, perhaps most easily seen in Galicia, known as the "least Sovietized" region within the whole Union (Hrytsak 2000).

In fact, the experience of Ukraine in seeing both its political and economic institutions heavily centralized was a key difference from Poland's experience. In Poland before the Partitions, and to a large extent after it, political and economic power may have been concentrated in the nobility, but it was fragmented across a rambunctious lot prone to taking up arms in defense of the law as they saw it. Even where antimarket institutions were in place, as in the spread of serfdom, it was held in place only on a local scale across a contiguous territory, allowing for some competition across nobles and pockets of liberty. By contrast, Ukraine saw great diversity in application of certain institutions, due to the fragmented nature of Ukraine's territory, but there was a consistent trend towards unifying power and direction of these institutions. From the hetmanate's attempts to control trade to the Russian move towards communal rights and the Ukrainian SSR's control of every facet of politics and the economy, institutions became increasingly a matter of elite determination rather than market needs. Even reforms that were beneficial for labor markets and private property in Ukraine, such as the emancipation of serfs, came from above (and from a foreign land!) in an unexpected manner, leaving little experience of just *how* to develop an institution. Hundreds of years of top-down institutional imposition had robbed the country of any ability to create bottom-up institutions, at least formal or large-scale ones. This problem was to be manifest in the biggest geopolitical and economic shift of our time, the dissolution of the Soviet Union, which was also in some sense exogenously given to Ukraine by fourteen other republics. How then could an independent Ukraine build the institutions that it had manifestly little experience with?

References

Alexander, J.T. (1988). *Catherine the Great: Life and Legend*. Oxford: Oxford Paperbacks.

Allen, W. E. D. (2014). *The Ukraine*. Cambridge: Cambridge University Press.

Andrusiak, J. (1935). The Ukrainian Movement in Galicia. *Slavonic and East European Review*, 14(40), pp. 163–175.

Antonovych, M. (2010). Implementation of international human rights norms in Ukrainian legislation. *Annual Survey of International & Comparative Law*, 3(1), pp. 1–17.

Babirad-Lazunin, V. (2013). Development of the customs statistics in Ukraine: Historical aspects. *Вісник Київського національного університету ім. Тараса Шевченка. Серія: Економіка [Bulletin of Taras Shevchenko National University of Kyiv: Economics]*, 3, pp. 12–17.

Backus III, O. P. (1963). Reply. *Slavic Review*, 22(3), pp. 450–455.

Badalova, O. (2013). State executive service at the time of Kievan Rus. *Public Policy and Economic Development*, 4, pp. 80–85.

Ball, A. (1984). Lenin and the question of private trade in Soviet Russia. *Slavic Review*, 43(3), pp. 399–412.

Bandera, V. N. (1963). The New Economic Policy (NEP) as an economic system. *Journal of Political Economy*, 71(3), pp. 265–279.

Banerji, A. (1997). *Merchants and Markets in Revolutionary Russia, 1917–30*. Basingstoke: Palgrave Macmillan.

Baran, A. (1982). Review: George Gajecky, "The Cossack Administration of the Hetmanate." *Journal of Ukrainian Studies*, 7(2), p. 87.

Barnett, V. (2014). M. Kh. Reutern and tariff reform in Russia. *Œconomia. History, Methodology, Philosophy*, 4(1), pp. 17–27.

Baten, J., and Szoltysek, M. (2014). *A golden age before serfdom? The human capital of Central-Eastern and Eastern Europe in the 17th-19th centuries*. Max Planck Institute for Demographic Research Working Paper No. WP-2014-008.

Blum, J. (1960). Russian agriculture in the last 150 years of Serfdom. *Agricultural History*, 34(1), pp. 3–12.

(1964). *Lord and Peasant in Russia.* New York: Atheneum Books.

Bocheński, A. (1937). *Między Niemcami a Rosją* [Between Germany and Russia]. Warsaw: Ośrodek Myśli Politycznej.

Boemeke, M. F., Feldman, G. D., and Glaser, E. (1998). *The Treaty of Versailles: A Reassessment after 75 Years.* Cambridge: Cambridge University Press.

Borzecki, J. (1996). The Union of Lublin as a factor in the emergence of Ukrainian national consciousness. *Polish Review,* 41(1), pp. 37–61.

Braudel, F. (1982). *Civilization and Capitalism, 15th–18th Century: The Perspective of the World.* Oakland: University of California Press.

Brunt, L. (2004). Nature or nurture? Explaining English wheat yields in the industrial revolution, c. 1770. *Journal of Economic History,* 64(1), pp. 193–225.

Chernina, E., Dower, P. C., and Markevich, A. (2014). Property rights, land liquidity, and internal migration. *Journal of Development Economics,* 110, pp. 191–215.

Chynczewska-Hennel, T. (1986). *Świadomość narodowa szlachty ukraińskiej i kozaczyzny od schyłku XVI do połowy XVII w.* [National consciousness among the Ukrainian nobility and the Cossacks, from the close of the 16th century to the mid-17th century]. *Harvard Ukrainian Studies,* 10(3/4), pp. 377–392.

Clement, H. (1999). Economic aspects of Ukrainian-Russian relations. In Spillman, K. R., Wenger, A., and Mueller, D. (eds.), *Between Russia and the West: Foreign and Security Policy of Independent Ukraine.* New York: Peter Lang, pp. 281–302.

Conquest, R. C. (1987). *The Harvest of Sorrow.* Oxford: Oxford University Press.

Crisp, O. (1976). *Studies in the Russian Economy before 1914.* Basingstoke: Macmillan.

Crowley, S. (1994). Barriers to collective action: Steelworkers and mutual dependence in the former Soviet Union. *World Politics,* 46(4), pp. 589–615.

Curtis, G.E. (1996). *Russia: A Country Study.* Washington, DC: Federal Research Division of the Library of Congress.

De Beauplan, G.L.V. (1990). *Description d'Ukrainie qui sont plusieurs provinces du Royaume Pologne.* Cambridge: Ukrainian Research Institute of Harvard University. Original imprint Rouen, 1660.

De Jong, E. H. (1985). Customs duties. In Ferdinand, F. J., Feldbrugge, J. M., Van den Berg, G. P., and Simons, W. B. (eds.), *Encyclopedia of Soviet Law.* Leiden, the Netherlands: Brill Publishing, p. 230.

Dewey, H. W., and Kleimola, A. M. (1984). Russian collective consciousness: The Kievan roots. *Slavonic and East European Review,* 62(2), pp. 180–191.

Dmytryshyn, B. (1960). The economic content of the 1767 nakaz of Catherine II. *American Slavic and East European Review,* 19(1), pp. 1–9.

Dolukhanov, P. (2014). *The Early Slavs: Eastern Europe from the Initial Settlement to the Kievan Rus.* New York: Routledge.

Dormois, J.-P., and Lains, P. (2006). *Classical Trade Protectionism 1815–1914.* New York: Routledge.

Dzera, O. (2012). Development of Institute of Right of Ownership. *Law of Ukraine: Legal Journal,* 5–6, pp. 26–43.

Engelstein, L. (1993). Combined underdevelopment: Discipline and the law in Imperial and Soviet Russia. *American Historical Review,* 98(2), pp. 338–353.

Eudin, X. J. (1941). The German occupation of the Ukraine in 1918. *Russian Review,* 1(1), pp. 90–105.

Fischer, D. H. (1996). *The Great Wave: Price Revolutions and the Rhythm of History*. Oxford: Oxford University Press.

Finkel, E., Gehlbach, S., and Olsen, T. D. (2015). Does reform prevent rebellion? Evidence from Russia's emancipation of the serfs. *Comparative Political Studies*, 48(8), pp. 984–1019.

Fisher, A. W. (1978). *The Crimean Tatars*. Palo Alto, CA: Hoover Institution Press.

(1979). The Ottoman Crimea in the mid-seventeenth century: Some problems and preliminary considerations. *Harvard Ukrainian Studies*, 3(1), pp. 215–226.

Frank, A. (2006). Galician California, Galician Hell: The Peril and Promise of Oil Production in Austria-Hungary. *Bridges*, 10 (June). Available at http://ostaustria .org/bridges-magazine/volume-10-june-29-2006/item/1172-galician-california-gali cian-hell-the-peril-and-promise-of-oil-production-in-austria-hungary. Accessed June 8, 2016.

Frost, R. I. (1986). 'Initium Calamitatis Regni'? John Casimir and monarchical power in Poland-Lithuania, 1648–68. *European History Quarterly*, 16(2), pp. 181–207.

(2000). *The Northern Wars: War, State and Society in Northeastern Europe 1558–1721*. New York: Routledge.

Gajecky, G. (1978). *The Cossack Administration of the Hetmanate*. Cambridge: Harvard Ukrainian Research Institute Press.

Gel'man, V. (2004). The unrule of law in the making: The politics of informal institution building in Russia. *Europe-Asia Studies*, 56(7), pp. 1021–1040.

Gillula, J. (1983). *The Reconstructed 1972 Input-Output Tables for Eight Soviet Republics*. Washington DC: U.S. Department of Commerce.

Gleason, G. (1992). The federal formula and the collapse of the USSR. *Publius: The Journal of Federalism*, 22(3), pp. 141–163.

Goldblatt, H. (1986). Orthodox Slavic heritage and national consciousness: Aspects of the East Slavic and South Slavic national revivals. *Harvard Ukrainian Studies*, 10 (3/4), pp. 336–354.

Goldsmith, R. W. (1961). The economic growth of tsarist Russia 1860–1913. *Economic Development and Cultural Change*, 9(3), pp. 441–475.

Gordon, Linda (1983). *Cossack Rebellions: Social Turmoil in the Sixteenth-Century Ukraine*. Albany: State University of New York Press.

Grossman, G. (1989). The Second Economy: Boon or hindrance to reforms in the First Economy. In Gomulka, S., Ha, Y-C., and Kim, S-W. (eds.), *Economic Reforms in the Socialist World*. New York: M. E. Sharpe, pp. 79–96.

Guthier, S. L. (1979). The popular base of Ukrainian nationalism in 1917. *Slavic Review*, 38(1), pp. 30–47.

Halperin, C. J. (1987). *Russia and the Golden Horde: The Mongol Impact on Medieval Russian History*. Bloomington: Indiana University Press.

Healy, J. (2003). *Central Europe in flux: Germany, Poland and Ukraine, 1918–1922*. PhD thesis, University of Glasgow.

Heller, M. A. (1998). The tragedy of the anticommons: Property in the transition from Marx to markets. *Harvard Law Review*, 111(3), pp. 621–688.

Hessler, J. (1998). A postwar perestroika? Toward a history of private enterprise in the USSR. *Slavic Review*, 57(3), pp. 516–542.

(2004). *A Social History of Soviet Trade: Trade Policy, Retail Practices, and Consumption, 1917–1953*. Princeton, NJ: Princeton University Press.

Himka, J. P. (1979). Priests and peasants: The Greek Catholic pastor and the Ukrainian national movement in Austria, 1867–1900. *Canadian Slavonic Papers*, 21(1), pp. 1–14.

(1982). Young radicals and independent statehood: The idea of a Ukrainian nation-state, 1890–1895. *Slavic Review*, 41(2), pp. 219–235.

(1993). The Revolution of 1905. In Kubijovyč, V. (ed.), *The Encyclopedia of Ukraine, Vol. 4*. Toronto: University of Toronto Press.

(1998). *Religion and Nationality in Western Ukraine: The Greek Catholic Church and the Ruthenian National Movement in Galicia, 1870–1900*. Oxford: Oxford University Press.

Hisrich, R. D., Bowser, K., and Smarsh, L. S. (2006). Women entrepreneurs in the Ukraine. *International Journal of Entrepreneurship and Small Business*, 3(2), pp. 207–221.

Holubnychy, V., and Ohloblyn, O. (1993). Tariffs. In Struk, D. H. (ed.), *Encyclopedia of Ukraine, Volume 5*. Alberta: Canadian Institute of Ukrainian Studies.

Horbulin, V. P., Byelov, O. F., and Lytvynenko, O. V. (2010). *Ukraine's National Security: An Agenda for the Security Sector*. Münster: LIT Verlag.

Hoszowski, S. (1954). *Les prix à Lwow*. Paris: Sevpen.

Howe, A. (1997). *Free Trade and Liberal England, 1846–1946*. Oxford:Clarendon Press.

Hrushevsky, M. (2012). *History of Ukraine-Rus'*. Vol. 6, *Economic, Cultural, and National Life in the Fourteenth to Seventeenth Centuries*. Edmonton: Canadian Institute of Ukrainian Studies Press.

Hrytsak, Y. (2000). Lviv: A multicultural history through the centuries. *Harvard Ukrainian Studies*, 24(1/4), pp. 47–73.

Jancec, M. (2013). *Do less stable borders lead to lower levels of political trust? Empirical evidence from Eastern Europe*. Mimeo, University of Maryland. Available at http://papers.ssrn.com/sol3/papers.cfm?abstract_id=2148773. Accessed June 8, 2016.

Kahan, A., and Hellie, R. (1985). *The Plow, the Hammer, and the Knout: An Economic History of Eighteenth-Century Russia*. Chicago: University of Chicago Press.

Kamiński, A. (1975). Neo-serfdom in Poland-Lithuania. *Slavic Review*, 34(2), pp. 253–268.

(1977). The Cossack experiment in *szlachta* democracy in the Polish-Lithuanian Commonwealth: The Hadiach (Hadziacz) union. *Harvard Ukrainian Studies*, 1(2), pp. 178–197.

Kappeler, A. (2014). *The Russian Empire: A Multi-Ethnic History*. New York: Routledge.

Katchanovski, I. (2005). Small nations but great differences: Political orientations and cultures of the Crimean Tatars and the Gagauz. *Europe-Asia Studies*, 57(6), pp. 877–894.

Katchanovski, I., Kohut, Z. E., Nebesio, B. Y., and Yurkevich, M. (2013). *Historical Dictionary of Ukraine*. Lanham, MD: Scarecrow Press.

Kedrovskyi, V. (1936). *Rizhske Andrusovo, spomini pro rosiisko-pol's'ki m irovi perehovori v 1920 r.* [Andrusovo at Riga, Memoirs from the Russian-Polish Peace Negotiations in 1920]. Winnipeg: Ukrainian Publishing Association of Canada.

Khodarkovsky, M. (2002). *Russia's Steppe Frontier: The Making of a Colonial Empire, 1500–1800*. Bloomington,: Indiana University Press.

Khristyuk, P. (1921). *Zamitki i materiyaly do istorii ukrainskoi revolyutsii, 1917–1920* [Notes and materials on the history of the Ukrainian Revolution]. Three vols. New York: Chartoriyskyh Publishers.

Kirimli, H. (1998). Diplomatic relations between the Ottoman Empire and the Ukrainian Democratic Republic, 1918–21. *Middle Eastern Studies*, 34(4), pp. 201–239.

Knowles, L. C. A. (2013). *Economic Development in the Nineteenth Century: France, Germany, Russia and the United States*. New York: Routledge.

Kohut, Z. E. (1986). The development of a Little Russian identity and Ukrainian nation-building. *Harvard Ukrainian Studies*, 10(3–4), pp. 559–576.

Komlos, J. (2014). *The Habsburg Monarchy as a Customs Union: Economic Development in Austria-Hungary in the Nineteenth Century*. Princeton, NJ: Princeton University Press.

Korostelina, K. V. (2013). Mapping national identity narratives in Ukraine. *Nationalities Papers*, 41(2), pp. 293–315.

Korzhov, G. (1999). Historical and cultural factors of entrepreneurship re-emergence in post-socialist Ukraine. *Polish Sociological Review*, 128, pp. 503–532.

Kotilaine, J.T. (2003). Competing claims: Russian foreign trade via Arkhangelsk and the eastern Baltic ports in the 17th century. *Kritika: Explorations in Russian and Eurasian History*, 4(2), pp. 279–311.

  (2005). *Russia's Foreign Trade and Economic Expansion in the Seventeenth Century: Windows on the World*. Leiden, the Netherlands: Brill Publishing.

Kramer, M. (2014). *Why did Russia give away Crimea Sixty Years Ago?* Cold War International History Project e-Dossier No. 47, the Wilson Center. https://www.wilsoncenter.org/publication/why-did-russia-give-away-crimea-sixty-years-ago. Accessed October 19, 2015.

Krasnozhon, L. (2004). Lessons of privatization: Property rights in agricultural land in Ukraine. *Economic Education Bulletin*, 45(5), pp. 123–136.

Kuzio, T. (2001). Identity and nation-building in Ukraine: Defining the "Other." *Ethnicities*, 1(3), pp. 343–365.

Kuzmany, B. (2011). Center and periphery at the Austrian-Russian Border: The Galician border town of Brody in the long nineteenth century. *Austrian History Yearbook*, 42, pp. 67–88.

Lamis, A. P. (1978). Some observations on the Ukrainian national movement and the Ukrainian revolution, 1917–1921. *Harvard Ukrainian Studies*, 2(4), pp. 525–531.

Lavigne, M. (1992). Trade policies in the USSR. In Salvatore, D. (ed.), *Handbook of National Trade Policies*. Westport, CT: Greenwood Press.

Ledeneva, A. (1998). *Russia's Economy of Favour*. Cambridge: Cambridge University Press.

Leonard, C. S. (1993). *Reform and Regicide: The Reign of Peter III of Russia*. Bloomington: Indiana University Press.

  (2011). *Agrarian Reform in Russia: The Road from Serfdom*. Cambridge: Cambridge University Press.

Lerman, Z. (2001). Agriculture in transition economies: From common heritage to divergence. *Agricultural Economics*, 26(2), pp. 95–114.

Leslie, R. F. (1955). Politics and economics in Congress Poland, 1815–1864. *Past and Present*, 8, pp. 43–63.

Lieven, D. (1995). The Russian Empire and the Soviet Union as imperial polities. *Journal of Contemporary History*, 30(4), pp. 607–636.

Litwin, H. (1987). Catholicization among the Ruthenian nobility and assimilation processes in the Ukraine during the years 1569–1648. *Acta Poloniae Historica*, 55, pp. 57–83.

Łobodowski, J. (1980). A Polish view of Polish-Ukrainian influences. In Potichnyj, P. J. (ed.), *Poland and Ukraine: Past and Present*. Edmonton: Canadian Institute of Ukrainian Studies Press, pp. 99–106.

Lotots'kyi, O. H. (1934). *Storinky mynuloho 3*. Warsaw: Ukrains'kyi naukovyi instytut.

Lukowski, J., and Zawadzki, H. (2006). *A Concise History of Poland*. Cambridge: Cambridge University Press.

Magocsi, P. (2010). *A History of Ukraine: The Land and Its Peoples*. Toronto: University of Toronto Press.

Markus, V., and Struminsky, B. (1984). The Black Hundreds. *The Encyclopedia of Ukraine*, Vol. 1. Toronto: University of Toronto Press.

Marples, D. R. (1984). The kulak in post-war USSR: The west Ukrainian example. *Soviet Studies*, 36(4), pp. 560–570.

(1985). The Soviet collectivization of Western Ukraine, 1948–1949. *Nationalities Papers*, 13(1), pp. 24–44.

Martin, J. (1995). *Medieval Russia, 980–1584*. Cambridge: Cambridge University Press.

Mathijs, E., and Swinnen, J. F. (1998). The economics of agricultural decollectivization in East Central Europe and the former Soviet Union. *Economic Development and Cultural Change*, 47(1), pp. 1–26.

McFaul, M. (1996). The allocation of property rights in Russia: The first round. *Communist and Post-Communist Studies*, 29(3), pp. 287–308.

Melnichuk, I. A. (2014). The appearance of the 'third power:' The change of the Ukrainian political elite in the XVIth century. *International Journal of Recent Scientific Research*, 5(3), pp. 618–621.

Metzer, J. (1974). Railroad development and market integration: The case of tsarist Russia. *Journal of Economic History*, 34(3), pp. 529–550.

Miller, J. (1983). The Polish nobility and the renaissance monarchy: The 'execution of the laws' movement: Part one. *Parliaments, Estates, and Representation*, 3(2), pp. 65–87.

Millward, R. (1982). An economic analysis of the organization of serfdom in Eastern Europe. *Journal of Economic History*, 42(3), pp. 513–548.

Moore, L., and Kaluzny, J. (2005). Regime change and debt default: The case of Russia, Austro-Hungary, and the Ottoman Empire following World War One. *Explorations in Economic History*, 42(2), pp. 237–258.

Moshenskyi, S. (2008). *History of the Weksel*. New York: Xlibris Books.

Myronenko, O. (2013). Law of the hetmanate (second half of XVII–XVIII century). *Law of Ukraine: Legal Journal*, 1, pp. 187–220.

Nadel-Golobič, E. (1979). Armenians and Jews in medieval Lvov: Their Role in oriental trade 1400–1600. *Cahiers du monde russe et soviétique*, 20(3/4), pp. 345–388.

Nafziger, S. (2008). Communal institutions, resource allocation, and Russian economic development: 1861–1905. *Journal of Economic History*, 68(2), pp. 570–575.

(2015). Communal property rights and land redistributions in late tsarist Russia. *Economic History Review*, Early View on-line, http://onlinelibrary.wiley.com/doi/10.1111/ehr.12167/abstract. Accessed November 4, 2015.

O'Brien, C. B. (1949). Agriculture in Russian war economy in the later seventeenth century. *American Slavic and East European Review*, 8(3), pp. 167–174.

Ostrowski, D. G. (2000). Muscovite adaptation of steppe political institutions: A reply to Halperin's objections. *Kritika: Explorations in Russian and Eurasian History*, 1 (2), pp. 267–304.

Paszkiewicz, H. (1983). *The Rise of Moscow's Power*. New York: Columbia University Press.

Pejovich, S. (1969). Liberman's reforms and property rights in the Soviet Union. *Journal of Law and Economics*, 12(1), pp. 155–162.

(2012). The effects of the interaction of formal and informal institutions on social stability and economic development. *Journal of Markets & Morality*, 2(2), pp. 164–181.

Pintner, W. M. (1970). The social characteristics of the early nineteenth-century Russian bureaucracy. *Slavic Review*, 29(3), pp. 429–443.

Pipes, R. (1990). *The Russian Revolution*. New York: Vintage Books.

Plank, T. E. (1996). The essential elements of judicial independence and the experience of pre-Soviet Russia. *William & Mary Bill of Rights Journal*, 5(1), pp. 1–74.

Plateris, A. (1965). Codification of the law in the Grand Duchy of Lithuania. *Lituanus*, 11 (2), http://www.lituanus.org/1965/65_2_03_Plateris.html. Accessed June 24, 2015.

Portal, R. (1966). The industrialization of Russia. In Habakkuk, H. J. and Postan, M. (eds.), *The Industrial Revolutions and After: Incomes, Population and Technological Change*. Cambridge: Cambridge University Press, pp. 801–872.

Pritsak, O. (1977). The origin of Rus'. *Russian Review*, 36(3), pp. 249–273.

(1986). Kiev and all of Rus: The fate of a sacral idea. *Harvard Ukrainian Studies*, 10(3/4), pp. 279–300.

(1998). The first constitution of Ukraine (5 April 1710). *Harvard Ukrainian Studies*, 22, pp. 471–496.

Pritsak, O., and Reshetar Jr., J. S. (1963). The Ukraine and the dialectics of nation-building. *Slavic Review*, 22(2), pp. 224–255.

Raiser, M. (2001). Informal institutions, social capital, and economic transition: reflections on a neglected dimension. In Cornia, G. A. (ed.), *Transition and Institutions: The Experience of Gradual and Late Reformers*. Oxford: Oxford University Press, pp. 218–239.

Reshetar Jr., J.S. (1952). *The Ukrainian Revolution, 1917–1920*. Princeton, N.J.: Princeton University Press.

Riasanovsky, N. (2000). *A History of Russia*. Oxford: Oxford University Press.

Rodrigues, D. (2010). The Polish-Lithuanian commonwealth: A new look on a peculiar type of federalism. *Regioninės Studijos*, (5), pp. 121–130.

Rowell, S.C. (2014). *Lithuania Ascending: A Pagan Empire within East-Central Europe, 1295–1345*. Cambridge: Cambridge University Press.

Rudnytsky, I. L. (1963). The role of the Ukraine in modern history. *Slavic Review*, 22(2), pp. 199–216.

(1977). The Ukrainian national movement on the eve of the First World War. *East European Quarterly*, 11(2), pp. 142–154.

(1980). Gajecky, the Cossack administration of the hetmanate. *Canadian Journal of History*, 15(1), pp. 114–116.

(1987a). Polish-Ukrainian relations: The burden of history. In Rudnytsky (ed.), *Essays in Modern Ukrainian History*. Edmonton: Canadian Institute of Ukrainian Studies Press, pp. 49–76.

(1987b). Soviet Ukraine in historical perspective. In Rudnytsky (ed.), *Essays in Modern Ukrainian History*. Edmonton: Canadian Institute of Ukrainian Studies Press, pp. 463–476.

Sawczak, P. (2004). Europe as object of aversion and desire: Cultural antinomies in Gogol's 'Taras Bul' ba'. *Australian Slavic and East European Studies*, 18)1–2), pp. 17–39.

Schulze, M. S. (2007). Regional income dispersion and market potential in the late nineteenth century Hapsburg Empire. London School of Economics and Political Science, Department of Economic History Working Paper No. 22311.

Sedlar, J.W. (2011). *East Central Europe in the Middle Ages, 1000–1500*. Seattle: University of Washington Press.

Skinner, B. (2005). Borderlands of faith: Reconsidering the origins of a Ukrainian tragedy. *Slavic Review*, 64(1), pp. 88–116.

Smolka, S. (1917). *Les Ruthénes et les problémes religieux du monide russien* [The Ruthenians and religious problems in the Russian world]. Bern: Ferdinand Wyss Publishers.

Solchanyk, R. (1986). Chernobyl: The political fallout in Ukraine. *Journal of Ukrainian Studies*, 11(1), pp. 20–34.

(2000). *Ukraine and Russia: The Post-Soviet Transition*. New York: Rowan & Littlefield Publishers.

Smith, G. B. (1996). *Reforming the Russian Legal System*. Cambridge: Cambridge University Press.

Snyder, T. D. (2010). *Bloodlands: Europe Between Hitler and Stalin*. New York: Basic Books.

Stampfer, S. (2003). What actually happened to the Jews of Ukraine in 1648? *Jewish History*, 17(2), pp. 207–227.

Stone, D.Z. (2001). *The Polish-Lithuanian State, 1386–1795*. Seattle: Washington University Press.

Struve, K. (2008). Citizenship and national identity: The peasants of Galicia during the 19th Century. In Wawrzeniuk, P. (ed.), *Societal Change and Ideological Formation among the Rural Population of the Baltic Area 1880–1939*. Huddinge, Sweden: Södertörns högskola, pp. 75–94.

Subtelny, O. (1980). Russia and the Ukraine: The difference that Peter I made. *Russian Review*, 39(1), pp. 1–17.

(2009). *Ukraine: A History*. Fourth ed. Toronto: University of Toronto Press.

Swinnen, J. F., and Heinegg, A. (2002). On the political economy of land reforms in the former Soviet Union. *Journal of International Development*, 14(7), pp. 1019–1031.

Sysyn, F. E. (1980). Ukrainian-Polish relations in the seventeenth century: The role of national consciousness and national conflict in the Khmelnytsky Movement. In Potichnyj, P. J. (ed.), *Poland and Ukraine: Past and Present*. Edmonton: Canadian Institute of Ukrainian Studies Press, pp. 58–82.

(1982). Regionalism and political thought in seventeenth-century Ukraine: The nobility's grievances at the Diet of 1641. *Harvard Ukrainian Studies*, 6(2), pp. 167–190.

(1986). Concepts of nationhood in Ukrainian history writing, 1620–1690. *Harvard Ukrainian Studies*, 10(3/4), pp. 393–423.

(1991). The reemergence of the Ukrainian nation and Cossack mythology. *Social Research*, 58(4), pp. 845–864.

(2003). The Khmel'nyts'kyi Uprising: A characterization of the Ukrainian revolt. *Jewish History*, 17(2), pp. 115–139.

Szporluk, R. (1997). Ukraine: From an imperial periphery to a sovereign state. *Daedalus*, 126(3), pp. 85–119.

Tazbir, J. (1982). Polish national consciousness in the sixteenth-eighteenth centuries. *Acta Polonica Historica*, 46, pp. 47–72.

Thaden, E. C. (2014). *Russia's Western Borderlands, 1710–1870*. Princeton, NJ: Princeton University Press.

Tkach, A. (1968). *Istoriia kodyfikatsii dorevoliutsiinoho prava Ukraïny* [The history of pre-revolutionary codification of laws in Ukraine]. Kyiv: Nauka Publishers.

Trethewey, R. (1974). The establishment of serfdom in Eastern Europe and Russia. *American Economist*, 18(1), pp. 36–41.

Van Tielhof, M. (2002). *The "Mother of All Trades": The Baltic Grain Trade in Amsterdam from the Late 16th to the Early 19th Century*. Leiden, the Netherlands: Brill Publishing.

Velychenko, S. (1989). Tsarist censorship and Ukrainian historiography, 1828–1906. *Canadian-American Slavic Studies*, 23(4), pp. 385–408.

(1995). Identities, loyalties and service in imperial Russia: Who administered the borderlands? *Russian Review*, 54(2), pp. 188–208.

Volin, L. (1943). The Russian peasant and serfdom. *Agricultural History*, 17(1), pp. 41–61.

Von Hagen, M. (1995). Does Ukraine have a history? *Slavic Review*, 54(3), pp. 658–673.

Wallerstein, I. (1972). Three paths of national development in sixteenth-century Europe. *Studies in Comparative International Development (SCID)*, 7(2), pp. 95–101.

(1974). *The Modern World System*. Vol. 1: *Capitalist Agriculture and the Origins of the European World-Economy in the Sixteenth Century*. Bradford, UK: Emerald Group Publishing.

Wandycz, P. S. (1969). The Treaty of Riga: its significance for interwar Polish foreign policy. *Polish Review*, 14(4), pp. 31–36.

Wanner, C. (2010). *Burden of Dreams: History and Identity in Post-Soviet Ukraine*. University Park: Penn State Press.

Waterbury, J. (1999). The long gestation and brief triumph of import-substituting industrialization. *World Development*, 27(2), pp. 323–341.

Wedel, J. R. (2003). Clans, cliques and captured states: Rethinking "transition" in Central and Eastern Europe and the former Soviet Union. *Journal of International Development*, 15(4), pp. 427–440.

Weickhardt, G. G. (1993). The pre-Petrine law of property. *Slavic Review*, 52(4), pp. 663–679.

Weinberg, R. (1993). *The Revolution of 1905 in Odessa: Blood on the Steps*. Bloomington,: Indiana University Press.

Williams, B. G. (2001). *The Crimean Tatars: The Diaspora Experience and the Forging of a Nation*. Leiden, the Netherlands: Brill Publishing.

Williams, S. F. (2013). *Liberal Reform in an Illiberal Regime: The Creation of Private Property in Russia, 1906–1915*. Palo Alto, CA: Hoover Institution Press.

Winiecki, J. (1990). Why economic reforms fail in the Soviet system – A property rights-based approach. *Economic Inquiry*, 28(2), pp. 195–221.

World Customs Organization (2003). *World History of Customs and Tariffs*. Brussels: World Customs Organization.

Wortman, R. S. (2011). *The Development of a Russian Legal Consciousness*. Chicago: University of Chicago Press.

Wright, H. (1945). Poland and the Crimea Conference. *American Journal of International Law*, 39(2), pp. 300–308.

Yekelchyk, S. (2007). *Ukraine: Birth of a Modern Nation*. Oxford: Oxford University Press.

5

The Transition of Poland and Ukraine: Two Roads Diverge

To this point, we have explored several hundred years of institutional development in two geographically contiguous countries, exploring the slow currents of institutional genesis and change in Poland and Ukraine. Historically, given the close connections between the two countries, including the existence of much of Right Bank Ukraine within the Polish-Lithuanian Commonwealth, we would expect the institutional development of the two to be very closely related. And indeed, for a brief period in the sixteenth century, the institutional outcomes of the Polish-Lithuanian Commonwealth and the Ruthenians across both political and economic institutions were very similar, with a constrained monarchy, growth of noble liberty, application of poor labor market institutions, some basis for private property, and a healthy development of trade and financial institutions.

Unfortunately, the changing incentives of both political and market actors in the two countries from this point onward led to very different arrangements in the political and economic institutions of Poland and Ukraine. In particular, the continuous influence of exogenous shocks, war, and global economic trends placed institutions in the region on different paths. A divergence in institutional development, especially in regard to basic market institutions of trade and property rights but also more visibly in political institutions, was already evident by the seventeenth century and the Cossack rebellion against the Poles. This divergence was accelerated by the absorption of Ukraine into tsarist Russia and then the Partitions of Poland, with institutional development subsequently following the example set by each occupying power. Throughout the eighteenth and nineteenth centuries, looking at it from an economic standpoint, the marginal costs of continuing indigenous institutions (especially in the political sphere) were made far too high by the empires controlling

Polish and Ukrainian land. Thus, institutional development was forced into small-scale and informal modes, generally in reaction to formal institutions but in some cases in support of them. While similarities continued to persist in some institutions due to a shared heritage, for the most part Poland's three Partitions created a very different patchwork of economic institutions than Ukraine's under Russian rule.

However, this multifaceted divergence, reflecting as it did the external influence of three empires (and also, it must be noted, different strains of thought in each country), appeared to be only a hiatus in the convergence of Polish and Ukrainian institutions from the vantage point of the twentieth century. The cataclysm of 1914 to 1918 (out of which Poland was reborn) and especially the leveling of Poland and Ukraine during the Second World War appeared to erase many of the differences institutionally between the two countries by leaving them (superficially) *tabula rasa*. In particular, by 1946 both Poland and Ukraine were brought together under the Soviet bloc as socialist nations, with a planned economy and all of the prefabricated institutions that this entailed. While Ukraine had a head start in communist institutions and was actually a constituent republic of the Soviet Union, the same institutional structure was overlaid on both countries: socialist, rather than private, property; trade monopolized by the state; financial institutions that were bookkeeping and credit allocation mechanisms rather than intermediaries; labor institutions that were also part of the state; and a political system that allowed for only one party, which ostensibly represented the interests of everyone in the country. With only small exceptions noted above related to cultural and social institutions, Ukraine and Poland were forced into the same institutional box and, as we will see, saw similar economic outcomes.

The end of communism as a political force in the late twentieth century changed everything once again, as the economic institutions that accompanied the Soviet occupation of Eastern Europe were manifestly unsuited for facilitating a market economy. In fact, as I have noted elsewhere (Hartwell 2013a), the process of transition that the nations of Central and Eastern Europe (CEE) and the former Soviet Union (FSU) started at various dates from 1989 to 1992 was in its essence concerned with institutional change, removing these central planning institutions in favor of those that would allow for free market relations. In this sense, improved economic outcomes, ranging from higher GDP per capita to greater availability of consumer goods, were just second-order to the process of institutional change; this point was somewhat misunderstood in the economics profession, especially during the first decade, that without institutional change, there was no "transition." And given the all-pervasive nature of the communist state, it would take a massive reorientation of political as well as economic institutions to successfully transition from the planned economy to the market. Given this basic methodological point, the reality it entailed was the daunting task for Poland and Ukraine of starting all over again in the process of formal institution building.

This chapter will tie together the historical view of the previous chapters with a new examination of the process of institutional change in Poland and Ukraine during the crucial years of transition. As I noted in Chapter 1, the economics profession is now in wide agreement that "institutions matter," even if there is some disagreement on what shape these institutions take. With empirical work in transition showing just *how much* particular institutions matter (Hartwell 2013a), it is crucial to understand that the wide divergence in economic outcomes and the contrast between Ukraine and Poland circa 2015 can be directly traced to their institutional divergence, a divergence that did not begin in 1989. Much as the communists discovered at various times from 1921 to 1947, neither country started transition with a blank institutional slate (a point that the previous four chapters have emphatically underlined). Indeed, if this book were written in 1956, we would still see that the historical experience of economic and political institutions in the two countries had colored the adoption of communist institutions and was influencing outcomes under communism. And whereas the communist period appeared to have thoroughly homogenized the institutions of Poland and Ukraine by the 1980s, communism lasted for only forty-two years in Poland and (depending on the dating based on the Civil War years) approximately seventy-one years in Ukraine, meaning that the long institutional history prior to the First World War must have played some part.

With this in mind, the transition process in Central and Eastern Europe did not represent so much the "end of history," in Fukuyama's (1989) memorable phrase, but the return of it, especially in Central and Eastern Europe. But, as we also have noted throughout the book, the path-dependent nature of institutional evolution means that no outcomes were preordained, merely harder or easier to attain. Even today, the creation of market-friendly institutions can be achieved, albeit at a much higher cost than if the institutional memory had already been present . . . or if the correct path had been followed from the outset of transition. The questions addressed in this chapter are thus, as noted earlier, how did the policies pursued during this transitional period build upon or break with the past institutional experience of the two countries? With such a momentous economic transformation at hand, what were the strategies that Poland and Ukraine undertook to manage the reformation of institutions – political and economic, formal and informal? And, finally, how did the development of these specific institutions affect the eventual economic outcomes that we see today?

INITIAL INSTITUTIONAL AND ECONOMIC CONDITIONS

Despite Poland being an independent country and Ukraine a constituent republic of the Soviet Union, the two countries had remarkably similar economic situations at the beginning of transition (Table 5.1), perhaps attributable to the institutional homogeneity imposed from the Soviet Union. Indeed, in GDP statistics alone (although subject to numerous errors and under-reporting of the formal contributions of the private sector in Poland), Poland and Ukraine had seen similar growth rates prior to starting transition and it appeared that Ukraine was almost *better-*situated than Poland in terms of GDP per capita levels. Other macroeconomic and structural factors were in Ukraine's favor, as Ukraine was bequeathed a lower internal and external macroeconomic imbalance, concentrated mainly on fiscal policies, than Poland faced after its decade of debt (Fischer and Gelb 1991). Similarly, Ukraine had both a "moderate" level of natural resource wealth (according to de Melo et al. 2001) and extensive integration with the resource infrastructure of the Soviet Union/ Russia, an economic lifeline that Poland did not have and which, from the vantage point of 1992, appeared to be a positive rather than a negative. Finally, Ukraine's level of industrialization was slightly higher than

Table 5.1 *Initial Conditions in the Two Countries*

	Poland	Ukraine
Transition year	1990	1992
1989 GDP per capita (PPP, constant 1989 US$)	$5150	$5680
Urbanization (% of population) in 1990	62%	67%
Average GDP growth, %, 1985–1989	2.8%	2.4%
Exports, % of GDP 1990	26.2%	27.6%
Private Sector as % of GDP, 1989	30%	10%
Share of Industry in total employment, transition year	28.6%	30.2%
Infant mortality rate, 1989, per 1000 live births	15.6	16.8

Sources: EBRD Structural Indicators, World Bank WDI Database, de Melo *et. al* (2001).

Poland's while still having more agricultural (arable) land than the entire surface area of Poland; encompassing both the black earth of the agricultural zones and the extensive coal reserves of the Donbas, both of which had been inefficiently utilized during the Soviet era, it appeared that Ukraine merely needed an influx of foreign investment and foreign know-how to make these natural advantages work in its favor.

From an institutional standpoint, however, as shown in the previous three chapters, such an assessment on the favorability of Ukraine was not as readily apparent at the outset of transition. In terms of *political institutions*, one could have made the argument that Ukraine was only marginally better off in some aspects, and handicapped in others. On the plus side, Poland had gone through the trauma of martial law in 1981, a mere eight years before the start of transition, while Ukraine avoided the major disruptions seen in other Soviet republics in the late 1980s (as in Armenia, Azerbaijan, Estonia, Georgia, and Lithuania). However, the reason that martial law was declared was because there was a well-organized and well-supported political opposition in Poland, one that already had enough support to threaten the monopoly of power that communists held. By contrast, in Ukraine, there was almost no indigenous political opposition due to the fact that Ukraine was governed not from Kyiv, but from Moscow some 758 kilometers away. With no seat of power in Ukraine, the "most talented Ukrainians regularly moved to Moscow, which offered the best careers as well as more intellectual freedom"; any talk that did occur of opposition to the Communist Party within Ukraine's borders instead centered on "national revival" and avoided discussions of democracy or alternative to communism (Åslund 2009:30).

Similarly, the situation with *economic institutions* also had some divergence between Poland and Ukraine even during Soviet times, intimately connected with the political differentiation between the two countries. Indeed, although both countries were under communist dictatorships directed from Moscow, the mere fact that Ukraine was part of the Soviet Union meant that it was under the yoke of communist central planning for much longer, having a three-decade head start on Poland (or at least two decades, if one considers the 1920s and the NEP as a time of relatively liberal economic institutions). Not only was the time spent under central planning longer, but the extent of economic centralization within the USSR in general was much higher than those countries merely in the Soviet bloc (Fischer and Gelb 1991); a telling sign of this is shown in Table 5.1, where we can see the estimated share of the private sector in GDP during the first year of transition was three times higher in Poland than in Ukraine.

Moreover, as de Melo et al. (2001) show, the macroeconomic distortions of the USSR may have been smaller in the aggregate and when including fiscal and budget policies, but in certain areas they were much higher inside the Soviet Union than outside of it:

- The black market premium on the exchange rate, reflecting the difference between the official rate and what it was traded at in the shadow economy, was "merely" 277 percent in Poland. While seemingly still rather high, the Polish black market premium was over 6 times lower than the premium in Ukraine (calculated at 1,828 percent for the whole Soviet Union);

- Similarly, despite having similar monetary policy institutions, as the headquarters of the planned economy for all of Central and Eastern Europe, the Soviet Union had additional responsibilities in centralized credit creation, i.e. in creating the credits to be pushed around the entire communist space. This responsibility meant that repressed inflation (calculated as percent change in the real wage less the percent change in real GDP over 1987–1990) was almost twice as high in Ukraine/Soviet Union (25.7 percent) as it was in Poland (13.6 percent);

- Finally, as de Melo et al. (2001) hint at, the fact that Ukraine was part of a larger political apparatus rather than its own sovereign nation meant that basic economic institutions such as a central bank or customs administration, even in its Soviet simulacra guise, also simply did not exist. There was no Ukrainian central bank or Ukrainian customs in addition to no Ukrainian leadership, meaning these economic institutions also had to be built rather than adapted, at the same time that political institutions were being built.

The sum total of these distortions was a much less advantageous position for Ukraine than for Poland at the outset of transition, a reality borne out by the economic outcomes during the first years of change. Indeed, early transition research from Åslund et al. (1996) was able to explain large swathes of the differences in output decline and unemployment from 1989 to 1995 by the inclusion of a dummy variable for the former Soviet Union, capturing the specific institutional distortions in money creation and the longer history of communism as a political system.

One area where the result appears to have been a draw was in the area of trade institutions, where both Poland and Ukraine were subsumed into the Council for Mutual Economic Assistance (COMECON) bloc. But even here, the extent of integration into the communist foreign trade institution varied across countries, and especially between Poland and Ukraine. As Blazyca (2001) noted, Poland's trade patterns exhibited schizophrenia due to COMECON, as its exports within the Soviet-dominated bloc made it a relatively advanced producer of engineering services, but it acted more as a developing country with the West, exporting basic commodities and raw materials. Yet, despite this schizophrenia, there was a definite trend away from the COMECON bloc in Poland over time in line with its previous institutional orientation towards the West: according to data provided in Winiecki (2000), Poland had the highest percentage of exports "westbound" of all countries of Central and Eastern Europe as of 1988 (44.7 percent), lower than its high of 62.7 percent in 1928 but still comprising nearly half of all of its exports even under communism. As noted in the previous chapter, Ukraine did not have such a Western orientation even before the Soviet Union, and, indeed, most of Ukraine's "exports" were in fact internal to the Soviet Union rather than external even within COMECON. Ukraine was also much more heavily dependent upon this trade, as de Melo et al. (2001) shows, with a ratio of CMEA imports and exports to GDP nearly three times the size of the same metric as Poland (23.8 percent versus 8.4 percent). It was not even until the late 1980s that foreign trade began to be liberalized throughout the entire USSR, but mismanagement of enterprise reform meant that large state-owned enterprises drove trade as a rent-seeking device, also harming Ukraine's institutional development (Åslund 2009).

These initial institutional conditions, taking into account just the legacy of communism, already show the divergence between Ukraine and Poland even under a common institutional framework. However, the all-pervasive nature of communism, and especially its domination of economic institutions with political ones, may have subsumed the institutional rifts between the two countries, rendering them unable to make a significant difference to economic outcomes (as shown in Table 5.1). But once this system was removed, there was a much higher probability of economic divergence, unless specific, concrete, and actionable steps were taken to re-orient the institutions of each country towards capitalism. To an outside observer, it appeared plausible in the heady days of 1992 that both countries could enact these steps: Poland was gripped by the enormity of its task but was optimistic for the future, while Ukraine appeared to finally put the Soviet legacy behind it and have a chance to re-orient itself back towards the West politically and economically. What actually transpired in this first decade of transition, and how the institutional divergence widened during the second, is the subject of the rest of this chapter.

LAYING THE GROUNDWORK FOR INSTITUTIONAL CHANGE

As hinted at in the previous chapters dealing with the institutional history of Poland and Ukraine, the process of transition in the late 1980s was just that, a process, but a unique one in its scale and scope. Indeed, the fact that a large number of countries were attempting to change their institutional structures at exactly the same time and in the same direction was unprecedented in economic history. Moreover, the transition process soon moved from small-scale, formal, and controlled economic liberalization into an actual multifaceted *transformation*, a broad-based push for reform across all fronts simultaneously, including all institutions (political and economic) and across all types of policies. This reality meant that the accelerated process beginning in 1989 for Poland and 1991 for Ukraine was unlike any of the previous institutional transformations we saw in the previous two chapters: the Partitions of Poland left much of the institutional structure of the country intact, and Ukraine was only slowly absorbed into the Russian Empire, meaning a slow extension of some institutions onto ground where they may have never formally existed. Indeed, the only parallel to the transition from communism to capitalism may have been the transition *to* communism, which also attempted to eradicate the previous formal and informal institutions that existed in each country. In this endeavor, as we have seen, communism was not entirely successful, as informal property rights and trade persisted and even formal institutions suffered reversals in the need to stave off starvation. Transition was then not only a way to build or rebuild institutions for a market economy, but also a need to remove cancerous institutions that had no reason to exist under capitalism.

The transformation from communism to capitalism came to encompass three separate attributes, all interlinked and yet distinct, to accomplish this broader goal:

1. *Economic Liberalization,* or the removal of communist-era barriers and prohibitions within the economy, including most importantly the freeing of prices.

2. *(Macro)economic Stabilization,* or "Type I" policies, removing macroeconomic imbalances left over from communism and shifting to prudent capitalist macroeconomic policies. In practice, as Åslund et al. (1996) noted, stabilization focused on breaking the back of inflation after prices had been freed, ensuring that they reached market-determined levels without the additional distortion of

monetary shenanigans and inflationary expectations. However, stabilization also referred to containing pressures on the government's finances and returning a country somewhat rapidly to growth (Blejer and Škreb 2006).[1]

3. *Structural Change*, or "Type II" policies, fashioning the longer-term institutional reform that has been the focus of this book. This facet, focused mainly on legal frameworks, built on the liberalization of the economy and its stability and was necessarily supported (or cast adrift) by commitment to these other aspects of transition.

The intertwined nature of these various aspects makes it difficult to speak of any one aspect in isolation, as each facet of transition contributed to the others. This "fuzzy" nature of transition, with the process being subjected to constant feedback, reverse causality, and endogeneity, was one of the reasons that econometric modeling of the transition process was so difficult in the early years, a true chicken and egg problem if there ever was one. However, the *inputs* for each attribute can be differentiated, in terms of policy levers and actions taken to reach these outcomes, and this is where we must begin.

As noted in the previous two chapters for Poland and Ukraine, liberalization had already slowly begun during the 1980s in all of the communist countries of Central and Eastern Europe (CEE) and the former Soviet Union (FSU), with the possible exception of Albania. Tentative and tightly controlled economic liberalization in Poland and Ukraine (the USSR) in the economic sphere had begun in earnest in the mid-1980s as a way to cope with the obvious economic failings of communism. However, as noted in the previous two chapters, this aspect of liberalization was more connected with institutional liberalization than the neoclassical form of liberalization, as trade institutions and somewhat small-scale property rights were allowed to form. The economic liberalization envisaged during the transformation encompassed this institutional change but also focused on releasing the communist economy from its shackles wholesale, with the replacement of the centrally planned system of allocation with the price mechanism of the market. Price liberalization was thus the *sine qua non* of transition, replacing administratively determined "prices" with market-determined ones in a parallel of the political transition (more on this below). Given that markets cannot operate without prices, this also

---

[1] It should go without saying that the bar was set high for these transition economies to go straight to prudent policies, when some nominally capitalist countries in the West had avoided these very same policies for years.

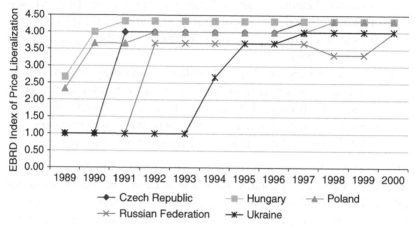

Figure 5.1 Price Liberalization, Selected Countries, 1989–2000
Source: EBRD Transition Indicators, various years.

meant that price liberalization was not only an essential component of transition, but it was the necessary first step, without which nothing else could proceed.

Poland was one of the fastest reformers in price liberalization, having started lifting administrative prices on food and rationing while still under communism, with a modest price reform in 1982 and a more comprehensive one in August 1989 (Kondratowicz and Okólski 2013). Further price liberalization occurred just before the stabilization plan of January 1990, so that by the time the first of the year arrived, "most of the remaining price controls on consumer and producer goods were removed, leaving only about 5 percent of consumer prices and 5 percent of producer prices subject to control" (Sachs and Lipton 1990:114). By 1991, Poland was only behind Hungary in terms of the extent of its price liberalization and well into the macroeconomic stabilization portion of its transition (however, Poland did not reach the level of full price liberalization, as measured by the European Bank for Reconstruction and Development (EBRD), until 1998 – see Figure 5.1). This rapid reform also allowed for the lifting of nearly all trade restrictions by 1990, including enabling any economic entity the freedom to import or export, "giving Poland an extremely liberal trade regime compared both to its past and to world standards" (Murrell 1993:128). The lowering of trade barriers helped to import global prices, providing a "rational price system for traded goods" (Fischer and Gelb 1991:96), and adding an additional automatic stabilizer to the price mechanism within Poland (by incentivizing exporters and increasing competition internally). While the USSR was still discussing the outline of how it should move politically, Poland had already made huge strides in its economic liberalization, accompanying price liberalization with "price rationalization," or the diminution of subsidies at the same time (Kondratowicz and Okólski 2013).

In contrast, Ukraine was slow to attempt even this basic step of liberalization as, when it was attempted, it was piecemeal and often reversed. Indeed, "until the end of 1994, Ukraine had not had a sustained attempt at economic liberalization . . . . state-imposed restrictions, interventions and distortions in the foreign exchange, trade, and pricing regimes, were extreme over much of the late-1991 to 1994 period" (Kaufmann and Kaliberda 1996:86). Even in October 1994, new president Kuchma noted in his presidential address that price "reform" would be implemented via a "government-regulated and con-trolled process," promising three years after the fact to think about allowing for free prices depending "on the actual economic and social situation"; as Shen (1996:66) notes, however, by the time that this speech was given, much of price determination was already beyond the hands of the Ukrainian government, as price deregulation in Russia had already taken control of Ukraine's prices (due to the tight integration that still existed and the widespread use of the ruble in Ukraine). The fact that, even as late as on the cusp of 1995, Ukrainian politicians were not convinced that price liberalization was such a good idea is very telling, an issue that will be explored below.

In addition to liberalization, and accompanying (and in many ways preceding) the building of institutions, was the very real need for economic stabilization, in order to correct the gross imbalances that the communist economy engendered. In reality, it is somewhat of a folly to speak of "stabilization" while undergoing a process that is, by its inherent nature, destabilizing; if stabilization had been the over-arching goal of policy makers in Poland and Ukraine in the late 1980s, such a disruptive process as transformation, let alone liberalization, would never have been attempted. Instead, the process of stabilization, generally referring to the macroeconomic situation, referred to mini-mizing the disruption that was to come as part of the transition (Kornai's (1994) "transformational recession") rather than exacerbat-ing it. And as a prerequisite for economic growth, the stabilization process could also allow the mediating institutions necessary for the market to take root.

Oddly enough, with apparent agreement on the most difficult and crucial aspect of the transition, the creation of the correct formal institutions, disagreements emerged on the means to achieve this transformation, centered on stabilization and liberalization. The proper policies to undertake these two facets of transition, and especially the speed and sequencing of these reforms, were to prove the most contentious in early debates over transition, resulting in the facile "shock therapy" versus "gradualism" debate. While this argument has been decisively settled for the transition economies of the region (see Hartwell (2013a) for a summary and postmortem of the debate), from the vantage point of the beginning of transition, both gradualist approaches and rapid liberalization appeared to be valid alternatives for reaching the desired institutional changes to leave communism behind.

Gradualist arguments, typified in the writings of former Polish finance minister Grzegorz Kołodko (2004), believed that the time-inconsistency of institution-building *vis-à-vis* macroeconomic policies meant that old institutions should be preserved while new ones are being built, in order to avoid precipitous drops in output (Popov 2000). In regard to stabilization and liberalization, this meant that both of these facets of transition should be undertaken slowly, especially where aggregate uncertainty regarding the outcome of transition is high and reversal costs are present (Roland 2000); slower policies that allowed for institutional adjustment were to be preferred to rapid reforms that brought about a deep recession. Conversely, proponents of shock therapy "highlight[ed] the interdependence, mutually supportive and interactive character of economic relationships," arguing that "reforms should be introduced simultaneously" (Marangos 2002:44); in practical terms, this meant that institutional change could only come about with fast liberalization, allowing institutions to grow in the environment they would have to compete in, rather than keeping in place the failed institutions of the past and encouraging further distortions from a dual-track economy (Marangos 2003). Output declines from the changeover would be inevitable, but they would be short lived and actually beneficial, as expectations would adjust only in an environment of radical change (Balcerowicz et al. 1997), allowing for institutions to grow.

It is here, on the battleground of stabilization and liberalization policies, where the first signs of divergence between the CEE countries and those of the FSU began to emerge in the early period of transition (approximately 1989 to 1994). In particular, the pace of stabilization in

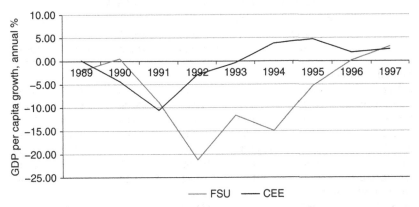

Figure 5.2 Economic Depression and Recovery in CEE and FSU Countries in Early Transition
Source: World Bank WDI Indicators. CEE includes Bulgaria, Czech Republic, Hungary, Poland, and Slovakia, FSU includes all ex-Soviet republics apart from the Baltic States.

countries that were west of Kyiv appeared to go much faster and much further than those to the east, with the CEE countries (mostly) taking the shock therapy route and the FSU taking a much longer time to stabilize and liberalize; measured by the resumption of GDP growth (Figure 5.2), it took the CEE countries approximately two years from the start of transition before growth resumed, while in the FSU countries it was nearly four years. Moreover, Figure 5.2 shows the relative depth of the trough in each region, which was much lower in the FSU countries than in CEE both at the outset of transition and subsequently (Brenton et al. (1997) estimate the total output decline in the FSU over 1989 to 1994 at 40.9 percent of 1989 GDP, while in the CEE it was a relatively mild 26.5 percent). Similarly, Tables 5.2a and 5.2b show the inflation experience across the region; taken from Åslund et al. (1996) and using their classification for "gradual" and "radical" from the mid-1990s, one can see that inflation was quickly broken in the "radical reforming" economies, albeit settling at levels that were high for Western economies in the 1990s (Table 5.2a), while in the FSU and gradual reformers (Table 5.2b), it persisted even years after transition. This macroeconomic failure necessarily contributed to the output decline and, as we will see later, also harmed the formation of new market institutions.

While these results in the aggregate across regions show a trend in the relative merits of fast versus slow reforms, the outcomes between Poland

Table 5.2a *Inflation Outcomes by Type of Reform*

	Year of Peak	Level at Peak	Level in Next Year	Level 2 Years Later	Level in 1994	Level in 1995
Radical reformers						
Poland	1990	586.00	70.30	43.00	32.20	31.70
Czech Republic	1991	56.70	11.10	20.80	10.20	10.00
Slovakia	1991	61.20	10.10	23.00	14.00	11.40
Albania	1992	225.90	85.00	28.00	28.00	9.30
Estonia	1992	1069.00	89.00	48.00	48.00	30.00
Latvia	1992	951.20	109.00	36.00	36.00	27.40
AVERAGE		**491.67**	**62.42**	**33.13**	**28.07**	**19.97**
Gradual reformers						
Romania	1993	256.00	131.00	33.40	131.00	33.40
Hungary	1991	34.20	22.90	22.50	19.00	29.00
Bulgaria	1991	333.50	82.00	72.80	89.00	70.00
Lithuania	1992	1020.30	390.20	72.00	72.00	25.00
Russia	1992	1353.00	896.00	220.00	220.00	184.00
Moldova	1992	1276.00	789.00	327.00	327.00	25.40
Belarus	1994	2200.00	.	.	2200.00	703.10
Ukraine	1993	4735.00	842.00	342.00	842.00	342.00
Kazakhstan	1994	1980.00	.	.	1980.00	177.10
Uzbekistan	1994	746.00	.	.	746.00	254.00
Turkmenistan	1993	3102.00	2400.00	2500.00	2400.00	2500.00
Georgia	1994	18000.00	.	.	18000.00	163.90
Armenia	1994	5458.00	.	.	5458.00	179.00
Azerbaijan	1994	1500.00	.	.	1500.00	535.70
Tajikistan	1993	2195.00	452.00	240.00	2195.00	240.00
Kyrgyz Republic	1993	1208.70	280.00	48.60	280.00	48.60
AVERAGE		**2837.36**	**628.51**	**387.83**	**2278.69**	**344.39**

Source: Åslund et al. (1996) and author's calculations.

and Ukraine serve as a microcosm of the entire debate, further driving home the differences across reform strategies. Poland in particular was the poster child for shock therapy, as the small and piecemeal macroeconomic reforms in the direction of a market economy in the late 1980s were supplanted by a broad series of economic stabilization policies that set the basis for institutional reforms. Set in motion by Finance Minister and Deputy Premier Leszek Balcerowicz, the "Balcerowicz Plan" of January 1990 had eleven separate components (as noted by Papava 1996:253):

Table 5.2b *Inflation Outcomes by Geography*

	Year of Peak	Level at Peak	Level in Next Year	Level 2 Years Later	Level in 1994	Level in 1995
Former Soviet Union						
Russia	1992	1353.00	896.00	220.00	220.00	184.00
Moldova	1992	1276.00	789.00	327.00	327.00	25.40
Belarus	1994	2200.00	.	.	2200.00	703.10
Ukraine	1993	4735.00	842.00	342.00	842.00	342.00
Kyrgyz Republic	1993	1208.70	280.00	48.60	280.00	48.60
Kazakhstan	1994	1980.00	.	.	1980.00	177.10
Uzbekistan	1994	746.00	.	.	746.00	254.00
Turkmenistan	1993	3102.00	2400.00	2500.00	2400.00	2500.00
Georgia	1994	18000.00	.	.	18000.00	163.90
Armenia	1994	5458.00	.	.	5458.00	179.00
Azerbaijan	1994	1500.00	.	.	1500.00	535.70
Tajikistan	1993	2195.00	452.00	240.00	2195.00	240.00
Estonia	1992	1069.00	89.00	48.00	48.00	30.00
Latvia	1992	951.20	109.00	36.00	36.00	27.40
Lithuania	1992	1020.30	390.20	72.00	72.00	25.00
AVERAGE		**3119.61**	**694.13**	**425.96**	**2420.27**	**362.35**
Central and Eastern Europe						
Poland	1990	586.00	70.30	43.00	32.20	31.70
Czech Republic	1991	56.70	11.10	20.80	10.20	10.00
Slovakia	1991	61.20	10.10	23.00	14.00	11.40
Romania	1993	256.00	131.00	33.40	131.00	33.40
Hungary	1991	34.20	22.90	22.50	19.00	29.00
Bulgaria	1991	333.50	82.00	72.80	89.00	70.00
Albania	1992	225.90	85.00	28.00	28.00	9.30
AVERAGE		**221.93**	**58.91**	**34.79**	**46.20**	**27.83**

Source: Åslund et al. (1996) and author's calculations.

1. Raising prices to world market level, accepting the inflationary effects of such action.
2. Constraining income growth in inflationary conditions.
3. Restricting money supply and raising interest rates.
4. Encouragement of saving via increases in interest rates on cash and other deposits.
5. Reductions in budgetary expenditure through reduction in government investment and elimination of subsidies to unprofitable enterprises.
6. Issuing government bonds to finance the state budget deficit.

7. Regulation of the tax system and its unification.
8. Establishing a single rate of exchange for the zloty and establishing convertibility of the zloty in the domestic market.
9. Introducing a common customs tariff in order to restrict imports and stimulate exports.
10. Providing social assistance to the population within the limits of budgetary prudence.
11. Breaking up monopolistic enterprises and rejecting state intervention in the activities of competitive enterprises.

This plan, a mixture of liberalization, stabilization, and structural change activities, was designed to put a quick end to the inflationary pressures unleashed by price liberalization, while enabling Poland to return to growth. While literally thousands of pages have already been written on the successes (and shortcomings) of the Plan, and here is not the place to re-examine this body of work, some issues need to be noted regarding its effect on stabilization. Its impact was immediate, in that inflation dropped nearly 510 percentage points from 1990 to 1991 while the decline in GDP was relatively mild, at slightly less than 20 percent, with the bulk of this decline happening in 1990 (approximately 11.6 percent in this one year, according to Åslund et al. (1996)). By 1995, the level of output of Poland was almost at its 1989 levels, and even this number is likely to be understated due to the proliferation of the private sector (which tended to be undercounted in official statistics in the early transition). Even where public support may have wavered and it appeared that the Polish economy was stubbornly refusing to adapt instantaneously to the reforms, "continued absence of a viable alternative to economic liberalism as a transition strategy" meant that even reactionary political parties had no choice but to continue the reforms (Slay 1993:238).[2]

Beyond the effect that the Plan had on macroeconomic aggregates, another crucial aspect of the Plan that has been somewhat overlooked is its comprehensive nature, addressing nearly every facet of the distortions that were created under communism. Utilizing a clever strategy that built off social and cultural institutions that had survived the Communist Party

---

[2] Reading some of the early post-mortems on Poland's stabilization in the present-day, especially Slay's (1993) missive, offers no end of mirth at just how misguided criticism at the time was. From the vantage point of approximately two years of stabilization, many economists (and especially sociologists and political scientists) were hastily pointing out that the transition had failed and was too extreme. In following years, these same researchers were to shift gears and say that institutions were neglected in the policies, implicitly arguing that the transition was not extreme enough.

(including a bold move to make the złoty convertible and unify exchange rates), the Plan created a series of reforms that seemed *irrevocable*. As noted below in a more theoretical framework, the stabilization process and its air of permanence created expectations that these reforms would succeed (setbacks were just that, setbacks rather than flaws that challenged the viability of the transition); this in turn oriented institutional development towards a world that included these reforms rather than a world that did not (this approach was also adopted in Estonia, which, in one sense, had even more radical reforms than Poland). Indeed, the stabilization reforms fed into the institutional reform process, as, while political turnover was high in the early governments of the new Poland, there was little sense that communism was a viable alternative or could make a comeback. Similarly, survey data from the 1990s showed that the perception of property rights (to take an example of an important institution) was growing throughout the country (Johnson et al. 2002). Even with a slow-moving privatization process, new enterprises sprang up that rendered the state-owned concerns irrelevant. The fast-moving reforms of 1989 and 1990 in Poland set the country upon a different path, and institutional arrangements adapted accordingly.

By contrast, and in line with the rest of the former Soviet Union, Ukraine saw a difficult stabilization process, with constant "fire-fighting" in the early years against recurring (or, more accurately, continuous) macroeconomic crises. As de Ménil and Woo (1994:9) noted, "Ukraine offers a pure case study of what happens to a transition economy when reform is delayed." With only partial price liberalization in the early years, stabilization was less an attempt to contain the inflation associated with free-market prices than an attempt to hold a hybrid communist-capitalist system from collapsing under the weight of its internal contradictions. De Ménil (2000:57) accurately called this period "stabilization without liberalization," a period where structural reforms were ignored and "the day of reckoning continued to be postponed." Havrylyshyn et al. (1994:356) catalogued these failures as "incomplete price liberalization, the maintenance of substantial export taxes, little or no privatization and few attempts to close or restructure loss-making public enterprises." In regard to the most egregious of these, the government's reach continued to include administrative allocation of resources, rather than letting the market sort it out, and as late as 1993, "quotas and other quantitative and tax measures continued to restrict more than 70 percent of all exports" (de Ménil 2000:52). Shen (1996) notes that the vast majority of the price increases that occurred during the period of 1992–1993 were administratively determined, meaning that the Ukrainian government was not only impeding liberalization, but also was arbitrarily undermining stabilization.

This lack of reform extended into other areas, as valuable institutions such as monetary oversight went neglected entirely (Table 5.2a shows that inflation reached a high of 4,375 percent in 1993). Authorities instead utilized monetary policy as a way to cover fiscal profligacy, not even attempting to reduce budgetary expenditure in the aftermath of the break-up of the Soviet Union (Åslund 1995). Havrylyshyn et al. (1994:356) note that this profligacy started early, as "in 1992, off-budget subsidies and capital transfers ... amounted to 16% of GDP. Combined with a 62% shortfall in planned VAT revenues, this led to a budget deficit of 28% of GDP." Privatization did not help to bring in additional money, nor did it create mass ownership, as "Ukraine opted for a slow discretionary approach, which favored incumbent managers [so that] by the end of 1994, only 11,000 enterprises had been privatized" (Åslund 1995:129). Unlike Poland, which had explicitly laid out a plan to specifically avoid these issues during the transition, Ukraine's stabilization attempted to ease the pain of transition (as well as enrich privileged individuals) through business as usual, undertaking the most gradual of transitions. It wasn't until the end of 1994 that a liberalization and stabilization program was finally agreed upon, with budgetary subsidies dramatically reduced (but not ended) and price liberalization (despite Kuchma's pledge to regulate this process) coming to fruition in a rather accelerated manner. As Åslund et al. (1996) note, Ukraine was the latest of the reformers throughout the former Soviet Union or Central and Eastern Europe, with its year of "most intense reform" (1994) coming after all other ex-Soviet Republics apart from Turkmenistan (and Figure 5.1 shows that price liberalization did not reach the level of Poland in 1991 until 1997). Not included in this assessment was the fact that the intensity of the reform in Ukraine was also much less than all CEE countries and many FSU countries.

These different experiences in liberalization and stabilization were to color the institutional evolution of each country in the transition space, with special impact on Poland and Ukraine. Indeed, such a divergence in policies between two countries that had shared a common institutional heritage can be traced to these issues. As we have stressed, however, the era of stabilization and liberalization was a mere three to four years out of the history of either country, a mere blip when compared to the centuries previous. Thus, the development of institutions in Poland and Ukraine may have been shaped by the (lack of a) stabilization process, but it is more likely that the stabilization and liberalization process was also colored by the history of institutions in each country: how did political institutional evolution, both pre- and post-communism, alter the calculus of timing of liberalization and stabilization? This endogeneity of reform was to be reinforced by the subsequent paths that the various institutions, both political and economic, in Poland and Ukraine took onward from this point. This is the issue we will now turn to.

POLITICAL INSTITUTIONS: THE MORE THINGS CHANGE?

As we have seen throughout this book, the development of political institutions in both Poland and Ukraine over their history had a demonstrable impact on the development of economic institutions, as well as economic policy. From the imposition of serfdom as a labor market institution by nobles to the restriction of trade by tsars and the freeing of property rights in Poland, political institutions were to play a large part in setting the rules of the game of economic institutions, at least at the formal level. Given the interplay between the two sets of institutions during the previous centuries, it would be folly to expect that political processes, never totally subsumed during the communist era, would not exert an influence on the parallel process of economic institution-building or reform. The only question was, of course, what type of influence this would be.

However, there are more interesting and situation-specific reasons as to why the transformation of political institutions in the CEE and FSU countries would be inextricably linked with the evolution of economic institutions. In the first instance, the entire basis of the economic system of communism was tied into one political institution, the monopoly of the Communist Party over every facet of life. Although there was small-scale liberalization throughout the communist bloc in the 1980s, it was not until the erosion of this political monopoly that the economic transition actually became a *transformation*. That is, the transition process only became broad, widespread, and comprehensive, across such a broad front of institutions and countries, when the political barriers to transition collapsed or withdrew; economic transition only began when the political sphere allowed it to. In some countries, this political withdrawal did not occur, and hence economic changes remained frozen in the Soviet era; one only need look at the "new" governments of Turkmenistan and Uzbekistan post-1992, where it was decided that transition was a fate to be avoided (thus seeing political independence but very little political or economic institutional transition). But elsewhere, either from pressure internal to the Party (the Soviet Union) or external to it (Poland), the start of the transformation process was a deliberate and conscious choice.

As time progressed, the transition process shifted to being driven not only by the absence of formal political institutions, but through the creation of new formal and informal political institutions. This brief period of political creation in many transition countries also set the tone for policies regarding the creation of economic institutions; in fact, the extent of formal political *influence* in the development of economic institutions appears to be directly correlated with the extent of formal political institutional *change*. The reason for this should be abundantly clear from a theoretical perspective, as the outset of transition offered a small and rapidly closing political window in which both macroeconomic policies and institutions could have been reoriented, created, or abolished altogether. This time, termed "extraordinary politics" by Balcerowicz (1995:311), was characterized "among the political elites and the populace at large [by] a stronger-than-normal tendency to think and to act in terms of the common good."

However, markets, attitudes, and especially politicians, do not stand still for long, with this time of extraordinary politics soon falling prey to the normal jockeying of the political process. Thus, momentous changes such as broad-based institutional reform had only a small timeframe in which to be enacted, changes that were more likely to occur if political institutions were also in a state of flux (that is, if there was less "normal jockeying" to return to). Without established political parties or political interests, it was more likely that tough political decisions could have been made regarding stabilization, liberalization, and structural change, rather than in a scenario where political leaders were clinging to power as all other institutions changed around them. Indeed, in many countries, stabilization represented a political trade-off of economic pain inflicted today, but finishing relatively quickly, versus economic pain spread out over twenty-five years or more, but which lessened political pain for the party in power. Where there was more continuity in power and more political spoils to lose, it was less likely for political institutions to voluntarily undertake the economic change necessary, a course that would then beget worse economic institutions.

Given this theoretical foundation, the importance of political institutional change on the transition process becomes readily apparent, and it is here where we begin our examination of Poland's and Ukraine's institutional changes since the end of communism. In this, we are somewhat aided by the fact that the easiest differences to spot between the two countries are often in the political institutions, in their dynamic processes and outcomes, as well as the reality that the political process immediately following transition was tumultuous in both Poland and in Ukraine. However, a brief overview of the overall political institutions in the two countries during transition reveals a divergence immediately, as there was far more continuity of leadership in the newly independent Ukraine than across the border at the outset of the transformation. Indeed, unlike Poland, which saw large-scale change in its politicians (and rapid political turnover in the first four years), the new state of Ukraine was governed by the same man who led it at the end of communism, Leonid Kravchuk (the head of state for the Ukrainian SSR), and would continue to be until 1994. This continuity did not stop with the head of government, for, while Poland was moving rapidly forward on a broad front of political and economic change, Ukraine's former communist party members remained in key positions throughout the government during these crucial early years. This continuity of personalities is the key difference in Ukraine's political transition versus Poland's, as the timing of post-communist elections, number of cabinets, and cabinet duration was exactly the same for the two countries during the first decade of transition (Table 5.3).

The Semi-Presidential Trap

This obvious divergence in political make-up has its roots in many of the political institutions that were fashioned during the changeover from communism to democracy. Indeed, the diverging outcomes in terms of political turnover are interesting precisely due to the fact that the overarching political institutional framework of the two countries has been basically the same since the withdrawal of the Communist Party. The form of government fashioned in both Poland and Ukraine on the eve of transition was a semi-presidential system, where the president is elected by popular vote, but does not form the government directly; instead, the president asks for parliamentary authority to confirm the prime minister, who then in turn forms a cabinet (a more precise definition of semi-presidentialism, and the debates surrounding it, are found in Elgie 1999). The two systems are not entirely identical, as Poland officially has "both the Council of Ministers and the President ... vested with the highest executive power," although, in reality, "it is the Council of Ministers led by the Prime Minister that

Table 5.3 *Duration of Cabinets in Postcommunist CEE/FSU,*
1991–2002

	Number of Cabinets since 1991	Average longevity of Cabinet (months)
President-parliamentary		
Ukraine	9.00	15.30
Russia	7.00	19.70
Kazakhstan	6.00	23.00
Average	**7.33**	**19.33**
Premier-presidential		
Lithuania	11.00	12.60
Moldova	8.00	17.30
Poland	9.00	15.30
Romania	7.00	19.70
Average	**8.75**	**16.23**
Parliamentary		
Czech Republic	5.00	27.60
Estonia	9.00	15.30
Hungary	5.00	27.60
Latvia	9.00	15.30
Slovakia	6.00	23.00
Average	**6.80**	**21.76**

Source: Protsyk (2003).

constitutes the centre of executive power" (Raciborski 2007:21); conversely, Ukraine has a "more symmetrical distribution of dismissal powers between president and parliament characteriz[ing] the president-parliamentary constitutional framework" (Protsyk 2003:1078). However, both systems create two poles within the government, dividing power between the president and the parliament and granting leeway to both to enact policy.

The manner in which the system works in practice, and even the reason for choosing such a semi-presidential system, provides us with our first clue to the political outcomes in the two countries, as the reasoning behind the system was very different in Poland and in Ukraine. Semi-presidentialism is generally designed to ensure checks and balances even within the executive branch, providing a constraint against concentration of power but also allowing for outsiders to enter the process (Elgie 2004) – a very important consideration in post-communism. As we have seen, the entire history of Polish political institutions from 1386 through to 1795 was of continuous decentralization from the king to the nobility, weakening the central authorities and preferring to keep political power dispersed in order to not harm economic interests. Given this reality, it would stand to reason that, after the extreme centralization under Piłsudski and communism, such a constraining system would also be preferred for the transition away from communism. In fact, the precise issues of semi-presidentialism that have been cited in the political science literature as a reason to avoid the system (including worries about divided rule, "cohabitation" of political parties in the prime minister's and president's offices, and worries about direct mandates) all may have appeared attractive to the architects of Poland's political transition.

The adoption of semi-presidentialism in Poland was not done in so calculated a manner, however, as McMenamin (2008:2) notes that "Polish semi-presidentialism [was] the result of a series of highly political decisions taken under very different and unforeseen circumstances." A desire to retain centralized power was still the goal of the communists as late as 1989, and during the Roundtable Talks of 1989 they advanced the idea of a strong executive (a president) elected by the *Sejm*; this formulation was done because the communists had been granted a guarantee of 65 percent of seats in the *Sejm* in the upcoming June elections, and assumed they would have a solid majority to effectively allow Jaruzelski to remain in power. As a concession to the opposition, who were wary of the continuation of a strong executive, the "Communists agreed (indeed, even suggested during the Roundtable talks) to establish the Senate, chosen in free elections, as an institutional guarantee against possible shift of balance of power into the President's hands" (Jasiewicz 2000:105–106). In this way, the Polish government would have a modicum of checks and balances, even if the Communist Party retained the office of the presidency and avoided direct electoral competition in the early years of transition (Olson 1993).

However, the confidence of the communists in Poland (as elsewhere in CEE) was misplaced (Lijphart 1992), as the parliamentary elections in June 1989 brought Tadeusz Mazowiecki into power as the first non-communist prime minister in over forty years. The electoral landslide against the ruling Communist Party created a strong anticommunist majority in the *Sejm* (many of whom had defected from communist splinter parties), thus killing the idea of a parliamentary election for the president. With political parties still being formed, reformed, disbanded, and merged (and Solidarity refusing to create its own political party and instead splintering into rival factions, see Gill (2003)), it appeared that direct election of the president was a sound alternative to the parliamentary procedure, as it would rely on the personality of the candidate rather than a coherent platform and party apparatus. More important in terms of its acceptance, political calculation by the main candidates for the presidency (Mazowiecki and Lech Wałęsa) led each of them to believe that they would emerge victorious, and thus they each endorsed direct election as a way to secure their own path to power (Rapaczynski 1991). With such support, the *Sejm* voted to amend the Polish constitution and allowed for direct elections.

A strong form of semi-presidentialism, with a powerful president in addition to an indirectly-elected Prime Minister, was to be the prevailing form of government in Poland from 1990 to 1997, as the systemic balancing act appeared to bring effective leaders into government while still restraining the president from communist-era-like powers. This system also combined two attributes of the Second Republic, or rather one attribute that was present in the 1920s and 1930s and one that was lacking: in Lech Wałęsa, Poland had a charismatic leader projecting the "goodwill of the people" as his mandate (similar to Piłsudski but with much less experience), while postcommunist Poland also had a *Sejm* that was still finding its footing but had a popular mandate formed around a common dislike (the failed policies of the past). And while the semi-presidential system was blamed for cabinet instability, especially over 1991–1993 (Roper 2002), the reality is that the Polish political system was simply undergoing a transition, forming coalitions and parties out of whole cloth. In such a situation, instability was perhaps preferred rather than the stability of continuity. Similarly, while McMenamin (2008:1) asserts that "the conflicting legitimacies generated by semi-presidentialism delayed but did not prevent, or seriously threaten, democratic consolidation in Poland," I would argue instead that the process of semi-presidentialism, as a way of coping with the lack of established parties and in order to keep all parties of the Roundtable in agreement, was a *necessary* step on the way to democratic consolidation.

But Poland's political instability was not due to semi-presidentialism, nor was Poland's successful political transition. As noted above, and as Elgie (2004) pointed out, semi-presidentialism has its own major flaws in gridlock and divisiveness, while Lijphart (2004:102) notes that "semi-presidential systems actually make it possible for the president to be even more powerful than in most pure presidential systems." All of these issues could have damaged Poland quite easily, if it hadn't been for agreement on broad principles undertaken before quibbling on the details emerged. As Jasiewicz (2000:108) correctly pointed out, in Poland,

> *the parties who signed the Roundtable Accord, uncertain about the outcome of the agreed-upon elections, apparently understood that their best political strategy would be to achieve consensus regarding not so much specific regulations (which could not be perfect, as the fate of the National List indicates), but the general rules of the game, and to accept mutual commitment to play by these rules. Essential here was the collective nature of the bargaining process and of mutual guarantees extended by one party to another. Both parties indeed played by the rules.*

McMenamin (2008:1) seconded this point, admitting that the ground-work for the Polish success had been laid "before the introduction of semi-presidentialism [as] Polish elites had already established a firm consensus on democracy, which was buttressed by consensus on the economic system and international relations." Such success was also enabled by the reality of political competition in Poland and the fact that the old guard was thoroughly and utterly repudiated: by the summer of 1990, there were no remaining communist ministers in government, and Jaruzelski had resigned the presidency to make way for new elections, meaning that the Polish political scene was virtually *tabula rasa* (Gill 2003). In fact, the wipeout of the communists in 1989 meant that they were continually supportive of the new system, as a directly elected presidency was the only way in which they were likely to influence Polish politics.

Finally, a reason why the semi-presidential system did not cause the havoc in Poland that it has elsewhere was that it did not last that long, at least in its strong form. This was due to other political institutional changes that were occurring at the same time underneath the surface, the most important being the shift to proportional representation (PR). Olson (1993:430) notes that proportional representation was opposed by the Communists, even though it might have "aggregated votes from around the country to give the PUWP at least some small share of Senate seats. But that method would have required a formal acknowledgment of rival organized political parties, a step neither side even proposed at the Roundtable early in the transition process." With the electoral wave sweeping aside the Communists in 1989, however, negotiations for the Electoral Law of 1991, necessary for the next set of *Sejm* elections, had settled on a consensus that proportional representation was a desirable step forward for Polish democracy (Raciborski 2007). However, the first experiment with PR in 1991 was far too similar to the problems that had plagued the Second Republic, in that the highly fragmented *Sejm*, unable to attain a consensus to overcome President Lech Wałęsa's veto, chose the "most proportional of the PR systems" that had no electoral threshold and favored smaller parties (Benoit and Hayden 2004:410). This system had the same effect as in the 1920s, producing a *Sejm* consisting of small and fragmented parties, requiring at least seven parties to form a governing coalition (ibid.).[3] It was only during negotiations for the modern "Small Constitution" (see below) that the larger parties in the *Sejm* were able to band together and support the introduction of thresholds and a much tighter proportional formula; this approach had the desired effect of winnowing down the number of parties in the parliament (Sydorchuk 2014).

With fewer and stronger political parties in parliament, led by their own personalities and coalescing around definite platforms, a pervasive worry developed that the office of president was too powerful *vis-à-vis* the *Sejm* (and, by extension, these parties). Thus, the previous consensus in favor of a semi-presidential system with a powerful, directly elected president began to shift *en masse*, enabled in some part (I would argue) by the cabinet instability that characterized Poland's early transition; with little hope to remain in power in the cabinet for an extended period of time, each political actor had the incentive to see a weaker president to ensure that power did not become unbalanced. Such a reality actually did occur with the presidential elections in 1995, as "Alexander Kwaśniewski was elected for the office against all odds . . . [meaning] the head of the Constitutional Committee and a fervent opponent of the model of a robust presidency became the President-elect" (Wyrzykowski and Ciele 2006:257). With political calculations shifting against a powerful president, and in line with Polish history, constitutional reforms in 1997 (see below) vitiated the role of the president and made Poland a stronger (yet still mixed) parliamentary model (Forestiere 2010). In this manner, the presidency became a more ceremonial role with power vested in the *Sejm*, a direct link to Poland's long history of political institutional evolution. As we will see, this has not eliminated the risk to the Polish political system, but it has reduced such risk substantially.

---

[3] This reality occurred despite the fact that Poland was a much more homogenous (ethnically) country than in the 1920s, a result of the Soviet Union's ethnic cleansing policies after the Second World War. Thus, the different small national minority parties that splintered the *Sejm* (and created a disincentive for collaboration during the Second Republic) were not problematic because they were minorities, but because the system allowed for so much fragmentation.

By contrast, the experience in Ukraine was not as sanguine as in Poland, as the former Soviet country saw all of Elgie's (2004) warnings about the dangers of semi-presidentialism in divided societies come true. Like the rest of the former Soviet Union (with the notable exception of the Baltics), Ukraine also embraced the semi-presidential system in its transition away from one-party rule, although, as in Poland, the choice was made as a political calculation by Communists on the basis of a "situational factor of conceived political power gain" (Christensen et al. 2005:213), a fair assessment given the events leading up to transition in 1990. Indeed, Ukraine's political transition began before Ukraine even became an independent country, as (relatively) free elections to the Ukrainian Verkhovna Rada (the Supreme Soviet, soon to become the parliament) occurred in 1990. These elections, enabled by a change in the law of 1989 that allowed for the direct election of deputies, represented both a resounding victory for the Communists, who walked away with 75 percent of the seats that were voted upon (331 out of 442), and the opposition, which finally had legal standing in the legislature.

With a popular mandate, something that had not been seen in Ukraine since 1918 (and even then for only a short time), and a declaration of sovereignty approved, the Rada moved to "the forefront of creating a legal and administrative structure for a sovereign state" (Magocsi 2010:722). The next step in this political transformation came in July 1991, a month before Ukraine left the Soviet Union, with the establishment of the office of the president; as Boban (2007:164) notes, as "the Constitution of the Ukrainian SSR of 1978 did not envisage the institution of the president of the republic," such a change needed to be "introduced by the constitutional novella of 5 July 1991." This amendment to the Basic Law created the post of president of the Ukrainian SSR, a designation that was changed on August 24, 1991, with Ukraine's declaration of independence, to president of Ukraine. It appeared that the building blocks of political institutions for an independent Ukraine were prepared in advance of actual independence, a move to be applauded for its foresight and prudence.

However, the actual move to independence over the rest of 1991 continued to expose difficulties in the design of brand-new political institutions in an environment that was unfamiliar with them. The office of the president was somewhat undefined in the Acts of July 1991 concerning its creation, which focused mainly on the role of the president in defense of Ukraine against external (mainly Soviet) attempts to vitiate sovereignty (Wolczuk 2001). Timmermans (1998) notes that the wrangling on the precise delineation of powers between the president and the Rada started almost immediately upon the creation of the institution, as the two Articles in the 1978 Constitution dealing with the distribution of powers were amended a combined sixteen times through 1994. In fact, from the outset, the president was at a decided disadvantage as compared to the Rada, which retained its extensive powers from the Soviet era: in particular, the president was unable to dismiss the Rada on his own initiative, forced "to obtain parliamentary consent for both the appointment and dismissal of the Prime Minister," and, in certain circumstances, could see decisions suspended by the Rada or vetoes overridden by a simple majority (Wolczuk 2001:84).

The weakness of the presidency was exacerbated by the Rada's avoiding reforms of its own, thus "crudely graft[ing]" a new institution (the presidency) onto an unreconstructed Soviet parliamentary system (Wolczuk 2001:85). Unlike Poland, the Rada remained a unitary institution, as despite debate on separating the parliament into two chambers, it remained a monolithic, 450-seat deliberative body (Magocsi 2010). Moreover, Wolczuk (2001:85) also points out that the Rada members were allowed to keep their positions in local councils after independence, resisting the pressure to become a professional legislature, a reality of "tinkering with the odd bits of the institutional framework [which] led to a paralyzing confusion on the delineation of power at the center and local level." Finally, even when the Rada did wield its power to obstruct, as in the case of parliament rejecting a president's candidate for prime minister there was little sense of what happened next. As Sydorchuk (2014) correctly pointed out, if such a rejection came to pass, there was no contingency for filling the post, and the process had to start over from the beginning.

There was little time to ponder these mechanical questions, for events accelerated quickly in late 1991, from Ukraine's declaration of independence in August 1991 to the presidential elections at the end of the year. On December 1, 1991, Communist Party ideologist and Chairman of the Supreme Soviet Leonid Kravchuk was elected as the first president of Ukraine in with 61.6 percent of the vote, buoyed by the unified support of the left and the disorganized efforts of the right (Åslund 2009). While we will discuss Kravchuk's indecisiveness in regard to the formation of economic institutions below, there is a belief amongst Ukrainian scholars that either Kravchuk wanted to keep the powers of the presidency limited (Protsyk 2003) or he actually wanted "stronger presidential power, but had little understanding of how to use his constitutional powers"

(Sydorchuk 2014:125). However, this assertion was not apparent in the early years of his presidency, as constitutional amendments in March 1992, a mere three months after Kravchuk's election, transformed the office of the presidency into a chief executive, giving Kravchuk "extensive executive powers" including the appointment of heads of local administrations (Wolczuk 2001:113). Kravchuk used these powers to try and create a rival center to the Cabinet of Ministers (a *Duma*, created in early 1992 and abolished by the end of the year due to an outcry from the Rada) as part of a reform of the executive branch, as well as pushing back against the opposition Rada with the threat of military force (similar to Yeltsin in Russia) in 1993 (Way 2005a). Similarly, Kravchuk had some success in 1992 in keeping Prime Minister Vitold Folkin under control, thus limiting pushback from the Rada (Sydorchuk 2014); he was not as effective in silencing protests from the media, and "demonstrated a readiness to use extra-legal and anti-democratic means to stay in power and to limit criticism," including trying "both to limit anti-governmental media and to crack down on opposition ... put[ting] pressure on newspapers and television stations that aired criticism of the administration" (Way 2005b:193). If the political institution of the presidency was designed to be weak prior to transition, throughout 1992 the first president sought to rectify this by aggrandizing powers to himself in a manner common across the post-Soviet space (Way 2005a).

Indeed, Kravchuk's problem in developing the political institution of the presidency may not have been that he wanted a limited presidency, but that he himself wanted broader powers to forge broad consensus in the system. Nearly every scholar (Åslund 2009, Protsyk 2004, Sydorchuk 2014, Wolczuk 2001) notes that Kravchuk was first and foremost concerned with compromise, a character trait that translated into his being overwhelmed by the magnitude of changes that were needed in the political and economic institutions of the country. In this, he vacillated between conciliatory nation-building and the firm hand of the communist autocrat who would close the Rada if it suited the country's needs (something that Kravchuk admitted in his memoirs and notes that was only stopped because the minister of the interior resisted). Thus, his "efforts directed at reforming the various tiers of government were largely seen as ineffective, further weakening his ability to negotiate with parliament over the figure of prime minister" (Protsyk 2004: 740). Moreover, Kravchuk not only weakened the presidency further, he also failed to build other institutions such as political parties, preferring to be seen as above the fray; this led him to also avoid dissolving the pretransition Rada in 1991, which left him with a Rada dominated by Communists who had been elected by the same populace that wanted to keep the USSR intact (Wilson 1997).

Surprisingly, at this point, Ukraine was still moving in the direction of Poland, as Kravchuk's choice for prime minister in 1992–1993, Leonid Kuchma, was able to undercut the president and waged a successful campaign to unseat him in 1994. Kuchma had been instrumental in weakening the presidency further during his time in the Rada, convincing members to transfer to his cabinet emergency powers for six months regarding the economy (Åslund 2009) and "demand[ing] the subordination of the National Bank, Anti-Monopoly Committee, and the State Property Committee to the Cabinet, along with the dual subordination of the local state administration (to the cabinet of ministers and the president)" (Wolczuk 2001:132). Indeed, Kuchma's conceptualization of the presidency (while he was prime minister) was similar to what it actually evolved into in Poland, a more ceremonial post that left policy making to the Rada (more along the lines of Germany than of France). Kravchuk fought back against these moves in 1993, even submitting a draft law that would make the cabinet directly subordinate to the president, but he did not have the ability in the fractured Rada to push such a measure through (Kubicek 2001). Political stalemate thus ruled the day, delaying economic reform and squandering precious time to build the political institutions necessary for a modern market economy.

Constitutional Change and Constraining the Executive

Once Kuchma was elected president, his ideas regarding the ceremonial nature of the presidency shifted dramatically. President Kuchma, ruling for eleven years (1994–2005) used the divided nature of parliament to strengthen his own rule and place in power prime ministers who followed the will of the president, rather than the will of the legislature (Protsyk 2003). In practice, the "dual executive" became a concentrated presidential system, an institutional shift of power in the exact opposite direction to the first four years of independent Ukraine, where the Rada had ruled supreme. Such a shift, given that it concerned the most fundamental of political institutions in the country, could only have been accomplished by changing the rules of the game; that is, by rewriting the constitution of Ukraine. In this sense, we can see another early divergence in political institutions between Ukraine and Poland.

As noted in earlier chapters, a constitution is a fundamental political institution, laying out the relationship of other institutions to each other and the distribution of political power in the country. However, the experience of Ukraine and Poland in creating (or following) such a document was patchy at best, given that the constitutional revolution occurred while both countries were partitioned amongst others. The Polish Constitution of 1791 was perhaps one of the most complete and inspiring political documents to be fashioned in the CEE region, but even it was never fully realized, as Poland disappeared from the map shortly thereafter. Similarly, the Constitution of Hetman Pylyp Orlyk in 1710, although not a true constitution in the modern sense of the word, was composed just after the hetmanate was crushed by Russia and thus had little chance of being implemented. Even the subsequent constitutions that both Poland and Ukraine labored under, the successive Soviet constitutions from 1936 and 1978, were of an entirely different stripe from those that came before (and would come after), outlining the obligations of the citizens to the government rather than the other way around.[4] Thus, in transitioning from a one-party to a pluralist democracy, it was imperative to change this "founding document" as quickly as possible, to reflect the changed circumstances and need for different rules of the game.

Of course, constitutional change also expressed deeper political factors and was reliant on other political institutions, a reality that surfaced in both countries; in fact, it is undeniable that, in the transition case, constitutional change was a lagging indicator for other political institutional changes. Indeed, constitutional changes in transition economies often came about after a period of experimentation with different political arrangements, with codification in law only coming about after various methods had been attempted. This was exactly the case in Poland, where experimentation with the semi-presidential system from 1989 to 1997 led to various tweaks and adjustments of the rules of the game. Starting, as all transition economies did, under the old Soviet Constitution (in Poland's case, under the

---

[4] U.S. President Ronald Reagan famously noted in his State of the Union speech to Congress in 1987 that "I've read the constitutions of a number of countries, including the Soviet Union's. Some are surprised to hear that they have a constitution, and it even supposedly grants a number of freedoms to its people. Many countries have written into their constitutions provisions for freedom of speech and freedom of assembly. Why is U.S. Constitution so exceptional? The difference is so small that it almost escapes you, but it's also so great it tells you the whole story in just three words: We the people. In those other constitutions, the Government tells the people of those countries what they're allowed to do. In our Constitution, we the people tell the government what it can do, and it can do only those things listed in that document and no others. Virtually every other revolution in history has just exchanged one set of rules for another set of rules. Our revolution is the first to say the people are the masters & the government is their servant."

amendments of 1982 to the 1952 Constitution), changing the fundamental document of governance meant a series of small-scale constitutional amendments in 1989 and 1990. Led by a Constitutional Commission comprising the interests present at the Roundtable Talks (including the Communists), these amendments ranged from the cosmetic (changing the name of the country, removing references to communism) to the substantial, including reinstating the bicameral legislature, freeing the courts from state prosecutor's offices, and, as noted, strengthening the power of the presidency and allowing for direct elections. A mini–constitutional crisis in 1991, precipitated by the tug of war over the powers of the presidency *vis-à-vis* the prime minister, led to the formation of a new Commission (without the Communists) to substantially replace the amended Soviet constitutions (Cole 1998); this resulted in the so-called Small Constitution of 1992, which balanced the power between the *Sejm* and the president and further defined legislative and executive relations, including the appointment of the prime minister and the responsibility for foreign affairs (Elster 1993). The Small Constitution, as noted above, also tightened up the proportional representation system in the *Sejm*, allowing for a less fragmented legislature (Benoit and Hayden 2004).

However, the Small Constitution was merely a placeholder for broader changes, given that it focused exclusively on the political institutional arrangements of the Polish government, and had no mention of the relationship of the citizen to the state (Cole 1998). President Wałęsa attempted to rectify this in November 1992 through the submission of a Charter of Rights and Freedoms, modeled on the Bill of Rights in the U.S. Constitution, but the dissolution of the *Sejm* led to the tabling of his motion and referral back to the Constitutional Commission (Elster 1993). The process to fashion a complete and new constitution took a further five years after the approval of the Small Constitution, but the 1997 Constitution that did emerge was a comprehensive document that addressed civil liberties, economic freedom, and the arrangement of political institutions in the new Poland (Cole 1998). As noted above, the 1997 Constitution circumscribed the powers of the presidency, especially in regard to the formation of cabinets, and both limits and clearly spells out (an omission from earlier drafts) the conditions under which the president can dissolve the *Sejm*.

Other portions of the 1997 Polish Constitution were not so clear-cut, representing a "bundle of compromises" that combined elements of liberalism, agrarianism, and Christian democracy in an attempt to smooth over divisions in Polish society; as Spiewak (1997:89) notes, the slow speed of constitutional reform may have missed an opportunity to reform political institutions as swiftly as the economic institutions were transformed by the Balcerowicz Plan. Leaving aside the fact that institutions transform at different paces and some have a maximum speed at which they *can* transform (Balcerowicz 1994a and Hartwell 2013a), the approach to constitutional change in Poland actually built a basis of legitimacy for the new constitution. As Garlicki (1997) notes, the constraining functions of the 1997 Constitution were informed by the ever-present fear of strong executives in Poland, including (in his conception) both Piłsudski and the fascist governments of the 1930s and the brash style of Wałęsa in the 1990s. I would argue that the 1997 Constitution, as shown in Chapter 2, was also informed by a much longer history of constraining the executive, encapsulated in noble liberty and the moves of the *szlachta* from 1386 to 1795. Building on this tradition, the constitution that did emerge eight years after transition began tapped into Poland's previous experience regarding the executive, providing a line of continuity with precommunist Poland.

Perhaps more important, this continuity was combined with the reality that there was little precedence for such a political changeover as Poland was undertaking, and thus experimentation in operationalizing the philosophy of the constrained executive was necessary. After all, there was neither hereditary nobility nor private armies as in the Commonwealth to keep the king in line (nor was there a king!), and precious little experience of modern democratic institutions. The alterations to political institutions made during the tumultuous period of 1989–1997, with some attributes being discarded as unworkable and others added, were thus necessary to reach an effective political institutional system in an atmosphere of uncertainty. Indeed, without such an iterative approach to the constitutional process, broken institutions might have been enshrined in law at an early stage and made very difficult to change. Similarly, the need to have the Communists' participation in early 1989 as part of the political transition process means it is not certain that more radical steps could have been taken in the constitutional modification process. Given this reality, and in tandem with the swift reform of economic institutions, Poland's 1997 Constitution represented a step forward for the legitimacy and the arrangement of the country's political institutions (Cole 1998).

While Ukraine had a similar iterative process for constitutional change as in Poland, "constitution drafting was one of the main political challenges that the political class of the newly independent state could not properly address for several years after the breakdown of the Soviet Union" (Protsyk 2005a:24). As noted earlier, Ukraine's founding document for its first five years was the 1978 Soviet Constitution of the Ukrainian SSR, with amendments made in 1990 to remove articles related to the economic system, state budgets, and state plans of economic development (Timmermans 1998). That same year, a Constitutional Committee was formed to revise the Soviet Constitution, advocating for an abolishment of the Soviet parliamentary approach (in a form of radicalism worthy of Spiewak's (1997) recommendations); however, a majority group of Communist parliamentarians (the so-called Group of 239) blocked such a radical plan and instead guided the move towards semi-presidentialism with amendments in 1991 to create a weak and neutered presidency and in 1992 to further limit the powers of the office to central administrative functions, as noted above (Boban 2007). As Wolczuk (2001:93) notes, this political deadlock by the Communists in the Rada led to an iterative process that never fully repudiated the old political institutions, merely tacking on new institutions to the old:

> As the constitutional debates revealed, the Soviet institutional framework "made sense" to the communist majority, including the national-communists. However, it was not "fit" to secure sovereignty, which was best served by the presidency, which, thus, was added to the system. So while the opposition principally repudiated the Soviet legacy on moral grounds, the Soviet ideological and institutional model— anchored in the cognitive framework of the communist elites—provided a baseline for defining the constitutional framework of the "sovereign" Ukraine. Other models played a subsidiary role. This resulted in the hybrid (presidential-soviet) institutional framework envisaged by the Concept of the new constitution and was followed by half-hearted and inconsistent institutional reform.

Indeed, an important point in the divergence of Poland and Ukraine must be noted again here, for it is crucial for understanding the subsequent path of political institution-building. In Poland, Communists were included in Roundtable Talks as a matter of legitimacy, but once the elections pushed the Communists out of power, constitutional reform and institution-building occurred on a very different path. This was confirmed quickly a mere two years later, as elections in 1991 ensured that the country was moving away from its communist past. In Ukraine, by contrast, the parliamentary elections in 1990 ensured that an obstructionist majority was in place not just at the time of transition but even beyond; combined with the longer terms afforded to Rada members than in the Polish *Sejm* and Kravchuk's unwillingness to dissolve the parliament, the Communists (the only party with a functioning party apparatus) were able to stymie even the political institutional experimentation that was occurring in Poland. This obstruction was exacerbated by what Kubicek (1994) called Ukraine's "delegative democracy," where elections were the only real interaction Ukrainians had with the political process. Lacking any interest in day-to-day politicking, average Ukrainians were not able to influence policy in the long pause between parliamentary or presidential elections, nor were they able to bring pressure to bear to push crucial reforms. This was even more problematic given that Ukraine exhibited what Way (2005c:131) has called "competitive authoritarianism, a civilian nondemocratic regime with regularly held elections that are competitive but extremely unfair."

With this reality frozen in place, constitutional debate from 1992 to 1995 took place in a poisoned atmosphere, giving rise to two separate yet simultaneous phenomena taking place. First, on the formal level, Ukraine began to experiment with various combinations of power under its existing constitutional arrangement, producing draft constitutions in 1992 and 1993 by the Constitutional Commission. These drafts, displaying a strongly pro-presidential stance and shifting power to the president, failed to gain any support in the Rada due to Kravchuk's lack of a power base in the parliament (Timmermans 1998). In fact, the only constitution that was prepared at this time was in Crimea, where a "Russian movement" produced a constitution calling itself independent; this constitution was rejected by the Rada in Kyiv and instead a compromise constitution was enacted in September 1992, noting Crimea's special status within Ukraine but firmly placing it as part of the country (Sasse 2014). At the same time as these formal mechanisms were failing, in a mirror of what was happening in the Ukrainian economy (and almost as extensive), politics became increasingly informal, as Kravchuk circumvented the institutional paralysis by calling on his Soviet skills to get things done. Such mechanisms were not unique to Kravchuk, as "both President Kravchuk and the Verkhovna Rada usually preferred informal methods of reaching their political aims, often leaving constitutional mechanisms aside. As a result, control over the executive switched from one institution to another, being conditioned not by existing constitutional rules, but by regular fluctuations in the constellation of power among the main actors" (Sydorchuk 2014:127).

With little incentive to work within formal institutions, parties outside of the Communists remained weak. This was partly attributable to the fact that the Communists utilized their organizational advantage to leverage support, keeping their party organization mostly intact even during the period when they were nominally illegal (from November 1991 to March 1993). Holdar (1995:112) noted that "the continued dominance of the former Communist Party *nomenklatura* in party politics in Ukraine" was also a key factor in the Party's reign, as personalities that the populace was familiar with combined with the fact that "no powerful popular movements or parties have been able or willing to seriously challenge this dominance." Beyond the Communist Party's strength, there was a conscious decision by the main actors in Ukrainian politics to not cultivate formal parties; both Kravchuk and Kuchma "seem to have felt that attaching their names to such organizations offered few immediate political benefits" (Way 2005b:196). With Kravchuk already operating in a highly informal manner, formal party organizations failed to find leadership and could provide no challenge to the Communists. Finally, the voting mechanism in use in Ukraine during transition also encouraged independents to stand for the Rada, unaffiliated with any party, as "the Soviet majoritarian electoral system [was] left largely intact . . . and what revisions [were] made have not been conducive to encouraging multi-party democracy" (Birch 1995:94). Not surprisingly, the Communist parties continued to support the majoritarian approach via the Electoral Law of 1993, seeing as it left their opposition fragmented.

It was not until 1994 and Kravchuk's calling for simultaneous parliamentary and presidential elections that the stalemate had any chance of being broken. Unfortunately, in regard to the parliamentary side, the desired outcome of a more focused Rada was not reached, as "unlike in Poland, the new legislative elections did not lead to a better structured parliament, as they were conducted on the basis of the majoritarian electoral system, which brought to the new parliament a large number of independent candidates" (Sydorchuk 2014:125). In fact, with the country's economy in tatters and little progress to show in the political arena, the election reflected an aversion to change, with the left-wing parties (the Communists and the Socialists) winning the largest plurality (the Communist Party only recently having been re-legalized). As Åslund (2009:64) noted, "the parliamentary elections . . . amounted to a protest vote against the disastrous economic management and overly nationalistic policies by the odd combination of the left and the business community." In this sense, lack of institutional change, in some sense obstructed by the parliament itself, worked wonders for the old guard, as it allowed them to claim that reform was a failure and the only way forward for an independent Ukraine was to return to the

Soviet institutional model, with gradual and limited economic reforms (Birch 1995).

On the presidential side, however, there was a clear shift, but also not for the better, as former prime minister Kuchma was able to rally support from both nationalists and communists to handily defeat his former co-executive in the second round of voting. Kuchma's election victory showed the first signs of Ukraine's reversion to its institutional difficulties of the past (and in particular the eighteenth century), as voting patterns in eastern Ukraine and Crimea were diametrically opposed to the cities of western Ukraine (Table 5.4). Kuzio (2005a:170) notes that it really was only the eastern, Russophone portion of Ukraine that was politically inactive between elections, as there was a vibrant civil society in western Ukraine;

Table 5.4 *Support of Presidential Candidates by Region, 1994*

Region	Kravchuk(%)	Kuchma(%)
West		
Lviv	93.8	3.9
Ternopil	94.8	3.8
Ivano-Frankovsk	94.5	3.9
overall average	83.8	13.9
Center		
Zhytomyr	55.6	41.6
Kyiv (oblast)	58.3	38.4
Kyiv (city)	59.7	35.6
Kirvohad	45.7	49.7
Cherkasy	50.8	45.7
overall average	47.3	49.2
South		
Crimea	8.9	89.7
Sevastopol	13.5	92.0
Odessa	29.2	66.8
Kherson	32.0	64.6
overall average	25.7	73.2
East		
Donetsk	18.5	79.0
Dnipropetrovsk	29.7	67.8
Luhansk	10.1	88.0
Kharkiv	25.9	71.0
Overall average	22.2	75.3

Source: Based on data from Wolczuk (2001).

however, the east's eager participation in elections (especially in 1994) tipped the balance in their favor, as "the 'nationalist' candidate, incumbent president Leonid Kravchuk, won only west of the Dnipro river in central Ukraine while his opponent, Leonid Kuchma, won most votes east of the Dnipro river." Kuchma openly portrayed himself as a champion of the south and the east, "capitaliz[ing] on the resentment over the influence of Western Ukrainian elites on Kyiv's policies and call[ing] for an end to the 'reign of Galician nationalism'" (Wolczuk 2001:139). For the most part, Kravchuk was perceived as anti-Russian, a key part of his strategy to ensure Ukrainian independence and sovereignty, a sharp contrast to Kuchma's explicit pro-Russian tilt, which found great support amongst Russian-speakers in the south and east, turning the election into a context between Russophones and Ukrainophones (Kuzio 2005b). Thus, as in other times in Ukraine's history, the western and eastern regions, and their wishes to pull in different directions, had a large and deleterious effect on political institution-building.

Kuchma's resounding victory gave him leeway to push through many of the presidential-strengthening measures that Kravchuk had wanted, albeit in service of Kuchma and his coterie. In 1995, President Kuchma signed a "Constitutional Agreement" with the Rada that moved the country closer to pure presidentialism, forcing compromise via intimidation and threatening to call a constitutional referendum and dissolve the Rada (Protsyk 2005a). The Agreement laid the basis for the 1996 Constitution (and actually set a deadline for constitutional reform), but the Constitution stopped short of all of the transfers to the presidency that the Agreement envisioned: in particular, the "President obtained the power to appoint a number of important officials ... according to his own consideration, namely, without any consultation with or approval by the other organs of power [but the constitution] practically deprived the president of the prerogative to dissolve the parliament, which was necessary to gain the parliamentary majority's support" (Matsuzato 2005:52). Åslund (2009:86) described the shift as follows: "on the whole, Ukraine moved from political disorganization to excessive presidential powers" with the new constitution leaving "many key questions to be determined by law."

Indeed, the removal of power to dismiss the parliament, while at the same time bringing the power to appoint the cabinet of ministers to the presidency, meant that much of the actual exercise of power was hazy and not constitutionally determined. As Protsyk (2003:1086) noted, "a compromise over the distribution of constitutional powers was achieved only after a prolonged period of political confrontation and deadlock.

The difficulty with which the principal political actors arrived at this compromise implied that the institutional status quo would be subjected to further tests." The person who did the bulk to this testing was Kuchma for, as Sydorchuk (2014:131) notes, "during his time in office, Kuchma did his best to expand his executive and legislative powers. In order to reach this aim, he used different strategies and, unlike Kravchuk, tried to squeeze as much as possible from his formal power. In his relations with prime ministers, he extensively used his constitutional powers to appoint loyal members of the cabinet, thus eroding the prime ministers' leadership, and quickly dismissed heads of cabinet if the latter challenged the president's dominance."

The time Ukraine spent under Kuchma is now seen as, quite possibly, the very point at which Ukraine's transition went off-track and the divergence with Poland widened. Over 1997–2004, Poland adjusted to the new rules of the game from its constitution and set about moving toward a more parliamentary system of government, readying its legal apparatus for EU Accession (see more on this in the next chapter). Indeed, the history of Polish political institutions from this point onward is one of maintenance and normal politics, with shifts in policy and politics (including the return of the left in the 2000s and their annihilation by the parties of the right by the end of the decade) but little change in fundamental institutions. As Rodrik (2000:13) rightly noted (and in a theme we will explore more below), "perhaps one reason that a 'big bang' worked for Poland is that this country had already defined its future: it wanted to be a 'normal' European society, with full membership in the European Union. Adopting European institutions wholesale was not only a means to an end; it was also the ultimate objective the country desired." Thus, once European political institutions were in place, there was no longer a need to tinker with them or rearrange the power structure, as the goal was achieved.

On the other hand, Ukraine was moving in the opposite direction towards a purely presidential system of concentrated power. Despite heroic leaps forward in stabilizing the country economically (also see below), the development of political institutions began a quick descent, subordinating the machinery of government to the power of one man (Whitmore 2005). Even before the ink was dry on the 1996 Constitution, Kuchma was attempting to extend his own powers beyond what the constitution allowed, "relying on the omni-powerful machine of executive government" to push for continued constitutional reforms that would secure "a constitutionally stronger presidency" (Protsyk 2003:1087). The most blatant (formal) attempt during his long presidency to secure these expanded powers came in April 2000, when Kuchma called for a Constitutional

Referendum to severely strip the Rada of its own responsibilities and bring Ukraine more in line with Russia's superpresidential powers (Wilson 2001), which Kuchma no doubt eyed with envy. In particular, Kuchma wanted the Ukrainian people to express a vote of no confidence in the Rada and support his adamant belief that constitutional amendments could be enabled via referenda; this point was noted by the Council of Europe to be unconstitutional, as "the 1996 Constitution clearly states that amendments require a two-thirds vote in parliament, to be followed by a ratification by referendum," a process that was by-passed in favor of moving directly to the referendum (Arel 2001:56). In addition to these broader themes, the referendum was to ask the Ukrainian people four specific initiatives:

1. To abolish parliamentary immunity to prosecution (making it easier to target parliamentarians for criminal wrongdoing, real or imagined);
2. To create a second chamber of parliament, akin to the United States Senate, that represented regional interests in Kyiv (Arel 2001);
3. To reduce the number of deputies in the Rada from 450 to 300; and
4. Give Kuchma the power he sought from 1994 to 1996 to dissolve parliament if no majority was created after one month, or if a budget was not passed within three months.

Despite "the referendum receiv[ing] suspiciously high, Soviet-like levels of endorsement of 89.7, 81.8, 89.06 and 84.78 percent respectively for all four questions" (Kuzio 2002), the Rada refused to budget and implement these proposals, showing that some checks and balances were still in place. Indeed, as Protsyk (2005:25) correctly stated, "the saga of constitutional reform in 2000 lasted for almost a year and revealed the worst aspects of Kuchma's increasingly authoritarian regime –intimidation, bribery, and falsification. It ended without any tangible results, due to the lack of legislative support for the presidential initiative." Moreover, evidence came to light in late 2000 that the vote tally had been falsified in both the referendum and in the presidential election in 1999 (which Kuchma won by almost a twenty-point margin over his communist rival Petro Symonenko), calling into doubt even the one political institution that appeared to work, however flawed, in Ukraine (Popson 2002).[5]

---

[5] The vote was tainted in more than one way. As Åslund (2009) relates, Kuchma wanted a virtual replay of Yelstin's 1996 win in Russia, meaning a plausible (but not actually threatening) Communist opponent who could be defeated in the second round. Oligarchs bankrolled Symonenko and made sure that he received enough support to make it through to the second round before Kuchma was able to single-handedly "rescue" Ukraine from

The lack of success from Kuchma in aggregating more power formally was counterbalanced by his acquisition of political power via informal means. The overall weakness of the state apparatus in Ukraine, with a bureaucracy barely reconstructed from the Soviet period (and often staffed by the same people), meant that Kuchma could not lord over the country by himself without assistance. As noted about the 1999 elections, the growing power of oligarchs, enriched by economic reform but still beholden to the Ukrainian state's ever-present hand in the economy, was growing steadily in the late 1990s (more on this below), and Kuchma relied on informal arrangements and support from this emerging oligarchic class. As Way (2005a:250) noted:

Because of the extraordinarily weak rule of law in these countries, such reform did not create a Western-style autonomous business class but instead created a group of very rich "oligarchs" who continued to depend on government connections. In Moldova under Petru Lucinschi, Russia under Yeltsin, and Ukraine under Kuchma, executives sought to use such dependence to buy support from individual oligarchs while playing off different groups against one another. Yet such a strategy, in the absence of strong pro-presidential (formal or informal) political organization, proved unreliable in the medium term.

This unreliability was shown in the appointment and subsequent dismissal of Prime Minister Viktor Yushchenko over 1999 to 2001. Yushchenko, a popular former chairman of the National Bank of Ukraine, was promoted by the oligarchy as a way to stave off Ukraine's looming financial disaster; born in Sumy in eastern Ukraine but firmly a believer in Ukrainian nationalism, his economic liberalism appeared to be an excellent way for Kuchma and the oligarchs to preserve their "investment" while not lessening the reins of power (Åslund 2009). However, it was only four months into his term before Yushchenko's reforms began to lessen the rents that the oligarchs had depended upon, and by April 2001, there was enough of a majority in the Rada to push him out the door (ibid.). Kuchma may himself have been threatened by Yushchenko's popularity and was more than happy to dismiss him (with the immediate economic threat already gone), but the oligarchy's ability to influence the process showed just how weak Kuchma had become as the wealth of the oligarchs increased (Sedelius and Berglund 2012).

---

the Communists. This apparent election, which in reality had been decided in advance, is an example of what I called Ukraine's institutional simulacra, the false reality put in place to deceive, which then takes on a life of its own (Hartwell 2015).

In addition to reliance on oligarchs, Kuchma also utilized the levers of state to control one of the most important institutions in a democracy, free and independent media. Way (2005c) notes that, despite the nominal privatization of the country's major media outlets in 1995, the government still retained informal control over the two major Ukrainian television stations, while Kuchma's son-in-law oversaw another three; in total, these five stations may have had as much as 75 percent of the market, making opposition to Kuchma highly unlikely to be broadcast. Indeed, one of the most notorious events to occur during Kuchma's presidency was the disappearance and murder of journalist Heorhii Gongadze, an act that opposition leaders claimed was ordered by Kuchma himself. A series of audio recordings from Kuchma's bodyguard Mykola Melnychenko were revealed by opposition deputy Oleksandr Moroz, and these recordings, authenticated in the following months, appeared to back, if not the direct responsibility of Kuchma, then a pattern of malfeasance within the executive branch that would lead to such an occurrence (Arel 2001). While Kuchma's popularity plummeted, the intimidation or murder of additional journalists continued, as did mass censorship of most media outlets, including direct instructions on what not to report (Dyczok 2006).

For the rest of Kuchma's presidency, political institutional development stagnated, in general resting on informal intimidation and deals rather than use of parliamentary procedure, with this state of affairs enlivened by brazen attempts to aggrandize more power. Indeed, Protsyk (2004) notes that the use of presidential decrees by Kuchma caught up to Russia during his first term, tapering off in the second term but still in excess of 200 per year, the majority concerned with shaping the political system to his advantage. Rather than rely on a Rada that came to mistrust him as allegiances shifted, Kuchma relied on the powers of his office and the oligarchs. The next substantive move he made to thoroughly reform the political institutional system in Ukraine, however, was a complete reversal of his entire political career to this point, coming as Kuchma saw his mandated two terms coming to an end. Sparked by a desire to anoint a successor to carry on his work, as well as a need to guarantee that the spoils would not end (as well as protect himself from any possible prosecution or worse), Kuchma suddenly reversed course and sought to weaken the power of the presidency in his wake. With his former prime minister Yushchenko polling as the likely next president, Kuchma pursued a two-track strategy: first, to weaken the office of the presidency via a series of constitutional amendments that shifted power back to the Rada. These amendments, Kuchma protested, would move Ukraine from a semi-presidential system based on a presidential-parliamentary axis to one that was parliamentary-presidential, closer to the Polish model than the Russian one (Christensen et al. 2005) and bringing Ukraine in line with European models. While this assertion was undeniably true, and the move was one that was long overdue in Ukraine, his ulterior motives were quite transparent and led to a defeat of his proposed revised constitution in April 2004 (Åslund 2009).

Once the first track of his strategy appeared to be a dead-end, Kuchma shifted to his second track, anointing a successor and ensuring that this person would win the 2004 presidential election even if "mass fraud and corruption" was necessary (Christensen et al. 2005:217). The man selected to succeed Kuchma was Viktor Yanukovych, an *apparatchik* from the Donetsk oblast and former street thug "who hardly conversed but gave orders," a man who was not above attaining the presidency by illicit means (Åslund 2009:160). Despite opinion polls showing clear preference for Yushchenko, as the elections at the end of the year neared, the fighting became much more dirty and dangerous; the most notorious attempt to steal the election was the attempted poisoning of Yushchenko by the State Security Service (SBU) with dioxin (Volodarsky 2013), a tragedy that left Yushchenko's youthful face disfigured, prematurely aged, and partially paralyzed. As Kuzio (2005a:30) noted, "the poisoning was subconsciously seen as a reprise of the assassination of four émigré nationalist leaders by the Soviet secret services between 1926 and 1959. For those who supported Yushchenko, the attempt proved that Ukraine's ruling elite had not changed since the Soviet era." Subsequent evidence has come to light that the Russian successor to the KGB, the FSB, was well aware of the attempt on Yushchenko's life, and may have even been implicated in a second, aborted attempt to remove Yushchenko via a bomb in a car owned by Russians and with Russian license plates (Kuzio 2005c). This was not the first, nor most certainly was it the last, time that Russia attempted to intervene in the development of independent Ukraine's political institutions (see below).

With Yushchenko surviving the poisoning, the state apparatus instead reverted to another time-honored tradition, and sought to steal the election, a blatant ploy that resulted in the Orange Revolution. The Orange Revolution has been amply covered elsewhere, and this is not the place to revisit the vast scholarship surrounding the event, nor is the actual campaign of the two main candidates our core concern. Instead, the main issues to be considered here are, first, the reality that the simulacrum of elections was insufficient in creating democracy in Ukraine without other supporting institutions – institutions that (mostly) appeared to have not evolved past their Soviet heritage. In particular, the brazen nature of the attempt to subvert the voting process was a direct challenge to all constraints that had been built up since the fall of communism and revealed the inefficacy of the Rada, the constitution, and even large portions of the executive branch. Secondly, the turmoil surrounding the 2004 elections left the Ukrainian nation even more divided along its recurring east-west fault line, leading to political issues that refuse to be resolved even today. And finally, the Orange Revolution also led to changes in the constitution, ironically in line with those championed by Kuchma in April 2004, which limited the power of the presidency.

In regard to the first point, the fact that the Kuchma and Yanukovych apparatus felt that they had a reasonable chance of stealing the election showed just how immature the political system of constraint was in Ukraine. Years of attempting to formalize presidential powers, only to be rebuffed, left Kuchma to rely on his informal bullying and intimidation tactics, bypassing the weak organs of the state or, even worse, subordinating them in service of political ends. Unfortunately for Yanukovych, the bureaucracy had so degenerated under Kuchma that the once-powerful vote-rigging machine of the Soviets could not even produce a convincing win for the chosen candidate. Instead, the weakness of Ukrainian political institutions shone through, as attempted vote fraud (including delays in announcing final tallies) in the first round could not produce anything more than a statistical dead heat, with Yushchenko receiving 39.9 percent of the vote to Yanukovych's 39.3 percent (Åslund 2009). The inelegance of the state's ability to defraud its people became more pronounced in the second round, where "widespread instances of voter fraud includ[ed] the illegal expulsion of opposition representatives from election commissions, multiple voting by busloads of people, absentee ballot abuse, and an extraordinary high number of mobile ballot box votes" (Tucker 2007:538). In fact, the two institutions that did appear to work in this instance were the Rada, which voted to invalidate the results of the second round of voting at the end of November 2004, and the Supreme Court, which annulled the run-off and accepted the claims of conspiracy (Karatnycky 2005).

As for our second point on the continuing partition of Ukraine, even with a tainted ballot, the results of the election showed that the east-west divide of Ukraine persisted and had in fact widened. In the first round,

Yanukovych won 71 percent of the vote in the east and Yushchenko won 78 percent of the vote in the west (Åslund 2009). This reality, which reflected each candidate's platform, as Yushchenko was unabashedly pro-NATO and pro-West, while Yanukovych was decidedly anti-NATO and pro-Russian (actually being advised by Russians during the campaign, with a strategy to play off fears in eastern Ukraine of western Ukraine's "domination"; see Kuzio (2011a)). Indeed, while Yushchenko was careful to focus his campaign on repudiating Ukraine's past, Yanukovych played directly into the Soviet strain of paranoia, disparaging Yushchenko (in echoes of today) as a "'Nazi,' a 'nationalist,' and an 'American puppet'" (Kuzio 2006a:52). This divide was only exacerbated after the fraudulent second round was invalidated by the Ukrainian Constitutional Court and Yushchenko was declared the victor in December 2004: as Osipian and Osipian (2006:504) note, "46.5 percent of respondents in the South and 54.1 percent of respondents in the East consider[ed] the Orange Revolution as a *coup d'état* either organized with Western support or prepared by political opposition." This perception is ironic, given that it was precisely in the Donbas where the bulk of the electoral fraud occurred. It is important here to quote Karatnycky (2005:36) in full on this point:

When the polling stations had first closed, the Central Election Commission (CEC) had reported that voter turnout in Ukraine's Russian-speaking eastern districts was consistent with the nationwide average of 78 to 80 percent. But four hours later, after a prolonged silence, the election commission radically increased the east's turnout figures. The eastern Donetsk region – Yanukovych's home base – went from a voter turnout of 78 percent to 96.2 percent overnight, with support for Yanukovych at around 97 percent. In neighboring Luhansk, turnout magically climbed from 80 percent at the time the polls closed to 89.5 percent the next morning, with Yanukovych winning 92 percent or more of the votes. Indeed, in several eastern districts, turnout was as much as 40 percent greater than during the first round of the presidential election three weeks before. This "miraculous" last-minute upsurge was responsible for approximately 1.2 million new votes – well over 90 percent of which went to the regime's favorite, giving him enough for a comfortable 800,000-vote margin of victory.

Finally, the aftermath of the Orange Revolution showed a form of compromise with the Yanukovych factions, as President-elect Yushchenko (as a last resort to avoid further social conflict, see D'Anieri (2005)), agreed to adopt the constitutional changes that Kuchma had been pushing for earlier in the year. As Protsyk (2005a:26) noted, the changes allowed the Rada to obtain "greater control over cabinet appointments and over the appointment and dismissal of the heads of other governmental agencies; it was given the exclusive right to dismiss the cabinet; its term in office was extended from four to five years; and the speaker of parliament was designated to assume the duties of the president should the incumbent leave office before the end of his term." In an odd turn of political posturing, the coalition that fought the Orange Revolution neutered itself once it came into power, handing over more power to the parliament, although there was a political calculation that the one year before the shift of powers came into effect would be enough for Yushchenko to build broad-based support (Karatnycky 2005).

This belief proved to be mistaken, and the hopes of the Orange Revolution, with its mobilization of the people and the unified front presented against the formal political institutions of the country, were not realized. One of the most intractable problems that Ukraine has encountered is the institutional rot at the heart of its bureaucracy. In reality, political institutional change is of course about much more than just the executive or the central government, especially in a transition country. However, this does not mean that the struggles at the top of the system did not filter through to the rest of the institution-building in these countries, as, indeed, it was to play a large role in determining the political apparatus. In Ukraine especially, the result of the continual uncertainty about the direction of political reform during the Kravchuk presidency and then the centralization of power under Kuchma created two effects that unfortunately led to the same result.

The first effect was related to the uncertainty and collapse of the state administrative system under Kravchuk, which created a void of power at the lower levels of bureaucracy and unclear lines of authority. There was no clarity of policy. This void forced administrators to find their own, more nefarious, ways to cope, as well as to find ways to justify their own hold on power under the Kravchuk administration. Much as there were informal political maneuvers in the Soviet bureaucracy in order to "get things done," and much as this tradition survived at the highest levels of the Ukrainian government during the time of constitutional uncertainty, it would be folly to think such practices did not occur at the lower levels of administration. This translated directly into corruption, as it did in the Soviet Union, with informal payments and bargaining necessary to undertake actions that were already mandated by law. One would think that the extreme centralization under Kuchma would remove these informal mechanisms; however, the shift of power to the executive branch created an extensive new set of incentives for rent-seeking, thereby institutionalizing corruption as a potent lever of government. This second effect also solidified the most

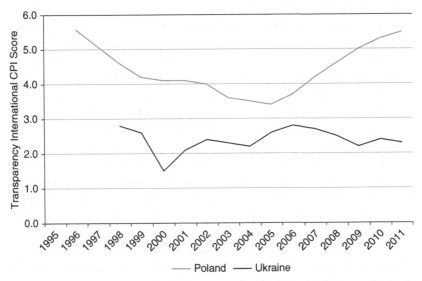

Figure 5.3 Transparency International Rating of Corruption in Ukraine and Poland
Source: Transparency International

crippling of Ukraine's institutional malaises (at least politically), the wide-spread corruption in Ukraine's public administration, making corruption the default option, rather than an aberration. In fact, Darden (2001) noted that the all-pervasiveness of corruption in Ukraine actually reinforced the move towards presidential control of the economy and helped President Kuchma consolidate power. Thus, what was born of uncertainty became a desired outcome of the ruling elite.

This swing towards corruption can be seen in the data, as Figure 5.3 shows the well-known Transparency International Corruption Perceptions Index (CPI) for both Ukraine and Poland (with higher scores indicating a perception of less corruption). As transition economies, perhaps Poland and Ukraine may have expected a greater incidence of corruption than in the West, with administrative levers still being developed, the rule of law gradually coming into existence, and the precise delineation of the state and its proper purview gradually crystallizing. In the case of Poland, it appeared that the transition away from the corrupt Soviet mind-set was much more successful, although not necessarily a complete triumph. Kojder (2004) accurately points out that an ill-defined legal framework for lobbying encourages some aspects of corruption, as did the trend towards discretionary decision making at the local and regional level. Adding to this list,

Gwiadza (2008) detailed the party patronage system over 2001 to 2006, noting that the appointment system of civil servants was a main area where parties attempted to reward their supporters, a problem inherent in many advanced democracies and in no way limited to Poland. High-level scandals in the 2000s, including at the Ministry of Defense and the Ministry of Communication, in tandem with the governing Democratic Left Alliance's (SLD) implication in the Rywin affair, created a perception that corruption was endemic to the postcommunist political system in Poland (McManus-Czubińska et al. 2004). Prodded by the EU and seeking to counter these perceptions, a powerful anticorruption commission was created under the Law and Justice (PiS) presidency from 2005–2007, a mechanism that was also seen as actually being used to pressure political opponents rather than root out malfeasance (Gadowska 2010).

However, while the perception of corruption was on the rise, as shown in Figure 5.3, there was paradoxically a decreasing *reality* of corruption, at least in the lower levels of the bureaucracy and in everyday life in Poland. This reality was shown clearly in the European Bank for Reconstruction and Development's (EBRD) "Life in Transition" survey in 2006, where the overwhelming number of respondents said that they pay no "irregular payments" to public institutions (EBRD 2006), a result that was repeated in 2011. Even in the midst of the SLD's political troubles, Poles were clear to note to pollsters that politicians, parliamentarians, activists, and even local leaders were the most corrupt of any institutions in Poland (Kubiak 2004). Thus, the continuing struggle against corruption within Poland comes against actors using the political system for their own gain *counter to* the formal institutional structure. That is, the system is not structured to enable corruption (apart from the aforementioned patronage), and the constant exposure and prosecution of corruption in Poland remains a powerful deterrent. In this vein, even though the PiS-led Anti-Corruption Bureau may have subtlely contributed to an uptick in corruption (that is, the use of political power to pursue one's opponents), the perception that corruption was being addressed as a concern at the highest levels lessened the perception of corruption in Poland (as shown in Figure 5.3). Finally, the most powerful check on corruption in Poland appears to be the ballot box, as Slomczynski and Shabad (2012) have shown that there is a clear correlation between the perception of the corruption of a party and the likelihood of a voter voting against that party. In this sense, while there may be an instinct to grab what one can while in power, the perception of this corruption is harshly punished by the voters at the subsequent election.

Despite these travails, corruption in Poland never reached the depths of Ukraine, as there was little perception that the ordinary policeman or little old woman working the counter at the social security service (ZUS) was expecting a bribe. This was the complete opposite from the state of play in Ukraine. By any metric, Ukraine has consistently been ranked one of the most corrupt countries in the world (and certainly the most corrupt country in Europe), seeing a brief improvement during the Orange Revolution but settling back into place under Yanukovych's administration. Corruption was so entrenched that, as Lovasz (2014) notes, not even the Swedish chain Ikea could enter Ukraine due to the immense bribes expected. Ironically, the driving force of corruption in Ukraine has been the police, an institution that has lost its sense of mission since independence and has gone from safeguarding the party apparatus to safeguarding itself and its patrons (Hartwell 2015). In fact, the Soviet institutional legacy is strong in the police for, as Shelley (1998) noted, policemen that had worked the Soviet apparatus were more likely to be active in illicit and illegal activities, due to the simple fact that they had more opportunities to do so. But the scourge of corruption did not just reside at the chief level, as bribery, illegal payments, and intimidation pervaded the police force in Ukraine (Beck and Chistyakova 2004), with one audit revealing nearly 30,000 suspicious cases that were either concealed or (unjustifiably) declined to prosecute from the police side (Beck 2005). And, of course, it was one manifestation of the myriad of police organizations, the SBU, which was complicit with the Russian attempt to assassinate or incapacitate a popular presidential candidate in 2004; as we will see, it was another version of the police, the *Berkut* (special police) which saw a growing "Putinization" during Yanukovych's rule after 2010 (Kuzio 2012a) and which, ultimately, fired on protestors at Maidan, killing one hundred. In fact, the actions of the *Berkut* were so notorious in the lead-up to Euromaidan, that Marat (2014) named them and the rest of Ukraine's police force "public enemy number one."

This breakdown of the state beneath the executive and emergence of the predatory bureaucracy was one of the few political institutions that did not, unfortunately, exhibit volatility during Ukraine's halting transformation. And with all strata of political institutions implicated in the crimes, there was little reason for the rest of society to accept that a rule of law existed; thus, corruption reached into all manner of institutions, including the labor market (Round et al. 2008) and higher education (Osipian 2009).

It was only a matter of time before this institutional rot brought the system down and forced Ukraine to start again.

Revolution Reborn: 2010 and Maidan

As Poland's political institutions had settled into the normal routine of political infighting and electioneering during this time, Ukraine's basic institutions were still in turmoil, especially given the disappointing record of the Orange Revolution in attaining long-lasting institutional change. Again, the failure of the Orange Revolution has been covered elsewhere, as the internecine bickering between Yushchenko and his on-again, off-again prime minister Yulia Tymoshenko produced paralysis and an inability to make good on the promises of the revolution. Constitutional change at precisely the wrong moment rendered the executive unable to push through the major changes needed in the economic sphere, and the global financial crisis of 2008 sent Ukraine into a deep slump. The inability of the leadership team in Ukraine to address these and other fundamental issues such as corruption, combined with a possibly unrealistic goal of EU accession, set the stage for the return of a Kuchma-era actor who knew exactly what he wished to do with the powers of the presidency. The election of Yanukovych in 2010 rang the death knell for the revolution, ushering in another institutional change or, rather, the return of a previous change, with the reversal of the 2004 Constitution in 2010.

The man at the center of the Orange Revolution and who attempted to steal the elections of 2004, Viktor Yanukovych, won a mostly fair fight in the presidential campaign of 2010 against Tymoshenko. As Kudelia (2014:21) notes, "Yanukovych spent his first year in office laying the groundwork for autocratic rule. In doing so, he helped to transform Ukraine's minimalist electoral democracy into an electoral authoritarian system." In fact, once Yanukovych's election was confirmed, a month later in the Rada his "Party of the Regions" (with support from the Communists) "suddenly changed the law on parliamentary procedures to allow individual deputies from other factions to join a governing coalition. As a result, the Party of Regions was able to create a new coalition with a slim majority" (Haran 2011:97). With this majority in the Rada, Yanukovych had a united front in both major power centers, meaning he could act with little constraints. One of the first acts, in addition to passing a law on local elections that cleverly barred Tymoshenko's party from competing (Valasek 2010), was to push for

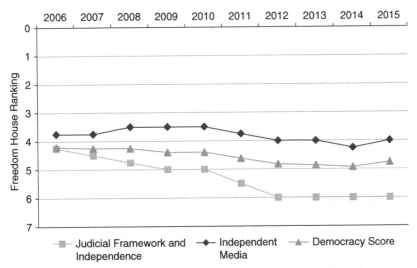

Figure 5.4 Deterioration of Political Freedom under Yanukovych
Source: Freedom House Nations in Transit Report, various years. Freedom House rankings are given on a scale of 1 to 7, with higher numbers representing poorer outcomes.

obtaining the rights that Kuchma had had during his presidency. In this he was aided and abetted by changes made to the judiciary, which was becoming increasingly a rubber stamp and subordinate to the executive branch or political winds (Trochev 2010). In fact, data from Freedom House, measuring the judicial independence of Ukraine, shows the increasing politicization of the judiciary, which unfortunately was underway already during the Orange Revolution (Figure 5.4). In fact, as Figure 5.4 shows, the decline of judicial independence in Ukraine occurred at a much more rapid pace than assaults on the media, while helping to bring down Ukraine's overall democracy score.

The drop in judicial independence allowed Yanukovych to push through the constitutional reforms he desired without having to bother with such niceties as parliamentary procedure or building of consensus. Instead, in September 2010 the Constitutional Court, widely seen as acting at the behest of the president, "declared that the 2004 constitutional reform had been adopted with procedural violations and thus ordered all state organs to bring their acts into conformity with the 1996 constitution" (Sydorchuk 2014:140), therefore transferring to Yanukovych all the authority that Kuchma had exercised. Indeed, combined with an additional move in July 2010, where a new law on the

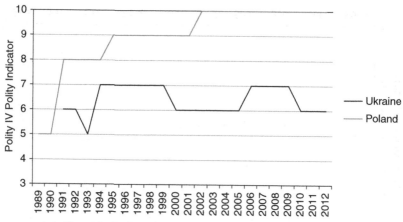

Figure 5.5 Polity IV "Polity" Score for Poland and Ukraine
Source: Polity IV Database.

judiciary gave the "Supreme Council of Justice (where the president, not the judges, de facto dominates) the right to appoint and dismiss judges from their positions" (Haran 2011:97), Yanukovych was able to wrest power back from the Rada, exercise dominion over the judiciary, and increase the powers of the presidency far beyond those that Kuchma formally held. He was not shy about use of this power, either, as by 2011 "more than thirty criminal investigations were running against members of the opposition" (Sedelius and Berglund 2012:40). In the span of a few months, Yanukovych had erased Ukraine's semi-presidential past and moved the country to a presidential system, moving the country closer to Russia's political system at the same time it was moving closer into Russia's policy orbit.

The divergence in presidential authority between Poland and Ukraine, enshrined in their constitutions in the mid-1990s and continually on the move in Ukraine, translated into divergences in democratic consolidation in each country. An illustration of the size of this divergence can be seen in Figure 5.5, which compares the democratic development of the two countries from 1989 to 2012 as shown in the much-utilized Polity IV "Polity" ranking. The Polity ranking places a country on a scale from –10 to 10, with –10 representing a full autocracy and 10 a full democracy, and is used to show the openness of the political process and how political actors are able to influence the system. As Figure 5.5 shows, Poland is currently ranked as a full democracy and has been since 2002 (reflecting changes in the administrative structure of the country and the formulae used for proportional representation; see Mansfeldová 2011). Perhaps more importantly, Poland made consistent strides towards a more open political system throughout its transition, with no reform reversals and a continual move towards more participation in the political system. While Ukraine appears to not be that far behind Poland (especially in 1994, as only one point separated the two countries), Ukraine has instead seen stagnation, ranking consistently between a 6 and a 7 as political progress stalled. For every leap forward, as in 1993 at the onset of transition, there has been backtracking, as in 1999, when Kuchma attempted to reform the constitution again, and 2009, as part of the electoral campaign; in short, there was no consistent move towards democracy and instead a history of political uncertainty and institutional volatility.

A key issue to be noted in looking at aggregate indicators such as the Polity IV index is that it measures the ability of actors to enter the system, for example, through elections. As noted above, in the case of Ukraine, the mere presence of elections was not necessarily a good indicator of the evolution of the overall political institutional system, especially if they occurred in an atmosphere of intimidation or led to regressive institutional policies. A better way to explore political institutional evolution would be examining the way in which the system constrains the executive, either institutionally or via the constitution. Previous work (Hartwell 2013a) has established that executive constraints are one of the most important indicators econometrically for positive economic outcomes in transition, and thus examining how the political system provides for such constraints gives an excellent sense of how political institutions evolved from the end of communism.

Figure 5.6 shows this evolution via the Polity IV subindicator on "executive constraints," which catalogues "the extent of institutionalized constraints on the decision-making powers of chief executives" on a scale from 1 to 7, with higher numbers meaning more constraints.[6] Tracking the changes noted above in the move away from presidentialism (in Poland) and the move towards centralization of power (Ukraine), Figure 5.6 shows that Poland had two major leaps to constrain the executive levers of government, reaching the maximum constraints in 1995 during the debates on the new constitution and retaining them thereafter. In fact, the interesting thing of note in these ratings is, once again, that it appears

---

[6] See the Polity IV user's manual, available on-line at http://www.systemicpeace.org/inscr/p4manualv2015.pdf.

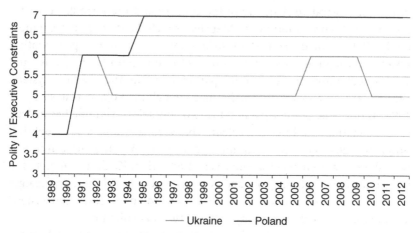

Figure 5.6 Executive Constraints, 1989–2012
Source: Polity IV Database.

that the constitution followed the re-arrangement of political institutions in the country rather than laying out the ground rules; that is, it was a codification of reality rather than a creator of that same reality. By 1995, the president in Poland had already been constrained; it was not until 1997 that this constraint and the institutional mechanisms surrounding it were enshrined in law. In many ways, this is also the exact opposite of what occurred with Poland's 1791 Constitution, generally taken as a beacon of liberalism. In this case, the constitution described the ideal that Poland was to strive for, an ideal never reached due to partition. By contrast, the 1997 Constitution showed that the optimal outcome (given compromises and other political constraints) had been attained and was thus able to be enshrined.

This same reality is shown in Figure 5.6 for Ukraine, albeit in the other direction. While Ukraine did not have a constitution until 1996, the diminution of executive constraints was already well underway by 1992 (under Kravchuk and Kuchma's prime ministerial term) and remained at this level until a glimmer of hope during the Orange Revolution in 2005 and the adoption of the 2004 Constitution. Once again, this ranking of executive constraints reflects the reality on the ground, and not necessarily constitutional vacillations, as the implementation of the Constitution of 1996 had no effect on the power structure that had already been established. Moreover, the unshackling of constraints on Yanukovych in 2010 could be attributable to the change in the constitution, the power he assumed over the judiciary, the change in parliamentary laws, or any other decree during this year in favor of increasing his authority. Regardless, the trend in Poland has been to greater constraints on the executive, while Ukraine has stalled its institutional evolution, due mainly to the personalities that were in charge.

Another interesting fact can be garnered from a glance at Figure 5.6, namely the correlation regarding executive constraints that comports with our reading of history in the previous chapter: periods where Ukraine was ruled by those from the eastern portions correspond with stronger executives, while the time of "Galician nationalism" (in Kuchma's phrase) produced much more constrained executives. Put another way, the areas that were under Russian rule the longest also produced executives that were much more likely to aggrandize power in their own hands and centralize the apparatus of the state. President Yanukovych, the man who grew up poor and wanted to break of his poverty, was born in Yenakiieve, a city in the Donetsk oblast that is only eighty-eight kilometers from the Russian border via the most direct route, while Leonid Kuchma is from Chernihiv oblast, a mere forty-five kilometers from Russia (to the north) and an area under Russian domination since the Russo-Polish war in 1654. While history may not be destiny, in the instance of Ukraine, it appears that the institutional influence of the Russian Empire played a major role in the development of modern-day Ukrainian institutions.

Kuchma and Yanukovych were not only successful at increasing their own power at the expense of the rest of the country, they were also successful at building nonstate institutions to enable this quest for power. In particular, the party apparatus that these men built, the Party of Regions, is notable for being a successful device for facilitating the election (through whatever means) of eastern politicians. The early years of Ukrainian independence saw the uneven development of political parties, mainly because of Kravchuk's decision to disaffiliate himself, the continued organizational strength of the Communist Party, and the single-member district plurality system that Ukraine had in place in 1994, which encouraged independents to stand for the Rada (Ishiyama and Kennedy 2001). There also was little popular clamor for political parties, as surveys conducted from 1996 to 1998 in Ukraine found that a full 26 percent of the population felt political parties were not necessary for the functioning of a democracy (Holmberg 2003).

This situation had begun to change by the 2000s, as Ukraine shifted towards a mixed electoral system in 1998 and 2002, allocating half of its seats to proportional representation while retaining the single-member

voting scheme (Ferrara et al. 2005). President Kuchma was also instrumental in helping parties to develop, although his only attempt at party-
building, the "For a United Ukraine" party, disintegrated after the 2002
Rada election (and he himself "feared concentrating too much power in
any single organization" (Way 2005b:196)). It was through more indirect
channels that he spurred on party-building as, sensing the usefulness of
organized support in the very institution he was trying to undercut, he
"established patronage relations with a loose group of pro-presidential
parties in parliament and created a relatively institutionalized system of
blackmail to keep allies in line" (Way 2005a:249). However, this loose
affiliation of interests and, in particular, Kuchma's constant playing off of
even his supporters against each other, was not sustainable as a political
strategy, as many of his allies and many oligarchs deserted him just before
the 2004 elections. In fact, as Way (2005b:198) highlights, "Kuchma's
active encouragement of multiple pro-presidential parties allowed political
leaders to gain the organizational and financial resources for future opposition activity." Thus, perhaps not in the manner he intended, Kuchma also
helped to foster the party system.

But where Kuchma may have only indirectly contributed to political
party building, without a doubt Viktor Yanukovych had a much more
direct hand in building the Party of Regions into the main success story for
political institutions in Ukraine. The party was founded in Donetsk in late
2000 by then-head of the tax administration (and future prime minister
under Yanukovych) Mykola Azarov (Way 2005c), and survived through
the defection of former Communist Party members and supporters from
2002 onward, promising a similar "programmatic support for social-
populist programs, thereby freezing the influence of Soviet political culture" (Kuzio 2011a:223). Yanukovych's ability to network with oligarchs,
especially Rinat Akhmetov, the second-richest man in the postcommunist
realm at that time (Karatnycky 2005), put him on their radar but also
garnered critical support for building the party's organization. Indeed,
while Yanukovych lost some luster after the Orange Revolution, Kudelia
(2014:20) notes that it was the Party of Regions that brought Yanukovych's
"political career back from the dead and lofted him to power by turning out
the vote in his largely Russian-speaking eastern base." With the law on local
elections of 2010 (noted above) shifting back to "a mixed proportional-
majoritarian system for *rayon* (district) and *oblast* (regional) *radas*
(councils)" (Haran 2011:101), combined with the fact that the party had
continued Kuchma's legacy by "unabashedly [buying] deputies" during the
presidency of Yushchenko (Åslund 2009:219), Yanukovych was able to

enjoy one-party rule in Ukraine under the Donbass clan after his election. Thus, while the ultimate outcomes of the success of the Party of Regions may not have been conducive to Ukraine's further development, there is no denying that it became a powerful institution in its own right (as Figure 5.7, detailing the 2012 Rada elections, shows).

Our analysis of the political institutional changes in Ukraine and Poland would not be complete without explaining the denouement of Ukraine's political institution-building from the present day, encapsulated in the "Revolution of Dignity" at Maidan in late 2013 and early 2014. While we have mostly focused on the formal political institutions of the country in transition, the informal gathering of civil society has played an important role in two political events in Ukraine's recent history, the protests accompanying the Orange Revolution and the large-scale revolution that occurred on Maidan. In both cases, the protests erupted as a counter to formal political institutions, and both protests occurred to counter one man specifically, Viktor Yanukovych (Onuch (2015) calls these protests "extra institutional political behavior"). Though the issue of the EU Association Agreement was a spark for this flame (see below), the protests rapidly metastasized into an all-encompassing dissatisfaction against the corruption and personal rule of the Yanukovych regime. Moreover, the decentralized nature of the protests and the active discouragement of professional politicians from joining the cause showed an apolitical approach to resolving political institutional issues (Diuk 2014). And where the Orange Revolution blocked a fraudulent event from becoming reality, the Maidan Revolution had an even bigger impact, in that it ousted a sitting authoritarian. Coming on the heels of the disappointment felt after the Orange Revolution, the events at Maidan were even more striking (Onuch 2015).

The eventual ouster of Yanukovych in February 2014 and his flight to Russia once again gave hope for the consolidation of a representative democracy in Ukraine. The issue of political institutional development has once again been brought to the fore, as, in an eerie echo of the Orange Revolution, the Rada reinstated the 2004 Constitution in February 2014, with 386 of 450 deputies voting in favor. New presidential elections followed in May 2014 after Yanukovych was formally removed by the Rada, bringing to power Petro Poroshenko, an oligarch from the extreme southwest of Ukraine, near the Moldovan and Romanian borders, who was inaugurated in June. One institutional issue that new President Poroshenko attempted to neutralize quickly, overcoming the legacy of past mistakes, was dissolving the old Yanukovych Rada in August 2014

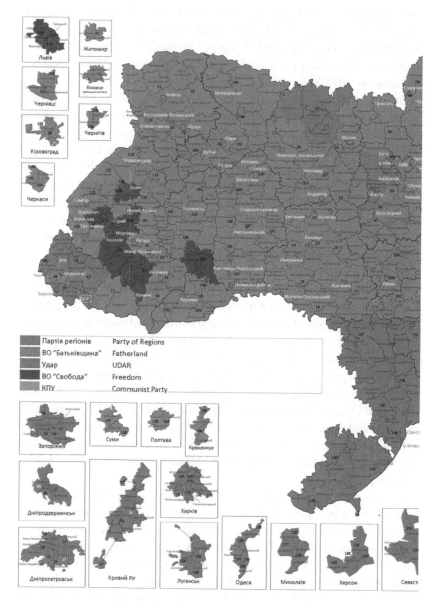

Figure 5.7 Results of the Rada Elections, 2012
Source: Central Election Commission of Ukraine website (www.cvk.gov.ua).
Licensed under the Creative Commons Attribution-Share
Alike 3.0 Unported license.

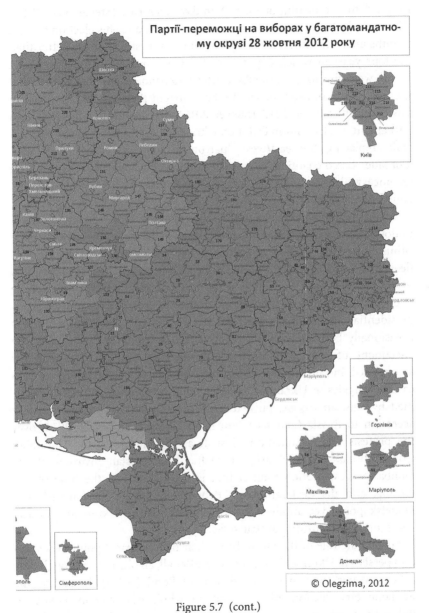

Figure 5.7 (cont.)

in a bid to "de-institutionalize" Yanukovych's rule (Stepanenko 2014). Although the move came two and a half months after his election and six months after Yanukovych's last plane out, it was still a far cry better than the four years in which deputies of the Communist Party of the Soviet Union were able to sit in the Rada after independence; more important, if the move had not been made, the then-current Rada would have been in power until October 2017 (Shevel 2015). Reconstituting the Rada via parliamentary elections in October, Ukraine saw yet again a major political shift, replacing the east/west "patronage machines" somewhat with a broader-based coalition "where the ruling Poroshenko Bloc depends on an uneasy alliance with the activist nationalists of the People's Front" (Burilkov 2015:1).

While the implementation of the changes of the 2004 Constitution have undoubtedly removed some of the power of the new presidency, Prime Minister Arseniy Yatsenyuk (who was elected prime minister after the fleeing of Yanukovych and again in the October parliamentary elections) has in reality been subordinate to the new president, who is still seen by many as the political force in Ukraine. More worryingly, as semi-presidential institutional arrangements are wont to do, Poroshenko has occasionally been at odds with Yatsenyuk, a reality that can affect the enactment of crucial economic reforms (see below). The need for a concerted and united effort has been highlighted by the echoes of even earlier struggles in Ukrainian independence, as Crimea, effectively occupied by Russian troops, pushed forward with a referendum regarding accession to Russia (and secession from Ukraine) in March 2014, over the protests and invalidation of such a referendum by the Ukrainian Constitutional Court. Shortly thereafter, the Russian invasion of the Donbas, a slow-motion tragedy that is still ongoing at the time of this writing, and the declaration of "People's Republics" in Luhansk and Donetsk posed yet another challenge to the entire Ukrainian political and economic institutional structure.

Finally, the role of the oligarchs as their own informal political institution persists in Ukraine (Poroshenko is, after all, an oligarch, although only a "second-tier" one in the assessment of Pond (2015)). In reality, the parliamentary elections of 2014 and the whole Euromaidan movement did not remove the oligarchs, as power was transferred from the clan of oligarchs formerly known as "the family" surrounding Yanukovych to other oligarchs such as Ihor Kolomoyskyi of Dnipropetrovsk and Oleh Bakhmatyuk. As Kononczuk (2015) notes, to a large extent, the Rada is still dependent upon the influence of oligarchs, and any concerted effort to break their power directly will create more tension. Moreover, Pond (2015:62) stresses that the oligarchs and Ukraine in general have gotten complacent, as "corruption as usual has resumed, albeit with fewer pots of state gold to plunder [and] the will to root out corruption and implement tough reform of Ukraine's post-Soviet kleptocracy is ebbing proportionately." Given these major challenges, it remains to be seen if Ukraine's new semi-presidential system can survive a time that calls for "extraordinary politics" or if Ukraine is merely repeating the same institutional mistakes of the Orange Revolution and once again has missed its political opportunity.

In conclusion, and on the whole, the political institutions of Ukraine today appear to be in much worse shape than those of Poland, as Poland has used the past twenty-five years to develop and converge with Western European institutions, constrain the executive, and overcome its communist past. Ukraine, on the other hand, is starting over again but with an additional two and a half decades' worth of political infighting and scars, a difficult challenge to surmount even for a country not in the midst of an invasion. Whether or not Ukraine can reverse the course it was on from 2010 to 2014 and become more like Poland, or the broader EU, politically is still an open question, contingent on the outcome of the Russian invasion and other exogenous factors such as the EU, NATO, and Russia's own internal weaknesses. However, one area that could determine Ukraine's future political path, a factor that is very much under Ukraine's control, is if it successfully completes the economic transition. Indeed, the evolution of political institutions in both Poland and Ukraine since 1989 has already had a demonstrable effect on the true goal of transition, the development of economic institutions, which then feed back into political change. It is to this point that we now turn, to understand how economic institutions reached their current point in Poland and Ukraine.

ECONOMIC INSTITUTIONS AND BUILDING THE MARKET

Economic institutional development in the transition process followed a similar but slightly different process from the development of political institutions, in terms of the mechanisms utilized and the policies put in place, perhaps due to the heterogeneous nature of economic institutions versus political ones. In all cases, however, the development of economic institutions in transition proceeded along two tracks: first, a positive one, in the sense that enabling legislation and policies were put in place by governments to consciously create specific institutions (so-called Type II policies), while the second track was negative, in that the removal of barriers (such as eliminating the prohibition of private property) was to allow for the spontaneous creation of supporting institutions. In fact, these two separate-yet-intertwined approaches also targeted different facets of institutional development, as the positive track targeted formal institutions (changing the machinery of the central government) while the negative track created the space for informal institutions to emerge. In many ways, both of these tracks were necessary for each particular institution, not only to be created but to put down roots, be accepted in society, and flourish in the new institutional reality of post-communism.

While perhaps the most visible manifestation of Poland and Ukraine's differences through the transition process has been in the process of political institution-building, a similar powerful dynamic has occurred with the evolution of the economic institutions needed to create a market economy. Indeed, in many ways, the development of economic institutions in Poland and Ukraine has diverged far more than political institutions, a reality that can be seen across the institutional spectrum, from property rights to the financial system, over the first two decades of transition (Table 5.5). On every transition indicator measured by the European Bank for Reconstruction and Development (EBRD), Poland has an absolute advantage in cumulative outcomes over Ukraine. Moreover, the change in institutions from the year before transition began also shows that Poland has gone faster and further in its reforms than Ukraine; in fact, where the cumulative change in Table 5.5 has been bigger for Ukraine, as in small-scale privatization and price liberalization, this is only because Poland had already begun some tentative liberalization before formal transition began. Thus, Poland may not have gone as far because it already had begun the journey. Even in financial sector institutions, where Poland has always been a laggard behind other transition countries (such as the Czech Republic or Estonia), there is a clear difference between the journey traveled by the two countries. And while these differences may appear small given the scaling of the indicators (from 1 to 4.33), it is important to note that, if they were normalized on a scale of 0 to 100, Poland's difference in large-scale privatization and bank reform would be 22 percent better than Ukraine, while governance and enterprise restructuring would see an absolute difference of 30 percent more improvement in Poland than Ukraine.

The purpose of this section, as in 3 and 4, will thus be to examine how these divergences occurred in the most important economic institutions, and how these institutions were influenced by the political institutions we

Table 5.5 *EBRD Transition Indicators, 2012 and Change over Transition*

	Poland		Ukraine	
	2012	**Change**	**2012**	**Change**
Large-scale privatization	3.67	2.67	3.00	2.00
Small-scale privatization	4.33	2.33	4.00	3.00
Governance and enterprise restructuring	3.67	2.67	2.33	1.33
Price liberalization	4.33	2.00	4.00	3.00
Trade & Forex system	4.33	3.33	4.00	3.00
Competition Policy	3.67	2.67	2.33	1.33
Bank Reform and Interest Rate Liberalization	3.67	2.67	3.00	2.00

Source: EBRD. "Change" refers to the change in the indicator from the year before transition began (Poland = 1989, Ukraine = 1991) through 2012. Each indicator is measured on a scale from 1 to 4.33.

just detailed in the previous section. As we will see, the presence of political volatility or (more accurately) stagnation makes the building of economic institutions incredibly difficult, a reality that can cripple an economy and render the idea of "transition" meaningless.

Property Rights

As noted in Chapter 3, the fundamental basis of a market economy and the key economic institution needed to move from communism to capitalism was that of property rights, with the right to acquire, manage, transfer, and dispose of assets forming the building block upon which all other economic institutions rest. Explicitly outlawed in the Soviet system, with its prohibition enshrined in the socialist constitutions of the twentieth century, the actual tolerance of private property (as shown in Chapters 3 and 4) was different between Poland and Ukraine, with Poland having much more of its economy devoted to private commerce. However, these initial conditions were by no means a guarantee of the successful development of property rights or the failure to develop these rights. As an example of this reality, one only needs to consider that Estonia, Bulgaria, and Slovenia all had approximately the same amount of private commerce to GDP (10 percent, according to the EBRD; see Hartwell (2013a)) as Ukraine at the outset of transition, higher than estimates for the Czech Republic or Hungary; in fact, the private sector share of employment at the beginning of transition was 25.8 percent in Ukraine versus a paltry 5.9 percent in

Bulgaria and 7 percent in Czechoslovakia. Thus, even more so than the political institutional development we just surveyed, the evolution of economic institutions depended both on the policies pursued at the outset of transition and the longer, historical experience with private property.

Despite this caveat, the experience of property rights–building over transition has resulted in a much steadier, and higher, level of property rights for Poland than for Ukraine throughout the entire transition period. This reality can be seen through a quantification of property rights, using two separate economic proxies: one that examines the inputs to property rights and the other which examines the outputs (or, more accurately, outcomes). The first metric focuses on property rights as a function of the legislation related to ownership of property and its threat of expropriation from the government, on the assumption that a formal legal framework that protects rights from expropriation will actually translate through to secure property rights. Using a subjective approach, that is, through expert evaluation of the legislative frameworks of each country, the International Country Risk Guide (ICRG) tabulates an "investor protection" score on a scale from 0 to 12 over three subcomponents (contract viability, payment delays, and repatriation), with higher scores indicating more secure property rights. Using this metric, we can see the monthly changes in the legislative framework surrounding property rights, confirming that Poland has tended to this economic institution much better than Ukraine in linear time (Figure 5.8). Poland has consistently scored between a 10 and 12 (the highest ranking) since 2000, apart from some substantial backsliding during the Eurozone crisis and in regard to pension "reform" (noted above) that has only just begun to recover. On the other hand, Ukraine has stalled at an 8, achieved during the Orange Revolution (in line with a theory advanced by Markus (2015a), as we will see below) and not since repeated, with reductions in contract viability driving the decline of the overall score since 2008. As of the last date in this dataset, June 2014, Ukraine was rated a 6, a level that Poland last saw in June 1995, after sixty-five months of transition.

Perhaps even more interesting, Poland has gone at a much more rapid pace than Ukraine, even when you consider their pace at similar points in transition. Figure 5.9 shows the same investor protection metric harmonized to "transition time": in this case, I have set month zero as the month that the country started its transition, with every month thereafter numbered. We are somewhat handicapped here by the fact that Ukraine's ICRG data does not start until April 1998, or approximately seventy-five months

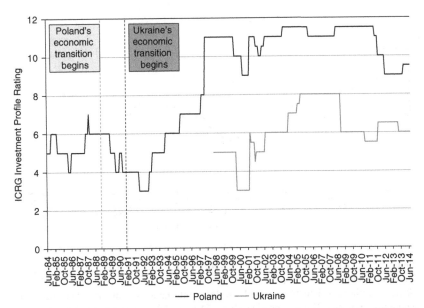

Figure 5.8 Property Rights in Poland and Ukraine: Investor Protection, Monthly, 1984
to 2014
Source: ICRG Database. Data only available for Ukraine from April 1998 onward.

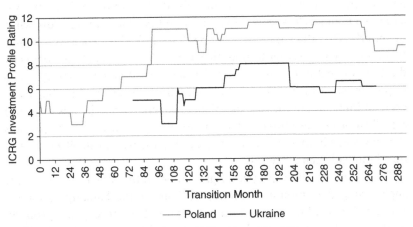

Figure 5.9 Investor Protection Harmonized in Transition Time
Source: Author's calculations based on the ICRG Database. Economic transition is
coded as beginning in January 1990 for Poland and January 1992 for Ukraine. Data
caveat noted above still applies.

Figure 5.10 Property Rights in Poland and Ukraine (Contract-Intensive Money), in Transition Time
Source: Author's calculations based on IMF International Financial Statistics data. Economic transition time is coded as above. Data for Ukraine begins in December 1992 on an annual basis and monthly from January 1996 onward.

after transition began (Ukraine's transition is dated as starting in January 1992), but even with this gap we can still discern that Ukraine has moved much more slowly than Poland. By month 75, Ukraine was a full two points below where Poland was at that stage of transition, while by month 200, rather than converging, the gap had widened to 5 points. It is also very interesting to note that Figure 5.10 shows almost perfectly the time of "extraordinary politics," where broad-based property rights improvements can be pushed through, before regular politics begins to exert an influence; in the case of Poland, property rights (by this measure) actually took between three and four years to begin a steady ascent, perhaps showing some immediate retrenchment after the pain of stabilization and transition had been achieved.

The second proxy for property rights comes at the issue from a different angle, using the amount of money held inside the banking sector (as a proportion of all money), on the assumption that more secure property rights mean that people are happier to keep their money in banks. This indicator, known as "contract-intensive money," has risen to prominence as a handy indicator of *realized* property rights, introduced by Clague et al. (1996) and used *inter alia* by Dollar and Kraay (2003), Knack et al. (2003), Fortin (2010), Compton and Giedeman (2011), and Hartwell (2013a).

Rather than focusing on the legislative framework, which could suffer from poor implementation and administrative capacity (especially in a transition context, where other supporting institutions are in flux), contract-intensive money tracks human behavior in response to institutional changes and thus gives us an objective indicator for property rights.

Figure 5.10, calculating this indicator based on IMF data and harmonized to transition time, shows that Poland's performance has also been consistently better than Ukraine, with far fewer fluctuations than the legislative inputs would suggest. In fact, despite twenty-three years of independence, Ukraine's realized property rights in late 2015 are still below the level that Poland's were in January 1990, when Poland's transition began. The largest drops in property rights in Ukraine occurred during the first five years, the time at which it may have been easiest to institute broad-based rights, with increases only happening in a period that corresponded with the onset of the Orange Revolution (again confirming Markus 2015a); however, the ascension of Viktor Yanukovych and the response to global financial crisis put the country back to where it was before the Revolution by July 2009 (month 211 of transition). While property rights actually climbed somewhat during Yanukovych's tenure, likely due to the perception of stability he engendered and the absence of political fighting, the emergence of Euromaidan and the uncertainty and volatility it created about what was to come next brought property rights back to a level last seen in 2011 (after most of Yanukovych's egregious power grabs were completed). But simply put, and holding everything else equal, Ukrainians have not trusted the government or the economic system enough to keep their money in Ukrainian banks, preferring to keep it under the mattress or (for those with the means), outside of the country.

The policies behind these broader numbers for each country are even more interesting for the story of institutional development, as they clearly show how the divergence in property rights came to be. In regard to Poland, as was shown in Chapter 3, there was a longer history of property rights, even throughout the Soviet period; as Polischuk (1997:86) notes in echoing our earlier chapters, "in Poland, agriculture and many services remained private throughout the period of communist control, and the economic system remained relatively less centralized than those of its neighbors." However, our earlier examination also showed that (as in other countries), so long as there have been property rights, there has been a history of political influence on the development of those rights (especially during the period of *szlachta* democracy in the 1600s and 1700s). The challenge for Poland's transition would be to secure the benefits of property rights but avoid the difficulties seen during the years of the Commonwealth and in the Second Republic, where unconstrained executives at various levels had the ability to threaten these rights.

It appeared that Poland solved this conundrum at an early stage by removing the government as much as possible from commerce. The basis for property rights in postcommunist Poland began as part and parcel of the economic transition even before the political transition began, with the passage of the Economic Activity Act in December 1988 putting private sector firms on "firmer legal footing," guaranteeing equal legal treatment of all forms of ownership, setting the basis for privatizing state assets, and, most important, enshrining the concept that "everything not explicitly prohibited is permitted" (Slay 2014:78). The success of this approach towards property rights could be seen in the outcomes it created, with 294,000 (formal) private-sector firms established in 1989 alone, a time that saw a momentous political changeover as well (Mroz 1991).

Building on this early success, and as with economic stabilization, the Polish government in transition worked swiftly to create the basis for a market economy: as Sachs (1992:7) said, "the crucial steps of establishing free trade, market pricing according to the forces of supply and demand, key aspects of commercial law and private property rights, and the end of state orders and central planning, were introduced in Poland in the space of a few weeks at the end of 1989 and the beginning of 1990." Following on the legal framework of the Economic Activity Act, the means used to accomplish this achievement was the implementation of the policy principles of the Balcerowicz Plan at the beginning of 1990. Although, as noted above, the Plan did not have an explicit point dealing with property rights (concerned as it was with macroeconomic stabilization), its last point, pledging to refrain from state intervention, was a crucial stepping stone to the emergence of private commerce by creating limitations to the state. With the state pulling back from ownership and the principles of free entry into the marketplace codified in legislation and administration, Poland saw a total of one million new private firms created from 1990 to 1993 (Gomułka and Jasinski 1994). Perhaps most heartening, comprehensive firm-level data from Roberts and Thompson (2003) shows that, even accounting for the disruptive nature of transition, Poland saw firm entry and exit typical of mature market economies during this period. In fact, the only inhibitor to firm entry during the first decade of transition, as it is elsewhere in the world, came about from state-owned firms competing in the same marketplace, but with the resources and guarantees of the state behind them.

This fact brings us to the next stage of Poland's development of property rights, and that is the sometimes thorny issue of privatization. Unfortunately, the idea of privatization has been all-too-frequently treated as a necessary and sufficient step for the creation of property rights in transition, an association that has besmirched the overall concept of property rights when privatization went wrong. In reality, privatization is neither necessary nor sufficient for the creation and protection of property rights, whether in transition or elsewhere, as privatization represents a way to transfer existing assets to private hands. As Shleifer (1994:109) put it, "transferring asset control rights from bureaucrats to firm insiders and shareholders does not, in itself, establish full property rights. The problem of protecting private control rights and enforcing contracts is not solved simply by transferring these rights from politicians: the solution is only delayed." An additional point to consider is that, as typified in the collective farms (*kolkhozes*) of Soviet agriculture, state assets under communism were created as part of a hugely inefficient economic process that drained capital from elsewhere in the economy. Large state-run industrial combines and mega-factories, created as part of a five-year plan to industrialize rapidly, do not represent market-determined outcomes but rather political whims. Thus, the idea of transferring these assets "back" to the private sector is somewhat of a misnomer, because no private sector in the world would have produced them.[7] The key facet of property rights creation in regard to enterprises is thus not merely removing some means of production from the hands of the state, but lifting the prohibitions on the creation of new capital and allowing for the emergence of new businesses and growth of the private sector.

In contrast to the quick legal and societal moves towards private property, the transfer of assets via privatization proceeded much more slowly in Poland. With the Economic Activity Act and follow-up legislation opening up the Polish market to firm entry (and, importantly, exit), Poland took a much more lackadaisical approach to large-scale privatization than other countries of Central and Eastern Europe, such as the Czech Republic or Russia. Poland had already begun liberalizing the state-owned firms as

---

[7] In an ideal market, the state would not have any "assets," but the fact that the state may attempt to run a business as a going concern is immaterial for property rights (unless the state-run enterprise is not subjected to competition, in which case it can become problematic).

early as 1981 under the Law of Economics of State-Owned Enterprises. The Law, coming as it did during a relative thaw in Poland's socialist state (and immediately preceding martial law), gave firms considerable autonomy, allowing them to "select sources of supply, make assortment decisions, market their product, and even decide how to invest retained profits," as well as sharing power between managers and workers' councils (Wellisz and Iwanek 1993:346). Additional small-scale waves of economic liberalization in 1983 replaced industrial production targets with a system of contracts and orders, while by 1986 state enterprises were allowed to enter into joint ventures with foreign investors; this was followed by additional portions of the Economic Activity Act in 1988 that allowed for "spontaneous privatization," permitting state-owned enterprises to constitute themselves as joint-stock companies (Rondinelli and Yurkiewicz 1996).

However, once the political transition began, formal mass privatization slowed as vested interests, mainly in the labor force and aided and abetted by politicians, arrayed against the transfer of state assets. In July 1990, the new Solidarity government passed the State Enterprises Privatization Act, allowing for ownership change via either transformation of an enterprise into a business corporation or privatization through liquidation (Mroz 1991). Initially focusing on selling the best assets via share sales (but with the Treasury holding a minority stake, in order to prevent ownership concentration), the early public offerings were accompanied by the creation of the Warsaw Stock Exchange to facilitate the transfer of shares in these companies. But even with this addition of a new financial institution to expedite the ownership transfer, the sales of firms proceeded at a disappointing pace (Rondinelli and Yurkiewicz 1996). The coalition government of Prime Minister Jan Olszewski came to power at the end of 1991, promising to halt the economic pain, and while this had little effect on economic stabilization efforts (Balcerowicz 1994c), it did lead to a halt in privatization. By 1992, a total of 2,478 state-owned firms had begun the privatization process, but only 668 had graduated and been struck from the register of state-owned businesses (Slay 2014), a far cry from the Mazowiecki government's plan to have more than half of state assets transferred to private owners by 1993 (Mroz 1991).

These political developments also put a damper on plans for mass privatization along the lines of other transition economies, plans that had been in the developmental stage since June 1991. Little progress was made until 1993, when the Law on the National Investment Funds and their

Privatization was adopted, using Investment Funds rather than direct distribution of shares as the vehicle for privatization. Estrin et al. (2000:2) noted that the Polish choice of investment funds was done deliberately "in order to eliminate or at least alleviate both the potential loss of corporate governance and other disadvantages such as reduced access to capital and management," but even here there were major delays in setting up these funds, with the first beginning to operate only in late 1995. Ironically, after all the wrangling in creating the funds, there was immediate public backlash that was swept away; as Lewandowski (1997) notes, despite a February 1996 referendum against extending the mass privatization program, by November 1996, 95 percent of the adult population of Poland had received certificates that were then transformed into shares of the investment funds by July 1997 (Estrin et al. 2000). Through this approach, a further 512 large and medium-sized enterprises were eventually privatized (ibid.).

As Woodruff (2004:91) has noted, the slow pace of privatization of the largest firms led to difficulties in restructuring firms due to entrenched interests at the firm level. In particular, state-owned enterprises retained workers' councils, an institutional innovation popular in Poland under communism, that acted as co-managers, with the power to "hire and fire the manager, determine managers' compensation, and clear all important strategic and even operating decisions" (Pinto et al. 1993:215). This concentration of power of course made "workers' councils ... very strong within enterprises, because previously it seemed that only market socialism reform was feasible [but] now the workers' councils tend to be factors of resistance in the transition to markets" (Åslund 1994:54). Woodruff (2004:91) put it more explicitly, noting that "Polish reformers focused more on the macroeconomy, and found themselves in a long political stalemate over privatization to restore microeconomic control. Privatization proceeded slowly, effectively on a case-by-case basis, with stakeholders granted a *de facto* veto over how privatization occurred." Attempts were made from very early on in the privatization process to undercut this reality, with the Law of Economics of State-Owned Enterprises amended in 1990 to allow state-owned firms the right to suppress the workers' councils on the way to privatization; however, such an approach only worked with the political will to take on labor, a difficult undertaking for a government headed by a president from the country's first and largest labor union (Rondinelli and Yurkiewicz 1996). The reality in many firms was as shown in Estrin et al. (1995:144), with "instances of workers vetoing restructuring or privatization plans, scaring off potential foreign investors, and reducing managerial pay markedly."

Given this state of events, insider privatization became the only successful means of privatization during the first three years of Poland's transition, with 617 of the 668 firms privatized by the end of 1992 (over 92 percent) done via liquidation (effectively a management buy-out; see Slay 2014). However, as the transition process continued in Poland, the need for privatizing these state-owned "dinosaurs" became less and less important from an institutional standpoint, as the continual entry of new firms had rendered many of the largest firms obsolete; in the words of Rondinelli and Yurkiewicz (1996:157), "the greatest contributions to Poland's economic transformation may well have been those reforms that simply allowed entrepreneurs to take over state-controlled small businesses or to create their own small- and medium scale enterprises without undue restrictions and controls."[8] If the state-owned enterprises had remained as the only game in town, with protected monopolies in their area of interest and state-directed prohibition against competition, it was highly likely that the SOEs would have remained both valuable for their owners and problematic for society. As it stood, these enterprises were eroded from below by new entrants into the market, making them less desirable as "assets" in a market economy.

Moreover, the competition created by firm entry also eventually forced changes in state-owned firms, mainly through the incentives competition provided for workers to restructure. Once the reality had hit that transformation of the firm was necessary, it became, like other decisions made on the workers' councils, one of consensus that then took on a life of its own. As Woodruff (2004:83) notes, the institutional process that could have blocked change became a motivator for change, once it was thrust upon them by exogenous forces:

Privatization and the transition to corporate form generally could occur only after potential shareholders and stakeholders had reached a bargained agreement. The allocation of property rights was part and parcel of a larger accommodation about the future of the firm – a positive-sum game, and one in which contesting property rights would risk the gains from cooperation. Thus, the form of privatization in Poland ensured that those in a position to challenge shareholders' property rights were embedded in relationships that encouraged them not to do so.

---

[8] Of course, state-owned enterprises continued to have a real economic cost, especially to the fiscal stance of Poland, but institutionally they were immaterial to blocking the development of property rights.

This reality contributed one additional bright spot to the privatization process in Poland, and that was the fact that ownership never became very concentrated with privileged insiders during the changeover from communism to capitalism. Indeed, when compared with Ukraine, Russia, or Kazakhstan, Poland is exceptional in its lack of an oligarchic class (in fact, it is very tough to even find the term "oligarch" applied to Poles during the transition period, mainly because they do not exist). The erosion of the value of state-owned firms removed the ability of the state to extract rents from the privatization process, while the relative dispersion of management in the existing firms (typified in workers' councils) also meant an inability for insiders to coalesce in favor of action; in short, workers could block privatization, but they could not formulate plans to use their insider abilities to obtain assets on the cheap. The lack of valuable state assets in Poland, coupled with management dispersion, thus prevented the emergence of a class of businessmen, rich from insider privatizations and leveraging these assets into political power. And while it is undeniable that Poland had its own difficulties in insider information and "sweetheart deals" made during the privatization period, it never reached the scale of Ukraine or Russia (Wedel 2003), with major corporate scandals during the transition concerned with disclosure rather than massive fraud or violence (Woodruff 2004).[9] Without a political class jealously guarding its own property rights investment (much as the *szlachta* did under the Commonwealth, and, as we will see below, the oligarchs of Ukraine still do today), Poland post-1989 was able to avoid localized property rights in favor of broader access to the market and better contract enforcement. The avoidance of an oligarchy in Poland has been perhaps the greatest guarantor of a property rights–based system.

The construction of formal property rights in Poland in the early years of transition faced an additional key obstacle (as in other Central European countries, but curiously absent in Ukraine and points east), that of restitution, or restoring properties seized during the Communist era to their original owners. Restitution was and is a very problematic issue in regard to the institution of property rights, as it raises questions about not only the process involved in the granting of rights, but also how these rights can be passed on, the duration of said rights, the question of formal versus

---

[9] Commenting on the corporate governance differences between Poland and Russia, Woodruff (2004) noted that the firm caught up in a disclosure scandal would have been the paragon of good behavior in Russia, where issues such as blocking shareholders from attending meetings were more the order of the day.

informal property rights, and how to resolve a situation when property rights are in conflict. It is this last point that was to prove the thorniest issue in transition, as no matter how these conflicts were resolved, it would imply a hierarchy of property rights: either the property rights of owners from the 1920s were paramount, in which case I had to give up the flat my family had been living in since the 1950s, or the property rights codified post-communism took precedence, meaning the land I just purchased during privatization was mine and did not belong to the original family that held title to it in 1928 (no matter what documents they produced). Similarly, there were often cases in which formal property rights were challenged by informal rights (especially in agricultural land), a situation that Verdery (1994) suggested meant land ownership in transition is flexible "to such a degree that there is an almost unlimited elasticity between the formal cadastre and informal land tenure" (Harvey 2006:296). Thus, restitution faced its own conundrum, as any large-scale restitution process required such highly detailed local knowledge and tradition as to make a large-scale generalization of the process impracticable.

In one sense, restitution issues in Poland were not as problematic as in the Soviet Union or even in Southern Europe, due to the relatively small amount of collectivization of agriculture that occurred during Soviet times. With private ownership (formally and informally) already well established (Brada 1996), there was less of a need to carefully delineate property rights in rural areas, nor was there an urgency to return what had been stolen. On the other hand, Poland had some traits that made restitution even more difficult than in the Soviet Union, due mainly to the dual occupations of the Nazis and the Soviets. The Second World War, having been fought for a large time on Polish soil, meant that land had changed hands several times during the 1930s and 1940s, leading to a multiplicity of claims to the same piece of land or immovable asset. Moreover, Poland itself was moved in its entirety to the west at the end of the war, meaning that any question of restitution could re-open the issue of how to handle the expropriation from Germans in the lands of western Poland (which until recently had been eastern Germany). Finally, the communist expropriations, done on the basis of decree in 1946, were often undertaken on the determination of the authorities that a certain building or piece of land had been "abandoned"; reversing such a determination a half-century after the fact would be very difficult to prove indeed.

The peculiarities of Poland's situation, especially regarding the long history of claims that would potentially need to be adjudicated, meant that finding an appropriate mechanism that was also politically acceptable was incredibly problematic, as "literally dozens of bills" introduced in the *Sejm* in the early 1990s went down to defeat (Youngblood 1995:646). The only area where there was rapid agreement on a broad-based restitution occurred in conjunction with religious institutions, as Poland swiftly enacted a Law on the Relation of the State to the Catholic Church in 1989 to allow for restitution of church property seized by the communists (amendments to the law allowed for select other churches to also claim restitution). According to the U.S. State Department (2007), by the end of 2006, the Catholic Church had filed 3,063 claims for restitution (of which 2,959 had been concluded), broken down as:

- 1,420 claims settled by agreement between the church and the party in possession of the property (in practice, this tended to be either the central government or local government);
- 932 properties returned to the church through decision of the commission on property restitution, which rules on disputed claims; and
- 632 claims rejected by the same commission in favor of the current owner of the property.

Similarly, the Lutheran Church filed a much smaller number of claims for 1,200 properties, of which 842 cases were heard, 228 were solved via negotiations, and 136 of which were restored by order of the commission. Given its much smaller reach in the country, only 486 claims were filed on behalf of the Orthodox Church, of which 215 were closed in full or in part by the end of 2006.

In regard to expanding this restitution across other strata of society, however, Poland struggled to find a solution, as "issues of who should benefit and what levels of financial compensation could and should be afforded . . . proved extremely intractable" (Blacksell and Born 2002:182). Indeed, a bill on restitution that actually made it through the Rada in 2001 was vetoed by President Kwaśniewski on the grounds that it would have had too dire an impact on the fiscal situation of the government, and by the time Poland had acceded to the European Union in 2004, it and Lithuania were the only countries to not have in place comprehensive restitution legislation (Polanska 2014). Instead, as noted above as a possible reality given the nature of the issue, the restitution debate was solved piecemeal and on a case-by-case basis. In addition to the law on churches, decrees were issued in the early years of transition returning land to unions and charity organizations if expropriated after the war (Glock et al. 2007) or rescinding expropriations if the former owner had fought for Poland at the end of World War II and was subsequently punished by the communists for doing so (Skapska and Kadylo, 2000). But by 2012, the government of Poland was reduced to stating publicly "that claimants of property that ha[d] been taken over during socialism should use the Polish legal system to pursue their claims, at the same time making it clear that the ambition to pass a restitution or compensation law is inexistent" (Polanska 2014:415). This approach has continued to the present day, with the normal legal system used as the mechanism to settle property rights disputes rather than passing supra-legal measures as elsewhere in transition.

While there is little quantification of the contribution of restitution to the development of property rights in Poland, there is a case to be made that the uncertainty regarding restitution may have dampened some forms of investment; as Harvey (2006:300) notes, "as long as Poland lacks a restitution law to regulate the return of private property seized or expropriated before, during, or after the Second World War, the ambiguity arising over a potential return of land causes anxiety and tempers many people's desire for improvement of the land and buildings they live in or use." However, this uncertainty may have been mitigated somewhat by the establishment of an effective judicial system in Poland capable of adjudicating competing claims. We have treated the judiciary in Ukraine above, as well as the judiciary under communism, as a political institution, a fact that is undoubtedly correct given both the context of its functioning during this time (under the control of the executive), as well as its stated purpose (to apply and interpret legislation). Given the broadness of the legislative body of work that a country's judiciary must interpret and the panoply of cases that may appear before it, it is thus natural to think of the judiciary as a crucial political institution, concerned with the distribution of power in a polity. But in reality, the enforcement of contracts, a crucial component of property rights, is done at a formal level only via the court system, meaning that the judiciary also plays an important role as an economic institution. Accepting this reality, the establishment of an effective judiciary, independent of political pressure and acting as a counterbalance to other arms of government, was another success story of Poland's institutional transition, a luxury that countries to the east such as Ukraine did not have – nor, indeed, even appeared to desire (as seen in the previous section). And as a key supporting institution for the administration of property rights, the presence of an independent judicial system has been crucial for Poland's broader economic institutional development.

As with its other economic institutions, legal reforms, "including the creation of administrative and constitutional courts and the reduction of the power of the *Prokuratura*, preceded the democratic transition" (Magalhães 1999:50). As early as 1985, just emerging from martial law, the creation of a *Trybunał Konstytucyjny* (Constitutional Tribunal) allowed the idea of "judicial review" to enter the vernacular, even if such a review process was still highly controlled by the Communist Party (Brzezinski 1993). The Tribunal was empowered to "adjudicate certain claims separate from the legislative function of government" (Koslosky 2009:209), starting a tentative process that would separate the role of the judiciary from the whims of the executive branch. Indeed, once the democratic transition began, "after 1989, [the Tribunal] interpreted newly created constitutional provisions to compel the executive and legislative branches to abide by certain unwritten rules of justice, fairness, and equity" (Brzezinski and Garlicki 1995:13). At the same time, in order to insulate the internal mechanisms of the judiciary (such as promotions and disciplinary powers) from outside influence, the High Judicial Council was formed in 1989 and codified in the Constitution in 1997; representing the judiciary before the other branches of government, the Council gave the judicial system equal footing before the executive and the *Sejm* (Bobek 2008).

These excellent institutional steps towards creating an independent judiciary were met with some resistance in the early years of transition, as there were attempts by both the executive and the *Sejm* to purge the judiciary of communist appointees who may have served the state too slavishly. One of the first moves pushed by the first postcommunist government was to remove the high bureaucracy of the judiciary, especially in the Ministry of Justice, a step that was seen as desirable for ensuring noncommunist and democratic oversight of the entire system (Piana 2009). However, the growing power of the nascent Judicial Council, coupled with political infighting in the *Sejm* and public concerns about political pressure being used to settle scores rather than improve the judiciary, led to the defeat of more egregious purge attempts in 1990 and 1991, including those that targeted the judiciary itself rather than its executive oversight mechanisms (Walicki 1997).[10] By 1992, in a parallel of the privatization process, the government instead turned its energies to fashioning the institutional constraints on the judiciary and facilitating entry of new judges, thus reforming the institutional framework in which

---

[10] This was an eerie premonition of what was to happen during the first PiS government; see below.

the judiciary operated and eroding surviving communist-era judges with new entrants (Magalhães 1999).

These early moves in institutional reform have made Poland's judicial system after communism fiercely independent of the government, a reality codified in the 1997 Constitution removing the *Sejm*'s ability to override the decisions of the Constitutional Tribunal (Schwartz 1998). Since that time, the evidence of independence has been impressive: amongst transition economies (with the notable exception of Estonia), Poland has the highest score on the World Economic Forum's indicator of "judicial independence" (4.1 out of 7).[11] By another metric, that of *de jure* judicial independence shown in Feld and Voigt (2003), Poland's score (0.693) is almost exactly at the EU-15 average (0.695), and is higher than the scores for the Netherlands, France, or Sweden. Finally, Bodnar and Bojarski (2012) note that the high number of acquittals and a growing number of times that the executive branch has lost a court case strongly indicates the nonpolitical nature of Poland's judiciary. This reality has persisted even during the period of 2005 to 2007, when the Law and Justice Party (*Prawo i Sprawiedliwość* or *PiS* for short) exerted strong political pressure on the judiciary and attempted to re-institute some of the veto powers of the executive, including packing the Constitutional Court with its supporters (Bodnar and Bojarski 2012).

The process of creating the judiciary was not entirely smooth, and issues still remain in Poland regarding judicial institutions, the relation to other political institutions, and their own internal functioning. As late as 2003, on the eve of EU accession, the EU was lamenting "poor court organization, burdensome procedures, [and] long delays" in the judiciary, and the issue of long delays or undue length of court cases has persisted to this day (Bodnar and Bojarski 2012; Open Society Institute 2002:427). Interesting work from Kantorowicz and Garoupa (2014) also shows that the voting records of judges in modern-day Poland are swayed by the judges' own political preferences and the identity of the petitioner, suggesting that more effective institutional mechanisms might be needed to constrain the personalities of judges. This does not mean an increase in executive oversight however, which, while scaled back considerably from the dreams of PiS, still has inappropriate influence on the composition and funding of

---

[11] Estonia, as is true on so many levels, far outclasses any of its postcommunist brethren with a ranking of 19 on judicial independence, far ahead of Poland's rank of 54. Estonia also has much higher levels of property rights as measured by contract-intensive money, consistently scoring around 0.96 to 0.98.

training of judges, especially through control of the purse strings (Piana 2009). Finally, Bodnar and Bojarski (2012) note that elections to the Supreme Administrative Court and appointments to the Constitutional Court are not as transparent as they should be, also allowing susceptibility to political influence (as is happening in Poland at the time of writing of this chapter in December 2015).

Despite these issues, Poland's judiciary has helped to keep property rights in transition on a fairly even keel since 1989 (as shown in Figure 5.10). Crucially, the independence of the judiciary and its reference to constitutional law meant that the judiciary was able to "curb legislative and bureaucratic arbitrariness in the post-Communist era," a necessary check on the executive branch and a key way to create the rule of law in Poland (Koslosky 2009:219). When combined with a sound legal structure for supporting property rights and a legacy of restitution that is smaller than elsewhere in the postcommunist world, it is apparent that Poland has had impressive success in a short time in building the crucial foundation for a market economy. As in all countries, however, the price of property rights is eternal vigilance, and even with (or perhaps because of) accession to the EU in 2004, recent moves in Poland have called into question the desire of the political class to avoid infringing these rights. In particular, moves to renationalize the pension system in 2013 and 2014 in order to stabilize the government's finances, done by an ostensibly center-right government, was seen as a blatant move against property rights over financial instruments. As Naczyk and Domonkos (2015:8) note, "by late 2013, the ... government reversed pension privatization even further by making private pension accounts voluntary, by transferring all state bonds owned by second pillar funds into the social security institution, and by banning the funds from investing in any state securities." It may be rather early to detect effects of the "reform" on the evolution of property rights in Poland, but empirical work done by Hagemejer et al. (2015:833) comparing the pension changes to a scenario of no change finds that "the shortsightedness of the governments imposes welfare costs." Whether a fiscally strapped government in future is more likely to infringe upon property rights is an open question, one that will determine Poland's growth path for the next twenty-five years.

In contrast to Poland's on-again, off-again love affair with property rights, Ukraine and its leaders maintained a much more consistent disdain for this building block of a market economy. Indeed, the history of property rights in postcommunist Ukraine tracks the development of its political institutions, as it does in many countries around the world; after all, executive constraints are a large determinant of the actual administration of property rights, with constrained executives lacking the power to expropriate or plunder, and countries that have higher constraints on the executive generally (but not always) show a correlation with better property rights in both legal framework and in execution. Given this reality, it is little wonder that the expansion of presidential powers under Kuchma and Yanukovych corresponded with a decline in broad-based property rights, even if it showed an increase in the property "rights" of a few well-connected oligarchs.

The legalization of private property in Ukraine faced resistance from the outset, perhaps a foreseeable outcome in a country where the Communist Party still retained power in the legislature and was in charge of the constitutional drafting process. While various land legislation was drafted even before Ukraine was independent, including the law "On Land Reform" in 1990, new legislation clarifying types of land ownership and laying out a framework for privatizing land (both from 1992) did not depart dramatically from the Soviet model (merely adding private property as just another type of property). This hesitance to embrace private property continued in a much more formal process, the drafting of the Constitution, which saw "the drafters intend[ing] to give the Constitution some rigidity ... by additions restricting forms of property and human rights" (Ludwikowski 1996:90). This was typified in one of the first drafts of the constitution from 1992, where it was noted that "the exercise of the right of ownership must not contradict the interests of society as a whole or of individual natural persons and legal entities," a formulation that opened the door for all manner of transgressions in the name of "society" (Ellis 1994). Additional drafts in 1993 not only retained these provisions but also envisioned additional administrative mechanisms consistent with limited property rights; as Ludwikowski (1993:183) noted, the retention of special economic courts, "which in a socialist state handled disputes between state enterprises, state farms and cooperatives and operated more like courts of arbitration than regular courts, confirms that the drafters still anticipate that the state will administer a vast area of public property."

With the finish line in sight, and after five years of uncertainty regarding the extent of property rights protection in Ukraine, debate surrounding the 1996 version of the constitution found increased resistance from the Communists and other parties of the left. In particular, the Communists wanted the constitution to both reflect all types of property (including the Russian "collective" property, as noted in Chapter 4) as well as "moralizing" on the responsibilities and limits of private property in Ukraine (eventually encapsulated in Article 13 of the final 1996 document; see Wolczuk 2001). But, as Wolczuk (2001) notes, even with the compromises and watering down the "inviolable" right to property, resistance continued until the actual vote, until the right of private property was enshrined in Article 41 with additional limitations. Indeed, although the Article begins with the assertion that "everyone shall have the right to own, use, or dispose of his property and the results of his intellectual or creative activities," the rest of the Article and elsewhere in the constitution contains caveats, exclusions, and, most important, the threat of revocation. As Futey (1996:30) correctly notes,

many of the protections seemingly guaranteed in these articles have been curtailed with "claw-back" provisions in which nullifying qualifications are introduced. Article 157, for example, states as a general proposition that the Constitution may not be changed to restrict rights and freedoms. In addition, Article 22 provides that constitutional rights and freedoms may not be abolished. Article 41 initially echoes this idea by stating that the right of private property is inviolable. The article goes on, however, to note that the right of private property is "granted on the basis of, and within limits determined by, law." Thus, a simple majority of Parliament can enact a statute that fundamentally alters constitutionally guaranteed property rights. Article 41, indeed, would allow the Verkhovna Rada to circumvent the two-thirds majority required for amending the Constitution, as well as the Article 157 prohibition on limiting rights.

This constriction of the right to private property (even in the constitution) became the hallmark of Ukraine's transition, rather than the begrudging nod made to property rights at the beginning of Article 41. This can be seen most strongly in the treatment of rural and agricultural land, where there may have been a theoretical right to property, but legislative obstacles and constraints made the exercise of this right nearly impossible. During the interim period between the collapse of the Soviet Union and the 1996 Constitution, Ukraine undertook a mass privatization of rural land in stages, starting at the end of 1991 and carrying through to 1995. While the constitutional debates raged, interim legislation stepped in to fill the gap, with the Law On the Forms of Land Ownership from 1992 establishing three types of land ownership, either "public, collective (common) [or] private." This classification, a non-negotiable belief of the Communists and leftists in the Rada (who rejected constitutional drafts for insufficient protection of communal property; see Wolczuk (2001)) and an intermediary step of land ownership for the former *kolkhozes* (collective agricultural enterprises), thus resurrected the tsarist-era conception of "communal property rights" and preserved it across the country (instead of leaving it in Left-Bank Ukraine, where it was most prevalent during the nineteenth century). In practical terms this meant that "collective and state farmland is distributed equally per capita among collective farm members or state farm employees in the form of paper shares or certificates," a move that "does not imply physical allocation of land plots corresponding to the shares ... [as] despite the allocation of land shares to individual members, the land remains in joint cultivation pending further restructuring decisions by those 'share owners'" (Swinnen 1999:639). Moreover, this move allowed for the preservation of the communist-era institution of the collective farm, an institution that had been created in Ukraine on the basis of starvation and mass execution; rather than forcing such institutions to disband and then (as it should be in a market system) reform themselves in any way they saw fit voluntarily, the legal system froze the institution in place.

This protection of communist institutions was further enabled by additional restrictions, the most egregious being a six-year moratorium on land sales enacted in 1992 (Krasnozhon 2011a). In December 1992, then–prime minister Kuchma attempted to overturn via a government resolution On Privatization of Land Plots, focused on small private plots but keeping the moratorium on selling farm land. Regardless of the political cover Kuchma tried to engender via this caveat, the Communist-dominated Rada overturned the decision in January 1993, meaning that former *kolkhozes* remained in "collective" hands (Csáki and Lerman 1997), in addition to the many state-owned farms (*sovkhozes*) that persisted through the first decade of transition (Table 5.6). The combined effect of this myriad of restrictions was a significant divergence in land plot-size, with the creation of thousands of small private land plots with an average size of 22.6 hectares in 1992 (Bogovin 2006), and the retention of both collective agricultural enterprises/*kolkhozes* and *sovkhozes* with an average size of over 3,000 hectares (World Bank 1994a).[12] In fact, after two years of land reform, by 1994, there were still eighty-seven collective farms and eighty-two state-owned farms that had over 9,500 hectares of land apiece, with the vast majority of collective farms (1,350) and state-owned farms (246) holding between 1,500 to 2,000 hectares apiece (Bouzaher et al. 1994). By early 1996, even with a "free" transfer of land (that is, from the state to

---

[12] This trend has continued unabated through to the present day, although it has improved since 1999. For example, in the Zhitomir oblast, as of 2009, 80% of the farms were up to 100 hectares in size, with the plurality being from 0–50 hectares (Strohm et al. 2010).

Table 5.6 *Number of Agricultural Producers in Ukraine by Legal Type, 1991–1998*

Legal form	1991	1994	1996	1998
Sovkhoz	2,438	2,000	1,520	1,120
Kolkhoz	8,354	2,680	450	231
Collective agricultural enterprises	–	7,385	7,344	6,676
Farmer unions	–	178	1,159	903
Agricultural co-operatives	–	320	486	486
Joint-stock companies	–	184	295	627
Limited-liability companies	–	–	–	665
Private farm enterprises	80	27,700	34,800	35,500

Source: Lissitsa and Odening (2005).

the collective or individuals without any requirement of payment), the land reserve that had been allocated for transfer had only been halfway completed, with 40 percent of this approximately 3.1 million hectares transferred going to collective farms (Lerman 1999).

Eppinger (2015:879) notes that there may have been a constituency for private property rights and land reform in Ukraine, a silent support that was expressed in the presidential election of 1999: "land share distribution clearly correlated with voter preference. In areas where the certificates had been issued, incumbent president Leonid Kuchma was the clear winner; in areas where directors managed to withhold them, Communist Party candidate Petro Symonenko, who opposed privatization, won overwhelmingly." With the agricultural sector in Ukraine collapsing as a result of macroeconomic instability and uncertain property rights, President-elect Kuchma attempted to reinvigorate land reform (and, by extension, private property rights) with the issuance of a Presidential Decree in December 1999. As Allina-Pisano (2004:561) noted, "the decree acknowledged malfeasance in past attempts at reform, including administrative delays in the documentation of land shares and registration of private farms," a welcome admission that still missed the heart of the problem, the restriction of transfer or sale of land. In order to remedy the perceived issues of the land reform, the Decree fashioned a process that "essentially forced the conversion of the share certificates into physical land plots, which could then be withdrawn by a simplified procedure and used to establish a new individual farm or to enlarge an existing household plot" (Lerman and Sedik 2007:6). These physical plots, approximately 4.2 hectares in size, on average, created approximately 7 million new land owners, while also finally starting the restructuring of the collectives into more market-oriented forms, with the distribution of land settling at approximately half private/half public from 2000 onward (ibid.).

Despite the bureaucratic zeal with which the Decree was carried out throughout 2000, the process of land reform only increased the power of the former *kolkhoz* managers (Allina-Pisano 2004), due to the fact that the supporting laws regarding disposal of property were not in place. It was to take an additional year until the Rada passed a new Land Code, reinforcing the idea of private ownership in land, setting out the constitutional arrangement of land regulations, and delineating types of land (as well as putting in place an additional five-year implementation period, beginning in 2002; see Eppinger (2015)). However, the Land Code, as a piece of legislation under the restrictive constitution, also continued to erect barriers to the exercise of property rights. In the first instance, individuals who wished to own more than 100 hectares of land in general needed to obtain permission from the State Land Agency, a situation that created opportunities for rent-seeking and artificially constricted the acquisition of private land. But perhaps more insidiously, and with much more staying power, the Land Code was accompanied by a moratorium on the sale of agricultural land, creating an additional burden for the 74 percent of land classified as "private" in Ukraine.

The land sale moratorium was structured to prohibit a farmer trading or selling any land that was deemed "arable" under the Code, with the sale and purchase or transfer of privately owned land explicitly prohibited if used for commercial agricultural production or individual farming activity. These restrictions on land sales curtailed the ability of Ukrainian farmers to exercise their property rights, in essence specifically denying property rights to an entire class of people; more accurately, the moratorium eschewed the communal property approach of late tsarist Russia to return to an even earlier economic model, the old land practices of serfdom under the Russian Empire, where the farmer was inextricably bound to the land. This reality has been shown in labor mobility data from the World Bank (2012), as Ukraine was estimated to have one of the least mobile labor forces in Central and Eastern Europe, let alone the world (Macours and Swinnen 2005 also note that relatively soft budget constraints in collective enterprises has meant that layoffs are not necessary, and thus workers tend to stay put). With no ability to sell the land, the farmer did not have a choice to garner the proceeds from the land and move elsewhere, and thus became tethered to a region. There is also evidence that this lack of ability to move to other regions meant that farmers kept their land but transitioned from the formal agricultural sector to an informal, salaried position, leaving the land to lay fallow and no longer being accurately classified as "farmers" (Duryea et al. 2006).

In a classic Catch-22 situation, the land moratorium has also reduced the ability of the farmer to improve the land that he must retain, as the inability to collateralize the land has meant that the development of agricultural financing in Ukraine was stunted. Financial institutions, as we will see, were already in a tenuous state in Ukraine during this time, and the development of lending for small farms (even mortgage lending), with little credit history and no collateral, was strenuously avoided in favor of (only) large agro-players (Csáki and Lerman 1997); as Krasnozhon (2011a:133) noted, "the crucial issue of mortgage financing remains unresolved as long as the moratorium on land sales stays effective." This lack of financial intermediation for farms then also fed back into the problem of labor mobility, as lack of mortgage lending created a major deterrent to workers moving within Ukraine, as there was no guarantee they could find a new domicile in the region they wanted to move (World Bank 2012). And, in a final insult, without the ability to transfer the land or improve it, Ukrainian farmers found themselves incredibly disadvantaged *vis-à-vis* larger (and sometimes politically connected) agricultural concerns, leading to "land grabs" carried out under fraudulent means but with the full complicity of Ukrainian politicians (Visser and Spoor 2011). Not only could farmers not use their full complement of property rights, but corruption could render these rights useless at any time.

The land sale moratorium has exposed the reality that the development of property rights should be paramount in transition, especially when one looks at the other economic and institutional distortions it facilitated. In particular, the sale moratorium and prohibitions on agricultural land ownership skewed the development of enterprises in what should have been the fastest-growing sector of the Ukrainian economy, the agricultural sector. In order for agricultural (or other) businesses to acquire land for their operations, they must acquire a lease to the land, given that sale or transfer is not possible (Articles 33 and 35 of the Land Code discuss leases). As the land sale moratorium continued in place (it was extended in 2005, 2008, and 2012 by the Rada and the current moratorium was set to expire on January 1, 2016 but was once again renewed), the Ukrainian government begrudgingly allowed businesses the ability to hold leases for up to fifty years, a timeframe that is seen as being equivalent to owning the land (Razumkov Centre 2011). In reality, however, right before the Euromaidan revolution, 90 percent of all agricultural land in Ukraine was on a year-to-year lease, with leases of 4.7 million privately owned parcels of land renewed annually (Nizalov 2014, based on data from the State Agency on Land Resources). This constant turnover of lease re-registration meant that not only was there little-to-no incentive for agri-businesses or farmers to invest in the leased land, but also that economic resources on the order of US$90 million are wasted annually in time and labor costs of registration (ibid.). And even with the lease work-around, accessing land remained a complex and time-consuming process, which took businesses up to as much as two years; moreover, as with many other aspects of business operations in Ukraine, obtaining rights to land use required first procuring permissions at various government levels. Moreover, Ukrainian agribusinesses were strenuous in emphasizing that the land acquisition process allows for many opportunities for rent-seeking behavior, given the extensive involvement of bureaucrats at all points along the lease procurement and registration continuum.[13] While there continue to be worries amongst Ukrainians that a free land market would result in rapid consolidation of land (or "forcing" people to sell), a poll taken in 2012 showed that only 7 percent of the population responded positively to the moratorium (Mischenko 2012).

Finally, the restrictions on land disposal for Ukrainian farmers were problematic enough, but they also had a highly protectionist and nationalistic streak to them, as prohibitions in regard to foreigners were made even more stringent than those facing Ukrainians. The Land Code (Article 22, item 5) already explicitly prohibited ownership of agricultural land by "foreigners, stateless individuals, foreign legal entities or foreign countries [these prohibitions on] ownership also extend to foreign businesses and states," with the only transaction in agricultural land that is permitted (actually compelled) for foreigners arises in the case of inheritance of an agricultural plot; in such an instance, the foreign entity is forced to "alienate" (dispose of) the land within one year's time, as per the Land Code Articles 81 and 82, or face judicial termination of their ownership. Foreigners are, in theory, allowed to own nonagricultural land (Article 82) for purposes related to agriculture, such as agro-processing located further away from the growing area, but only as an adjunct to purchasing non-movable assets located on said land. This creates an odd disincentive to investment, as purchase of or building a factory creates a right to own land, and not the other way around. Finally, if a foreign entity wishes to purchase

---

[13] I heard these concerns personally during conversations with various agricultural producers on an OECD mission in Kyiv in May 2015.

state-owned nonagricultural land, a complicated process is prescribed in the Land Code which must be approved by the Cabinet of Ministers for *each* such transaction. In this manner, property rights infringements were spread to both Ukrainians and foreigners alike.

The issues connected with protecting and exercising property rights on agricultural land in Ukraine had several parallels in other parts of the Ukrainian economy, mainly centered around (but not exclusively concerning) the mass privatization process of the 1990s. Unfortunately, along with Russia, Ukraine became the poster child of the "privatization means property rights" argument noted above, a reality made more problematic by the fact that the privatization process in Ukraine became a means to limit property rights of new entrepreneurs rather than creating them (in the words of Pivovarsky (2003:15), privatization "took place in an economic environment that did not lend institutional support to minority shareholders or investors in general"). A key reason behind the deleterious effect of privatization in Ukraine was that the process of "de-socializing" assets went through several false starts, with each reversal allowing for retrenchment of vested interests, an expansion of political influence, and a move further away from market-determined outcomes. As an illustration of Ukraine's path to privatization, Figure 5.11 shows Ukraine's progress in "large-scale" privatization (i.e., large state-owned firms) as compared to Poland, scaled by transition year (that is, with both countries rescaled to

Figure 5.11 Large-Scale Privatization in Poland and Ukraine
Source: EBRD Transition Indicators.

show the progress in comparable time from transition). As the figure shows, Poland began its process of privatization in the first year of transition, while for Ukraine it did not begin in any appreciable sense until year 3 (1995 in real time), when it caught up to Poland's level. However, that same year of transition, Poland initiated another round of privatization that pulled it further away from Ukraine (noting, as we did above, that Poland's progress was even relatively slow compared to other transition economies). The gap once again narrowed after the ninth year of Ukraine's transition, but, proving the dynamic nature of institutional development, Poland once again undertook privatization reforms in its nineteenth year of transition, leading to another widening gap with Ukraine. Thus, after early quick steps to divest itself of state-owned enterprises, a long period of consolidation in Poland led to more reforms. By contrast, Ukraine's delayed reforms led to smaller, incremental gains over a longer period, while even the gains of the Orange Revolution did not translate to any progress in these economic reforms.

The actual policies behind these headline numbers illustrate just how the privatization process was wielded to expand property rights for a select few. From the outset, even before Ukraine became independent, it underwent what Krasnozhon (2011a) termed the "*nomenklatura* privatization"; from 1987 to 1991, as throughout the Soviet Union, there was a devolution of power to managers, who then used their position of power over assets, that is, as director of a *kolkhoz* or manager of a large industrial firm, to acquire at least the use of these assets, if not outright ownership.[14] Despite such an inauspicious start to the process of transferring assets, once Ukraine became independent, the gears shifted towards mass privatization on the Russian model, but such a process (as with so many other aspects of the economic transition) did not begin to take shape until the end of Kravchuk's term in 1993 and 1994. A large-scale privatization program was put together in 1994 that "optimistically provided for privatization of 1,300 large and midsize enterprises and about 9,000 small scale objects" over two waves at the beginning and middle of the year, but by end-1994, only 650 entities had been up for sale to outsiders, as opposed to existing employees and managers (Frishberg 1995). With the election of a new Rada in July 1994, the process ground to

---

[14] Referring to this process as incipient privatization rather than "property rights" is thus a more accurate term, as it was acquiring an asset somewhat illicitly for private use; in many cases, because the route chosen to acquire the asset was dubious, there was little security of rights to that asset.

a halt with the passage of the On Perfection of the Privatization Mechanism in Ukraine and Intensifying the Control of Its Conduct resolution forbidding privatization by cash sales of medium and large enterprises until politicians could decide which firms were not to be sold (Snelbecker 1995).

Indeed, although the privatization process finally reached critical mass from 1995 to 1997, as with the exercise of property rights, the privatization process became a contest of political wills to see who could extract the most benefit. The Rada was first to chime in during 1995 by excusing particular companies from the harsh rigors of privatization, "declar[ing] 6,100 enterprises to be 'strategic' and, therefore, ineligible for privatization" (Buck et al. 1996:46). At the same time, as Kudelia (2012:420–421) notes, "Kuchma personally oversaw privatization of all key industrial assets which was largely completed by the end of his first term. Although some privatization deals provided property to those who had no direct connection to the president, new owners often found themselves under pressure from Kuchma's business cronies." Buck et al. (1996:46) also note that Kuchma played the strategic card as well, as "in October 1995 the government made the decision to cut by half the target of 8,000 privatizations for 1995." Without an incentive to change their Soviet-era ways, the overhaul of existing firms in Ukraine stalled, as shown in Figure 5.12, and only changed in response to sustained political pressure. Once again scaled to reflect transition years, Figure 5.12 shows that Poland, as a comparator to

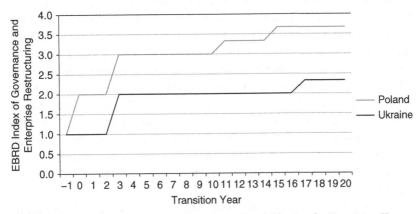

Figure 5.12 Enterprise Restructuring in Poland and Ukraine, by Transition Year
Source: EBRD Transition Indicators and author's calculations. Economic transition is coded as beginning in 1990 for Poland and 1992 for Ukraine.

Ukraine, actually saw widespread governance reforms before the transformation even started, showing perhaps the influence of informal institutions as the formal institutions began to break down. On the other hand, Ukraine's first set of enterprise reforms in the third transition year (between 1994 and 1995 in real time), forced through as part of the privatization process but highly incomplete, remained in place for well over a decade before any other changes were made. With large-scale uncertainty about property rights, and continuing capture of the commanding heights by political elites and bureaucracy, needed structural reforms at the enterprise level stalled.

Moreover, the slow pace of enterprise restructuring (Figure 5.12) in Ukraine as compared to Poland, combined with the fact that the economy still relied on the Soviet-era capital, meant that when privatization did take place, insiders were more able even than in Russia to take advantage of their insider status to acquire shares in their companies (Frydman et al. 1993) – in short, that *nomenklatura* privatization never really ended. The only progress made in selling off state-owned firms that occurred from 1992 to 1994 was the divestiture of 1,240 medium and large-scale enterprises via lease buyouts by managers and employees (Elborgh-Woytek and Lewis 2002). This inevitably resulted in "large-scale shareholding by managers and workers, some dispersed outsider shares and block holding by domestic entities, and substantial levels of state ownership" (Brown et al. 2006:72). More important, the insider privatizations led to a small-scale, yet widespread, informal system of property rights, with only those with local knowledge able to understand the corporate culture within a firm and actually implement effective restructuring; for foreigners, walking into a system of little effective legal contract enforcement and a culture of overstaffing and underworking would have rendered restructuring attempts futile (Åslund 2009). Thus, the political nature of the privatization process created a very odd type of privatized firm, one that would combine the Soviet institutional past with the dysfunctional institutional system that was arising in 1990s Ukraine. Property rights then became very situation-specific, enmeshed in a complex cultural web but undoubtedly small-scale, relying on trust, knowledge of the other operators, and backed by credible threats of force or sanctions.

In fact, given this reality, the only type of owner who could get things done in such an environment of unreconstructed enterprises turned out to be wealthy (and politically connected) Russians and Ukrainians, the so-called oligarchs, who became an economic institution unto themselves.

The rise of the oligarchy, as in Russia, was connected almost exclusively with the privatization process, although not necessarily the privatizations of the late 1990s. In fact, the oligarchs have their roots beginning with the *nomenklatura* privatization of the late 1980s, arising from the *nomenklatura* class and using their positions of privilege in an egalitarian society to acquire large amounts of capital; once privatization of larger state-owned assets began in the mid-to-late-1990s, they were able to leverage this capital acquired before the Soviet Union fell, in tandem with their insider knowledge, to purchase the industrial combines of the Soviet era at low prices (Matuszak 2012). This second phase in which the oligarchs truly became plutocrats (Åslund 2007), as with many of the distortions that became entrenched in Ukraine during its transition, occurred as a direct result of Kuchma's "personal rulership," where "rent-seekers and rent-givers ... forged an alliance aimed at preserving the current state of affairs" (Puglisi 2003:99). Given that Ukraine's heavy Soviet industry was concentrated in the east of the country, generally in the Donetsk and Luhansk Oblasts and the region surrounding Dnipropetrovsk, it was here where the oligarchs became concentrated, with Kuchma acting as "arbiter between the emerging oligarchic groups" (Matuszak 2012:14).

Shelley (1998:649) expresses the popular view of privatization in Ukraine, both inside the country and in the West, noting that "hijacking of the privatization process by organized crime and corrupt officials has resulted in a highly polarized society. Instead of an emergent middle class, Ukraine now has a small, extremely rich, new elite and a large, impoverished population." Åslund (2005a) argues that this is not quite right, noting that before 2000, the oligarchs made their money trading in gas, which continues to suffer from major distortionary policies but was not subjected to any sort of privatization. For our purposes, and more accurately, the emergence of the oligarchy in Ukraine is interesting because of the stratification of property rights it created, with only the enormously wealthy able to secure their property. In fact, as noted earlier, Ukrainian oligarchs were a modern-day *szlachta*, although they did not wax on poetically about the liberty that should be given to their noble lineage or about constraint of the executive and the right to take up arms against a tyrant. Instead, they were a group of wealthy landowners and business owners, localized in a certain territory, who wanted a much weaker central power in order to preserve their own privileges. In fact, the situation in Ukraine was exactly as Sonin (2003:715) modeled it, as "the ability to maintain private protection systems ma[de] the rich natural opponents of public property rights and preclude[d] grass-roots demand to drive the development of the market-friendly institution." Åslund (2005a) shows how the oligarchs established their own private security firms and, in an acknowledgment of the continued influence of politics in Ukraine, how they acquired state services, political influence, or politicians themselves (Yanukovych stands out as one of their acquisitions) to protect their property. In this sense, the development of hard-fought and expensive property rights on their assets was seen as an investment, and thus there was little need to develop external rights-guaranteeing institutions (which might not do the job as effectively or, worse, come into clash with the oligarchs' own enforcement mechanisms).[15] The parallels with the *szlachta* in the Commonwealth era are uncanny; moreover, given the indigenous nature of the Ukrainian oligarchs, it could also be said that they achieved the goal of the Cossack rebellion of 1654, in that the Polish nobility was replaced, not with an egalitarian society of free men, but a ruling class of Ukrainians.

This reality also led oligarchs into the public eye during the 2004 presidential elections, as many of the Donetsk and Luhansk-based clans (primary amongst them Rinat Akhmetov) sought to bankroll the candidate most likely to protect their own property rights; figures suggest that Yanukovych attempted to raise $600 million for his campaign, a sum equal to the amount spent by U.S. president George W. Bush in 2000 and with half of it raised from Ukrainian oligarchs (Åslund 2005b). But even with Yanukovych's defeat and the inauguration of market-friendly Yushchenko, Markus (2015a) argues that the Orange Revolution did not improve property rights protection in Ukraine and actually worsened it. Noting how difficult it is to expand property rights in an environment where the state has already arrayed against them (and not even considering that this has been a consistent theme in Ukraine's institutional history), Markus (2015a) correctly notes that the Orange Revolution committed the president of Ukraine into protecting broad-based property rights, mainly through the constraining of the office of the president via the constitutional

---

[15] Indeed, Guriev and Sonin (2009) develop a model of dictators and oligarchs, showing that weak dictators do not limit rent-seeking while strong dictators are able to eliminate rent-seeking and overthrow oligarchs in pursuit of their own ends. In this dynamic game, the elimination of rent-seeking is Parteo optimal, but if the oligarchs are powerful enough and supporting institutions weak enough, the weak dictator emerges as the preferred strategy. This is also a plausible explanation for Kuchma's term in Ukraine, as the banding together of oligarchs outside the Donbas enabled Yushchenko to ascend, even though these same oligarchs had supported Kuchma throughout his second term (Way 2005a). In this way, the oligarchs were also opposed to each other; it was just that one coalition of oligarchs was able to dominate in this instance.

changes of 2004. However, the continuation of the myriad of rules and restrictions on entrepreneurs, combined with the lack of any substantial diminution of the size of the state, meant that lower-level bureaucrats became more empowered to be corrupt, demand bribes, or use their office as a means of extortion. Much as with the late stages of the Soviet Union, once the political authority at the top eroded but the institutional mechanisms below had not been swapped out, the entire edifice was in danger of toppling under its own bureaucratic weight.

Moreover, the Orange Revolution created a problematic process that struck at the heart of property rights, a process that is still contemplated in Ukraine today: "re-privatization." Re-privatization, a cause championed by Prime Minister Yulia Tymoshenko, assumed that many of the privatizations that occurred under Kuchma were problematic and sold below market price, and thus confiscation of these assets for resale was necessary. As Åslund (2005b:344) noted, "in the world at large, populism has long focused on macroeconomics, but in Ukraine it is concentrating on property rights, posing a dangerous and long-lasting threat to the economy." Indeed, the issue of re-privatization was a direct strike at property rights, no matter how ill-gotten, as it confirmed that the state could take away such rights on a whim. In this issue, as many others, Tymoshenko was clearly no unquestioning friend of property rights and instead was more concerned with feeding the state apparatus: she noted in an interview in 2005 that she felt that the largest enterprises should remain under state control to "give the state as their owner wonderful profits" (Yatsenko 2005), and on re-privatization she was willing to sacrifice the development of property rights to rectify previous injustices in the privatization process to the tune of several hundred million more dollars in the government's coffers. President Yushchenko wisely replaced Tymoshenko as prime minister near the end of 2005 with Yuri Yekhanurov, a technocrat who promptly cancelled re-privatization and instead negotiated a "peace agreement" with companies felt to have benefited improperly from privatization (Markus 2015a). Despite this about-face, the damage was done, as the government's promises to re-privatize actually confirmed the oligarchs' greatest fears and justified their need for both private property rights and a say in the political process. The oligarchs soon drifted away from Yushchenko and his party (Our Ukraine) in the Rada, fearing he was too weak even to protect broader property rights (much less their own), instead backing Tymoshenko (perhaps trying to ensure that they would not be re-privatized if she should come to power) and, of course, Yanukovych (Matuszak 2012).

The continued in-fighting of the "orange" politicians, the questionable commitment of some of the group to property rights (e.g., Tymoshenko), and the failure to reform Ukraine's economy, perhaps even more so than the privatization process, had a deleterious effect on the perception of property rights in Ukraine that then spread to other institutions. As Markus (2015a) notes,

The failure of the Orange Revolution to secure the property rights of Ukraine's middle class may answer the puzzle of the democratically sanctioned rollback of achieved freedoms, signified by the election of Yanukovych to presidency in 2010 – i.e., the puzzle of revolution's ultimate implosion, contrary to the euphoric predictions of Western social scientists and policymakers alike. . . .. Among the interviewed entre-preneurs of all political convictions, the revolution's negative impact on PR security seemed to have discredited democratic institutions.

This reality could be seen most prominently in Tymoshenko's approach to re-privatization. As Paskhaver and Verkhovodova (2007:21) correctly stated, "Reprivatization processes under Tymoshenko's direction were carried out in a demonstrably inflexible way. As far as one could tell from the indictments handed down, the purchasers of state property were declared guilty beforehand, rather than the government agencies that sold the property." Thus, a government that came to power promising secure property rights for all, and that in many ways did undertake such a program even where it was unpopular (e.g., Yushchenko taking a stand against re-privatization), ended up undercutting property rights and even democracy due to its inability to carry through substantial institutional change.

Yanukovych's election, as with political institution-building, was also a setback for the expansion of property rights in Ukraine, although the degradation of property rights was not uniformly the case during Yanukovych's presidency. In particular, following the highly publicized and highly politicized trial of Tymoshenko, Yanukovych undertook a series of property rights reforms in 2010 designed by the western consultancy McKinsey in order to improve Ukraine's rankings in the World Bank's "Doing Business" rankings; unfortunately, as Markus (2015b) notes, this was done mainly because the changes in paying taxes or other facets of the rankings did not require democracy or other supporting institutions. And it was these supporting institutions that suffered greatly during the rest of Yanukovych's term, allowing for the continuance of privatized corruption (Markus 2015a), the favoring of oligarchs over broad-based reforms, and the elimination of judicial independence (Krasnozhon 2013). In fact, rather than build institutions to support property rights, as in the Soviet times, the state took measures to protect itself from the people. A prime example of this was Yanukovych's championing of the continuation of the moratorium on forced sales of state property for companies with more than a 25 percent ownership share by the state; in place since 2001 and a direct contributor to the stalled privatization process (Figure 5.12), Law No. 4901-VI of 2013 easily passed the Rada, continuing the prohibition of asset seizures from state-owned firms (Meleshevich and Forstein 2014). In this manner, Ukraine took a step back from both imposing hard budget constraints on state-owned firms (if there was no threat of seizure of forfeiture in event of bankruptcy, there was no reason to fear bankruptcy) and from creating a level playing field (state firms thus becoming advantaged *vis-à-vis* private firms).

The destruction of the delicate balancing act of Ukrainian institutions came together in the shift from Yanukovych's allegiance to the Donetsk clan, who made up the bulk of his government from 2010 to 2011, to "the Family." The Family was the colloquial name given to the even more insidious group of Yanukovych associates and actual family members who utilized the power of the state to acquire resources in a much more blunt and nonsubtle manner than the oligarchs of old. As Satter (2014:7) described it,

The usual scenario was for representatives of Yanukovych or his son to offer to buy an attractive business at a price far below what it was worth. If the offer was refused, the next step was to use force. The first move was to send in inspectors – fire inspectors, sanitation inspectors, the police, tax inspectors – to find violations, both real and imaginary, and impose fines so draconian that it was impossible to continue long in business. And if that wasn't enough, the victim could be arrested on trumped-up charges. The depredations of Alexander Yanukovych were such that many people started taking over businesses by saying that they represented him when in fact they didn't even know him. The brand was sufficiently powerful that people were afraid to risk a confrontation. Soon, the biggest oligarchs in Ukraine were Yanukovych, the members of his family, and those like Rinat Akhmetov who were already oligarchs and friendly to Yanukovych. Akhmetov, for example, was Yanukovych's early sponsor and patron.

With the president explicitly utilizing the powers of his office to directly expropriate businesses and threaten property rights, the breakdown of the Ukrainian state was complete. As Riabchuk and Lushnycky (2015:48) noted, Yanukovych "usurped all power, accumulated gargantuan resources via corruption schemes, destroyed the court system, encroached thoroughly on civil liberties and violated human rights." In such an environment, "the conditions necessary for this rapid concentration of wealth by those who exercised political power meant that there could be no reliable legal mechanisms to protect individual rights, including property rights" (Satter 2014:7). In reality, Yanukovych had bypassed the state mechanism entirely, making property rights dependent upon his own whim; in this manner, he had achieved power beyond that sought by Kravchuk and Kuchma, subordinating the state's existing apparatus to protect his own property (which happened to be anything he desired).

As of the writing of this book (December 2015), the trend for property rights in Ukraine post-Yanukovych has not become apparent. Indeed, the Russian invasion in Crimea, Donetsk, and Luhansk is unlikely to change the protection of property rights in those regions, as they were predisposed by history and by practice to already eschew property rights in favor of "might makes right." Thus, even an outright invasion by Russian troops is unlikely to worsen the approach to property rights in the industrial east or Crimea, merely to keep it frozen in place. In the other portions of Ukraine, those perhaps subjected more to the "Galician nationalism" that Kuchma warned the country about, there is more hope to turn away from the approach to property rights characterized by "the Family" and towards broader property rights. Early signs have not been encouraging, however, as the land sale moratorium remains in place and little progress has been made in reducing the power of the state (Orttung 2015), with the post-Maidan leadership worried about the precarious state of the government's finances and the macroeconomic imbalances that threaten to erupt into financial crisis. As Markus (2015a) notes, "runaway predation by unaccountable state agents will remain a formidable obstacle to the country's development, an obstacle that should be addressed head-on, lest the events of 2004 and 2014 must repeat themselves in 2024."

Foreign Trade and Commercial Institutions

As the previous section shows, the formation of property rights in the transition in Central and Eastern Europe entailed the creation or spontaneous generation of a great number of supporting institutions, including judicial institutions, financial institutions (in the case of privatization), and small-scale agricultural institutions. This simple fact makes property rights one of the most important institutions in an instrumental sense for a country's economic transformation: beyond the fact that property rights are crucial for a market economy, the reality is that their protection necessitates a broad spectrum of institutions to develop simultaneously, and thus working towards property rights helps to advance the transformation on a broad front. It also means, however, that achieving property rights protection is more difficult, precisely because several institutions need to reform concurrently.

An additional supporting institution that we touched upon in Chapters 3 and 4 is, in reality, another side of the right to engage in commerce, namely foreign trade. Once the right to owning property within a country's boundaries has been established and, more important, defended, the extension of these rights to trade across borders appears to be a natural progression. However, from a political economy standpoint, the development of foreign trade and other commercial institutions has rarely been so clear-cut, and while a country may have developed property rights, there is no guarantee that it will be so dedicated to defending the right to engage in foreign trade (on the other hand, it is virtually unheard of for a country to have excellent trade institutions and poor property rights). From a transition perspective, developing trade institutions would also require a concerted effort to remove the shackles and barriers imposed by communism, where trade was the monopoly of the state, a process that would require more political will than merely allowing for the right to own property. In short, where developing property rights required, at the outset, removing a simple prohibition that was often already violated informally, allowing for foreign trade required a much larger dismantling of the state apparatus, fostering businesses with the acumen to compete internationally, and standing aside as commerce bloomed and trade changed the structure of the economy.

The approach of Poland and Ukraine to this challenge was characterized by differences across three specific dimensions: in pace of change, in the choice of instruments for carrying out trade policies, and in each country's institutional relationship to the external environment. In regard to pace of reforms, as with other economic institutions, Poland went much more quickly than Ukraine, removing the prohibitions against trade in one fell swoop and sweeping away foreign trade restrictions along with other similar distortions all at once. Indeed, foreign trade and commercial liberalization were included as part of the Balcerowicz Plan, making the right to trade a fundamental piece of the institutional transition as the foreign trade monopoly of the Soviet era was eliminated. Unlike Ukraine (as we will see), Poland dramatically eliminated export and import subsidies, decreased absolute tariff levels by the second half of 1990, and drastically removed quotas and qualitative restrictions during its first year of liberalization (Winiecki 2003), as well as restoring the złoty to full international convertibility in order to allow the growth of both exports and imports (Berg and Sachs 1992). The swift and decisive manner in which the Soviet-era institutions were eliminated from the economy, when coupled with external events such as the collapse of the COMECON (CMEA) trade bloc, created a solid basis for trade and business institutions to grow as part of a market economy after the transformational recession had been completed. As the World Bank (1994b) notes, by late 1990, Poland had one of the most liberal trade regimes in Europe, if not the world.

The second area of difference with Ukraine was the focus of Polish trade institutions and policies on formal trade barriers and tariffs rather than nontariff barriers and administrative burdens, an approach that was very important in minimizing corruption at the borders (Kamiński 1999). While trade policy was utilized to advantage domestic industries at times, the trade policies of Poland were not designed to advantage specific *individuals*, a major difference from Ukraine (as we will see). This did not mean that the transition to the use of tariffs was necessarily smooth from the outset, nor does it mean that tariff rates were not utilized in a capricious and political manner: as is usually the case in relation to trade, the time of extraordinary politics ended fairly rapidly and domestic interests reasserted themselves in the trade realm. In fact, after the rapid institutional successes of 1990 resulting in an import boom (Rodrik 1994), by 1991 the agricultural lobby (followed by some industrialists) were pushing for a strong turn back to protectionism, finding themselves harmed by international competition (Balcerowicz et al. 1997) and seeing their access to Western markets not proceeding at quite the desired pace (Rodrik 1994). But while the agricultural lobby may have failed in its first attempt to influence trade policy, industrial producers had more success as protectionism reasserted itself by 1992, with the Polish government ratcheting rates on specific manufactures, including personal computers and automobiles (Gács 1994). These changes came on the back of a previous substantial adjustment of customs tariffs in August 1991, where "most duty rates ranged between 10 per cent and 40 per cent, with 70 per cent of tariff lines in the 15 per cent category" (GATT 1992). The impetus behind this original realignment was less due to protectionist pressures and more to fiscal ones, as the government sought to tap the revenue stream of goods entering the country and accordingly raised average tariffs from 5. 5 percent to 18.4 percent in 1992 (also the reason behind an imports surcharge from 1993 to 1996; see Kamiński (1999)); additionally, with an eye on eventual EU membership, the government may have also adjusted the tariff rates as a strategic move, to create a bargaining chip for future multilateral negotiations (Hare 2001).

Poland has also not been immune to the siren song of nontariff barriers, a point made by Kamiński (1999), who noted that the percentage of coverage of nontariff measures in Poland was a staggeringly low 3.2 percent in 1996 but was on the rise due to both technical regulations from the EU (Brenton et al. 2001) and the domestic use of technical standards and licensing. In particular, the Certification Law, introduced in 1997, required testing on a panoply of imports, while safety certificates issued by foreign governments were no longer recognized. As Kamiński (1999:18) noted, "the refusal to accept foreign firms' self-certification of conformance to domestic standards forces producers from other countries to undertake lengthy testing procedures in designated units. This has created problems not only for foreign companies but also for Polish exporters, as governments in EU countries do not recognize Polish safety certificates. This requires further testing and often at considerable cost," at the same time helping to save the Soviet dinosaur "testing" facilities who had a monopoly on certification in Poland. Due to an outcry from the EU and opposition from business, the law was replaced by a new Law on Conformity Assessment in April 2000, which aligned Poland with EU legislation regarding certification, technical barriers to trade, and mutual recognition (OECD 2002); an additional benefit of the long and protracted process that led to this outcome was repeated interactions between the EU and Poland, helping to forge a consensus on international best practice and educate Polish lawmakers on what was permissible under EU law (Preston and Michonski 1999). Additional ad hoc restrictions, including quotas on textiles, alcohol, and raw animal hides came and went over the period 1994 to 1999 (WTO 2000), mainly as the Democratic Left Alliance (SLD) attempted to placate its allies on the left and pander to various domestic interests. Similarly, a report by Pelkmans et al. (2000:34) charged that "bribes and other corruptive favors are endemic in Poland because widespread licensing prevents economic freedoms from being enjoyed automatically," focusing on the sometimes-difficult business environment in the country. With the move towards EU accession, however, many (albeit not all) of these nontariff barriers were forced to fall by the wayside.

Indeed, external trade institutions played a substantial (if not *the* most substantial) role in guiding the development of Poland's trade institutions, providing discipline to the reform process (Preston 1998). In an odd aberration, Poland had already belonged to the General Agreement on Tariffs and Trade (GATT), the precursor to the World Trade Organization (WTO), becoming the first planned economy to accede in 1967 (Douglass 1972). As a result of this, Poland already had some experience with international rule-bound trade institutions, even as the external situation of Poland was dictated by Moscow and by the exigencies of its own socialist planning. With the start of transition, additional external trade institutions began to influence Poland's trade strategies, as the Polish government signed an Association Agreement with the European Economic Community (EEC) in December 1991, followed by free trade agreements with the European Free Trade Area (EFTA) and Central European Free Trade Area (CEFTA). As the largest and most advanced trade bloc, the evolution of Polish trade institutions and policies during the transition became guided almost exclusively by the process of EU accession, a process that was kick-started by the 1991 Association Agreement and which accelerated with the full implementation of the Agreement in 1994, the application of Poland for membership submitted on April 5, 1994, and the convening of accession negotiations in March 1998.[16] Combined with the EFTA and CEFTA agreements, coming into force at various times over 1992 to 1994, approximately 75 percent of Poland's trade flows at that point were covered by trade treaties, offering substantial market access with areas that were very recently closed off to Polish goods (World Bank 1994b). And as a result of this rapid move towards international and supranational trade institutions, Poland's tariff policies quickly stabilized, especially in regard to imports (Balcerowicz et al. 1997), and were brought down substantially from their pre-EU levels (Fidrmuc et al. 2001). According to Goh and Javorcik (2007:343), "in 1999, the average Polish tariff on imports from the EU, the European Free Trade Association (EFTA), and Central European Free Trade Agreement (CEFTA) countries was brought down to 6.5 percent, as compared to the most-favored-nation (MFN) rate of 15.6 percent and the 34.6 percent rate applied to non-WTO members."

---

[16] The entire Association Agreement came completely into force in 1994, but the trade-related provisions were effective as of 1992.

Alongside this continuous lowering of tariffs came a dramatic reorientation of trade towards the EU and its Member States. The collapse of the CMEA bloc, as with every member, hurt the Polish economy, severing trade links that had been built up as a matter of plan over many years, not only with Russia but even within Central Europe; Kolankiewicz (1994) notes that trade amongst the CEE CMEA countries declined 59.5 percent for Poland over 1985 to 1992, while trade with the West increased 52.3 percent from 1989 to 1992, even before the Association Agreement came into place. Slay (2000) notes that the Agreement did indeed accelerate Poland's reorientation westward, as the share of Polish imports from the EU went from 33.8 percent in 1989 to 63.9 percent in 1996, and exports increased from 32.1 percent to 66.3 percent over the same timeframe. By the eve of Accession in 2003, imports from the EU accounted for 69.6 percent of all Polish trade, while exports had reached 81.9 percent, a number that actually decreased in later years as Poland diversified its trade beyond the EU.[17] Beyond the macroeconomic aggregates, at the industrial level, Polish firms were also integrating into value chains in Europe, as shown by Dunin-Wasowicz et al. (2002) in their study of the automobile industry in Poland. At the same time that this integration was occurring, and perhaps due to the concurrent Accession processes taking place in the region, Poland rebuilt its trade with the so-called Visegrad Four countries, although to a much smaller extent, showing 7.7 percent of its exports heading to the CEE in 2002 (Allard 2009). It was not until after EU accession that Polish trade, buoyed by its new institutional affiliation, began to turn back to Russia, increasing to 4.4 percent of all exports by 2005, according to the Polish Statistical Office (GUS).

One area where the Polish experience, and in particular the EU influence, did *not* allow for the creation of liberal trade institutions, however, as already noted, was in agriculture. The issue of the agricultural lobby, given its central place in the Polish economy, has recurred throughout the past twenty-five years, with agricultural producers arguing for protection, subsidies, and other preferential trade treatment at the expense of consumers and other producers. And while they were not successful in 1991 at pushing their agenda for increased protection, they have had relatively more success in the years since, especially in the setting of tariff rates. In fact, as Goh and Javorcik (2007) note, the odd arrangement that Poland had as a centrally planned economy in GATT resulted in a similarly odd

---

[17] Numbers based on data from Eurostat database, available at http://ec.europa.eu/eurostat/data/database.

loophole when it came to tariff protections in agriculture, as Poland's nonmarket nature meant a basis needed to be found for estimating tariff equivalents of its nontariff barriers on trade; this process resulted in Poland taking the EU's levels of tariffs on agriculture, leaving the country after its shedding of communism with high barriers in the agricultural sector (still at a simple average applied most favored nation (MFN) rate of 34.2 percent in 1999). Additional protectionist measures were introduced by the left-wing government in 1994 in the form of variable import levies on eight separate groups of agricultural products, including poultry, meat, and vegetable oils (Drabek and Brada 1998), hoping to stifle competition from the former Soviet countries (including Ukraine) who had demonstrable capabilities in these products. Nontariff barriers also clustered in the agricultural realm, as the power of the agricultural lobby meant that food and beverages and live animals for meat were subjected to a large number of quotas and qualitative restrictions throughout the 1990s (Kamiński 1999). Even in the move towards free trade within the region, as typified in the CEFTA agreement, agricultural products remained a sticking point for integration, with a large number of both tariff and quota barriers amongst the signatories "actually more restrictive than that found in the EU's Common Agricultural Policy (CAP)" (Medvec 2009).[18]

In fact, when considering the impact of external forces on Poland's institutional development in trade, the reality remains that the EU has not had the success in forcing institutional change that has happened elsewhere in the Polish economy. The reason behind this is simple, namely that the EU is a poor model for agriculture in general, given its own protectionist impulses and the policy abomination that is the Common Agricultural Policy. In truth, Poland did converge institutionally with the European model in regard to its agricultural trade institutions, but that convergence did not actually mean that Poland was coming close to economically sane policies or fostering the most appropriate trade institutions for a market economy. Poland, as a major agricultural producer, cast in its lot with the EU and all that entailed. However, the experience of agriculture should not detract from the overall Polish experience in liberalizing its trade institutions.

---

[18] The one saving grace, perhaps, was that Poland did not make full use of its entitlements under WTO membership to support the agricultural sector with subsidies and price supports. As Buckwell and Tangermann (1999) noted, Poland was only utilizing 8.3 percent of its WTO allowance as of 1998, the period of its most intensive protectionism.

Agriculture remains problematic for every country in the world (as evidenced by U.S. and EU trade policies), and expecting Poland not only to converge with but actually leap-frog these countries in terms of liberalization (and in two decades' time) may have been unrealistic. Taken on the whole, then, the move towards the EU and, more importantly, the adoption of liberalized trade institutions improved Poland's trade outcomes with the entire world, laying the foundation for market-determined trade flows and competitiveness. Despite setbacks and difficulties with domestic politics, the swift nature of the transition and the enticement of external institutions helped to move Poland's trade institutions along a positive path.

This experience was in stark contrast with Ukraine, which is continuing to see difficulties in its trade institutions mostly of its own making. As with other institutions we have examined and will examine in this chapter, Ukraine tends to dominate the discussion of foreign trade institutional development, mainly as a primer in how *not* to build the appropriate institutions for a market economy. Similar to Poland, trade was always a large part of Ukraine's economic activity during the Soviet era; however, as Ukrainian trade was dictated by central planners in Moscow, this meant that (unlike Poland), Ukraine's trade was almost exclusively oriented towards Russia and the rest of the Soviet Union. Indeed, the exigencies of Soviet planning meant that approximately 82 percent of the Ukrainian SSR's trade was concentrated in the other republics of the Soviet Union (Tarr 1994), with Russian-Ukrainian trade making up two-thirds of all inter-republic trade within the USSR by the late 1980s (Woehrel 1993). Moreover, keeping in line with the Soviet style of trade management, Ukraine was assigned its own area of specialization (not determined by the market and tenets of comparative advantage) and was tapped to become the USSR's main supplier of heavy industry and, to a lesser extent, agriculture: by the late 1980s, Ukraine's economy was heavily concentrated in industrial production (making up 69 percent of all production), especially machine-building (33 percent of production), which was then "exported" throughout the rest of the Soviet Union (Woehrel 1993).[19] But despite this "success" in orienting the Ukrainian economy towards the rest of the Union, Ukraine still managed to run a persistent trade deficit, especially if one priced Ukrainian goods at world market prices rather than distorted internal prices, importing much more from the other

---

[19] Woehrel (1993) also notes that Ukraine produced 20 percent of the Soviet Union's agriculture by 1988.

republics, especially in regard to energy (Kiss and Sidenko 1992). Facing the reality that "Ukraine's industry [was] old (even relative to other Soviet republics) and badly in need of investment" (Johnson et al. 1993:925), Ukraine was ill-poised to make the leap towards international competitiveness when the transition began.

Unfortunately, the development of Ukraine's trade institutions after independence was characterized by many of the same flaws inherent in the other economic institutions examined in this chapter, with the most prominent flaw being the interference of political institutions in the determination of trade. In fact, trade institutions showed much less of a transition in Ukraine away from the Soviet model than other economic institutions, primarily property rights; given that property rights did not ostensibly exist in the Soviet Union, creating such rights (even fragile and tenuous ones) meant a substantial investment to cobble together a formal institution on the basis of small-scale and informal customs. On the other hand, a transition away from the Soviet model of trade merely required the abolition of the plan and the removal of government from the process, as was done in neighboring Poland. But in a land where market-determined comparative advantage was a foreign concept, as in Ukraine of 1991, the choice of building trade institutions that could compete internationally on their own terms may have appeared to be the more difficult path than leaving Soviet-era controls in place. In fact, with political costs to be borne from institutional change (a reality faced by politicians in all countries when it comes to trade) and, more importantly, the benefits to be reaped from the political class from maintaining the status quo, it was perhaps understandable that Ukrainian politicians chose the path of least resistance. And without political incentives to alter Ukraine's path, the trade institutions that did emerge after independence appeared to be carrying on the same Soviet spirit of directed trade and tight administrative control, failing to build the basis of growth for the future and crippling Ukrainian businesses.

This mind-set, of continued political control of a key economic institution, was established most clearly in the foundation law on trade, the Law on Foreign Economic Activities, passed in the Ukrainian SSR in April 1991 by the majority Communists but still the governing legislation of Ukraine today.[20] The Law appears to set a firm foundation for trade, allowing for

---

[20] As of the time of writing of this chapter, the law had been amended twenty-five times, with further amendments proposed in December 2015 in order to mirror sanctions by Russia on Ukrainian trade.

the "exclusive right of the people of Ukraine to perform foreign economic activities in Ukraine on an independent basis following the laws in force on the territory of Ukraine" (Article 2) and noting that "interference of the state bodies into foreign economic activities of its entities in cases when it is not stipulated by this Law, including adoption of subordinate legislation which creates unfavorable conditions worse than those established in this Law, shall be deemed limitation of the right to perform foreign economic activities and therefore shall be prohibited" (Article 5). However, beginning with Article 8, a long and vague list of times when the state can intervene in economic relations is elucidated, with several chapters afterwards laying out customs regulations, antidumping rules (curiously a main theme of the Law), and other issues such as the mandatory distribution of foreign currency proceeds (Article 12). Perhaps more interesting, the Law goes far beyond laying out the rules for export and import to encompass a huge number of peripheral subjects, ranging from trade fairs to leasing operations to employment of foreigners to currency auctions and cross-border contracts, staking a claim to the government's involvement in each sphere. This approach, coming as it does from a Soviet legal background, continues the Soviet style of legislation, where issues not expressly allowed are prohibited, and thus the legislation must take care to be comprehensive in its allowances.

With such a basic document governing trade, it is little wonder that policies surrounding the development of trade institutions reverted to Soviet type and continued the state's reach in the realm of foreign trade. The broad powers given to the state for regulating trade in Article 8 were almost immediately utilized under Kravchuk as part of the nation-building project to ensure that Ukraine's trade relations went as the country appeared to need them. Indeed, not satisfied with merely dictating the content of trade, the newly independent Ukrainian authorities also sought to control its direction: "after the legacy of Soviet rule, and the inability of Ukraine and Russia to cooperate in the early days of independence, Ukraine enacted an economic program in 1992 explicitly aimed at breaking trade ties with Russia" (D'Anieri 1999:106). As part of this overarching goal, "rather than laying down guidelines and principles and combining an obligation to establish free-market institutions with federal cooperation, aim[ed] to conclude a series of bilateral economic agreements with the other republics (particularly Russia) as a way of settling the details of this cooperation that [were] most in dispute" (Kiss and Sidenko 1992:65). While the reduction of reliance on Russia as a source of trade would have been welcome, the reality of Ukraine's infrastructure (and especially the lack of its own energy resources) meant that it was likely to be tied to Russia in the short term as trade relations re-oriented themselves; unlike property rights or other economic institutions, trade institutions themselves could have undergone a "big bang" transition, but this would not necessarily have resulted in a swift change in trade *outcomes*. It was on this point that the Ukrainian leadership was confused, as a concerted effort to liberalize trade would likely have led to the same outcome, that is, a move away from Russian goods, as the dilapidated industry of the east was replaced by newer and more appropriate economic structures forced by international competition. But by trying to force the change in outcomes without a break with the underlying institutions, the Kravchuk administration was merely using the same command-and-control approach for different goals, ironically clinging on to Soviet tenets of trade while Russia was liberalizing (as Tedstrom (1995) noted).

The fruits of this policy were seen in the rapid decline in trade across the board, as, from 1991 to 1992, Ukrainian exports to the (now) ex-Soviet republics fell by 32 percent, with imports of non-energy goods also plummeting 28 percent (Havrylyshyn 1994). The move away from the planned markets of the Soviet Union was accompanied by a drop in trade in general as the country experienced its transformational recession, with the share of exports in Ukraine's GDP dropping from approximately 35.7 percent in 1988 to 25.9 percent by 1993, along with a drop in imports 37.9 to 26.2 percent over the same time period (Freinkman et al. 2004). Important for understanding today's issues, the Russian-reliant east of Ukraine, notably the Donbas, suffered greatly during this period as its antiquated industry realistically had no other markets than Russia. From a political economy standpoint, this severing of trade links also increased the calls from industry for protection and/or subsidies: as Drabek (1996:734) noted, then–prime minister Marchuk called for protectionist trade policies in 1995 amidst rising calls for bailouts from 240 "strategic" enterprises (which were funded via monetary means, see below).

This inauspicious debut of Ukraine's trade policy showed the difficulty of dismantling the old centrally planned trade links by directive from above. Unfortunately, this mind-set also persisted into the building of new trade institutions, which was also halted by continued political interference, directives from the state, and, above all, a huge burden of administration. The Ukrainian approach to trade has been quite unlike other developed countries, where the primary tool for control of trade flows are tariff structures or the tax system, as Ukraine has instead

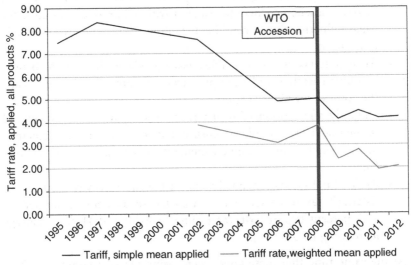

Figure 5.13 Overall Tariff Rates in Ukraine, 1995–2012
Source: World Bank World Development Indicators and author's calculations.

continued to rely on a large number of nontariff barriers (NTBs), including licensing, quotas, and permissions, to influence trade patterns. Indeed, formal trade barriers have been on a steady downward path in Ukraine (Figure 5.13), mainly as a result of Ukraine's move towards the World Trade Organization (WTO), a long journey that began in 1993 and concluded in 2008, and towards the EU, a journey which began in 1994 and is still ongoing. The story of these formal barriers is inextricably linked with these international trade institutions, and will form the basis for the rest of this section.

WTO accession in particular has been a guiding point for the evolution of Ukraine's formal barriers to trade, as the country has been willing, in the longer term, to bargain away tariff rates in hopes of obtaining greater access to other countries' markets (Eremenko et al. 2004). This road has not been easy, however, as there was a heated and unnecessarily prolonged debate in Ukraine on the desirability of WTO accession (generally related to fears about import competition, see Landrich 2004) that led to stagnation in the 1990s on movement towards accession (Åslund 2009). Despite beginning the process of accession in 1993, a working party was not established until 1995, at the same time that Ukraine was instituting a panoply of formal barriers to trade, including (according to Åslund 2003):

- Import tariffs (by weight) for sugar of approximately 100 percent, linked to a scheme where the state distributed production quotas for sugar refineries, thus controlling the inflow of sugar and who was able to utilize it;
- An export tax on animal hides was introduced in 1995 to benefit Ukrainian leather and shoe producers, keeping their goods inside the country for higher prices;
- Similarly, an export tariff of 30 percent on scrap metal was introduced in the mid-1990s in order to ensure that adequate supplies remained in the country for Ukrainian metalworkers (a policy that patently failed);
- Agricultural goods remained some of the most heavily (and inconsistently) taxed goods, with sunflower seeds being subjected to a 17 percent export tariff (according to Åslund 2003, to encourage its refining in Ukraine).

At the same time that these goods were being taxed, a complex web of agricultural subsidies was instituted that comprised up to 22 percent of all transfers to the agro-food industry in 1998; as the OECD (2004:27) noted, "income measures in 1996–1999 were extremely nontransparent, creating favorable conditions for administrative discretion, abuse, and rent seeking." Despite the plethora of subsidies, the macroeconomic instability and administrative barriers to trade (in tandem with property rights difficulties) led to a decline in agricultural production of 39 percent from 1991 to 2000 (Zorya and von Cramon-Taubadel 2002).

These various policies, at times at loggerheads but underpinned by state administrative control of trade, only abated somewhat during the term of Viktor Yushchenko as prime minister in 2000, which helped to accelerate the WTO process by adopting laws needed for accession (Åslund 2009). After the Orange Revolution, the pace quickened even more substantially, with bilateral protocols quickly signed during 2005 and 2006, and nearly 95 percent of tariff lines in "sensitive products" and 98 percent of service lines agreed upon by mid-2005 (de Souza et al. 2006). Ukraine finally acceded to the organization on May 16, 2008, a full fifteen years after beginning its journey, with trade legislation such as the April 2008 law On Ratification of the Protocol on Ukraine Accession to the World Trade Organization specifying changes to Ukraine's trade regime in line with WTO commitments. Similarly, the Cabinet of Ministers Instruction #1570-p from December 2008, "On approving the plan of urgent measure to meet Ukraine's commitments under WTO membership," also attempted to create a more tangible roadmap for changes in the trade policy of the country.

At the policy level, overall tariff rates have come down since entry into the WTO, as shown in Figure 5.13, with a simple tariff rate across all products averaging 4.4 percent since 2008, in addition to improvements in FTA negotiations and at least legislative approximation of customs at the EU border (Gawrich et al., 2010). However, the WTO has proven to be less of a binding constraint on Ukraine's protectionist tendencies than hoped, especially in regard to agriculture, where government intervention refuses to die. As recently as 2012 the Ukrainian government announced its intent to renegotiate tariff bindings on over 350 products that were agreed upon as part of accession (Auyezov and Miles 2012), a move that was thwarted after an international outcry (leading Ukraine to revise its submission in May 2014). And even the new Yatsenyuk government soon after Euromaidan publicly stated that it reserves the right to initiate a review of its customs duties under the WTO over a three-year period, starting from January 1, 2015. Even with several changes of power and the external constraints of the WTO, Ukraine's political institutions appear to continue to be heavily involved in the development of trade, a reality that has not worked for the better.

The use of trade as a political instrument, as well as a possible impetus for institutional evolution, can also be seen in the ongoing relationship of Ukraine to the European Union. In fact, it is helpful to note here that Ukraine's trade policy institutions have been shaped by strong exogenous forces, even if the WTO's influence has been very slow in filtering through. Unlike Poland, which had a steady pull of institutional convergence due to the EU accession process (which it was single-mindedly moving towards), Ukraine has been torn in two directions by the prospect of EU accession but also by the trade initiatives of the Russian Federation and its former country-mates in the Soviet Union. Of course, the trade infrastructure of Ukraine was already oriented towards Russia, hence the difficulties that were visited upon Ukraine (noted above) when an abrupt re-orientation away from the country was embarked upon in 1992. After the rapid decline in trade during this first year of independence, Ukraine sought to repair some of its trade links by negotiating bilateral free trade agreements (FTAs) with all members of the newly-formed Commonwealth of Independent States (CIS), apart from Tajikistan and Uzbekistan (Roberts and Wehrheim 2001). The CIS remains the main forum of trade integration within the post-Soviet space, with relations amongst members having stabilized after the 1998 Russian crisis, while additional trade initiatives within the region floundered during the first decade-and-a-half of transition (Zhukov and Reznikova 2007).[21] In fact, even the CIS has experienced its own delays in trade integration, as it agreed upon creating a free-trade area in 1994 but did not see this come into reality until 2011 due to delays in ratification by the Russian Duma. Ukraine has been an active participant in these CIS agreements, but has repeatedly tried to keep further attempts at integration within the CIS framework at arms' length: as D'Anieri (1999: 133–134) noted, "the main goal of Ukraine in the fall of 1991 was to ensure the demise of the Soviet Union, so to the extent that the CIS represented a continuation of Soviet institutions, it represented an institution to be feared, not welcomed."

This point of view remained prevalent even after Kuchma made a *volte-face* during his presidency to acknowledge that Russia and Ukraine were "doomed to live in friendship" (quoted in Åslund 2009:102), and thus greater trade integration with the Russian Federation, if not necessarily desirable, was at least unavoidable in the short term. But, as the two largest members of the CIS, Russia and Ukraine have often been at loggerheads regarding trade under the CIS umbrella (as well as under the Treaty on Friendship, Cooperation, and Partnership signed in 1997 and ratified in 1998). In many ways, this was inevitable, as both countries have treated trade as a potential political weapon, with extensive state intervention in trade and their main exporting industries, meaning that the institutional basis for trade as politics by other means was already set. This use of trade has manifested itself in the active use of "contingent temporary protection" measures against each other in order to favor specific industries and prohibit certain imports (Freinkman et al. 2004), as well as the use of frequent trade embargoes and restrictions by Russia to express displeasure with the way political winds may be blowing in Kyiv.

Russia first used trade in this manner towards Ukraine early in the transition, repeatedly reducing or threatening to cut off energy supplies to Ukraine entirely from 1992 to 1994, in response to Ukraine's chronic arrears. While cutting off a customer who refuses to make payments is established as an appropriate action for a producer, Russia's use of trade quickly went beyond these early maneuvers, with trade threats leveraged in 1994 in a bid to obtain ownership of Ukrainian gas and oil facilities (D'Anieri 1999). As the 1990s progressed, Kyiv and Moscow often played

---

[21] Additional initiatives including Ukraine, such as the so-called GUAM organization (comprised of Georgia, Ukraine, Azerbaijan, and Moldova, hence the name) created in 1997, remain more talking shops than serious motivators for trade liberalization.

tit-for-tat in trade battles, including Ukraine's unilateral imposition of quotas on goods such as electric filaments and canvas in 1999, which resulted in Russia slapping antidumping sanctions on Ukrainian metal pipes (Freinkman et al. 2004). The use of trade escalated after the 2004 presidential elections and the Orange Revolution in a nonstop frenzy of accusations, some of which appeared to be karmic retribution: indeed, Ukraine received some of its own medicine in 2006, as "Russia tightened the rules of border crossing for Ukrainian border residents who carry agricultural products to Russia for sale. Before, up to 500 kg was allowed according to the simplified rules; according to the new rules, an official registration and license for export is required for such commercial activities," an approach that had found favor in Kyiv but was now to prove painful for Ukrainian small businesses (Zhurzhenko 2007:80). Additional measures, such as a ban on exports of livestock products to Russia on grounds of violating Russian veterinary legislation, appeared merely as a punitive move against Yushchenko, as Ukraine was Russia's biggest source of dairy products (Shportyuk and Movchan 2007).[22] "Gas wars" also renewed in the era of Orange, as two separate major economic conflagrations in 2006 and 2009 highlighted the use of gas pricing to disadvantage countries that were seen as moving away from Moscow's orbit (Pirani et al. 2009). While the election of Viktor Yanukovych led to a diminution of trade tensions between the two countries, due to Yanukovych's pro-Russian stance, a "low grade trade war" was still in effect even in 2011, as Russia pushed to collect a supposed $400 million debt from Tymoshenko's government (Spechler and Spechler 2013).

But while Russia was still utilizing its myriad of sticks, it was also introducing a carrot into the recipe, hoping to woo Ukraine and orient its trade towards the Russian-led "Eurasian Economic Union" (EaEU). The EaEU began life in concept in 2003 as the Single Economic Space (SES) comprised of Russia, Kazakhstan, Belarus, and Ukraine, but began to gather steam with the creation of a common tariff in 2009 and enactment of a Customs Union in 2010 amongst three of the four (Hartwell 2013b). Ukrainian leadership had always been wary of the SES concept, much as it was of the CIS (see above), but while Kuchma supported the idea in principle as a hedge against economic uncertainty, the Orange Revolution brought to power leaders who were much more interested in what the EU had to offer (Nygren 2007). From an economic standpoint, as

---

[22] By this point, Russia had expanded its use of trade as a weapon to several other countries, including most notably Georgia and Moldova.

well, simulations of trade using gravity models showed that Ukraine already was perhaps slightly overperforming in its trade with the other SES countries, and thus moves towards a customs union would likely not be beneficial (Shepotylo 2009).

It was not until Yanukovych came to power in 2010 that Ukraine was seen as seriously contemplating joining the Customs Union, a point that was raised at a joint press conference in November 2010 with Russian president Dmitry Medvedev (Bureiko 2013). But even with the tilt towards Russia that Yanukovych represented, at this point the EU appeared to be a more likely choice for Ukraine, as Yanukovych continued to insist in public upon a simple free trade agreement between the Customs Union and Ukraine rather than Ukrainian accession (Shumylo-Tapiola 2012). It was only as the move to the EU became more likely that Russia began to rely, once again, on pressure on Ukraine, starting with higher customs duties on Ukrainian products in 2011 and culminating in summer 2013 with a series of embargoes and lengthy customs procedures to convince Ukraine that it was better to be inside the EaEU rather than outside of it (Delcour and Wolczuk 2015). Feeling incredible heat from Russia and likely calculating it was in his own personal interest to cast his lot with Russia, Yanukovych backed Ukraine out at the last minute from signing the EU Association Agreement (more on this below) and threw his support behind the EaEU. While Yanukovych had been negotiating as early as 2010 to sell Ukraine's oil and gas infrastructure to Russia's Gazprom (Cameron and Orenstein 2012), the sell-out of the EU path came with a much steeper price, as Yanukovych accepted a treaty with Russia that nearly halved the price of gas imports and committed Russia to purchasing $15 billion worth of Ukrainian Eurobonds.[23] By this time, however, "Moscow's pressure on Ukrainian president Victor Yanukovych" had already resulted "in average Ukrainians and the elite rallying around the EU integration flag – if only to gain leverage vis-à-vis Russia" (Charap and Troitskiy 2013:57). The turn towards the EaEU thus precipitated the Maidan protests and eventually led to Ukraine moving much closer to the EU than to the EaEU, without Viktor Yanukovych. The EaEU similarly went ahead as planned without Ukraine on January 1, 2015, adding new members Armenia and Kyrgyzstan over the following eight months.

---

[23] See coverage of the deal from the BBC, "Russia Offers Ukraine Major Economic Assistance," December 17, 2013 (http://www.bbc.com/news/world-europe-25411118) and on Interfax Ukraine, "Ukraine to issue Eurobonds; Russia will purchase $15 bln, says Russian finance minister," same day, at http://en.interfax.com.ua/news/economic/182491.html.

Perhaps somewhat ironically, Ukraine had turned away from a supranational trade institution that was much closer to its own internal trade institutions, in order to tap a far greater market, a choice that would involve a need for undertaking the delayed institutional transformation in trade. This other institutional suitor for Ukraine, the European Union, was also involved with Ukraine from near the beginning of transition, as Ukraine was one of the first transition economies to sign a Partnership and Cooperation Agreement (PCA) with the EU in 1994 (although it did not come into force until 1997, see Åslund (2009), and the EU's Member States did not ratify it until 1998). The PCA, designed to be valid for ten years, "provide[d] reciprocal, legally binding commitments to ensure a dynamic development of two-way trade and investment flows [and laid] the foundation for broad economic, financial, social and cultural co-operation" (Schneider 2001:68). In tandem with technical assistance provided through the Technical Aid to the Commonwealth of Independent States (TACIS) program, the PCA was meant to demonstrate the EU's commitment to supporting democracy and market reforms in the east, albeit to a much lower extent than it was doing in Central Europe. In fact, much like the early CIS agreements, the PCA did not contain clauses establishing a free trade agreement, only an "evolutionary clause" that stipulated that such an FTA was possible and that, under the PCA, the two parties could discuss such movement (Hillion 2007). Moreover, unlike the EU accession process, which was underway as early as 1994 (for Poland), the PCAs never envisioned themselves as a path to EU membership, being explicitly crafted as a substitute for the membership track that other CEE countries were on (Kuzio 2006b). While other countries were signing Association Agreements, laying out the path for harmonization with the body of European law, the CIS countries were to settle for the vaguer tenets of the PCA.

A further shortcoming to note about the PCA was that, while it was excellent as a foundation statement of principles for the relations between the two partners, the PCA was less concrete on what needed to be done in order to reform Ukraine's trade institutions, lacking an action plan or mechanisms to help push further cooperation, as well as placing Ukrainian commodities at a much lower level of trade preferences than other agreements the EU had in place at the time (Shportyuk and Movchan 2007). Indeed, a major criticism of the PCA, as well as the EU's approach to Ukraine in general after the Orange Revolution and Euromaidan, was that it took an overly technocratic approach to the reform of trade institutions (as well as democracy promotion; see Dimitrova and Dragneva (2009)), focusing on the processes occurring within Ukraine rather than holistically looking at the institutions themselves. Ignored in the PCA was the fact that institutions are more than just the procedures that occur within an organization; they are the sum total of the external institutional environment, cultural factors, and prevailing "meta-rules" of the game (e.g., markets versus planning). By focusing narrowly on procedural issues rather than assisting broader cultural changes, the EU missed a valuable opportunity to help Ukraine reform. And, as seen in the trade sphere in this section, this meant that Ukraine continued along its old path of centralized trade control while denying that the EU was anything more than just a competing trade bloc (a pillar of Kuchma's vaunted and incoherent "multivector foreign policy," which attempted to establish good relations with all; see Kuzio (2006b) and Åslund (2009)).[24]

Much as with other reforms in Ukraine, once the initial hurdle of stabilization – in this case, the signing of the PCA – had been surmounted, not much else occurred to drive the country forward. To be fair, the stagnation of the EU-Ukraine relationship from the signing of the PCA to the Orange Revolution was not entirely (or even mostly) Ukraine's fault, as the EU dragged its feet repeatedly on further cooperation; as Kuzio (2006b:89) noted at the time, "under Kuchma, because both Russia and Ukraine were experiencing democratic regression, Western fears of offending Russia were more legitimate. The EU often used the argument that it could not invite Ukraine into membership negotiations without also inviting Russia." Having just absorbed ten new Member States, the largest number to ever enter simultaneously, in the 2004 wave of accession (and with a further two slated to accede in 2007), even the shift in Ukraine after the Orange Revolution could not catch the EU's attention. This reality was directly counter to Schneider's (2001:69) assertion that the "provisions of the PCA [we]re clearly designed to be only a stage in the rapprochement between Ukraine and the EU so that the evolution of the relationship would primarily depend on the way Ukraine would handle its political and economic transition to a democratic society and functioning market economy"; the Orange Revolution proved that the overall transition, after years of regression, was now on track, but even at this point, the EU was unable to extend further benefits (Kuzio (2006b) also notes that the failure of EU constitutional referenda contributed to the crisis atmosphere in Brussels). With the PCA lapsing, the EU shifted first towards

---

[24] Gawrich et al. (2010) also make the point that Kuchma was interested in the EU insofar as it would help to legitimize his own rule.

a "Common Strategy" in 1999, a procedure that was greeted with much disappointment in Kyiv, as it once again avoided an Association Agreement and also failed to deliver on a timeframe for an FTA (White et al. 2002). Ultimately, the EU crafted the European Neighborhood Policy (ENP) in 2003, an approach that was more tangible than the PCA in that it contained a tailored action plan for Ukraine and the promise of a new bilateral agreement that would initiate a comprehensive FTA between the two (Hillion 2007). Unfortunately, this instrument also fell short of Ukraine's desires after the Orange Revolution, placing Ukraine at the same level of importance as northern African states, Israel, and Russia (Kuzio 2006b), and still delaying the signing of an Association Agreement until some unspecified time in the future. Sasse (2008) also noted that, while more action-oriented than the PCAs, the ENP Action Plans remained vague, with little sense of what "success" would look like in measuring the institutional and administrative changes in Ukraine. Once again, at a crucial juncture in Ukraine's institutional development, the incentives from the EU that could have helped force these institutional changes were pushed down the road.

An area where the EU (as well as the United States) was active actually occurred outside of the EU umbrella, as the EU granted Ukraine "market economy" status in 2006 and championed Ukraine's accession to the WTO. Despite the hesitancy surrounding the opening of Ukraine's markets that even Yushchenko and Tymoshenko displayed, the country's accession to the WTO then created a basis from which discussions on a Deep and Comprehensive Free Trade Agreement (DCFTA) could finally be launched, in order to expand market access to the EU (Dimitrova and Dragneva 2009). By the time WTO accession became a reality in 2008, the foundation had already been laid for increased trade cooperation, mainly because the structural changes in the Ukrainian economy (no matter how slight) had returned growth to Ukraine and led to the EU leapfrogging Russia as Ukraine's largest trading partner. The Eastern Partnership program followed in 2009, setting Ukraine on the path for conclusion of a DCFTA, the purpose of which was to expedite Ukraine's approximation of EU trade legislation while at the same time lowering still-existing formal barriers to trade between the two partners. Indeed, as part of the agreement, Ukraine and the EU pledged to eventually eliminate nearly all of their trade duties (99.1 percent of Ukraine's import duties and 98.1 percent of the EU's by value are projected to be scrapped), although not every line item tariff will be immediately dismantled. Indeed, there is a long transition period envisaged for some goods under a "special regime," such as passenger cars and agricultural goods (which make up 27 percent of the EU's imports from Ukraine, as shown in Movchan and Shportyuk (2012)). Unfortunately, this long transition period, as with other economic institutional reforms that Ukraine has been hesitant to undertake, will likely be less beneficial for the development of both Ukraine's trade institutions and its economy than if the tariff regimes had been abolished entirely and immediately, in line with trade theory and practice (and as noted at the beginning of the transition by Havrylyshyn (1994)).

The slow pace of the EU in dealing with Ukraine meant that the negotiations for a DCFTA, as well as an Association Agreement (AA), occurred just as Ukraine was taking a step back from its wholeheartedly pro-EU stance and towards a more "balanced" approach, as practiced by Kuchma. Indeed, the DCFTA and AA procedures only gathered momentum after Viktor Yanukovych had been elected president, a reality that placed Yanukovych in a delicate situation as the prospect of the AA "raised a furor in the Kremlin" (Åslund 2013:1). Negotiations continued throughout 2011 and 2012 on the DCFTA, but the competing bloc of the EaEU made it clear that Ukraine had to choose one or the other, as the tariff schedules for the two trade groupings were (at least at that point) incompatible (Havilk 2014). Additional analyses by experts connected with the EaEU (specifically the Eurasian Development Bank (2012)) predicted catastrophe for the Ukrainian economy if it sided with the EU, noting the benefits of cheaper gas and how this would feed Ukrainian industry in an expanded EaEU. Moreover, the EU, always having a larger interest in Ukraine's democratization than necessarily its economic institutional reform, in December 2012 made the signing of the AA contingent on "complying with international standards of electoral practice, ending selective justice [i.e. the imprisonment of Tymoshenko], and 'implementing the reforms defined in the jointly agreed Association Agenda'" (Sherr 2013:5). This move towards creating a scorecard for Ukraine's institutional reforms put unprecedented power in the hands of the EU over a non–Member State, a move that Yanukovych likely felt was too difficult to satisfy, given his own proclivities. Thus, despite the fact that an AA was the long-term goal of Ukrainian foreign policy since Kravchuk, and with the pressure from Moscow noted above, Yanukovych pulled Ukraine out of the long-awaited Vilnius Summit at the end of November 2013 and cancelled the signing of the AA. In practical terms, the effect this would have had on trade would be the raising of Ukraine's external tariffs in line with the common EaEU tariff, meaning a higher cost on goods coming from Ukraine's largest trade partner (the EU), with a dismantling of tariffs with Belarus, Kazakhstan, and Russia. However, this reality was not to be, as the Euromaidan protests and toppling of Yanukovych reinvigorated the AA process, and the DCFTA was signed in June 2014 and entered into force in January 2016.

While formal barriers to trade, manifested as tariffs, have been on a steady path downward as part of the myriad of multilateral and bilateral negotiations that Ukraine has undertaken since independence, the prevalence of nontariff barriers (NTBs) has increased substantially and remains a threat to Ukraine's growth. Unlike Poland, which utilized tariffs as a lever of industrial policy, Ukraine has relied on NTBs, with their prevalence being the greatest manifestation of the institutional difficulties that Ukraine faces in developing trade. The various barriers to trade that Ukraine has enacted are both legion and multifaceted; a handy guide to the various NTBs is provided by Movchan and Shportyuk (2008) as being in one of three categories:

1. "Hard," or outright barriers to trade including quotas, licenses, and antidumping or competition-related barriers.
2. "Health," including sanitary and phytosanitary (SPS) regulations, technical standards, mandatory certification, and (important for agriculture) veterinary inspections.
3. "Customs," the administrative and paperwork requirements from the Customs Service at the border, including prepayment of customs fees and taxes before release of a shipment.

Over the past twenty-five years, Ukraine has made substantial use of each of these categories, but especially favored hard NTBs in the run-up to WTO accession. Unlike most countries, who tend to favor exports as an engine of growth but restrict imports on the misperception that imports will create hardships, Ukraine has been an equal opportunity discriminator, with a complex array of export controls maintained "to simply maintain opportunities for bureaucrats to extract rents from exporters" (Kamiński 1996:394). Indeed, politicians and bureaucrats have been instrumental as a lobby to retain restrictions on trade, a pattern that manifested itself in the years of economic crisis, as "in Ukraine in 1992 and 1993, hyperinflation and undervaluation of the *karbovanets* (the new national currency) paradoxically intensified domestic pressures for export restrictions, as political leaders argued that restrictions were necessary to prevent neighbors from massively buying underpriced Ukrainian products to the detriment of Ukrainian consumers" (Havrylyshyn 1994:176).[25] The extent of the state's involvement in such restrictions is shown by Kaufmann (1994), who calculated an "export restriction index" for Ukraine, showing that by the third quarter of 1993, approximately 95 percent of all exports from Ukraine were subjected to a quota or license regime (and at no point did this index dip below 70 percent – in fact, the number of restrictions increased as the economic crisis deepened). This is not to say that the Ukrainian authorities did not use NTBs in order to discriminate against foreign imports, as this trend was also particularly pronounced in the first decade of transition (Bodenstein et al. 2003) and continues to persist to this day.

Hard NTBs to trade (like their formal counterpart, tariff barriers) have diminished somewhat as a result of Ukraine's WTO membership but have not entirely disappeared. For example, a resolution by the Cabinet of Ministers in October 2006 to license grain exporters on the grounds of "food security" was quickly transformed in November of that year into a quota system, after resistance emerged from judicial entities and private actors within Ukraine (Crane and Larrabee 2007). This subsequent quota system, called "ineffective, inefficient, and non-transparent" by the World Bank country office (Cramon and Raiser, 2006), led to price rises in flour and bread and created a powerful deterrent to investment in the grain industry (as grain storage facilities, a capital-intensive investment, were already overwhelmed with unused grain stores that legally could not be exported). As part of Ukraine's accession to the WTO, it appeared that the quota system was finally finished, but in October 2010, the Cabinet of Ministers resurrected it with a further resolution requiring quotas and licenses for exporting grain (Krasnozhon 2011b). Eventually, the restrictions on grain exports that were established in 2010–2011 were transformed into export taxes and transformed again in 2012 into a "voluntary" Memorandum of Understanding (MoU) process (Götz et al. 2013). The MoU system, still in place today, is a way for the government (in the guise of Ministry of Agrarian Policy and Food) to set the extent of grain supply and export quantities in collaboration with major grain producers, a procedure that creates additional opportunities for rent-seeking and the stifling of competition.

---

[25] A similar anecdote is recalled in Åslund (2009:71), where he recounts then-president Kuchma arguing vehemently against the lifting of export restrictions by noting, "Don't you understand that the whole country will be empty!"

Quotas also still exist in areas considered crucial to national security, an expansive definition that allows the imposition of import quotas for steel pipes.

On the whole, however, accession to the WTO shone a spotlight on hard NTBs in Ukraine and forced, if not their abolition, then their adaptation into different forms. In reality, the difficulties in Ukraine's trade structure have shifted towards health and customs NTBs, especially in regard to sanitary and phytosanitary (SPS) barriers that create administrative difficulties in obtaining permission from state agencies to export. These SPS barriers are especially severe in the agricultural sphere, as Ryzhenkov et al. (2013) estimated that the 2,280 tariff lines of agricultural and related products in 2012 faced approximately 46,000 instances of non-tariff measures. A preliminary catalogue of Ukraine's NTBs, provided by Taran (2008:13) and focusing on the agricultural sector, notes that the most frequent measures utilized include:

- *Health:* mandatory certification across several goods, various SPS and technical barriers to trade (TBT) measures, state registration and permits for certain imports (e.g., pesticides), customs controls, discretionary and automatic licensing, and high certification and licensing fees.
- *Customs:* export duties (as noted above), export licensing, and "mandatory exportation of certain products processed under 'give-and-take' schemes."
- *State monopolies of certain goods:* including the export of ethyl alcohol and electricity, the import of natural gas (a major source of corruption), regulation of certain types of narcotics, and sole responsibility for export of arms and military equipment.

Disaggregating the extent of barriers further by sector, Ryzhenkov et al. (2013) note that live animals continue to face the highest amount of NTBs, likely due to the high phytosanitary constraints placed on import of livestock, while edible meat and fish also experienced approximately 10,000 separate nontariff measures combined in 2012 (Figure 5.14). Given the sensitive nature of these food and animal exports, and the desired increase in trade with the EU, it is unlikely that the number of NTBs will be decreasing in the near future. Additionally, Jakubiak et al. (2009) highlight the prevalence of TBTs in Ukraine, noting that 91.4 percent of the firms they interviewed needed to satisfy technical regulations just to sell on the Ukrainian market (as opposed to 92.8 percent who

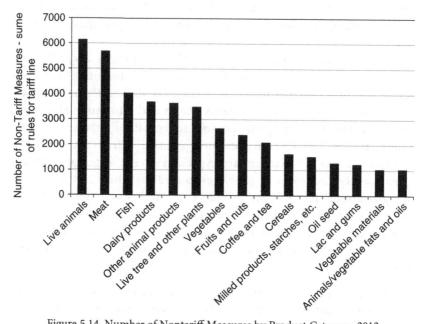

Figure 5.14 Number of Nontariff Measures by Product Category, 2012
Source: Ryzhenkov et al. (2013)

needed to satisfy standards to export to the EU); this incredibly high number of firms requiring technical permissions just to trade domestically perhaps suggests that the regulatory burden on Ukrainian businesses is impermissibly high.

Beyond SPS and health and safety concerns, the administrative barriers to trade at the border remain onerous. The customs administration of Ukraine has been highly resistant to change, even with WTO accession and substantial technical assistance from the European Union, World Bank, and USAID, and the overall pervasiveness of paperwork, formal procedures, and informal corruption at the borders (all couched in a framework of repeated interactions with state agencies) slows down the process of trade demonstrably and remains a source of rent-seeking behavior. This reality can be seen in a slew of research materials concerned with the business climate in Ukraine, starting with a report from the USAID BIZPRO project on export activities of Ukrainian companies (BIZPRO 2005), which found that nearly 22 percent of companies in the early 2000s considered customs procedures to be problematic, with a further 12.6 percent noting procedures and permits were the biggest issue to

Table 5.7 *Trading Across Borders in Ukraine, 2015*

Indicator	Ukraine	Europe & Central Asia	OECD
Documents to export (number)	8	7	4
Time to export (hours)	29	23.6	10.5
Cost to export (US$ per container)	1,880.00	2,154.50	1,080.30
Cost to export (deflated US$ per container)	1,880.00	2,154.50	1,080.30
Documents to import (number)	9	8	4
Time to import (days)	28	25.9	9.6
Cost to import (US$ per container)	2,455.00	2,435.90	1,100.40
Cost to import (deflated US$ per container)	2,455.00	2,435.90	1,100.40

Source: World Bank Doing Business 2015.

overcome while exporting. Similarly, a study by my own institute, the Center for Social and Economic Research (CASE) in Warsaw (Jakubiak et al. 2009), using a comprehensive questionnaire administered in 2004–2005, found that testing procedures for export to the EU were perceived as onerous, mainly because testing needed to be done on goods in both Ukraine and the EU (32 percent of respondents from small firms noted this as an issue). Porto (2005) also found that shipment across Ukraine from Moldova and other CIS countries in 2003 added approximately 4.34 percent of the total value of a shipment in additional costs, with the largest portion of these costs attributable to payments to customs officers (1.17 percent of value), border troops (0.48 percent of value), and border police (0.18 percent of value).

This state of affairs has unfortunately persisted to the present day, as evidenced by the World Bank's Doing Business report, which, for 2016 notes that Ukraine remains 109th in the world in "trading across borders" (up from 154th in 2015, see Table 5.7). The World Economic Forum's "Global Competitiveness Report" shows similar stagnation, as, in 2007–2008, the last year before accession, Ukraine was ranked 123rd (out of 131 countries) in the world in "prevalence of trade barriers," a number that improved slightly to 116th out of 140 in the 2015–2016 edition of the Report. While there is hope that the extensive barriers to trade, encapsulated in the myriad of permissions and corruption, will be removed via the DCFTA and the post-Maidan government, the institutional rot in agencies such as the Customs Administration will take some time to thoroughly remove.

The consequence of the continued prevalence of all types of NTBs, as well as other modes of state intervention into trade (especially taxation), has been the entrenchment of the unofficial economy in Ukrainian life. The shadow, grey, second, or informal economy (also known in some circles as "black markets") began under communism as a way to cope with the failings of socialist planning and the prevalence of shortages engendered by these economic institutions.[26] Estimates of the size of the informal economy throughout the entire USSR ranged from an exceedingly low bound of 10 percent, likely during the Stalinist years of repression, to a high of 40 percent during the stagnant Brezhnev and Andropov years and with the loosening of the Communist Party's grip under Gorbachev (Brezinski 1985); for Ukraine specifically, Johnson et al. (1997) estimate that the informal economy made up 12 percent of the republic's net material product in 1989, a similar size to other republics of the USSR, but had reached 25.6 percent by 1991. And although "participation in the second economy [was] a contravention of socialist morality [where] individual wants reign supreme ... leading to the rise of ostentation and conspicuous consumption," the small-scale and informal markets of Ukraine fulfilled a valuable role especially in food distribution but also in the provision of needed consumer goods (O'Hearn 1980:231).

The transition away from these communist economic institutions should have obviated the need for a large and economically significant black market, as the legalization of private commerce would have brought business into the light. However, while this occurred in other countries such as Poland, which saw the "black market" disappear during the transition as legitimate commerce was made legal, the countries of the former Soviet Union, especially Ukraine, saw the shadow economy actually expand. This state of affairs was due to a combination of factors inherited from the late Soviet period, as the authorities became less able to control all facets of economic life, but yet still continued to churn out rules and regulations regarding commerce and the manner in which it was to be conducted. In such a situation, incentives were high to avoid entering the official economy and incurring the myriad of costs that might make economic activity uneconomical, and the lack of administrative capacity of the government meant there were cracks that businesses could slip through. During the transformational recession and even beyond, much

---

[26] Russ Roberts of George Mason University has remarked accurately on several occasions that there are no such things as "black" markets; there are only markets.

as under communism, the shadow economy also fulfilled a valuable role in keeping economies moving, for, as a colleague of mine once noted about a similarly situated country as Ukraine (Azerbaijan, where I worked from 2010 to 2011), "if every law on the books is adhered to, this country would simply grind to a halt."[27] To put it another way, Åslund (2009) correctly pointed out that the reason that Poland did not have such problems with the informal economy was that most of its economy was already legal: without an extensive array of prohibitions, by definition any business apart from narcotics and weapons dealing was "official." Such a luxury did not exist in Ukraine after independence, much less before.

The economic crisis accompanying transition and the tightening of control over the economy was the first event to conspire to push commerce into the shadows in Ukraine, as regulatory burdens and tax changes especially accompanying the independence of the country, coupled with hyperinflation and macroeconomic mismanagement, led to a huge spike in underground activities (Thiessen 2003). Kaufmann (1994:63) noted that "a survey of private traders indicated that the share of their business outside of the official economy rose from 25 percent in 1992 to close to 75 percent in March 1994," while Johnson et al. (1997) estimated that, by 1995, the unofficial economy accounted for as much as 50 percent of Ukraine's GDP, or the same amount as the official economy. Even changes in tax rates, noted as the number one reason for the prevalence of the shadow economy, had little success in bringing this economy into the light, as tax changes in the late 1990s had only a modest effect on the size of the economy, showing that the regulatory burdens on commerce remained the driving factor (Thiessen 2003). Illustrative work on petty ("suitcase") traders in the Carpathian Mountains by Williams and Baláž (2002) reinforces this broader conclusion, with their research showing how the institutional basis for suitcase trade, laid in the late Soviet era, expanded after independence as petty traders used new regulations as an opportunity to find new markets and avenues around these rules. Moreover, the pervasiveness of the regulatory burden in Ukraine has meant that it is difficult to characterize the "typical" shadow economy participant, as small-scale traders came from all strata of society. Participation in the shadow economy in Ukraine has also not been limited to small-scale traders, as even when businesses operated in the official economy, they utilized dubious practices to escape the grabbing hand of government and hide their activities (Solomon and Foglesong 2000). One widespread example of

---

[27] Thanks are due to this unnamed colleague, who understood the value of incentives.

this was shown in Åslund (2009:167), as a spike in VAT fraud in exports in 2004 was precipitated by "Yanukovych's tax people decid[ing] to make a killing before the deluge"; anticipating a capricious response from the state in tax enforcement, businesses made rational decisions to falsify invoices rather than call attention to their (otherwise legal) activities. Similarly, many formal businesses in Ukraine during the 2000s employed workers informally to avoid taxation and other labor regulation scrutiny or paid their employees two separate incomes, one formal and one "envelope" or cash as a supplement that was beyond the reach of authorities (Williams and Round 2008).

The end result of the institutional moves against commerce and trade by the Ukrainian government has been a persistent influence of the shadow economy over the past twenty-five years, consistent across all metrics that have been proposed to measure the underground economy. Indeed, comparing these several different approaches to estimating the size of the informal economy in Ukraine, Bochi and Povoroznyk (2014) find that it has been remarkably resilient over the past twelve years, with estimates using Schneider's (2005) methodology showing the shadow economy hovering around 40 to 45 percent of GDP; estimates by the State Statistical Service are much lower, at nearly 18 percent of the economy, while electricity output methods pioneered by Kaufmann and Kaliberda (1996) are closer to 30 to 35 percent of the economy. As a comparison with its neighbors, using the Schneider (2005) method, Ukraine's informal economy in 2012 was almost double that of Poland's (44 percent to 25 percent) and a full 3.26 times higher than estimates for Germany at 13.5 percent (Vinnychuk and Ziukov 2013). The effects of this persistent underground economy have also had long-lasting effects on Ukraine's institutional development, as noted by Kuzio (2011b:94):

> An unwillingness to tackle corruption can be seen in the persistence over two decades of a permanent shadow economy roughly equal to half the economy.... A country with half of its economy in the underground inevitably experiences a large influence of political corruption over the political system and high levels of influence of organized crime over business. The shadow economy acts as a large, nontransparent source of funding for political parties during election campaigns.

In conclusion, even post-Maidan, Ukraine's trade and commercial institutions exhibit severe structural problems derived from an unwillingness to relinquish political control over economic processes. While it appears that Ukraine's foreign trade policy has finally chosen the path of liberalization with the Deep and Comprehensive Free Trade Area (DCFTA) starting its implementation in 2016, it is unknown if the institutions surrounding trade and commerce can reform to operate in a market environment. An advantage of the DCFTA is, in addition to eliminating nearly all of the tariff barriers between the EU and Ukraine, it will also allow for harmonization of NTBs and other "WTO-plus" provisions, such as trade in services, investment, procurement, and secondary regulations (Sushko et al. 2012). Moreover, the target of EU accession, not on the table for Ukraine, did allow for the convergence with European institutions for trade by the CEE countries in the 1990s – although Poland liberalized its trade institutions entirely endogenously – and it is possible that such an external goal can help to rally political will in Kyiv. However, the opportunity of WTO accession already has slipped by in terms of liberalizing Ukrainian trade institutions, and the delays in implementing the DCFTA (coupled with the EU's own on-again, off-again relationship with free trade) may not be enough to overcome decades, if not centuries, of the command-and-control mind-set. Similarly, for issues such as business regulation, the power rests with the Ukrainians themselves to make the necessary changes to lessen state intervention, but again, optimism for such a change may not survive the reality of Ukrainian history.

Monetary Institutions

Outside of the realm of property rights and trade and commerce, other economic institutions were also being built or spontaneously being created during the transition; one of these crucial institutions, non-existent during the communist era but with a pedigree before communism, included monetary institutions. Monetary institutions occupy a central place in modern market economies, not so much for their necessity (a large literature on free banking, including de Soto (1995), Hülsmann (1996), and Murphy (2013) questions the need for central banks), but for the reality that, if they are operated improperly, they have the capacity to ruin an entire economy. This final section will take a look at the monetary institutions of the region during the economic transformation and how their evolution resulted in better or worse economic outcomes in Poland and Ukraine.

In regard to monetary institutions, both Poland and Ukraine benefitted from beginning their transition at a time when the economics profession was reaching a consensus on the optimal institutional structure for conducting monetary policy. Indeed, while Poland and Ukraine were transitioning, a wealth of data and research was being produced regarding the effectiveness of central bank independence (CBI), the notion that monetary policy authorities should be insulated from political pressures. Early research on the conduct of monetary policy focused on "dynamic inconsistency theories of inflation" (Kydland and Prescott 1977), where a theoretical short-term boost to employment from inflation would offer a powerful enticement (often utilized) for policy makers to generate this inflation. To fight this suboptimal "equilibrium," one had to either limit the incentives for inflation, or, even more importantly, to tackle the issue head-on and remove the power to create this inflation. The original debate in this literature centered around the first option (limiting incentives), focusing on the issue of "rules versus discretion," and how limiting the discretion of an individual policy maker to inflate the money supply could be done through the creation of "binding" monetary rules (Barro and Gordon 1983). However, the notable conclusion of much of the work on policy rules was, no matter how well-crafted they were, policy makers could always fall prey to the political process (and their own incentives that derived from that process).

Thus, with people fallible and political pressures omnipresent, it was more important to shift away from the personalities running the monetary system and focus instead on the design of the institutions themselves (the second option). Research from Alesina (1988); Grilli, Masciandaro, and Tabellini (1991); and Cukierman (1992) thus posited that *de jure* independence led to more beneficial macroeconomic outcomes: further broken down, independence could be divided into two components, "goal independence" and "instrument independence" (Debelle and Fischer 1995), with "a central bank that is given control over the levers of monetary policy and allowed to use them has *instrument independence;* a central bank that sets its own policy goals has *goal independence*" (Fischer 1995:202). This distinction has also been fleshed out in the literature in regard to the desirability of one form of independence *vis-à-vis* the other. In Rogoff's (1985) framework, a conservative central banker would have both goal and policy independence, but the need for accountability means that it would be desirable for a polity to give a central bank instrument independence but remove goal independence (the entire point of imposing inflation aversion in an institutional framework).

Even with technical assistance from international organizations and the theoretical and empirical guidance of economists, designing such an independent monetary authority was difficult for countries such as Poland and Ukraine that had little modern experience of monetary policy. In this,

Poland perhaps had an edge due to its institutional memory before communism. The National Bank of Poland (*Narodowy Bank Polski* or NBP), as an institution and as noted in Chapter 3, had been operating continuously in Poland since its chartering in 1924 as the Bank of Poland, but had been re-constituted as a Soviet-style monobank in 1945 (when it was renamed NBP). During the communist era, as noted above, the central bank functioned as a clearinghouse for payments and the credit allocation mechanism for the entire economy, as well as overseeing the dismantling of the zloty as a controvertible currency. Given the importance of the monobank to the entire socialist system, there was almost no move towards liberalization before the democratic transition gained momentum, with a large array of foreign exchange restrictions in place and only slow and halting liberalization beginning in 1987 regarding holding of foreign currency (Chrabonszczewska 1994). The "new" NBP was created out of the monobank structure at the beginning of 1989 under the National Bank Act and the Banking Law for commercial banks, simultaneously with the creation of Poland's financial sector institutions; as part of the disentangling of the state from the financial sector, nine commercial banks were hived out of the monobank, with the NBP remaining as the sole monetary authority in the new democratic Poland (Kowalski et al. 1999). After Poland's elections and as an accompaniment to the broader-based liberalization reforms, the Act was revised at the end of 1989 and combined with an action plan for transforming the NBP into a modern central bank in January 1990 (Ugolini 1996).

The new NBP faced several pressing issues as, with every other transition economy (including Ukraine, as we will see), Poland suffered from severe monetary distortions accrued during communism, distortions that were exposed once rapid price liberalization was pursued after 1990. The largest was repressed inflation, a phenomenon that was part and parcel of the communist system; in fact, Nuti (1989:107) noted at the start of the transition to capitalism that inflation was rampant in Poland during the transition to communism and under communist rule, as "retail prices in Poland increased by 62.4% between 1946 and 1949, and again by 78.5% in 1950–53." While there was a period of relative price stability from 1957 to 1972 (as there was also in Western economies), Poland then saw open inflation in the 1970s and 1980s, driven by wage increases and higher retail prices, with retail prices increasing 101 percent in 1982 alone (ibid.). With Poland's high foreign debts and budget deficits during the 1980s, and a central bank firmly under control of the Party, the only way to finance these deficits became by use of the printing press, a weakness common not only to socialist states but one responsible for creating a huge monetary overhang (Commander 1992). In fact, Balcerowicz (1994c:74) notes that "repressed inflation in Poland was far more dramatic [at the beginning of the transition] than in Hungary and Czechoslovakia and similar to that in Bulgaria and Romania." Thus, the NBP was faced with latent inflation, held down only by an administered price system which was failing in setting prices, due to the piecemeal liberalization also undertaken in the 1980s. Last but not least, as Gottschalk and Moore (2001:25) note, "inflationary pressures were aggravated by pervasive wage-price indexation and the absence of hard budget constraints on unreformed enterprises," meaning that the NBP's attempts to fight inflation would be hampered by the very same wage structure that was responsible for inflation in the 1980s.

The stabilization of inflation in Poland after the freeing of prices is a story told extensively elsewhere, with Lipton and Sachs (1990) providing an excellent view from the inside and Poznanski (2012) providing a more recent and comprehensive overview. It is important to note, as we did at the beginning of this chapter, that inflationary stabilization followed a similar process to other facets of macroeconomic stabilization, in that it was done quickly and with a conscious design to prevent long-term toleration of inflation (Balcerowicz 1994c). Compared to other transition countries, Poland's inflation levels peaked much earlier (in 1989, a full year before Hungary and four years before Ukraine), following a restrictive monetary policy to wring out excess liquidity combined with full internationalization of the currency (Lane 1992). For our purposes, and from the institutional standpoint, the NBP at this time had substantial instrument independence, a reality that it took advantage of in implementing Poland's inflation stabilization program; as Huerski et al. (2003) point out, the NBP's anti-inflationary policy shifted in its use of instruments over the period 1991 to 1994, from a fixed zloty exchange rate as the nominal anchor (Lane 1992) to an administrative credit ceiling in 1992 to normal interest rate policy and open market operations from 1993 onward (Brzozowski 2004).

However, given the need for stabilization and the imperatives of transition (as well as fighting the persistent inflation shown in 1993 and 1994), the NBP had little goal independence, as all policies undertaken by the government were facing in the same direction as the NBP. In fact, the original Act on the National Bank from 1989 gave the NBP a dual mandate, charging it with both "strengthening the national currency and cooperating in the implementation of national economic policy" (Myślak 2013:175). Based on this mandate, and using some of the most common indicators for measuring central bank independence – the index devised by Cukierman, Webb, and Neyapti (1992, hereafter CWN) – we can see that central bank independence remained rather low in Poland until reforms in 1997 and 1998 that greatly increased the independence of the NBP. Indeed, Huterski's et al. (2003) calculations updating CWN put Poland's index of legal independence at 0.72 (out of 1) in 1994, increasing to 0.75 in 1997, 0.86 in 1998, and 0.95 in 1999. Other indices are not as favorable to Poland's central bank independence, such as Dincer and Eichengreen (2014), but all agree that the trend in independence has been on a gradual upward trajectory (Jurek and Marszałek 2008).

Indeed, a jump in independence between 1997 and 1998, captured in the Huterski et al. (2003) ranking, is attributable to several developments. In the first and most important instance, a new Act on the National Bank was passed in August 1997 and came into force on January 1, 1998, greatly increasing the independence of the central bank in both goals and instruments, and restructuring the organization of the NBP (Huterski et al. 2003). One of the key provisions of the Act was the creation of a Monetary Policy Council, similar to the Board of Governors of the Federal Reserve in the United States, with members serving a term of six years, longer than anyone would serve in the government and thus building in some insulation from political pressure (Myślak 2013). At the same time, the Act also prohibited central bank lending to the government (Huterski et al. 2003), a codicil that was delayed in its implementation for a year but also served to sever political links between the NBP and the government (and was a far cry from the proposal from the left-wing parties in the *Sejm*, who wanted the NBP to be able to "purchase government securities from the Treasury during a single financial year to a total amount not exceeding 5% of the estimated budgeted revenue for the year" (Myślak 2013:175). Finally, in regard to financial-sector development in Poland, the Act removed all restrictions on foreign banks, creating new supervisory authority in the NBP to oversee financial institutions (Havrylchyk 2006).

As part of its evolution in monetary policy, and also in preparation for EU accession, the NBP shifted towards an inflation-targeting regime after 1999, adopting its own goals independent of the government (Gottschalk and Moore 2001). In this, the NBP was aided by various international institutions, which had their own interest in keeping the NBP independent and on-track as part of the EU accession process; in fact, Epstein (2005:188) claims that World Bank consultant Robert Clarke "provided the commentary, language, and arguments for the NBP to defend itself against political pressure." However, perhaps explaining the disagreement in central bank independence rankings noted above, just because the NBP had legal independence did not mean that there was no pushback against the Bank's monetary policy independence, as two bills introduced in the *Sejm* in 2001 attempted to curtail the NBP's independence and make it more supportive of the government's economic policy (Myślak 2013). The attempts were defeated, not least after Leszek Balcerowicz made an impassioned plea in the *Sejm* calling the bills a "retreat from adjusting Polish law to EU standards" and casting doubt on if the government wanted the opposition to have more power over monetary policy when they inevitably came to power (Balcerowicz 2002). The defeat of the amendments in 2001 and 2002 only temporarily halted, but did not stop, the push towards greater governmental control over the bank. In 2005, after Poland had been in the EU for a year, another bill was pushed in the *Sejm* to both force the bank to support the government's economic policies and allow for the dismissal of the head of the NBP if the *Sejm* did not accept the report of the Monetary Policy Council (the bill also called for reducing the size of the Council, from nine members to six). This approach, bringing parliamentary procedure to the central bank (in effect, allowing for dismissal after a vote of no confidence in the president), while novel, unnecessarily blurred the lines of responsibility between the NBP, the executive, and the legislature, and the bill was defeated in 2007 when a parliamentary committee found the proposals to be illegal (Myślak 2013).

The NBP, in an attempt to circumvent additional moves to curtail its independence, has instead attempted to improve its transparency, including publication of staff inflation projections (starting in 2004) and the minutes of Council meetings (beginning in 2007), in addition to improving communications with the public (Łyziak 2013). Additional measures taken during this time also skirted the obligations of Poland in reference to its EU accession, as the fact that "draft monetary policy guidelines may be subject to forwarding to the Council of Ministers and the Minister of Finance" is not in line with the Treaty establishing the European Commission or the Statute of the European System of Central Banks (Bini Smaghi 2008:450). In general, however, the institutional mechanisms within the NBP have been very successful in insulating Council members from political pressure, a fact borne out by empirical analysis from Vivyan (2010); this work shows that parties in power nominate Council members based on their ideological similarity, but in practice, no matter the candidate nominated, it is very difficult to shift the voting position of these candidates once they are approved. In this manner, the independence of the NBP rests in its ability to integrate outsiders into the mission of the Bank.

Despite a successful history of gradually increasing central bank independence and, especially, defeating inflationary outcomes, the monetary policy institutions in Poland are at a crossroads. In the first instance, a debate now rages in Poland regarding the eventual adoption of the euro as the national currency, and whether or not the country is a) ready for it and b) willing to go the route of Finland, Ireland, Greece, or Spain in giving up its monetary independence for an uncertain future. Indeed, could it be possible that Poland would follow the same path as Germany, that is, a country with a history of effective monetary institutions and a strong currency that gave it up in the name of "Europe" and is now subjected to a policy of weakness and inflation-by-design? Such an eventuality, of surrendering the hard-won institutional gains of postcommunism, is perhaps ironically championed by the same institution that contributed to those gains, namely the NBP, while it is opposed by a clear majority of Poles: 76 percent of those polled in October 2014 were against Poland's joining the Eurozone, with 38 percent very opposed and 38 percent mildly opposed, according to German research firm GfK (Bermingham 2014). Whether or not the institutional apparatus of the NBP is subsumed to the European Central Bank (as it must be, sooner or later, according to Poland's terms of accession) and how such a transfer of institutional sovereignty takes place will be crucial for determining the path of Poland's economy in the future.

The second issue regarding monetary institutions in Poland, before any potential loss of institutional sovereignty, is the actual degree of independence of the NBP from the government, at least in terms of this independence being a two-way street. A scandal erupted in 2014, with NBP Governor Marek Belka caught on tape in July 2013 openly discussing with the interior minister the removal of then–finance minister Jacek Rostowski in exchange for an easing of monetary policy before the election (Brinded 2014). While the episode caused a major outcry in the *Sejm* and in the popular press, the NBP's vaunted independence won in 2002 and 2005 meant that Belka could not be ousted by the government of Prime Minister Tusk unless he was gravely ill (and, indeed, Tusk publicly supported Belka as speaking out of "concern for the country"). This prohibition did not mean that the government could not investigate the possibility of attempted undue influence of a government minister, but Tusk and his government instead focused its energies on an investigation on who was responsible for the taping of the conversation (Radio Poland 2014). This sordid episode, and the manner in which the government appeared to curry favor with the NBP, has highlighted the possibility that central banks may have insulated themselves so much from political pressure that they themselves are now the source of pressure on government, especially in Poland. This issue, an unexplored one in the economics literature, needs further research, but it will be interesting to see how it plays out in a transition context. If a central bank can demand changes in government and link its monetary policies to personnel in the executive branch, it is a clear sign that the institutional constraints to the bank may not be as well designed as previously thought.

It is highly unlikely that such problems will manifest themselves in Ukraine, given the fact that the country started much later in the process of building an independent central bank and has moved much more slowly than Poland. Technically, Ukraine also had a history of central banking (even longer than in Poland): in 1917, on the eve of independence, the Central Rada passed a law "On transformation of the Kiev office of the Russian State Bank into the Ukrainian State Bank," uniting the former Russian State Bank, the Noble Land Bank, and the Peasant Land Bank (Katchanovski et al. 2013). The Ukrainian State Bank was charged with creating a new national currency, distinct from the Russian ruble (which Ukraine had been utilizing since the seventeenth century), and began issuing *karbovanets* in 1917 and amalgamating them into *grivna* (the precursor of the modern *hryvnia*, with 100 *karbovanets* to a *grivna*) in 1918 (Kuzniatsou 2008). However, the constant change of leadership in Ukraine and the proliferation of money that accompanied the Russian Civil War made it impossible for the State Bank to effectively operate as a sovereign entity, especially given that there was no "nation" for it to supply (Khodjakov 2014). The brief monetary experiment of a national currency ended in 1921 as the Russian ruble returned in large quantities with the Bolshevik armies, and by 1922 as the Soviet Union instituted a major currency reform to institutionalize the ruble in the Ukrainian SSR. From this point, lasting from 1922 to 1987, the State Bank was abolished in favor of the *Gosbank* (USSR State Bank), a situation that made Ukraine highly dependent on Moscow for any financial decisions, as there were no branches of *Gosbank* in Kyiv (Kibita 2013). In the 1980s, tentative moves were made under *perestroika* to constitute the National Bank of Ukraine (NBU) as a republic branch of *Gosbank*, but with no ability to issue currency and no regulatory functions over the economy, becoming merely a bank on par with five other state-owned institutions in Ukraine (such as the State Savings Bank and the Bank of Industry; see Shen (1996)).

It was not until March 1991, several months before independence, that the Rada passed a law endowing the NBU with the responsibilities of a normal modern central bank, and the NBU was established as a new entity in July of that year (Åslund 2009). Unfortunately, the design of the NBU did not differ substantially from the functions of the Soviet central bank system, in that the NBU was almost entirely subordinated to the Communist-dominated Rada and the president and had little (if any) independence. Indeed, Maliszewski (2000) notes that Ukraine's central bank independence through its first decade was the lowest of any country in the entire transition space, as the 1991 Act granted neither goal nor instrument independence, a problem compounded by the fact that the NBU's budget (as well as monetary policy) had to be approved by the Rada. Schwödiauer et al. (2006) quantified this (lack of) independence using the CWN (1992) methodology, showing that the NBU scored lowest on facets related to the total lack of limitations on lending to the government and regarding the head of the Bank (especially in regard to dismissal of the president and the lack of any prohibitions on the president from holding another office in government); as Lybek (1999) noted, the 1991 Law did not actually stipulate the term for which the Bank president was supposed to serve.

The issue of lack of independence was exacerbated by issues regarding the issuance of currency: Ukraine was doubly handicapped due to its long history of subservience under Russia, making central banking a missing part of the country's institutional memory, but also due to its long history of reliance on other country currencies rather than its own. Despite, as just noted, the brief experiment with an independent currency from 1918 to 1921, the Ukrainian lands had actually moved from using gold to złoty to rubles in a fairly seamless transition over its history, with the foray into currency over three years an infinitesimal speck compared to the long experience of reliance on foreign monetary institutions. Thus, designing a national currency for a newly independent state would require additional effort, as it would have to be created entirely from scratch. This left Ukraine in an odd position during the beginning of its transformation, having the role of issuer of credit rubles (to enterprises and banks) but without the authority to issue cash rubles, as this still solely resided at the Central Bank of the Russian Federation in Moscow (Petryk 2006).

With such a distortion of incentives (the ability to issue unlimited credit but without having to redeem it in cash), the NBU promptly "started issuing virtually unlimited amounts of ruble credits at low interest rates, which guaranteed hyperinflation" (Åslund 2009:3). Indeed, "high inflation was a defining feature of Ukraine's experience" (Lissovolik 2003:2), as the Communist-dominated Rada stymied attempts at reform and the NBU was utilized as a way to generate cheap credits for failing Soviet-era institutions. This political push peaked in spring 1993, as the parliament pushed back against Prime Minister Kuchma's economic stabilization attempts and voted to have the NBU provide direct credit to collective farms and "needy" enterprises (Wolchik 2000). From 1992 to 1993, nearly 100 percent of the government's budget deficit was financed by the NBU, along with "direct credits to the coal industry during the miners' strikes in Donbas, credits to the agro-industrial sector, [and] for mutual settlements," (Petryk 2006:6), a reality that caused the money supply to jump 20 percent and inflation to peak at over 10,000 percent in December 1993. As the central bank independence literature predicted, lack of independence had translated into a populist legislature and presidential aspirants using the NBU to create bursts of inflation and large-scale lending to the government, a ploy utilized to obscure real structural problems in the Ukrainian economy. In the words of Viktor Yushchenko (2000:79), former head of the Central Bank and then–prime minister, "the first years of independence were characterized by attempts to plug financial gaps hastily by pouring out meaningless money."

As an additional distortion to the economy, the NBU's behavior under the thumb of the Rada from 1991 to 1994 had a negative effect on inflationary expectations, as businesses began to price in ever-higher inflation into their own calculations. Indeed, the Ukrainian economy soon became wise to the strategies of the NBU, with Kaufmann (1994:60) noting that "an announcement of monetary emission by the National Bank of Ukraine (NBU) would be quickly interpreted by economic agents as an imminent inflationary surge"; while this did no good for the economy, it did help enhance "understanding of the link between monetary emission and inflation [so that] a constituency for monetary restraint gradually emerged." This also created a healthy distrust of the government's own figures, as "government-provided economic information was widely distrusted. The only reliable source of information about inflation which was broadly available to firms and households was the changing price level itself" (Kravchuk 1998:65). Even when the government did provide information, it came far too late in a world in flux, as "money aggregates [were] calculated and published by the NBU with a considerable time lag, normally 45 days" (Volosovych 2002:294). Schwödiauer et al. (2006) went even further as to note that the experience of hyperinflation in Ukraine in the early 1990s may have helped coalesce public opposition to inflation, as the excess of the ruling party and the untrustworthiness of the NBU galvanized support for harder monetary policies. However, as with so many of Ukraine's economic institutions, this opposition was unable to dramatically influence the day-to-day workings of the NBU within the first decade of independence.

A key reason for this was that, even though the NBU was not independent in dealing with the government and mostly was required to slavishly follow government directives, it had no such shackles in dealing with the public. And, much as the rest of the economy and the government's approach to it, the NBU retained a command-and-control approach towards the monetary and financial sectors, with "administrative control by the National Bank of Ukraine (NBU) over foreign currency purchases ... requiring vetting, registration, and prepayment of contracts. Further, additional limitations have been imposed on companies' holding of hryvnia settlement accounts. Also, there are short time limits to settle export payments" (Kaufmann 1997:244). Indeed, rather than handling a unified exchange rate (which was somewhat successful in early 1993 but then reversed), the NBU presided over several different exchange rates while holding monopoly power as the manager of auctions for foreign exchange, a position that also created rent-seeking opportunities (Wolchik 2000). At the same time, credit was tightly controlled and "all of the credit resources continued to be allocated administratively by the National Bank of Ukraine [with] nearly 98 percent of credits ... lent to two commercial banks – Agrobank 'Ukraina' and 'Prominvestbank' – at interest rates that were several times lower than the official discount rate of 240 percent" (Pynzenyk 1994:199). In short, the NBU was in place to assist the government of Ukraine with its economic policies, but by no means was it there to assist in making the economy better as viewed from the private sector. In fact, the financial policy implemented by the NBU remained highly protectionist, closed, centrally planned, and, for lack of a better word, Soviet. There is no other way to describe the lack of institutional reform in this key institution over the first decade of transition, as the NBU was a tool of government policy and patently unable to reform.

The continued macroeconomic issues engendered by the NBU also created major problems in transitioning to a new currency: while, as noted above, the ruble acted as a de facto currency that the NBU abused in issuing credit, the Russian Central Bank undertook reforms in 1992 that made it much more difficult for CIS countries to settle their currency accounts and helped the Russians to control their monetary supply (Petryk 2006). Moreover, a point of pride for Kravchuk in state-building was to introduce a new Ukrainian currency; this also became a macroeconomic imperative and issue of policy sovereignty, as the Ukrainian economy's rubleization meaning that Ukraine was beholden to Russia's attempts at price liberalization even as it forsook its own (Shen 1996). Following these issues, a new currency, named the *karbovanets* in a nod to the last currency issued by an independent Ukraine, was issued in November 1992. Unfortunately coming in lieu of instead of accompanying price liberalization, the new currency only fueled the hyperinflation of 1993. As noted above, the Ukrainian economy became savvy rather quickly on inflationary expectations, meaning that "Ukraine showed evidence of such *karbovanets*-avoiding behavior throughout the early 1990s [and this] flight from money – effectively a reduction in demand for money balances – reduce[d] the inflation tax base, which necessitate[d] increasingly large monetary emissions in order to reap an equivalent amount of inflation tax revenue" (Kravchuk 1998:58). As de Ménil (1997:493) noted, Ukrainians wanted currency, just not their own, as "when one adds to the unofficial supply of US bills, an already large volume of official, hard currency banking deposits (806 million dollars' worth in March 1996), one arrives at an estimate of the share of foreign currencies in the total money supply of between 56 and 73 per cent." It took until 1996 that a concerted effort by the NBU, including credit ceilings, re-unification of the exchange rate, and improvement of the system of interbank settlements, allowed the macroeconomic stability for the introduction of the new and improved *hryvnia* at an exchange rate of 100,000 to 1 with the *karbovanets* (Petryk 2006).[28]

Even with the monetary reform, as with the constitution, several attempts were made to reform the Law on the NBU over an eight-year span beginning in 1991, but these reforms failed to garner much political support for turning off the monetary spigot. It was not until the Law on the National Bank of Ukraine was passed in May 1999, accompanied

---

[28] Yushchenko (2000:81) also notes that "It would not have been wise to introduce our new permanent national money at a time when hyperinflation would have immediately destroyed its credibility. When hyperinflation was over, it then took some time to create a sufficient degree of confidence to ensure acceptance of the hryvnia."

by a full liberalization of the exchange rate after the imposition of capital controls during the Russian crisis of 1998, when the NBU moved towards some semblance of independence (Yushchenko 2000). The key driver of this independence was the prohibition of direct lending to the government by the NBU, along with the prohibition on the president of the NBU holding any other government offices (this was coupled with a lengthening of the term of the head of the NBU to five years). Underscoring the changes under the Law, Schwödiauer et al. (2006) rated central bank independence in Ukraine from 1999 to 2005 as 0.73 (out of 1) on the Cukierman scale, a 135 percent improvement over its score of 0.31 from 1991 to 1999. Moreover, at this point, the NBU began to exert some influence over the government, as former NBU head Yushchenko moved over to become prime minister under Kuchma.

On the heels of these changes and the long-delayed macroeconomic stabilization, Ukraine saw its first growth in the early 2000s. Unfortunately, while the NBU was better insulated from political *pressures*, it was not protected from the same political *volatility* that has plagued Ukraine. After it took a decade for the institutional apparatus of the NBU to finally be put in place, the exigencies of the rest of the Ukrainian institutional system began to intrude and create difficulties in the maintenance of monetary policy. As Duenwald et al. (2005:6) noted, "during the tumultuous presidential elections in late 2004, the National Bank of Ukraine (NBU) lost about one-fourth of its international reserves, and liquidity pressures emerged for the banking system when households withdrew 17 percent of their total deposits." Additional moves towards a fixed exchange rate were seen by some as too tight to cope with the continued macroeconomic pressures that Ukraine faced (Petryk 2006), while the fiscal pressures accompanying the Yushchenko government and especially the threat of re-privatization continued to stymie the investment climate, making it much more difficult for the NBU to remain as guarantor of the hryvnia and simultaneously fight inflation. At the same time, while the NBU had statutory independence (and much as was to happen after 2010 in the Rada), Yushchenko (as a former NBU Head) and the then-head of the NBU were very close throughout the Orange presidency; this reality meant that Yushchenko had much influence over NBU policy and exerted undue influence, with "rent-seeking pressure on the National Bank from the presidential secretariat continu[ing] until the end of Yushchenko's presidency" (Kudelia 2012:424).

Ironically, while the global financial crisis gave Ukraine another huge blow, erasing many of the growth gains of the early 2000s via inflation, the NBU showing its own independent streak in resetting a lower peg to the U.S. dollar in 2011 (Barisitz and Fungáčová 2015). However, the cozy relationship between the NBU and the presidency evidenced during the Orange Revolution was to return during the Yanukovych presidency, as NBU head Serhiy Arbuzov was one of Yanukovych's "Family" and well-known for his tight connections with other Yanukovych cronies (Kuzio 2012b). Indeed, much as during Yushchenko's term, during the entirety of the Yanukovych presidency there was far less overt pressure on the NBU, with the NBU instead using its relationship with the executive to carve out its own sphere of influence; Stewart (2013:207) relates the tale of Arbuzov authoring "a draft law in which he proposed exempting the NBU from its obligation to follow public procurement procedures when managing foreign exchange reserves or printing money," a situation where "an extremely high-ranking government official has clearly indicated his willingness to meddle with the public procurement rules and to do so to benefit the agency he himself was running." Since the main instrument political institutions utilized to influence the economy (and to enrich themselves) was either the budgetary process or administrative fiat, the pressures on the NBU came from normal monetary moves rather than from direct political influence. This is not to say that the NBU did not pursue its own goals independently of the government, as Åslund (2013:7) noted that, when global bond prices started rising in 2013, "the National Bank of Ukraine pursued ever stricter currency regulations and high interest rates, which have killed investment and economic growth but brought inflation to zero." However, much as with the rest of the government under Yanukovych, an additional mandate for enrichment of high-ranking NBU staff appeared to have been added to its mandate to fight inflation and stabilize the currency.

With Yanukovych's deposal and the return of crisis economics to Ukraine, as of the writing of this chapter, the NBU has continued to function as an independent monetary authority but has faced its most difficult challenge yet, managing the stability of the currency in the face of foreign invasion, loss of Crimea, and promised but as-yet-unmaterialized reforms. The loss of the fairly rigid exchange rate peg due to the crisis was caused by rapid loss of confidence in the Ukrainian government to manage the crisis, coupled with capital flight in the face of possible Russian invasion; much as was done in 2008, the NBU instituted capital controls in 2014 to staunch this flight and prevent monetary collapse (Barisitz and

Fungáčová 2015). While the capital controls were now, as before, a blunt instrument that enabled further administrative meddling in the economy, the bigger challenges to the Ukrainian economy will be fought on other fronts than monetary policies. At the very least, the signals from the Poroshenko government are that the NBU will remain an independent institution, even though the goals of the NBU in staving off systemic collapse comport with the government's own goals of retaining Ukrainian sovereignty. It will take some time to see if the NBU can survive in a prolonged crisis situation, as the political pressure for easing may be unbearable should the Russian invasion continue, and the example of the Orange Revolution shows that not all reform-minded governments actually support central bank independence. In this case, the short institutional history of central bank independence may once again be overwhelmed by the forces of history.

PRELIMINARY CONCLUSIONS

In one sense, much as the earlier chapters were unbalanced in favor of Poland, due to Ukraine's lack of independence or viability as a sovereign entity, this chapter on transition was also unbalanced, but in favor of Ukraine. This was unfortunately not due to Ukraine being inherently more interesting, but because Poland appeared to get many of its institutions right at a very early stage of the transition process. Indeed, by relative measures (including distance from the start of transition or compared against each other), Poland has outperformed Ukraine in institutional change by huge margins. This is not to say that Poland is the exemplar of institutional change, as, when compared to other countries or examined in absolute levels, the country has many more improvements to make, as in property rights or business freedom/commercial institutions. As shown in my earlier work (Hartwell 2013a), Poland has also actually seen some slippage in its institutions from the heady early days of transition, as normal political processes began to erode economic freedoms. On the whole, however, and considering the history of Poland in the twentieth century, under siege, under occupation, and under communism, Poland made remarkable progress in building economic institutions.

In contrast to Poland, which saw economic and political reforms working hand in hand to shift expectations and thus engender a new institutional reform path, Ukraine was not as successful in its own economic institutional reforms. For the vast majority of the transition period, Ukraine retained a system that relied on government planning and intervention, retarding any institutional development in the long term in favor of short-term gains for the primary political actors in the system. Instead of bold moves towards a market economy, Ukraine's transition incrementally pushed the market back into the unofficial economy, with little progress on any of the economic institutions needed to actually start (much less complete) a transition. In many ways, even the building blocks of transition were pushed off to a later date, as stabilization came later than elsewhere, and only in a most tenuous manner; when time came to face the multiple institutional crises that were plaguing the country, some tape, string, and a new coat of paint were applied to old institutions but no substantive changes were made until the edifice collapsed. In short, where we may see failures in Poland's transitional policies, for every misstep Poland made it appears that Ukraine made three. This incomplete transition, and the continued resistance to "allowing" the necessary economy institutions to flourish (see, for instance, the continued agricultural land sale moratorium) may be a theme recurring from the country's past, but it has large ramifications for the future as well.

Taking the recent experience of the two countries into account, the next, and final, chapter will try to derive some conclusions on the interplay of political and economic institutions in the post-transition landscape of Central and Eastern Europe. Is the weight of history a burden that these two countries cannot escape? Or do the events of recent years mean that path-dependent institutions have a rare opportunity to find a new path?

References

Alesina, A. (1988). Macroeconomics and Politics. *NBER Macroeconomics Annual.* Cambridge: MIT Press, pp. 13–62.

Allard, C. (2009). *Competitiveness in Central-Europe: What Has Happened Since EU Accession?* IMF Working Papers No. 09/121.

Allina-Pisano, J. (2004). Sub rosa resistance and the politics of economic reform: Land redistribution in post-soviet Ukraine. *World Politics*, 56(4), pp. 554–581.

Arel, D. (2001). Kuchmagate and the demise of Ukraine's geopolitical bluff. *East European Constitutional Review*, 10(2/3), pp. 54–59.

Åslund, A. (1994). Comment on "Macropolicies in Transition to a Market Economy: A Three-Year Perspective," by Balcerowicz and Gelb. *World Bank Economic Review*, 8(suppl. 1), pp. 45–55.

(1995). Eurasia letter: Ukraine's turnaround. *Foreign Policy*, 100, pp. 125–143.

(2003). *A Foreign Trade Policy Strategy for Ukraine.* Kyiv: United Nations Development Programme.

(2005a). Comparative Oligarchy: Russia, Ukraine and the United States. *CASE Network Studies and Analyses*, No. 296.

(2005b). The economic policy of Ukraine after the Orange Revolution. *Eurasian Geography and Economics*, 46(5), pp. 327–353.

(2007). *How Capitalism Was Built: The Transformation of Central and Eastern Europe, Russia, and Central Asia.* Cambridge: Cambridge University Press.

(2009). *How Ukraine Became a Market Economy and Democracy.* Washington DC: Peterson Institute for International Economics.

(2013). *Ukraine's Choice: European Association Agreement or Eurasian Union?* Petersen Institute for International Economics Policy Brief No. 13–26.

Åslund, A., Boone, P., Johnson, S., Fischer, S., and Ickes, B. W. (1996). How to stabilize: lessons from post-communist countries. *Brookings Papers on Economic Activity*, 1, pp. 217–313.

Auyezov, O., and Miles, T. (2012). Ukraine denies protectionism as 58 nations attack WTO tariffs plan. Reuters, www.reuters.com/article/2012/10/16/us-ukraine-wto-idUSBRE89F16C20121016. Accessed January 12, 2016.

Balcerowicz, L. (1994a). Economic transition in central and Eastern Europe: Comparisons and lessons. *Australian Economic Review*, 27(1), pp. 47–59.

(1994b). Poland. In Williamson, J. (ed.), *The Political Economy of Policy Reform*. Washington DC: Peterson Institute for International Economics.

(1994c). Transition to the market economy: Poland, 1989–93 in comparative perspective. *Economic Policy*, 9(19), pp. 72–97.

(1995). *Socialism, Capitalism, Transformation.* Budapest: Central European University Press.

(2002) *Wystąpienie prof. Leszka Balcerowicza w debacie sejmowej w sprawie projektów nowelizacji ustawy o NBP* [Speech given by Professor Leszek Balcerowicz in the parliamentary debate on the draft amendment to the Act on the NBP]. Available on-line at: http://www.nbp.pl/home.aspx?f=aktualnosci/wiadomosci_2002/sejm_230502.html. Accessed June 8, 2016.

Balcerowicz, L., Blaszczyk, B., and Dąbrowski, M. (1997). The Polish way to the market economy, 1989–1995. In Woo, W. T., Parker, S., and Sachs, J. D. (eds.), *Economies in Transition: Comparing Asia and Europe.* Cambridge, MA: MIT Press, pp.131–160.

Barisitz, S., and Fungáčová, Z. (2015). *Ukraine: Struggling banking sector and substantial political and economic uncertainty.* Bank of Finland Institute for Economies in Transition (BOFIT) Policy Brief No. 2/2015.

Barro, R. J., and Gordon, D. B. (1983). Rules, discretion and reputation in a model of monetary policy. *Journal of Monetary Economics*, 12(1), pp. 101–121.

Beck, A. (2005). Reflections on policing in post-soviet Ukraine: A case study of continuity. *The Journal of Power Institutions in Post-Soviet Societies*, 2, http://pipss.revues.org/294.

Beck, A., and Chistyakova, Y. (2004). Closing the gap between the police and the public in post-Soviet Ukraine: a bridge too far? *Police Practice and Research*, 5(1), pp. 43–65.

Benoit, K., and Hayden, J. (2004). Institutional change and persistence: the evolution of Poland's electoral system, 1989–2001. *Journal of Politics*, 66(2), pp. 396–427.

Bermingham, F. (2014). Poland's people 'do not want to join the euro.' *International Business Times*, October 22.

Berg, A., and Sachs, J. (1992). Structural adjustment and international trade in Eastern Europe: The case of Poland. *Economic Policy*, 7(14), pp. 118–173.

Bini Smaghi, L. (2008). Central bank independence in the EU: From theory to practice. *European Law Journal*, 14(4), pp. 446–460.

Birch, S. (1995). The Ukrainian parliamentary and presidential elections of 1994. *Electoral Studies*, 14(1), pp. 93–99.

(2008). Ukraine: Presidential power, veto strategies and democratization. In Elgie, R., and Moestrup, S. (eds.), *Semi-presidentialism in Central and Eastern Europe*. Manchester: Manchester University Press, pp. 219–238.

BIZPRO (2005). *Export Activities of Ukrainian Companies*. Kyiv: USAID.

Blacksell, M., and Born, K. M. (2002). Private property restitution: the geographical consequences of official government policies in Central and Eastern Europe. *The Geographical Journal*, 168(2), pp. 178–190.

Blazyca, G. (2001). Poland's place in the international economy. In Rapacki, R., and Blazyca, G. (eds.), *Poland Into the New Millennium*. London: Edward Elgar Publishing.

Blejer, M., and Škreb, M. (2006). Stabilization after five years of reform: Issues and experiences. In Blejer, M., and Škreb, M. (eds.), *Macroeconomic Stabilization in Transition Economies*. Cambridge: Cambridge University Press.

Boban, D. (2007). "Minimalist" concepts of semi-presidentialism: are Ukraine and Slovenia semi-presidential states? *Politička misao*, 44(5), pp. 155–177.

Bobek, M. (2008). The fortress of judicial independence and the mental transitions of the Central European judiciaries. *European Public Law*, 14(1), pp. 99–123.

Bochi, A., and Povoroznyk, V. (2014). *Shadow Economy in Ukraine: Causes and Solutions*. Kyiv: International Centre for Policy Studies.

Bodenstein, T., Plümper, T., and Schneider, G. (2003). Two sides of economic openness: non-tariff barriers to trade and capital controls in transition countries, 1993–2000. *Communist and Post-Communist Studies*, 36(2), pp. 231–243.

Bodnar, A., and Bojarski, Ł. (2012). Judicial independence in Poland. In Siebert-Fohr, A. (ed.), *Judicial Independence in Transition: Strengthening the Rule of Law*. Berlin: Springer, pp. 667–738.

Bogovin, A.V. (2006). *Ukraine: Country Pasture/Forage Resource Profile*. Rome: Food and Agriculture Organization (FAO), available on-line at: www.fao.org/ag/agp/AGPC/doc/Counprof/PDF%20files/Ukraine.pdf. Accessed February 26, 2015.

Bouzaher, A., Carriquiry, A., and Jensen, H. H. (1994). *The Structure of Ukrainian Agriculture: Comparative Efficiency and Implications for Policy Reform*. Center for Agricultural and Rural Development (CARD), Iowa State University, Staff Report 94-SR 72.

Brada, J. C. (1996). Privatization is transition–Or is it? *Journal of Economic Perspectives*, 10(2), pp. 67–86.

Brenton, P., Gros, D., and Vanadille, G. (1997). Output decline and recovery in the transition economies: causes and social consequences. *Economics of Transition*, 5(1), pp. 113–130.

Brenton, P., Sheehy, J., and Vancauteren, M. (2001). Technical barriers to trade in the European Union: importance for accession countries. *JCMS: Journal of Common Market Studies*, 39(2), pp. 265–284.

Brezinski, H. (1985). The second economy in the Soviet Union and its implications for economic policy. In Gaertner, W., and Wenig, A. (eds.), *The Economics of the Shadow Economy*. Berlin: Springer, pp. 362–376.

Brinded, L. (2014). Poland's central bank governor marek belka refuses to quit despite leaked tape scandal. *International Business Times*, June 17.

Brown, J. D., Earle, J. S., and Telegdy, A. (2006). The productivity effects of privatization: Longitudinal estimates from Hungary, Romania, Russia, and Ukraine. *Journal of Political Economy*, 114(1), pp. 61–99.

Brzezinski, M. F. (1993). The emergence of judicial review in Eastern Europe: The case of Poland. *The American Journal of Comparative Law*, 41(2), pp. 153–200.

Brzezinski, M. F., and Garlicki, L. (1995). Judicial review in post-communist Poland: The emergence of a Rechtsstaat. *Stanford Journal of International Law*, 31, pp. 13–59.

Brzozowski, M. (2004). *Identifying central bank's preferences: the case of Poland*. Göteborg University. School of Business, Economics and Law Working Papers in Economics No. 143.

Buck, T., Van Frausum, Y., and Wright, M. (1996). The process and impact of privatization in Russia and Ukraine. *Comparative Economic Studies*, 38(2–3), pp. 45–69.

Buckwell, A., and Tangermann, S. (1999). Agricultural policy issue of European integration: The future of direct payments in the context of Eastern Enlargement and the WTO. *MOCT-MOST: Economic Policy in Transitional Economies*, 9(3), pp. 229–254.

Bureiko, N. (2013). The Cooperation Between the EU and Ukraine in the Period of Intensifying Integration Processes in the Post-Soviet Area. *EURINT Proceedings*, 1, pp. 364–373.

Burilkov, A. (2015). *Oligarch vs. Nationalist: Ukraine's 2014 Parliamentary Elections*. German Institute of Global and Area Studies (University of Leibnitz) Focus Paper No. 2.

Cameron, D. R., and Orenstein, M. A. (2012). Post-Soviet Authoritarianism: The Influence of Russia in Its "Near Abroad." *Post-Soviet Affairs*, 28(1), pp. 1–44.

Charap, S., and Troitskiy, M. (2013). Russia, the West and the integration dilemma. *Survival*, 55(6), pp. 49–62.

Chrabonszczewska, E. (1994). Convertibility and the exchange-rate regime in Poland. *Russian and East European Finance and Trade*, 30(6), pp. 28–39.

Christensen, R. K., Rakhimkulov, E. R., and Wise, C. R. (2005). The Ukrainian Orange Revolution brought more than a new president: What kind of democracy will the institutional changes bring? *Communist and Post-Communist Studies*, 38(2), pp. 207–230.

Clague, C., Keefer, P., Knack, S., and Olson, M. (1996). Property and contract rights in autocracies and democracies. *Journal of Economic Growth*, 1(2), pp. 243–276.

Cole, D. H. (1998). Poland's 1997 Constitution in Its Historical Context. *Saint Louis-Warsaw Transatlantic Law Journal*, 1, pp. 1–43.

Commander, S. (1992). Inflation and the transition to a market economy: an overview. *The World Bank Economic Review*, 6(1), pp. 3–12.

Compton, R. A., and Giedeman, D. C. (2011). Panel evidence on finance, institutions and economic growth. *Applied Economics*, 43(25), pp. 3523–3547.

Cramon, S.V., and Raiser, M. (2006). *The Quotas on Grain Exports in Ukraine: ineffective, inefficient, and non-transparent*. World Bank Country Office Ukraine Note, no. 38596, www-wds.worldbank.org/external/default/WDSContentServer/WDSP/IB/2007/02/09/000310607_20070209130442/Rendered/PDF/385960ENGLISH0UA0Wheat0quota01PUBLIC1.pdf. Accessed December 22, 2015.

Crane, K., and Larrabee, F. S. (2007). *Encouraging Trade and Foreign Direct Investment in Ukraine.* Santa Monica, CA: Rand Corporation.

Csáki, C., and Lerman, Z. (1997). *Land reform in Ukraine: the first five years.* World Bank Discussion Paper No. 371, August.

Cukierman, A. (1992). *Central Bank Strategy, Credibility, and Autonomy.* Cambridge: MIT Press.

Cukierman, A., Webb, S., and Neyapti, B. (1992). Measuring the Independence of Central Banks and its Effect on Policy Outcomes. *World Bank Economic Review,* 6(3), pp. 353–398.

D'Anieri, P. (1999). *Economic Interdependence in Ukrainian-Russian Relations.* Albany: State University of New York Press.

(2005). What has changed in ukrainian politics? Assessing the implications of the orange revolution. *Problems of Post-Communism,* 52(5), pp. 82–91.

Darden, K. (2001). Blackmail as a tool of state domination: ukraine under kuchma. *East European Constitutional Review,* 10(2/3), pp. 67–71.

De Melo, M., Denizer, C., Gelb, A., and Tenev, S. (2001). Circumstance and choice: The role of initial conditions and policies in transition economies. *The World Bank Economic Review,* 15(1), pp. 1–31.

De Ménil, G. (1997). The volatile relationship between deficits and inflation in Ukraine, 1992-1996. *Economics of Transition,* 5(2), pp. 485–497.

(2000). From Hyperinflation to Stagnation. In Åslund, A., and De Ménil, G. (eds.), *Economic Reform in Ukraine: The Unfinished Agenda.* New York: M.E. Sharpe, pp. 49–77.

De Ménil, G., and Woo, W.T. (1994) Introduction to a Ukrainian debate. *Economic Policy,* 9(supplement), pp. 9–15.

De Soto, J. H. (1995). A critical analysis of central banks and fractional-reserve free banking from the Austrian school perspective. *The Review of Austrian Economics,* 8(2), pp. 25–38.

De Souza, L. V., Schweickert, R., Movchan, V., Bilan, O., and Burakovsky, I. (2006). Now so near, and yet still so far: Relations between Ukraine and the European Union. In de Souza, L.V., and Havrylyshyn, O. (eds.), *Return to Growth in CIS countries.* Berlin: Springer, pp. 144–190.

Delcour, L., and Wolczuk, K. (2015). Spoiler or facilitator of democratization? Russia's role in Georgia and Ukraine. *Democratization,* 22(3), pp. 459–478.

Dimitrova, A., and Dragneva, R. (2009). Constraining external governance: interdependence with Russia and the CIS as limits to the EU's rule transfer in the Ukraine. *Journal of European Public Policy,* 16(6), pp. 853–872.

Dincer, N. N., & Eichengreen, B. (2014). Central bank transparency and independence: updates and new measures. *International Journal of Central Banking,* March, pp. 189–253.

Diuk, N. (2014). Finding Ukraine. *Journal of Democracy,* 25(3), pp. 83–89.

Dollar, D., and Kraay, A. (2003). Institutions, trade, and growth. *Journal of Monetary Economics,* 50(1), pp. 133–162.

Douglass, A. I. (1972). East-West Trade: The Accession of Poland to the GATT. *Stanford Law Review,* 24(4), pp. 748–764.

Drabek, Z. (1996). The stability of trade policy in the countries in transition and their integration into the multilateral trading system. *The World Economy,* 19(6), pp. 721–745.

Drabek, Z., and Brada, J. C. (1998). Exchange rate regimes and the stability of trade policy in transition economies. *Journal of Comparative Economics*, 26(4), pp. 642–668.

Duenwald, C. K., Gueorguiev, N., and Schaechter, A. (2005). *Too much of a good thing? Credit booms in transition economies: The cases of Bulgaria, Romania, and Ukraine.* International Monetary Fund Working Paper No. 05/128.

Dunin-Wasowicz, S., Gorzynski, M., and Woodward, R. (2002). Integration of Poland into EU global industrial networks: the evidence and the main challenges. Centre for the Study of Economic & Social Change in Europe, UCL School of Slavonic & East European Studies Working Paper No. 16.

Duryea, S., Marquéz, G., Pagés, C., Scarpetta, S., and Reinhart, C. (2006). For better or for worse? Job and earnings mobility in nine middle-and low-income countries. *Brookings Trade Forum*, pp. 187–209.

Dyczok, M. (2006). Was Kuchma's censorship effective? Mass media in Ukraine before 2004. *Europe-Asia Studies*, 58(2), pp. 215–238.

Elborgh-Woytek, M. K., and Lewis, M. M. (2002). *Privatization in Ukraine: Challenges of assessment and coverage in fund conditionality.* International Monetary Fund Policy Discussion Paper No. 02/7.

Elgie, R. (1999) The Politics of Semi-presidentialism. In Elgie, R. (ed.) *Semi-Presidentialism in Europe.* Oxford: Oxford University Press, pp. 1–21.

(2004). Semi-presidentialism: concepts, consequences and contesting explanations. *Political Studies Review*, 2(3), pp. 314–330.

Ellis, M. (1994). Drafting Constitutions: Property Rights in Central and Eastern Europe. *Yale International Law Journal*, 19(1), pp. 196–201.

Elster, J. (1993). Constitution-making in Eastern Europe: Rebuilding the boat in the open sea. *Public Administration*, 71(1–2), pp. 169–217.

Eppinger, M. E. (2015). Property and Political Community: Democracy, Oligarchy, and the Case of Ukraine. *The George Washington International Law Review*, 47(4), pp. 825–891.

Epstein, R. (2005). Diverging effects of social learning and external incentives in Polish central banking and agriculture. In Schimmelfennig, F., and Sedelmeier, U. (eds.), *The Europeanization of Central and Eastern Europe.* Ithaca, NY: Cornell University Press, pp. 178–198.

Eremenko, I., Mankovska, N., and Dean, J. W. (2004). Will WTO membership really improve market access for Ukrainian exports? In Burakovsky, I., Handrich, L., and Hoffmann, L. (eds.), *Ukraine's WTO Accession: Challenge for Domestic Economic Reforms.* Heidelberg: Physica-Verlag HD, pp. 167–188.

Estrin, S., Gelb, A., and Singh, I. (1995). Shocks and adjustment by firms in transition: A comparative study. *Journal of Comparative Economics*, 21(2), pp. 131–153.

Estrin, S., Nuti, D. M., and Uvalic, M. (2000). The impact of investment funds on corporate governance in mass privatization schemes: czech republic, poland and slovenia. *MOCT-MOST: Economic Policy in Transitional Economies*, 10(1), pp. 1–26.

Eurasian Development Bank (2012). *Comprehensive Assessment of the Macroeconomic Effects of Various Forms of Deep Economic Integration of Ukraine and the Member States of the Customs Union and the Common Economic Space.* Astana: Centre for Integration Studies Report No. 1.

European Bank for Reconstruction and Development (2006). *Life in Transition Survey 2006*. London: EBRD Press.

Feld, L. P., and Voigt, S. (2003). Economic growth and judicial independence: cross-country evidence using a new set of indicators. *European Journal of Political Economy*, 19(3), pp. 497–527.

Ferrara, F., Herron, E.S., and Nishikawa, M. (2005). *Mixed Electoral Systems: Contamination and Its Consequences*. Basingstoke: Palgrave Macmillan.

Fidrmuc, J., Huber, P., and Michalek, J. J. (2001). Poland's accession to the European Union: Demand for protection of selected sensitive products. *MOST: Economic Policy in Transitional Economies*, 11(1), pp. 47–70.

Fischer, S., and Gelb, A. (1991). The Process of Socialist Economic Transformation. *Journal of Economic Perspectives*, 5(4), pp. 91–105.

Forestiere, C. (2010). Political Volatility and Governance in East Central Europe. *Slavic Review*, 69(4), pp. 903–924.

Fortin, J. (2010). A tool to evaluate state capacity in post-communist countries, 1989–2006. *European Journal of Political Research*, 49(5), pp. 654–686.

Freinkman, L., Polyakov, E., and Revenco, C. (2004). *Trade performance and regional integration of the CIS countries*. World Bank Working Paper No. 38.

Frishberg, A. (1995). Privatization in the Ukraine. *International Business Lawyer*, 23(6), pp. 251–257.

Frydman, R., Rapaczynski, A., and Earle, J.S. (1993). *The Privatization Process in Russia, Ukraine, and the Baltic States*. Oxford: Oxford University Press.

Frye, T. (1997). A Politics of Institutional Choice Post-Communist Presidencies. *Comparative Political Studies*, 30(5), pp. 523–552.

Fukuyama, F. (1989). The end of history? *The National Interest*, Summer, pp. 3–18.

Futey, B. A. (1996). Comments on the Constitution of Ukraine. *East European Constitutional Review*, 5(2–3), pp. 29–34.

Gács, J. (1994). Trade Liberalization in the CSFR, Hungary, and Poland: Rush and Reconsideration. In Gács, J., and Winckler, G. (eds.), *International Trade and Restructuring in Eastern Europe*. Heidelberg: Springer Physica-Verlag, pp. 123–151.

Gadowska, K. (2010). National and international anti-corruption efforts: the case of Poland. *Global Crime*, 11(2), pp. 178–209.

Garlicki, L. L. (1997). The presidency in the new Polish constitution. *Eastern European Constitutional Review*, 6(2–3), pp. 81–89.

GATT (General Agreement on Tariffs and Trade)(1992). *Draft Report of the Working Party on the Renegotiation of the Terms of Accession of Poland*. Geneva: GATT Secretariat.

Gawrich, A., Melnykovska, I., and Schweickert, R. (2010). Neighbourhood Europeanization through ENP: the case of Ukraine. *Journal of Common Market Studies*, 48(5), pp. 1209–1235.

Gill, G. (2003). *Democracy and Post-Communism: Political Change in the Post-Communist World*. New York: Routledge.

Glock, B., Häussermann, H., and Keller, C. (2007). Social and spatial consequences of the restitution of real estate. In Stanilov, K. (ed.), *The Post-Socialist City*. Dordrecht: Springer Netherlands, pp. 191–214.

Goh, C. C., and Javorcik, B. S. (2007). Trade protection and industry wage structure in Poland. In Harrison, A. (ed.), *Globalization and Poverty*. Chicago: University of Chicago Press, pp. 337–372.

Gomułka, S., and Jasinski, P. (1994). Privatisation in Poland 1989–1993: Policies, Methods and Results. In Estrin, S. (ed.), *Privatisation in Central and Eastern Europe*. London: Longmans, pp. 218–251.

Gottschalk, J., and Moore, D. (2001). Implementing inflation targeting regimes: The case of Poland. *Journal of Comparative Economics*, 29(1), pp. 24–39.

Götz, L., Goychuk, K., Glauben, T., and Meyers, W. H. (2013). *Export restrictions and market uncertainty: Evidence from the analysis of price volatility in the Ukrainian wheat market*. Annual Meeting of Agricultural and Applied Economics Association, August 4–6, Washington, DC.

Grilli, V., Masciandaro, D., and Tabellini, G. (1991). Political and Monetary Institutions and Public Financial Policies in the Industrial Countries. *Economic Policy*, 6(13), pp. 341–392.

Guriev, S., and Sonin, K. (2009). Dictators and oligarchs: A dynamic theory of contested property rights. *Journal of Public Economics*, 93(1), pp. 1–13.

Gwiazda, A. (2008). Party patronage in poland the democratic left alliance and law and justice compared. *East European Politics & Societies*, 22(4), pp. 802–827.

Hagemejer, J., Makarski, K., and Tyrowicz, J. (2015). Unprivatizing the pension system: the case of Poland. *Applied Economics*, 47(8), pp. 833–852.

Handrich, L. (2004). Ukraine on the way to WTO membership. In Burakovsky, I., Handrich, L., and Hoffmann, L. (eds.), *Ukraine's WTO Accession: Challenge for Domestic Economic Reforms*. Heidelberg: Physica-Verlag HD, pp. 1–2.

Haran, O. (2011). From Viktor to Viktor: democracy and authoritarianism in Ukraine. *Demokratizatsiya*, 19(2), pp. 93–110.

Hare, P. (2001). Trade policy during the transition: lessons from the 1990s. *The World Economy*, 24(4), pp. 433–452.

Hartwell, C.A. (2013a). *Institutional Barriers in the Transition to Market: Explaining Performance and Divergence in Transition Economies*. Basingstoke: Palgrave Macmillan.

(2013b). A Eurasian (or a Soviet) Union? Consequences of further economic integration in the Commonwealth of Independent States. *Business Horizons*, 56(4), pp. 411–420.

(2015). Baudrillard Goes to Kyiv: Institutional Simulacra in Transition. *Journal of Economic and Social Thought*, 2(2), pp. 92–105.

Harvey, F. (2006). Elasticity between the cadastre and land tenure: Balancing civil and political society interests in Poland. *Information Technology for Development*, 12 (4), pp. 291–310.

Havlik, P. (2014). Vilnius eastern partnership summit: milestone in EU-Russia relations–not just for Ukraine. *Danube*, 5(1), pp. 21–51.

Havrylchyk, O. (2006). Efficiency of the Polish banking industry: Foreign versus domestic banks. *Journal of Banking & Finance*, 30(7), pp. 1975–1996.

Havrylyshyn, O. (1994). Reviving Trade amongst the Newly Independent States. *Economic Policy*, 9(19), pp. 172–190.

Havrylyshyn, O., Miller, M., Perraudin, W., Aven, P., and von Hagen, J. (1994). Deficits, inflation and the political economy of Ukraine. *Economic Policy*, 9(19), pp. 354–401.

Hillion, C. (2007). Mapping-Out the New Contractual Relations between the European Union and Its Neighbours: Learning from the EU–Ukraine 'Enhanced Agreement'. *European Foreign Affairs Review*, 12(2), pp. 169–182.

Holmberg, S. (2003). Are political parties necessary? *Electoral Studies*, 22(2), pp. 287–299.

Hülsmann, J. G. (1996). Free banking and the free bankers. *The Review of Austrian Economics*, 9(1), pp. 3–53.

Huterski, R., Nicholls, R., and Wiśniewski, Z. (2003). Central Bank Independence in Poland. In Harrison, B., and Healey, N. (eds.), *Central Banking in Eastern Europe*. New York: Routledge, pp. 193–223.

Ishiyama, J. T., and Kennedy, R. (2001). Superpresidentialism and political party development in Russia, Ukraine, Armenia and Kyrgyzstan. *Europe-Asia Studies*, 53(8), pp. 1177–1191.

Jakubiak, M., Maliszewska, M., Orlova, I., Rokicka, M., and Vavryschuk, V. (2009). *Non-tariff barriers in Ukrainian export to the EU*. Warsaw: Center for Social and Economic Research (CASE) Network Report No. 68.

Jasiewicz, K. (2000). Dead ends and new beginnings: the quest for a procedural republic in Poland. *Communist and Post-Communist Studies*, 33(1), pp. 101–122.

Johnson, D.C., Albergo, G., Green, D., Mitchell, J.K., Myachin, V., Sagers, M., Sellers, E.M., and Vanous, J. (1993). Recent Economic Development in the 15 Former Soviet Republics. In Kaufman, R. F., and Hardt, J. P. (eds.), *The Former Soviet Union in Transition*. Armonk, New York: M.E. Sharpe, pp. 913–949.

Johnson, S., Kaufmann, D., and Shleifer, A. (1997). The unofficial economy in transition. *Brookings Papers on Economic Activity*, 2, pp. 159–239.

Johnson, S., McMillan, J., and Woodruff, C. (2002). Property Rights and Finance. *American Economic Review*, 92(5), pp. 1335–1356.

Jurek, M., and Marszałek, P. (2008). Monetary and exchange rate policy in Poland after 1990–relationship and prospects of coordination. *Poznan University of Economics Review*, 8(2), pp. 26–48.

Kamiński, B. (1996). Factors Affecting Trade Reorientation of the Newly Independent States. In Kamiński, B. (ed.), *Economic Transition in Russia and the New States of Eurasia*. Armonk, NY: M.E. Sharpe, pp. 384–416.

(1999). *The EU factor in the trade policies of Central European countries*. World Bank Policy Research Working Paper No. 2239.

Kantorowicz, J., and Garoupa, N. M. (2014). An Empirical Analysis of Constitutional Review Voting in the Polish Constitutional Tribunal, 2003–2014. Rotterdam Institute of Law and Economics (RILE) Working Paper Series, (2014/08).

Karatnycky, A. (2005). Ukraine's Orange Revolution. *Foreign Affairs*, 84(2), pp. 35–52.

Katchanovski, I., Kohut, Z.E., Nebesio, B.Y., and Yurkevich, M. (2013). *Historical Dictionary of Ukraine*. Lanham, MD: Scarecrow Press.

Kaufmann, D. (1994). Diminishing Returns to Administrative Controls and the Emergence of the Unofficial Economy: A Framework of Analysis and Applications to Ukraine. *Economic Policy*, 9(19), pp. 52–69.

(1997). The missing pillar of a growth strategy for Ukraine: reforms for private sector development. In Lenain, P., and Cornelius, P. (eds.), *Ukraine: Accelerating the transition to market.* Washington DC: International Monetary Fund, pp. 234–274.

Kaufmann, D., and Kaliberda, A. (1996). Integrating the unofficial economy into the dynamics of post-socialist economies. In Kaminski, B. (ed.), *Economic Transition in Russia and the New States of Eurasia, Vol. 8.* New York: M.E. Sharpe, pp. 81–120.

Khodjakov, M.K. (2014). *Money of the Russian Revolution: 1917–1920.* Newcastle-on-Tyne: Cambridge Scholars Publishing.

Kibita, N. (2013). *Soviet Economic Management Under Khrushchev: The Sovnarkhoz Reform.* New York: Routledge.

Kiss, K., and Sidenko, V. R. (1992). Ukraine on the Way toward Economic Stabilization and Independence. *Eastern European Economics,* 31(2), pp. 65–93.

Knack, S., Kugler, M., and Manning, N. (2003). Second-generation governance indicators. *International Review of Administrative Sciences,* 69(3), pp. 345–364.

Kołodko, G. W. (2004). *Transition to a market system: Gradualism versus radicalism.* Transformation, Integration and Globalization Economic Research (TIGER), Kozminski University, Working Paper No. 60.

Kojder, A. (2004). Corruption in Poland: symptoms, causes, scope and attempted counter-measures. *Polish Sociological Review,* 146, pp. 183–202.

Kolankiewicz, G. (1994). Consensus and competition in the eastern enlargement of the European Union. *International Affairs,* 70(3), pp. 477–495.

Kondratowicz, A., and Okólski, M. (2013). The Polish Economy on the Eve of the Solidarity Take-over. In Kierzkowski, H., Okólski, M., and Wellisz, S. H. (eds.), *Stabilization and Structural Adjustment in Poland.* New York: Routledge, pp. 7–28.

Konończuk, W. (2015). *Oligarchs after the Maidan: the old system in a 'new' Ukraine.* Center for Eastern Studies (OSW) COMMENTARY, February 16.

Kornai, J. (1994). Transformational Recession: The Main Causes. *Journal of Comparative Economics,* 19(1), pp. 39–63.

Koslosky, D. R. (2009). Toward an Interpretative Model of Judicial Independence: A Case Study of Eastern Europe. *University of Pennsylvania Journal of International Law,* 31(1), pp. 203–255.

Kowalski, T., Staniszewska, D., and Wihlborg, C. (1999). Institutional and Macroeconomics Developments and Operational Efficiency of Polish Banks in 1994-1997. *Raporty. Opracowania. Referaty/Akademia Ekonomiczna w Poznaniu,* 10, pp. 154–175.

Krasnozhon, L.O. (2011a). Property rights and farm efficiency: evidence from Ukraine. *Economic Change and Restructuring,* 44(4), pp. 279–295.

(2011b). Robbing the breadbasket. *Kyiv Post,* May 26, www.kyivpost.com/opinion/op-ed/robbing-the-breadbasket-306124.html.

(2013). Political economy of agricultural market reform in ukraine: "good bye lenin." *Journal of Private Enterprise,* 29(1), pp. 119–140.

Kravchuk, R. S. (1998). Budget deficits, hyperinflation, and stabilization in ukraine, 1991–96. *Public Budgeting & Finance,* 18(4), pp. 45–70.

Kubiak, A. (2004) *Opinia publiczna i poslowie o korupcji. Raport z badan* [Public Opinion on Corrupt: A Research Report].Warsaw: Program Przeciw Korupcji.

Kubicek, P. (1994). Delegative democracy in Russia and Ukraine. *Communist and Post-Communist Studies*, 27(4), pp. 423–441.

(2001). The limits of electoral democracy in Ukraine. *Democratization*, 8(2), pp. 117–139.

Kudelia, S. (2012). The sources of continuity and change of Ukraine's incomplete state. *Communist and Post-Communist Studies*, 45(3), pp. 417–428.

(2014). The house that Yanukovych built. *Journal of Democracy*, 25(3), pp. 19–34.

Kuzniatsou, S. (2008). Symbolism of money: finances and historical consciousness of Ukraine, Lithuania and Belarus. *Палітычная сфера* [Political Sphere], 11, pp. 89–100.

Kuzio, T. (2002). Parliamentary Elections in the "Blackmail State". *Prism*, 8(1), available on-line at: www.jamestown.org/single/?tx_ttnews%5Btt_news%5D=20270&no_cache=1#.VmMGn_mDGko. Accessed June 8, 2016.

(2005a). Regime type and politics in Ukraine under Kuchma. *Communist and Post-Communist Studies*, 38(2), pp. 167–190.

(2005b). From Kuchma to Yushchenko Ukraine's 2004 presidential elections and the Orange revolution. *Problems of Post-Communism*, 52(2), pp. 29–44.

(2005c). Russian policy toward Ukraine during Elections. *Demokratizatsiya*, 13(4), pp. 491–517.

(2006a). Everyday Ukrainians and the Orange Revolution. In Åslund, A., and McFaul, M. (eds.), *Revolution in Orange: The Origins of Ukraine's Democratic Breakthrough*. Washington, DC: Carnegie Endowment for International Peace, pp. 45–68.

(2006b). Is Ukraine part of Europe's future? *Washington Quarterly*, 29(3), pp. 89–108.

(2011a). Soviet conspiracy theories and political culture in Ukraine: Understanding Viktor Yanukovych and the Party of Regions. *Communist and Post-Communist Studies*, 44, pp. 221–232.

(2011b). Political Culture and Democracy: Ukraine as an Immobile State, *East European Politics and Societies*, 25(1), pp. 88–113.

(2012a). Berkut Riot Police Used to Falsify Ukrainian Parliamentary Elections. *Eurasia Daily Monitor*, 9 (209), available on-line at: www.jamestown.org/single/?tx_ttnews%5Btt_news%5D=40108&no_cache=1#.VmaLzfmDGko. Accessed December 7, 2015.

(2012b). Russianization of Ukrainian National Security Policy under Viktor Yanukovych. *The Journal of Slavic Military Studies*, 25(4), pp. 558–581.

Kydland, F., and Prescott, E. (1977). Rules rather than discretion: the inconsistency of optimal plans. *Journal of Political Economy*, 85(3), pp. 473–490.

Lane, T. D. (1992). Inflation stabilization and economic transformation in Poland: The first year. *Carnegie-Rochester Conference Series on Public Policy*, 36, pp. 105–155.

Lerman, Z. (1999). Land Reform and Farm Restructuring in Ukraine. *Problems of Post-Communism*, 46(3), pp. 42–55.

Lerman, Z., and Sedik, D. J. (2007). *Productivity and Efficiency of Corporate and Individual Farms in Ukraine*. Paper prepared for presentation at the American Agricultural Economics Association Annual Meeting, July, available on-line at: http://ageconsearch.umn.edu/bitstream/9985/1/sp07le04.pdf. Accessed December 11, 2015.

Lewandowski, J. (1997). The political context of mass privatization in poland. In Lieberman, I. W., Nestor, S., and Desai, R. M. (eds.). (1997), *Between State And Market: Mass Privatization In Transition Economies*. Washington DC: World Bank Publications, pp. 35–39.

Lijphart, A. (1992). Democratization and constitutional choices in Czecho-Slovakia, Hungary and Poland 1989–91. *Journal of Theoretical Politics*, 4(2), pp. 207–223.

(2004). Constitutional design for divided societies. *Journal of Democracy*, 15(2), pp. 96–109.

Lissitsa, A., and Odening, M. (2005). Efficiency and total factor productivity in Ukrainian agriculture in transition. *Agricultural Economics*, 32(3), pp. 311–325.

Lissovolik, M. B. (2003). *Determinants of inflation in a transition economy: The case of Ukraine*. International Monetary Fund Working Paper No. 3/126.

Lovasz, A. (2014). Dashed Ikea Dreams in Ukraine Show Decades Lost to Corruption. *Bloomberg News*, March 31, 2014, available on-line at: www .bloomberg.com/news/2014-03-30/dashed-ikea-dreams-in-ukraine-show-dec ades-lost-to-corruption.html. Accessed December 5, 2015.

Ludwikowski, R.R. (1993). Constitution making in the countries of former Soviet dominance: Current development. *Georgia Journal of International and Comparative Law*, 23(2), pp. 155–267.

(1996). *Constitution-making in the Region of Former Soviet Dominance*. Durham, NC: Duke University Press.

Lybek, M. T. (1999). *Central Bank Autonomy, and Inflation and Output Performance in the Baltic States, Russia, and Other Countries of the Former Soviet Union, 1995–1997*. International Monetary Fund Working Paper 99/4.

Łyziak, T. (2013). *A note on central bank transparency and credibility in Poland*. Warsaw: National Bank of Poland Economic Institute.

Macours, K., and Swinnen, J. F. (2005). Agricultural labor adjustments in transition countries: The role of migration and impact on poverty. *Applied Economic Perspectives and Policy*, 27(3), pp. 405–411.

Magalhães, P. C. (1999). The politics of judicial reform in Eastern Europe. *Comparative Politics*, 32(1), pp. 43–62.

Magocsi, P. (2010). *A History of Ukraine: The Land and Its Peoples*. Toronto: University of Toronto Press.

Maliszewski, W. S. (2000). Central bank independence in transition economies. *Economics of Transition*, 8(3), pp. 749–789.

Mansfeldová, Z. (2011). Central European Parliaments over Two Decades–Diminishing Stability? Parliaments in Czech Republic, Hungary, Poland, and Slovenia. *The Journal of Legislative Studies*, 17(2), pp. 128–146.

Marangos, J. (2002). The political economy of shock therapy. *Journal of Economic Surveys*, 16(1), pp. 41–76.

(2003). Was shock therapy really a shock? *Journal of Economic Issues*, 37(4), pp. 943–966.

Marat, E. (2014). Ukraine's Public Enemy Number One: The Police. *Foreign Policy*, January 24, available on-line at: http://foreignpolicy.com/2014/01/24/ukraines-public-enemy-number-one-the-police/. Accessed December 8, 2015.

Markus, S. (2015a). Sovereign Commitment and Property Rights: the Case of Ukraine's Orange Revolution. *Studies in Comparative International Development*, On-line first, pp. 1–23.

(2015b). *Property, Predation, and Protection*. Cambridge: Cambridge University Press.

Matsuzato, K. (2005). Semipresidentialism in ukraine: institutionalist centrism in rampant clan politics. *Demokratizatsiya*, 13(1), pp. 45–58.

Matuszak, S. (2012). *The Oligarchic Democracy: The Influence of Business Groups on Ukrainian Politics*. OSW Studies, No. 42, Center for Eastern Studies (Warsaw).

McManus-Czubińska, C., Miller, W. L., Markowski, R., and Wasilewski, J. (2004). Why is corruption in Poland "a serious cause for concern?" *Crime, Law and Social Change*, 41(2), pp. 107–132.

McMenamin, I. (2008). *Semi-Presidentialism and Democratisation in Poland*. Working Papers in International Studies, Centre for International Studies. Dublin City University, No. 2. Available at http://doras.dcu.ie/612/1/semi-presidentialism_poland_2008.pdf.. Accessed June 8, 2016.

Medvec, S. E. (2009). The European Union and expansion to the East: Aspects of accession, problems, and prospects for the future. *International Social Science Review*, 84(1–2), pp. 66–83.

Meleshevich, A., and Forstein, C. (2014). Bringing human rights home: the challenge of enforcing judicial rulings in Ukraine and Russia. *Indiana International & Comparative Law Review*, 24(2), pp. 269–311.

Millard, F. (2006). Poland's politics and the travails of transition after 2001: The 2005 elections. *Europe-Asia Studies*, 58(7), pp. 1007–1031.

Mischenko, M. (2012). Public opinion on land policy and land reform in ukraine. *National Security and Defence*, No. 1, pp. 3–24.

Movchan, V. and Shportyuk, V. (2008), *Effects of non-tariff protectionism in Ukraine: sector aspects*, Paper prepared for the Tenth Annual Conference of the European Trade Study Group (ETSG), September, www.etsg.org/ETSG2004/Papers/Movchan.pdf.

(2012). *EU-Ukraine DCFTA: the Model for Eastern Partnership Regional Trade Cooperation*. Warsaw: Center for Social and Economic Research (CASE) Network Studies & Analyses No.445.

Mroz, B. (1991). Poland's economy in transition to private ownership. *Europe-Asia Studies*, 43(4), pp. 677–688.

Murphy, R. H. (2013). A comparative institutional analysis of free banking and central bank NGDP targeting. *Journal of Private Enterprise*, 29(1), pp. 25–39.

Murrell, P. (1993). What is shock therapy? What did it do in Poland and Russia? *Post-Soviet Affairs*, 9(2), pp. 111–140.

Myślak, E. (2013). Selected aspects of the independence of the National Bank of Poland in the context of Polish political practice. *Przegląd Politologiczny*, 3, pp. 173–182.

Naczyk, M., and Domonkos, S. (2015). The financial crisis and varieties of pension privatization reversals in Eastern Europe. *Governance*, 29(2), pp. 167–184.

Nizalov, D. (2014). Land Moratorium: Guess who benefits from the status quo? *VoxUkraine*, September 8, http://voxukraine.blogspot.com/2014/09/landmoratorium-guess-who-benefits-from.html. Accessed February 26, 2015.

Nuti, D. M. (1989). Hidden and repressed inflation in Soviet-type economies: definitions, measurements and stabilization. In Davis, C., and Charemza, W. (eds.), *Models of Disequilibrium and Shortage in Centrally Planned Economies.* Dordrecht: Springer Netherlands, pp. 101–146.

Nygren, B. (2007). *The Rebuilding of Greater Russia: Putin's Foreign Policy towards the CIS Countries.* New York: Routledge.

O'Hearn, D. (1980). The consumer second economy: size and effects. *Europe-Asia Studies,* 32(2), pp. 218–234.

OECD (2002). *OECD Reviews of Regulatory Reform: Poland, From Transition to New Regulatory Challenges.* Paris: OECD.

(2004). *Achieving Ukraine's Agricultural Potential.* Paris: OECD.

Olson, D. M. (1993). Compartmentalized competition: the managed transitional election system of Poland. *The Journal of Politics,* 55(2), pp. 415–441.

Onuch, O. (2015). The Maidan past and present: Euromaidan and the Orange Revolution. In Marples, D., and Mills, F. V. (eds.), *Euromaidan: Analyses of a Civil Revolution.* New York: Ibidem Press, pp. 27–56.

Open Society Institute (2002). *Monitoring the EU Accession Process: Corruption and Anti-Corruption Policy: The Accession Monitoring Program.* Available on-line at: www.opensocietyfoundations.org/sites/default/files/euaccesscorruptionpolish trans_2002060_0.pdf. Accessed December 17, 2015.

Orttung, R. W. (2015). Property, predation, and protection: piranha capitalism in Russia and Ukraine. *Eurasian Geography and Economics,* 56(2), pp. 220–221.

Osipian, A. L. (2009). Corruption and reform in higher education in Ukraine. *Comparative and International Education/Éducation Comparée et Internationale,* 38(2), pp. 104–122.

Osipian, A.L., and Osipian, A.L. (2006). Why Donbass votes tor Yanukovych: Confronting the Ukrainian Orange Revolution. *Demokratizatsiya,* 14(4), pp. 495–517.

Papava, V. (1996). The georgian economy: from 'shock therapy' to 'social promotion'. *Communist Economies and Economic Transformation,* 8(2), pp. 251–267.

Paskhaver, A., and Verkhovodova, L. (2007). Privatization before and after the Orange Revolution. *Problems of Economic Transition,* 50(3), pp. 5–40.

Pelkmans, J., Gros, D., and Ferrer, J. N. (2000). *Long-Run Economic Aspects of the European Union's Eastern Enlargement.* The Hague: WRR Scientific Council for Government Policy.

Petryk, O. (2006). History of monetary development in Ukraine. *Bank i Kredyt,* 37, pp. 3–24.

Piana, D. (2009). The power knocks at the courts' back door: two waves of postcommunist judicial reforms. *Comparative Political Studies,* 42(6), pp. 816–840.

Pinto, B., Belka, M., Krajewski, S., and Shleifer, A. (1993). Transforming state enterprises in Poland: Evidence on adjustment by manufacturing firms. *Brookings Papers on Economic Activity,* 1, pp. 213–270.

Pirani, S., Stern, J. P., and Yafimava, K. (2009). *The Russo-Ukrainian gas dispute of January 2009: a comprehensive assessment.* Oxford: Oxford Institute for Energy Studies.

Pivovarsky, A. (2003). Ownership concentration and performance in Ukraine's privatized enterprises. *IMF Staff Papers,* 50(1), pp. 10–42.

Polanska, D. V. (2014). Urban policy and the rise of gated housing in post-socialist Poland. *GeoJournal*, 79(4), pp. 407–419.

Polishchuk, L. (1997). Missed markets: implications for economic behavior and institutional change. In Nelson, J. M., Tilly, C., and Walker, L. (eds.), *Transforming Post-Communist Political Economies*. Washington, DC: National Academies Press, pp. 80–101.

Pond, E. (2015). Will ukraine snatch defeat from the jaws of victory? *Survival*, 57(6), pp. 59–68.

Popov, V. (2000). Shock therapy versus gradualism: the end of the debate (explaining the magnitude of transformational recession). *Comparative Economic Studies*, 42(1), pp. 1–57.

Popson, N. (2002). Where does europe end? *The Wilson Quarterly*, Summer, pp. 13–19.

Porto, G. G. (2005). Informal export barriers and poverty. *Journal of international Economics*, 66(2), pp. 447–470.

Poznanski, K.Z. (2012). Poland's transition to capitalism: shock and therapy. In Poznanski, K. Z. (ed.), *Stabilization and Privatization in Poland: An Economic Evaluation of the Shock Therapy Program*. Heidelberg: Springer Business, pp. 15–42.

Preston, C. (1998). Poland and EU membership: Current issues and future prospects. *Journal of European Integration*, 21(2), pp. 147–168.

Preston, C., and Michonski, A. (1999). *Negotiating Regulatory Alignment in Central Europe: The Case of the Poland EU European Conformity Assessment Agreement*. Sussex European Institute Working Paper No. 31.

Protsyk, O. (2003). Troubled semi-presidentialism: stability of the constitutional system and cabinet in Ukraine. *Europe-Asia Studies*, 55(7), pp. 1077–1095.

(2004). Ruling with decrees: presidential decree making in russia and ukraine. *Europe-Asia Studies*, 56(5), pp. 637–660.

(2005a). Constitutional politics and presidential power in kuchma's ukraine. *Problems of Post-Communism*, 52(5), pp. 23–31.

(2005b). Prime ministers' identity in semi-presidential regimes: Constitutional norms and cabinet formation outcomes. *European Journal of Political Research*, 44(5), pp. 721–748.

Puglisi, R. (2003). The rise of the Ukrainian oligarchs. *Democratization*, 10(3), pp. 99–123.

Pynzenyk, V. (1994). Ukrainian economic reforms: reflections on the past and the future. *Economic Policy*, 9(19), pp. 198–204.

Raciborski, J. (2007). Forming government elites in a new democracy: The case of Poland. *Communist and Post-Communist Studies*, 40(1), pp. 17–40.

Radio Poland (2014). Police detain businessman in 'Tape Affair' scandal. June 24, available on-line at: www.thenews.pl/1/9/Artykul/174568,Police-detain-businessman-in-Tape-Affair-scandal.

Rapaczynski, A. (1991). Constitutional politics in poland: a report on the constitutional committee of the polish Parliament. *The University of Chicago Law Review*, 58(2), pp. 595–631.

Razumkov Centre (2011). Cadastral system in ukraine: the state and prospects. *National Security and Defence*, No. 6, pp. 2–27.

Riabchuk, M., and Lushnycky, A.N. (2015). Ukraine's third attempt. In Stepanenko, V., and Pylynskyi, Y. (eds.), *Ukraine after the Euromaidan: Challenges and Hopes.* Oxford: Peter Lang, pp. 47–58.

Roberts, B. M., and Thompson, S. (2003). Entry and exit in a transition economy: the case of Poland. *Review of Industrial Organization*, 22(3), pp. 225–243.

Roberts, M., and Wehrheim, P. (2001). Regional trade agreements and WTO accession of CIS countries. *Intereconomics*, 36(6), pp. 315–323.

Rodrik, D. (1994). Foreign trade in Eastern Europe's transition: early results. In Blanchard, O. J., Froot, K. A., and Sachs, J. D. (eds.), *The Transition in Eastern Europe, Volume 2: Restructuring.* Chicago: University of Chicago Press, pp. 319–356.

(2000). Institutions for high-quality growth: what they are and how to acquire them. *Studies in Comparative International Development*, 35(3), pp. 3–31.

Roland, G. (2000). *Transition and Economics: Politics, Markets and Firms.* Cambridge, MA: MIT Press.

Rondinelli, D. A., and Yurkiewicz, J. (1996). Privatization and economic restructuring in Poland: an assessment of transition policies. *American Journal of Economics and Sociology*, 55(2), pp. 145–160.

Roper, S. D. (2002). Are all semi-presidential regimes the same? A comparison of premier-presidential regimes. *Comparative Politics*, 34(3), pp. 253–272.

Round, J., Williams, C. C., and Rodgers, P. (2008). Corruption in the post-Soviet workplace: the experiences of recent graduates in contemporary Ukraine. *Work, Employment & Society*, 22(1), pp. 149–166.

Ryzhenkov, M., Galko, S., Movchan, V., and Radeke, J. (2013). *The impact of the EU-Ukraine DCFTA on agricultural trade.* Institute for Economic Research and Policy Consulting (IER) Policy Paper 01/2013, www.ier.com.ua/files/publications/News/2013/PolPap_01–2013_DCFTA_eng.pdf. Accessed December 12, 2016.

Sachs, J. (1992). The economic transformation of Eastern Europe: the case of Poland. *Economics of Planning*, 25(1), pp. 5–19.

Sachs, J., and Lipton, D. (1990). Creating a market economy in Eastern Europe: The case of Poland. *Brookings Papers on Economic Activity*, 1, pp. 75–147.

Sasse, G. (2008). The European neighbourhood policy: Conditionality revisited for the EU's Eastern neighbours. *Europe-Asia Studies*, 60(2), pp. 295–316.

(2014). The new 'ukraine:' a state of regions. In Hughes, J., and Sasse, G. (eds.), *Ethnicity and Territory in the Former Soviet Union: Regions in Conflict.* New York: Routledge, pp. 69–100.

Satter, D. (2014). How the ukraine crisis arose – and why? *Hungarian Review*, 5(3), pp.6–9.

Schneider, F. (2005). Shadow economies around the world: what do we really know? *European Journal of Political Economy*, 21(3), pp. 598–642.

Schneider, K. (2001). The Partnership and Co-operation Agreement (PCA) between Ukraine and the EU—idea and reality. In Hoffman, L., and Möllers, F. (eds.), *Ukraine on the Road to Europe.* Heidelberg: Springer Physica-Verlag, pp. 66–78.

Schwartz, H. (1998). Eastern Europe's Constitutional Courts. *Journal of Democracy*, 9(4), pp. 100–114.

Schwödiauer, G., Komarov, V., and Akimova, I. (2006). *Central Bank Independence Accountability and Transparency: The Case of Ukraine.* Otto-von-Guericke University Magdeburg FEMM Working Paper Series No. 30.

Sedelius, T., and Berglund, S. (2012). Towards presidential rule in ukraine: hybrid regime dynamics under semi-presidentialism. *Baltic Journal of Law & Politics*, 5(1), pp. 20–45.

Shelley, L. (1998). Organized crime and corruption in Ukraine: impediments to the development of a free market economy. *Demokratizatsiya*, 6(4), pp. 648–663.

Shen, R. (1996). *Ukraine's Economic Reform: Obstacles, Errors, Lessons.* Westport, CT: Greenwood Publishing Group.

Shepotylo, O. (2009). Gravity with zeros: estimating trade potential of CIS countries. Unpublished working paper, available at: https://www.researchgate.net/profile/ Oleksandr_Shepotylo/publication/228239819_Gravity_with_Zeros_Estimating_ Trade_Potential_of_CIS_Countries/links/00b49526d0dac25ac8000000.pdf. Accessed December 13, 2016.

Sherr, J. (2013). *Ukraine and Europe: Final Decision?* London: Chatham House.

Shevel, O. (2015). The parliamentary elections in Ukraine, October 2014. *Electoral Studies*, 39, pp. 159–163.

Shleifer, A. (1994). Establishing property rights. *World Bank Economic Review*, 8 (suppl. 1), pp. 93–116.

Shportyuk, V. and V. Movchan (2007). *Regional integration choice for Ukraine: between the EU and Russia.* Kyiv: Institute for Economic Research and Policy Consulting.

Shumylo-Tapiola, O. (2012). *Ukraine at the Crossroads: Between the EU DCFTA & Customs Union.* IFRI Russie.NEI Report No. 11, April.

Skapska, G., and Kadylo, J. (2000). *Regulation of Restitution as a Part of polish Transformation.* Working Paper 4. Plymouth: Media Services.

Slay, B. (1993). The dilemmas of economic liberalism in Poland. *Europe-Asia Studies*, 45(2), pp. 237–257.

——— (2000). The Polish economic transition: outcome and lessons. *Communist and Post-Communist Studies*, 33(1), pp. 49–70.

——— (2014). *The Polish Economy: Crisis, Reform, and Transformation.* Princeton, NJ: Princeton University Press.

Slomczynski, K., & Shabad, G. (2012). Perceptions of political party corruption and voting behaviour in Poland. *Party Politics*, 18(6), pp. 897–917.

Solomon Jr, P. H., and Foglesong, T. S. (2000). The two faces of crime in post-soviet ukraine. *East European Constitutional Review*, 9(3), pp. 72–76.

Snelbecker, D. (1995). The political economy of privatization in ukraine. *CASE Network Studies and Analyses* No. 59.

Sonin, K. (2003). Why the rich may favor poor protection of property rights. *Journal of Comparative Economics*, 31(4), pp. 715–731.

Spechler, M. C., and Spechler, D. R. (2013). Russia's lost position in Central Eurasia. *Journal of Eurasian Studies*, 4(1), pp. 1–7.

Spiewak, P. (1997). Battle for a Constitution. *Eastern European Constitutional Review*, 6(2–3), pp. 89–96.

Stewart, S. (2013). Public procurement reform in Ukraine: the implications of neopatrimonialism for external actors. *Demokratizatsiya*, 21(2), 197–214.

Stepanenko, V. (2014). Civil society and deinstitutionalization in post-Maidan Ukraine. *Ukrainian Society: Monitoring of Social Changes*, 1(15), pp. 75–84.

Strohm, K., Tovstopyat, A., and Walther, S. (2010). *The Ukrainian farm UA2500ZH in the context of its region.* Presentation to the Cash Crop Conference 2010,

Perth, Australia, available on-line at: www.agribenchmark.org/fileadmin/ Dateiablage/B-Cash-Crop/Conferences/2010/Presentations/Poster_Ukraine_final .pdf. Accessed February 26, 2015.

Sushko, O., Zelinska, O., Khorolskyy, R., Movchan, V., Solonenko, I., Gumeniuk, V., and Triukhan, V. (2012). *EU-Ukraine Association Agreement: Guideline for Reforms.* KAS Policy Paper No.20, Konrad Adenauer Stiftung, Kyiv.

Swinnen, J. F. (1999). The political economy of land reform choices in Central and Eastern Europe. *Economics of Transition,* 7(3), pp. 637–664.

Sydorchuk, O. (2014). The impact of semi-presidentialism on democratic consolidation in Poland and Ukraine. *Demokratizatsiya,* 22(1), pp. 117–144.

Taran, S. (2008). *A paper detailing the types of non-tariff barriers encountered in the EU and New Border Countries and their impact on trade.* Paper produced for the "EU Eastern Neighbourhood: Economic Potential and Future Development" Project, www.case-research.eu/sites/default/files/A%20paper%20detailing%20the% 20types%20of%20non-tariff%20barriers%20encountered%20in%20the%20EU% 20and%20New%20Border%20Countries%20and%20their%20impact%20on% 20trade.pdf. Accessed December 11, 2016.

Tarr, D. G. (1994). The terms-of-trade effects of moving to world prices on countries of the former Soviet Union. *Journal of Comparative Economics,* 18(1), pp. 1–24.

Tedstrom, J. E. (1995). Ukraine: a crash course in economic transition. *Comparative Economic Studies,* 37(4), pp. 49–67.

Thiessen, U. (2003). The impact of fiscal policy and deregulation on shadow economies in transition countries: the case of Ukraine. *Public Choice,* 114(3–4), pp. 295–318.

Timmermans, W. (1998). Constitution Developments in Ukraine. In Müllerson, R.A., Fitzmaurice, M., and Andenæs, M. T. (eds.), *Constitutional Reforms and International Law in Central and Eastern Europe.* Leiden, the Netherlands: Martinus Nijhoff Publishers, pp. 37–58.

Trochev, A. (2010). Meddling with justice: competitive politics, impunity, and distrusted courts in post-orange Ukraine. *Demokratizatsiya,* 18(2), pp. 122–147.

Tucker, J. A. (2007). Enough! Electoral fraud, collective action problems, and post-communist colored revolutions. *Perspectives on Politics,* 5(3), pp. 535–551.

Ugolini, P. (1996). *National Bank of Poland: The Road to Indirect Instruments.* Washington DC: International Monetary Fund.

US State Department (2007). *Property Restitution in Central and Eastern Europe.* Available on-line at: http://2001-2009.state.gov/p/eur/rls/or/93062.htm. Accessed December 16, 2015.

Valasek, T. (2010). *Ukraine turns away from democracy and the EU.* Centre for European Reform (CER) Briefing Paper, available on-line at: http://cer-staging .thomas-paterson.co.uk/sites/default/files/publications/attachments/pdf/2011/ pb_ukraine_eu_valasek_oct10-193.pdf. Accessed December 7, 2015.

Verdery, K. (1994). The elasticity of land: Problems of property restitution in Transylvania. *Slavic Review,* 53(4), pp. 1071–1109.

Vinnychuk, I., and Ziukov, S. (2013). Shadow economy in Ukraine: modelling and analysis. *Business Systems & Economics,* 3(2), pp. 141–152.

Visser, O., and Spoor, M. (2011). Land grabbing in post-soviet eurasia. the world's largest land reserves at stake. *Journal of Peasant Studies,* 38(2), pp. 299–324.

Vivyan, N. (2010). Testing for partisan behaviour in independent central banks: an analysis of voting in the National Bank of Poland. Paper prepared for the 2010 Annual Meeting of the American Political Science Association. Available on-line at: www.uio.no/english/research/interfaculty-research-areas/democracy/news-and-events/events/conferences/2010/papers/Vivyan-TestingForPartisanBehaviour-2010.pdf. Accessed December 19, 2015.

Volodarsky, B. (2013). *The KGB's Poison Factory*. Barnsley, UK: Frontline Books.

Volosovych, V. (2002). The feasibility of monetary targeting in Ukraine. In Cramon-Taubadel, S., and Akimova, I. (eds.), *Fostering Sustainable Growth in Ukraine*. Berlin: Springer-Verlag, pp. 289–301.

Walicki, A.S. (1997). Transitional justice and the political struggles of post-communist poland. In McAdams, A. J. (ed.), *Transitional Justice and the Rule of Law in New Democracies*. Notre Dame: University of Notre Dame Press, pp. 185–238.

Way, L. A. (2005a). Authoritarian state building and the sources of regime competitiveness in the fourth wave: the cases of Belarus, Moldova, Russia, and Ukraine. *World Politics*, 57(2), pp. 231–261.

(2005b). Rapacious individualism and political competition in Ukraine, 1992–2004. *Communist and Post-Communist Studies*, 38(2), pp. 191–205.

(2005c). Kuchma's failed authoritarianism. *Journal of Democracy*, 16(2), pp. 131–145.

Wedel, J. R. (2003). Clans, cliques and captured states: rethinking 'transition' in Central and Eastern Europe and the former Soviet Union. *Journal of International Development*, 15(4), pp. 427–440.

Wellisz, S., and Iwanek, M. (1993). The Privatization of the Polish Economy. *Eastern Economic Journal*, 19(3), pp. 345–354.

White, S. L., McAllister, I., and Light, M. (2002). Enlargement and the new outsiders. *Journal of Common Market Studies*, 40(1), pp. 135–153.

Whitmore, S. (2005). State and Institution Building under Kuchma. *Problems of Post-Communism*, 52(5), pp. 3–11.

Williams, A. M., and Baláž, V. (2002). International Petty Trading: Changing Practices in Trans–Carpathian Ukraine. *International Journal of Urban and Regional Research*, 26(2), pp. 323–342.

Williams, C. C., and Round, J. (2008). Retheorizing the Nature of Informal Employment Some Lessons from Ukraine. *International Sociology*, 23(3), pp. 367–388.

Wilson, A. (1997). Ukraine: two presidents and their powers. In Taras, R. (ed.), *Postcommunist Presidents*. Cambridge: Cambridge University Press, pp. 67–105.

(2001). Ukraine's new virtual politics. *East European Constitutional Review*, 10(2/3), pp. 60–68.

Winiecki, J. (2000). Solving foreign trade puzzles in post-communist transition. *Post-Communist Economies*, 12(3), pp. 261–278.

(2003). *Transition Economies and Foreign Trade*. New York: Routledge.

Woehrel, S.J. (1993). Political-Economic Assessments: Ukraine. In Kaufman, R. F., and Hardt, J. P. (eds.), *The Former Soviet Union in Transition*. Armonk, New York: M.E. Sharpe, pp. 961–970.

Wolchik, S.L. (2000). *Ukraine: The Search for a National Identity*. Lanham, MD: Rowan & Littlefield.

Wolczuk, K. (2001). *The Moulding of Ukraine: The Constitutional Politics of State Formation.* Budapest: Central European University Press.

Woodruff, D. M. (2004). Property rights in context: Privatization's legacy for corporate legality in Poland and Russia. *Studies in Comparative International Development,* 38(4), pp. 82–108.

World Bank (1994a). *Ukraine: The Agriculture Sector in Transition.* Washington, DC: World Bank Press.

(1994b). *Poland: Policies for Growth with Equity.* Washington DC: World Bank Press.

(2012). *In Search of Opportunities: How a More Mobile Workforce Can Propel Ukraine's Prosperity.* Washington DC: World Bank, https://openknowledge .worldbank.org/bitstream/handle/10986/12268/NonAsciiFileName0.pdf? sequence=1. Accessed February 26, 2015.

World Economic Forum (2015). *Global Competitiveness Report 2015–16.* Geneva: World Economic Forum.

WTO (2000). *Trade Policy Review: Poland, 2000.* Geneva: WTO.

Wyrzykowski, M., and Cielen, A. (2006). Presidential Elements in Government Poland: semi-presidentialism or 'rationalised parliamentarianism'? *European Constitutional Law Review,* 2(2), pp. 253–267.

Yatsenko, N (2005). *'Posevnaya': Do, posle, i vmesto* ['Sowing': Before, After, and Instead of]. *Zerkalo nedeli,* April 16–22.

Youngblood, W. R. (1995). Poland's struggle for a restitution policy in the 1990s. *Emory International Law Review,* 9(2), pp. 645–673.

Yushchenko, V. (2000). Monetary policy in the transition to a market economy. *Russian and East European Finance and Trade,* 36(1), pp. 78–96.

Zhukov, S., and Reznikova, O. (2007). Economic integration in the post-Soviet space. *Problems of Economic Transition,* 50(7), pp. 24–36.

Zhurzhenko, T. (2007). Ukraine's Border with Russia before and after the Orange Revolution. In Malek, M. (ed.), *Die Ukraine: Zerrissen zwischen Ost und West?* Vienna: Schriftenreihe der Landesverteidigungsakademie, pp. 63–90.

Zorya, S., and von Cramon-Taubadel, S. (2002). *When Will Ukraine be a Global Player on World Agricultural Markets?* Paper prepared for presentation at the Xth EAAE Congress 'Exploring Diversity in the European Agri-Food System', Zaragoza (Spain), 28–31 August. Available on-line at: http://ageconsearch.umn.edu/bit stream/24912/1/cp02zo17.pdf. Accessed January 12, 2016.

6

Conclusion – The *Why* of Divergence

The year in which I started this book, 2014, marked the twenty-fifth anniversary of the "official" and broad-based start of Poland's journey towards becoming a democracy and a market economy, and it can be said with some certainty that the path has been a successful one. Poland's per capita GDP in 2012 was $10,573 (in constant 2005 US dollars), with the country safely ensconced in such supranational institutions as the OECD, NATO, and the European Union. Rather than lurching from crisis to crisis (political or economic), Poland saw the creation of a regular and functional market democracy, with free and fair elections, regular change of government, steady economic growth, and, following the global financial crisis of 2007–2008, a record of macroeconomic performance that became the envy of Europe. From martial law and the debt crises of the 1980s, to the deep trough of the transformational recession, Poland underwent a remarkable economic and political turnaround that few would have predicted.

In contrast, Poland's large eastern neighbor has seen a starkly different path. The current turmoil and war in Ukraine has only served to highlight the seriousness of the country's underlying economic situation. After twenty-two years of independence, the country's per capita GDP in 2012 was only slightly over US$2,000, five times less than Poland despite starting from nearly the same initial conditions, and this gap was to widen even further in 2014 and 2015. Burrowing down beneath this headline number, the country's economy has faltered in nearly every attribute, with a fiscal situation best described in 2014 as "bankrupt" and the smallest of transitions economy-wide away from its Soviet, heavy-industry past. Looking at the Ukraine of late 2013, one would be hard-pressed to highlight a success of Ukraine's transition, and certainly nothing that would make one think (as we noted in the introduction) that the system could provide for its people in the manner that Viktor Yanukovych lived. Ukraine's road to transition has instead been marked by delays in needed reforms leading to and exacerbating severe economic turbulence, including banking and currency crises in 1998–99 and from 2008 to the present. Additionally, the long-delayed political transition resulted in rampant corruption, cronyism at the highest levels, and a fragile state apparatus that has finally collapsed in places. From the days of 10,000 percent inflation in 1993 to the plummeting hryvnia and scramble for IMF loans in 2014 and 2015, the country appeared to be trapped in a suboptimal equilibrium of perpetual crisis.

This book has shown that this divergence in economic outcomes between Poland and Ukraine, and the prospect of continued divergence, can be traced exclusively to the development (or lack thereof) of their political and economic institutions since the transition away from communism began in 1989 and 1991. Of course, as the rest of this book has shown in regard to Poland and Ukraine, one cannot only look at recent manifestations of institutions in order to understand institutional influence on the economy. Indeed, given that the transition process encompasses only twenty-five or so years out of several hundred years of development of the countries of Central and Eastern Europe, we have delved deep into the history of Ukraine and Poland to try and ascertain the source of the current economic and political institutions in each country: in short, if institutions are path dependent, what determined the path that they ultimately traversed? In particular, we have drawn a connection between broader institutional changes, the evolution of "rules of the game" in several different and particular spheres, and economic results, illustrating how the long historical memories of institutions, combined with recent reforms, have impacted the transition experience of two similarly situated countries. With such an expansive approach and so many topics to cover, this book cannot have offered anything but a broader overview of institutional development, as the nuances of many particular institutions, alas, must be left for another time, better suited to a lifetime of scholarly journal articles than a larger tome such as this. However, across the broad swath of institutions that we have examined in the previous chapters, tangible lessons can be derived for the future of Poland and Ukraine, as well as for other countries that face a similar transition in political and economic institutions. As a corollary to the rest of this work, which examines the *how* of economic divergence, this conclusion will summarize our results on the *why*.

UNDERSTANDING INSTITUTIONAL CHANGE
AND THE WHY OF DIVERGENCE

In regard to political institutions, looking over the post-transition institutional development in the political sphere, we can see that both Poland and Ukraine drew on their precommunist histories, whether consciously or unconsciously. Poland saw its institutions post-1989 fashioned in the long history of "noble liberty" and the Second Republic, focused on limiting the power of the executive and elevating the democracy of the *Sejm* above all. Some successes of the Polish experience after transition stand out immediately: the inclusion of Communists in the original Roundtable Talks was necessary for legitimacy, but more importantly, the dissolution of the *Sejm* once the Communists were defeated helped to start the country off with fewer obstructions. This move, which may have appeared "radical" at the time, was a more sustainable route than the Ukrainian experience, where the Communists hung on and obstructed reforms both political and economic. Similarly, Poland experimented with a strong executive right when it was crucial, a decided departure from its historical experience: during the Commonwealth years, the relative strength of the executive to wage war and the strength of the nobles was never fully curtailed, and the Second Republic fell after five years to a coup, long after the basic institutions should have been in place. Unlike these missteps, post-transition Poland had a strong executive with broad popular support at the outset, a president who was gradually curtailed in his power as necessary economic reforms were implemented, culminating in the Constitution of 1997. Indeed, the lesson perhaps to be derived from this examination is that Poland succeeded because its political progress was continual and sustained towards executive constraints. Avoiding the half-measures that could create their own serious obstacles to completing reforms, and with prudent measures to ensure that the *Sejm* did not remain fragmented, Poland learned from its past and adapted.

Poland is by no means the perfect example of political transition (as can be seen from recent developments, see below), as it also benefitted from many other advantages in the informal institutional realm, which helped the process of formal institutional reform go much more smoothly. The fact that the population was engaged and mobilized in 1989 meant that there was a significant backlash against the Communists, one that translated into shifting the electoral map in favor of democracy. As noted earlier, the populace was also willing to wield the power of the ballot in order to punish parties perceived as corrupt, meaning that a measure of accountability was in place to also constrain politicians, a reality that has continued through the elections of 2015. Additionally, Poland had a bright and eager team of Ministers to undertake the economic reform, and in this they were given a free hand by President Wałęsa, who chose to focus on other issues or supported the reforms (explicitly, in some aspects, or implicitly, by refusing to criticize them; see Balcerowicz (1994)). Finally, Poland's Partitions did have some influence in electoral calculus (the most recent elections of 2015 prove this), but they did not unduly influence the formation of institutions; the portions of eastern Poland that were once part of Russia are for the most part now in Ukraine (and represent the most liberal parts of that country), and even Warsaw has retained its cosmopolitan worldview. In this sense, the Soviet move of Poland to the west may have been more than geographical, perhaps spiritual as well.

By contrast, the tale of Ukraine and its political institutions was a tale of improper timing, missed opportunities, and a true return to Cossack ways. Where Poland rapidly experimented with various means to constrain the executive, but left enough executive power to undertake the reforms needed during the time of "extraordinary politics," Ukraine saw a weak executive retained from the Soviet system and a long struggle by the president to take back power. Indeed, in the political institutional reform seen in Ukraine since 1991, there is a sense that the past was never actually left behind. Instead, there was rather a repeat of the Cossack rebellion from 1654 to 1657, when Ukraine left the Polish orbit to enter into Moscow's gravitational pull. As noted in previous chapters, the point of the Cossack rebellion and the ensuing hetmanate was not to create an egalitarian democracy, but to replace the Polish nobles with an indigenous class of nobles. In many ways, the history of Ukraine's political institutions in the postcommunist era has done the exact same thing: the early institutional policies of the Kravchuk regime were much like the policies of the Hetmanate in the seventeenth century, as under first president Leonid Kravchuk, Ukrainians took over the Soviet system rather than replacing it, substituting rapacious leaders from Moscow with home-grown ones from Donetsk and Velykyi Zhytyn.[1]

Seen in this historical lens, the lack of reform of political institutions in Ukraine makes perfect sense, as does the continued development of a corrupt bureaucratic state, which helped to both solidify the elites in

---

[1] It would seem that the motto of post-Soviet Ukraine has been "you can't exploit us! Only WE can exploit us!"

power and to keep the bureaucracy in check via its dependence on the prevailing power structure. The reality of Ukraine after 1991 was a fusing of the Cossack desire to have Ukrainian nobility with the institutional mechanisms of the corrupt tsarist (and Soviet) empire, creating an effective machine to serve political elites and no one else. In fact, the lack of executive constraints led to the system becoming so ossified and impene-trable by the average Ukrainian that periodic bursts of street protests were needed to break the elites' hold on the political process. This is not a cycle that engenders political stability, nor does it lead to development of appropriate economic institutions. And it was not a strategy that ensured the political unity of Ukraine, as both the Orange Revolution and the Maidan Revolution of Dignity were vilified by elites in the Donbas and their Russian enablers as some odd sort of fascism that wanted freer expression and a bigger market economy.

The entire Ukrainian experience thus raises the question, when is the appropriate moment to constrain the executive? It appears from Poland and other countries (even the United States) that Ukraine missed its opportunity long ago; this does not mean that it can never be reclaimed, as many countries have successfully limited their executives even after they have been in power for a long time. But so many missed opportunities in political institutional reform have already passed, from the Rada which survived until 1994 to Kravchuk's gyrations between consensus-building and attempting to concentrate power in the office of the presidency, to Kuchma's bypassing of the system entirely and the lost promise of the Orange Revolution. These roads not taken from 1991 to 1994 (and then again from 2004 to 2010) have made it much harder for the "correct" institutions to ever be built: half-hearted political reform in constraining the executive as was done in Ukraine entrenched interests against reform, leading to more difficulties in carrying out the next set of reforms or an even easier time in backsliding. In short, if you haven't left the past that far behind, it is much easier to throw the car in reverse and reach it once again. The ongoing war in the Donbas also makes it more difficult to erect executive constraints at this point in time, as the public looks for a decisive military leader to organize the armed forces and the defense of the realm.

On the other hand, the experience of Polish history shows that it is not the office of the executive per se that should be the focus of restraint, but all forms of executive power (including that vested in legislative authorities). My previous work (Hartwell 2013) found that not only are more executive constraints correlated with better economic outcomes in transition, but also that more developed legislatures were correlated with *worse* economic outcomes. As I conjectured at the time and still believe, this is likely due to the development of political institutions in advance of economic ones, institutions that are predicated on sharing the pie across society before the pie has even been baked (or, in the case of transition, the ingredients put together). With politicians in both the executive and the legislature attempting to spend and distribute the proceeds of an economy in flux, incentives are drastically altered, and political connections become much more important than market ones. Given this reality, the focus for the future in Ukraine, as well as in Poland, should not just be on formally limiting the power of the chief executive, but in removing the influence of government from the economy in general. This was the main goal of the transition from communism, and it remains unfinished business.

Indeed, our analysis of economic institutions over the past four centuries in Ukraine and Poland shows just how political institutions stunted the development of major economic institutions. Of course, the immense diversity of economic institutions, plus their reliance on each other, makes it more difficult to draw blanket conclusions as easily as we can with political ones. But the consistent theme of political interference is undeniable: as an economist, it pains me to admit it, but the evidence (over the past twenty-five years especially, but also far beyond the transition period) seems to show that political institutions predominated over and determined the path of economic institutions in both countries. With the political system in both countries subjected to random and internally generated shocks, it became difficult for economic institutions to develop to their fullest, a problem that Poland was mostly able to surmount (but has now reared its head again, see below) but that Ukraine has been unable to escape.

Moreover, the continual influence of political institutions and their role in derailing the development of economic institutions (especially throughout Ukraine's history) directly calls into question the undue emphasis that has been placed on economic policies in the economics literature (as well as challenging the optimism expressed by politicians in their role in generating positive economic outcomes). This is especially true in regard to the transition from communism, where macroeconomic stabilization is often discussed as the be-all and end-all of transition. In reality, policies can only be enacted within an institutional framework, originating from some (usually formal and usually political) institutions, becoming enmeshed in others, and being implemented by still others. This state of affairs means that policies can only have their desired effect a) if they are resonant with the institutional framework they occur under (i.e., if there is will) and b) if the prevailing institutions within the system have the ability to implement these policies. Where there is no alignment between institutional capacity, institutional will, and policies, or if policies are not in line with institutional incentives, policies become the weak link that must give way. This was entirely true in regard to stabilization, as policies to undertake macroeconomic stabilization without institutional reform meant that all "stabilization" was bound to be temporary (as the policy of stabilization itself was not resonant with prevailing institutions). This could be seen most clearly in Ukraine's early transition experience, where stabilization was needed to give the political class in Ukraine some breathing space, but the incentive for the medium-term was not to stabilize but to keep the economy in a state of flux. Focusing on stabilization without a change of institutions did not alter this incentive, and thus did not alter economic outcomes, a reality that makes the debate between "gradualism" and "shock therapy" seem all the more facile.

Beyond the early stages of macroeconomic stabilization and its relationship to the institutional environment, the analysis of the previous five chapters has demonstrated the importance of institutional alignment and broad-based institutional change in sustaining the transition process for the long term. Even beneficial, pro-market policies in transition failed due to lack of institutional change, the presence of countervailing institutions, or the lack of reform across key institutions with the power to block policies. Indeed, one of the reasons that Poland was successful in its transition was that it pursued a strategy that was predicated on swift macroeconomic *and* institutional reforms (while Ukraine delayed on both), creating momentum for political institutions to accept the economic institutions as a given. By placing institutional reforms such as trade liberalization, enabling private commerce and property rights, and creating a stable currency at the forefront of the stabilization process, the stabilization policies in Poland themselves began to seem *irrevocable*. This then created expectations for the success of these policies and in turn helped to push forward to institutional development that was also occurring (this approach was also adopted in Estonia, which, in one sense, had even more radical reforms than Poland). While political turnover was high in the early governments of the new Poland, there was little sense that communism was a viable economic alternative that could make a comeback, with survey data from the 1990s showing that the positive perception of property rights (to take an example of an important institution) was growing throughout the country (Johnson et al. 2002). Indeed, despite hardship in terms of declining industrial production (a hardship which would have paled in comparison to no reforms), the communist system was left behind as new institutions supplanted communist-era ones. Even with a slow-moving privatization process, new enterprises sprang up that rendered the state-owned concerns irrelevant. The fast-moving reforms of 1989 and 1990 in Poland set the country upon a different path, and institutional arrangements adapted accordingly.

On the contrary, an environment where major institutions survived to act as a representative of the old institutional order, as typified in Ukraine's early transition, doomed even the most meaningful economic policies to failure. Moreover, the policies implemented in Ukraine (and elsewhere in the former Soviet Union) in the early years of transition that avoided institutional changes only helped to ossify the barriers in place against future institutional reforms. Rather than focusing on the mediating mechanisms for facilitating transition, the early policies of the Ukrainian government were focused on constructing nationalist symbols, neglecting economic institutions as political symbolism was crafted instead. In the words of Åslund (2009:35) regarding Leonid Kravchuk, the first president, "he had a minimal political agenda, essentially consisting of the establishment of the Ukrainian state and amicable foreign relations as well as his maintenance of power ... [but] Kravchuk had no clue about economic policy." As noted in the introduction and in Hartwell (2015), this meant erecting the façade of a market democracy while avoiding building the house behind it, leaving Ukraine as its own Potemkin state.

With the trappings of institutional change but no reality behind it, the Soviet economic system had no incentives to leave and instead began to cohabitate with increased corruption, uneven progress towards both political and economic reform, and a populace that now finds itself being increasingly manipulated by outside powers simply because the alternatives have not been seen as ever achievable. While many of the prescriptions of researchers such as Joseph Stiglitz, who once claimed that institutions were "neglected" in transition, have been proven demonstrably wrong (Hartwell 2013), one theme has been proven right; in fact, one would only need to look at Ukraine's experience to find some vindication for the view that institutions were neglected. Where Poland worked to quickly put in place the building blocks of what would become market institutions, Ukraine instead resisted the difficult transition of institutions in favor of incremental tinkering of the Soviet apparatus. Not surprisingly, with institutions neglected, cultural and societal attitudes remained mired in the communist past. Economic institutions could not grow in poisoned soil with overbearing gardeners.

An important point to note at this juncture is that swift reforms, either policy or institutional, are no guarantee against either bad policy or reversals; they just make the likelihood of bad policy coming into existence less likely, increasing transaction costs for patently deleterious policies that would advantage one group against all. A germane example is the recent pension "reform" in Poland, which comes after twenty years of a successful market economy but was (and remains) a direct threat to the idea of property rights. In early 2014, the Polish government seized nearly US$51 billion of private pension holdings in the country's second pillar and shifted it back into the first pillar, at the same time considerably easing (on paper) the government's fiscal position. Despite all of the progress Poland has made in basic economic institutions, this policy still moved quickly into law and was approved by the Constitutional Tribunal, showing perhaps that there are no ironclad checks and balances against bad policy if everyone is on board. But this is no argument against Poland's institutional reforms, as, after twenty-five years, some political give-and-take is inevitable. A more salient question to ask would be, if Poland's institutional reforms had not occurred, would such a move to grab pension assets even have been possible? That is, could there even have been privately invested pension assets in a functioning and liquid capital market? Institutional regression is worrying, but it should not take our eyes off the terrain that has already been covered. Indeed, in a more volatile and slowly (or barely) reformed state like Ukraine, the political and economic institutions of the country were continuously shaped by an environment of distortions, proving how difficult it is to shape institutions that facilitate the market economy without being subjected to that same market economy. Put simply, institutions reflect their external environment, and without the incentives for institutions to change, they would not. This is the true tragedy of Ukraine, not that bad policy occurred repeatedly, but that, due to the institutional stagnation, it was the default option.

Finally, as noted throughout this book, exogenous pressures on institutional development in both Ukraine and Poland have been enormous throughout history, exerting a strong influence on the transition process comparable to the Partitions era in Poland and Ukraine's absorption into Russia. While we have mentioned several times already the importance of Russia and the European Union in the transition process, a brief look at the channels in which both actors worked is important for understanding where Poland and Ukraine are today economically. In the first instance, as Chapters 2 through 5 showed, the external influence of West and East on institution-building in the two countries has been a constant over the past four hundred years, perhaps even more pronounced in the nineteenth century and during partition than today. But empirical evidence cited in these chapters has also shown that this influence has persisted and been carried forth in the current institutions of both countries, a fact that shows that the east-west divide currently seen in Ukraine and Poland is a real and consistent challenge for institutional stability. The problems of the Donbas and its orientation towards Russia did not begin in March 2014, but can be traced back hundreds of years; the ramifications this has for economic institutions at the local and national level could thus be larger than currently imagined.

While it is simplistic to think of Russia and the EU as opposite poles, exerting a pull on Poland and Ukraine in one direction or the other, the reality is that this is precisely what has occurred over the past five centuries. Currently, the EU remains perhaps the biggest external influence in the region; after all, it was Yanukovych's failure to sign the Association Agreement with the EU that triggered the protests that led to his downfall. The EU exerts such a powerful influence due to its large economy (its combined nominal GDP may be larger than the United States) and proximity, but the EU has always been seen as more than a trade institution. Associated with free-market values and political liberalism, a distinct contrast from the Soviet times, the EU was the "other," a stark rejoinder to Soviet central planning and a beacon for the once-shackled countries of the east. This association provided the countries of Central and Eastern Europe with an institutional blueprint, a target to achieve in order to (presumably) reach the same economic outcomes as found in Brussels, Copenhagen, or Berlin. As Schimmelfennig and Sedelmeier (2004) conjecture, the EU was a conduit for "rule transfer," a way to not necessarily import institutions but to import the adherence to rule-based mechanisms on which institutions can grow. This overpowering pull towards Europe was most pronounced in Poland, transcending even party affiliation or location within the country, as Szczerbiak (2004) noted that the popular support for EU accession in Poland survived even the dislike of the then-current government. Whereas the EU may have some (serious) issues with its own institutions, as well as the way it influences institutional development in member countries (more on this below), it was a clear and preferred alternative to remaining in the Russian orbit.

While the accession to the EU provided Poland with a concrete goal and a blueprint for how to get there, Ukraine's accession to the EU was always less assured, if simply for the fact that EU accession was more uncertain; that is, the EU itself was less clear to Ukraine if accession was actually an achievable goal or not. This uncertainty of EU intent, encapsulated in the PCA in lieu of an AA and the demonstrable lower financial assistance offered to Ukraine (Russia was the prime recipient of EU technical assistance funds by a substantial margin), offered less of an external incentive for Ukrainians to go against their recent institutional past. Without the EU to aspire to, EU-affiliated institutional reforms such as rule of law, open democracy, an independent judiciary, or (relatively) free trade were not incorporated into Ukraine's economic policy making in the early years of transition, left behind on the road to nation-building and the capture of the state by powerful interests. Of course, one can argue that such institutional reforms were never really on the table, as Wolczuk (2004) has correctly noted that Ukrainian leaders (Kuchma above all) wanted "integration without Europeanization." But without a concerted effort to bring the same sort of rule transfer that occurred in Central Europe, there is less of an external influence on Ukraine's institutional development. Moreover, once the EU enlarged in 2004, Ukraine became the first country left out, moved to the borders of the EU as Poland was the westernmost non-German border of the Iron Curtain; as Grabbe (2000:519) noted, "EU border policies are raising new barriers to the free movement of people and goods that inhibit trade and investment between candidates and their non-applicant neighbors. There is a risk that the EU could end up giving the central and east European (CEE) countries the benefits of westward integration with their richer neighbors at the high cost of cutting ties with their poorer neighbors in the east." In short, the EU moved closer to Ukraine while Ukraine had moved no closer to the EU. And while the exact contribution of the EU to institutional development in Poland and the effect its absence had in Ukraine is impossible to fully quantify, as the events of December 2013 show, the EU still held symbolic power in Kyiv that likely could have made a difference if utilized earlier.

THE FUTURE OF INSTITUTIONS IN POLAND AND UKRAINE

When all of these factors are taken into account, across economic, political, and external institutions, it is plain to see that the economic divergence of Poland and Ukraine was not preordained, even though the weight of history did play a part in the transition. The choices made by the government and people of Poland from 1989 onward made a huge contribution to the country's successful transition, forcing institutional change and putting in place the building blocks of a market economy. But these choices and the entire transition experience were conditioned by the experience of the Polish-Lithuanian Commonwealth from 1386 to 1795, as well as the experience of Poland under Partition, its independence, and under Nazi and Communist rule. While some institutions were able to survive each of these historical events in various forms (for example, trade and financial institutions), others needed to be shaped and formed entirely from scratch or refurbished in such a manner that the institution was unrecognizable (the office of the president stands out as such a change). And of course, in many ways the transition is still ongoing, as some institutions that were incompletely built through centuries of the Commonwealth (such as property rights) have shown themselves to be more crucial for a market economy than a monarchy or quasi-fascist state; thus, institutions that may have been neglected in earlier economic and political systems will require more effort in order to bring them to fruition.

Seen from this vantage point, the transition in Poland is incomplete, but this is true in every country, as institutions are a dynamic and shifting part of the economic landscape, and thus "transition" is a constant and ongoing process. However, a few hundred kilometers to the east of Warsaw, the transition is not only incomplete in Ukraine in terms of attaining the institutions necessary for a market economy, it is far behind Poland in terms of position and pace. The experience of Ukraine since the transition from communism to capitalism began is also a function of its history, as the key economic institutions that should have influenced the economic transition either never blossomed (property rights) or were deliberately stunted in their growth (foreign trade). This state of affairs, a recurrent theme in Ukraine's economic development across centuries, can be traced directly to the retention of outdated political institutions, mainly a political system that favored the centralization of political and economic authority. While such a political institution may have had some success in earlier years in forging the nation-state as an independent entity, in terms of fostering the market economy it was an unmitigated failure for Ukraine.

Given this reality, where do Ukraine and Poland go from here in their institutional development? As promised in Chapter 1, the historical look at the institutional development in Central and Eastern Europe should suggest some recommendations for the two countries going forward. This is somewhat more difficult than it appears due to the idiosyncrasies of institutions themselves, specifically their semipermanent nature. Indeed, perhaps one of the most frustrating aspects of institutional analysis is the reality that institutional change is difficult to implement on a broad scale. Institutional continuity is, as we have seen in our historical analysis, a key trait in the history of nations or people, as institutions can persist even as governments come and go and even in times where the state doesn't exist (as seen in the Partitions period). Beyond the extraordinary circumstances of building national institutions without a state, just shifting a specific institution is a difficult task due to the knowledge and inertia embedded in an institutional structure; even "bad" institutions embody a certain economic rationale, be it the distribution of power or maintaining a balance between "winners" and "losers," and even changes in formal institutions may not result in different outcomes if informal ones persist (Acemoglu and Robinson 2008). In addition, and as noted throughout this book, there also may be a limit to the speed that one institution can actually change, with one institution taking years (if not centuries) to adapt and evolve, another changing fairly rapidly, and still others appearing to change somewhat quickly but actually seeing a substantial amount of time pass until institutional and economic outcomes are affected.[2] This reality complicates policy making, as politicians tend to be focused solely on these economic outcomes and not on the process of change, leading to policy overshoot and disruption. A prime example of this can be seen in our examination of institutions in transition in Chapter 5, encapsulated in the first president of Ukraine attempting to sever the trade links with Russia rather than creating the institutional environment that would allow those links to disappear on their own. Finally, institutional change is difficult given the reliance of institutions on each other, a trait exemplified by property rights and their reliance on judicial mechanisms or (as just noted) the slow process involved in forging trade links. In order to change a singular institution, the overall institutional environment must be receptive to such changes, for if certain institutions remain to block progress, such as communist-era political institutions or Soviet-era trade institutions, even the best-laid plans will come to naught.

---

[2] This point is brilliantly made in a paper by Pierre-Guillaume Méon and Khalid Sekkat that I had the pleasure of discussing at the Allied Social Sciences Association (ASSA) meetings in 2016. Entitled, "A Time to Throw Stones, a Time to Reap: How Long Does it Take for Democratic Reforms to Improve Institutional Outcomes?" this as yet-unpublished work draws a distinction between changes in institutions (in their example, democratic accountability) and institutional outcomes, which take longer to be perceived.

This broad array of obstacles to change does not mean that institutions, at least formal ones, cannot change abruptly, it just means that such change is unlikely at any given moment. But while economists (and political scientists and sociologists) focus on the semipermanence of institutions as one of their defining characteristics, the truth is that they are also very highly path-dependent. This dependence, personified by the reliance of institutions on their external environment, means that it may paradoxically be easier to undertake a systemic institutional change, having an institutional environment that is changing across all of its facets, rather than waiting for gradual and evolutionary changes in one institution. Given that even small-scale institutional change is so dependent upon the broader institutional environment, it is easy to see how scaling up to a large-scale change of institutions can appear even more daunting . . . and yet, despite these obstacles, such a change actually occurred *twice* within the twentieth century, from capitalism to communism and back again. However, the driving force for these changes was also related to the external environment, as the bubble of a country's institutional system became pierced by exogenous events that could not be ignored. This can be seen clearly in the First World War's contribution to the collapse of tsarist Russia, and the way that this cleared a path for socialism to conquer Russia and eventually a sizeable portion of the world, as well as in the Soviet release of Eastern Europe in 1989, which enabled capitalism and a monumental change in institutions around the globe.[3] In fact, such a seismic shift in the external environment of an institutional system forced domestic changes in a manner that might never have occurred endogenously; the radical and disruptive nature of this path to institutional change is very rarely chosen by a polity consciously (much less championed by an existing political party), as revolutionary change tends not to be the preferred choice of the median voter. It is for this reason that the transition period was so crucial for putting in place the foundations of a market economy (Balcerowicz's (1995) heralded time of "extraordinary politics"), as it was precisely a rapidly closing window to effect institutional change for the better. Such opportunities do not arise very often in the life of a nation, if they occur at all.

---

[3] The Soviet release of its empire was of course also not endogenously determined, but was a combination of a broad range of factors, including the collapsing economy, conflict in Afghanistan, and the pressure put on Soviet leadership by U.S. president Ronald Reagan.

This fact is precisely why the events of early 2014, coming only twenty-five years after the major, broad-based wave of institutional reform known as "transition," managed to surprise the world so much. The Maidan protests in Ukraine and the ousting of Viktor Yanukovych, the personi-fication of the old institutions that had bedeviled Ukraine's economic progress, forced open the window that had only cracked slightly in 1991 and that had been nailed shut in 1992. After several centuries of political subordination to foreign powers (including three centuries of subservience to Moscow), Ukraine finally appeared, as of February 2014, to have a chance to change the path of its institutions and move them towards a different equilibrium. In fact, the dramatic events at Euromaidan proved several things about the state of institutions in Ukraine, especially in light of Ukrainian history. Perhaps the most important was the capacity of Ukrainian society and people to organize themselves without the hand of the state; indeed, Maidan was a reaction to the state's oppressive hands and the formal political institutions that had failed the country for so long, and showed the power of informal institutions to challenge the status quo. Without coherent goals or leaders at the outset, the protestors at Maidan organized themselves into effective microsocieties, taking care of needs such as food, shelter, and medical attention when necessary.[4] Even more strikingly, the Maidan protestors rejected *all* of the representatives of the current political class, mocking opposition leaders Vitali Klitschko and Oleh Tyahnybok when they attempted to sell a compromise with President Yanukovych as a way to end the impasse.[5] No one was spared, not even soon-to-be Prime Minister Arseniy Yatsenyuk, who was regarded with "deep suspicion" due to his association with the old regime, nor former Prime Minister Yulia Tymoshenko, released from jail on the day Yanukovych fled, who addressed crowds in Maidan that evening and was greeted with derision for her part in enabling Yanukovych's rise.[6]

---

[4] An excellent retelling of this spontaneous order can be found in Evgeny Afineevsky's incredible documentary, "Winter on Fire," which has in-depth and on-the-ground footage of Maidan as it happened.

[5] For an account of this meeting, see "Kyiv Protesters Jeer Truce Offer, Build More Barricades," *Radio Free Europe/Radio Liberty*, January 24, 2014. Available at www.rferl .org/content/ukraine-protest-standoff-truce-rejected/25239418.html.

[6] On Yatsenyuk, see David Blair, "Ukraine's Maidan protesters: 'The revolution is not finished yet'," *Daily Telegraph*, April 23, 2014; on Tymoshenko, see Shaun Walker, "Yulia Tymoshenko is back centre stage in Ukraine – but not all want her there," *The Guardian*, February 23, 2014.

Thus, Maidan showed that, even with centuries of highly centralized political rule and the active suppression of some economic institutions, the ability to self-organize remained intact and spontaneous institutions could still appear. But even though this small-scale institutional revolution had major ramifications, the longer-term impact of Maidan on the institutional development of Ukraine, in regard to both political and economic institutions, remains uncertain. The change of leaders, as shown in the May 2014 presidential elections and the Rada elections of October 2014, resulted in a definite change of course towards the EU, but the actors involved were mainly career politicians who had already been involved in politics. Would they be able to shed the system they had prospered under for so long for an uncertain future? Poland's experience showed that such a political transition could be done, but Ukraine had already had the failure of the first transition and the failure of the Orange Revolution as precursors, making this attempt less likely to succeed (a fact that the Maidan protestors were well aware of). Additionally, many economic institutions, as shown in the previous chapter, have been untouched by post-Maidan reform, as issues such as the moratorium on sale of agricultural land unconscionably remains in place and other institutions such as the judiciary prove resistant to change. Institutional reforms have begun in Ukraine and moved away from the stagnation of the Yanukovych era, but they may have moved at too slow a pace to reach the terminal velocity necessary to escape the immense countervailing forces at play.

The largest of these countervailing forces is of course the war in the Donbas. The Russian invasion has created a safe haven for the discredited institutions of the past on Ukrainian soil, supporting the "People's Republics" from similarly dysfunctional institutions from elsewhere in the world. An exposé in the German newspaper *Bild* from January 2016 detailed the extent of the linkages between institutions in Russia, Russian-held territory outside of Russia, and the self-proclaimed authorities in Donetsk and Luhansk.[7] Beyond the physical support of regular Russian military personnel and equipment, the article focused on how the Russian government was bringing money into the "People's Republics" in Eastern Ukraine; apart from simply driving cash across the porous border in "humanitarian convoys," a tactic done purely for public relations, the Russian government also utilized banks from the Russian-occupied region

---

[7] Crimea, as formally a part of the Russian Federation after its annexation in 2014, required no such subterfuge for budgetary transfers.

of Abkhazia in Georgia to "divert billions of rubles from the [Russian] state budget and other sources and to redesignate them" for the Donbas.[8] In this manner, the Russians have utilized existing financial linkages from an area held by force (and unrecognized by the world) to support and consolidate their own hold on another institutional void of their own making. And financial institutions that may have been less-than-optimal in Ukraine's recent past were now hijacked entirely and connected to other external institutions for the purpose of bypassing the prevailing political institutional order and establishing a new one.

In addition, beyond the transmission of money, the Russian troops in the Donbas have also brought with them an ideological defense of Soviet institutions, establishing "People's Republics" that are characterized by tightly centralized and militarized leadership unbound by rule of law. A distinct contrast to the move towards rulebound institutions that Kyiv attempted to undertake beginning in February 2014, the "People's Republics" and the annexed region of Crimea are in danger of becoming like other "frozen conflicts" in the post-Soviet space. On the political side, this means a return to the Soviet traditions of erecting institutional simulacra, creating a façade of a particular institution – most commonly, this means holding "elections" that are either highly fraudulent or decided well in advance – but with no reality behind the institution apart from what the powers-that-be desire (Hartwell 2015). This has already been seen with the hastily conducted "referendum" in Crimea in March 2014, a throwback to the election that precipitated the Orange Revolution, where a constructed "theatrical narrative" under the eye of Russian soldiers somehow proved that Crimea was united (between 95 and 97 percent in favor!) in leaving Ukraine and joining Russia (Bobick 2014). Similarly, referenda in Luhansk and Donetsk in May 2014, while shown to be doctored and patently false (Gentile 2015), were utilized by Russian politicians as an expression of the will of the people.

The triumph of the image over reality, of the repetition of what is patently false in hopes of having it accepted as true, has horrible consequences for the creation of new political institutions, and, as practiced elsewhere in the ex-Soviet realm, it has resulted in the constitution of

---

[8] Julian Röpcke, "How Russia finances the Ukrainian rebel territories," *Bild*, January 16, 2016. Available at www.bild.de/politik/ausland/ukraine-konflikt/russia-finances-donbass-44151166.bild.html.

a lawless land governed only by might; such a political entity is character-ized by disappearances, political violence, arbitrary assassination, and a disruption of even the most basic bonds of human trust, just as was seen during the first two decades of the Soviet Union and as witnessed in the brutal wars in Chechnya (Politkovskaya 2003).[9] There is already evi-dence of murders of dissidents not toeing the Moscow line in occupied Crimea, especially amongst the Crimean Tatars, who have been most vocal in protesting the Russian annexation; people such as Islam Dzhepparov, Dzhevdet Islamov, Vasyl Chernysh, and Timur Shaimardanov remain missing while others such as Reshat Ametov and Stanislav Karachevsky were murdered for their beliefs (Zayets et al. 2015). The extension of Russian political institutions to the peninsula is not quite complete, leaving a sizeable political institutional void, but it is telling which institutions have been transferred as a priority, mainly the FSB (secret police). In the occu-pied Donbas, where not even formal Russian control has been acknowl-edged, the size of the institutional void is larger, as is the extension of the informal Russian approach to the statelets. This approach also relies heavily on FSB and military "justice."

In regard to the economic institutions in Crimea and the Donbas, the Russian invasion also means a return to the state-led planned approach of the Soviet Union, although tempered by the crony capitalism of post-Soviet Russia. As Åslund (2016) summarized,

in the second half of 2014, the occupied Donbas went through terrible destruction. Russian engineering troops blew up bridges and factories were subject to extensive artillery fire. All banks and ATM machines were looted and banking ceased. Most shops closed, leaving little but grocery stores. Rebels plundered or seized small, medium-sized and state enterprises, while big private enterprises, largely owned by Rinat Akhmetov's DTEK and Metinvest, were protected by the Kremlin. They continue to operate according to Ukrainian law in Ukrainian currency and pay Ukrainian taxes. Their workers have to go to ATM machines in free Ukraine to collect their salaries.

The results of such a policy in a war zone have been predictable: the GDP of the Donbas collapsed in 2014 and through 2015, with the National Bank of Ukraine quoting figures that show industrial production down by 40 percent in Luhansk and over 30 percent in Donetsk (NBU 2015),

---

[9] Politkovskaya was murdered in 2006 in Moscow in her apartment building in a contract-style killing. Long known for her exposés of corruption of those in power in Russia, and especially critical of the Putin regime, questions still remain over the chain of command that led to her killing. It was perhaps not coincidental that she was killed on Putin's fifty-fourth birthday.

while only one-third of the inhabitants of the region have regular work.[10] Unwilling to shoulder the burden of a territory that it no longer physically controls, Kyiv has cut off pensions to the region, a situation further enabled by the destruction of financial institutions in the region (as noted above and in Motyl (2015)). Where economic institutions do remain, they have been mostly nationalized and subordinated to the war effort or parceled out to separatist leaders, further exacerbating the economic decline.[11] In an environment such as this, it is highly unlikely that the necessary economic institutions for a market economy will emerge, an approach that may, ironically, be dangerous for the occupiers; Zhukov (2015) details that "rebellion" took hold the strongest in regions that were dependent upon dilapidated industries with heavy ties to Russia, that is, where the costs of rebellion were low and economic self-interest was high. However, the war itself has "returned many parts of the [Donbas] region to a pre-industrial state," meaning that even the aging industries no longer exist, shuttered by the reality of war (ibid.). Such a state of affairs, especially when it impacts individuals directly as through violation of property rights, could turn support away from the Russian model of institutions and create support for the prowestern government (Coupé and Obrizana 2015).

However, the external environment, once seemingly somewhat favorable to Ukraine's institutional reforms, has also cooled. The continuing Russian invasion of Luhansk and Donetsk highlights the ancient divide of the country, as well as adding additional challenges to long-delayed institutional change. In the first instance, the conflict has remained a convenient excuse for non-reform-minded politicians to avoid such radical steps as removing energy subsidies, the existence of which has provided the greatest bonanza of corruption in the country (Åslund 2009), under the guise of national unity (although some reforms have regardless moved on). Similarly, reform of the civil service and the still-substantial state-owned companies has been postponed due to the fears that putting more people on the unemployment queue would weaken

---

[10] See "Лише третина жителів окупованого Донбасу живе на доходи від постійної роботи – соціолог" [Only one-third of inhabitants of occupied Donbas live on income from regular work – sociologist], *UNIAN* Press Agency, March 30, 2015, available at www.unian.ua/politics/1061590-lishe-tretina-jiteliv-okupovanogo-donbasu-jive-na-dohodi-vid-postiynoji-roboti-sotsiolog.html.

[11] See Röpcke, "How Russia finances the Ukrainian rebel territories."

support for the government and the conflict. However, in reality, delays in reforms are not likely to result in a better outcome for Ukraine in the conflict or economically, and more likely will result in "an opportunity for oligarchic groups to restore their rule [and] .... as has happened twice previously in Ukraine, result in an authoritarian figure taking presidential office" (Minakov 2015). Such an outcome must be avoided if Ukraine's institutions are to transcend their Soviet past.

In addition to the excuse that the conflict has given the champions of the status quo, the war in the Donbas has also put pressure on the country's economic institutions from several different angles. The trade disruptions emanating from the Russian embargo are the most obvious manifestation, the maneuvers of Russia regarding the quasi-state of Transnistria in-between Moldova and Ukraine has also had an impact on Ukrainian trade institutions, creating opportunities for rent-seeking and illicit trade (Michael and Polner 2008) that can undermine the move towards Europe. Indeed, the EU itself also remains an enigma in its attitude towards Ukraine's institutional reforms, as its on-again/off-again dedication to Ukraine has not provided the same beacon for institutional change that it once did for Poland. Given that the Association Agreement provides no promise of eventual EU accession, it can be argued that the AA represents a form of external governance without long-term reward (apart from the sizeable institutional gains). At the same time, the unwillingness of the EU to offer any but the most milquetoast of sanctions on Russia also exposes the deep divide among Member States on the correct way of dealing with Ukraine's issues. Also, while the Deep and Comprehensive Free Trade Agreement (DCFTA) is back on track after being postponed by the EU in September 2014 and is being implemented as of January 1, 2016, it is only being provisionally implemented, meaning a slow unrolling of tariffs and formal barriers to trade and less of an impact in the short term that is necessary. And perhaps most troublingly for Ukraine, in January 2016 the Dutch government announced that a referendum would be held in April on the AA, a political move that had less to do with the resistance of the Dutch to Ukraine and more about a rising wave of euro-skepticism. It is this wave that has hampered the institutional reforms in Ukraine substantially, as the confident and assured EU of the early 1990s has been replaced by an unsure and unstable entity; if the EU cannot help its own members to grow, what would be the point of Ukraine aspiring to such a goal?

It is this same issue, the continuing crisis of identity amongst the EU's institutions, that has also impacted Poland in recent years. In a final coda regarding the impermanence of institutions, one need only look to Ukraine's western border to see how dynamic institution-building really is, as Poland in 2016 is showing the difficulties of sustaining institutional reform. As of the writing of this chapter, Poland has seen its first majority government since the end of communism, with the Law and Justice Party (*Prawo i Sprawiedliwość* or *PiS* for short) taking power at the end of 2015. PiS had held power in Poland before, first in a coalition government from 2005 to 2007 in what was widely regarded as a disastrous term, characterized by friction with the EU; in a much-publicized tiff regarding voting rights for Poland in the EU, then–prime minister Jaroslaw Kaczyński argued that Poland should have much more influence for its population would have been higher if not for the Germans and their actions during World War Two (Orenstein 2015). The impetus for the PiS victory this time around was a growing disillusionment with the governing Civic Platform (*Platforma Obywatelska* or *PO*), in power for eight years but widely seen as arrogant, out-of-touch, and far too pro-EU. The Eurozone crisis and Greek bailout also gave the Polish public pause, as Polish elites (especially in PO) insisted that euro adoption would be going ahead on schedule despite the large numbers of Poles that are against jettisoning the złoty. Coupled with the growing refugee crisis and the EU's trademark heavy-handedness in trying to override national sovereignty, the Euroskeptic sentiment in Poland was rising in late 2015, albeit from very low levels: a Pew Research Center poll of attitudes towards the EU showed 72 percent of Poles with a favorable attitude, the highest of any country surveyed (Stokes 2015). Drawing support from the south and east of the country, PiS were able to ride this general wave of discontent with internal and external factors into a landmark electoral victory.

However, recent moves by PiS have resurrected the long-standing Polish fear of centralized executive power (as well as highlighting the fragility of postcommunist institutions), as PiS has attempted to exert political pressure on several Polish institutions across the spectrum in a bid to consolidate its own power. In moves that historian Adam Zamoyski has called "pure Soviet-style politics," the Constitutional Tribunal (a bridge from communist institutions to the present) had its internal procedures amended by legislative fiat, with a bill that passed the *Sejm* requiring supermajority voting for passage and fixing rules for a larger quorum in order to function.[12] Similarly, additional laws have been passed in the *Sejm* affording the government more say in the (already) state-run media outlets, an approach that is in line with previous Polish governments but appears to be much cruder and straightforward than moves undertaken by the prior ruling party, Civic Platform. Despite former prime minister Donald Tusk being ensconced as the president of the European Council, perhaps the greatest sign of Poland's integration into the EU, the EU has threatened Poland with sanctions for these institutional moves (thus lending some credibility to the PiS view that Brussels is too dictatorial and imposing). The sum total of these initiatives has been a downgrade by Standards and Poors (S&P) of Polish government debt and a continuing war of words between Warsaw and Brussels, with few constructive moves to suggest a way out of the stalemate.[13] As it is too early in the term of Prime Minister Beata Szydło to tell what the future may bring, it is perhaps sufficient to note here that continued fighting between Warsaw and Brussels also weakens the case for "Europe" in the eyes of Ukraine.

And it is this issue that is perhaps the most problematic for institutional change in both Poland and Ukraine. Over the past six years, institutional reform in Central and Eastern Europe has come to be strongly identified with external forces, a situation that may be grounded in fact and of course in history, but does not tell the whole story. While institutional reforms may be influenced by this trade grouping or that country (as they were over Poland and Ukraine's long history), these reforms are not synonymous with one side or the other; put another way, while the EU may offer a series of institutions that are qualitatively and quantitatively better than those offered by Russia for facilitating a market economy, they may not necessarily be ideal or perfect. The EU is not the wellspring of good institutions. Institutional reforms such as property rights protection or liberalization of foreign trade are not dependent upon the EU for their implementation, as both Poland and Ukraine are sovereign entities and, barring catastrophe, will remain so. To associate proper economic institutions exclusively with

---

[12] Adam Zamoyski, writing in "Symposium: Is Poland a failing democracy?" *Politco.com*, January 13, 2016, available at www.politico.eu/article/poland-democracy-failing-pis-law-and-justice-media-rule-of-law/.

[13] Even the financial markets realize the root cause of this downgrade. As Manolis Davradaki, economist at Axa, said about the downgrade, "this is all about the institutions. The country's economic situation is still positive and does not warrant this downgrade." Quoted in Elaine Moore and Roger Blitz, "Poland sell off follows S&P rating cut," *Financial Times*, January 18, 2016.

the EU may have helped to provide a goal at the outset of transition, but the reality is that even EU membership may have diminishing institutional returns, especially noting that the EU today is not the same as the EU of even 2004 when Poland acceded. Instead, institutional reforms should be thought of as an endogenous process that may be informed by exogenous forces but that no longer needs to be exclusively the purview of external factors.

Thus, the recommendations given to both countries are similar, as Ukraine needs to accelerate its institutional reform while Poland needs to step back from its current path and revitalize its own institutional liberalization. As I showed in earlier work (Hartwell 2013), Poland and now Ukraine need to recapture the spirit of transition that surrounded 1989 and 1991, going beyond the ossified EU and going far beyond the retrograde Russian experiment to forge more open and more liberal institutions. Just as Poland once had the most liberal trade regime in the world, it should strive for that again, as well as seek to complete the transition in its business environment and with property rights that have languished for too long. Similarly, Ukraine should be focused on removing the shackles that have held it back for hundreds of years, fostering the conditions in which fundamental economic institutions can grow with a minimum of political interference. While, given the frozen conflict in the east, the institutional reforms that Ukraine needs to undertake may seem dwarfed by the existential threat posed by the Russian invasion, the opportunities provided by Maidan are still there and need to be seized, to create a much stronger Ukraine able to resist external aggression. Institutional reform, as a dynamic process, often influences economic outcomes only in the medium and longer term; given this reality, there is no time like the present to build the institutions that will ensure better economic outcomes in the future.

References

Acemoglu, D., and Robinson, J. A. (2008). Persistence of power, elites, and institutions. *American Economic Review*, 98(1), pp. 267–293.

Åslund, A. (2009). *How Ukraine Became a Market Economy and Democracy*. Washington DC: Peterson Institute for International Economics.

(2016). New Russian Management of the Donbas Signifies Putin May Be Ready to Negotiate. *New Atlanticist*, Atlantic Council Blog, January 4. Available at: http://www.atlanticcouncil.org/blogs/new-atlanticist/new-russian-management-of-the-donbas-signifies-putin-may-be-ready-to-negotiate. Accessed January 19, 2016.

Balcerowicz, L. (1994). Poland. In Williamson, J. (ed.), *The Political Economy of Policy Reform*. Washington DC: Peterson Institute for International Economics.

(1995). *Socialism, Capitalism, Transformation*. Budapest: Central European University Press.

Bobick, M. S. (2014). Separatism redux: Crimea, Transnistria, and Eurasia's de facto states. *Anthropology Today*, 30(3), pp. 3–8.

Coupe, T., and Obrizan, M. (2015). Violence and political outcomes in Ukraine— Evidence from Sloviansk and Kramatorsk. *Journal of Comparative Economics*, online first, October.

Gentile, M. (2015). West oriented in the East-oriented Donbas: a political stratigraphy of geopolitical identity in Luhansk, Ukraine. *Post-Soviet Affairs*, 31(3), pp. 201–223.

Grabbe, H. (2000). The sharp edges of Europe: extending Schengen eastwards. *International Affairs*, 76(3), pp. 519–536.

Hartwell, C. A. (2013). *Institutional Barriers in the Transition to Market: Explaining Performance and Divergence in Transition Economies*. Basingstoke: Palgrave Macmillan.

(2015). Baudrillard goes to kyiv: institutional simulacra in transition. *Journal of Economic and Social Thought*, 2(2), pp. 92–105.

Johnson, S., McMillan, J., and Woodruff, C. (2002). Property Rights and Finance. *American Economic Review*, 92(5), pp. 1335–1356.

Michael, B., and Polner, M. (2008). Fighting corruption on the transdnistrian border: lessons from failed and new successful anti-corruption programmes. *Transition Studies Review*, 15(3), pp. 524–541.

Minakov, M. (2015). Ukraine is caught between war and reform. *OpenDemocracy.net*, November 27, available online at: https://www.opendemocracy.net/od-russia /mikhail-minakov/ukraine-is-caught-between-war-and-reform. Accessed January 19, 2016.

Moytl, A.J. (2015). Out of Kiev's Hands: Why Ukraine's failing Donbass region is becoming a big headache for Russia. *Foreign Policy*, May 4, available online at: http://foreignpolicy.com/2015/05/04/out-of-kievs-hands/.

National Bank of Ukraine (2015). *Аналіз економічного стану України* [Analysis of Economic Situation in Ukraine]. Kyiv: National Bank of Ukraine. online at www .bank.gov.ua/doccatalog/document?id=4972952. Accessed January 19, 2016.

Orenstein, M.A. (2015). Paranoid in Poland: How Worried Should the West be About the Law and Justice Party's Victory? *Foreign Affairs*, November 1, available online at: https://www.foreignaffairs.com/articles/poland/2015-11-01/paranoid-poland. Accessed January 19, 2016.

Politkovskaya, A. (2003). *A Small Corner of Hell: Dispatches from Chechnya*. Chicago: University of Chicago Press.

Schimmelfennig, F., and Sedelmeier, U. (2004). Governance by conditionality: EU rule transfer to the candidate countries of Central and Eastern Europe. *Journal of European Public Policy*, 11(4), pp. 661–679.

Stokes, B. (2015). *Faith in European Project Reviving (But Most Say Rise of Eurosceptic Parties Is a Good Thing)*. Washington DC: Pew Research Center.

Szczerbiak, A. (2004). History trumps government unpopularity: The June 2003 Polish EU accession referendum. *West European Politics*, 27(4), pp. 671–690.

Wolczuk, K. (2004). *Integration without Europeanisation: Ukraine and its policy towards the European Union*. European University Institute Working Paper RSCAS No. 2004/15.

Zayets, S., Matviichuk, O., Pechonchyk, T., Svyrydova, D., and Skrypnyk, O. (2015). *The Fear Peninsula: Chronicle of Occupation and Violation of Human Rights in Crimea*. Kyiv: Ukrainian Helsinki Human Rights Union.

Zhukov, Y. M. (2015). Trading hard hats for combat helmets: The economics of rebellion in eastern Ukraine. *Journal of Comparative Economics*, online first, October.

Index